Dr. Rudolph Masciantonio

DICAEARCHUS
OF MESSANA

Rutgers University Studies
in Classical Humanities

Series Editor: William W. Fortenbaugh

Advisory Board: Dimitri Gutas
                        Pamela M. Huby
                        Eckart Schütrumpf
                        Robert W. Sharples

On Stoic and Peripatetic Ethics: The Work of Arius Didymus, volume I

Theophrastus of Eresus: On His Life and Work, volume II

Theophrastean Studies: On Natural Science, Physics and Metaphysics, Ethics, Religion and Rhetoric, volume III

Cicero's Knowledge of the Peripatos, volume IV

Theophrastus: His Psychological, Doxographical, and Scientific Writings, volume V

Peripatetic Rhetoric After Aristotle, volume VI

The Passionate Intellect: Essays on the Transformation of Classical Traditions presented to Professor I.G. Kidd, volume VII

Theophrastus: Reappraising the Sources, volume VIII

Demetrius of Phalerum: Texts, Translation and Discussion, volume IX

Dicaearchus of Messana: Text, Translation, and Discussion, volume X

DICAEARCHUS OF MESSANA

TEXT, TRANSLATION, AND DISCUSSION

RUTGERS UNIVERSITY STUDIES
IN CLASSICAL HUMANITIES

VOLUME 10

WILLIAM W. FORTENBAUGH
ECKART SCHÜTRUMPF
EDITORS

TRANSACTION PUBLISHERS
NEW BRUNSWICK (U.S.A.) AND LONDON (U.K.)

Library of Congress Catalog Number: 2001023965
ISBN: 0-7658-0093-4
Printed in the United States of America

Library of Congress Cataloging-in-Publication Data

Dicaearchus of Messana: text, translation, and discussion / edited by William
    Fortenbaugh, Eckart Schütrumpf.
        p.   cm. —(Rutgers University studies in classical humanities ; v. 10)
    Includes bibliographical references and index.
    ISBN 0-7658-0093-4 (cloth : alk. paper)
    1. Dicaearchus, Messenius, 4th cent. B.C. 2. Philosophy, Ancient.
    I. Fortenbaugh, William W. II. Schütrumpf, Eckart. III. Series.

B557. D344 2001
185—dc21   2001023965

Professor Trevor J. Saunders
Scholar, Colleague and Friend
1934–1999
In Memoriam

Contents

Preface   ix

Contributors   xi

1. Dicaearchus of Messana: The Sources,
   Text and Translation   1–142
   David C. Mirhady

2. Dicaearchus on the Soul and on Divination   143–73
   Robert W. Sharples

3. Dicaearchus' Philosophy of Mind   175–93
   Victor Caston

4. *Principes Sapientiae*: Dicaearchus' Biography of
   Philosophy   195–236
   Stephen A. White

5. Dicaearchus' Historical Anthropology   237–54
   Trevor J. Saunders

6. Dikaiarchs Βίος Ἑλλάδος und die Philosophie des vierten
   Jahrhunderts   255–77
   Eckart Schütrumpf

7. Dikaiarchs Bios Hellados und Varros De vita populi
   Romani   279–310
   Wolfram Ax

8. The *Controversia* between Dicaearchus and
   Theophrastus about the Best Life   311–28
   Pamela M. Huby

9. Neues aus Papyrus-Hypotheseis zu verlorenen
   Euripides-Dramen   329–41
   Wolfgang Luppe

10. La Tradizione Papirologica di Dicearco   343–52
   Tiziano Dorandi

11. The Geographical Work of Dikaiarchos   353–72
   Paul T. Keyser

Index of Ancient Sources for Articles 2–11   373–89

Preface

This volume is the tenth in the series Rutgers University Studies in Classical Humanities. The majority of the preceding volumes have been concerned with Theophrastus of Eresus, the pupil of Aristotle and his successor as head of the Peripatetic School. With Volume IX a new direction was taken. We turned our attention to the colleagues and successors of Theophrastus and produced a volume devoted to Demetrius of Phalerum. The volume includes a new edition of the fragments of Demetrius, text and facing translation, as well as essays which discuss issues of special interest. The present volume, no. X, continues this work. It is devoted to Diaearchus of Messana, who, like Theophrastus, was a pupil of Aristotle. Again the volume includes text, translation and essays. Future volumes will continue this focus. No. XI will be a collection of essays concerning Eudemus of Rhodes. It will be followed by Volume XII on Lyco, Aristo of Ceos and Hieronymus of Rhodes, and by Volume XIII on Heraclides Ponticus. The last two volumes will contain not only essays but also new editions of the fragments.

Earlier versions of the essays appearing in this volume were presented at a conference held at the University of Colorado at Boulder. We are grateful for the space and funding which was provided by the College of Arts and Sciences of the university. In addition, we wish to acknowledge the editorial assistence provided by Jennifer Faulkner of Rutgers University and the prepartation of camera ready copy by Diane Smith of Waco, Texas.

One participant in the Boulder conference was Professor Trevor Saunders of Newcastle on Tyne. He had already contributed to Volume VIII on Theophrastus; now a second contribution of his is appearing in this volume on Dicaearchus. Sadly, Trevor died during the interval between the Boulder conference and the publication of this volume. He was a special person: a good scholar, a man of great integrity, always fun to be with and a friend of Project Theophrastus. To his memory we dedicate the edition of Dicaearchus and the several essays contained in this volume.

WWF and ES
September 2000

Contributors

Wolfram AX, Institut für Altertumskunde der Universität zu Köln, Albertus-Magnus-Platz, 50923 Köln, Germany

Victor CASTON, Department of Philosophy, University of California at Davis, Davis CA 95616-8673, USA

Tiziano DORANDI, UPR 76, CNRS, 7 rue G. Moquet, BP 8, F-94801 Villejuif Cedex, France

Pamela M. HUBY, 33A Barton Road, Harlington, Beds LU5 6LG, England

Paul T. KEYSER, IBM Thomas Watson Research Center, POB 218, Yorktown NY 10598, USA

Wolfgang LUPPE, Institut für Klassische Altertumswissenschaften, Martin-Lüther-Universität, 06099 Halle-Wittenberg, Germany

David C. MIRHADY, Department of Humanities, Simon Fraser University, Burnaby BC V5A 1S6, Canada

Trevor J. SAUNDERS†, formerly Department of Classics, University of Newcastle upon Tyne, Newcastle upon Tyne NE1 7RU, England

Eckart SCHÜTRUMPF, Department of Classics, University of Colorado, Campus Box 248, Boulder CO 80309, USA

Robert W. SHARPLES, University College London, Department of Greek and Latin, Gower Street, London WC1E 6BT, England

Stephen A. WHITE, Department of Classics, University of Texas, Austin TX 78712–1181, USA

1

Dicaearchus of Messana
The Sources, Text and Translation

David C. Mirhady

CONTENTS

INTRODUCTION	3
TEXTS	6
Titles **1**	6
Life and Writings **2–12**	10
Psychology **13–32**	16
Philosophical Biography **33–52**	30
Cultural History **53–85**	56
Politics **86–88**	88
Contests, Literary Criticism **89–111**	90
Hypotheses **112–115B**	110
Geography **116–127**	114
CONCORDANCES	124
INDEX OF TEXTS AND PASSAGES	128
INDEX OF NAMES AND PLACES	138

INTRODUCTION

The methodology of this collection follows that established in the FHS&G edition of Theophrastean material,[1] beginning with a list of titles of works ascribed to Dicaearchus and continuing with texts relating to his life, writings, thought and influence. Almost without exception, the fundamental criterion for inclusion has been that Dicaearchus is named in the text. This collection also shares many things with that of Wehrli, but the order is significantly different in some areas, and much more contextual material has been included with many of the texts. Moreover, since we have no clear evidence that indicates that Dicaearchus wrote discrete works on divination, Homeric questions, or a collection of sayings, there are no separate sections on these matters.

The list of titles **1** is conceived very broadly to include all passages that describe Dicaearchus' writings, whether or not the description actually constitutes a title. **2–12** deal with Dicaearchus' life and writings. These texts locate him within the Peripatos **5** (cp. **53** for his inclusion in the Academy), as a student of Aristotle **2**, **4** and contemporary of Aristoxenus **3**. He was, however, not in agreement with Aristotle on all things **6**. He was a good teacher, citizen and human being **7–8**. Several texts that mention his writings without mentioning doctrine are also included here **9–12**.

Those texts that deal with psychology **13–32** are arranged in such a way that varying understandings of Dicaearchus' doctrine are collected together. (Like other Peripatetics', his views are said to have been at odds with Plato's **13**.) Those texts that portray him as an "eliminativist," as denying the existence of the soul, come first **14–20**, followed by those that see him embracing some sort of "epiphenomenalist" position **21–29**. Whether the soul is characterized as a "harmony" **21A–22**,

---

[1] *Theophrastus of Eresus: Sources for his Life, Writings, Thought and Influence.* Edited and Translated by William W. Fortenbaugh, Pamela M. Huby, Robert W. Sharples and Dimitri Gutas, et al. Leiden: Brill, 1992.

3

simply a "quality" or an "arrangement" of the body **23–24**, Dicaearchus is said in all of the sources to have denied the substantiality or causative function of the soul, a point made particularly in **25–26**, so that his position is materialist **27**, like that of the Epicureans **28–29**. On the other hand, and somewhat paradoxically, he is said to recognize a faculty of divination through dreams and madness **30A–31C**, although rejecting the utility of divination **32**.

There is little indication beyond **1** no.5 (*On Lives*) that Dicaearchus actually wrote a discrete work on philosophical biography, but the direction of the texts that deal both with the life of a philosopher in general and with specific philosophers' lives encourages having a section incorporating these matters **33–52**. Dicaearchus is portrayed as advocating a life of action rather than mere contemplation **33–34**, and this theme seems to be maintained throughout these texts, which embrace wisdom only when it has some practical value. Accordingly, Dicaearchus is said to reject impractical ideals with regard to friendship **35**, and to have prized the Seven Wise Men not for their wisdom, but for their practical sense and legislative abilities **36–37**. His discussion of whether the ancient poets and singers were wise appears to belong in this context **39**. The philosophers on whom Dicaearchus appears to have focused were Pythagoras **40–42**, Socrates **43–45** and Plato **46–49**, as well as Plato's students **50–51**. The proverb concerning learning pottery on a wine-jar **44** seems as if it may be related to the description of Socrates **43**.

The largest number of texts in the collection deal with cultural history **53–85**. Most of these stem, or appear to stem, from his *Life of Greece* **53–77**. In that work, Dicaearchus appears to have begun with human origins **53–57** before discussing ancient Egypt **58–59**, Chaldaea **60–61**, and perhaps Media **62**. Several texts that relate to mythical figures and foundation myths of Greek cities are gathered here **63–70**, as is one relating to Italy **71**. Then come texts relating to early musical practices and dancing **72–74** and several relating to historical times, right up to Philip of Macedon **75–77**. Finally, there are grouped a wide range of texts that are ascribed to other works that also seem to relate to cultural history **78–85**.

The smallest section deals with politics **86–88**, although there are several texts that mention titles that are political **9–11C**.

The texts dealing with contests and literary criticism **89–104** indicate Dicaearchus' further interest in music, beyond what appears in **72–74**.

Dicaearchus appears concerned in these texts with the relationship between poetry and wisdom **89, 91**, although he is also interested in issues of performance **93**, textual variations in Homer **94**, and ethical questions in poetry **95**. With regard to dramatic contests, he appears to have been interested in various aspects of the dramatic productions **99–104**. Most of the texts relating to *On Alcaeus* **105–111** derive from a single source and discuss the game of cottabus **105–109**. While two others relate to Alcaeus **110–111**, they do not name the work.

Four texts relate Dicaearchus by name to the massive amount of material contained in the *Hypotheses* or *Summaries* now associated with him, **112–115A**. They appear to consist of only the title and a short plot summary rather than any details of date or production, which he dealt with in other texts (see **99–104**).

The final group of texts deals with geography **116–127**. These touch on the measurement of mountains **118–120**, the sphericity of the earth **121–122**, mapping the Mediterranean **123–125**, the Nile River **126** and tides **127**.

I have received the help of many people in the preparation of this edition. My thanks are due to Tiziano Dorandi, Bill Fortenbaugh, Pamela Huby, Dirk Obbink, Bob Sharples, Diane Smith, Peter Stork, and the Dean of the Faculty of Humanities at the University of Calgary. Eckart Schütrumpf organized the conference in Boulder when this project was only just begun and read the entire text through with a keen eye near its completion. To him are owed special thanks.

Tabula inscriptionum

1 Tabula inscriptionum

1 Περὶ ψυχῆς] Plutarchus, Adv. Colotem 14 1115A = **13**; Cicero, Ad
   Atticum 13.32.2 = **11B** (utrosque); Cicero, Ad Atticum 13.33.2 =
   11C (titulum add. Lambinus)

2 Sermo Corinthi habitus tribus libris] Cicero, Tusculanae disputationes 1.21 = **19**

3 Lesbiaci libri, tres libri] Cicero, Tusculanae disputationes 1.77 =
   27

4 Epistula ad Aristoxenum] Cicero, Ad Atticum 13.32.2 = **11B**

5 Περὶ βίων] Diogenes Laertius, Vitae 3.4 = **47** (ἐν πρώτῳ)

6 Antiquitates] Hieronymus, Adv. Jovinianum 2.13 = **56B** (in libris)

7a ʽΕλλάδος βίος, ἐν βιβλίοις γʹ] Suda, s.v. Δικαίαρχος = **2**;
   Stephanus Byzantius, Ethnica, s.v. Χαλδαῖοι = **60** (ἐν πρώτῳ);
   Stephanus Byzantius, Ethnica, s.v. Δώριον = **63** (κατὰ τὸ πρῶτον);
   scholion in Apollonii Rhodii Argonautica 4.272–4 = **58** (ἐν αʹ);
   scholion in Apollonii Rhodii Argonautica 4.276 (ms. L) = app. **59**
   (ἐν βʹ); Hypothesis in Euripidis Medeam 25–7 = **62**
 b Περὶ τοῦ τῆς ʽΕλλάδος βίου] Athenaeus, Deipnosophistae 14.39
   636C = **72** (ἐν τοῖς); Athenaeus, Deipnosophistae 13.5 557B = **77**
   (ἐν τρίτῳ)
 c ʽΕλληνικὸς βίος] scholion in Apollonii Rhodii Argonautica 4.272–
   4 (ms. P) = **58** (ἐν βʹ); Varro, De re rustica 1.2.16 = **55** (Graeca
   Vita)
 d Περὶ τῆς ʽΕλλάδος] Zenobius 5.23 = **57** (ἐν τοῖς)
 e ʼΑναγραφὴ τῆς ʽΕλλάδος] Codex Parisinus Graecus, Supplementum 443 = **12**
 f Descriptio Graeciae] Hieronymus, Adv. Jovinianum 2.13 = **56B**

8a Περὶ τῆς εἰς Τροφωνίου καταβάσεως] Athenaeus, Deipnosophistae
   13.67 594E = **81** (ἐν τοῖς); cf. Lampriae tabulam librorum Plutarchi
   181, ubi eadem inscriptio invenitur

Titles

1   List of titles

1   *On the Soul*] Plutarch, *In Reply to Colotes* 14 1115A = **13**; Cicero, *To Atticus* 13.32.2 = **11B** ("both"); Cicero, *To Atticus* 13.33.2 = **11C** (Lambinus added the title)

2   Dialogue set at Corinth, 3 books] Cicero, *Tusculan Disputations* 1.21 = **19**

3   *Lesbian Books,* 3 books] Cicero, *Tusculan Disputations* 1.77 = **27**

4   *Letter to Aristoxenus*] Cicero, *To Atticus* 13.32.2 = **11B**

5   *On Lives*] Diogenes Laertius, *Lives* 3.4 = **47** ("in the first book")

6   *Antiquities*] Jerome, *Against Jovinian* 2.13 = **56B** ("in the books")

7a *Life of Greece,* in 3 books] Suda, on *Dicaearchus* = **2**; Stephen of Byzantium, *Place-Names,* on *Chaldaeans* = **60** ("in the first book"); Stephen of Byzantium, *Place-Names,* on *Dorium* = **63** ("according to the first book"); Scholion on Apollonius of Rhodes' *Argonautica* 4.272–4 = **58** ("in book one"); Scholion on Apollonius of Rhodes' *Argonautica* 4.276 (ms. L) = app. **59** ("in book two"); Hypothesis to Euripides' *Medea* = **62**

b   *On the Life of Greece*] Athenaeus, *The Sophists at Dinner* 14.39 636C = **72** ("in the books"); Athenaeus, *The Sophists at Dinner* 13.5 557B = **77** ("in the third book")

c   *Greek Life*] Scholion on Apollonius of Rhodes' *Argonautica* 4.272–4 (ms. P) = **58** ("in the second book"); Varro, *On Farming* 1.2.16 = **55** (*Greek Life*)

d   *On Greece*] Zenobius 5.23 = **57** ("in the books")

e   *Description of Greece*] Cod. Parisinus Gr., Supplement 443 = **12**

f   *Description of Greece*] Jerome, *Against Jovinian* 2.13 = **56B**

8a *On the Descent into (the Cave) of Trophonius*] Athenaeus, *The Sophists at Dinner* 13.67 594E = **81** ("in the books"); cf. the Lamprias Catalogue of Plutarch's works 181, where the same title is found

b Εἰς Τροφωνίου κατάβασις] Athenaeus, Deipnosophistae 14.48 641E = **80** (ἐν πρώτῳ)

c Κατάβασις] Cicero, Ad Atticum 13.32.2 = **11B** (librum); Cicero, Ad Atticum 13.33.2 = **11C**

d Trophoniana narratio] Cicero, Ad Atticum 6.2.3 = **79**

9 Περὶ τῆς ἐν Ἰλίῳ θυσίας] Athenaeus, Deipnosophistae 13.80 603A = **83**

10 De interitu hominum, liber] Cicero, De officiis 2.16 = **78**

11a Πολιτικὸς σύλλογος, Olympiae habitus] Cicero, Ad Atticum 13.30.2 = **10**

b Ὀλυμπικός] Athenaeus, Deipnosophistae 14.12 620D = **85**

12 Τριπολιτικός] Cicero, Ad Atticum 13.32.2 = **11B**; Athenaeus, Deipnosophistae 4.19 141A = **87**

13a Πολιτεία Σπαρτιατῶν] Suda, s.v. Δικαίαρχος = **2**
   b Πελληναίων] Cicero, Ad Atticum 2.2.2 = **9**
   c Κορινθίων] Cicero, Ad Atticum 2.2.2 = **9**
   d Ἀθηναίων] Cicero, Ad Atticum 2.2.2 = **9**

14 Περὶ Διονυσιακῶν ἀγώνων] Scholion in Aristophanis Aves 1403 = **99** (ἐν τῷ)

15 Περὶ μουσικῶν ἀγώνων] Suda, s.v. σκολιόν = **89** (ἐν τῷ); scholion in Aristophanis Nubes 1364c = **90**, ubi verbum ἀγώνων ab editoribus additum est

16 Παναθηναϊκός] Scholion in Aristophanis Vespas 544b = **84**

17a Ὑποθέσεις τῶν Εὐριπίδου καὶ Σοφοκλέους μύθων] Sextus Empiricus, Adv. mathematicos 3.3 = **112**; cf. Hypothesis in Rhesum = **114**
   b Ὑπόθεσις Ἀλκήστιδος] Hypothesis in Euripidis Alcestem (codex Laurentianus) = **115A**

b *Descent into (the Cave) of Trophonius*] Athenaeus, *The Sophists at Dinner* 14.48 641E = **80** ("in the first book")

c *Descent*] Cicero, *To Atticus* 13.32.2 = **11B** ("the book"); Cicero, *To Atticus* 13.33.2 = **11C**

d *Trophonian Story*] Cicero, *To Atticus* 6.2.3 = **79**

9 *On the Sacrifice at Ilium*] Athenaeus, *The Sophists at Dinner* 13.80 603A = **83**

10 *On Human Destruction,* book] Cicero, *On Duties* 2.16 = **78**

11a *Political Dialogue,* (set at Olympia)] Cicero, *To Atticus* 13.30.2 = **10**

b *Olympic (Dialogue)*] Athenaeus, *The Sophists at Dinner* 14.12 620D = **85**

12 *Three-City (Dialogue)*] Cicero, *To Atticus* 13.32.2 = **11B**; Athenaeus, *The Sophists at Dinner* 4.19 141A = **87**

13a *Constitution of the Spartans*] Suda, on *Dicaearchus* = **2**

b *(Constitution) of the Pellenaeans*] Cicero, *To Atticus* 2.2.2 = **9**

c *(Constitution) of the Corinthians*] Cicero, *To Atticus* 2.2.2 = **9**

d *(Constitution) of the Athenians*] Cicero, *To Atticus* 2.2.2 = **9**

14 *On Dionysiac Contests*] Scholion on Aristophanes' *Birds* 1403 = **99** ("in the")

15 *On Musical Contests*] Suda, on *skolion* = **89** ("in the"); Scholion on Aristophanes' *Clouds* 1364c = **90**, where the word 'Contests' has been added by the editors

16 *Panathenaic (Dialogue)*] Scholion on Aristophanes' *Clouds* 544b = **84**

17a *Summaries of the Plots of Euripides and Sophocles*] Sextus Empiricus, *Against the Mathematicians* 3.3 = **112**; cf. *Hypothesis to Rhesus* = **114**

b *Hypothesis to Alcestis*] Hypothesis to Euripides' *Alcestis* (Laurentian codex) = **115A**

18 Περὶ Ἀλκαίου] Athenaeus, Deipnosophistae 11.4 461A = **105**; Athenaeus, Deipnosophistae 15.5 667B = **107**; Athenaeus, Deipnosophistae 15.7 668E = **108** (ἐν τῷ)

19 Περίοδος γῆς] Ioannes Lydus, De mensibus 4.107 = **126**

20 Tabulae] Cicero, Ad Atticum 6.2.3 = **79**

21 Καταμετρήσεις τῶν ἐν Πελοποννήσῳ ὀρῶν] Suda, s.v. Δικαίαρχος = **2**

Vita et Scripta

2 Suda, s.v. Δικαίαρχος (no. 1062, LG t.1 pars 2 p.93.30–94.4 Adler)

Φειδίου, Σικελιώτης, ἐκ πόλεως Μεσσήνης, Ἀριστοτέλους ἀκουστής, φιλόσοφος καὶ ῥήτωρ καὶ γεωμέτρης. Καταμετρήσεις τῶν ἐν Πελοποννήσῳ ὀρῶν, Ἑλλάδος βίον ἐν βιβλίοις γ'. οὗτος ἔγραψε τὴν πολιτείαν Σπαρτιατῶν· καὶ νόμος ἐτέθη ἐν Λακε-δαίμονι καθ' ἕκαστον ἔτος ἀναγινώσκεσθαι τὸν λόγον εἰς τὸ τῶν   5 Ἐφόρων ἀρχεῖον, τοὺς δὲ τὴν ἡβητικὴν ἔχοντας ἡλικίαν ἀκρο-ᾶσθαι. καὶ τοῦτο ἐκράτει μέχρι πολλοῦ.

1 Σικελιώτης : Σικελειώτης *AFV*   Μεσσήνης: Μεσήνης *VM*   7 ἐκράτει: ἐκράτησε *M cp. V*

3 Suda, s.v. Ἀριστόξενος (no. 3927, LG t.1 pars 1 p.357.12–14 Adler)

γέγονε δὲ ἐπὶ τῶν Ἀλεξάνδρου καὶ τῶν μετέπειτα χρόνων, ὡς εἶναι ἀπὸ τῆς ρια' ὀλυμπιάδος. σύγχρονος Δικαιάρχῳ τῷ Μεσσηνίῳ.

4 Anonymus, Vita Aristotelis Latina 46–7 (AABT p.157.13–17 Düring)

47   et mortuus est in Calchide … dimisit autem filium Nicomachum et filiam Pithaida, proprios autem discipulos Theofrastum, Phaniam,

18 *On Alcaeus*] Athenaeus, *The Sophists at Dinner* 11.4 461A = **105**;
Athenaeus, *The Sophists at Dinner* 15.5 667B = **107**; Athenaeus,
The Sophists at Dinner 15.7 668E = **108** ("in the")

19 *Circuit of the Earth*] John of Lydia, *On Months* 4.107 = **126**

20 *Accounts*] Cicero, *To Atticus* 6.2.3 = **79**

21 *Measurements of the Mountains of the Peloponnesus*] Suda, on
Dicaearchus = **2**

Life and Writings

2 Suda, on *Dicaearchus* (no. 1062, *LG* v.1 part 2 p.93.30–94.4 Adler)

(Son of) Pheidias, a Sicilian from the city of Messana, a student
of Aristotle, philosopher, rhetorician and geometrician. *Measurements of the Mountains in the Peloponnesus*, *Life of Greece* in 3
books. He wrote the *Constitution of the Spartan*s, and a law was
established in Lacedaemon each year to read the text to the council
of ephors, and the young were also to listen. And this was in force
for a long time.

3 Suda, on *Aristoxenus* (no. 3927, *LG* v.1 part 1 p.357.12–14 Adler)

(Aristoxenus) lived at the time of Alexander and those following him, so that he was from the 111th Olympiad.[1] A contemporary to Dicaearchus the Messanian.

[1] I.e., *c.* 332 B.C.

4 Anonymous, *Latin Life of Aristotle* 46–7 (*AABT* p.157.13–17
Düring)

47   And (Aristotle) died in Chalcis… He also[1] left behind a son
Nicomachus and daughter Pithais, as well as his personal students

Eudimium, Clitum, Aristoxenum et Dicearchum.

1–3 *Anonymus, Vita Aristotelis Marciana 196 (p.6.32 et 77.30–2 Gigon)*　2
*Theophrastus, 10 no.2 FHS&G　Phanias, fr. 6 Wehrli　3 Aristoxenus, fr. 65
Wehrli*

2 et filiam Pithaida: et alteram (filiam *nonnulli*) phytiandam *c*　2–3 *discipulorum
nomina turbata in multis mss.*　3 Dicearchum: dircatum *a²* : dircum *b³ alii alia*

5　Cicero, De finibus 4.79 (BT p.155.7–14 Schiche)

　　quam illorum tristitiam atque asperitatem fugiens Panaetius nec
acerbitatem sententiarum nec disserendi spinas probavit fuitque in
altero genere mitior, in altero illustrior semperque habuit in ore
Platonem, Aristotelem, Xenocratem, Theophrastum, Dicaearchum,
ut ipsius scripta declarant. quos quidem tibi studiose et diligenter　5
tractandos magnopere censeo.

1 *Panaetius, fr. 55 van Straaten, fr. 79 Alesse*　4 *Theophrastus, 56 FHS&G*

6　Themistius, 23 Sophistes 285C (BT t.2 p.79.8–12 Schenkel et al.)

　　Κηφισοδώρους δὲ καὶ Εὐβουλίδας καὶ Τιμαίους ⟨καὶ⟩
Δικαιάρχους καὶ στρατὸν ὅλον τῶν ἐπιθεμένων Ἀριστοτέλει τῷ
Σταγειρίτῃ πότ' ἂν καταλέξαιμι εὐπετῶς, ὧν καὶ λόγοι
ἐξικνοῦνται εἰς τόνδε τὸν χρόνον, διατηροῦντες τὴν ἀπέχθειαν
καὶ φιλονεικίαν;　5

1 καὶ *Re*　2 Δικαιάρχους] Δημοχάρεις *Luzac*

7　Cicero, Epistulae ad Atticum 8.4.1 (BT t.1 p.294.14–16 Shackleton
Bailey)

　　Dicaearchum mehercule aut Aristoxenum diceres arcessi,
non unum hominem omnium loquacissimum et minime aptum

Theophrastus, Phanias, Eudimius, Clitus, Aristoxenus and Dicaearchus.

[1] Besides his will and writings.

5   Cicero, *On Ends* 4.79 (*BT* p.155.7–14 Schiche)

Avoiding their (sc. the Stoics') austerity and roughness, Panaetius approved of neither the severity of their opinions nor the thorns of their disputation, and in the former he was milder and in the latter more lucid, and always had Plato, Aristotle, Xenocrates, Theophrastus and Dicaearchus on his lips, as his own writings show. And these men especially I strongly recommend you to study attentively and diligently.

6   Themistius, 23 *Sophist* 285C (*BT* v.2 p.79.8–12 Schenkel et al.)

I might easily recount men like Cephisodorus[1] and Euboulides[2] and Timaeus[3] and Dicaearchus[4] and a whole army of those who have attacked Aristotle the Stagirite. Their words survive into this time, maintaining their odium and love of strife.

[1] Cephisodorus, a student of Isocrates, defended his teacher against Aristotle's attacks (DH, *De Isoc.* 18); he criticized Aristotle on other grounds also (Athen. *Deipn.* 2.56 60D).
[2] Euboulides of Miletus' attacks on Aristotle are recorded by Athenaeus, *Deipn.* 7.50 354C.
[3] The hostility of the historian Timaeus toward Aristotle is criticized by Polybius, *Histories* 12.11.
[4] Some have thought that Themistius confused Dicaearchus with Demachares. See Huby, p. 312 n.2, in this volume.

7   Cicero, *Letters to Atticus* 8.4.1 (*BT* v.1 p.294.14–16 Shackleton Bailey)

By Hercules, you would say that I was summoning Dicaearchus or Aristoxenus, not the one man (Dionysius)[1] most garrulous of all

ad docendum.

2 non unum hominem *Purser* : novi unum hominem *s* : non unum *EOR* : non unum hominum *bm*

8   Cicero, Ad Atticum 2.12.4 (BT t.1 p.69.6–12 Shackleton Bailey)

Dicaearchum recte amas. luculentus homo est et civis haud paulo melior quam isti nostri ἀδικαίαρχοι. . . . . καὶ Κικέρων ὁ φιλόσοφος τὸν πολιτικὸν Τίτον ἀσπάζεται.

9   Cicero, Ad Atticum 2.2.2 (BT t.1 p.53.21–54.5 Shackleton Bailey)

Πελληναίων in manibus tenebam et hercule magnum acervum Dicaearchi mihi ante pedes exstruxeram. o magnum hominem, et unde multo plura didiceris quam de Procilio. Κορινθίων et ᾿Αθηναίων puto me Romae habere. mihi crede (sed ego te hoc doceo?) mirabilis vir est. ῾Ηρώδης, si homo esset, eum potius legeret 5 quam unam litteram scriberet.

4 crede *(Lambinus)* (sed scilicet *olim) Shackleton Bailey scripsit* : credes (h̄ēdes *M*, heredes *M*) lege ΩΖ   te *om.* Δ hoc *HNRbds* : h(a)ec *GMm*

10   Cicero, Ad Atticum 13.30.2 (BT t.2 p.545.15–16 Shackleton Bailey)

volo aliquem Olympiae aut ubivis habitum πολιτικὸν σύλλογον more Dicaearchi familiaris tui.

1 Olympiae aut ubivis habitum *Schmidt* : Olympia aut ubi visum *codd.* : habitum *om. Shackleton Bailey*

11A Cicero, Ad Atticum 13.31.2 (BT t.2 p.546.9–11 Shackleton Bailey)

Dicaearchi quos scribis libros sane velim mi mittas, addas etiam Καταβάσεως.

and least able to teach.

[1] M. Pomponius Dionysius was an ungrateful former teacher of Cicero's son. See also **79** n.2.

8   Cicero, *To Atticus* 2.12.4 (*BT* v.1 p.69.6–12 Shackleton Bailey)

You are right to like Dicaearchus. He is a splendid human being and a citizen by no means a little better than those *adikaiarchoi* (unjust rulers) of ours.[1] ... And Cicero the philosopher salutes the statesman Titus.

[1] Cicero is referring to the Triumvirs, Caesar, Pompey and Crassus, whose grip on power had shut Cicero out of active political life.

9   Cicero, *To Atticus* 2.2.2 (*BT* v.1 p.53.21–54.5 Shackleton Bailey)

I was holding in my hands (the constitution) of Pellene and I had piled up an ungodly large heap (of books) of Dicaearchus before my feet. What a great man! You would learn much more from that source than from Procilius.[1] I think I have (his constitutions) of Corinth and Athens at Rome. Believe me, (but am I teaching you this?) the man is a marvel. Herodes,[2] if he were a (sensible) human being, would rather read him than write a single letter.

[1] From Varro (*LL* 148.154) and Pliny (*NH* 8.4) we learn that Procilius wrote on Roman topography and antiquities.
[2] Herodes was a mentor of M. Cicero. Apparently he wanted to write about Cicero's consulship.

10   Cicero, *To Atticus* 13.30.2 (*BT* v.2 p.545.15–16 Shackleton Bailey)

I want to write a sort of political dialogue, set at Olympia or wherever you like, in the manner of your intimate Dicaearchus.

11A Cicero, *To Atticus* 13.31.2 (*BT* v.2 p.546.9–11 Shackleton Bailey)

Please send me the books of Dicaearchus, about which you wrote, and add the *Descent*.

11B Cicero, Ad Atticum 13.32.2 (BT t.2 p.547.16–19 Shackleton Bailey)

Dicaearchi Περὶ ψυχῆς utrosque velim mittas et Καταβάσεως. Τριπολιτικὸν non invenio et epistulam eius, quam ad Aristoxenum misit. tris eos libros maxime nunc vellem, apti essent ad id quod cogito.

2 *cf. Joseph., Contra Apionem 1.220 = 70,I Wehrli*

2 et epistolam *Victorius*: te epistola *PΔ*

11C Cicero, Ad Atticum 13.33.2 (BT t.2 p.549.14–15 Shackleton Bailey)

Dicaearchi librum accepi et Καταβάσεως exspecto.

1 Περὶ ψυχῆς *posuit Lambinus post* librum

12   Codex Parisinus Graecus, Suppl. 443 (GGM t.1 p.243a19 Müller)

Δικαιάρχου Ἀναγραφὴ τῆς Ἑλλάδος.

De Anima

13   Plutarchus, Adversus Colotem 14 1115A (BT t.6.2 p.189.7–19 Pohlenz et Westman)

καὶ πρῶτόν γε τὴν ἐπιμέλειαν καὶ πολυμάθειαν τοῦ φιλοσόφου σκεψώμεθα, λέγοντος ὅτι τούτοις τοῖς δόγμασι τοῦ
Πλάτωνος ἐπηκολουθήκασιν Ἀριστοτέλης καὶ Ξενοκράτης
καὶ Θεόφραστος καὶ πάντες οἱ Περιπατητικοί. ποῦ γὰρ ὢν τῆς
ἀοικήτου τὸ βιβλίον ἔγραφες, ἵνα ταῦτα συντιθεὶς τὰ ἐγκλήματα 5
μὴ τοῖς ἐκείνων συντάγμασιν ἐντύχῃς μηδ' ἀναλάβῃς εἰς χεῖρας Ἀριστοτέλους τὰ Περὶ οὐρανοῦ καὶ τὰ Περὶ ψυχῆς,
Θεοφράστου δὲ τὰ Πρὸς τοὺς φυσικούς, Ἡρακλείδου δὲ τὸν
Ζωροάστρην, τὸ Περὶ τῶν ἐν Ἅιδου, τὸ Περὶ τῶν φυσικῶς
ἀπορουμένων, Δικαιάρχου δὲ τὰ Περὶ ψυχῆς; ἐν οἷς πρὸς τὰ 10
κυριώτατα καὶ μέγιστα τῶν φυσικῶν ὑπεναντιούμενοι τῷ

11B Cicero, *To Atticus* 13.32.2 (*BT* v.2 p.547.16–19 Shackleton Bailey)

I would like you to send Dicaearchus' two books *On the Soul* and *Descent*. I am not finding the *Three-City*[1] *(Dialogue)* and his letter, which he sent to Aristoxenus. I would like these three books especially now (since) they touch on what I am considering.

[1] Or: *Dialogue on Three Constitutions*, cf. G.J.D. Aalders H. Wzn, *Die Theorie der gemischten Verfassung im Altertum*, Amsterdam 1968, 73 n.5.

11C Cicero, *To Atticus* 13.33.2 (*BT* v.2 p.549.14–15 Shackleton Bailey)

I have received Dicaearchus' book (*On the Soul*) and am expecting the *Descent*.

12 Paris Codex, Greek supplement 443 (*GGM* v.1 p.243a19 Müller)

Dicaearchus' *Description of Greece*.[1]

[1] The work has been shown to be by a Dionysius, son of Kalliphon. See the paper by Keyser in this volume.

Psychology

13 Plutarch, *In Reply to Colotes* 14 1115A (*BT* v.6.2 p.189.7–19 Pohlenz and Westman)

And first let us consider the carefulness and wide learning of the philosopher (Colotes), when he says that these doctrines of Plato were followed by Aristotle and Xenocrates and Theophrastus and all the Peripatetics. In what uninhabited region did you write the book, so that when you put together these accusations you did not come across their compositions or take into your hands Aristotle's *On Heaven* and *On the Soul*, Theophrastus' *In Reply to the Natural Philosophers*, Heraclides' *Zoroaster, On the Underworld*, and *On Difficulties in Natural Philosophy*, and Dicaearchus' *On the Soul*? In these works they are continually at variance with Plato and wrangling (with him) in relation to the greatest and most important mat-

Πλάτωνι καὶ μαχόμενοι διατελοῦσι.

1–12 Theophrastus, 245 FHS&G   *4–12 Heraclides, fr. 68, 71 Wehrli*

8 Ἡρακλείδου *Reiske*: ἡρκλείτου *FB*

14 Cicero, Tusculanae disputationes 1.24 (BT p.229.24–5 Pohlenz)

quid de Dicaearcho dicam, qui nihil omnino animum dicat esse?

15 Cicero, Tusculanae disputationes 1.41 (BT p.238.8–17 Pohlenz)

Dicaearchum vero cum Aristoxeno aequali et condiscipulo suo, doctos sane homines, omittamus, quorum alter ne condoluisse quidem umquam videtur, qui animum se habere non sentiat, alter ita delectatur suis cantibus, ut eos etiam ad haec transferre conetur. ἁρμονίαν autem ex intervallis sonorum nosse possumus, quorum   5 varia compositio etiam harmonias efficit pluris, membrorum vero situs et figura corporis vacans animo quam possit harmoniam efficere non video.

3 animum] animam *Wehrli*

16 Cicero, Tusculanae disputationes 1.51 (BT p.243.11–13 Pohlenz)

Dicaearchus quidem et Aristoxenus, quia difficilis erat animi quid aut qualis esset intellegentia, nullum omnino animum esse dixerunt.

1 Dicaearchus : dice archus *X*

17 Cicero, Academici libri 2.124 (BT p.89.19–21 Plasberg)

tenemusne, quid sit animus? ubi sit? denique sitne an, ut Dicaearcho visum est, ne sit quidem ullus?

1 an *Lambinus*: aut *AB*   1–2 Dicaearcho A^2NB^2 : dicet archo B^1 : dicect A^1

ters in natural philosophy.

14 Cicero, *Tusculan Disputations* 1.24 (*BT* p.229.24–5 Pohlenz)

What shall I say about Dicaearchus, who says that the mind is nothing at all?

15 Cicero, *Tusculan Disputations* 1.41 (*BT* p.238.8–17 Pohlenz)

But let's ignore Dicaearchus, with his contemporary and fellow-student Aristoxenus, even though they were learned men. The one appears never to have felt grief, since he was not aware he had a soul;[1] the other is so pleased by his own songs that he tries to apply them even to (philosophy). Certainly we can recognize the *harmonia* resulting from the intervals of tones: their varying arrangement creates a greater number of musical modes. But I do not see what harmony the positioning of the limbs and the shape of the body, void of soul,[1] can create.

[1] Cicero here uses the masculine form, *animus*, which is translated "mind" elsewhere. See the paper of Sharples, p. 148 n.22, in this volume.

16 Cicero, *Tusculan Disputations* 1.51 (*BT* p.243.11–13 Pohlenz)

Indeed, since it was difficult to comprehend what the mind was or what sort of thing it was, Dicaearchus and Aristoxenus said that there was no mind at all.

17 Cicero, *Academics* 2.124 (*BT* p.89.19–21 Plasberg)

Do we grasp what the mind is? Where it is? Finally, does it exist or is it really not anything, as it appeared to Dicaearchus?

18 Sextus Empiricus, Pyrrhoniae hypotyposes 2.31 (BT t.1 p.71.28–72.2 Mutschmann et Mau)

ὅτι δὲ ἀκατάληπτός ἐστιν αὕτη, δῆλον ἐντεῦθεν· τῶν περὶ
ψυχῆς διαλαβόντων, ἵνα τὴν πολλὴν καὶ ἀνήνυτον μάχην
παραλίπωμεν, οἱ μὲν μὴ εἶναι τὴν ψυχὴν ἔφασαν, ὡς οἱ περὶ τὸν
Μεσσήνιον Δικαίαρχον, οἱ δὲ εἶναι, οἱ δὲ ἐπέσχον.

1 ἐντεῦθεν *om. EAB*   4 Μεσσήνιον: μεσήνιον *G*: messanensem *T*

19 Cicero, Tusculanae disputationes 1.21 (BT p.228.2–15 Pohlenz)

Dicaearchus autem in eo sermone, quem Corinthi habitum tribus
libris exponit, doctorum hominum disputantium primo libro multos
loquentes facit; duobus Pherecratem quendam Phthiotam senem,
quem ait a Deucalione ortum, disserentem inducit, nihil esse omnino
animum et hoc esse nomen totum inane frustraque animalia et 5
animantes appellari, neque in homine inesse animum vel animam
nec in bestia, vimque omnem eam, qua vel agamus quid vel sentiamus, in omnibus corporibus vivis aequabiliter esse fusam nec
separabilem a corpore esse, quippe quae nulla sit, nec sit quicquam
nisi corpus unum et simplex, ita figuratum, ut temperatione naturae 10
vigeat et sentiat.

1 Dicaearchu: dice archus *KRV*: dicaearcŭs *G´*   4–5 omnino animum] animum
omnino *K*

20 Atticus Platonicus, fr. 7.9–10 (CB p.63.16–20 des Places) =
Eusebius, Praeparatio evangelica 15.9.10

οὐ γὰρ ἡ ψυχή, φησίν, ἀλλ᾽ ὁ ἄνθρωπός ἐστιν ὁ τούτων
10 ἕκαστον ἐνεργῶν, ἡ ψυχὴ δ᾽ ἀκίνητος οὕτως. τοιγαροῦν ἑπόμενος
Δικαίαρχος, καὶ τ᾽ ἀκόλουθον ἱκανὸς ὢν θεωρεῖν, ἀνήρηκε τὴν
ὅλην ὑπόστασιν τῆς ψυχῆς.

1 *Aristoteles, De anima 1.4 408b13–15*   3–4 *cf. Plutarchus, De lib. et aegr. 5*
54.18–19

1 φησίν *ID*: φασίν *OVN*   2 ἀκίνητος οὕτως. τοιγαροῦν *codd.*: ἀκίνητος.
τούτῳ γὰρ ἐπόμενος *Stephanus*

18 Sextus Empiricus, *Outlines of Pyrrhonism* 2.31 (*BT* v.1 p.71.28–72.2 Mutschmann and Mau)

That it (the soul) is non-apprehensible is clear from the following: of those who have taken up discussion concerning the soul—so that we may avoid the long and endless battle—some said that there is no soul, like those associated with the Messanian Dicaearchus, others (have said) that there is (a soul), and others have withheld (judgment).

19 Cicero, *Tusculan Disputations* 1.21 (*BT* p.228.2–15 Pohlenz)

However, in the first book of the dialogue, which is set in Corinth in three books, Dicaearchus has many of the learned men who are in debate speak. In the (other) two (books) he introduces a certain Pherecrates, an old man from Phthia who, he says, was descended from Deucalion. (Pherecrates) argues that the *animus* (mind) is nothing at all, that the term is entirely empty and that it is pointless to use the terms *animalia* (animate creatures) and *animantes* (ensouled creatures). There is neither in man, an *animus* (mind) or *anima* (soul), nor in a beast. All the force by which we do or feel anything is spread equally in all living bodies. It is inseparable from the body, for it is nothing (by itself) nor is there anything except a body, single and plain, so configured that it has strength and feeling by means of a natural blending.

20 Atticus the Platonist, fr. 7.9–10 (*CB* p.63.16–20 des Places) = Eusebius, *Preparation for the Gospels* 15.9.10

For it is not the soul, says (Aristotle), but the man that actualizes each of these (mental processes), and the soul is in this way un-
10 moved. Dicaearchus followed accordingly, and since he was competent at observing what was entailed (sc. in Aristotle's view), he rejected the entire existence of the soul.

21A Nemesius, De natura hominis 2 (BT p.17.1–10 Morani)

Θαλῆς μὲν γὰρ πρῶτος τὴν ψυχὴν ἔφησεν ἀεικίνητον καὶ
αὐτοκίνητον, Πυθαγόρας δὲ ἀριθμὸν ἑαυτὸν κινοῦντα, Πλάτων
δὲ οὐσίαν νοητὴν ἐξ ἑαυτῆς κινητὴν κατὰ ἀριθμὸν ἐναρμόνιον,
Ἀριστοτέλης δὲ ἐντελέχειαν πρώτην σώματος φυσικοῦ,
ὀργανικοῦ, δυνάμει ζωὴν ἔχοντος, Δικαίαρχος δὲ ἁρμονίαν τῶν   5
τεσσάρων στοιχείων ἀντὶ τοῦ κρᾶσιν καὶ συμφωνίαν τῶν
στοιχείων. οὐ γὰρ τὴν ἐκ τῶν φθόγγων συνισταμένην, ἀλλὰ τὴν
ἐν τῷ σώματι θερμῶν καὶ ψυχρῶν καὶ ὑγρῶν καὶ ξηρῶν
ἐναρμόνιον κρᾶσιν καὶ συμφωνίαν βούλεται λέγειν. δῆλον δὲ
ὅτι καὶ τούτων οἱ μὲν ἄλλοι τὴν ψυχὴν οὐσίαν εἶναι λέγουσιν.   10
Ἀριστοτέλης δὲ καὶ Δικαίαρχος ἀνούσιον.

1 6 [Plutarchus], De placitis philosophorum 4.2.5 898B–C (BT t.5.2.1 p.115.11–
20 Mau) et Stobaeus, Anthologium 1.49.1a (t.1 p.318.19–320.3 Wachsmuth), quibus
locis nomen Dicaearchi in codd. legitur; Theodoretus, Graecarum affectionum
curatio 5.18 (BT p.126.22–127.4 Raedner) ubi tamen nomen Clearchi legitur   1
Thales, FVS 11A22a   2 Platon, cf. Timaeus 43a   3 Aristoteles, De anima
2.1 412a27   5 Hermias, Irrisio gentilium philosophorum 2 (DG p.651.13
Diels), quo loco nomen Dicaearchi pro nomine Deinarchi inseruit Diels

5 et 11 Δικαίαρχος Matthaei: Δείναρχος codd. et Morani   6–7 ἀντὶ τοῦ—
στοιχείων βDP Alf.arm.: om. KF   9 κρᾶσιν] τάξιν K

21B Nemesius, De natura hominis 2 (BT p.22.19–22 Morani)

ἐπειδὴ δὲ καὶ Δικαίαρχος ἁρμονίαν ὡρίσατο τὴν ψυχὴν καὶ
Σιμμίας ἀντιλέγων τῷ Σωκράτει τὴν ψυχὴν ἁρμονίαν ἔφασκεν
εἶναι, λέγων ἐοικέναι τὴν μὲν ψυχὴν ἁρμονίᾳ τὸ δὲ σῶμα λύρᾳ,
ἐκθετέον τὰς λύσεις τούτου τὰς ἐν τῷ Φαίδωνι Πλάτωνος
κειμένας.   5

4 Platon, Phaedo 91E et 93A

1 Δικαίαρχος: Δείναρχος codd. et Morani

22 Meletius, De natura hominis, De anima (Anecdota Graeca Oxon.
t.3 p.145.3–11 Cramer)

Δικαίαρχος δὲ ἁρμονίαν ὡρίσατο τὴν ψυχὴν εἶναι καὶ λύραν

21A Nemesius, *On Human Nature* 2 (*BT* p.17.1–10 Morani)

First, Thales said the soul was ever moving and self-moving: Pythagoras (said it was) number moving itself; Plato (said that it was) mental substance moved of itself in harmony according to number; Aristotle (said that it was the) first actuality of a natural, organic body, having life potentially. Dicaearchus[1] (said that it was) a harmony of the four elements, meaning by this the mixture and concord of the elements. For he does not mean the (harmony) created from sounds, but rather the harmonious mixture and concord in the body of hot, cold, wet and dry (constituents). It is clear that the others say that the soul is a substance, but Aristotle and Dicaearchus (say that it is) non-substantial.

[1] In both instances where the name "Dicaearchus" appears in this text, the manuscripts actually say "Deinarchus." Theodoretus, who provides a parallel text, gives the name as "Clearchus," while [Plutarch] and Stobaeus give "Dicaearchus." See the paper of Sharples, p.145–6 n.10, in this volume.

21B Nemesius, *On Human Nature* 2 (*BT* p.22.19–22 Morani)

Since Dicaearchus[1] defined the soul as a harmony and Simmias, when contradicting Socrates, asserted that the soul was a harmony, saying that the soul was like a harmony and the body like a lyre, it is necessary to set out (Socrates') solutions, which are in Plato's *Phaedo*.

[1] As in **21A**, the manuscripts of this text actually say "Deinarchus."

22 Meletius, *On Human Nature, On the Soul* (Anecdota Graeca Oxon. v.3 p.145.3–11 Cramer)

Dicaearchus defined the soul as a harmony and the body as a

τὸ σῶμα· ἀλλ' ἡ ἁρμονία ἐπιδέχεται τὸ μᾶλλον καὶ ἧττον, τῷ χαλᾶσθαι καὶ ἐπιτείνεσθαι· ψυχὴ δὲ ψυχῆς οὐκ ἔστι μᾶλλον καὶ ἧττον· ἀλλ' οὐδὲ αὐτὴ ἑαυτῆς· οὐκ ἄρα ἁρμονία ἡ ψυχή. ἔτι ἡ ψυχὴ ἀρετὴν καὶ κακίαν ἐπιδέχεται καὶ ἁρμονία   5 εὐαρμοστίαν καὶ ἀναρμοστίαν οὐκ ἐπιδέχεται, οὐκ ἄρα ἡ ψυχὴ ἁρμονία· ἔτι ἡ ψυχὴ τῷ ἐπιδέχεσθαι τὰ ἐναντία παρὰ μέρος, οὐσία ἐστὶ καὶ ὑποκείμενον· ἡ δὲ ἁρμονία ποιότης, καὶ ἐν ὑποκειμένῳ· οὐκ ἄρα ἁρμονία ἡ ψυχή.

1 Δικαίαρχος: Δείναρχος codd. et Cramer   5 ἁρμονία: ἁρμονίαν Cramer

23 Iamblichus, De anima ap. Stobaeum, Anthologium 1.49.32 (t.1 p.366.25–367.9 Wachsmuth)

τινὲς μὲν τῶν Ἀριστοτελικῶν αἰθέριον σῶμα τὴν ψυχὴν τίθενται· ἕτεροι δὲ τελειότητα αὐτὴν ἀφορίζονται κατ' οὐσίαν τοῦ θείου σώματος, ἣν ἐντελέχειαν καλεῖ Ἀριστοτέλης, ὥσπερ δὴ ἐν ἐνίοις Θεόφραστος, ἢ τὸ ἀπογεννώμενον ἀπὸ τῶν θειοτέρων γενῶν ὅλων, ὥσπερ ἄν τις νεωτερίσειεν ἐν ταῖς ἐπινοίαις· ἢ τὸ   5 συγκεκραμένον τοῖς σώμασιν, ὥσπερ οἱ Στωικοὶ λέγουσιν· ἢ τὸ τῇ φύσει συμμεμιγμένον ἢ τὸ τοῦ σώματος ὂν ὥσπερ τὸ ἐψυχῶσθαι, αὐτὴ δὴ μὴ παρὸν τῇ ψυχῇ ὁπωσοῦν ὑπάρχειν, οἷα δὴ λέγεται περὶ ψυχῆς παρὰ Δικαιάρχῳ τῷ Μεσσηνίῳ.

3 Theophrastus, 269 FHS&G   6–8 Plutarchus, De lib. et aegr. 5 54.12–13

3 ἐντελέχειαν Heeren: ἐνδελέχειαν FP   8 ἐψυχῶσθαι Wachsmuth: ἐμψυχῶσθαι FP   δὴ Wachsmuth: δὲ FP   ὁπωσοῦν proposuit Wachsmuth: ὥσπερ FP   ὑπάρχειν Wachsmuth: ὑπάρχον FP

24 Sextus Empiricus, Adversus mathematicos 7.348–9 (t.2 p.80.6–12 Mutschmann)

ἐχρῆν καὶ τὴν διάνοιαν, εἴπερ διακριτική ἐστι τοῦ ἀληθοῦς καὶ τοῦ ψεύδους, πολλῷ πρότερον τῇ ἑαυτῆς φύσει συνεπι-βάλλειν δι' ἥν, οὐσίᾳ τῇ ἐξ ἧς ἐστι, τόπῳ τῷ ἐν ᾧ πέφυκε, τοῖς
349 ἄλλοις ἅπασιν. οὐ πάνυ δέ γε τὰ τοιαῦτα συνορᾶν δύναται, εἴγε οἱ μὲν μηδέν φασιν εἶναι αὐτὴν παρὰ τὸ πῶς ἔχον σῶμα,   5 καθάπερ ὁ Δικαίαρχος, οἱ δὲ εἶναι μὲν ἔλεξαν, οὐκ ἐν τῷ αὐτῷ

lyre. But harmony allows the more and less by slackening and tightening; and soul is not more and less than soul; but it is also not (more or less) than itself, so soul is not a harmony. Moreover, soul allows excellence and badness, and harmony does not allow harmoniousness and non-harmoniousness, so soul is not a harmony. Moreover, by allowing opposites in turn soul is a substance and subject. But harmony is a quality and (it is) in a subject; so soul is not a harmony.

23 Iamblichus, *On the Soul*, in Stobaeus, *Anthology* 1.49.32 (v.1 p.366.25–367.9 Wachsmuth)

Some of the Aristotelians suppose that the soul is a body made of ether; others define it as perfection in accordance with the substance of the divine body, which Aristotle calls 'actuality'—so, in some places, Theophrastus—or the product of all the more divine kinds, as if modernising their notions; or (they say that it) is what is mixed with bodies, just as the Stoics say, or (that it is) what is blended by nature, or (that it is) the (quality) of the body like 'having been ensouled', it not actually being possible for the soul itself to exist in any way at all, which are the sorts of things said about the soul by Dicaearchus the Messanian.

24 Sextus Empiricus, *Against the Professors* 7.348–9 (v.2 p.80.6–12 Mutschmann)

If it is capable of distinguishing truth and falsity, the mind must much earlier be aware of its own nature by which [it exists], the substance out of which it exists, the place where it naturally exists 349 and all the rest. But it cannot comprehend such things at all, if indeed some, such as Dicaearchus, say that there is no mind beyond body in a certain state, while others agree that it exists, but

δὲ τόπῳ περιέχεσθαι.

5 *cf. Plutarchus, De lib. et aegr. 5 54.15*

---

1 διακρτική: διακριτικόν ς   2–3 φύσει συνεπιβάλλειν–ᾧ *codd.* : φύσει
ἐπιβάλλειν, συνεπιβάλλειν δὲ τῇ οὐσίᾳ, ἐξ ἧς ἐστι, τῷ τόπῳ ἐν ᾧ *Kayser*   3
δι᾽ ἣν οὐσίᾳ *Gen.* : διονουσία *NEL* : δι᾽ ὃν οὐσίᾳ ς   4 τὰ *om.* ς   5 εἶναί
φασιν *N*   6 ἔλεξαν *NLE*: ἔλεγον ς   7 τόπῳ ς : τούτῳ *NLE*

25 Tertullianus, De anima 15.1–3 (CC Series latina, pars 2 p.801.4–17
Waszink)

    in primis an sit aliqui summus in anima gradus vitalis et
sapientalis, quod ἡγεμονικόν appellant, id est principale, quia si
negetur, totus animae status periclitatur. denique qui negant
2 principale, ipsam prius animam nihil censuerunt. Messenius aliqui
Dicaearchus, ex medicis autem Andreas et Asclepiades, ita 5
abstulerunt principale, dum in animo ipso volunt esse sensus, quo-
3 rum vindicatur principale … sed plures et philosophi adversus
Dicaearchum, Plato, Strato, Epicurus, Democritus, Empedocles,
Socrates, Aristoteles et medici …

7–8 adversus Dicaearchum] adverdi cae arcum *A*   9 Socrates] Xenocrates
Diels

26 Simplicius, In Aristotelis Categorias 8b25 (CAG t.8 p.216.12–15
Kalbfleisch)

    οἱ ἀπὸ τῆς Ἐρετρίας ἀνήρουν τὰς ποιότητας ὡς οὐδαμῶς
ἐχούσας τι κοινὸν οὐσιῶδες, ἐν δὲ τοῖς καθ᾽ ἕκαστα καὶ
συνθέτοις ὑπαρχούσας. καὶ Δικαίαρχος δὲ ἀπὸ τῆς αὐτῆς αἰτίας
τὸ μὲν ζῷον συνεχώρει εἶναι, τὴν δὲ αἰτίαν αὐτοῦ ψυχὴν ἀνήρει.

3 δὲ *om. A*

27 Cicero, Tusculanae disputationes 1.77 (BT p.256.23–7 Pohlenz)

    acerrime autem deliciae meae Dicaearchus contra hanc immor-
talitatem disseruit. is enim tres libros scripsit, qui Lesbiaci vocantur

not that it is contained in the same place.[1]

[1] That is, some say that it exists outside the body while others say it exists throughout the entire body.

25   Tertullian, *On the Soul* 15.1–3 (*CC Latin Series*, part 2 p.801.4–17 Waszink)

In particular, (there is the question) whether there is some highest level in the soul pertaining to life and wisdom, which they call "hegemonic," i.e., ruling, since if it be denied, the whole status of the soul is in jeopardy. In short, those who deny that there is a ruling part (of the soul) have first determined that the soul itself is
2   nothing. A certain Messanian, Dicaearchus, and of the physicians Andreas and Asclepiades, rejected the ruling part in this way, while they want the senses, whose ruling part it is claimed to be, to be in
3   the mind itself ... But most, including the philosophers, are against Dicaearchus: Plato, Strato, Epicurus, Democritus, Empedocles, Socrates, Aristotle, and of the physicians ...

26   Simplicius, *Commentary on Aristotle's* Categories 8b25 (*CAG* v.8 p.216.12–15 Kalbfleisch)

The Eretrians[1] rejected the qualities on the grounds that they have nothing substantial in common at all, but exist in things that are particulars and compounds. For the same reason Dicaearchus agreed that the "living creature" exists, but rejected its cause, soul.

[1] Founded by Menedemus (D.L. 2.125–44), the Eretrians represented a continuation of the school of Elis.

27   Cicero, *Tusculan Disputations* 1.77 (*BT* p.256.23–7 Pohlenz)

But my favourite, Dicaearchus, has written most incisively against this immortality (of the mind). For he wrote three books,

quod Mytilenis sermo habetur, in quibus volt efficere animos esse mortales.

28 [Galenus], De historia philosophica 24 (DG p.613.14–16 Diels)

θνητὴν μὲν ψυχὴν ὁ Ἐπίκουρος καὶ Δικαίαρχος ᾠήθησαν, ἀθάνατον δὲ Πλάτων καὶ οἱ Στωικοί.

1 Δικαίαρχος *Camerarius*: Δίαρχος *AB*: Diocles *N (versio Latina)*

29 Lactantius, Institutiones divinae 7.13.7 (CSEL t.19 pars 1 sec.2 p.627.1–9 Brandt)

falsa est ergo Democriti et Epicuri et Dicaearchi de animae disolutione sententia. qui profecto non auderent de interitu animarum mago aliquo praesente disserere, qui sciret certis carminibus cieri ab inferis animas et adesse et praebere se humanis oculis videndas et loqui et futura praedicere, et si auderent, re ipsa et documentis prae-   5 sentibus vincerentur. sed quia non pervidebant animae rationem, quae tam subtilis est, ut oculos humanae mentis effugiat, interire dixerunt.

1–2 *Zeno Veronensis, Tractatus 1.2.4 (CCSL t.22 p.15.27–9 Löfstedt)*

6 rationem: ratione *H*

30A [Galenus], De historia philosophica 105 (DG p.639.27–9 Diels)

Ἀριστοτέλης καὶ Δικαίαρχος τοὺς ὀνείρους εἰσάγουσιν, ἀθάνατον μὲν τὴν ψυχὴν οὐ νομίζοντες, θείου δέ τινος μετέχειν.

1 Δικαίαρχος *Diels*: Δίαρχος *codd.*   2 νομίζοντες: νομίζονται *B*

30B [Plutarchus], De placitis philosophorum 5.1 904E (BT t.5.2.1 p.134.1–3 Mau)

Ἀριστοτέλης καὶ Δικαίαρχος τὸ κατ᾽ ἐνθουσιασμὸν μόνον παρεισάγουσι καὶ τοὺς ὀνείρους, ἀθάνατον μὲν εἶναι οὐ νομίζοντες τὴν ψυχήν, θείου δέ τινος μετέχειν αὐτήν.

1 *Aristoteles, cf. Parva naturalia = De divinatione in somno 2 463b14–16*

which are called 'Lesbian' because the dialogue is set at Mytilene, in which he wishes to show that minds are mortal.

28   Pseudo-Galen, *History of Philosophy* 24 (*DG* p.613.14–16 Diels)

Epicurus and Dicaearchus[1] thought that the soul was mortal, but Plato and the Stoics (thought it was) immortal.

[1] The name "Dicaearchus" has been restored from "Diarchos."

29   Lactantius, *Divine Institutes* 7.13.7 (*CSEL* v.19 part 1 sec.2 p.627.1–9 Brandt)

Therefore the view of Democritus and Epicurus and Dicaearchus concerning the dissolution of the soul is false. They would not dare to discuss the perishing of souls in the presence of some magician, who knew that souls are summoned from the underworld by specific charms and come to us and present themselves to be seen by human eyes and speak and predict future events—and if they dared, they would be defeated by the fact itself and the proofs there before them. But since they did not succeed in seeing the make-up of the soul, which is so fine that it escapes the eyes of the human mind, they said that it perished.

30A Pseudo-Galen, *History of Philosophy* 105 (*DG* p.639.27–9 Diels)

Aristotle and Dicaearchus[1] admit dreams, not because they think that the soul is immortal, but that it shares something divine.

[1] The name "Dicaearchus" has been restored from "Diarchus."

30B Pseudo-Plutarch, *On the Opinions of the Philosophers* 5.1 904E (*BT* v.5.2.1 p.134.1–3 Mau)

Aristotle and Dicaearchus admit only that (sort of divination) that is according to inspiration and dreams, since they do not believe the soul to be immortal but that it shares in something divine.

31A Cicero, De divinatione 1.5 (BT p.4.11–13 Giomini)

Dicaearchus Peripateticus cetera divinationis genera sustulit, somniorum et furoris reliquit.

31B Cicero, De divinatione 1.113 (BT p.65.3–7 Giomini)

nec vero umquam animus hominis naturaliter divinat, nisi cum ita solutus est et vacuus, ut ei plane nihil sit cum corpore, quod aut vatibus contingit aut dormientibus. itaque ea duo genera a Dicaearcho probantur et ut dixi[1] a Cratippo nostro.

[1] I.e., in *De div.* 1.5.

31C Cicero, De divinatione 2.100 (BT p.124.25–125.3 Giomini)

haec me Peripateticorum ratio magis movebat et veteris Dicaearchi et eius qui nunc floret Cratippi, qui censent esse in mentibus hominum tamquam oraclum aliquod, ex quo futura praesentiant, si aut furore divino incitatus animus aut somno relaxatus solute moveatur ac libere.   5

1 haec *Giomini* : ac *V*

32 Cicero, De divinatione 2.105 (BT p.127.2–4 Giomini)

at nostra interest scire ea quae eventura sint. magnus Dicaearchi liber est, nescire ea melius esse quam scire.

1 scire] scire *ex* scribere *V*

De Vita Philosophica

33 Cicero, Ad Atticum 2.16.3 (BT t.1 p.74.5–12 Shackleton Bailey)

nunc prorsus hoc statui, ut quoniam tanta controversia est Dicaearcho familiari tuo cum Theophrasto amico meo, ut ille tuus

31A Cicero, *On Divination* 1.5 (*BT* p.4.11–13 Giomini)

Dicaearchus the Peripatetic rejected all the other forms of divination, but left those from dreams and madness.

31B Cicero, *On Divination* 1.113 (*BT* p.65.3–7 Giomini)

Indeed, the human mind never divines naturally, except when it is so loosened and empty that it has absolutely nothing to do with the body, which occurs to either mantics or dreamers. And so two kinds (of divination) are approved by Dicaearchus and by our Cratippus, as I said.[1]

[1] In *On Divination* 1.5, above (following our excerpt), Cicero also identifies Cratippus' views with those of Dicaearchus.

31C Cicero, *On Divination* 2.100 (*BT* p.124.25–125.3 Giomini)

This reasoning of the Peripatetics used to move me somewhat, that of Dicaearchus of old and Cratippus, who is popular now. They think there is in the minds of men, as it were, some oracle, from which they foresee future events, if either the soul is excited by a divine madness or if it is relaxed by sleep and moved loosely and freely.

32 Cicero, *On Divination* 2.105 (*BT* p.127.2–4 Giomini)

But (the Stoics say) it matters to us to know what will happen. There is a large book of Dicaearchus, (which says) it is better not to know these things than to know (them).

Philosophical Biography

33 Cicero, *To Atticus* 2.16.3 (*BT* v.1 p.74.5–12 Shackleton Bailey)

At present I have fully resolved, that, since the controversy between your intimate Dicaearchus and my friend Theophrastus is so

τὸν πρακτικὸν βίον longe omnibus anteponat, hic autem τὸν θεωρητικόν, utrique a me mos gestus esse videatur. puto enim me Dicaearcho adfatim satis fecisse; respicio nunc ad hanc familiam 5 quae mihi non modo ut requiescam permittit sed reprehendit quia non semper quierim.

2 *Theophrastus, 481 FHS&G*

34 Cicero, Ad Atticum 7.3.1 (BT t.1 p.246.24–247.6 Shackleton Bailey)

ac primum illud, in quo te Dicaearcho adsentiri negas, etsi cupidissime expetitum a me est et te approbante, ne diutius anno in provincia essem, tamen non est nostra contentione perfectum: sic enim scito, verbum in senatu factum esse numquam de ullo nostrum, qui provincias obtinuimus, quo in iis diutius quam ex senatus 5 consulto maneremus, ut iam ne istius quidem rei culpam sustineam, quod minus diu fuerim in provincia, quam fortasse fuerit utile.

1 *cf. Cic. Ad Att. 7.1*

2 est *Wisenberg*: sit Ω   et *om. H*   te approbante *HC*: ap- *NORM*: ap- te δ

35 Plutarchus, Quaestiones convivales 4 Praef. 659E–660A (BT t.4 p.117.6–16 Hubert)

τοῦ Πολυβίου Σκηπίωνι παραινοῦντος Ἀφρικανῷ μὴ πρότερον ἐξ ἀγορᾶς ἀπελθεῖν ἢ φίλον τινὰ ποιήσασθαι τῶν
F   πολιτῶν, φίλον δεῖ μὴ πικρῶς μηδὲ σοφιστικῶς ἀκούειν ἐκεῖνον τὸν ἀμετάπτωτον καὶ βέβαιον, ἀλλὰ κοινῶς τὸν εὔνουν· ὥσπερ ᾤετο χρῆναι Δικαίαρχος εὔνους μὲν αὑτῷ παρασκευάζειν 5
660   ἅπαντας, φίλους δὲ ποιεῖσθαι τοὺς ἀγαθούς. φιλία γὰρ ἐν χρόνῳ πολλῷ καὶ δι᾽ ἀρετῆς ἁλώσιμον· εὔνοια δὲ καὶ χρείᾳ καὶ ὁμιλίᾳ καὶ παιδιᾷ πολιτικῶν ἀνδρῶν ἐπάγεται, καιρὸν λαβοῦσα πειθοῦς φιλανθρώπου καὶ χάριτος συνεργόν.

3 *cf. [Arist.], MM 2.11 1209b12*

great that that man of yours puts the active life far ahead of all others, while this (friend of mine prefers) the contemplative life, I may appear to practise the rule of both. For I think that I have sufficiently satisfied Dicaearchus; now I am looking back toward this school (the Epicurean), which not only permits me to be at leisure, but criticizes (me) since I have not always been at rest.

34   Cicero, *To Atticus* 7.3.1 (*BT* v.1 p.246.24–247.6 Shackleton Bailey)

But first on that point in which you claim not to agree with Dicaearchus: even if it was sought most desirously by me, with your approval, not to be in a province longer than a year,[1] nevertheless it was not brought about through my own effort; for you should know that no word was ever said in the senate concerning any of us who got provinces, that we should stay in them longer than was commanded by the senate, so that now I should take no blame for that business of yours because I was in the province less long than might have been useful.

[1] Cicero was governor in Cilicia from summer 51 to summer 50.

35   Plutarch, *Table Talk* 4 Pref. 659E–660A (*BT* v.4 p.117.6–16 Hubert)

When Polybius advises Scipio Africanus not to leave the marF ketplace before having made a friend of one of the ctizens, one must not understand "friend" narrowly and pedantically as unfailing and sure, but more widely, as someone with goodwill, just as Dicaearchus thought it necessary to make all people well disposed
660 to oneself, but to make the good people one's friends. For friendship is won over great time and through virtue; but goodwill comes about through business, social contact and cultural gatherings with people in the city, when one takes the opportunity for benevolent persuasion and sharing favors.

36 Codex Vaticanus 435, Πλουτάρ〈χου ἢ〉 Κεκιλίου ἀποφθέγματα
Ῥωμαϊκά (Hermes t.27 [1892] p.119.37–120.26 Arnim)

οὐκ ἐβούλοντο οἱ παλαιοὶ Ῥωμαίων, ὦ Σήβωσε ἀνδρῶν
ἄριστε, σοφοὶ εἶναι δοκεῖν, ὅθεν οὐδὲ ἐθήρων τὴν δόξαν
δεινότητι λόγων ἢ περιττοῖς καὶ πιθανοῖς ἀποφθέγμασιν, οἷς
ἐχρήσαντο Ἑλλήνων τινές, ἃ διαβεβόηται χρησμῶν εἶναι
δοκοῦντα ἤδη πιστότερα, μηδὲν ἄγαν, καὶ ἕπου θεῷ, καὶ χρόνων 5
φείδου, καὶ γνῶθι σαυτόν, καὶ ἐγγύα πάρα δ᾽ ἄτα καὶ ἄλλα τούτοις ἐοικότα, ἴσως μὲν καὶ ὠφέλιμα τοῖς πειθομένοις, ἔχοντα δέ
τι ἐν τῷ βραχεῖ τῆς ἀποδόσεως ἡδὺ καὶ προσκλητικόν.
Δικαιάρχῳ δὲ οὐδὲ ταῦτα σοφῶν εἶναι ἀνδρῶν δοκεῖ, μὴ γὰρ δή
γε τοὺς πάλαι λόγῳ φιλοσοφεῖν. ἀλλ᾽ εἶναι τὴν σοφίαν τότε γοῦν 10
ἐπιτήδευσιν ἔργων καλῶν, χρόνῳ δὲ λόγων ὀχλικῶν γενέσθαι
τέχνην. καὶ νῦν μὲν τὸν πιθανῶς διαλεχθέντα μέγαν εἶναι δοκεῖν
φιλόσοφον, ἐν δὲ τοῖς πάλαι χρόνοις ὁ ἀγαθὸς μόνος ἦν
φιλόσοφος, εἰ καὶ μὴ περιβλέπτους καὶ ὀχλικοὺς ἀσκοῖτο λόγους.
οὐ γὰρ ἐζήτουν ἐκεῖνοί γε εἰ πολιτευτέον οὐδὲ πῶς, ἀλλ᾽ 15
ἐπολιτεύοντο αὐτοὶ καλῶς, οὐδὲ εἰ χρὴ γαμεῖν, ἀλλὰ γήμαντες
ὃν δεῖ τρόπον γαμεῖν ταῖς γυναιξὶ συνεβίων. ταῦτα ἦν, φησίν,
ἔργα ἀνδρῶν καὶ ἐπιτηδεύματα σοφῶν, αἱ δὲ ἀποφθέγξεις αὗται
πρᾶγμα φορτικόν. τοιούτους πείθομαι καὶ τοὺς ὑμετέρους
γενέσθαι πατέρας· εἶναι γὰρ ἀγαθοὶ ἐβούλοντο καὶ τούτου τοῖς 20
ἔργοις ἐφικνοῦντο· στρογγύλας δ᾽ ἀποφθέγξεις καὶ καλλιρ-
ρήμονας ὥστε περιττοὺς εἶναι δοκεῖν οὔτ᾽ ἐπετήδευον οὔτε
ἐγίγνωσκον. οἵοις μέντοι λογισμοῖς ἕκαστα ἔπραττον, τοιούτοις
καὶ λόγοις περὶ αὐτῶν ἐχρῶντο, οὐκ εἰς βραχὺ συνηγμένοις,
ἀλλὰ καλοῖς, εἰ τὸν νοῦν σκέπτοιτό τις, μὴ ἐπιδεικτικῶς 25
ἐξετάζων ἀλλ᾽ ἐπὶ τὴν χρείαν ἕκαστα ἀνάγων.

1 Σήβωσε *Dittenberger; Egermann (Sitz.ber. Wien. Ak. 214 p.53.1)*: Σίβοσσε *cod.*
15 ἐκεῖνοι *Arnim*: ἐκεῖ *cod.*   17 συνεβίων *Arnim* : συνεβίουν *cod. et Wehrli*
φησίν *Arnim*: φασίν *cod.*   20 τούτου *Arnim*: τούτων *cod.*   22 περιττοὺς]
περιττὰς *White*

37 Diogenes Laertius, Vitae philosophorum 1.40 (OCT t.1 p.16.21–6
Long)

περὶ δὴ τῶν ἑπτά—ἄξιον γὰρ ἐνταῦθα καθολικῶς κ᾽ἀκείνων
ἐπιμνησθῆναι—λόγοι φέρονται τοιοῦτοι. Δάμων ὁ Κυρηναῖος,

36 Vatican Codex 435, Plutarch's or Caecilius' *Roman Sayings*
    (*Hermes* v.27 [1892] p.119.37–120.26 Arnim)

The ancient Romans, Sebosus my fine fellow, did not wish to be
considered wise, so they did not pursue a reputation through cleverness of speeches or exceptional and persuasive sayings, which
some of the Greeks used and which have commonly been thought
to be regarded as even more credible than oracles, e.g. 'nothing in
excess', 'obey god', 'save time', 'know thyself', 'stand surety and
suffer greatly' and others similar to these—perhaps they are even
beneficial to those who obey them, and they do have something in
their shortness of expression that is pleasant and inviting. But to
Dicaearchus not even these are reputed to be by wise men, since
the ancients did not do philosophy with speech. Indeed (he thought)
that wisdom at that time was the practice of good deeds, but in time
the craft of popular speeches developed. Nowadays the one who
speaks persuasively appears to be a great philosopher, but in ancient times only the good man was a philosopher, even if he did not
create admired and popular speeches for himself. For (the ancients)
did not enquire whether they should practise politics or how, although they themselves did practise politics nobly, (nor did they
enquire) whether it was necessary to marry, but having married in
the manner in which they were supposed to marry, they lived together with their wives. These, he says, were the deeds of men and
the practices of the wise, but these proverbializings are a vulgar
matter. I believe your ancestors were also this way. For they wished
to be good and they achieved this by their deeds, but they neither
practised nor knew pithy and elegant sayings coined for the sake of
appearing exceptional. Indeed, like the reasons they used each time
they acted, so also were the words they used about them; they were
composed not for brevity, but they were noble—if one examines
their content, not by investigating their presentation but by recalling their usefulness on each occasion.

37 Diogenes Laertius, *Lives of the Philosophers* 1.40 (*OCT* v.1 p.16.21–
    6 Long)

Concerning the seven—for it is right to mention them in general
here—the following sorts of statements are made: Damon of Cyrene,

γεγραφὼς Περὶ τῶν φιλοσόφων, πᾶσιν ἐγκαλεῖ, μάλιστα δὲ τοῖς
ἑπτά· Ἀναξιμένης δέ φησι πάντας ἐπιθέσθαι ποιητικῇ. ὁ δὲ
Δικαίαρχος οὔτε σοφοὺς οὔτε φιλοσόφους φησὶν αὐτοὺς   5
γεγονέναι, συνετοὺς δέ τινας καὶ νομοθετικούς.

4 *Anaximenes, FGrH 72 F22*   4–5 *cf. Plato, Prot. 342a–343c et Cic., De am.*
2.7

38 Diogenes Laertius, Vitae philosophorum 1.41 (OCT t.1 p.17.9–18
Long)

στασιάζεται δὲ καὶ περὶ τοῦ ἀριθμοῦ αὐτῶν. Λεάνδριος μὲν
γὰρ ἀντὶ Κλεοβούλου καὶ Μύσωνος Λεώφαντον Γοργιάδα,
Λεβέδιον ἢ Ἐφέσιον, ἐγκρίνει καὶ Ἐπιμενίδην τὸν Κρῆτα·
Πλάτων δὲ ἐν Πρωταγόρᾳ Μύσωνα ἀντὶ Περιάνδρου· Ἔφορος
δὲ ἀντὶ Μύσωνος Ἀνάχαρσιν· οἱ δὲ καὶ Πυθαγόραν προσ-   5
γράφουσιν. Δικαίαρχος δὲ τέσσαρας ὡμολογημένους ἡμῖν
παραδίδωσι, Θαλῆν, Βίαντα, Πιττακὸν, Σόλωνα. ἄλλους δὲ
ὀνομάζει ἕξ, ὧν ἐκλέξασθαι τρεῖς, Ἀριστόδημον, Πάμφυλον,
Χίλωνα Λακεδαιμόνιον, Κλεόβουλον, Ἀνάχαρσιν, Περίανδρον.

3 *Epimenides, FGrH 492 F16*   4 *Plato, Protagoras 343a*   *Ephorus, FGrH*
70 *F182*

———————
1 Λεάνδριος *codd.* : Μαιάνδριος *Keil*   2 Γοργιάδα *Reiske* : γορσιάδα *BP¹* :
alii alia

39 Philodemus, De musica, PHerc. 1572, fr. 2.20–39 (Ricerche sui
Papiri Ercolanesi 1 [1969] 239a2–11 Rispoli)

... ἐξ ὧν δὲ παρατίθετ[αι]
[Δικ]αιάρχου λάβοι τις ἂν ὅσ[α βού-]
[λετ]αι πρὸς τὴν ἐνεστηκυ[ῖ-]
αν] ὑπόθεσιν [ἢ] τὸ τοὺς πα-
[λα]ιοὺς καὶ σοφὸν τὸν ὠ⟨ι⟩δὸ[ν]   5
νο]μίζειν, ὡς εἶναι δῆλον
[ἐκ] τοῦ παρὰ τῆι Κλυταιμνή-
[στραι κατ]αλειφθέντος· καὶ
[μάλιστ]α γνῶναί φασιν, ὅ[[δ]]ς [ἄν]
[τι τ]ούτων ἀκούση[ι], δι' οὗ γε   10

who wrote *On the Philosophers*, attacks everyone, but especially the seven; Anaximenes says that they all did poetry; Dicaearchus says that (the seven wise men) were neither wise men nor philosophers, but intelligent people and capable lawmakers.

38   Diogenes Laertius, *Lives of the Philosophers* 1.41 (*OCT* v.1 p.17.9– 18 Long)

There is dispute also about the number of (the seven wise men). Leandrius includes Leophantus, son of Gorgias, from Lebedus or Ephesus, and Epimenides of Crete in place of Cleobulus and Myson; Plato in the *Protagoras* includes Myson instead of Periander; Ephorus includes Anacharsis instead of Myson; others add Pythagoras also. Dicaearchus reports to us four who are agreed upon: Thales, Bias, Pittacus, and Solon. He names six others of whom three (he says) are to be selected, Aristodemus, Pamphylus and Chilon the Lacedaemonian, Cleoboulus, Anacharsis, and Periander.

39   Philodemus, *On Music*, *PHerc.* 1572, fr. 2.20–39 (*Ricerche sui Papiri Ercolanesi* 1 [1969] 239a2–11 Rispoli)

. . . from what he (Diogenes of Babylon) cites from Dicaearchus, one might derive as much as one wants for the present supposition: The ancients thought that the singer was also wise, as is clear from the one left with Clytemnestra; and they say that whoever hears any of these things recognizes this especially. Through him (the

[συμ]φωνεῖται καὶ πλείο-
[σι παρίσ]τα[τ]αι τὸ πρὸ⟨ς⟩ ταῖς ἄλ-
[λαις δυνάμ]εσιν τὸ μέλος καὶ
[στάσεων κ]αὶ ταραχῶν εἰ-
[ναι κ]αταπ[α]υστικόν, ὡς ἐπὶ   15
[τῶν ἀνθρώ]πων καὶ τῶν ζώι-
[ων φαίν]ε⟨σ⟩θαι καταπραυνο-
[μένω]ν· διὸ καὶ τὸν Ἀρχίλο-
[χον λ]έγειν "κηλῶ⟨ν⟩ται δ᾽ ὅτις
[ἀστ]ῶν ἀοιδαῖς."   20

5 cf. Philodem., De musica, PHerc. 225, fr. 22.13–20 (CE 19 [1989] 133 Delattre)
7–8 cf. Hom., Od. 3.267   18–19 Archilochus, fr. 253 West

2 Δικ]αίαρχου restituit Kemke   19 κηλῶ⟨ν⟩ται Gigante: κηλῶται pap. :
κηλεῖται Rispoli

40 Porphyrius, Vita Pythagorae 18–19 (CB p.44.1–45.3 des Places)

ἐπεὶ δὲ τῆς Ἰταλίας ἐπέβη καὶ ἐν Κρότωνι ἐγένετο, φησὶν ὁ
Δικαίαρχος, ὡς ἀνδρὸς ἀφικομένου πολυπλάνου τε καὶ περιττοῦ
καὶ κατὰ τὴν ἰδίαν φύσιν ὑπὸ τῆς τύχης εὖ κεχορηγημένου, τήν
τε γὰρ ἰδέαν εἶναι ἐλευθέριον καὶ μέγαν χάριν τε πλείστην καὶ
κόσμον ἐπί τε τῆς φωνῆς καὶ τοῦ ἤθους καὶ ἐπὶ τῶν ἄλλων   5
ἁπάντων ἔχειν, οὕτως διαθεῖναι τὴν Κροτωνιατῶν πόλιν, ὥστ᾽
ἐπεὶ τὸ τῶν γερόντων ἀρχεῖον ἐψυχαγώγησε πολλὰ καὶ καλὰ
διαλεχθείς, τοῖς νέοις πάλιν ἡβητικὰς ἐποιήσατο παραινέσεις
ὑπὸ τῶν ἀρχόντων κελευσθείς, μετὰ δὲ ταῦτα τοῖς παισὶν ἐκ τῶν
διδασκαλείων ἀθρόοις συνελθοῦσιν, εἶτα ταῖς γυναιξί, ⟨ἐπεὶ⟩   10
καὶ γυναικῶν σύλλογος αὐτῷ κατεσκευάσθη.

19   γενομένων δὲ τούτων μεγάλη περὶ αὐτὸν ηὐξήθη δόξα, καὶ
πολλοὺς μὲν ἔλαβεν ἐξ αὐτῆς τῆς πόλεως ὁμιλητὰς οὐ μόνον
ἄνδρας ἀλλὰ καὶ γυναῖκας ὧν μιᾶς γε Θεανοῦς καὶ διεβοήθη
τοὔνομα, πολλοὺς δ᾽ ἀπὸ τῆς σύνεγγυς βαρβάρου χώρας   15
βασιλεῖς τε καὶ δυνάστας. ἃ μὲν οὖν ἔλεγε τοῖς συνοῦσιν οὐδὲ
εἰς ἔχει φράσαι βεβαίως· καὶ γὰρ οὐδ᾽ ἡ τυχοῦσα ἦν παρ᾽ αὐτοῖς
σιωπή. μάλιστα μέντοι γνώριμα παρὰ πᾶσιν ἐγένετο πρῶτον μὲν
ὡς ἀθάνατον εἶναί φησι τὴν ψυχήν, εἶτα μεταβάλλουσαν εἰς
ἄλλα γένη ζώων, πρὸς δὲ τούτοις ὅτι κατὰ περιόδους τινὰς τὰ   20

singer), at any rate, song is made concordant and provides to rather many, in addition to its other powers, a damper on strife and distur- bances, as is seen both with regard to humans and animals, which are soothed (by it). For this reason Archilochus says, "each citizen is beguiled by songs."

40 Porphyry, *Life of Pythagoras* 18–19 (*CB* p.44.1–45.3 des Places)

Dicaearchus says that when (Pythagoras) arrived in Italy and came to be in Croton—as a man who had arrived after wandering far, was exceptional and was well endowed in his personal nature by fortune, for he had a great and free-born physique, much charm and beauty in his voice, character and everything else—he had such an effect on the city of the Crotoniates that after he had influenced the council of the elders with many fine arguments, he made ad- dresses suitable for their age in turn to the young, when bidden by the councillors, and after this to the children gathered in groups from the schools, then to women, when an assembly of women was created for him.

19   When these things happened, fame grew great around him and he won over many followers from this city, not only men but also women, one of whom, Theano at least, made a famous name for herself, and also many from the neighbouring non-Greek territory, both kings and rulers. What he said to those with him, however, it is not possible for anyone to say exactly, for there was no ordinary silence among them. However, it was especially well-known by all, first, that he said that the soul is immortal, then, that it transmi- grates into other kinds of animals, and in addition that what hap-

γενόμενά ποτε πάλιν γίνεται, νέον δ' οὐδὲν ἁπλῶς ἔστι, καὶ ὅτι
πάντα τὰ γινόμενα ἔμψυχα ὁμογενῆ δεῖ νομίζειν. φαίνεται γὰρ
εἰς τὴν Ἑλλάδα τὰ δόγματα πρῶτος κομίσαι ταῦτα Πυθαγόρας.

1–24 *FVS 14A8a*

5 ἐπὶ *(bis)*] ἀπὸ *Nauck*   10 ⟨ἐπεὶ⟩ *supplevit Westermann* : *om. des Places*   19
φησὶ *BM* : φασὶ *VLW*   21 γενόμενά *Westermann* : γινόμενά *codd.*   22 φαίνε-
ται] φέρεται *Nauck et des Places*

41A Porphyrius, Vita Pythagorae 56–7 (CB p.63.4–64.1 des Places)

Δικαίαρχος δὲ καὶ οἱ ἀκριβέστεροι καὶ τὸν Πυθαγόραν φασὶν
παρεῖναι τῇ ἐπιβουλῇ. Φερεκύδην γὰρ πρὸ τῆς ἐκ Σάμου
ἀπάρσεως τελευτῆσαι. τῶν δ' ἑταίρων ἀθρόους μὲν τετταράκοντα ἐν οἰκίᾳ τινὸς παρεδρεύοντας ληφθῆναι, τοὺς δὲ
πολλοὺς σποράδην κατὰ τὴν πόλιν ὡς ἔτυχον ἕκαστοι   5
διαφθαρῆναι. Πυθαγόραν δὲ κρατουμένων τῶν φίλων τὸ μὲν
πρῶτον εἰς Καυλωνίαν τὸν ὅρμον σωθῆναι, ἐκεῖθεν δὲ πάλιν εἰς
Λοκρούς. πυθομένους δὲ τοὺς Λοκροὺς τῶν γερόντων τινὰς ἐπὶ
τὰ τῆς χώρας ὅρια ἀποστεῖλαι. τούτους δὲ πρὸς αὐτὸν
ἀπαντήσαντας εἰπεῖν · "ἡμεῖς, ὦ Πυθαγόρα, σοφὸν μὲν ἄνδρα   10
σε καὶ δεινὸν ἀκούομεν. ἀλλ' ἐπεὶ τοῖς ἰδίοις νόμοις οὐθὲν
ἔχομεν ἐγκαλεῖν, αὐτοὶ μὲν ἐπὶ τῶν ὑπαρχόντων πειρασόμεθα
μένειν, σὺ δ' ἑτέρωθί που βάδιζε λαβὼν παρ' ἡμῶν εἴ του
κεχρημένος [τῶν ἀναγκαίων] τυγχάνεις." ἐπεὶ δ' ἀπὸ τῆς τῶν
Λοκρῶν πόλεως τὸν εἰρημένον ἀπηλλάγη τρόπον, εἰς Τάραντα   15
πλεῦσαι. πάλιν δὲ κἀκεῖ παραπλήσια παθόντα τοῖς περὶ
Κρότωνα εἰς Μεταπόντιον ἐλθεῖν. πανταχοῦ γὰρ ἐγένοντο
μεγάλαι στάσεις, ἃς ἔτι καὶ νῦν οἱ περὶ τοὺς τόπους μνημονεύ-
ουσί τε καὶ διηγοῦνται, τὰς ἐπὶ τῶν Πυθαγορείων καλοῦντες.
[Πυθαγόρειοι δ' ἐκλήθησαν ἡ σύστασις ἅπασα ἡ συνακολου-   20
57 θήσασα αὐτῷ.] ἐν δὲ τῇ περὶ Μεταπόντιον καὶ Πυθαγόραν αὐτὸν
λέγουσι τελευτῆσαι καταφυγόντα ἐπὶ τὸ Μουσῶν ἱερόν, σπάνει
τῶν ἀναγκαίων τεσσαράκοντα ἡμέρας διαμείναντα.

4 *cf. Iamblichus, De vita Pyth. 249; Plut., De genio Socratis 13 583A*

4 παρεδρεύοντας] συνεδρεύοντας *Nauck*   5 ἕκαστοι *Usener* : εἰς ἄστυ *codd.*
7 τὸν *Rittershusius* : τὴν *codd.*   14 τῶν ἀναγκαίων *expunxit Cobet*   20–1
Πυθαγόρειοι—αὐτῷ *secl. Nauck*

pens happens again at some time according to certain cycles, that, in short, there is nothing new, and that it is necessary to believe that all ensouled beings are of the same kind. For it appears that Pythagoras was the first to bring these teachings into Greece.

41A Porphyry, *Life of Pythagoras* 56–7 (*CB* p.63.4–64.1 des Places)

Dicaearchus and the more accurate reporters say that Pythagoras was present during the conspiracy. For Pherecydes died before ejection from Samos. Forty of his companions were caught sitting gathered at someone's house, but most perished scattered across the city, wherever each happened to be. When his friends were overwhelmed, Pythagoras at first reached refuge safely at Caulonia, and from there went to Locri. When the Locrians discovered this, they sent some of the elders to the borders of their territory. Approaching him, they said, "Pythagoras, we hear that you are a wise and crafty man. But since we have no accusation to make on the basis of our laws, we ourselves shall attempt to remain within the present (arrangements). But you, take from us if you happen to have need of something and go somewhere else." When he left the city of Locri in the aforesaid way, he sailed to Tarentum. There again he had experiences very similar to those at Croton, and went to Metapontum. For everywhere there were great revolutions, which they recall and discuss even now in those places, calling them the (revolutions) in the time of the Pythagoreans. [And the entire group
57 following him was called Pythagorean.] They say that Pythagoras died, because of a lack of necessities, in the area around Metapontum, having fled to the temple of the Muses and remained there forty days.

41B Diogenes Laertius, Vitae philosophorum 8.40 (OCT t.2 p.410.11–
13 Long)

φησὶ δὲ Δικαίαρχος τὸν Πυθαγόραν ἀποθανεῖν καταφυγόντα
εἰς τὸ ἐν Μεταποντίῳ ἱερὸν τῶν Μουσῶν, τετταράκοντα ἡμέρας
ἀσιτήσαντα.

1–3 cf. Themistius, 23 Sophistes 285b

1 καταφυγόντα BP: ἀποφυγόντα F

42 Gellius, Noctes Atticae 4.11.14 (OCT t.1 p.178.26–179.3 Marshall)

Pythagoram vero ipsum sicuti celebre est Euphorbum primo
fuisse dictasse, ita haec remotiora sunt his, quae Clearchus et
Dicaearchus memoriae tradiderunt, fuisse eum postea Pyrandrum,
deinde Aethaliden deinde feminam pulcra facie meretricem cui
nomen fuerat Alco.   5

2 Clearchus, fr. 10 Wehrli

3 Pyrandrum Wehrli: pirrandum vel pyrrandum codd. meliores: Pyrrum Hertz et
Marshall   4 Aethaliden Hosius alii: thalidena vel talidena codd.

43 Plutarchus, An seni sit gerenda res publica 26 796C–797A (BT
t.5.1 p.53.17–54.28 Hubert et Drexler)

παρὰ πάντα δὲ ταῦτα χρὴ μνημονεύειν, ὡς οὐκ ἔστι πολιτεύεσθαι μόνον τὸ ἄρχειν καὶ πρεσβεύειν καὶ μέγα βοᾶν ἐν
ἐκκλησίᾳ καὶ περὶ τὸ βῆμα βακχεύειν λέγοντας ἢ γράφοντας, ἃ
οἱ πολλοὶ τοῦ πολιτεύεσθαι νομίζουσιν, ὥσπερ ἀμέλει καὶ
D φιλοσοφεῖν τοὺς ἀπὸ τοῦ δίφρου διαλεγομένους καὶ σχολὰς ἐπὶ 5
βιβλίοις περαίνοντας. ἡ δὲ συνεχὴς ἐν ἔργοις καὶ πράξεσιν
ὁρωμένη καθ᾽ ἡμέραν ὁμαλῶς πολιτεία καὶ φιλοσοφία λέληθεν
αὐτούς. καὶ γὰρ τοὺς ἐν ταῖς στοαῖς ἀνακάμπτοντας περιπατεῖν
φασίν, ὡς ἔλεγε Δικαίαρχος, οὐκέτι δὲ τοὺς εἰς ἀγρὸν ἢ πρὸς
φίλον βαδίζοντας. ὅμοιον δ᾽ ἐστὶ τῷ φιλοσοφεῖν τὸ πολι- 10
τεύεσθαι. Σωκράτης γοῦν οὔτε βάθρα θεὶς οὔτ᾽ εἰς θρόνον
καθίσας οὔθ᾽ ὥραν διατριβῆς ἢ περιπάτου τοῖς γνωρίμοις
τεταγμένην φυλάττων, ἀλλὰ καὶ παίζων ὅτε τύχοι καὶ συμπίνων

41B Diogenes Laertius, *Lives of the Philosophers* 8.40 (*OCT* v.2 p.410.11–13 Long)

Dicaearchus says that Pythagoras died after having fled to the temple of the Muses at Metapontum, after he had starved for forty days.

42 Gellius, *Attic Nights* 4.11.14 (*OCT* v.1 p.178.26–179.3 Marshall)

Just as is very well known, Pythagoras said that he had previously been Euphorbus, but what is more obscure than this, which Clearchus and Dicaearchus have committed to record, is that he was later Pyrander, then Aethalides and then a woman prostitute with a beautiful face whose name was Alco.

43 Plutarch, *Old Men in Public Affairs* 26 796C–797A (*BT* v.5.1 p.53.17–54.28 Hubert and Drexler)

Above all it is necessary to recall that practising politics not only consists in holding office, going on embassies, shouting in the assembly and raving like a bacchant around the speaker's platform when speaking or proposing a law. That is what most think is char-
D acteristic of politics, just as they assume that those who discourse from a chair and write lectures in books are doing philosophy. But they overlook the regular practice of politics and philosophy that is daily seen alike in deeds and actions. For they say that those who are promenading up and down in the stoas are 'doing peripatetics', as Dicaearchus used to say, but those who stroll in the country or to a friend are not. Doing politics is like doing philosophy.[1] Socrates, at any rate, did philosophy, but he did not set up benches or sit on a throne. He did not keep a set time for conversing with his students

καὶ συστρατευόμενος ἐνίοις καὶ συναγοράζων, τέλος δὲ καὶ
[συν]δεδεμένος καὶ πίνων τὸ φάρμακον ἐφιλοσόφει, πρῶτος 15
E ἀποδείξας τὸν βίον ἅπαντι χρόνῳ καὶ μέρει καὶ πάθεσι καὶ
πράγμασιν ἁπλῶς ἅπασι φιλοσοφίαν δεχόμενον. οὕτω δὴ
διανοητέον καὶ περὶ πολιτείας, . . . τὸν δὲ κοινωνικὸν καὶ
φιλάνθρωπον καὶ φιλόπολιν καὶ κηδεμονικὸν καὶ πολιτικὸν
ἀληθῶς, κἂν μηδέποτε τὴν χλαμύδα περίθηται, πολιτευόμενον 20
ἀεὶ τῷ παρορμᾶν τοὺς δυναμένους, ὑφηγεῖσθαι τοῖς δεομένοις,
συμπαρεῖναι τοῖς βουλευομένοις, διατρέπειν τοὺς κακο-
πραγμονοῦντας, ἐπιρρωννύναι τοὺς εὐγνώμονας, φανερὸν εἶναι
μὴ παρέργως προσέχοντα τοῖς κοινοῖς μηδ᾽ ὅπου σπουδή τις ἢ
παράκλησις διὰ τὸ πρωτεῖον εἰς τὸ θέατρον βαδίζοντα καὶ τὸ 25
βουλευτήριον, ἄλλως δὲ διαγωγῆς χάριν ὡς ἐπὶ θέαν ἢ
797 ἀκρόασιν, ὅταν ἐπέλθῃ, παραγινόμενον, ἀλλά, κἂν μὴ
παραγένηται τῷ σώματι, παρόντα τῇ γνώμῃ καὶ τῷ πυνθάνεσθαι
τὰ μὲν ἀποδεχόμενον τοῖς δὲ δυσκολαίνοντα τῶν πραττο-
μένων. 30

7 ὁμαλῶς Coraes: οὐδαμῶς codd.   9 φασίν XJ῾γφα: φησίν Jy   15 συν
del. Wyttenbach   16 χρόνῳ καὶ μέρει ΒΠ: μέρει χρόνῳ O: μέρει χρόνου
dub. Man.: χρόνῳ del. Drexler

44 Zenobius, Epitome collectionum Lucilli Tarrhaei et Didymi 3.65
(CPG t.1 p.73.6–13 Leutsch et Schneidewin)

ἐν πίθῳ τὴν κεραμείαν μανθάνω· παροιμία ἐπὶ τῶν τὰς
πρώτας μαθήσεις ὑπερβαινόντων, ἁπτομένων δὲ εὐθέως τῶν
μειζόνων. ὡς εἴ τις μανθάνων κεραμεύειν, πρὶν μαθεῖν πίνακας
ἢ ἄλλο τι τῶν μικρῶν πλάττειν, πίθῳ ἐγχειροίη. Δικαίαρχος δέ
φησιν ἕτερόν τι δηλοῦν τὴν παροιμίαν, οἱονεὶ τὴν μελέτην ἐν 5
τοῖς ὁμοίοις ποιεῖσθαι, ὡς κυβερνήτης ἐπὶ τῆς νηὸς καὶ ἡνίοχος
ἐπὶ τῶν ἵππων.

5–7 cf. Arist., NE 2.1 1102a32–b12

1–7 Hesychius, Lexicon, s.v. ἐν πίθῳ (no. 3276 t.1 p.107.31–108.2 Latte)   1 cf.
Plato, Gorgias 514e6, Laches 187b et [Plut.], Prov. Alex. 112

1 μανθάνω] μανθάνεις B   3 μειζόνων] μεγάλων καὶ τελείων Hesychius
6 ὁμοίοις: οἰκείοις Hesychius   7 τῶν ἵππων: τοῦ ἵππου Hesychius

or walking with them. He did philosophy just as he happened to play and drink with them, serve in the military and share the market-place, and in the end, as he was imprisoned and drank poison.

E He was the first to demonstrate the life at all times and in every part, in all that he experienced and all that he did, that embraced philosophy without qualification. Surely we must have the same thoughts about politics . . . that the community-spirited, humane, patriotic, concerned and political individual, even if he never wears a *chlamys*, is always truly politically active by advising those in power, guiding the needy, standing by those in deliberation, converting those doing wrong, and supporting those with good judgments; he clearly does not give (only) casual attention to public concerns, and whenever some serious matter arises, or a summons, he does not go to the theater and to the council, because of the first prize, being there for the sake of entertainment with no purpose, as

797 if (he were) at a performance or recitation, but, even if he cannot be there physically, he is present in thought and interest, approving some of the things being done and showing displeasure at others.

[1] Since Dicaearchus speaks approvingly of the ancients who identified wisdom with the practice of doing good deeds (see **36**.11), it seems that by *homoion* he means a closer identificaiton than we might assume: for Dicaearchus doing philosophy and politics appear not just similar, but one and the same. Cf. **44**.4–7.

44 Zenobius, *Summary of the Collections of Lucillus Tarrhaeus and Didymus* 3.65 (*CPG* v.1 p.73.6–13 Leutsch and Schneidewin)

I learn pottery on a wine-jar: A saying referring to those who skip over their first lessons and immediately attempt greater things. For example, if someone is learning to do pottery and before learning how to form tablets or some other small object tried his hand at a wine-jar. Dicaearchus says that the saying means something else, such as getting practice in similar things, as a helmsman on a ship and a charioteer with horses.

45 Plutarchus, Quaestiones convivales 8.2 719A–B (BT t.4 p.262.19–263.7 Hubert)

οὐ γάρ τί που καὶ θεὸς δεῖται μαθήματος οἷον ὀργάνου στρέφοντος ἀπὸ τῶν γενητῶν καὶ περιάγοντος ἐπὶ τὰ ὄντα τὴν διάνοιαν· ἐν αὐτῷ γὰρ ἔστιν ἐκεῖνα καὶ σὺν αὐτῷ καὶ περὶ αὐτόν. ἀλλ' ὅρα μή τι σοι προσῆκον ὁ Πλάτων καὶ οἰκεῖον αἰνιττόμενος λέληθεν, ἅτε δὴ τῷ Σωκράτει τὸν Λυκοῦργον ἀναμιγνὺς οὐχ 5 ἧττον ἢ τὸν Πυθαγόραν ⟨ὡς⟩ ᾤετο Δικαίαχος. ὁ γὰρ Λυκοῦργος
B οἶσθα δήπουθεν ὅτι τὴν ἀριθμητικὴν ἀναλογίαν, ὡς δημοκρατικὴν καὶ ὀχλικὴν οὖσαν, ἐξέβαλεν ἐκ τῆς Λακεδαίμονος, ἐπεισήγαγεν δὲ τὴν γεωμετρικήν, ὀλιγαρχίᾳ σώφρονι καὶ βασιλείᾳ νομίμῃ πρέπουσαν· ἡ μὲν γὰρ ἀριθμῷ τὸ ἴσον ἡ δὲ 10 λόγῳ τὸ κατ' ἀξίαν ἀπονέμει.

3 ἐκεῖνα *Valckenaer*: ἐκείνῳ *codd. et Hubert*   6 ὡς *supplevit Osann*

46A Philodemus, Academicorum historia, PHerc. 1021, col. 1.1–43 (p.148.1–150.13 Gaiser)

"... ἐνδε[χ]ομενων [μὲ]ν ἐπανεκαίνισε πάλιν ἅπασαν,
τήν τ' ἐ[παίδο]υσ[αν δι]ὰ τοῦτ'
ἐν τοῖς [λ]όγοις εὐρυθμίαν
προσέλαβεν, αὐτὸς δὲ πολ-   5
λὰ ἐπεισηνέγκατο ἴδ[ια, δι' ὧ]ν
–εἴ γε διὰ παρρη[σίας δεῖ τ]ὰ γ[ε]-
νόμενα λέγειν–πλ[εῖστον]
δὴ τῶν πάντων [ἀνθρ]ώ-
πων οὗτος εὔξησε[ν φ]ιλο-   10
σοφίαν καὶ κατέλυσ[ε]. προ-
[ετ]ρέψατο μὲγ γὰρ ἀπε[ίρ]ου[ς]
ὡς εἰπεῖν ἐπ' αὐτὴν διὰ
τῆς ἀναγραφῆς τῶν λ[ό]-
[γω]ν. ἐπιπολ[α]ίως δὲ καί   15
[τινας] ἐπο[ίησ]ε φιλοσοφεῖν
φανερὰν ἐκτρέ[πων] εἰ[ς]
τρί[βον]. φησὶ δ' ὅτι '[θεὸς τὸν ἀ]-
[ριθμὸν] καὶ τὴ[ν τ]ῶν ἄσ[τρων]

45 Plutarch, *Table Talk* 8.2 719A–B (*BT* v.4 p.262.19–263.7 Hubert)

For a god surely has no need at all for mathematics as some instrument for turning his mind away from created things and directing it around to what really exists. For those things exist in him, with him and regarding him. But see whether Plato, without your notice, may enigmatically have suggested something proper and familiar to you, since he mixed Lycurgus no less than Pythagoras with Socrates, <as> Dicaearchus thought. For I suppose you know
B that Lycurgus expelled the arithmetic model from Lacedaemon as being democratic and mob-oriented. He introduced the geometric, since it fits a temperate oligarchy and a lawful monarchy. For the one distributes equality by number, the other an amount according to worth by means of proportion.

46A Philodemus, *History of the Academics*, *PHerc.* 1021, col. 1.1-43 (p.148.1–150.13 Gaiser)[1]

"... Out of what he received, (Plato) renewed (philosophy) again entirely, and added the pleasant rhythm that accompanies it in his dialogues on account of this.[2] But he himself introduced many of his own thoughts, through which—since I must say frankly what happened—this man of all people most strengthened philosophy and subverted it. For he converted (so to speak) countless people to it through the recording of his dialogues. However, he also made some do philosophy superficially by diverting them onto a ready-made path. He says, 'god gave number and the sight of the stars as a guide for doing philosophy', so that those who neither learned

[ὄψιν τ]οῦ φιλ[οσ]οφεῖν ἐνδό-   20
σιμον ἔδω[κεν],' ὥστε μήτε [με]-
μαθηκότα[ς φα]σμάτων
τε μηδὲν μ[ήπ]οτ[ε βουλομέ]-
νους μαθε[ῖν οὐ] μόνον εἰς
τὸ τῶν φιλ[οδόξων αὐτ]οὺς   25
καταριθμε[ῖ πλῆθος, ἀ]λλὰ
καὶ π[λημμελεῖς νομίζει]. φα-
[νερῶς δ' ὁρμᾶν ἔ]ξεσ[τιν ε]ἰς
[τὴν τρίβον ἐκεί]νη[ν], ὅ[τι] σο-
[φῶς γέγραφε· 'χρ]ὴ τοὺ[ς] ἀν[θρ]ώ-   30
[πους τὸν Ἔρωτα τιμᾶν καὶ]
[τὰ ἐρωτικὰ διαφερόντως]
[ἀσκεῖν τῶι τ' Ἔρωτι πάντας]
ἀ[εὶ] πε[ί]θεσθαι,' [ὥσ]τε εἰς
ἐκεῖνο[ν π]αρασπώμε-   35
νο[ί] τι[νες] ἱκανὸν ἔχειν
πρόβλη[μ]α τῆς ἰδίας ἀμαθίας νομ[ίζ]ουσιν, μᾶλλον δὲ
ἀ[ρε]τ[ῆς κτῆσ]ιν, μόνοι τὴν
τοῦ γ[ενναίο]υ καὶ σοφωτά-   40
του διδ[ασκάλο]υ κατανοοῦν-
τες πα[ραίνεσιν.]" ὃ μὲν ἀπέ-
[δειξεν οὗτος αὐ]τοῦ κατα-

1–6 cf. Them., 26 318c–319a   18–27 cf. Plat., Resp. 7 522c–534e et 531d–
532d, Tim. 47a–c; Epinomis 976c-978b   30–4 cf. Plat., Symp. 212b

ante 1 οὕτω τὴν φιλοσοφίαν ἐκ τῶν Gaiser: ἐκ τῶν Mekler: διὰ τῶν Lasserre
1 [μὲ]ν Lasserre, Gaiser, Dorandi: [οὗ]ν Arnim et Mekler   3 ἐ[παίδο]υσ[αν
Gaiser: ἐ[λλείπο]υσ[αν Arnim, Mekler, Lasserre   8 πλ[εῖστον] Praechter et
Gaiser: πρ[ῶτος Gomperz, Mekler, Lasserre   11 κατέλυσ[ε Mekler, Dorandi,
Lasserre: κατήνυσ[ε Gaiser   15–16 καί | [τινας] Gaiser: κ. [ραι|θύμως
Mekler: [ραῖον] Lasserre   39 ἀ[ρε]τ[ῆς κτῆσ]ιν Gaiser: ἀ[μαρ]τ[άνουσ]ιν
Buecheler, Mekler, Lasserre

46B Philodemus, Academicorum historia, PHerc. 1021, col. Y.1–41
(p.152.1–154.7 Gaiser)

[γνοὺς τ]ὸ δὲ συνά[ψα]ς παρέγρα[ψε]·
"κα[τε]νενόητο δέ" φη[σ]ί "καὶ τῶν μα-

nor ever wanted to learn anything from heavenly signs (Plato) not only counted among those who loved simply appearance, but also thought offensive. But clearly it is possible to set people onto that ready-made path, because he has wisely written, 'it is necessary for people to honor Love and to cultivate the elements of Love especially and for everyone always to obey Love', so that those who are drawn to (Love) believe that they have a sufficient defense for their own lack of learning, or rather a store of virtue (such that) they alone understand the teaching of the noble and most wise teacher (Plato)."

This was one thing (Dicaearchus) pointed out in criticizing (Plato) . . .

[1] The Greekless reader of these texts should be alerted that the Greek text of Gaiser on which this translation is based includes many conjectures, only a few of which have gained widespread scholarly support (see Dorandi in this volume). Gaiser's conjectures do allow, however, a readability that is scarcely possible in the editions of more cautious editors.

[2] It is unclear what the "this" refers to. Gaiser suggests that it refers somehow to the combining of Pythagorean and Socratic philosophy. See **45**.

46B Philodemus, *History of the Academics*, *PHerc*. 1021, col. Y.1-41 (p.152.1–154.7 Gaiser)

And after he had connected the other part he (?)[1] wrote in addition: "much progress was also acknowledged," he said, "in math-

θημάτων ἐπίδοσις πολλὴ κατ᾽ ἐκεῖ-
ν[ον] τὸν χρόνον ἀρχιτεκτονοῦντο[ς]
μ[ὲ]ν καὶ προβλήματ[α] διδόντος τοῦ   5
Π[λ]άτωνος, ζητούντων δὲ μετὰ σπου-
[δῆ]ς αὐτὰ τῶν μαθηματικῶν. τοιγὰρ
[ταύ]τη(ι) [τὰ] περὶ μετρολογίαν ἦλθεν
[ἐπὶ κορυ]φὴν τότε πρῶτον καὶ τὰ περὶ
[τοὺς ὁρι]σμοὺς προβλήματα τῶν περὶ   10
Ε[ὔδο]ξον μεταστησάντων τὸν ἀ[φ᾽ Ἱπ]-
πο[κρά]τους ἀρχαισμόν. ἔλαβε [δὲ καὶ]
ἡ γε[ωμ]ετρία πολλὴν ἐπίδοσιν· ἐγε[ν]-
νήθ[η] γὰρ καὶ ἡ ἀνάλυσις καὶ τὸ περὶ
διορισμοὺς λῆμ[μα], καὶ ὅλω[ς] τὰ π[ερὶ]   15
[τ]ὴν γεωμετρίαν ἐπὶ πολὺ π[ρο]ήν[εγ]-
κ[ον· οὐ]δέν τε [ὀπ]τ[ικ]ὴ καὶ μη[χ]ανικ[ή]
[γ᾽ ἦσα]ν [ἀ]μ[ε]λεῖς. τὴν ἅπα[σαν δὲ] σ[υλ]-
λ[ο]γὴν τῶν το[ιού]τω[ν, ἐξ ἧς ἔσχον ὁ]-
[ν]ήσιμα συχνοὶ [τῶν σπε]ρμολόγων,   20
αὐτῶν ἕνε[κ᾽ ἐποίησ]αν· σχεδὸν γὰ[ρ]
ἦν φοιτητῶ[ν γένος] ἄλλο, καὶ τῶ[ν]
[γ]ε θερῶν τὸ ἰδ[ιωτικὸν] ἀνέλαβον.
[ο]ὖ μετα[λαβόντες δὲ τὰ πρά]γματ[α]
[ἴ]σην καὶ [κοινὴν σχολὴν ἦγον, κ]αὶ   25
τοῦτον τ[ὸν βίον τότε κατ]ελ[ά]βο[ν]-
[το] πρ[ῶτοι]· δι[είλοντο γὰρ] ἄλλο
[μὲν] ἀνθρώπω[ν ἐλευθέρων ἀ]ληθ[ι]-
[νὴ]ν συνουσία[ν κοινωνίαν τ᾽ εἶναι],
ἄ[λλο] δὲ Δάων καὶ [Γετῶν ἰσον]ομί[αν].   30
τἀ[λ]ηθ[ὲς δὲ] καὶ [πρ]ὸς τοῦτο [τὰ μαθή]-
μ[ατ᾽] ἀπήρτησαν τῶν ἀναγ[καί]ων·
οἳ γ[ὰ]ρ περὶ τῶν [ὀν]ησίμων [νο]ο]ῦσι, δ]ικαί-
ως ε[ἶ]ναι δοκοῦσιν οἰκοτριβές. [τῆι δὲ γρα]-
φικῆ[ι] δυνάμενος ὁ Πλάτων πολλ[οὺς ἐ]-   35
θάρ[συ]νε καὶ τῶν ἀπόντων τοῖς [βυβ]λίοι[ς].
ἰδιώτατ᾽—οἶδ᾽ οὖν—τῶν ἀπερηρει[κό]των
ἥ τε [Ἀξι]οθέα συνπαρεγέν[ετο, καὶ σ]οφή
γ᾽ οὖ[ν ἦ]ν ἀνδρὸς ἐπ᾽ ἀ[ρε]τῆ[ι πάντ᾽ἐπ]ι-
ν[οήσα]σα καὶ γνοῦσα, καὶ δὴ κοιν[ω]ν[ή]σ[α]-   40

ematics at that time, since Plato was designing and setting out problems and the mathematicians were investigating them seriously. Consequently, in this way the theory of measurement and the problems of definition first reached a high point then, once those associated with Eudoxus revised the older style of Hippocrates. Geometry also made much progress then; for the analytical method was created then and the auxiliary theorem regarding definitions, and, in general, they brought the practice of geometry a great step forward. And in no way were optics and mechanics ignored. They created the entire collection of such (inquiries) as these for their own sake, from which a great many scavengers took profit. For there was another sort among those in attendance, and they took a private interest in their rewards. Since they took no part in (public) affairs, they pursued an equal and shared scholarship, and they were at that time the first who attained this lifestyle. For they distinguished true communalism and sharing of free men from the equality of the Dacians and Getae.[2] They separated the truth and studies directed toward it from those pursuits necessary (for living). For those who think (only) about what is useful are justly considered like household servants. Through the power of his writing, Plato even inspired many at a distance with books. Most peculiarly—I am aware—among those who submitted themselves (to his writings), Axiothea joined in, and she was indeed a wise woman with regard to every quality of a man, since she reflected and understood, and in fact shared in wearing a worn-out cloak without a

[σα τοῦ τ]ρ̣ίβωνο[ς ἄ]νευ αἰσ[χύνης· ἐ]φοίτ[α]

2–18 cf. Procl., In primum Euclidis Elementorum librum, p.66.4–68.4 Friedlein
14 cf. Diog. Laert. 3.24 et Procl., In prim. Eucl. El. libr., p.211.18–23   34–6 cf.
Epist. Socraticorum 22.2   35–7 PHerc. 164, fr. 1 Dorandi

1 συνά[ψα]ς Gaiser: συνά[γω]ν Lasserre   1–2 παρέγρα[ψε] Ικα[τε] Gaiser:
παρέγρα|ψα [κατε] Dorandi

46C Philodemus, Academicorum historia, PHerc. 1021, col. 2.1–8
(p.157.1–8 Gaiser)

"... δὲ [ἄγνωστος τοῖς] ἄλλοις. [ὁ δὲ]
ἀτ[έλειαν ἐποίει φι]λανθ[ρ]ω-
πίαν [πᾶσι δ]ούς, ὅ[τι] προί[ε]-
το ἴσ[οι]ς ἴσα." τοιαῦτα γεγραφότο[ς Δ]ικαιάρχου, Φιλόχ[ο]-   5
ρος ἐν τῶι τῆς ʼΑτθ[ί]δ[ος] ἕ-
κτωι παρέ⟨ι⟩παι[σ]εν ἐπὶ τὸ [ὄνο]-
[μα τ]αῦτ'·

7 παρέ⟨ι⟩παι[σ]εν Mekler et Gaiser: παρέπιπτεν Croenert et Jacoby

47 Diogenes Laertius, Vitae philosophorum 3.4 (OCT t.1 p.122.13–
23 Long)

καὶ ἐπαιδεύθη μὲν γράμματα παρὰ Διονυσίῳ, οὗ καὶ
μνημονεύει ἐν τοῖς ʼΑντερασταῖς. ἐγυμνάσατο δὲ παρὰ
ʼΑρίστωνι τῷ ʼΑργείῳ παλαιστῇ ... εἰσὶ δ᾽ οἳ καὶ παλαῖσαί φασιν
αὐτὸν Ἰσθμοῖ, καθὰ καὶ Δικαίαρχος ἐν πρώτῳ Περὶ βίων, καὶ
γραφικῆς ἐπιμεληθῆναι καὶ ποιήματα γράψαι, πρῶτον μὲν 5
διθυράμβους, ἔπειτα καὶ μέλη καὶ τραγῳδίας.

1–2 Plato, Amatores 132A   2–4 cf. Apul., De Plat. 1.2

5 ἐπιμεληθῆναι ... γράψαι BP: ἐπεμελήθη ... ἔγραψε F

48 Diogenes Laertius, Vitae philosophorum 3.38 (OCT t.1 p.137.22–
5 Long)

λόγος δὲ πρῶτον γράψαι αὐτὸν τὸν Φαῖδρον. καὶ γὰρ ἔχειν

sense of shame. But she attended . . . "

¹ The consensus of most scholars (see Dorandi and White in this collection) is that despite Gaiser's intuitions, the source of this text is not Dicaearchus but Philip of Opus.

² Cultures considered uncivilized and servile by the Greeks.

46C Philodemus, *History of the Academics*, *PHerc.* 1021, col. 2.1-8 (p.157.1–8 Gaiser)

" . . . without being recognized by the others. (Plato) sometimes made a payment exemption, and was benevolent to everyone, because he freely gave 'equal for equals'." Although Dicaearchus has written these sorts of things, Philochorus in the 6th book of his *Atthis* mocked Plato's name, saying . . .

47 Diogenes Laertius, *Lives of the Philosophers* 3.4 (*OCT* v.1 p.122.13–23 Long)

(Plato) was taught his letters at the school of Dionysius, whom he also recalls in his *Rival Lovers*. He did gymnastics with Ariston of Argos the wrestler... There are others who say that he wrestled in the Isthmian games, like Dicaearchus in the first book *On Lives*, and that he practised painting and writing poetry, first dithyrambs, then also lyric poems and tragedies.

48 Diogenes Laertius, *Lives of the Philosophers* 3.38 (*OCT* v.1 p.137.22–5 Long)

There is an account that (Plato) wrote the *Phaedrus* first. For

μειρακιῶδές τι τὸ πρόβλημα. Δικαίαρχος δὲ καὶ τὸν τρόπον τῆς γραφῆς ὅλον ἐπιμέμφεται ὡς φορτικόν.

1 ἔχειν *B*: ἔχει *FP*

49 Cicero, Tusculanae disputationes 4.71 (BT p.398.1–5 Pohlenz)

atque horum omnium lubidinosos esse amores videmus: philosophi sumus exorti, et auctore quidem nostro Platone, quem non iniuria Dicaearchus accusat, qui amori auctoritatem tribueremus.

2 et] ex *G¹*

50 Diogenes Laertius, Vitae philosophorum 3.46 (OCT t.1 p.140.19–141.3 Long)

μαθηταὶ δ᾽αὐτοῦ... καὶ ἄλλοι πλείους, σὺν οἷς καὶ γυναῖκες δύο, Λασθένεια Μαντινικὴ καὶ ᾽Αξιοθέα Φλειασία, ἣ καὶ ἀνδρεῖα ἠμπίσχετο, ὥς φησι Δικαίαρχος.

1–2 *cf. Diogenes Laertius, Vitae 4.2*

2 Λασθένεια *Seminarii Basil. sodales*: Λανθάνεια *codd.*

51 Philodemus, Academicorum historia, PHerc. 164, fr. 22.1–7 = PHerc. 1021, col. 11.17–21 (p.179.15–21 et 225 Dorandi)

```
        ] υπ....[
      ]περασιακον .[
   Δικ]αίαρχός φησιν
   [.]ιοντα. ἄλλα τε
   δειξάμενος διὰ
   τόλμης ἔργα κα[λὰ
           ]εν[
```

In PHerc. 1021, col. 11.17–21 haec tantum leguntur: ἀ]ποδειξάμ[ενος ǀ διὰ τῆς τόλ]μης ἔργα κα[λὰ

the subject has something youthful about it. But Dicaearchus criticizes the whole manner of the writing on the grounds that it is vulgar.

49 Cicero, *Tusculan Disputations* 4.71 (*BT* p.398.1–5 Pohlenz)

But we see that the love poetry of all of these (Alcaeus, Anacreon,
Ibycus) is lustful: we philosophers have arisen, indeed under the
authority of our Plato—whom Dicaearchus criticizes not unjustly—
to give authority to love.

50 Diogenes Laertius, *Lives of the Philosophers* 3.46 (*OCT* v.1
p.140.19–141.3 Long)

Students of (Plato)… and many others, including two women,
Lastheneia of Mantinea and Axiothea of Phlius, who, Dicaearchus
says, used to wear men's clothing.

51 Philodemus, *History of the Academics*, *PHerc*. 164, fr. 22.1–7 =
PHerc. 1021, col. 11.19–21 (p.179.1–5 and 225 Dorandi)

. . .
. . .
. . . Dicaearchus says . . .
Because (Chaeron)[1] had demonstrated
other fine deeds through his
boldness . . .

---

[1] Chaeron, a student of Plato, is the subject of this part of Philodemus' work.

52 Philodemus, De Stoicis, PHerc. 155, fr. 15 (CE 12 [1982] 104.29 Dorandi)

καὶ Δ]ικαίαρχο[ς]
    ]κ[. .]ιτου βίου σημ[αί
νει   ]αριστ[

1–2 διὰ τοῦ Ἡρα]κ[λε]ίτου *Croenert*   3 Ἀριστ *Croenert*

De humana vita

53 Censorinus, De die natali 4.2–4 (BT p.4.18–5.10 Sallman)

  alii semper homines fuisse nec umquam nisi ex hominibus natos, atque eorum generi caput exordiumque nullum extitisse arbitrati sunt, alii vero fuisse tempus cum homines non essent, et his ortum
3 aliquem principiumque natura tributum. sed prior illa sententia, qua semper humanum genus fuisse creditur, auctores habet Pythagoran 5 Samium et Occelum Lucanum et Archytan Tarentinum omnesque adeo Pythagoricos. sed et Plato Atheniensis et Xenocrates et Dicaearchus Messenius itemque antiquae Academiae philosophi non aliud videntur opinati, Aristoteles quoque Stagirites et Theophrastus multique praeterea non ignobiles Peripatetici idem 10 scripserunt eiusque rei exemplum dicunt quo negant omnino posse reperiri, avesne ante an ova generata sint, cum et ovum sine ave et
4 avis sine ovo gigni non possit. itaque et omnium, quae in sempiterno isto mundo semper fuerunt futuraque sunt, aiunt principium fuisse nullum, sed orbem esse quendam generantium nascentiumque, in 15 quo unius cuiusque geniti initium simul et finis esse videatur.

6 *Occelus, FVS 48 A2*   *Archytas deest FVS 47*   7 *Plato, cf. Leges 6 781E7*
Xenocrates, fr. 59 Heinze   9 *Aristoteles, De gen. anim. 2.1 731b35–36*
Theophrastus, 185 FHS&G

---

5 creditur] traditur *Wehrli*   6 Occelum *Diels*: Ocellum *Canter et Sallman*:
occeium *CP alii codices habent alia*   Archytan *edd.* : adrenytan *CP*: architam
V: archita *I*   11 exemplum *Giusta*: exempla *codd.*   16 quo *Sallman*: quod
codd. edd.

52 Philodemus, *On the Stoics*, *PHerc.* 155, fr. 15 (*CE* 12 [1982] 104.29 Dorandi)

> . . . and Dicaearchus . . .
> of life indicates . . .

Cultural History

53 Censorinus, *About the Day of Birth* 4.2–4 (*BT* p.4.18–5.10 Sallman)

Some have thought that human beings have always existed and have never been born except from human beings, and that there has been no inception or origin of their species; others, however, (say) that there was a time when human beings did not exist, and that
3 some origin and beginning was assigned to them by nature. The former opinion, according to which the human race is believed to have existed always, has as its supporters Pythagoras of Samos and Occelus of Lucania and Archytas of Tarentum and absolutely all of the Pythagoreans. Moreover Plato the Athenian and Xenocrates and Dicaearchus of Messana and likewise the (other) philosophers of the Old Academy do not seem to have held a different opinion; and Aristotle of Stagira too and Theophrastus and many not undistinguished Peripatetics besides wrote the same. And as an illustration of this point they say that it is altogether impossible to find out whether birds or eggs were created first, since it is the case both that the egg cannot come to be without the bird and that the bird
4 cannot come to be without the egg. And so they say that of all the things that have always existed in this eternal universe and always will exist, there has been no beginning; rather, there is a certain cycle of those who produce and of those who are born, in which the beginning and the end of each and everything that is begotten seem to coincide.

54 Varro, De re rustica 2.1.3–9 (CB t.2 p.13.7–16.9 Heurgon)

   igitur, inquam, et homines et pecudes cum semper fuisse sit
necesse natura—sive enim aliquod fuit principium generandi
animalium, ut putavit Thales Milesius et Zeno Citieus, sive contra
principium horum exstitit nullum, ut credidit Pythagoras Samius et
Aristoteles Stagirites—necesse est humanae vitae a summa memoria   5
gradatim descendisse ad hanc aetatem ut scribit Dicaearchus, et
summum gradum fuisse naturalem, cum viverent homines ex iis re-
4 bus, quae inviolata ultro ferret terra; ex hac vita in secundam
descendisse pastoriciam e feris atque agrestibus, ut arboribus ac
virgultis [ac] decarpendo glandem, arbu[s]tum, mora, poma   10
colligerent ad usum, sic ex animalibus cum propter eandem utilitatem quae possent silvestria deprenderent ac concluderent et man-
suescerent. in quis primum non sine causa putant oves assumptas et
propter utilitatem et propter <p>laciditatem. maxime enim hae
natura quietae et aptissimae ad vitam hominum. ad cibum enim lacte   15
5 et caseum adhibitum, ad corpus vestitum et pelles attulerunt. tertio
denique gradu a vita pastorali ad agri culturam descenderunt, in qua
ex duobus gradibus superioribus retinuerunt multa, et quo descend-
erant, ibi processerunt longe, dum ad nos perveniret. etiam nunc in
locis multis genera pecudum ferarum sint aliquot, ab ovibus, ut in   20
Phrygia, ubi greges videntur conplures, in Samothrace caprarum,
quas Latine rotas appellant. sunt enim in Italia circum Fiscellum et
Tetricam montes multae. de subus nemini ignotum, nisi qui apros
non putat sues vocari. boves perferi etiam nunc sunt multi in
Dardanica et Maedica et Thracia, asini feri in Phrygia et <Ly>caonia,   25
equi feri in Hispania citeriore regionibus aliquot.
6   origo, quam dixi; dignitas, quam dicam. de antiquis inlustrissimus
quisque pastor erat, ut ostendit et Graeca et Latina lingua et veteres
poetae, qui alios vocant polyarnas, alios polymelos, alios polybutas;

54 Varro, *On Farming* 2.1.3–9 (*CB* v.2 p.13.7–16.9 Heurgon)

"Therefore," I said, "humans and domesticated animals must always have existed by nature—for whether there was some beginning of generation for animals, as Thales of Miletus and Zeno of Citium thought, or there existed no beginning for them, as Pythagoras of Samos and Aristotle of Stagira believed, human life must have come down by steps from the earliest history until our time, as Dicaearchus writes, and the earliest stage was natural, when humans lived from those things that the inviolate earth bore spon-

4 taneously. From this mode of life they must have descended to the second, pastoral mode, in which, by plucking from wild and woodland trees and shrubs acorns, arbutus berries and mulberries and (other) fruits, they made a store for (later) use. Likewise toward the same purpose, they captured such wild animals as they could and shut them up and tamed them. Among these they believe, not without reason, that sheep were gathered because of their usefulness and gentleness. For they were especially quiet by nature and fit very well with the human lifestyle. Milk and cheese were added to the (humans') food, and for clothing the body (the sheep) fur-

5 nished their skins. Finally, in the third stage they arrived from the pastoral life to the agricultural, in which they maintained many things from the previous two stages and then progressed for a long time in that stage in which they had descended until it arrived at our civilization. Even now in many places there are several kinds of wild herds, such as sheep, as in Phrygia, where many flocks are seen; in Samothrace (many flocks) of goats (are seen), which they call *rotae* in Latin.[1] There are indeed many of them in Italy around the mountains Fiscellus and Tetrica. Everyone knows about the wild pigs, except those who believe that wild boars are not properly called pigs. There are also many very wild bulls now in Dardania and Maedica and Thrace, wild asses in Phrygia and Lyconia and wild horses in some areas of Hither Spain.

6 I have spoken (so far) about the origin (of agriculture); I shall now speak of its dignity. From ancient times every famous man was a shepherd, as both the Greek and Latin shows and the older poets, who called some men 'rich in sheep,' others 'rich in goats'; and others 'rich in oxen'; they reported that the sheep themselves

qui ipsas pecudes propter caritatem aureas habuisse pelles 30
tradiderunt, ut Argis, Atreus quam sibi Thyesten subduxe queritur;
ut in Colchide <ad> Aeetam, ad cuius arietis pellem profecti regio
genere dicuntur Argonautae; ut in Libya ad Hesperidas, unde aurea
mala, id est secundum antiquam consuetudinem capras et oves,
[quas] Hercules ex Africa in Graeciam exportavit. eas enim <a> 35
7 sua voce Graeci appellarunt mela. nec multo secus nostri ab eadem
voce sed ab alia littera (vox earum non me sed be sonare videtur)
oves baelare vocem efferentes dicunt, e quo post balare extrita littera,
ut in multis. quod si apud antiquos non magnae dignitatis pecus
esset, in caelo describendo astrologi non appellassent eorum 40
vocabulis signa, quae non modo non dubitarunt ponere, sed etiam
ab iis principibus duodecim signa multi numerant, ab Ariete et Tauro,
cum ea praeponerent Apollini et Herculi. ii enim dei ea secuntur,
8 sed appellantur Gemini. nec satis putarunt de duodecim signis
sextam partem obtinere pecudum nomina, nisi adiecissent, ut 45
quartam tenere<n>t, Capricornum. praeterea a pecuariis addiderunt
Capram, Haedos, Canes. an non etiam item in mari terraque ab his
regiones notae [a pecore], in mari, quod nominaverunt a capris
Aeg<a>eum pelagus, ad Syriam montem Taurum, in Sabinis
Cantherium montem, <Bosporum> unum Thracium, alterum 50
9 Ci<m>merium? nonne in terris multa, ut oppidum in Graecia
Hippion Argos? denique non Italia a vitulis, ut scribit Piso?

1 pecudes *m*: pecu (pecd) *vel* pecua *ceteri codd.*   10 ac *expunxit Iucundus*
[s] *expunxit Politian.*   14 p *supplevit Politian.*   19 ad nos *Victorius*: annus
codd.   22 Latine rotas] platycerotae *Scaliger*: strepsicerotae *Schneider*   25
Lycaonia *Plinius*: chaonia *codd.*   32 ad Aeetam *Keil*: actam *codd.*   33 Libya
Politian.: libro *codd.*   35 quas *expunxit Gesner*   a *supplevit Ursinus*   46
n *supplevit Iucundus*   47 an non *Politian.*: anno *codd.*   48 regiones A^2:
regionibus VA^1bm, *edd.* -num *Iuc.*   a pecore *expunxit Gesner*   50 Bosporum
supplevit Politian.

55   Varro, De re rustica 1.2.15–16 (CB t.1 p.16.18–17.6 Heurgon)

certe, inquit Fundanius, aliud pastio et aliud agri cultura, sed
adfinis et ut dextra tibia alia quam sinistra, ita ut tamen sit quodam

had golden fleeces because of their value, like the one at Argos, which Atreus complains Thyestes stole for himself; or there was the one at Colchis belonging to Aeetes, in quest of whose fleece the Argonauts, of royal kind, are said to have voyaged. In Libya in the garden of the Hesperides there were golden *mala*, i.e. goats and sheep according to the ancient manner of speech, which Hercules took from Africa to Greece. For the Greeks called them *mela* from

7 the sound of their voice, and our people not very differently say that sheep *baelare* ('bah') when using their voice (their voice seems to sound 'b' not 'm') from which afterwards (we have) *balare* ('to bleat'), once a letter is removed, as in many words. But if among the ancients sheep and goats had not had great dignity, in describing the sky the astrologers would not have called the signs by their names, which they not only did, but many even enumerate the twelve beginning with them, from the Ram (Aries) and Bull (Taurus), which they place before Apollo and Hercules. For those gods follow them,

8 but they are called Gemini.[2] Not satisfied that a sixth of the twelve had the names of cattle they added Capricorn ('Goathorn') to make up a quarter. From the domestic animals, besides, they added the Goat, Kids and Dogs. Both by sea and on land are not areas known (as named) from these, by sea what they called the Aegean Sea from goats, in Syria Mount Taurus ('Bull'), Mount Cantherius ('Gelding') in the Sabine region, and both the Thracian and

9 Cimmerian Bosporus ('Cattle-crossing')? Are there not many places on land like the town in Greece called Horsey Argos? Finally, is not Italy from 'bulls', as Piso[3] writes?

[1] The text is corrupt here. *Rotae* would mean 'chariots'. What appears to be needed is some word like *oreobatae* (ὀρειβάται), 'mountain-ranging'.

[2] Like the other signs of the zodiac, the constellation Gemini ('Twins') was first identified by the Babylonians. In Greece they were usually identified with the Discouri, Castor and Pollux, or with Amphion and Zethus of Thebes, but their identification with Heracles and Apollo, who were half-brothers, was not unheard of.

[3] M. Pupius Piso was a politician and soldier active *c.* 83–60 B.C. "Italia" is derived from *vitulus*, "bull."

55   Varro, *On Farming* 1.2.15-16 (*CB* v.1 p.16.18–17.6 Heurgon)

"Certainly," said Fundanius,[1] "the shepherding of stock is one thing, agriculture another, but they are related as the right pipe of

62   Dicaearchus of Messana

modo coniuncta, quod est altera eiusdem carminis modorum
16 incentiva, altera succentiva. et quidem licet adicias, inquam,
pastorum vitam esse incentivam, agricolarum succentivam auctore 5
doctissimo homine Dicaearcho, qui Graeciae vita qualis fuerit ab
initio nobis ita ostendit, ut superioribus temporibus fuisse doceat,
cum homines pastoriciam vitam agerent neque scirent etiam arare
terram aut serere arbores aut putare; ab iis inferiore gradu aetatis
susceptam agri culturam. quocirca ea succinit pastorali, quod est 10
inferior, ut tibia sinistra dextrae foraminibus.

7 doceat *Vb*: docent *Am*   10 ea *Ursinus*: ei *codd.*   11 dextrae *Heurgon*:
addextre *A*: a dextrae *ceteri et Wehrli*

56A Porphyrius, De abstinentia ab esu animalium 4.2.1–9 (CB t.3 p.1.16–
4.7 Patillon et Segonds)

ἀρξώμεθα δ᾽ ἀπὸ τῆς κατὰ ἔθνη τινῶν ἀποχῆς, ὧν ἡγήσονται
τοῦ λόγου οἱ Ἕλληνες, ὡς ἂν τῶν μαρτυρούντων ὄντες
οἰκειότατοι. τῶν τοίνυν συντόμως τε ὁμοῦ καὶ ἀκριβῶς τὰ
Ἑλληνικὰ συναγαγόντων ἐστὶ καὶ ὁ Περιπατητικὸς Δικαίαρχος,
ὃς τὸν ἀρχαῖον βίον τῆς Ἑλλάδος ἀφηγούμενος τοὺς παλαιοὺς 5
καὶ ἐγγὺς θεῶν φησὶ γεγονότας, βελτίστους τε ὄντας φύσει καὶ
τὸν ἄριστον ἐζηκότας βίον, ὡς χρυσοῦν γένος νομίζεσθαι
παραβαλλομένους πρὸς τοὺς νῦν, κιβδήλου καὶ φαυλοτάτης
2 ὑπάρχοντας ὕλης, μηδὲν φονεύειν ἔμψυχον. ὃ δὴ καὶ τοὺς
   ποιητὰς παριστάντας χρυσοῦν μὲν ἐπονομάζειν γένος,   10
      ἐσθλὰ δὲ πάντα, λέγειν,
   τοῖσιν ἔην· καρπὸν δ᾽ ἔφερε ζείδωρος ἄρουρα
   αὐτομάτη πολλόν τε καὶ ἄφθονον· οἳ δ᾽ ἐθελημοὶ
   ἥσυχοι ἔργ᾽ ἐνέμοντο σὺν ἐσθλοῖσιν πολέεσσιν
3 ἃ δὴ καὶ ἐξηγούμενος ὁ Δικαίαρχος τὸν ἐπὶ Κρόνου βίον τοιοῦτον 15
εἶναι φησίν, εἰ δεῖ λαμβάνειν μὲν αὐτὸν ὡς γεγονότα καὶ μὴ
μάτην ἐπιπεφημισμένον, τὸ δὲ λίαν μυθικὸν ἀφέντας, εἰς τὸ διὰ

16 the flute is other than the left, yet in such a way that they are connected in a certain way, because the one is the lead, the other the accompaniment of the melodies of the same song." "Indeed, you may add," I said, "that the life of shepherding is the lead, agricultural the accompaniment, according to the authority of a most learned man, Dicaearchus, who has shown us in his *Life of Greece* what quality it had from its beginning. In the earlier times, he teaches, when people led a pastoral life they knew neither how to plough the earth nor how to plant trees nor how to prune. At a time later than this they took up agriculture. Therefore (agriculture) accompanies the pastoral life, because it is secondary, as the left pipe of the flute is to the stops of the right hand."

[1] C. Fundanius was Varro's father-in-law and one of the interlocutors in book one of *On Farming*.

56A Porphyry, *On Abstinence* 4.2.1–9 (*CB* v.3 p.1.16–4.7 Patillon and Segonds)

Let us begin with the abstinence (from eating meat) of some nations, of whom the Greeks will lead our discussion since they would be the most suitable witnesses. Among those, therefore, that have concisely and at the same time accurately composed an account of the affairs of the Greeks, there is included the Peripatetic Dicaearchus, who in narrating the ancient life of the Greeks says that the men of old, who were actually born close to gods, were naturally most excellent, and led the best life, so that they are regarded as a golden race, when compared with those of the present day, who consist of an adulterated and most vile matter; and they

2 killed no animate being. The truth of this, he also says, is attested by the poets, who call these ancients a Golden Race, and assert that

> All good things were theirs, the grain-giving fields of their own accord bore much fruit ungrudgingly. Willing and at peace, they enjoyed their possessions with many good things.

3 In explanation of this, Dicaearchus says that life under Cronus was of this kind—since it is necessary to accept that it did exist, that it has not been renowned to no purpose, but also, by laying aside

τοῦ λόγου φυσικὸν ἀνάγειν. αὐτόματα μὲν γὰρ πάντα ἐφύετο,
εἰκότως· οὐ γὰρ αὐτοί γε κατεσκεύαζον οὐθὲν διὰ τὸ μήτε τὴν
4 γεωργικὴν ἔχειν πω τέχνην μήθ᾽ ἑτέραν μηδεμίαν ἁπλῶς. τὸ δ᾽ 20
αὐτὸ καὶ τοῦ σχολὴν ἄγειν αἴτιον ἐγίγνετο αὐτοῖς καὶ τοῦ διάγειν
ἄνευ πόνων καὶ μερίμνης, εἰ δὲ τῇ τῶν γλαφυρωτάτων ἰατρῶν
ἐπακολουθῆσαι δεῖ διανοίᾳ, καὶ τοῦ μὴ νοσεῖν. οὐθὲν γὰρ εἰς
ὑγίειαν αὐτῶν μεῖζον παράγγελμα εὕροι τις ἂν ἢ τὸ μὴ ποιεῖν
περιττώματα, ὧν διὰ παντὸς ἐκεῖνοι καθαρὰ τὰ σώματα 25
ἐφύλαττον. οὔτε γὰρ τὴν τῆς φύσεως ἰσχυροτέραν τροφὴν ἀλλ᾽
ἧς ἡ φύσις ἰσχυροτέρα προσεφέροντο, οὔτε τὴν πλείω τῆς μετρίας
διὰ τὴν ἑτοιμότητα, ἀλλ᾽ ὡς τὰ πολλὰ τὴν ἐλάττω τῆς ἱκανῆς
5 διὰ τὴν σπάνιν. ἀλλὰ μὴν οὐδὲ πόλεμοι αὐτοῖς ἦσαν οὐδὲ
στάσεις πρὸς ἀλλήλους· ἆθλον γὰρ οὐθὲν ἀξιόλογον ἐν τῷ μέσῳ 30
προκείμενον ὑπῆρχεν, ὕπερ ὅτου τις ἂν διαφορὰν τοσαύτην
ἐνεστήσατο, ὥστε τὸ κεφάλαιον εἶναι τοῦ βίου συνέβαινεν
σχολήν, ῥᾳθυμίαν ἀπὸ τῶν ἀναγκαίων, ὑγίειαν, εἰρήνην, φιλίαν.
6 τοῖς δὲ ὑστέροις ἐφιεμένοις μεγάλων καὶ πολλοῖς περιπίπτουσι
κακοῖς ποθεινὸς εἰκότως ἐκεῖνος ὁ βίος ἐγίγνετο. δηλοῖ δὲ τὸ 35
λιτὸν τῶν πρώτων καὶ αὐτοσχέδιον τῆς τροφῆς τὸ μεθύστερον
ῥηθὲν "ἅλις δρυός," τοῦ μεταβάλλοντος πρώτου, οἷα εἰκός, τοῦτο
φθεγξαμένου.
7   ὕστερον ὁ νομαδικὸς εἰσῆλθεν βίος, καθ᾽ ὃν περιττοτέραν ἤδη
κτῆσιν προσπεριεβάλλοντο καὶ ζῴων ἥψαντο, κατανοήσαντες 40
ὅτι τὰ μὲν ἀσινῆ ἐτύγχανεν ὄντα, τὰ δὲ κακοῦργα καὶ χαλεπά.
καὶ οὕτω δὴ τὰ μὲν ἐτιθάσευσαν, τοῖς δὲ ἐπέθεντο, καὶ ἅμα ἐν
τῷ αὐτῷ βίῳ συνεισῆλθεν πόλεμος. καὶ ταῦτα, φησίν, οὐχ ἡμεῖς,
8 ἀλλ᾽ οἱ τὰ παλαιὰ ἱστορίᾳ διεξελθόντες εἰρήκασιν. ἤδη γὰρ
ἀξιόλογα κτήματα ἐνυπῆρχον, ἃ οἳ μὲν ἐπὶ τὸ παρελέσθαι 45
φιλοτιμίαν ἐποιοῦντο, ἀθροιζόμενοί τε καὶ παρακαλοῦντες
ἀλλήλους, οἳ δ᾽ ἐπὶ τὸ διαφυλάξαι. προϊόντος δὲ οὕτω τοῦ
χρόνου, κατανοοῦντες κατὰ μικρὸν ἀεὶ τῶν χρησίμων εἶναι
δοκούντων, εἰς τὸ τρίτον τε καὶ γεωργικὸν ἐνέπεσον εἶδος.

what is excessively mythical, to reduce it to natural terms based on reason. All things, therefore, are very reasonably said to have grown of their own accord; for men themselves did not procure anything because they were still unaquainted with the agricultural art, or, in fact, any other art. This very thing, likewise, was the cause of their being at leisure and living free from labours and care; and if it is proper to assent to the view of the most skillful physicians, it was also the cause of their being free from disease. For one could find no prescription which contributed more to their health than avoiding the production of excesses, from which those Greeks of old always preserved their bodies pure. For they neither consumed food that was stronger than their nature, but (only) such that their nature was stronger, nor more than is moderate because of its ready availability, but for the most part less than (we would consider) sufficient, on account of its scarcity. Moreover, they neither had wars nor dissensions against each other. For no reward worth mentioning was set before them, for the sake of which someone might begin such dissension, so that that life consisted mainly of leisure and rest from necessary occupations, together with health, peace and friendship. And, of course, to those in later times, who aspired after great things and fell into many evils, this ancient life became desirable. The simple and extemporaneous food of the early men is manifested in the saying that was afterwards used, "enough of oak," this adage being introduced by the man who first changed (his mode of living), as seems reasonable.

7   The pastoral life succeeded this, in which men began to procure superfluous possessions for themselves, and handle animals. They perceived that some of them were not in fact harmful, but others destructive and difficult, so they tamed the former and attacked the latter. At the same time, together with this life, war was introduced. And these things, says (Dicaearchus), are not asserted by us, but by those who have spoken after researching thoroughly ancient matters. For, as possessions were now worthwhile, some made it a point of honor to seize them (from others) by gathering themselves together and calling on each other (for help), but others (made it a point of honor) to protect (what they had). Time, thus, gradually proceeding, and men concerned evermore with what appeared to be useful, they entered the third, agricultural form of life.

9 ταυτὶ μὲν Δικαιάρχου τὰ παλαιὰ τῶν Ἑλληνικῶν διεξιόντος 50
μακάριόν τε τὸν βίον ἀφηγουμένου τῶν παλαιτάτων, ὃν οὐχ
ἧττον τῶν ἄλλων καὶ ἡ ἀποχὴ τῶν ἐμψύχων συνεπλήρου.
διὸ
πόλεμος οὐκ ἦν, ὡς ἂν ἀδικίας ἐξεληλαμένης· συνεισῆλθεν δὲ
ὕστερον καὶ πόλεμος καὶ εἰς ἀλλήλους πλεονεξία ἅμα τῇ τῶν
ζῴων ἀδικίᾳ. ὃ καὶ θαυμάζω τῶν τολμησάντων τὴν ἀποχὴν τῶν 55
ζῴων ἀδικίας μητέρα εἰπεῖν, τῆς ἱστορίας καὶ τῆς πείρας ἅμα
τῷ φόνῳ αὐτῶν τρυφήν τε καὶ πόλεμον καὶ ἀδικίαν συνεισελθεῖν
μηνυούσης.

11–14 *Hesiodus, Opera et dies 116–19*   37 *de proverbio* ἅλις δρυός *vid.*
Zenob. 2.40

19 μήτε *Reiske*: μήπω V   20 γεωργικὴν *Nauck*: γεωργίαν V   22 τῇ *Reiske*:
τι V   26–7 ἀλλ᾽... ἰσχυροτέρα *expunxit Nauck*   28 τῆς ἱκανῆς *expunxit*
Nauck   35 ἐγίγνετο V: ἐφαίνετο *Nauck*   40 προσπεριεβάλλοντο V:
προσπεριεβάλοντο *Nauck*   48 κατὰ μικρὸν *ante* ἀεὶ *traiecerunt Patillon et*
Segonds: ante οὕτω *habet* V

56B Hieronymus, Adversus Iovinianum 2.13 (PL t.23 col. 315.42–316.5
Migne)

   Dicaearchus in libris Antiquitatum et Descriptione Graeciae refert
sub Saturno (id est in aureo saeculo), cum omnia humus funderet,
nullum comedisse carnem, sed universos vixisse frugibus et pomis
quae sponte terra gignebat.

57 Zenobius, Epitome collectionum Lucilli Tarrhaei et Didymi 5.23
(CPG t.1 p.125.3–11 Leutsch et Schneidewin)

   μερὶς οὐ πνίγει. Δικαίαρχός φησιν ἐν τοῖς Περὶ τῆς Ἑλλάδος
ἐν τοῖς δείπνοις μὴ εἶναι σύνηθες τοῖς ἀρχαίοις διανέμειν
μερίδας. διὰ δὲ προφάσεις τινὰς ἐνδεεστέρων γενομένων τῶν
ἐδεσμάτων, κρατῆσαι τὸ ἔθος τῶν μερίδων, καὶ διὰ τοῦτο τὴν
παροιμίαν εἰρῆσθαι. τῶν γὰρ ἐδεσμάτων κοινῇ καὶ μὴ κατὰ 5
μέρος τιθεμένων τὸ πρότερον οἱ δυνατώτεροι τὰς τροφὰς τῶν
ἀσθενῶν ἥρπαζον, καὶ συνέβαινε τούτους ἀποπνίγεσθαι, μὴ
δυναμένους ἑαυτοῖς βοηθεῖν. διὰ τοῦτο οὖν ὁ μερισμὸς
ἐπενοήθη.

9   This is (what is said) by Dicaearchus when he narrates the ancient affairs of the Greeks and relates as blessed the life of the earliest people, to which abstinence from animal food contributed no
less than other things. Therefore there was no war, inasmuch as
injustice had been driven out. But later, together with injustice towards animals, came war and competition towards each other. That
is why I wonder at those who dare to say that abstinence from animals is the mother of injustice, since enquiry and experience reveal
that luxury, war and injustice came in together with their slaughter.

56B Jerome, *Against Jovinian* 2.13 (*PL* v.23 col. 315.42–316.5 Migne)

Dicaearchus in the books of *Antiquities* and *Description of
Greece* says that under Saturn, that is, in the golden age, when the
earth provided all things, no one ate meat, but all lived from the
fruits and vegetables that the earth bore spontaneously.

57 Zenobius, *Summary of the Collections of Lucillus Tarrhaeus and
Didymus* 5.23 (*CPG* v.1 p.125.3–11 Leutsch and Schneidewin)

"A portion does not choke." Dicaearchus says in the books *On
Greece* that at the meals it was not the custom for the ancients to
distribute portions. But when for some reasons shortages of meats
occurred, the custom of portions prevailed, and the saying was
coined because of this. For earlier, when meats were set out as common dishes and not in individual portions, the more powerful seized
the food from the weaker, and it happened that these choked to
death because they were not able to save themselves. For this reason then the portioning was contrived.

58 Scholion in Apollonii Rhodii Argonautica 4.272–4 (p.277.24–278.3 Wendel)

Δικαίαρχος δὲ ἐν α΄ Ἑλλάδος βίου Σεσόγχωσιν, καὶ νόμους αὐτὸν θεῖναι λέγει, ὥστε μηδένα καταλιπεῖν τὴν πατρῴαν τέχνην. τοῦτο γὰρ ὑπολαμβάνειν ἀρχὴν εἶναι πλεονεξίας. καὶ πρῶτόν φησιν αὐτὸν εὑρηκέναι ἵππων ἄνθρωπον ἐπιβαίνειν. οἱ δὲ ταῦτα τὸν Ὧρον, οὐ τὸν Σεχόγχωσιν.   5

1–2 *in fine scholii habet P* καὶ τοῦτο δέ φησι Δικαίαρχος ἐν β΄ Ἑλληνικοῦ βίου Σεσώστριδι μεμεληκέναι.   2 αὐτὸν *expunxit Wendel*

59 Scholion in Apollonii Rhodii Argonautica 4.276 (p.278.8–12 Wendel)

Δικαίαρχος δὲ ἐν α΄ μετὰ τὸν Ἴσιδος καὶ Ὀσίριδος Ὧρον βασιλέα γεγονέναι Σεσόγχωσιν. γίνεται δὲ ἀπὸ Σεσογχώσεως ἐπὶ τὴν Νείλου βασιλείαν ἔτη ͵βφ΄, ⟨ἀπὸ δὲ τῆς Νείλου βασιλείας ἐπὶ τὴν Ἰλίου ἅλωσιν ζ΄⟩, ἀπὸ δὲ τῆς Ἰλίου ἁλώσεως ἐπὶ τὴν α΄ Ὀλυμπιάδα υλς΄, ὁμοῦ ͵β ᐃμγ΄.   5

2 Σεσόγχωσιν—Σεσογχώσεως *L*: Σέσωστρις—Σεσώστριδος *P*   3 ἀπὸ— ἅλωσιν ζ΄ *supplevit Keil*: ἀπὸ δὲ τῆς Ἰλίου ἁλώσεως *L*: ἀπὸ τῆς Νείλου βασιλείας *P*   4 ͵βπμγ΄ *L*: ͵βπλς΄ *P*

sub finem scholii habet L Δικαίαρχος δέ φησιν ἐν β΄ Ἑλλάδος βίου Σεσόγχωσιν

60 Stephanus Byzantius, Ethnica, s.v. Χαλδαῖοι (p. 680.4–14 Meineke)

ἐκλήθησαν δὲ ἀπὸ Χαλδαίου τινός, ὡς Δικαίαρχος ἐν πρώτῳ τοῦ τῆς Ἑλλάδος βίου. τούτων δὲ συνέσει καὶ δυνάμει διάφορον γενόμενον τὸν καλούμενον Νίνον τὴν ὁμώνυμον αὐτῷ συνοικίσαι πόλιν. ἀπὸ δὲ τούτου τέταρτον ἐπὶ δέκα βασιλέα γενόμενον, ᾧ τοὔνομα Χαλδαῖον εἶναι λέγουσιν, ὅν φασι καὶ 5 Βαβυλῶνα τὴν ὀνομαστοτάτην πόλιν περὶ τὸν Εὐφράτην ποταμὸν κατασκευάσαι, ἅπαντας εἰς ταὐτὸ συναγαγόντα τοὺς

58 Scholium on Apollonius of Rhodes' *Argonautica* 4.272–4 (p.277.24–278.3 Wendel)

Dicaearchus in the first book of the *Life of Greece*[1] (calls him) Sesonchosis[2] and says that he established laws that no one should abandon his father's trade. For he assumed that this was the origin of greed. (Dicaearchus) says that he was the first man to discover mounting horses. Others (say) that Oros (Horus) did these things, not Sesonchosis.

[1] At the end of the scholium, P adds, "Dicaearchus in book 2 of *Greek Life* says Sesostris was responsible for this."
[2] One of the scholia reads "Sesostris," the version of his name that appears in Hdt. 2.102–10, which is a composite account of several Egyptian rulers of the Twelfth Dynasty (2040–1785) called Senwosret in Egyptian. In Egyptian propaganda "Sesostris" came to embody an ideal kingship.

59 Scholium on Apollonius of Rhodes' *Argonautica* 4.276 (p.278.8–12 Wendel)

In the first book[1] Dicaearchus says that after Oros (Horus), the son of Isis and Osiris, Sesonchosis became king. From Sesonchosis to the kingship of Nilus was 2500 years, <from the kingship of Nilus to the destruction of Ilium was 7 years>, from the capture of Ilium to the first Olympiad was 436 years, altogether 2943 years.

[1] Under this scholium L adds, "Dicaearchus in book 2 of *Life of Greece* (says) Sesonchosis."

60 Stephen of Byzantium, *Place-Names,* on *Chaldaeans* (p.680.4–14 Meineke)

They were named after a certain Chaldaeus, as Dicaearchus says in the first book of his *Life of Greece*. Of them the one called Ninus became outstanding in intelligence and power and settled a city named after himself. From this time, the fourteenth king was, they say, Chaldaeus by name, who they say built Babylon, the most renowned city, around the river Euphrates, collecting all those called

70   Dicaearchus of Messana

καλουμένους Χαλδαίους. λέγεται καὶ Χαλδαία χώρα. εἰσὶ δὲ
καὶ Χαλδαῖοι ἔθνος πλησίον τῆς Κολχίδος. Σοφοκλῆς
Τυμπανισταῖς· Κόλχος τε Χαλδαῖός τε καὶ Σύρων ἔθνος.   10

9 *Sophocles, fr. 638 Radt*

2 τούτων *Neue*: τούτῳ *vel* τοῦτον *codd.*

61 Eustathius, Commentarium in Dionysii perigetae orbis descrip-
tionem 767 (GGM t.2 p.350.34–44 Müller)

χώρα δὲ Ἀρμενίας ἡ Χαλδία, ἧς μέχρις ἡ Ποντικὴ βασιλεία.
τοὺς δὲ ἐκεῖσε Χάλδους λέγεσθαι ἐπικρατεῖ ἡ συνήθεια
δισυλλάβως, οὐ Χαλδαίους. Χαλδαῖοι γὰρ τρισυλλάβως οἱ ποτὲ
μὲν Κηφῆνες, ἀπὸ δὲ Περσέως Πέρσαι· Χαλδαῖοι κληθέντες ἀπό
τινος Χαλδαίου, ὅν φασι τέταρτον ἐπὶ δέκα, ἤγουν τεσσα-   5
ρεσκαιδέκατον, βασιλέα μετὰ Νίνον γενόμενον τὴν Βαβυλῶνα
οἰκίσαι, καὶ τοὺς συναχθέντας καλέσαι ἀφ᾽ ἑαυτοῦ Χαλδαίους.
λέγονται μέντοι παρά τινων καὶ οἱ περὶ τὴν Κολχίδα Χάλδοι
Χαλδαῖοι τρισυλλάβως, κατὰ Δικαίαρχον.

62 Hypothesis in Euripidis Medeam 27–9 (BT p.4.5–7 Van Looy)

τὸ δρᾶμα δοκεῖ ὑποβαλέσθαι παρὰ Νεόφρονος διασκευάσας,
ὡς Δικαίαρχος ⟨ἐν⟩ πρ⟨ώτῳ⟩ τοῦ τῆς Ἑλλάδος βίου καὶ
Ἀριστοτέλης ἐν ὑπομνήμασι.

1 *Neophron., fr. 15 TrGF Snell; cf. Suda, s.v.* Νεόφρων *et Diog. Laert. 2.134*   3
Aristot., fr. 635 Rose³

1 ὑποβαλέσθει] παραβαλέσθαι *Hn*   2–3 ὡς ... ὑπομνήμασι *om. Pet Ambros*
2 ⟨ἐν⟩ πρ⟨ώτῳ⟩ *Luppe (RhM 135 [1992] 94)*: ⟨ἐν   ⟩ *Van Looy*: ⟨ἐν ᾱ⟩ *vel sim.*
Klotz   τοῦ τῆς *W*: τοῦ τε *FHn*: περὶ τοῦ τε *A*

63 Stephanus Byzantius, Ethnica, s.v. Δώριον (p.251.6–9 Meineke)

πόλις μία τῶν τριῶν ὧν Ὅμηρος μνημονεύει "καὶ Πτελεὸν
καὶ Ἕλος καὶ Δώριον." Δικαίαρχος δὲ τέτταρας ταύτας εἶναί
φησι, καὶ Πτελέας, οὐ Πτελεὸν τὴν μίαν καλεῖ, κατὰ τὸ πρῶτον

Chaldaeans into the same spot. A land is also called Chaldaea, and there is a race (of people called) Chaldaeans near Colchis. Sophocles in the *Tympanistai:* "Colchian and Chaldaean and the race of Syrians."

61 Eustathius, *Commentary on Dionysius Periegetes'* Guide to the World 767 (*GGM* v.2 p.350.34–44 Müller)

Chaldia is a region of Armenia up to which the Pontic kingdom extends. According to customary usage, the people there are called "Chaldi," in two syllables, not Chaldaeans. For the "Chaldaeans," in three syllables, were once the "Cephenes," and then "Persians" after Perseus; the Chaldaeans were named after a certain Chaldaeus, who they say became the fourth after ten, i.e., the 14th, king after Ninus and settled Babylon. And he named those gathered Chaldaeans after himself. The Chaldi around Colchis are also said by some, however, to be "Chaldaeans" in three syllables, according to Dicaearchus.

62 Hypothesis to Euripides' *Medea* 27–9 (*BT* p.4.5–7 Van Looy)

(Euripides) appears to have passed off the play as his own, having reworked it (from an original) by Neophron, as Dicaearchus says in the first book of his *Life of Greece* and Aristotle in the *Memoranda*.

63 Stephen of Byzantium, *Place-Names*, on *Dorium* (p.251.6–9 Meineke)

One of the three cities that Homer mentions, "and Pteleum and Helus and Dorium." Dicaearchus says that these are four and he calls the one Ptelea, not Pteleum, according to the first book of the

τοῦ Βίου τῆς Ἑλλάδος βιβλίον.

1–2 *Hom., Il. 2.594*

2 τέτταρας dubitat *Meineke, qui proponit* Θετταλίας

64 Stephanus Byzantius, Ethnica, s.v. πάτρα (p.511.17–512.13
Meineke)

ἓν τῶν τριῶν παρ᾽ Ἕλλησι κοινωνίας εἰδῶν, ὡς Δικαίαρχος,
ἃ δὴ καλοῦμεν πάτραν φρατρίαν φυλήν. ἐκλήθη δὲ πάτρα μὲν
εἰς τὴν δευτέραν μετάβασιν ἐλθόντων ἡ κατὰ μόνας ἑκάστῳ
πρότερον οὖσα συγγένεια, ἀπὸ τοῦ πρεσβυτάτου τε καὶ μάλιστα
ἰσχύσαντος ἐν τῷ γένει τὴν ἐπωνυμίαν ἔχουσα, ὃν ἂν τρόπον   5
Αἰακίδας ἢ Πελοπίδας εἴποι τις. φατρίαν δὲ συνέβη λέγεσθαι
καὶ φρατρίαν, ἐπειδή τινες εἰς ἑτέραν πάτραν ἐδίδοσαν
θυγατέρας ἑαυτῶν. οὐ γὰρ ἔτι τῶν πατριωτικῶν ἱερῶν εἶχε
κοινωνίαν ἡ δοθεῖσα, ἀλλ᾽ εἰς τὴν τοῦ λαβόντος αὐτὴν συνετέλει
πάτραν, ὥστε πρότερον πόθῳ τῆς συνόδου γιγνομένης ἀδελφαῖς   10
σὺν ἀδελφῷ ἑτέρα τις ἱερῶν ἐτέθη κοινωνικὴ σύνοδος, ἣν δὴ
φρατρίαν ὠνόμαζον. καὶ πάλιν· ὥστε πάτρα μὲν ὅνπερ εἴπομεν
ἐκ τῆς συγγενείας τρόπον ἐγένετο μάλιστα τῆς γονέων σὺν
τέκνοις καὶ τέκνων σὺν γονεῦσι, φρατρία δὲ ἐκ τῆς τῶν ἀδελφῶν.
φυλὴ δὲ καὶ φυλέται πρότερον ὠνομάσθησαν ἐκ τῆς εἰς τὰς   15
πόλεις καὶ τὰ καλούμενα ἔθνη συνόδου γενομένης. ἕκαστον γὰρ
τῶν συνελθόντων φῦλον ἐλέγετο εἶναι.

2 φρατρίαν *RX*: φατρίαν *AV*   6 φατρίαν *Buttmann*: πατρίαν *codd.*   7
πάτραν *Buttmann*: φάτραν *vel* φράτραν *codd.*   12 φρατρίαν *Buttmann*:
πατρίαν *codd.*   14 τέκνων *Buttmann*: τέκνα *codd.*

65 Scholion in Homeri Iliadem 6.396 (t.1 p.244.3–10 Dindorf)

Γράνικος, οἱ δὲ Ἄτραμυς, Πελασγὸς τὸ γένος, ἀφίκετό ποτε
ὑπὸ τὴν ἐν τῇ Λυκίᾳ Ἴδην, καὶ πόλιν κτίσας ἐκεῖσε ἀφ᾽ ἑαυτοῦ
προσηγόρευσεν Ἀδραμύττιον. γεννήσας δὲ θυγατέρα Θήβην τῷ
ὀνόματι, παρὰ τὴν ἀκμὴν τοῦ γάμου ἔθετο γυμνικὸν ἀγῶνα καὶ
τὸν ταύτης γάμον τῷ ἀριστεύσαντι. Ἡρακλῆς δὲ κατ᾽ ἐκεῖνο   5
καιροῦ φανεὶς ἔλαβε τὴν Θήβην γυναῖκα, καὶ κτίσας πόλιν ὑπὸ
τὸ Πλάκιον καλούμενον ὄρος τῆς Λυκίας Πλακίαν Θήβην αὐτὴν

Life of Greece.

64 Stephen of Byzantium, *Place-Names,* on *patra* (p.511.17–512.13 Meineke)

One of the three forms of union among the Greeks, as Dicaearchus says, which we call *patra, phratria* and *phyle.* The kinship existing first for each person individually on coming into the second generation is called *patra*; it has its name from the oldest and strongest in the clan, as one might say Aeacidae or Pelopidae. There is said to be a *phatria* and *phratria* when some have given their daughters into another *patra.* For the woman who is given away no longer has a sharing in the rites of her father's people, but she contributes to the same *patra* as her husband, so that earlier, because of the longing of sisters for the meeting with a brother to occur, another shared meeting of rites was established, which they called a *phratria.* And again, the *patra* came about from kinship in the way we mentioned, especially of parents with children and children with parents, and the *phratria* from the siblings. A *phyle* and *phyletai* were earlier named from the association that came to become cities and what are called tribes. For each of (the groups) that came together used to be called a *phyle.*

65 Scholion on Homer, *Iliad* 6.396 (v.1 p.244.3–10 Dindorf)

Granicus, others (say) Atramys, a Pelasgian by race, came then to Mount Ida in Lycia, and having founded a city there called it Adramyttion after himself. After he had fathered a daughter named Thebe, when she was ready for marriage, he arranged an athletic contest and (promised) her in marriage to the best athlete. At that moment, Heracles appeared and took Thebe as his wife, and having founded a city under what is called the Placian mountain of

ἀπὸ τῆς γυναικὸς ἐκάλεσεν. ἡ ἱστορία παρὰ Δικαιάρχῳ.

1–8 cf. Erbse, p.197   3–7 cf. schol. in Hom. Il. 1.366C

1 Ἄτραμυς *Müller*: ἀτράμους *cod.*   7 Λυκίας] Κιλικίας *Müller*

66 Scholion in Euripidis Andromacham 1 (p.247.10–12 Schwartz)

τὴν ἐν Ἀσίᾳ λέγει Ὑπυπλάκιον Θήβην, ἧς Ἠετίων ἐβασίλευσεν. Δικαίαρχός φησιν ἐνθάδε ἀπόσπασμά τι τοῦ μετὰ τοῦ Κάδμου στόλου οἰκῆσαι.

2 ἀπόσπασμά τι τοῦ *Schwartz*: ἀποσπάσματι *MN*: ἀποσπάσαντα *O*   3 στόλου *omisit M*   οἰκῆσαι] οἰκῶν *NO*

67 Clemens Alexandrinus, Protrepticus ad Graecos 2.30.7 (GCS t.1 p.23.2–7 Stählin)

Δικαίαρχος δὲ σχιζίαν, νευρώδη, μέλανα, γρυπόν, ὑποχαροπόν, τετανότριχα.

68 Zenobius, Epitome collectionum Lucilli Tarrhaei et Didymi 4.26 (CPG t.1 p.91.4–6 Leutsch et Schneidewin)

Ἡράκλειος νόσος· Δικαίαρχός φησι τὴν ἱερὰν νόσον Ἡράκλειον ὀνομάζεσθαι. εἰς ταύτην γὰρ ἐκ τῶν μακρῶν πόνων περιπεσεῖν φασὶ τὸν Ἡρακλέα.

1–3 Par. Graec. Suppl.B474 (p.61.19–22 Leutsch et Schneidewin)

1 νόσος: ψώρα *B*   2 πόνων: πόρων *codex Atheniensis 1083 (S.B. München [1910] 22)*   3 φασὶ: *omisit codex Atheniensis 1083*

69 Phlegon, Mirabilia 4–5 (Paradoxographi Graeci p.130.24–131.20 Westermann)

ἱστορεῖ δὲ καὶ Ἡσίοδος καὶ Δικαίαρχος καὶ Κλείταρχος καὶ Καλλίμαχος καὶ ἄλλοι τινὲς περὶ Τειρεσίου τάδε. Τειρεσίαν τὸν Εὐήρους ἐν Ἀρκαδίᾳ [ἄνδρα] ὄντα ἐν τῷ ὄρει τῷ ἐν Κυλλήνῃ ὄφεις ἰδόντα ὀχεύοντας τρῶσαι τὸν ἕτερον καὶ παραχρῆμα

Lycia, he called it Placian Thebe after his wife. The story is in Dicaearchus.

66 Scholion on Euripides, *Andromache* 1 (p.247.10–12 Schwartz)

She (Andromache) means Hypoplacian Thebe, where (her father) Eetion was king. Dicaearchus says that a detachment of Cadmus' expedition settled there.

67 Clement of Alexandria, *Protreptic to the Greeks* 2.30.7 (*GCS* v.1 p.23.2–7 Stählin)

Dicaearchus (says) that (Heracles was) well defined, sinewy, dark, hook-nosed, somewhat bright-eyed and straight-haired.

68 Zenobius, *Summary of the Collections of Lucillus Tarrhaeus and Didymus* 4.26 (*CPG* v.1 p.91.4–6 Leutsch and Schneidewin)

Heraclean disease: Dicaearchus says that the sacred disease was called Heraclean. For they say Heracles fell ill as a result of it after his great labours.

69 Phlegon, *Miraculous Occurrences* 4–5 (*Greek Writers on Marvels* p.130.24–131.20 Westermann)

Hesiod, Dicaearchus, Clitarchus, Callimachus and some others report the following concerning Teiresias: Teiresias the son of Eueres, when he was in Arcadia (and) saw snakes mating on the mountain in Cyllene, wounded one of them and suddenly changed

μεταβαλεῖν τὴν ἰδέαν. γενέσθαι γὰρ ἐξ ἀνδρὸς γυναῖκα καὶ 5
μιχθῆναι ἀνδρί. τοῦ δὲ Ἀπόλλωνος αὐτῷ χρήσαντος, ὡς ἐὰν
τηρήσας ὀχεύοντας ὁμοίως τρώσῃ τὸν ἕνα ἔσται οἷος ἦν,
παραφυλάξαντα τὸν Τειρεσίαν ποιῆσαι τὰ ὑπὸ τοῦ θεοῦ ῥηθέντα
καὶ οὕτως ⟨ἀνα⟩κομίσασθαι τὴν ἀρχαίαν φύσιν.
Διὸς δὲ
ἐρίσαντος Ἥρᾳ καὶ φαμένου ἐν ταῖς συνουσίαις πλεονεκτεῖν 10
τὴν γυναῖκα τοῦ ἀνδρὸς τῇ τῶν ἀφροδισίων ἡδονῇ καὶ τῆς Ἥρας
φασκούσης τὰ ἐναντία, δόξαι αὐτοῖς μεταπεμψαμένοις ἐρέσθαι
τὸν Τειρεσίαν διὰ τὸ τῶν τρόπων ἀμφοτέρων πεπειρᾶσθαι. τὸν
δὲ ἐρωτώμενον ἀποφήνασθαι, διότι μοιρῶν οὐσῶν δέκα τὸν
ἄνδρα τέρπεσθαι τὴν μίαν, τὴν δὲ γυναῖκα τὰς ἐννέα. τὴν δὲ 15
Ἥραν ὀργισθεῖσαν κατανύξαι αὐτοῦ τοὺς ὀφθαλμοὺς καὶ
ποιῆσαι τυφλόν, τὸν δὲ Δία δωρήσασθαι αὐτῷ τὴν μαντικήν,
καὶ βιοῦν ἐπὶ γενεὰς ἑπτά.
5   οἱ αὐτοὶ ἱστοροῦσιν κατὰ τὴν Λαπίθων χώραν γενέσθαι
Ἐλάτῳ τῷ βασιλεῖ θυγατέρα, ὀνομαζομένην Καινίδα. ταύτῃ δὲ 20
Ποσειδῶνα μιγέντα ἐπαγγείλασθαι ποιήσειν αὐτὴν ὃ ἂν ἐθέλῃ,
τὴν δὲ ἀξιῶσαι μεταλλάξαι αὐτὴν εἰς ἄνδρα ποιῆσαί τε
ἄτρωτον. τοῦ δὲ Ποσειδῶνος κατὰ τὸ ἀξιωθὲν ποιήσαντος
μετονομασθῆναι Καινέα.

1 *Hesiodos, cf. fr. 275 Merkelbach et West*   *Clitarchus, FGrH 137 F 37*   2
Callimachus, fr. 576–7 Pfeiffer

1 Κλείταρχος] Κλέαρχος *Müller*   3 Εὐήρους *Meursius*: εὐμάρους *cod.*
ἄνδρα *expunxit Keller*   9 ἄνα *supplevit Nauck*   11 τῇ ... ἡδονῇ *Hercher*:
τῆς ... ἡδονῆς *cod. et Westermann*

70 Plutarchus, Theseus 32.5 (BT t.1.1 p.31.11–16 Ziegler)

ὁ δὲ Δικαίαρχος Ἐχέμου φησὶ καὶ Μαράθου συστρα-
τευσάντων τότε τοῖς Τυνδαρίδαις ἐξ Ἀρκαδίας ἀφ᾽ οὗ μὲν
Ἐχεδημίαν προσαγορευθῆναι τὴν νῦν Ἀκαδήμειαν, ἀφ᾽ οὗ δὲ
Μαραθῶνα τὸν δῆμον, ἐπιδόντος ἑαυτὸν ἑκουσίως κατά τι
λόγιον σφαγιάσασθαι πρὸ τῆς παρατάξεως.   5

1–3 *de Echemo, Stephanus Byzantius, Ethnica, s.v.* Ἐκαδήμεια, *et Hesychius,
s.v., Dicaearcho non nominato*

1 Ἐχέμου *codd. et Dorandi (CQ 38 [1988] 577)* : Ἐχεδήμου *anon. (Xylander?)
et Ziegler*

his form. For he became a woman instead of a man and slept with a man. When Apollo prophesied to him that if he should watch out for snakes mating and similarly wound one of them (the male) he (she) would again be such as he had been, Teiresias took care to do what the god had said and thus regained for himself his original nature. When Zeus was disputing with Hera and claiming that the woman got more sexual pleasure than the man in their sexual unions and Hera claimed the opposite, they decided to send for Teiresias to give his opinion since he had experienced both ways. When asked, he said that of the ten portions the man got one of pleasure, the woman nine. In her anger Hera darkened his eyes and made him blind, but Zeus gave him prophecy and made him live seven generations.

5   The same people report that in the land of the Lapiths a daughter was born to King Elatus, named Caenis. When Poseidon had intercourse with her and promised to do whatever she wished, she demanded he change her into a man and make her invulnerable. When Poseidon had done what was demanded, (her) name was changed to Caineus.

70 Plutarch, *Theseus* 32.5 (*BT* v.1.1 p.31.11–16 Ziegler)

But[1] Dicaearchus says that Echemus and Marathus of Arcadia fought then alongside the Tyndaridae, from the first of these (Echemus) the present Academy was named Echedemia, from the second the town of Marathon, since, according to a certain story, he voluntarily gave himself to be sacrificed before the line of battle.

---

[1] Plutarch has just said that the Academy was named for a hero named Academus.

71 [Demetrius], De elocutione 181–2 (CB p.52.11–22 Chiron)

κἂν μετροειδῆ δὲ ᾖ, τὴν αὐτὴν ποιήσει χάριν, λανθανόντως
δέ τοι παραδύεται ἡ ἐκ τῆς τοιαύτης ἡδονῆς χάρις. καὶ πλεῖστον
μὲν τὸ τοιοῦτον εἶδός ἐστι παρὰ τοῖς Περιπατητικοῖς καὶ παρὰ
Πλάτωνι καὶ παρὰ Ξενοφῶντι καὶ Ἡροδότῳ, τάχα δὲ καὶ παρὰ
Δημοσθένει πολλαχοῦ, Θουκυδίδης μέντοι πέφευγε τὸ εἶδος.   5
2 παραδείγματα δὲ αὐτοῦ λάβοι τις ἂν τοιάδε, οἷον ὡς ὁ
Δικαίαρχος· "ἐν Ἐλέᾳ," φησί, "τῆς Ἰταλίας πρεσβύτῃ δὴ τὴν
ἡλικίαν ὄντι." τῶν γὰρ κώλων ἀμφοτέρων αἱ ἀπολήξεις
μετροειδές τι ἔχουσιν, ὑπὸ δὲ τοῦ εἱρμοῦ καὶ τῆς συναφείας
κλέπτεται μὲν τὸ μετρικόν, ἡδονὴ δ᾽ οὐκ ὀλίγη ἔπεστι.   10

7 πρεσβύτῃ δὴ *Rademacher* : πρεσβύτ᾽ ἤδη *P. a.c.* : πρεσβύτην ἤδη *Pp.* :
πρεσβύτη ἤδη *M*   8 ὄντα] ὄντι *P et Rademacher*

72 Athenaeus, Deipnosophistae 14.39 636C–D (BT t.3 p.404.16–405.2
Kaibel)

ἦν γὰρ δή τινα καὶ χωρὶς τῶν ἐμφυσωμένων καὶ χορδαῖς
διειλημμένων ἕτερα ψόφου μόνον παρασκευαστικά, καθάπερ
τὰ κρέμβαλα. περὶ ὧν φησι Δικαίαρχος ἐν τοῖς Περὶ τοῦ τῆς
Ἑλλάδος βίου, ἐπιχωριάσαι φάσκων ποτὲ καθ᾽ ὑπερβολὴν εἰς
D τὸ προσορχεῖσθαί τε καὶ προσᾴδειν ταῖς γυναιξὶν ὄργανά τινα   5
ποιά, ὧν ὅτε τις ἅπτοιτο τοῖς δακτύλοις ποιεῖν λιγυρὸν ψόφον.
δηλοῦσθαι δὲ ἐν τῷ τῆς Ἀρτέμιδος ᾄσματι οὗ ἐστιν ἀρχή
    Ἄρτεμι, σοί μέ τι φρὴν ἐφίμερον
    ὕμνον ὑ⟨φαινέμ⟩εναι θεόθεν
    ἅδε τις ἀλλὰ χρυσοφά⟨ενν⟩α   10
    κρέμβαλα χαλκοπάρα⟨ι⟩α χερσίν.

8–11 *Alcman, fr. 60D Bergk*

8 ἐφίμερον *Wilamowitz* : ἐφίησιν *codd.*   9 ὑ⟨φαινέμ⟩εναι *Bergk* : υεναι *codd.*
10 χρυσοφά⟨ενν⟩α *Bergk* : χρυσοφανια *codd.*

73 Athenaeus, Deipnosophistae 1.25 14D–E (CB t.1 p.32.9–14
Desrousseaux)

ὀρχήσεις δ᾽ εἰσὶ παρ᾽ Ὁμήρῳ αἱ μέν τινες τῶν κυβιστητήρων,
αἳ δὲ διὰ τῆς σφαίρας. ἧς τὴν εὕρεσιν Ἀγαλλὶς ἡ Κερκυραία

71   Pseudo-Demetrius, *On Style* 181–2 (CB p.52.11–12 Chiron)

Even something like a meter will achieve the same delight,[1] and the delight of such pleasure steals in unnoticed. This form occurs most often in the Peripatetics, in Plato, in Herodotus, and often in Demosthenes, but Thucydides avoided the form.

2   One may take examples of this, e.g. what Dicaearchus says, "In Elea in Italy, when he was already advanced in age." The endings of the two parts have a certain metrical form, and while the metricality is concealed by the sequence and repetition of feet, the pleasure (that results) is not small.[2]

[1] I.e., as something properly metrical.
[2] For an account of the metrical qualities discussed here, see Chiron, p.119.

72   Athenaeus, *The Sophists at Dinner* 14.39 636C–D (*BT* v.3 p.404.16–405.2 Kaibel)

For of course besides wind instruments and those divided by strings there were other instruments, which are capable of providing only a loud noise, like the crembala. Concerning them, Dicaearchus says in the books *On the Life of Greece* that they were

D   a sort of instrument once exceedingly fashionable for women to dance and sing to; when one touched them with the fingers they made a ringing sound. It is clear in the hymn to Artemis which begins:

To you, Artemis, my heart impels me
to sing a lovely hymn from the gods
Here some other (plays) in her hands golden shining
crembala with bronzen sides.

73   Athenaeus, *The Sophists at Dinner* 1.25 14D–E (*CB* v.1 p.32.9–14 Desrousseaux)

Some of the dances in Homer are by tumblers, others are performed with a ball, the invention of which Agallis[1] the Corcyraean

γηραμματικὴ Ναυσικάᾳ ἀνατίθησιν ὡς πολίτιδι χαριζομένη,
E Δικαίαρχος δὲ Σικυωνίοις, Ἵππασος δὲ Λακεδαιμονίοις ταύτην
τε καὶ τὰ γυμνάσια πρώτοις.   5

1 κυβιστητήρων *edd.* : κυβιστήρων *codd.*

74 Plutarchus, Theseus 21.1–3 (BT t.1.1 p.18.22–19.3 Ziegler)

    ἐκ δὲ τῆς Κρήτης ἀποπλέων εἰς Δῆλον κατέσχε, καὶ τῷ θεῷ
θύσας καὶ ἀναθεὶς τὸ Ἀφροδίσιον ὃ παρὰ τῆς Ἀριάδνης ἔλαβεν,
ἐχόρευσε μετὰ τῶν ἠιθέων χορείαν, ἣν ἔτι νῦν ἐπιτελεῖν Δηλίους
λέγουσι, μίμημα τῶν ἐν τῷ Λαβυρίνθῳ περιόδων καὶ διεξόδων
ἔν τινι ῥυθμῷ παραλλάξεις καὶ ἀνελίξεις ἔχοντι γιγνομένην.   5
2 καλεῖται δὲ τὸ γένος τοῦτο τῆς χορείας ὑπὸ Δηλίων γέρανος, ὡς
ἱστορεῖ Δικαίαρχος. ἐχόρευσε δὲ περὶ τὸν Κερατῶνα βωμόν, ἐκ
3 κεράτων συνηρμοσμένον εὐωνύμων ἁπάντων. ποιῆσαι δὲ καὶ
ἀγῶνά φασιν αὐτὸν ἐν Δήλῳ καὶ τοῖς νικῶσι τότε πρῶτον ὑπ᾽
ἐκείνου φοίνικα δοθῆναι.   10

7–8 *cf. Plut., Mor.* 983E

75 Zenobius, Epitome collectionum Lucilli Tarrhaei et Didymi 6.16
(CPG t.1 p.166.6–9 Leutsch et Schneidewin)

    τάδε Μῆδος οὐ φυλάξει· Δικαίαρχός φησιν, ὅτι μελλούσης
τῆς Ξέρξου στρατείας γίνεσθαι οἱ Ἕλληνες ἀπογνόντες τῆς
σωτηρίας τὰς οὐσίας αὐτῶν ἀνήλισκον, ἐπιλέγοντες· Τάδε
Μῆδος οὐ φυλάξει.

1–4 *cf. Pausanias Atticista, s.v.*

1 φυλάξει] λαφύξει *Kassel (Hermes* 91 *[1963]* 57)

76 Plutarchus, Agesilaus 19.9 (BT t.3.2 p.217.17–21 Ziegler)

    ὁ μὲν οὖν Ξενοφῶν ὄνομα τῆς Ἀγησιλάου θυγατρὸς οὐ
γέγραφε, καὶ ὁ Δικαίαρχος ἐπηγανάκτησεν, ὡς μήτε τὴν
Ἀγησιλάου θυγατέρα μήτε τὴν Ἐπαμεινώνδου μητέρα
γινωσκόντων ἡμῶν.

grammarian ascribes to Nausicaa inasmuch as she favoured her
E own countrywoman. But Dicaearchus ascribes it to the Sicyonians, and Hippasus ascribes it, as well as gymnastics, to the Lacedaemonians first.

[1] Desrousseaux thinks this is perhaps a daughter of Agallias of Corcyra.

74 Plutarch, *Theseus* 21.1–3 (*BT* v.1.1 p.18.22–19.3 Ziegler)

When sailing from Crete (Theseus) put in at Delos. And after sacrificing to the god and setting up the image of Aphrodite that he got from Ariadne, he danced with his youths a dance which they say even now the Delians perform, an imitation of the paths around and out of the Labyrinth in a rhythm having releases and tightenings.
2 This kind of dance is called 'the crane' by the Delians, as Dicaearchus reports. Theseus danced around the altar Keraton,
3 which is constructed from all left horns. They say he also held a contest on Delos and palms were then given by him to the victors for the first time.

75 Zenobius, *Summary of the Collections of Lucillus Tarrhaeus and Didymus* 6.16 (*CPG* v.1 p.166.6–9 Leutsch and Schneidewin)

A Mede will not keep[1] these things: Dicaearchus says that when the campaign of Xerxes was about to come, the Greeks despaired for their own safety and destroyed their belongings, saying: "a Mede will not keep these things."

[1] Kassel has suggested the emendation 'devour'.

76 Plutarch, *Agesilaus* 19.9 (*BT* v.3.2 p.217.17–21 Ziegler)

Xenophon, then, has not written the name of the daughter of Agesilaus, and Dicaearchus was indignant that we know neither the daughter of Agesilaus nor the mother of Epaminondas.

77 Athenaeus, Deipnosophistae 13.5 557B (BT t.3 p.228.16–21 Kaibel)

Φίλιππος δ' ὁ Μακεδὼν οὐκ ἐπήγετο μὲν εἰς τοὺς πολέμους
γυναῖκας, ὥσπερ Δαρεῖος ὁ ὑπ' Ἀλεξάνδρου καταλυθείς, ὃς περὶ
τῶν ὅλων πολεμῶν τριακοσίας ἑξήκοντα περιήγετο παλλακάς,
ὡς ἱστορεῖ Δικαίαρχος ἐν τρίτῳ Περὶ τοῦ τῆς Ἑλλάδος βίου. ὁ
δὲ Φίλιππος αἰεὶ κατὰ πόλεμον ἐγάμει.   5

78 Cicero, De officiis 2.16–17 (OCT p.74.21–75.2 Winterbottom)

   est Dicaearchi liber De interitu hominum, Peripatetici magni et
copiosi, qui collectis ceteris causis eluvionis, pestilentiae, vastitatis,
beluarum etiam repentinae multitudinis, quarum impetu docet
quaedam hominum genera esse consumpta, deinde comparat, quanto
plures deleti sint homines hominum impetu, id est bellis aut   5
17 seditionibus, quam omni reliqua calamitate. cum igitur hic locus
nihil habeat dubitationis, quin homines plurimum hominibus et
prosint et obsint, proprium hoc statuo esse virtutis, conciliare animos
hominum et ad usus suos adiungere.

2–3 cf. Plato, Leg. 3 677a et Arist., Meteor. 351b12 et Polybius 6.5.5

───────────

5 aut *B*: et *B'*   7 nihil] nil *L*   8 proprium hoc *Z*: primum et hoc *X*

79 Cicero, Ad Atticum 6.2.3 (BT t.1 p.220.7–22 Shackleton Bailey)

   Peloponnesias civitates omnis maritimas esse hominis non
nequam sed etiam tuo iudicio probati Dicaearchi Tabulis credidi. is
multis nominibus in Trophoniana Chaeronis narratione Graecos in
eo reprehendit, quod mare tantum secuti sunt nec ullum in
Peleponneso locum excipit. cum mihi auctor placeret, etenim erat   5
ἱστορικώτατος et vixerat in Peloponneso, admirabar tamen et vix
accredens communicavi cum Dionysio; atque is primo est
commotus, deinde, quod de isto Dicaearcho non minus bene
existimabat quam tu de C. Vestorio, ego de M. Cluvio, non dubitabat
quin ei crederemus: Arcadiae censebat esse Lepreon quoddam   10
maritimum, Tenea autem et Aliphera et Tritia νεόκτιστα ei

77 Athenaeus, *The Sophists at Dinner* 13.5 557B (*BT* v.3 p.228.16–21 Kaibel)

Philip the Macedonian did not bring women into wars, as did the Darius deposed by Alexander, who (even) when making war concerning everything brought 360 concubines along, as Dicaearchus writes in the third book *On the Life of Greece*. But Philip always married in war.

78 Cicero, *On Duties* 2.16–17 (*OCT* p.74.21–75.2 Winterbottom)

There is a book *On Human Destruction* by Dicaearchus, a great and prolific Peripatetic. He collected all the other causes of destruction, flood, epidemic, famine, even sudden increases in the populations of wild animals by the onslaught of which, he teaches, certain tribes of humans have been entirely consumed. Then he makes a comparison of how many more humans have been destroyed by the onslaught of humans, that is, by war and revolu-
17 tions, than by every other calamity. Therefore, since this point offers no doubt but that humans both help and hurt humans most, I conclude that it is the peculiar function of (human) excellence to conciliate human minds and to join them to its service.

79 Cicero, *To Atticus* 6.2.3 (*BT* v.1 p.220.7–22 Shackleton Bailey)

I trusted the *Accounts* of a man, Dicaearchus, who is not worthless but who is approved even by your judgement, (who said) that all the Peloponnesian states were on the sea. In the *Trophonian Story* of Chaeron,[1] he criticizes the Greeks in many respects because they only pursued the sea, and he did not except any place in the Peloponnesus. Although he pleased me as an authority, for he was "most given to enquiry" and had lived in the Peloponnesus, I wondered still and, scarcely believing it, corresponded with Dionysius[2]; he also was shaken at first; then, because he approved of your Dicaearchus no less than you do of C. Vestorius[3] and I of M. Cluvius, he did not doubt that we should believe him: he thought Arcadia had a certain port (called) Lepreon, but Tenea, Aliphera

videbantur, idque τῷ τῶν νεῶν καταλόγῳ confirmabat, ubi mentio non fit istorum. itaque istum ego locum totidem verbis a Dicaearcho transtuli.

13–14 cf. Cic., De rep. 2.8

4 mare tantum *Orelli alii*: mare tam *codd.* : maritima *Shackleton Bailey*   7 accredens *Bosius*: adgredens, -iens *codd.*   8 de isto *Orelli alii* : cum de isto, de deo cum isto *alia codd.* : de deo isto *Shackleton Bailey*: de Chaerone isto Dicaearcho *Purser*

80 Athenaeus, Deipnosophistae 14.48 641E–F (BT t.3 p.417.9–14 Kaibel)

F Δικαίαρχος δ᾽ ἐν πρώτῳ τῆς Εἰς Τροφωνίου καταβάσεώς φησιν οὕτως· "ἥ γε τὴν πολλὴν δαπάνην ἐν τοῖς δείπνοις παρέχουσα δευτέρα τράπεζα προσεγένετο, καὶ στέφανοι καὶ μύρα καὶ θυμιάματα καὶ τὰ τούτοις ἀκόλουθα πάντα."

81 Athenaeus, Deipnosophistae 13.67 594E–595A (BT t.3 p.311.4–18 Kaibel)

F Δικαίαρχος δ᾽ ἐν τοῖς Περὶ τῆς εἰς Τροφωνίου καταβάσεώς φησι· "ταὐτὸ δὲ πάθοι τις ἂν ἐπὶ τὴν Ἀθηναίων πόλιν ἀφικνού-μενος κατὰ τὴν ἀπ᾽ Ἐλευσῖνος τὴν ἱερὰν ὁδὸν καλουμένην. καὶ γὰρ ἐνταῦθα καταστάς, οὗ ἂν φανῇ τὸ πρῶτον ὁ τῆς Ἀθηνᾶς ἀφορώμενος νεὼς καὶ τὸ πόλισμα, ὄψεται παρὰ τὴν ὁδὸν αὐτὴν 5 ᾠκοδομημένον μνῆμα οἷον οὐχ ἕτερον οὐδὲ σύνεγγυς οὐδέν ἐστι τῷ μεγέθει. τοῦτο δὲ τὸ μὲν πρῶτον, ὅπερ εἰκός, ἢ Μιλτιάδου φήσειεν ⟨ἂν⟩ σαφῶς ἢ Περικλέους ἢ Κίμωνος ἤ τινος ἑτέρου τῶν
595 ἀγαθῶν ἀνδρῶν εἶναι, ⟨καὶ⟩ μάλιστα μὲν ὑπὸ τῆς πόλεως δημοσίᾳ κατεσκευασμένον, εἰ δὲ μή, δεδομένον κατασκευά- 10 σασθαι. πάλιν δ᾽ ὅταν ἐξετάσῃ Πυθιονίκης τῆς ἑταίρας ὄν, τίνα χρὴ προσδοκίαν λαβεῖν αὐτόν;"

6–12 cf. Paus., 1.37.5 et Plut., Phoc. 22

3 κατὰ τὴν *Jacoby*: καὶ ταύτην A   4 φανῇ *Valckenar*: ᾗ A   ὁ τῆς Ἀθηνᾶς *Meineke* : εἰς Ἀθήνας A   8 ἄν *supplevit Kaibel*   9 καὶ *suppl. Kaibel*   10 δεδομένον *Kaibel* : δεδογμένον A

and Tritia appeared to him to be newly created, which he verified by the *Catalogue of Ships*, where there is no mention of them. And so I took over that passage from Dicaearchus verbatim.

[1] According to Paus. 9.40.5, Chaeron was the son of Apollo and Thero, after whom the Boeotian city of Chaeroneia was named. Dicaearchus apparently used the name for a character in his dialogue because of its Boeotian association.

[2] M. Pomponius Dionysius, a scholar and teacher, is praised by Cicero in *Ad Att.* 7.4.1.

[3] C. Vestorius and M. Cluvius were businessmen from Puteoli, which was formerly called Dicaearchia. Cicero is not serious; he considered both men to be uncultivated (*Ad Att.* 14.12).

80 Athenaeus, *The Sophists at Dinner* 14.48 641E–F (*BT* v.3 p.417.9–14 Kaibel)

F Dicaearchus in the first book of his *Descent into (the Cave) of Trophonius* says, "there was added the dessert, which causes great expense at the dinner party, wreaths, perfumes, incense, and all the things that go with them."

81 Atheneaeus, *The Sophists at Dinner* 13.67 594E–595A (*BT* v.3 p.311.4–18 Kaibel)

F Dicaearchus in the books *On the Descent into (the Cave) of Trophonius* says, "but a man would experience the same thing on arriving at the city of the Athenians on the road from Eleusis called the Sacred Way. For standing there where the temple of Athena and the citadel (i.e., the Acropolis) first appear, he will see built beside the road itself a monument such as no other, nor is any like it in size. At first he would likely say that it is clearly of Miltiades 595 or Pericles or Cimon, or some other noble man, and that certainly it had been set up publicly by the city, or, if not, that its erection had been allowed. But when he reflects on its being of a courtesan, Pythionike, what expectation (of the city) should he assume?

82 Scholion in Pindari Olympiacas 6.7b (BT p.155.24–156.2 Drachmann)

δι᾽ ἐμπύρων ἐν Ἤλιδι Ἰαμίδαι ἐμαντεύοντο. ἀφ᾽ ὧν τὸ γένος εἶχεν Ἀγησίας. τοῦ δὲ μαντείου τοῦ ἐν Ἤλιδι καὶ Δικαίαρχος μέμνηται.

1 Ἰαμίδαι] Ἰαμμίδι *b*

83 Athenaeus, Deipnosophistae 13.80 603A–B (BT t.3 p.330.4–10 Kaibel)

φιλόπαις δ᾽ ἦν ἐκμανῶς καὶ Ἀλέξανδρος ὁ βασιλεύς. Δικαίαρχος γοῦν ἐν τῷ Περὶ τῆς ἐν Ἰλίῳ θυσίας Βαγώου τοῦ
B εὐνούχου οὕτως αὐτόν φησιν ἡττᾶσθαι ὡς ἐν ὄψει θεάτρου ὅλου καταφιλεῖν αὐτὸν ἀνακλάσαντα, καὶ τῶν θεατῶν ἐπιφωνησάντων μετὰ κρότου οὐκ ἀπειθήσας πάλιν ἀνακλάσας   5
ἐφίλησεν.

1–6 cf. Plut., Alex. 67.4

84 Scholion in Aristophanis Vespas 544b (p.86.10–17 Koster)

θαλλοφόρους γὰρ ἔφη, βουλόμενος τοὺς γέροντας δηλῶσαι, ἐπειδὴ ἐν τοῖς Παναθηναίοις οἱ γέροντες θαλλοὺς ἔχοντες ἐπόμπευον. ὡς οὖν εἰς οὐδὲν ὄντων χρησίμων αὐτῶν ἔξω τοῦ θαλλοφορεῖν, οὕτως αὐτοὺς ἐπέσκωψεν. ὁ μέντοι Δικαίαρχος ἐν τῷ Παναθηναικῷ φησιν—οὐκ οἶδα ἐξ ὅτου—"ποτὲ καὶ τὰς γραῦς   5
ἐν τοῖς Παναθηναίοις ὑπειλῆφθαι θαλλοφορεῖν," πολλῶν ἀλλήλοις ὁμολογούντων ὑπὲρ τοῦ μόνους τοὺς πρεσβύτας θαλλοφορεῖν.

5 ἐξ ὅτου *post* ποτέ *ponendum esse censet Holwerda; sine ulla interpunctione ante* οὐκ *et post* ὅτου *Dindorf, Duebner, Wehrli*

85 Athenaeus, Deipnosophistae 14.12 620D (BT t.3 p.367.27–368.1 Kaibel)

τοὺς δ᾽ Ἐμπεδοκλέους Καθαρμοὺς ἐρραψῴδησεν Ὀλυμπίασι

82 Scholium on Pindar's *Olympian Ode* 6.7b (*BT* p.155.24–156.2
Drachmann)

The Iamidae used to divine through fires in Elis. Agesias
was their descendant. Dicaearchus also recalls the divination in
Elis.

83 Athenaeus, *The Sophists at Dinner* 13.80 603A–B (*BT* v.3 p.330.4–
10 Kaibel)

King Alexander was also madly in love with boys. Indeed,
Dicaearchus, in the work *On the Sacrifice at Ilium*, says that he
B was so overcome by Bagoas the eunuch that in view of the entire
theater he bent him over to kiss him passionately and then, when
the spectators shouted approval, he obliged and again bent him over
and kissed him.

84 Scholion on Aristophanes' *Wasps* 544b (p.86.10–17 Koster)

For he said "olive-shoot carriers" because he wished to show
that they were old men, since in the Panathenaiac (processions) the
old men used to process holding olive shoots. Indeed, inasmuch as
they (contributed) nothing that was useful outside of carrying olive
shoots, in this way he ridiculed them. However, Dicaearchus in the
Panathenaic (Dialogue) says—I do not know from what source—
"at some time the practice was taken up for old women also to
carry olive shoots in the Panathenaic (processions)," since many
agree with each other about only old men carrying olive shoots.

85 Athenaeus, *The Sophists at Dinner* 14 620D (*BT* v.3 p.367.27–368.1
Kaibel)

The rhapsodist Cleomenes performed the *Purifications* of

Κλεομένης ὁ ῥαψῳδός, ὥς φησιν Δικαίαρχος ἐν τῷ Ὀλυμπικῷ.

1–2 cf. Diog. Laert. 8.63, ubi Favorinus non Dicaearchus nominatur   1
Empedocles, FVS 31A12

Politica

86 Cicero, De legibus 3.14 (CB p.88.10–18 de Plinval)

nam veteres verbo tenus acute illi quidem, sed non ad hunc usum
popularem atque civilem de re publica disserebant. ab hac familia
magis ista manarunt Platone principe, post Aristoteles illustravit
omnem hunc civilem in disputando locum; Heraclidesque Ponticus
profectus ab eodem Platone; Theophrastus vero, institutus ab   5
Aristotele, habitavit ut scitis in eo genere rerum, ab eodemque
Aristotele doctus Dicaearchus huic rationi studioque non defuit.
post a Theophrasto Phalereus ille Demetrius, de quo feci supra
mentionem, mirabiliter doctrinam ex umbraculis eruditorum otioque
non modo in solem atque in pulverem, sed in ipsum discrimen 10
aciemque produxit.

4 Heracleides Ponticus, fr. 143 Wehrli   5 Theophrastus 591 FHS&G   7
Demetrius, 57 SOD; cf. Cic., De leg. 2.64–6

2 ab hac (hanc) familia] Academia Haupt et de Plinval

87 Athenaeus, Deipnosophistae 4.19 141A–C (BT t.1 p.319.25–320.17
Kaibel)

περὶ δὲ τοῦ τῶν φιδιτίων δείπνου Δικαίαρχος τάδε ἱστορεῖ ἐν
τῷ ἐπιγραφομένῳ Τριπολιτικῷ· "τὸ δεῖπνον πρῶτον μὲν ἑκάστῳ
χωρὶς παρατιθέμενον καὶ πρὸς ἕτερον κοινωνίαν οὐδεμίαν ἔχον·
B εἶτα μᾶζαν μὲν ὅσην ἂν ἕκαστος ᾖ βουλόμενος, καὶ πιεῖν πάλιν
ὅταν ᾖ θυμὸς ἑκάστῳ κώθων παρακείμενός ἐστιν. ὄψον δὲ ταὐτὸν   5
ἀεί ποτε πᾶσίν ἐστιν, ὕειον κρέας ἐφθόν, ἐνίοτε δ' ⟨οὐδ'⟩
ὁτιμενοῦν πλὴν †ὄψον† τι μικρὸν ἔχον σταθμὸν ὡς τέταρτον
μάλιστα καὶ παρὰ τοῦτο ἕτερον οὐδὲν πλὴν ὅ γε ἀπὸ τούτων
ζωμὸς ἱκανὸς ὢν παρὰ πᾶν τὸ δεῖπνον ἅπαντας αὐτοὺς παρα-

Empedocles at Olympia, as Dicaearchus says in the *Olympic Dialogue*.

Politics

86   Cicero, *On Laws* 3.14 (*CB* p.88.10–18 de Plinval)

For the old (philosophers) discussed the state intelligently, in so far as theory goes, but not, as here, with a view to things useful for the people and citizens. Those things (i.e. theoretical discussions) have been derived more from this school (the Academy) led by Plato. Afterwards Aristotle clarified the whole topic of politics in dialogues, as did Heraclides of Pontus, who also got his start from the same Plato. Indeed Theophrastus, who was instructed by Aristotle, spent his time, as you know, in this kind of subject, and Dicaearchus, who was taught by the same Aristotle, did not neglect this area of thought and discipline. Afterwards a student of Theophrastus, that Demetrius of Phaleron concerning whom I made mention above, admirably brought the teaching forward from the shadows and leisure of scholars not only into the sun and arena, but also into conflict itself and the line of battle.

87   Athenaeus, *The Sophists at Dinner* 4.19 141A–C (*BT* v.1 p.319.25–320.17 Kaibel)

Concerning the dinner of the messes (in Sparta) Dicaearchus reports the following in the work entitled *Three-City (Dialogue)*: "First the dinner is served to each individually, there being no shar-

B   ing with another. Then each (receives) a barley cake as large as he wishes, and drinks whenever he has desire, a cup being set beside each one. The same meat dish is always given to all, a piece of boiled pork, but sometimes <not> even that, but rather some small dish of meat having at most a quarter portion. And beyond that there is nothing else except the broth resulting from these things, which is sufficient to be sent around to all throughout the whole

πέμπειν, κἂν ἄρα ἐλάα τις ἢ τυρὸς ἢ σῦκον, ἀλλὰ κἄν τι λάβωσιν 10
c ἐπιδόσιμον, ἰχθὺν ἢ λαγὼν ἢ φάτταν ἤ τι τοιοῦτον. εἶτ᾽ ὀξέως
ἤδη δεδειπνηκόσιν ὕστερα περιφέρεται ταῦτα τὰ ἐπάικλα
καλούμενα. συμφέρει δ᾽ ἕκαστος εἰς τὸ φιδίτιον ἀλφίτων μὲν
ὡς τρία μάλιστα ἡμιμέδιμνα Ἀττικά, οἴνου δὲ χοεῖς ἕνδεκά
τινας ἢ δώδεκα, παρὰ δὲ ταῦτα τυροῦ σταθμόν τινα καὶ σύκων, 15
ἔτι δὲ εἰς ὀψωνίαν περὶ δέκα τινὰς Αἰγιναίους ὀβολούς."

6–8 cf. Plut., Lyc. 12   12–13 cf. Athen., 4.16–19 139B–141E

5 κώθων Casaubonus : καθ᾽ ὧν A   6 οὐδ᾽ ὀτιμενοῦν Schweighäuser : δε τι
μονον A   7 cruces pos. Wehrli   8 ἀπὸ τούτων A : ἀπὸ τούτου C

88 Photius, Bibliotheca 37 (CB t.1 p.22.20–30 Henry)

ἀνεγνώσθη Περὶ πολιτικῆς ὡς ἐν διαλόγῳ, Μηνᾶν πατρίκιον
καὶ Θωμᾶν ῥεφερενδάριον τὰ διαλεγόμενα εἰσάγον πρόσωπα.
περιέχει δὲ ἡ πραγματεία λόγους ἕξ, ἐν οἷς καὶ ἕτερον εἶδος
πολιτείας παρὰ τὰ τοῖς παλαιοῖς εἰρημένα εἰσάγει, ὃ καὶ καλεῖ
Δικαιαρχικόν. ἐπιμέμφεται δὲ τῆς Πλάτωνος δικαίως πολιτείας. 5
ἣν δ᾽ αὐτοὶ πολιτείαν εἰσάγουσιν ἐκ τῶν τριῶν εἰδῶν τῆς
πολιτείας δέον αὐτὴν συγκεῖσθαί φασι, βασιλικοῦ καὶ
ἀριστοκρατικοῦ καὶ δημοκρατικοῦ, τὸ εἰλικρινὲς αὐτῇ ἑκάστης
πολιτείας συνεισαγούσης, κἀκείνην τὴν ὡς ἀληθῶς ἀρίστην
πολιτείαν ἀποτελειούσης. 10

7–8 cf. Polybius, 6.3 et 10

2 εἰσάγον AM' : εἰσάγων M   7 δέον A : om. M   10 ἀποτελειούσης A'M' :
ἀποτελούσης A

Certamina, Ars critica

89 Suda, s.v. σκολιόν (no. 643, LG t.1 pars 4 p.382.28–383.3 Adler)

ἡ παροίνιος ᾠδή, ὡς μὲν Δικαίαρχος ἐν τῷ Περὶ μουσικῶν
ἀγώνων, ὅτι τρία γένη ἦν ᾠδῶν, τὸ μὲν ὑπὸ πάντων ᾀδόμενον,
⟨τὸ δὲ⟩ καθ᾽ ἕνα ἑξῆς, τὸ δ᾽ ὑπὸ τῶν συνετωτάτων ὡς ἔτυχε τῇ

dinner, and there may be some olive or cheese or fig, and if they get something added, it is a fish or a hare or a ring-dove or something of that sort. After they have quickly dined there are passed around the so-called *epaikla*. Each contributes to the mess about three Attic half medimni of barley, eleven or twelve pitchers of wine, and beyond this a measure of cheese and figs, and for the meat dish about twelve Aigenetan obols."

88 Photius, *Library* 37 (*CB* v.1 p.22.20–30 Henry)

There was read (a work) *On Political Theory* in dialogue form, introducing Menas the patrician and Thomas a referendarius as the characters in the discussion. The work contains six dialogues, in which (the author) introduces a different form of constitution from those discussed by the ancients, which he even called Dicaearchic.[1] He justly found fault with the *Republic* of Plato. They (the interlocutors) say that the constitution that they introduce must be combined from the three forms of constitution, the monarchical, aristocratic and democratic, each constitution contributing to it its pureness and perfecting what is truely the best constitution.

[1] This may have nothing to do with Dicaearchus; it may refer only to 'just rule' (*dikaia arche*); cf. Suda, s.v. *Dikaiarcheia*. Dicaearchus' name appears in a list of names of orators, historians and generals in Photius, *Library* 167.

Contests, Literary Criticism

89 Suda, on *scolion* (no. 643, *LG* v.1 part 4 p.382.28–383.3 Adler)

As Dicaearchus (says) in the work *On Musical Contests*, (*scolion*) was a drinking song. There were three kinds of songs, one was sung by all, another was sung by each individually one after another, and the last by the most quick-witted in order as it happened.

τάξει. ὃ δὴ καλεῖσθαι διὰ τὴν τάξιν σκολιόν.

1–4 *Pausanias Atticista, s.v., (no.16, p.209.18–20 Erbse) et scholion in Platonis Gorgiam 451e (p.134.1–4 Greene)*   2–4 cf. *Athen., Deipn. 15.49 694A–B, et Plut., Quaest. conv. 1 615A–C, ubi tamen non Dicaearchus sed Artemon nominatur*

3 τὸ δὲ *supplevit Wehrli post Hermann*

90 Scholion in Aristophanis Nubes 1364c (p.239.8–12 Koster)

Δικαίαρχος ἐν τῷ Περὶ μουσικῶν ⟨ἀγώνων⟩· "ἔτι δὲ κοινόν τι πάθος φαίνεται συνακολουθεῖν τοῖς διερχομένοις εἴτε μετὰ μέλους εἴτε ἄνευ μέλους, ἔχοντάς τι ἐν τῇ χειρὶ ποιεῖσθαι τὴν ἀφήγησιν. οἵ τε γὰρ ᾄδοντες ἐν τοῖς συμποσίοις ἐκ παλαιᾶς τινος παραδόσεως κλῶνα δάφνης ἢ μυρρίνης λαβόντες ᾄδουσιν."   5

1 ἀγώνων *supplevit Dindorf*   ἔτι *Hermann* : ἐπεὶ *codd.*

91 Zenobius, Epitome collectionum Lucilli Tarrhaei et Didymi 3.99 (CPG t.1 p.83.3–6 Leutsch et Schneidewin)

ἐκκέκοφθ᾽ ἡ μουσική· φησὶν ὅτι τῶν παλαιῶν ἐν τοῖς συμποσίοις φιλολόγων ζητήσει χρωμένων οἱ ὕστερον τὰς μουσουργοὺς καὶ κιθαρίστριας καὶ ὀρχήστριας ἐπεισήγαγον, ὅθεν τὴν καινοτομίαν τινὲς αἰτιώμενοι τῇ παροιμίᾳ ἐχρῶντο.

1–4 *Plutarchus 1.38, Apostolius 6.94*

1 ἐκκέκοφθ᾽] ἐκκεκοφ᾽ *L*   φησὶν ὅτι *codex Atheniensis 1083 (S.B. München 4 [1910] 22 Kugéas)*: omit. *L, Plut.*: φασὶν *P, Apostolius*   2 φιλολόγων *cod. Athen. 1083*: φιλολόγῳ *P*   4 ὅθεν … ἐχρῶντο *cod. Athen. 1083*: omit. *P*

92 Plutarchus, Non posse suaviter vivi secundum Epicurum 12 1095A (BT t.6.2 p.144.11–15 Pohlenz et Westman)

οὐ γὰρ ἂν ἐπῆλθεν αὐτοῖς εἰς νοῦν βαλέσθαι τὰς τυφλὰς καὶ νωδὰς ἐκείνας ψηλαφήσεις καὶ ἐπιπηδήσεις τοῦ ἀκολάστου, μεμαθηκόσιν, εἰ μηδὲν ἄλλο, γράφειν περὶ Ὁμήρου καὶ περὶ Εὐριπίδου, ὡς Ἀριστοτέλης καὶ Ἡρακλείδης καὶ Δικαίαρχος.

4 *Heraclides Ponticus, fr. 168 Wehrli*

This was called *scolion* on account of the order.[1]

[1] *Skolion* literally means "crooked." That is, there was no particular order.

90 Scholion on Aristophanes' *Clouds* 1364c (p.239.8–12 Koster)

Dicaearchus in the work *On Musical <Contests>*: "It still appears to be a common affectation associated with those performing either with a song or without a song, to hold something in their hand when doing their recitation. For from some old tradition those singing in the symposia take a twig of laurel or myrtle when they sing."

91 Zenobius, *Summary of the Collections of Lucillus Tarrhaeus and Didymus* 3.99 (*CPG* v.1 p.83.3–6 Leutsch and Schneidewin)

"Music[1] has been cut out:" (Dicaearchus)[2] says that while the ancient lovers of literature practiced inquiry at their symposia, those who came later introduced girls who sang, played the lyre, and danced. As a result, those who criticized the change used the saying.

[1] I.e. culture.
[2] This text appears in the *codex Atheniensis* 1083 immediately following **73**, **68** and **74**, each of which names Dicaearchus. Kugéas proposed that Dicaearchus be seen as the source for this text also. Cf. Kassel, *Hermes* 91 (1963).

92 Plutarch, *That Epicurus Actually Makes a Pleasant Life Impossible* 12 1095A (*BT* v.6.2 p.144.11–15 Pohlenz and Westman)

It would not have occurred to them to put into their minds those blind and toothless fingerings of and leapings upon wantonness if they had learned, if nothing else, to write about Homer and Euripides, as did Aristotle and Heraclides and Dicaearchus.

93 Anonymus Grammaticus Romanus, De notis veterum criticis 3 (Lexicon Vindobonense p.273.16–17 Nauck)

τὴν δὲ ποίησιν ἀναγινώσκεσθαι ἀξιοῖ Ζώπυρος ὁ Μάγνης Αἰολίδι διαλέκτῳ, τὸ δ᾽ αὐτὸ καὶ Δικαίαρχος. αἱ μέντοι ῥαψῳδίαι κατὰ συνάφειαν ἤβωντο, κορωνίδι μόνῃ διαστελλόμεναι, ἄλλῳ δ᾽ οὐδενί.

1 *Zopyrus, FGrH 494F 3*

3 ῥαψῳδίαι *Osannus* : ῥαψῳδείαι *cod.*   ἤβωντο] ἤνωντο *Osannus*

94 Apollonius Dyscolus, De pronomine 60B (t.1.1 p.48.1–11 Uhlig et Schneider)

ὅθεν τινές, πάλιν ἀγνοήσαντες τὸ μεταβατικόν, τὸ
αἴτει δ᾽ οἰωνόν, ἐὸν ἄγγελον
μεταγράφουσιν εἰς τὸ ταχὺν ἄγγελον, ἢ τὸν ἀγαθὸν
ἐκδέχονται. καὶ ἐπὶ θηλυκῆς
τὸν ξεῖνον πέμπωμεν ἐὴν ἐς πατρίδα γαῖαν   5
φασὶ δὲ καὶ τὸν Ἀρίσταρχον ἀσμένως τὴν γραφὴν τοῦ
Δικαιάρχου παραδέξασθαι, ἐν γὰρ ἁπάσαις ἦν τὸ
ἐῇ ἐν πατρίδι γαίῃ,
ὑπολαβόντα τὸ ἑαυτῆς νοεῖσθαι ἐκ τοῦ ἐῇ, δέον πάλιν ψιλῶς
μεταλαμβάνειν.   10

2 *Homerus, Ilias 24.292; cf. 24.296*   5 *Homerus, Odysseas 13.52*   9 *Homerus, Ilias 3.243–4* ὡς φάτο, τοὺς δ᾽ ἤδη κάτεχεν φυσίζοος αἶα / ἐν Λακεδαίμονι αὖθι, φίλῃ ἐν πατρίδι γαίῃ. Cf. *Apollon. Dysc., De Syntaxi 2.115*

4 θηλυκῆς *Skrzeczka* : αἰτιατικῆς *Ab*   7 παραδέξασθαι : ἀναδέξασθαι *A et Wehrli*   8 ἐῇ ἐν πατρίδι γαίῃ *b in var. lect.* : ἐὴν ἐς πατρίδα γαίην *Ab*   9 ἑαυτῆς *Naeke* : ἑαυτοῦ *Ab*

95 Scholion in Homeri Odysseam 1.332 (p.58.25–59.12 Dindorf)

αἰτιᾶται ἐκ τῶν ἐπῶν τούτων Δικαίαρχος τὴν παρ᾽ Ὁμήρῳ Πηνελόπην
ἡ δ᾽ ὅτε δὴ μνηστῆρας ἀφίκετο δῖα γυναικῶν,
στῆ ῥα παρὰ σταθμὸν τέγεος πύκα ποιητοῖο
ἄντα παρειάων   5

93 Anonymus Roman Grammarian, *Critical Notes on the Ancients* 3
(*Vienna Lexicon* p.273.16–17 Nauck)

Zopyrus of Magnesia thinks the poetry (of Homer) ought to be
sung in the Aeolic dialect and Dicaearchus (thinks) the same thing.
However, rhapsodic poetry had its vigour through repetition of the
same metrical foot and was distinguished by the ending alone, by
nothing else.

94 Apollonius Dyscolus, *On the Pronoun* 60 B (v.1.1 p.48.1–11 Uhlig
and Schneider)

For this reason, again, some who are ignorant of the change (of
the possessive adjective) rewrite
    ask for a bird of omen, *his* messenger
as '*swift* messenger', or they understand 'the *good*' (messenger). And with regard to the feminine
    let us send the stranger to *his* native land,
they say that even Aristarchus gladly accepted the reading of
Dicaearchus—for in all (copies) there was the (reading)
    in *her* native land—
since he supposed that '*her*' meant '*her own*', it requiring again
(only) a simple substitution.

95 Scholion on Homer, *Odyssey* 1.332 (p.58.25–59.12 Dindorf)

From these words Dicaearchus found fault with the Penelope in
Homer:
              When she reached the suitors, divine of women,
              She stood beside a pillar of the strongly made building,
              Before her cheeks.

καὶ τὰ ἑξῆς. οὐδαμῶς γὰρ εὔτακτον εἶναί φησι τὴν Πηνελόπην, πρῶτα μὲν ὅτι πρὸς μεθύοντας αὕτη παραγίνεται νεανίσκους, ἔπειτα τῷ κρηδέμνῳ τὰ κάλλιστα μέρη τοῦ προσώπου καλύψασα τοὺς ὀφθαλμοὺς μόνους ἀπολέλοιπε θεωρεῖσθαι. περίεργος γὰρ ἡ τοιαύτη σχηματοποιία καὶ προσποίητος, ἥ τε παράστασις τῶν 10 θεραπαινίδων ἑκάτερθεν εἰς τὸ κατ᾽ ἐξοχὴν φαίνεσθαι καλὴν οὐκ ἀνεπιτήδευτον δείκνυσι. φάμεν οὖν ὅτι τὸ καθόλου ἔθος ἀγνοεῖν ἔοικεν ὁ Δικαίαρχος. σύνηθες γὰρ παρὰ τοῖς ἀρχαίοις τὰς ἐλευθέρας γυναῖκας εἰς τὰ τῶν ἀνδρῶν εἰσιέναι συμπόσια.

96 Plutarchus, Non posse suaviter vivi secundum Epicurum 13 1096A (BT t.6.2 p.146.10–19 Pohlenz et Westman)

οὐκ ἦν δὲ πρὸς τὸ ἡδέως ζῆν ἐπιεικέστερον μύρα καὶ θυμιάματα δυσχεραίνειν ὡς κάνθαροι καὶ γῦπες, ἢ κριτικῶν καὶ μουσικῶν λαλιὰν βδελύττεσθαι καὶ φεύγειν· ποῖος γὰρ ἂν αὐλὸς ἢ κιθάρα διηρμοσμένη πρὸς ᾠδὴν ἢ τίς χορὸς "Εὐρύοπα κέλαδον ἀκροσόφων ἀγνύμενον διὰ στομάτων" φθεγγόμενος οὕτως 5 εὔφρανεν Ἐπίκουρον καὶ Μητρόδωρον, ὡς Ἀριστοτέλην καὶ Θεόφραστον καὶ Δικαίαρχον καὶ Ἱερώνυμον οἱ περὶ χορῶν λόγοι καὶ διδασκαλιῶν καὶ τὰ [δι᾽] αὐλῶν προβλήματα καὶ ῥυθμῶν καὶ ἁρμονιῶν;

1–2 cf. Theophrastus, CP 6.5.1   5 PMG fr. 1008 (adesp. 90)   6 Epicurus, fr. 512 Usener = 136 Arrighetti[2]   Aristoteles, fr. 99 Rose[3]   7 Theophrastus, 715 FHS&G   Hieronymus, fr. 26 Wehrli

6–7 ὡς—Δικαίαρχον om. Γ   8 διδασκαλιῶν] διδασκαλίαι Π   [δι᾽] αὐλῶν Pohlenz : διαυλιῶν Reiske : διαυλίων Apelt : περὶ αὐλῶν Wyttenbach

97 Zenobius, Epitome collectionum Lucilli Tarrhaei et Didymi 2.15 (CPG t.1 p.35.7–9 Leutsch et Schneidewin)

ἄειδε τὰ Τέλληνος· οὗτος ὁ Τέλλην ἐγένετο αὐλητὴς καὶ μελῶν ἀνυποτάκτων ποιητής. μέμνηται αὐτοῦ Δικαίαρχος ὁ Μεσσήνιος.

2 Δικαίαρχος Schottus : Δίαρχος codd.

and so on. He says that Penelope is by no means well-behaved, first, because she comes into the presence of drunk young men, then, because she covers the most beautiful parts of her face with the veil, she leaves her eyes alone to be seen. For such posturing is superfluous and pretentious, and the accompanying of the women servants on each side for the purpose of appearing outstandingly beautiful shows it was not unintended. However, we say that Dicaearchus seems to be ignorant of the general custom. For it was common among the ancients that the free women entered the men's symposia.

96 Plutarch, *That Epicurus Actually Makes a Pleasant Life Impossible* 13 1096A (*BT* v.6.2 p.146.10–19 Pohlenz and Westman)

With a view to living pleasantly, wouldn't it be more reasonable to feel disgust at sweet oil and burnt offerings, as do dung-beetles and vultures, rather than to loathe and avoid the talk of literary and musical critics? For what sort of *aulos* or cithara tuned for song or what chorus giving forth "far-sounding voice passed through expert mouths" could so have cheered Epicurus and Metrodorus as the discussions of choruses and the productions, and the problems concerning *auloi* (pipes) and rhythms and harmonies (cheered) Aristotle and Theophrastus and Dicaearchus and Hieronymus?

97 Zenobius, *Summary of the Collections of Lucillus Tarrhaeus and Didymus* 2.15 (*CPG* v.1 p.35.7–9 Leutsch and Schneidewin)

Sing the (story) of Tellen: This Tellen was a piper and composer of unruly songs. Dicaearchus of Messana mentions him.

98 Zenobius, Epitome proverbiorum Didymi Tarrhaei 2.100 (Mélanges de littérature grecque [1868] p.368.16–18 Miller)

τὸν αὐλητὴν αὐλεῖν· ταύτης μέμνηται Φιλήμων ὁ κωμικός. Δικαίαρχος δέ φησιν ὅτι αὐλητής τις ἐγένετο μὴ πάνυ τοῖς αὐλητικοῖς ἐμμένων νόμοις, ἀλλὰ παρακινῶν· ὅθεν εἰς παροιμίαν ἦλθεν ὁ λόγος.

1 *Philemon, PCG 7 F 183 KA*

3 νόμοις *CPG App. 4.94* : λόγοις *cod.*

99 Scholion in Aristophanis Aves 1403 (p.241a.41–7 Duebner)

Ἀντίπατρος δὲ καὶ Εὐφρόνιος ἐν τοῖς Ὑπομνήσασί φασι τοὺς κυκλίους χοροὺς στῆσαι πρῶτον Λᾶσον τὸν Ἑρμιονέα, οἱ δὲ ἀρχαιότεροι Ἑλλάνικος καὶ Δικαίαρχος Ἀρίονα τὸν Μηθυμναῖον, Δικαίαρχος μὲν ἐν τῷ περὶ Διονυσιακῶν ἀγώνων, Ἑλλάνικος δὲ ἐν τοῖς Καρνεονίκαις.   5

2 *Lasus, vid. fr. 703 Page*   2, 4 *Hellanicus, FGrH 4 F 86*   4–5 *cf. Arist., fr. 677 Rose³*

5 Καρνεονίκαις *Dahlmann* : Καρναικοῖς *vel* Κραναικοῖς *codd. et Duebner*

100 Vita Aeschyli 15 (TrGF t.3 p. 36.56–9 Radt)

ἐχρήσατο δὲ ὑποκρίτῃ πρώτῳ μὲν Κλεάνδρῳ, ἔπειτα καὶ τὸν δεύτερον αὐτῷ προσῆψε Μυννίσκον τὸν Καλχιδέα, τὸν δὲ τρίτον ὑποκριτὴν αὐτὸς ἐξεῦρεν, ὡς δὲ Δικαίαρχος ὁ Μεσσήνιος, Σοφοκλῆς.

2–3 *cf. Them., Or. 26 316d*   3–4 *cf. Diog. Laert. 3.56; cf. Arist., Poet. 4 1449a15–19*   4 *Sophocles, TrGF T98 Radt*

101 Hypothesis secunda Sophoclis Oedipodis tyranni (OCT p.109.20–3 Pearson)

ὁ Τύραννος Οἰδίπους ἐπὶ διακρίσει θατέρου ἐπιγέγραπται. χαριέντως δὲ Τύραννον ἅπαντες αὐτὸν ἐπιγράφουσιν ὡς ἐξέχοντα πάσης τῆς Σοφοκλέους ποιήσεως, καίπερ ἡττηθέντα

98 Pseudo-Zenobius, *Summary of the Proverbs of Didymus Tarrhaeus*
2.100 (*Mélanges de littérature grecque* [1868] 368.16–18 Miller)

"The piper pipes:" Philemon the comic poet mentions this saying. Dicaearchus says that there was a certain piper who did not
abide at all by the rules of piping, but violated them. This story
became a saying.

99 Scholion on Aristophanes *Birds* 1403 (p.241a.41–7 Duebner)

Antipater and Euphronius in the *Memoranda* say that Lasus of
Hermione first created circular choruses, but the older authors,
Hellanicus and Dicaearchus say it was Arion of Mythymna,
Dicaearchus (writing) in the work *On the Dionysiac Contests* and
Hellanicus in the *Carnean Victors*.

100 *Life of Aeschylus* 15 (*TrGF* v.3 p.36.56–9 Radt)

(Aeschylus) used Cleandros as first actor, and then added
Mynniscus of Kalchis to him as the second, and he himself in-
vented the third actor, but Dicaearchus the Messanian says it was
Sophocles.

101 Second *Hypothesis* of Sophocles' *Oedipus Tyrannus* (*OCT*
p.109.20–3 Pearson)

The *Oedipus Tyrannus* has been given this title (*Tyrannus*) in
order to distinguish it from the other. All graciously give it the
additional title *Tyrannus* as standing out above all Sophocles' work,

ὑπὸ Φιλοκλέους, ὥς φησι Δικαίαρχος. εἰσὶ δὲ καὶ οἱ πρότερον, οὐ τύραννον, αὐτὸν ἐπιγράφοντες, διὰ τοὺς χρόνους τῶν   5 διδασκαλιῶν καὶ διὰ τὰ πράγματα.

2 ἐπιγράφουσιν L: ἐπέγραφον *vulgo*   4 ὥς φησιν Δικαίαρχος *dubitat Luppe*
(*Hermes 119 [1991] 467–9*)

102 Plutarchus, De E apud Delphos 1 384D (BT t.3 p.1.4–8 Sieveking)

στιχιδίοις τισὶν οὐ φαύλως ἔχουσιν, ὦ φίλε Σαραπίων,
ἐνέτυχον πρῴην, ἃ Δικαίαρχος Εὐριπίδην οἴεται πρὸς Ἀρχέλαον
εἰπεῖν
    οὐ βούλομαι πλουτοῦντι δωρεῖσθαι πένης,
    μή μ᾽ ἄφρονα κρίνῃς ἢ διδοὺς αἰτεῖν δοκῶ.   5

2 *Euripides, fr. 969 Nauck²*   4–5 *cf. Menander, fr. 109b Kock*

103 Scholion in Platonis Apologiam 19C (p.421.16–20 Greene)

τρεῖς δ᾽ ἔσχεν υἱούς, Φίλιππον τὸν τοῖς Εὐβούλου δράμασιν
ἀγωνισάμενον, καὶ Ἀραρότα ἰδίοις τε καὶ τοῦ πατρὸς δράμασι
διηγωνισμένον, καὶ τρίτον, ὃν Ἀπολλόδωρος μὲν Νικόστρατον
καλεῖ, οἱ δὲ περὶ Δικαίαρχον Φιλέταιρον.

1–3 *PCG 3(2) T3.14–16 KA*   3–4 *cf. PCG 3(2) T1.55–7, T2.8–9, T7, T8 KA*
3 *Apollodorus, FGrH 244 F 75*

104 Hypothesis in Aristophanis Ranas 1(c) (p.114.26–9 Dover)

ἐδιδάχθη ἐπὶ Καλλίου ἄρχοντος τοῦ μετὰ Ἀντιγένη διὰ
Φιλωνίδου εἰς Λήναια. πρῶτος ἦν, Φρύνιχος β΄ Μούσαις,
Πλάτων τρίτος Κλεοφῶντι. οὕτω δὲ ἐθαυμάσθη τὸ δρᾶμα διὰ
τὴν ἐν αὐτῷ παράβασιν, ⟨καθ᾽ ἣν διαλλάττει τοὺς ἐντίμους τοῖς
ἀτίμοις καὶ τοὺς πολίτας τοῖς φυγάσιν⟩, ὥστε καὶ ἀνεδιδάχθη,   5

although it was beaten by Philocles, as Dicaearchus says. Some have also entitled it the *Earlier*, not *Tyrannus*, because of the chronology of the productions and because of the (dramatic) events.

102 Plutarch, *The E at Delphi* 1 384D (*BT* v.3 p.1.4–8 Sieveking)

My dear Serapion, I recently came upon some lines that were not too bad. Dicaearchus thinks Euripides addressed them to Archelaus:[1]

Poor as I am I do not wish to bestow a gift on a rich man
lest you judge me a fool or I appear in giving to demand (a
return).

[1] Archelaus was king of Macedon *c.* 413–399 and served as Euripides' patron after the playwright left Athens *c.* 408. It seems unlikely that the lines were taken from the play entitled *Archelaus*.

103 Scholion on Plato, *Apology* 19C (p.421.16–20 Greene)

(Aristophanes) had three sons, Philippus who competed with the plays of Eubulus, Araros who performed in his own and his father's plays, and a third, whom Apollodorus called Nicostratus, but those associated with Dicaearchus call Philetaerus.

104 *Hypothesis* to Aristophanes' *Frogs* 1(c) (p.114.26–9 Dover)

(The play) was produced when Callias was archon following Antigenes[1] by Philonides for the Lenaia. (Aristophanes) was first, Phrynicus second with *Muses*, and Platon third with *Cleophon*. The play was so admired because of its parabasis–through which (Aristophanes) reconciled the enfranchised to the disenfranchised and the citizens to the exiles–that it was produced again, as

ὡς φησι Δικαίαρχος.

1, 3–6 *Hypothesis Thomae Magistri (OCT t.2 p.102.16–19 Hall et Geldart)*   3–
4 *cf. Vit. Ar. (PCG 3(2) T1.35–9 KA)*

---

4 παράβασιν] κατάβασιν *Weil*   4–5 καθ᾽ ... φυγάσιν *suppl.* Wehrli e Thoma
Magistro

105 Athenaeus, Deipnosophistae 11.4 460F–461A (BT t.3 p.3.25–4.1
Kaibel)

ἄξιον δ᾽ ἐστὶ ζητῆσαι εἰ οἱ ἀρχαῖοι μεγάλοις ἔπινον ποτηρίοις.
461 Δικαίαρχος μὲν γὰρ ὁ Μεσσήνιος, ὁ Ἀριστοτέλους μαθητής, ἐν
τῷ Περὶ Ἀλκαίου μικροῖς φησιν αὐτοὺς ἐκπώμασι κεχρῆσθαι
καὶ ὑδαρέστερον πεπωκέναι.

106 Athenaeus, Deipnosophistae 15.2 666B–C (BT t.3 p.472.6–17
Kaibel

πρῶτον μὲν ἡ τῶν κοττάβων εὕρεσις Σικελική ἐστιν παιδιά,
ταύτην πρώτων εὑρόντων Σικελῶν, ὡς Κριτίας φησὶν ὁ
Καλλαίσχρου ἐν τοῖς Ἐλεγείοις διὰ τούτων
κότταβος ἐκ Σικελῆς ἐστι χθονὸς ἐκπρεπὲς ἔργον,
ὃν σκοπὸν ἐς λατάγων τόξα καθιστάμεθα.   5
Δικαίαρχος ⟨δὲ⟩ ὁ Μεσσήνιος, Ἀριστοτέλους μαθητής, ἐν τῷ
Περὶ Ἀλκαίου καὶ τὴν λατάγην φησὶν εἶναι Σικελικὸν ὄνομα.
c λατάγη δ᾽ ἐστὶν τὸ ὑπολειπόμενον ἀπὸ τοῦ ἐκποθέντος ποτηρίου
ὑγρόν, ὃ συνεστραμμένῃ τῇ χειρὶ ἄνωθεν ἐρρίπτουν οἱ παίζο-
ντες εἰς τὸ κοττάβιον.   10

2–9 *scholion in Aristophanis Pacem 1244 (p.176.9–16 Holwerda)*   2 Critias,
FVS 88B2   6 Alcaeus, fr. 462 Voigt

---

5 ἐς *Athen.* 28B: ἐκ *cod.*   6 δὲ *supplevit Wehrli*   7 λατάγην] λάταγα *schol.*
Aristoph.   8 ἀπὸ] ἐκ *schol. Aristoph.*

107 Athenaeus, Deipnosophistae 15.5 667B–C (BT t.3 p.474.23–475.4
Kaibel)

ἀγκυλοῦντα γὰρ δεῖ σφόδρα τὴν χεῖρα εὐρύθμως πέμπειν τὸν
κότταβον, ὡς Δικαίαρχός φησιν καὶ Πλάτων δ᾽ ἐν τῷ Διὶ [τῷ]

Dicaearchus says.

¹ I.e., 406/5 B.C.

105 Athenaeus, *The Sophists at Dinner* 11.4 460F–461A (*BT* v.3 p.3.25–4.1 Kaibel)

It is worth enquiring whether the ancients drank with large cups.
461   For Dicaearchus of Messana, a student of Aristotle, says in *On Alcaeus* that they used small cups and drank rather watery wine.

106 Athenaeus, *The Sophists at Dinner* 15.2 666B–C (*BT* v.3 p.472.6–17 Kaibel)

First of all, the discovery of the game of the *cottabos* is Sicilian, since the Sicilians were the first to discover it, as Critias, son of Callaeschrus, says in his elegies in the following words:
cottabos is the outstanding work of the land of Sicily, which we set up as a target for arrows made of drops (*latagai*) of wine.
Dicaearchus of Messana, a student of Aristotle, says in his *On*
C   *Alcaeus* that *latagê* as well is a Sicilian word. The *latagê* is the remaining moisture in an emptied cup, which the players flung up into the *cottabion* with a flick of the hand.¹

¹ Cf. scholium on Aristophanes' *Peace* 1244.

107 Athenaeus, *The Sophists at Dinner* 15.5 667B–C (*BT* v.3 p.474.23–475.4 Kaibel)

It is necessary to bend the arm very rhythmically when shooting the *cottabos*, as Dicaearchus says, and Platon in *Zeus Outraged.*

κακουμένῳ. παρακελεύεται δέ τις τῷ Ἡρακλεῖ μὴ σκληρὰν ἔχειν
c τὴν χεῖρα μέλλοντα κοτταβίζειν. ἐκάλουν δ' ἀπ' ἀγκύλης τὴν
τοῦ κοττάβου πρόεσιν διὰ τὸ ἐπαγκυλοῦν τὴν δεξιὰν χεῖρα ἐν 5
τοῖς ἀποκοτταβισμοῖς.

2 *Plato, PCG 7 F47 KA*

2 τῷ *expunxit Kaibel*   5 ἐπαγκυλοῦν *schol. Aristoph.* : ἀπαγκυλοῦν *codd.*
Athenaei

108 Athenaeus, Deipnosophistae 15.7 668D–E (BT t.3 p.478.12–15
Kaibel)

ὅτι δὲ ἐσπούδαστο παρὰ τοῖς Σικελιώταις ὁ κότταβος, δῆλον
E ἐκ τοῦ καὶ οἰκήματα ἐπιτήδεια τῇ παιδιᾷ κατασκευάζεσθαι, ὡς
ἱστορεῖ Δικαίαρχος ἐν τῷ Περὶ Ἀλκαίου.

3 *Alcaeus, fr. 462 Voigt*

109 Athenaeus, Deipnosophistae 11.58 479D–E (BT t.3 p.55.10–56.1
Kaibel)

Ἡγήσανδρος δ' ὁ Δελφὸς ἐν Ὑπομνήμασιν, ὧν ἀρχὴ "ἐν τῇ
ἀρίστῃ· πολιτείᾳ," φησίν· "ὁ καλούμενος κότταβος παρῆλθεν
εἰς τὰ συμπόσια τῶν περὶ Σικελίαν, ὥς φησιν Δικαίαρχος, πρῶτον
εἰσαγαγόντων. τοσαύτη δὲ ἐγένετο σπουδὴ περὶ τὸ ἐπιτήδευμα,
ὥστε εἰς τὰ συμπόσια παρεισφέρειν ἆθλα κοτταβεῖα καλούμενα. 5
εἶτα κύλικες αἱ πρὸς τὸ πρᾶγμα χρήσιμαι μάλιστ' εἶναι δοκοῦσαι
κατεσκευάζοντο, καλούμεναι κοτταβίδες. πρὸς δὲ τούτοις οἶκοι
E κατεσκευάζοντο κυκλοτερεῖς, ἵνα πάντες εἰς τὸ μέσον τοῦ
κοττάβου τεθέντος ἐξ ἀποστήματος ἴσου καὶ τόπων ὁμοίων
ἀγωνίζοιντο περὶ τῆς νίκης. οὐ γὰρ μόνον ἐφιλοτιμοῦντο βάλλειν 10
ἐπὶ τὸν σκοπόν, ἀλλὰ καὶ καλῶς †ἕκαστα αὐτῶν†. ἔδει γὰρ εἰς
τὸν ἀριστερὸν ἀγκῶνα ἐρείσαντα καὶ τὴν δεξιὰν ἀγκυλώσαντα
εὐρύθμως ἀφεῖναι τὴν λάταγα. οὕτω γὰρ ἐκάλουν τὸ πῖπτον ἐκ
τῆς κύλικος ὑγρόν. ὥστε ἔνιοι μεῖζον ἐφρόνουν ἐπὶ τῷ καλῶς

Someone advises Heracles not to hold his arm stiffly when about
C to shoot. They called the throwing of the *cottabos* 'from the bent
arm' from the 'bending' of the right arm in the *cottabos* games.

108 Athenaeus, *The Sophists at Dinner* 15.7 668D–E (*BT* v.3 p.478.12–
15 Kaibel)

That the *cottabos* was taken seriously among the Sicilians is
E clear from the practice of even fitting out special rooms for the
game, as Dicaearchus reports in his *On Alcaeus*.

109 Athenaeus, *The Sophists at Dinner* 11.58 479D–E (*BT* v.3 p.55.10–
56.1 Kaibel)

Hegesander of Delphi in his *Memoranda*, which begins, "in the
best form of government," says, "the (game) called *cottabos* was
introduced into their symposia, the Sicilians being the first to bring
it in, according to Dicaearchus. So great an interest was aroused in
the game that they even introduced prizes, called *cottabeia,* into
the drinking parties. Thereupon cups (*kylixes*) that were especially
adapted to the purpose were manufactured, and they were called
cottabides. In addition to this, circular rooms were constructed in
E order that when the *cottabos* was set up in the center, all might
compete for victory at an equal distance and from similar positions. For they were proud not merely to hit the mark, but also to
carry through each motion with good form. The player, leaning on
his left elbow, was obliged to bend his right arm and rhythmically
toss the *latax*; for that is what they called the liquid that fell from
the cup. Some people took more pride in playing *cottabos* well

κοτταβίζειν τῶν ἐπὶ τῷ ἀκοντίζειν μέγα φρονούντων.   15

1 *Hegesander, FHG 4.419*

9 τόπων ὁμοίων] καὶ ἐπὶ τῶν ὁμοίων *suspicatur Kaibel*   11 ἕκαστα αὐτῶν]
ἕκαστα ποιεῖν *Wilamowitz* : *cruces pos.*   *Wehrli*   12 τὴν δεξιὰν ἀγκυλώσαντα
Kaibel : τῇ δεξιᾷ κυκλώσαντα *codd.*   13 εὐρύθμως *Kaibel* : ὑγρῶς *codd.*
πῖπτον *A* : πίπτειν *E* : ῥιπτόμενον *proposuit Kaibel*

110 Athenaeus, Deipnosophistae 3.31 85F (BT t.1 p.198.14–24 Kaibel)

Καλλίας δ᾽ ὁ Μυτιληναῖος ἐν τῷ Περὶ τῆς παρ᾽ Ἀλκαίῳ
λεπάδος παρὰ τῷ Ἀλκαίῳ φησὶν εἶναι ᾠδὴν ἧς ἡ ἀρχή
Πέτρας καὶ πολιᾶς θαλάσσας τέκνον,
ἧς ἐπὶ τέλει γεγράφθαι
ἐκ δὲ παίδων χαύνοις φρένας, ἁ θαλασσία λεπάς.   5
ὁ δ᾽ Ἀριστοφάνης γράφει ἀντὶ τοῦ λεπὰς χέλυς καί φησιν οὐκ
εὖ Δικαίαρχον ἐκδεξάμενον λέγειν τὰς λεπάδας. τὰ παιδάρια
δὲ ἡνίκ᾽ ἂν εἰς τὸ στόμα λάβωσιν, αὐλεῖν ἐν ταύταις καὶ παίζειν.

1 *Callias, cf. Strabonem, 13.618*   *Alcaeus, fr. 359 Lobel et Page* 6 *Aristophanes
Byzantius, fr. 367 Slater*

5 ἐκ δὲ παίδων *Ahrens* : ἐκ λεπάδων *codd.*   6 λεπάς : χέλυς *cum germano
Alcaeo Wilamowitz; Diehl*   7 ἐκδεξάμενον *Valckenar.* : ἐκλεξάμενον *codd.*

111 Papyrus Oxyrhynchus 2506, fr. 6a, 77, 79, 137b (CPF pars 1 t.1.2
p.30–1 Montanari)

fr. 6a   δηκα..[
        προσα[
        υποδικα[
        ταυταμα[
        ριστοτε[5
        παρισταρ[
        τονυρ[.]..[
        π.[
        μη[
        κεφ[10

3 ὑπὸ Δικα[ιάρχου *proposuit Page*

than do people who pride themselves on hurling the javelin."

110 Athenaeus, *The Sophists at Dinner* 3.31 85F (*BT* v.1 p.198.14–24 Kaibel)

Callias of Mytilene, in the work *On the (Word) Limpet in Alcaeus*, says that there is an ode in the collection of Alcaeus' works that begins
Child of the rocks and of the hoary sea,
and at the end is written:
Limpet of the sea, swell the hearts of children,
Aristophanes writes 'tortoise' instead of 'limpet' and says that Dicaearchus had not understood well in saying 'limpets'. But when children put them to their mouths, they blow on them like a pipe and play tunes with them.

111 Papyrus Oxyrhynchus 2506, fr. 6a, 77, 79, 137b (*CPF* part 1 v.1.2 p.30–1 Montanari)

fr. 6a

by Dicaearchus (?)

Aristotle

fr. 77   — — —
        ].τ[.]λλ[
Φι]ττακο[
        ]νασυμφ[
        ]ην 'Αλκαιο[
        ].ρ ὑποδικ[5
        ]τον αλ.[
        ]ουτεφ[
        ]μου φον.[
        ]σ μελεδ[
        ]. αμα.[......].[10

5 ὑπὸ Δικ[αιάρχου *Page*

fr. 79   — — —
        ]νπρ.[
        ]αλλια[
        ]νεσ[
        ]κτιδ[
        ].αυτ[5
        ]καια[
        ].αρχ.[
        ]ονπ[
        ]οκι[
        ]τ.[10

6 Δι]καια[ρχ- *Page*

fr. 137b   — — —
        ]ον[
        ]ννεω[
        ]εταιεισ[
        ]τοισαλ[
        ]νεικοσ[5
        ]οδικαι[
        ]ηοσ[
        ]νοσπροσ[
        ]γυν^αι [
        ]οσεν [
        ].. γαρ [10

6 ὁ Δικαί[αρχος *Page*

fr. 77

Pittacus

Alcaeus
by Dicaearchus (?)

fr. 79

Dicaearchus (?)

fr. 137b

Dicaearchus (?)

Argumenta

112 Sextus Empiricus, Adversus Mathematicos 3.3 (BT t.3 p.107.11–17 Mau)

πολλαχῶς μὲν καὶ ἄλλως ὑπόθεσις προσαγορεύεται, τὰ νῦν δὲ ἀπαρκέσει τριχῶς λέγεσθαι. καθ᾿ ἕνα μὲν τρόπον ἡ δραματικὴ περιπέτεια, καθὸ καὶ τραγικὴν καὶ κωμικὴν ὑπόθεσιν εἶναι λέγομεν καὶ Δικαιάρχου τινὰς ὑποθέσεις τῶν Εὐριπίδου καὶ Σοφοκλέους μύθων, οὐκ ἄλλο τι καλοῦντες ὑπόθεσιν ἢ τὴν τοῦ 5 δράματος περιπέτειαν.

5 *Sophocles, TrGF T153 Radt*

113 Hypothesis Sophoclis Aiacis (OCT p.1.11–13 Pearson)

Δικαίαρχος δὲ Αἴαντος θάνατον ἐπιγράφει. ἐν δὲ ταῖς Διδασκαλίαις ψιλῶς Αἴας ἀναγέγραπται.

1–2 *Aristoteles, fr. 623 Rose³*

114 Hypothesis Rhesi 1.26 (BT p.4.3–12 Zanetto)

τοῦτο τὸ δρᾶμα ἔνιοι νόθον ὑπενόησαν ὡς οὐκ ὂν Εὐριπίδου· τὸν γὰρ Σοφόκλειον μᾶλλον ὑποφαίνει χαρακτῆρα. ἐν μέντοι ταῖς Διδασκαλίαις ὡς γνήσιον ἀναγέγραπται. καὶ ἡ περὶ τὰ μετάρσια δὲ ἐν αὐτῷ πολυπραγμοσύνη τὸν Εὐριπίδην ὁμολογεῖ. πρόλογοι δὲ διττοὶ φέρονται. ὁ γοῦν Δικαίαρχος ἐκτιθεὶς τὴν 5 ὑπόθεσιν τοῦ ῾Ρήσου γράφει κατὰ λέξιν οὕτως ⟨῾Ρῆσος, οὗ ἀρχή·⟩ "νῦν εὐσέληνον φέγγος ἡ διφρήλατος" καὶ * * * καὶ ἐν ἐνίοις δὲ τῶν ἀντιγράφων ἕτερός τις φέρεται πρόλογος, πεζὸς πάνυ καὶ οὐ πρέπων Εὐριπίδῃ.

2 *Sophocles, TrGF T129 Radt*   3 *Aristoteles, fr. 626 Rose³*

---

1 ὡς οὐκ ὂν Εὐριπίδου *HLPQ* : Εὐριπίδου δὲ μὴ εἶναι *V*   3 Διδασκαλίαις] διδασκαλίας *Zanetto haud recte*   4 *post* δὲ *habet A* ἐν αὐτῷ   5 Δικαίαρχος *Nauck* : δικαίαν *VLP* : *omit. Q*   ἐκτιθεὶς *V* : ἐπιτιθεὶς *LPC*   6 ῾Ρῆσος οὗ ἀρχή *supplevit Luppe* (ZPE 84 [1990] 11–13): *lacunam indicat Schwartz*   7 * * *: τ.ἐ. *supplevit Wilamowitz*   8 φέρεται *LPQ* : φαίνεται *V*

Hypotheses

112 Sextus Empiricus, *Against the Mathematicians* 3.3 (*BT* v.3 p.107.11–17 Mau)

> *Hypothesis* (summary) has been used in many other ways, but for the moment three ways of speaking are enough. According to one way, the *hypothesis* is the play's progression of incidents (*peripeteia*), just as we say that there is both a tragic and a comic *hypothesis*, and we speak of certain *Hypotheses of the Plots of Euripides and Sophocles* by Dicaearchus, calling a *hypothesis* nothing other than the progression of incidents of the play.

113 *Hypothesis* of Sophocles' *Ajax* (*OCT* p.1.11–13 Pearson)

> Dicaearchus entitles (the play) *Death of Ajax*. But in the *Catalogues of the Dramas* simply *Ajax* has been recorded.

114 *Hypothesis* of *Rhesus* 1.26 (*BT* p. 4.3–12 Zanetto)

> Some suspect that this play is inauthentic, that it is not by Euripides, for it appears to be more Sophoclean in character. In the *Catalogues of the Dramas*, however, it is recorded as genuine. The keen interest in astronomical matters in it confirms Euripides. There are double prologues. Indeed, Dicaearchus in setting down the *hypothesis* of the *Rhesus* word for word writes as follows <"Rhesus, which begins> 'now the chariot-born (goddess brings) moonlit splendour'" and ∗ ∗ ∗ and in some of the copies another prologue is reported which is entirely prosaic and uncharacteristic of Euripides.[1]

[1] The extant manuscripts of the play do not use either of the prologues cited by the *Hypothesis.*

115A Hypothesis Euripidis Alcestis (OCT t.1 p.33.3–14 Diggle)

ὑπόθεσις Ἀλκήστιδος Δικαιάρχου
Ἀπόλλων ἠτήσατο παρὰ τῶν Μοιρῶν ὅπως Ἄδμητος
τελευτᾶν μέλλων παράσχῃ τὸν ὑπὲρ ἑαυτοῦ ἑκόντα
τεθνηξόμενον, ἵνα ἴσον τῷ προτέρῳ χρόνον ζήσῃ. καὶ δὴ
Ἄλκηστις, ἡ γυνὴ τοῦ Ἀδμήτου, ἐπέδωκεν ἑαυτήν, οὐδετέρου   5
τῶν γονέων ἐθελήσαντος ὑπὲρ τοῦ παιδὸς ἀποθανεῖν. μετ' οὐ
πολὺ δὲ ταύτης τῆς συμφορᾶς γενομένης Ἡρακλῆς παρα-
γενόμενος καὶ μαθὼν παρά τινος θεράποντος τὰ περὶ τὴν
Ἄλκηστιν ἐπορεύθη ἐπὶ τὸν τάφον καὶ Θάνατον ἀποστῆναι
ποιήσας ἐσθῆτι καλύπτει τὴν γυναῖκα, τὸν δὲ Ἄδμητον ἠξίου   10
λαβόντα τηρεῖν. εἰληφέναι γὰρ αὐτὴν πάλης ἆθλον ἔλεγεν. μὴ
βουλομένου δὲ ἐκείνου ἀποκαλύψας ἔδειξεν ἣν ἐπένθει.

1 Δικαιάρχου *addidit Triclinius L*   2–12 *schol. in Platonis Symp. 179B*

115B Papyrus Oxyrhynchus 2457 (Philologus 126 [1982] 14 Luppe)

(Ἡρακλῆς) κα]τέλυσεν πα[ρὰ τῷ Ἀδμή-]
[τῳ. ὁ δ' ἔκρυψεν τὴν συ]μφοράν, ὅπ[ως αὐτὸν μὴ]
[ἀπελάσῃ, καὶ μεθ' ὑπερ]οχῆς αὐτ]ὸν ἐξένισεν.]
[ἐπεὶ δ' οὗτος ἰδὼν δεδ]ακρυμέν[ους τοὺς πε-]
[ρὶ τὸν Ἄδμητον ἔ]μαθεν παρ[ά τινος τὰ πε-]   5
[ρὶ τὴν Ἄλκηστιν, παρ]αγενόμεν[ος ἐπὶ τὸν]
[τάφον αὐτῆς ἐποίησε]ν τὸν Θάν[ατον ἀποστῆ-]
ναι. ἀνεβίω μὲν οὖν ἡ ν]εκρὰ καὶ τ[
[   ]λα ... [   ]
[τὴ]ν Ἄλκηστ[ιν   ]   10
ἐσθῆτι σ]υγκαλύ][ψας αὐτὴν]
[τὸν Ἄδμητον ἠξίωσ]ε λαβόντ[α τηρεῖν.]
[εἰληφέναι γὰρ αὐτὴ]ν πάλης ἆθ[λον ἔφησεν.]
[ἐκείνου δὲ τῆς συνεύ]νου χάριν τα[ύτην λα-]
[βεῖν μὴ βου.λομένου] ἐκκαλύψα[ς ἔδειξεν]   15
[ἣν ἐπ]ένθ[ει.]

2 ἔκρυψεν *vel* ἔκρυπτεν *Luppe*

115A_Hypothesis_ of Euripides' _Alcestis_ (_OCT_ v.1 p.33.3–14 Diggle)

Dicaearchus' _Hypothesis_ of _Alcestis_.

Apollo had asked from the Fates that Admetus, who was about to die, might provide someone willing to die on his behalf, so that he might live a time equal to what (he would have lived) before. However, Alcestis, the wife of Admetus, gave herself, since neither of his parents were willing to die for their son. Not long after this misfortune, Heracles came by and, after learning from a servant what happened concerning Alcestis, went to her grave and, having made Death restore the woman, dressed her in disguised clothing. Then he asked Admetus to take her to watch over; for he said that he had won her as a wrestling prize. But when (Admetus) did not wish (to take her), (Heracles) revealed her and showed that it was the woman he was mourning.

115B Papyrus Oxyrhynchus 2457 (_Philologus_ 126 [1982] 14 Luppe)

Heracles stayed at Admetus' palace, but Admetus hid his misfortune in order not to drive Heracles away, and gave him exaggerated hospitality. But when Heracles saw Admetus' attendants in tears and learned from one of them the news concerning Alcestis, he went to her grave and made Death restore her. The corpse did indeed come back to life and . . .

. . . he disguised Alcestis with clothing and demanded that Admetus take her to guard. For he said that he had won her as a wrestling prize. When, for the sake of his wife, Admetus did not wish to take her, Heracles revealed her and showed that she was the woman that he was mourning.

Geographia

116 Plinius in primo libro Naturalis historiae materiam ex Dicaearchi
scriptis in his libris componendis se desumpsisse asseverat:

lib. 2] NH 1.[2] (CB t.1 p.61.28 Beaujeu)
lib. 4] NH 1.[4] (CB t.1 p.64.8 Beaujeu)
lib. 5] NH 1.[5] (CB t.1 p.66.2 Beaujeu)
lib. 6] NH 1.[6] (CB t.1 p.67.34 Beaujeu)

117 Strabo, Geographica 1.1.1 (CB t.1 p.1.1–10 Lasserre)

τῆς τοῦ φιλοσόφου πραγματείας εἶναι νομίζομεν, εἴπερ ἄλλην
τινά, καὶ τὴν γεωγραφικήν . . . οἵ τε γὰρ πρῶτοι θαρρήσαντες
αὐτῆς ἅψασθαι τοιοῦτοί τινες ὑπῆρξαν, Ὅμηρός τε καὶ
Ἀναξίμανδρος ὁ Μιλήσιος καὶ Ἑκαταῖος ὁ πολίτης αὐτοῦ,
καθὼς καὶ Ἐρατοσθένης φησί καὶ Δημόκριτος δὲ καὶ Εὔδοξος   5
καὶ Δικαίαρχος καὶ Ἔφορος καὶ ἄλλοι πλείους. ἔτι δὲ οἱ μετὰ
τούτους, Ἐρατοσθένης τε καὶ Πολύβιος καὶ Ποσειδώνιος,
ἄνδρες φιλόσοφοι.

4 *Anaximander, FVS 12A6*   Hecataeus, FGrH 1 T 11a   5 *Democritus, FVS*
68B15   Eudoxus, fr. 273b Lasserre   6 *Ephorus, FGrH 70 T 19*   7
Posidonius, T75 Edelstein et Kidd

118 Plinius, Naturalis historia 2.162 (BT t.1 p.188.23–189.4 Mayhoff)

globum tamen effici mirum est in tanta planitie maris camp-
orumque. cui sententiae adest Dicaearchus vir in primis eruditus
regum cura permensus montis, ex quibus altissimum prodidit Pelion
MCCL passuum, ratione perpendiculi nullam esse eam portionem
universae rotunditatis colligens.   5

119 Geminus, Elementa astronomiae 17.5 (CB p.84.12–15 Aujac)

καὶ ἔστι μὲν τῆς Κυλλήνης τὸ ὕψος ἔλασσον σταδίων ιε΄, ὡς
Δικαίαρχος ἀναμεμετρηκὼς ἀποφαίνεται· τοῦ δὲ Ἀταβυρίου

Geography

116 Pliny in the first book of the *Natural History* says that he has taken material from Dicaearchus in composing the following books:

Book 2] *NH* 1.[2] (*CB* v.1 p. 61.28 Beaujeu)
Book 4] *NH* 1.[4] (*CB* v.1 p. 64.8 Beaujeu)
Book 5] *NH* 1.[5] (*CB* v.1 p. 66.2 Beaujeu)
Book 6] *NH* 1.[6] (*CB* v. 1 p. 67.34 Beaujeu)

117 Strabo, Geography 1.1.1 (*CB* v.1 p.1.1–10 Lasserre)

We believe that geography belongs to the activity of a philosopher, if any (activity) does. ... For the first to dare to touch upon it were people like Homer and Anaximander the Milesian and Hecataeus his fellow citizen, as Eratosthenes too says, and Democritus and Eudoxus and Dicaearchus and Ephorus and many others. Even after them there were philosophers like Eratosthenes, Polybius and Posidonius (doing geography).

118 Pliny, *Natural History* 2.162 (*BT* v.1 p.188.23–189.4 Mayhoff)

It is nevertheless amazing that in such a great level expanse of sea and fields a sphere is created. Dicaearchus supports this view, a man among the first in learning. Under the patronage of kings he measured the height of mountains and reported that the highest is Mount Pelion at 1250 paces. He concluded from the calculation of the vertical that this proportion amounted to nothing compared to the entire roundness (of the earth).

119 Geminus, *Elements of Astronomy* 17.5 (*CB* p.84.12–15 Aujac)

The height of Cyllene is less than fifteen stades, as Dicaearchus has shown by measurement. The vertical drop of Mount Ataburius

ἐλάσσων ἐστὶν ἡ κάθετος σταδίων η΄.

1 *cf. Strabonem 8.1*

2 Δικαίαρχος *AC* : Δικέαρχος Β   ἀναμεμετρηκὼς *Manitius* : ἀναμετρικῶς
codd.   Ἀταβυρίου *Pet.* : Σαταβυρίου *codd.*   3 η΄ *Aujac* : ,δ΄ *(?) ABC* : 10
(sic) Lat. transl.

120 Theon Smyrnaeus, De utilitate mathematicae (p.124.19–125.1
Hiller)

⟨δέκα δὲ σταδίων ἐστὶν ἡ⟩ τῶν ὑψηλοτάτων ὀρῶν πρὸς τὰ
χθαμαλώτατα τῆς γῆς ὑπεροχὴ κατὰ κάθετον, καθὰ Ἐρατοσθένης καὶ Δικαίαρχος εὑρηκέναι φασίν, καὶ ὀργανικῶς δὲ ταῖς
τὰ ἐξ ἀποστημάτων μεγέθη μετρούσαις διόπτραις τηλικαῦτα
θεωρεῖται.   5

1 *cf. Plutarchi Vitam Aemiliani 15*

1 δέκα . . . ἡ *supplevit Martin*

121 Martianus Capella, De nuptiis Philologiae et Mercurii 6.590–1
(p.292.16–293.3 Dick)

formam totius terrae non planam, ut aestimant, positioni qui eam
disci diffusioris assimulant, neque concavam, ut alii, qui descendere
imbrem dixere telluris in gremium, sed rotundam, globosam etiam
591   [sicut Secundus] Dicaearchus asseverat. namque ortus obitusque
siderum non diversus pro terrae elatione vel inclinationibus   5
haberetur, si per plana diffusis mundanae constitutionis operibus
uno eodemque tempore supra terras et aequora nituissent aut item,
si emersi solis exortus concavis subductioris terrae latebris abderetur.

3 *cf. Arist., De caelo 2.14 297a8*

4 sicut Secundus *(i.e. Plinius) ut glossema delevit Dick* : sicut secundum
Dicaearchum asseverant *Eyssh.*   5 elatione] elevatione *Wehrli*

is less than eight stades.

120 Theon of Smyrna, *Exposition of Mathematics* (p.124.19–125.1 Hiller)

The vertical difference between the highest mountains and the lowest points of the earth is less <than ten stades>, as Eratosthenes and Dicaearchus claim to have discovered. Such great amounts are observed mechanically by means of optical devices measuring the magnitudes from intervals.

121 Martianus Capella, *On the Marriage of Philology and Mercury* 6.590–1 (p.292.16–293.3 Dick)

The shape of the entire earth is not flat, as some suppose who liken it to the position of an expanded disk. Nor is it concave, as others (say), who have said that rain descends into the "lap of earth,"
591   but it is rounded, even spherical, as Dicaearchus had claimed. For the rising and the settings of the stars would not vary according to the elevation or inclinations of the earth if the activities of the heavenly firmament were spread out across flat surfaces and at one and the same time they shone above the lands and waters, or likewise, if the rising of the emerging sun were concealed by the concave shadows of the depressed land.

122 Agathemerus, Geographiae informatio, prooemion 2 (GRBS t.16 [1975] p.60.24–8 Diller)

οἱ μὲν οὖν παλαιοὶ τὴν οἰκουμένην ἔγραφον στρογγύλην, μέσην δὲ κεῖσθαι τὴν Ἑλλάδα καὶ ταύτης Δελφούς, τὸν ὀμφαλὸν γὰρ ἔχειν τῆς γῆς. πρῶτος δὲ Δημόκριτος, πολύπειρος ἀνὴρ, συνεῖδεν ὅτι προμήκης ἐστὶν ἡ γῆ, ἡμιόλιον τὸ μῆκος τοῦ πλάτους ἔχουσα. συνήνεσε τούτῳ καὶ Δικαίαρχος ὁ Περιπατητικός.   5

2 δὲ κεῖσθαι *Gronovius*: δ᾽ ἡγεῖσθαι *codd. et Diller*   3 Democritus, FVS 68A94

123 Agathemerus, Geographiae informatio, prooemion 5 (GRBS t.16 [1975] p.61.13–16 Diller)

Δικαίαρχος δὲ ὁρίζει τὴν γῆν οὐχ ὕδασιν, ἀλλὰ τομῇ εὐθείᾳ εὐκράτῳ ἀπὸ στηλῶν διὰ Σαρδοῦς Σικελίας Πελοποννήσου Ἰωνίας Καρίας Λυκίας Παμφυλίας Κιλικίας καὶ Ταύρου ἑξῆς ἕως Ἰμάου ὄρους. τῶν τοίνυν τόπων τὸν μὲν βόρειον, τὸν δὲ νότιον ὀνομάζει.   5

2 εὐκράτῳ *B* : ἀκράτῳ *edd.*   3 Ἰωνίας *del. Gronovius*

124 Strabo, Geographica 2.4.1–3 (CB t.1 p.70.5–73.2 Lasserre)

Πολύβιος δὲ τὴν Εὐρώπην χωρογραφῶν τοὺς μὲν ἀρχαίους ἐᾶν φησι, τοὺς δ᾽ ἐκείνους ἐλέγχοντας ἐξετάζειν Δικαίαρχόν τε καὶ Ἐρατοσθένη τὸν τελευταῖον πραγματευσάμενον περὶ γεωγραφίας καὶ Πυθέαν, ὑφ᾽ οὗ παρακρουσθῆναι πολλούς. ... πολὺ δέ φησι βέλτιον τῷ Μεσσηνίῳ πιστεύειν ἢ τούτῳ. ὁ μέντοι   5 γε εἰς μίαν χώραν τὴν Παγχαίαν λέγει πλεῦσαι, ὁ δὲ καὶ μέχρι τῶν τοῦ κόσμου περάτων κατωπτευκέναι τὴν προσάρκτιον τῆς
2 Εὐρώπης πᾶσαν ... Ἐρατοσθένη δὲ τὸν μὲν Εὐήμερον Βεργαῖον καλεῖν, Πυθέᾳ δὲ πιστεύειν, καὶ ταῦτα μηδὲ Δικαιάρχου πιστεύσαντος. τὸ μὲν οὖν μηδὲ Δικαιάρχου πιστεύσαντος   10 γελοῖον, ὥσπερ ἐκείνῳ κανόνι χρήσασθαι προσῆκον, καθ᾽ οὗ τοσούτους ἐλέγχους αὐτὸς προφέρεται. Ἐρατοσθένους δὲ εἴρηται ἡ περὶ τὰ ἑσπέρια καὶ τὰ ἀρκτικὰ τῆς Εὐρώπης ἄγνοια.

122 Agathemerus, *Sketch of Geography*, Proem 2 (*GRBS* v.16 [1975] p.60.24–8 Diller)

Therefore the ancients wrote that the inhabited region is circular, that Greece lay in its middle and Delphi in (Greece's) middle. For it holds the navel of the earth. Democritus, a very learned man, was the first to see that the earth is oblong, having a length one and a half times the width, and Dicaearchus the Peripatetic agreed with him.

123 Agathemerus, *Sketch of Geography*, Proem 5 (*GRBS* v.16 [1975] p.61.13–16 Diller)

Dicaearchus divides the earth not by waters, but by a straight, proportioned cut from the Pillars through Sardinia, Sicily, Peloponnesus, Ionia, Caria, Lycia, Pamphylia, Cilicia and Taurus in turn until Mount Imaus. In terms of these places, therefore, he applied the names North and South.

124 Strabo, *Geography* 2.4.1–3 (*CB* v.1 p.70.5–73.2 Lasserre)

In writing his geography of Europe, Polybius says he passes over the ancient geographers but examines those who criticize them, Dicaearchus and Eratosthenes, the last to have been active concerning geography, and Pytheas, by whom (Polybius says) many have been misled. ... (Polybius) says it is much better to believe (Euhemerus) the Messanian than (Pytheas). (Euhemerus), you see, claims that he sailed only to one country, Panchaea, whereas Pytheas claims that he saw for himself the whole northern region of Europe
2 up to the limits of the world... Eratosthenes calls Euhemerus a storyteller and he believes Pytheas, although not even Dicaearchus believed these things. However, that phrase "although not even Dicaearchus believed," is ridiculous; as if it were fitting for Eratosthenes to use that man as a standard, against whom he himself directs so many criticisms. Eratosthenes' ignorance concerning the western and northern parts of Europe has already been stated.

ἀλλ᾽ ἐκείνῳ μὲν καὶ Δικαιάρχῳ συγγνώμη, τοῖς μὴ κατιδοῦσι τοὺς τόπους ἐκείνους. Πολυβίῳ δὲ καὶ Ποσειδωνίῳ τίς ἂν 15 συγγνοίη; ἀλλὰ μὴν Πολύβιός γέ ἐστιν ὁ λαοδογματικὰς καλῶν ἀποφάσεις, ἃς ποιοῦνται περὶ τῶν ἐν τούτοις τοῖς τόποις διαστημάτων καὶ ἐν ἄλλοις πολλοῖς, ἀλλ᾽ οὐδ᾽ ἐν οἷς ἐκείνους ἐλέγχει καθαρεύων. τοῦ γοῦν Δικαιάρχου μυρίους μὲν εἰπόντος τοὺς ἐπὶ στήλας ἀπὸ τῆς Πελοποννήσου σταδίους, πλείους δὲ 20 τούτων τοὺς ἐπὶ τὸν Ἀδρίαν μέχρι τοῦ μυχοῦ, τοῦ δ᾽ ἐπὶ στήλας τὸ μέχρι τοῦ πορθμοῦ τρισχιλίους ἀποδόντος, ὡς γίνεσθαι τὸ λοιπὸν ἑπτακισχιλίους τὸ ἀπὸ πορθμοῦ μέχρι στηλῶν. τοὺς μὲν τρισχιλίους ἐᾶν φησιν, εἴτ᾽ εὖ λαμβάνονται εἴτε μή, τοὺς δ᾽ ἑπτακισχιλίους οὐδετέρως, οὐδὲ τὴν παραλίαν ἐκμετροῦντι, 25 οὔτε τὴν διὰ μέσου τοῦ πελάγους. ... προστεθέντων δὲ τῶν ἀπὸ τῆς Πελοποννήσου ἐπὶ τὸν πορθμὸν τρισχιλίων, οἱ σύμπαντες ἔσονται στάδιοι, αὐτοὶ ἐπ᾽ εὐθείας, πλείους ἢ διπλάσιοι ὧν Δικαίαρχος εἶπε· πλείους δὲ τούτων τοὺς ἐπὶ τὸν μυχὸν τὸν Ἀδριατικὸν δεήσει, φησί, τιθέναι κατ᾽ ἐκεῖνον.   30

3   ἀλλ᾽ ὦ φίλε Πολύβιε, φαίη τις ἄν, ὥσπερ τούτου τοῦ ψεύσματος ἐναργῆ παρίστησι τὸν ἔλεγχον ἡ πεῖρα ἐξ αὐτῶν, ὧν εἴρηκας αὐτός, ... οὕτως κἀκεῖνα ψεύσματά ἐστιν ἀμφότερα, καὶ ὁ Δικαίαρχος εἶπε, τὸ ἀπὸ πορθμοῦ ἐπὶ Στήλας εἶναι σταδίων ἑπτακισχιλίων, καὶ ὃ σὺ δοκεῖς ἀποδεῖξαι.   35

1 Polybius 34.1.1–6 Büttner et Wobst   3 Eratosthenes, fr. 2 Berger   4 Pythias, fr. 7a Mette   14 Posidonius, T25 Edelstein et Kidd

9 μηδὲ Meineke: δὲ μήτε codd. et Lasserre   10 μηδὲ Meineke: μήτε codd. 16 λαοδογματικὰς Tyrwhitt: ὅλας δογματικὰς Aω´   17 ποιοῦνται Groskurd: ποιρῖται Aω´

125 Strabo, Geographica 3.5.5 (CB t.2 p.87.11–13 Lasserre)

Δικαίαρχος δὲ καὶ Ἐρατοσθένης καὶ Πολύβιος καὶ οἱ πλεῖστοι τῶν Ἑλλήνων περὶ τὸν πορθμὸν ἀποφαίνουσι τὰς στήλας.

1 Polybius, 34.9.4

But while pardon may be allowed to him and Dicaearchus because they had not seen those regions, who would pardon Polybius and Posidonius? It is in fact Polybius who calls the statements made by them concerning the distances in those regions and many other regions 'folk wisdom', though he does not get clear (himself) the points which he criticizes. Now Dicaearchus estimates the distance from the Peloponnesus to the Pillars at ten thousand stadia, and (from the Peloponnesus) to the recess of the Adriatic sea at more than this, and when he reckons the part up to the Straights (of Sicily) at three thousand stadia, the rest from the Straights to the Pillars becomes seven thousand stadia. (Polybius) says that he disregards the three thousand—whether or not they are correctly accepted—but in no way does he allow the seven thousand, neither measuring by the shoreline nor through the middle of the sea. . . . If the three thousand from the Peloponnesus to the straight were added, the entire number of stades, those alone that follow a straight line, will be more than double what Dicaearchus said; and, says (Polybius), according to (Dicaearchus) the number of stades (from the Peloponnesus) to the recess of the Adriatic will need to be more than this.

3   But my dear Polybius, one might say, just as the test of these things, which you yourself have stated, furnishes the clear refutation of this falsity, . . . so also both those others are false, what Dicaearchus said, namely, that the distance from the Straight to the Pillars is seven thousand stades, and what you think you demonstrate.

125 Strabo, *Geography* 3.5.5 (*CB* v.2 p.87.11–13 Laserre)

Dicaearchus and Eratosthenes and Polybius and most of the Greeks represent the Pillars (of Heracles) as near the Strait (of Gibraltar).

126 Joannes Lydus, De mensibus 4.107 (BT p.147.1–3 Wünsch)

ἀλλὰ καὶ Δικαίαρχος ἐν Περιόδῳ γῆς ἐκ τῆς Ἀτλαντικῆς θαλάττης τὸν Νεῖλον ἀναχεῖσθαι βούλεται.

1–2 Seneca, Naturales quaestiones 4a fr. 6 (BT p.189.1–2 Hine); cf. Lucani Pharsalia 10.255–7

127 Stobaeus, Anthologium 1.38.2 (t.1 p.252.13–17 Wachsmuth)

⟨Δικαίαρχος ὁ Μεσσ⟩ήνιος ἡλίῳ καὐτὸς τὴν αἰτίαν ἀνατίθησι, καθ᾽οὓς μὲν ἂν τόπους γένηται τῆς γῆς πλημμύροντι τὰ πελάγη, ἐξ ὧν δ᾽ ἂν τύχῃ παραποστὰς ὑποσυνέλκοντι. ταῦτα δὲ συμβαίνειν περὶ τὰς ἑῴας καὶ τὰς μεσημβρινὰς ἐκκλίσεις.

1 Δικαίαρχος ὁ Μεσσ *Meineke, Diels* : ⟨Εὐ⟩ήνιος *Wachsmuth*: . . . . ηνιος *D*   4 περὶ *Meineke* : παρὰ *codd.*

126 John of Lydia, *On Months* 4.107 (*BT* p.147.1–3 Wünsch)

But even Dicaearchus in the *Circuit of the Earth* wants the Nile to takes its rise from the Atlantic ocean.

127 Stobaeus, *Selections* 1.38.2 (v.1 p.252.13–17 Wachsmuth)

(Dicaearchus) the Messanian also himself refers the cause to the sun, which causes the seas to overflow in whatever areas of the earth they are, and draws them away with itself from the places it recedes from on each occasion. These things occur around the morning and the noon shifts.

CONCORDANCES

F. Wehrli, *Die Schule des Aristoteles, Texte und Commentar,* Band 1:
Dikaiarchos Basel, Schwabe, 1967.2nd edition.

Mirhady	Wehrli	Mirhady	Wehrli	Mirhady	Wehrli	Mirhady	Wehrli
2	1	33	25	63	61	95	92
3	2	34	28	64	52	96	74
4	1, I	35	46	65	53	97	103
5	3	36	31	66	53, I	98	103, I
6	26	37	30	67	54	99	75
7	4	38	32	68	101	100	76
8	27	39	93	69	37–8	101	80
9	69	40	33	70	66	102	77
10	68	41A	34	71	39	103	83
11A–C	18a, 70,	41B	35a–b	72	60	104	84
	18c	42	36	73	62	105	98
12	117	43	29	74	85	106	95
13	5	44	100	75	102	107	96
14	8c	45	41	76	65	108	94
15	8d	46A	om.	77	64	109	97
16	8e	46B	om.	78	24	110	99
17	8f	46C	45	79	20	112	78
18	8b	47	40	80	19	113	79
19	7	48	42	81	21	114	81
20	8i	49	43	82	22	115A	82
21A–B	11,12a–d	50	44	83	23	115B	om.
22	12e	52	118	84	86	116	116
23	8k	53	47	85	87	117	104
24	8a	54	48	86	67	118	105
25	8h	55	51	87	72	119	106
26	8g	56A–B	49–50	88	71	120	107
27	9	57	59	89	88	121	108
28	10a	58	57a	90	89	122	109
29	10b	59	58a	91	om.	123	110
30A–B	13a–b	60	55	92	73	124	111
31A–C	14–16	61	56	93	90	125	112
32	17	62	63	94	91	126	113
						127	114

W	M	W	M	W	M	W	M
1	**2**	19	**80**	53,I	**66**	86	**84**
1,I	**4**	20	**79**	54	**67**	87	**85**
2	**3**	21	**81**	55	**60**	88	**89**
3	**5**	22	**82**	56	**61**	89	**90**
4	**7**	23	**83**	57a	**58**	90	**93**
5	**13**	24	**78**	57b	app.**58**	91	**94**
6	**11B**	25	**33**	58a	**59**	92	**95**
7	**19**	26	**6**	58b	app.**59**	93	**39**
8a	**24**	27	**8**	59	**57**	94	**108**
8b	**18**	28	**34**	60	**72**	95	**106**
8c	**14**	29	**43**	61	**64**	96	**107**
8d	**15**	30	**37**	62	**73**	97	**109**
8e	**16**	31	**36**	63	**62**	98	**105**
8f	**17**	32	**38**	64	**77**	99	**110**
8g	**26**	33	**40**	65	**76**	100	**44**
8h	**25**	34	**41A**	66	**70**	101	**68**
8i	**20**	35a	**41A**	67	**86**	101,I	**app.68**
8k	**23**	35b	**41B**	68	**10**	102	**75**
9	**27**	36	**42**	69	**9**	103	**97**
10a	**28**	37	**69**	70	**11B**	103, I	**98**
10b	**29**	38	**69**	70,I	**om.**	104	**117**
11	**21a**	39	**71**	71	**88**	105	**118**
12a	app.**21A**	40	**47**	72	**87**	106	**119**
12b	app.**21A**	41	**45**	73	**92**	107	**120**
12c	app.**21A**	42	**48**	74	**96**	108	**121**
12d	app.**21A**	43	**49**	75	**99**	109	**122**
12e	**22**	44	**50**	76	**100**	110	**123**
13a	**30A**	45	**46C**	77	**102**	111	**124**
13b	**30B**	46	**35**	78	**112**	112	**125**
14	**31A**	47	**53**	79	**113**	113	**126**
15	**31B**	48	**54**	80	**101**	114	**127**
16	**31C**	49	**56A**	81	**114**	115	**79**
17	**32**	50	**56B**	82	**115A**	116	**116**
18a	**11A**	51	**55**	83	**103**	117	**12**
18b	**11B**	52	**58**	84	**104**	118	**52**
18c	**11C**	53	**65**	85	**74**		

C. Müller, *Fragmenta Historicorum Graecorum.* vol. 2. pp. 225–68. Paris: Didot, 1848 (repr. 1975).

Müller	Mirhady	Müller	Mirhady	Müller	Mirhady	Müller	Mirhady
1	56A	20	9	39	101	58	119
2	56B	21	2	40	102	62	19
3	53	22	11B	41	103	63	23
4	54	23	87, 88	42	104	64	18, 20,
5	55	24	47	43	89		21A, 24,
6	57	25	48	44	90		25
7	58, 59	26	50	45	99	65	27
8	60, 61	27	45	46	84	66	29
9	64	28	37, 38	47	85	67	78
10	67	29	40	48	73	69	31A–B,
11	65	30	42, 69	49	74		32
12	63	31	41A	50	97	70	30B
13	70	32	41B	51	44	71	80
14	82	33	71	52	126	72	81
15	72	34	106–9	53	118, 121	73	79
16	62	35	105	54	122	74	35
17	76	36	110	55	123	75	43
18	77	37	100	56	124		
19	83	38	113	57	125		

Mirhady	Müller	Mirhady	Müller	Mirhady	Müller	Mirhady	Müller
2	21	35	74	55	5	71	33
9	20	37	28	56A	1	72	15
11B	22	38	28	56B	2	73	48
18	64	40	29	57	6	74	49
19	62	41A	31	58	7	76	17
20	64	41B	32	59	7	77	18
21A	64	42	30	60	8	78	67
23	63	43	75	61	8	79	73
24	64	44	51	62	16	80	71
25	64	45	27	63	12	81	72
27	65	47	24	64	9	82	14
29	66	48	25	65	11	83	19
30b	70	50	26	67	10	84	46
31A–B	69	53	3	69	30	85	47
32	69	54	4	70	13	86	67

Mirhady	Müller	Mirhady	Müller	Mirhady	Müller	Mirhady	Müller
87	72	95	33a	105	35	118	53
88	71	97	50	106	34	119	58
89	43	99	45	107	34	121	53
90	44	100	37	108	34	122	54
92	73	101	39	109	34	123	55
93	90	102	40	110	36	124	56
94	91	103	41	113	38	125	57
						126	52

INDEX OF TEXTS AND PASSAGES

	Wehrli	**Mirhady**
AGATHEMERUS (post saec. 1 ante Chr.)		
Geographiae informatio		
prooemion 2 (GRBS t.16 [1975] p.60.24–28 Diller)	109	**122**
prooemion 5 (GRBS t.16 [1975] p.61.13–16)	110	**123**
ANECDOTA GRAECA OXONIENSIA: vid. MELETIUS		
ANONYMUS		
Vita Aristotelis Latina (post saec 6 a.D.)		
46–7 (AABT p.157.13–17 Düring)	1,I	**4**
Vita Aristotelis Marciana (post saec. 6 a.D.)		
196 (p.6.32 et 17.30–2 Gigon)	app.1,I	app.**4**
ANONYMUS GRAMMATICUS ROMANUS		
De notis veterum criticis		
3 (Lexicon Vindobonense p.273.16–17 Nauck)	90	**93**
APOLLONIUS DYSCOLUS (saec. 2. a.D.)		
De pronomine		
60B (t.1.1 p.48.1–11 Uhlig et Schneider)	91	**94**
ATHENAEUS (nat. *c.* a.D. 200)		
Deipnosophistae		
1.25 14D–E (CB t.1 p.32.9–14 Desrousseaux)	62	**73**
3.31 85F (BT t.1 p.198.14–24 Kaibel)	99	**110**
4.19 141A–C (BT t.1 p.319.25–320.17)	72	**87**
11.4 460F–461A (BT t.3 p.3.25–4.1)	98	**105**
11.58 479D–E (BT t.3 p.55.10–56.1)	97	**109**
13.5 557B (BT t.3 p.228.16–21)	64	**77**

	Wehrli	Mirhady
13.67 594E–595A (BT t.3 p.311.4–18)	21	**81**
13.80 603A–B (BT t.3 p.330.4–10)	23	**83**
14.12 620D (BT t.3 p.367.27–368.1)	87	**85**
14.39 636C–D (BT t.3 p.404.16–405.2)	60	**72**
14.48 641E–F (BT t.3 p.417.9–14)	19	**80**
15.2 666B–C (BT t.3 p.472.6–17)	95	**106**
15.5 667B–C (BT t.3 p.474.23–475.4)	96	**107**
15.7 668D–E (BT t.3 p.478.12–15)	94	**108**

ATTICUS PLATONICUS: vid. EUSEBIUS

	Wehrli	Mirhady
fr. 7.9–10 (CB p.63.16–20 des Places)	8i	**20**

CENSORINUS (saec. 3 a.D.)
De die natali

	Wehrli	Mirhady
4.2–4 (BT p. 4.18–5.10 Sallman)	47	**53**

CICERO (106–43 a.C.)
Academici libri

	Wehrli	Mirhady
2.124 (BT p.89.19–21 Plasberg)	8f	**17**

Ad Atticum

	Wehrli	Mirhady
2.2.2 (BT t.1 p.53.21–54.5 Shackleton Bailey)	69	**9**
2.12.4 (BT t.1 p.69.6–12)	27	**8**
2.16.3 (BT t.1 p.74.5–12)	25	**33**
6.2.3 (BT t.1 p.220.7–22)	20	**79**
7.3.1 (BT t.1 p.246.24–247.6)	28	**34**
8.4.1 (BT t.1 p.294.14–16)	4	**7**
13.30.2 (BT t.2 p.545.15–16)	68	**10**
13.31.2 (BT t.2 p.546.9–11)	18a	**11A**
13.32.2 (BT t.2 p.547.16–19)	70	**11B**
13.33.2 (BT t.2 p.549.14–15)	18c	**11C**

De divinatione

	Wehrli	Mirhady
1.5 (BT p.4.11–13 Giomini)	14	**31A**
1.113 (BT p.65.3–7)	15	**31B**
2.100 (BT p.124.25–125.3)	16	**31C**
2.105 (BT p.127.2–4)	17	**32**

	Wehrli	Mirhady
De finibus		
4.79 (BT p.155.7–14 Schiche)	3	**5**
De legibus		
3.14 (CB p.88.10–18 de Plinval)	67	**86**
De officiis		
2.16–17 (OCT p.74.21–75.2 Winterbottom)	24	**78**
Tusculanae disputationes		
1.21 (BT p.228.2–15 Pohlenz)	7	**19**
1.24 (BT p.229.24–5)	8c	**14**
1.41 (BT p.238.8–17)	8d	**15**
1.51 (BT p.243.11–13)	8e	**16**
1.77 (BT p.256.23–7)	9	**27**
4.71 (BT p.398.1–5)	43	**49**
CLEMENS ALEXANDRINUS (c. a.D. 150–215)		
Protrepticus ad Graecos		
2.30.7 (GCS t.1 p.23.2–7 Stählin)	54	**67**
CODICES		
Parisinus Graecus		
supplementum 443 (GGM t.1 p.243a19 Müller)	117	**12**
Vaticanus		
435 (Hermes t.27 [1892] p.119.37–120.26 Arnim)	31	**36**
[DEMETRIUS] (saec. 1 ante Chr.–saec. 1 a.D.)		
De elocutione		
181–2 (CB p.52.11–22 Chiron)	39	**71**
DIOGENES LAERTIUS (saec. 3 a.D.)		
Vitae philosophorum		
1.40 (OCT t.1 p.16.21–6 Long)	30	**37**
1.41 (OCT t.1 p.17.9–18)	32	**38**
3.4 (OCT t.1 p.122.13–23)	40	**47**
3.38 (OCT t.1 p.137.22–5)	42	**48**
3.46 (OCT t.1 p.140.19–141.3)	44	**50**
8.40 (OCT t.2 p.410.11–13)	35b	**41B**

	Wehrli	Mirhady
EUSEBIUS (A.D. 265–339/40)		
Praeparatio evangelica		
15.9.10 (vid. ATTICUS)	8i	**20**
EUSTATHIUS (saec. 12 a.D)		
Commentarium in Dionysii periegetae orbis descriptionem		
767 (GGM t.2 p.350.34–44 Müller)	56	**61**
[GALENUS] (post. saec. 2 a.D.)		
Dc historia philosophica		
24 (DG p.613.14–16 Diels)	10a	**28**
105 (DG p.639.27–9)	13a	**30A**
GELLIUS, AULUS (c. a.D. 130–180)		
Noctes Atticae		
4.11.14 (OCT t.1 p.178.26–179.3 Marshall)	36	**42**
GEMINUS (saec. 1 ante Chr.)		
Elementa astronomiae		
17.5 (CB p.84.12–15 Aujac)	106	**119**
HERMIAS (saec. 2–6 a.D.)		
Irrisio gentilium philosophorum		
2 (DG p.651.13 Diels)	12d app.	**21A**
HESYCHIUS (saec. 5 vel 6 a.D.)		
Lexicon		
s.v. ἐν πίθῳ (no.3276, t.1 p.107.31–108.2 Latte)	app.100	app.**44**
HIERONYMUS (c. a.D. 350–420)		
Adversus Iovinianum		
2.13 (PL t. 23 col.315.42–316.5 Migne)	50	**56B**
IAMBLICHUS: vid. STOBAEUS		
IOANNES LYDUS (saec. 6 a.D.)		
De mensibus		
4.107 (BT p.147.1–3 Wünsch)	113	**126**

	Wehrli	Mirhady

LACTANTIUS (c. a.D. 240–320)
Institutiones divinae
    7.13.7 (CSEL t.19 pars 1 sec. 2 p.627.1–9 Brandt)   10b   **29**

MARTIANUS CAPELLA (saec. 4–5 a.D.)
De nuptiis Philologiae et Mercurii
    6.590–1 (p.292.16–293.3 Dick)   108   **121**

MELETIUS (saec. 7–9 a.D.)
De natura hominis
    De anima (Anecdota Graeca Oxon. t.3 p.145.3–11
    Cramer)   12e   **22**

NEMESIUS (saec. 4 a.D.)
De natura hominis
    2 (BT p.17.1–10 Morani)   11   **21A**
    2 (BT p.22.19–22)   11a   **21B**

PAPYRUS OXYRHYNCHUS
2506
    fr. 6a, 77, 79, 137b (CPF pars 1 t.1.2
    p.30–1 Montanari)   om.   **111**
2457
    (Philologus 126 [1982] 14 Luppe)   om.   **115B**

PAUSANIAS ATTICISTA (c. saec. 2 a.D.)
    s.v.σκολιόν (no. 16, p.209.18–20 Erbse)

PHILODEMUS (saec. 1 ante Chr.)
Academicorum historia
    PHerc. 164, fr. 1 Dorandi   app.**46B**
    PHerc. 164, fr. 22.1–7 (p.179.15–21, 225 Dorandi)   **51**
    PHerc. 1021, col. 1.1–43 (p.148.1–150.13 Gaiser)   **46A**
    PHerc. 1021, col. 2.1–8 (p.157.1–8)   45   **46C**
    PHerc. 1021, col. Y.1–41 (p.152.1–154.7)   **46B**

	Wehrli	**Mirhady**
De Musica		
PHerc. 1572, fr. 2.20–39 (Ricerche sui Papiri		
Ercolanesi 1 [1969] 239a2–11 Rispoli)	93	**39**
De Stoicis		
PHerc. 155, fr. 15 (CE 12 [1982] 104.29 Dorandi)	118	**52**
PHLEGON		
Mirabilia		
4–5 (Paradoxographi Graeci p.130.24–131.20		
Westermann)	37–38	**69**
PHOTIUS (c. a.D. 810–95)		
Bibliotheca		
37 (CB t.1 p.22.20–30 Henry)	71	**88**
PLINIUS (a.D. 23/24–79)		
Naturalis historia		
1.[2] (CB t.1 p.61.28 Beaujeu)	116	**116**
1.[4] (CB t.1 p.64.8)	116	**116**
1.[5] (CB t.1 p.66.2)	116	**116**
1.[6] (CB t.1 p.67.34)	116	**116**
2.162 (BT t.1 p.188.23–189.4 Mayhoff)	105	**118**
PLUTARCHUS (c. a.D. 46–120)		
Moralia		
De E apud Delphos		
1 384D (BT t.3 p.1.4–8 Sieveking)	77	**102**
Quaestiones convivales		
4 Praef. 659E–660A (BT t.4 p.117.6–16 Hubert)	46	**35**
8.2 719A–B (BT t.4 p.262.19–263.7)	41	**45**
An seni gerenda res publica		
26 796C–797A (BT t.5.1 p.53.17–54.28		
Hubert et Drexler)	29	**43**
Non posse suaviter vivi secundum Epicurum		
12 1095A (BT t.6.2 p.144.11–15 Pohlenz et Westman)	73	**92**
13 1096A (BT t.6.2 p.146.10–19)	74	**96**

	Wehrli	Mirhady
Adversus Colotem		
14 1115A (BT t.6.2 p.189.7–19 Pohlenz et Westman)	5	**13**
Vitae		
Agesilaus		
19.9 (BT t.3.2 p.217.17–21 Ziegler)	65	**76**
Theseus		
21.1–3 (BT t.1.1 p.18.22–19.3 Ziegler)	85	**74**
32.5 (BT t.1.1 p.31.11–16)	66	**70**
[PLUTARCHUS]		
De placitis philosophorum (saec. 2 a.D.)		
4.2.5 898B–C (BT t.5.2.1 p.115.11–20 Mau)	12a app.	**21A**
5.1 904E (BT t.5.2.1 p.134.1–3)	13b	**30B**
PORPHYRIUS (c. a.D. 232/3–305)		
Vita Pythagorae		
18–19 (CB p.44.1–45.3 des Places)	33	**40**
56–7 (CB p.63.4–64.1)	34, 35a	**41A**
De abstinentia ab esu animalium		
4.2.1–9 (CB t.3 p.1.16–4.7 Patillon et Segonds)	49	**56A**
SCHOLIA		
In Apollonii Rhodii Argonautica		
4.272–4 (p.277.24–278.3 Wendell)	57a	**58**
4.276 (p.278.8–12)	58a	**59**
In Aristophanis Aves		
1403 (p.241a.41–7 Duebner)	75	**99**
In Aristophanis Nubes		
1364c (p.239.8–12 Koster)	89	**90**
In Aristophanis Pacem		
1244 (p.176.9–16 Holwerda)	app.95	app.**106**
In Aristophanis Ranas		
Hypothesis 1 (c) (p.114.26–29 Dover)	84	**104**
In Aristophanis Vespas		
544b (p.86.10–17 Koster)	86	**84**
In Euripidis Alcestem		
Hypothesis (OCT t.1 p.33.3–14 Diggle)	82	**115A**

	Wehrli	Mirhady
In Euripidis Andromacham		
1 (p.247.10–12 Schwartz)	53,I	**66**
In Euripidis Medeam		
Hypothesis 27–9 (BT p.4.5–7 Van Looy)	63	**62**
In [Euripidis] Rhesum		
Hypothesis 1.26 (BT p.4.3–12 Zanetto)	81	**114**
In Homeri Iliadem		
6.396 (t.1 p.244.3–10 Dindorf)	53	**65**
In Homeri Odysseam		
1.332 (p.58.25–59.12 Dindorf)	92	**95**
In Pindari Olympiacas		
6.7b (BT p.155.24–156.2 Drachmann)	22	**82**
In Platonis Apologiam		
19c (p.421.16–20 Greene)	83	**103**
In Platonis Gorgiam		
451e (p.134.1–4 Greene)	app.88	app.**89**
In Sophoclis Aiacem		
Hypothesis (OCT p.1.11–13 Pearson)	79	**113**
In Sophoclis Oedipodem Tyrannum		
Hypothesis secunda (OCT p.109.20–3 Pearson)	80	**101**
SENECA, LUCIUS ANNAEUS (2 ante Chr.–a.D. 65)		
Naturales quaestiones		
4a fr. 6 (BT p.189.1–2 Hine)	app.113	app.**126**
SEXTUS EMPIRICUS (exeunte saec. 2 a.D.)		
Pyrrhoniae hypotyposes		
2.31 (BT t.1 p.71.28–72.2 Mutschmann et Mau)	8b	**18**
Adversus mathematicos		
3.3 (BT t.3 p.107.11–17 Mau)	78	**112**
7.348–9 (BT t.2 p.80.6–12 Mutschmann)	8a	**24**
SIMPLICIUS (saec. 6 a.D.)		
In Aristotelis Categorias		
8b25 (CAG t. 8 p.216.12–15 Kalbfleisch)	8g	**26**

	Wehrli	Mirhady
STEPHANUS BYZANTIUS (saec. 6 a.D.)		
Ethnica		
s.v. Δώριον (p. 251.6–9 Meineke)	61	**63**
s.v. πάτρα (p. 511.17–512.13)	52	**64**
s.v. Χαλδαῖοι (p.680.4–14)	55	**60**
STOBAEUS (saec. 5 a.D.)		
Anthologium		
1.38.2 (t.1 p.252.13–17 Wachsmuth)	114	**127**
1.49.1a (t.1 p.318.19–320.3)	12b app.**21A**	
1.49.32 (t.1 p.366.25–367.9) = IAMBLICHUS	8k	**23**
STRABO (c. 63 ante Chr.–a.D. 19)		
Geographica		
1.1.1 (CB t.1 p.1.1–10 Lasserre)	104	**117**
2.4.1–3 (CB t.1 p.70.5–73.2)	111	**124**
3.5.5 (CB t.2 p.87.11–13)	112	**125**
SUDA (exeunte saec. 10 a.D.)		
s.v. Ἀριστόξενος (no. 3927, LG t.1 pars 1		
p.357.12–14 Adler)	2	**3**
s.v. Δικαίαρχος (no. 1062, LG t.1 pars 2 p.93.30–94.4)	1	**2**
s.v. σκολιόν (no. 643, LG t.1 pars 4 p.382.28–383.3)	88	**89**
TERTULLIANUS (c. a.D. 160–225)		
De anima		
15.1–3 (CC Series latina, pars 2 p.801.4–17 Waszink)	8h	**25**
THEMISTIUS (c. a.D. 317–88)		
23 Sophistes		
285C (BT t.2 p.79.8–12 Schenkel et al.)	26	**6**
THEODORETUS (ineunte saec. 5 a.D.)		
Graecarum affectionum curatio		
5.18 (BT p.126.22–127.4 Raeder)	12c app.**21A**	

	Wehrli	**Mirhady**
THEON SMYRNAEUS (saec. 2 a.D.)		
De utilitate mathematicae		
(p.124.19–125.1 Hiller)	107	**120**
VARRO (116–27 ante Chr.)		
De re rustica		
1.2.15–16 (CB t.1 p.16.18–17.6 Heurgon)	51	**55**
2.1.3–9 (CB t.2 p.13.7–16.9)	48	**54**
VITA AESCHYLI		
15 (TrGF t.3 p.36.56–9 Radt)	76	**100**
ZENOBIUS (saec. 2 a.D.)		
Epitome collectionum Lucilli Tarrhaei et Didymi		
2.15 (CPG t.1 p.35.7–9 Leutsch et Schneidewin)	103	**97**
3.65 (CPG t.1 p.73.6–13)	100	**44**
3.99 (CPG t.1 p.83.3–6)	om.	**91**
4.26 (CPG t.1 p.91.4–6)	101	**68**
5.23 (CPG t.1 p.125.3–11)	59	**57**
6.16 (CPG t.1 p.166.6–9)	102	**75**
Epitome proverbiorum Didymi Tarrhaei		
2.100 (Mélanges de littérature grecque [1868]		
p.368.16–18 Miller)	103, I	**98**
ZENO VERONENSIS (SAEC. 4 a.D.)		
Tractatus		
1.2.4 (CCSL t.22 p.15.27–9 Löfstedt)	om.	app.**29**

INDEX OF NAMES AND PLACES

Academus   70 n.1
Academy   53, 70, 86
Admetus   115A, 115B
Adramyttion   65
Aeacidae   58
Aeetes   54
Aegean Sea   54
Aeschylus   100
Agallis of Corcyra   73
Agesias   82
Agesilaus   76
Alcaeus   49, 110
Alcestis   115A, 115B
Alexander the Great   3, 83
Aliphera   79
Anacharsis   38
Anacreon   49
Anaximander of Miletus   117
Anaximenes   37
Andreas and Asclepiades   25
Andromache   66
Antipater   99
Aphrodite   74
Apollo   54, 68, 79 n.1, 115A
Araros, son of Aristophanes   103
Arcadia   68
Archelaus of Macedon   102
Archilochus   39
Archytas of Tarentum   53
Argos   54
Argonauts   54
Ariadne   74
Aristarchus   94
Aristodemus   38

Ariston of Argos   47
Aristophanes of Athens   103, 104
-Frogs   104
Aristophanes of Byzantium   110
Aristotle   2, 4, 5, 6, 13, 20, 21A,
    23, 25, 30A, 30B, 53, 54, 67,
    86, 96, 105, 106, 111
-Catalogues of Dramas   114
-On Heaven   13
-On the Soul   13
-Memoranda   67
Aristoxenus   3, 4, 7, 11B, 15, 16
Armenia   62
Artemis   72
Mt. Ataburius   119
Athens   9, 81
Atlantic ocean   126
Atramys   65
Atreus   54
Axiothea   46B, 49

Bagoas   78
Babylon   60
Bias   38
Bosporus   54

Cadmus   66
Caecilius   37
-Roman Sayings   37
Callias of Athens   104
Callias of Mytilene   110
-On the (Word) Limpet in Alcaeus
    110
Callimachus   68

Caria   **123**
Caulonia   **41A**
Caenis/Caeneus   **68**
Caesar   **8** n.1
Mt. Cantherinus   **54**
Cephenes   **62**
Cephisodorus   **6**
Chaeron, character in Dicaearchus'
    Trophonian Story   **79** n.1
Chaeron, Academic   **51**
Chaldaea   **61, 62**
Chaldaeus   **61**
Chilon of Sparta   **38**
Cilicia   **123**
Cimon   **81**
Clearchus   **21a** n.1, **42**
Cleobulus   **38**
Cleomenes   **85**
Clitarchus   **68**
Clitus   **4**
Mt. Cluvius   **79**
Clytemnestra   **39**
Colchis   **54, 60**
Colotes   **13**
Corinth   **9, 19**
Crassus   **8** n.1
Cratippus   **31B, 31C**
Critias   **105**
Cronus/Saturn   **56A, 56B**
Croton   **40**
Mt. Cyllene   **68, 119**

Dacians   **46B**
Damon of Cyrene   **37**
-*On the Philosophers*   **37**
Dardania   **54**
Darius   **77**
Deinarchus   **21A** n.1, **21B** n.1
Delos   **4**
Delphi   **122**
Demetrius of Phaleron   **86**
Democritus of Abderra   **25, 29**, **122**

Demosthenes   **70**
Deucalion   **19**
Diogenes of Babylon   **39**
Dionysius, schoolmaster of Plato
    47
Dionysius, teacher of Cicero's son
    7 n.1, **79**
Dorium   **63**

Echedemus   **70**
Eetion   **66**
Elatus   **68**
Elea   **70**
Eleusis   **81**
Elis   **82**
Empedocles   **25, 84, 85**
-*Purifications*   **85**
Epaminondas   **76**
Ephesus   **38**
Ephorus   **38, 117**
Epicurus   **25, 28, 29, 96**
Epimenides   **38**
Eratosthenes   **117, 120, 124, 125**
Eretria, school of   **26**
Euboulides   **6**
Euboulus, comic poet   **103**
Eudimius   **4**
Eudoxus   **46B, 117**
Euhemerus   **124**
Euphrates   **60**
Euphronius   **99**
Euripides   **67, 102, 112, 114**
-*Alcestis*   **115A, 115B**
-*Medea*   **62**
-*Rhesus*   **114**

Mt. Fiscellus   **54**
Fundanius   **55**

Gemini   **54**
Getae   **46B**
Gibraltar/the Pillars   **123, 124, 125**

Gorgias   38
Granicus river   65

Hecataeus of Miletus   117
Hegesander of Delphi   109
-*Memoranda*   109
Hellanicus   99
Helus   63
Hera   68
Heracles   54, 65, 67, 68, 107, 115A, 115B
Heraclides of Pontus   13, 86, 92
-*Zoroaster*   13
-*On the Underworld*   13
-*On Difficulties in Natural Philosophy*   13
Herodes   9
Herodotus   70
Hesiod   56A, 68
Hesperides   54
Hieronymus   96
Hippasus   73
Hippocrates   46B
Homer   92, 117
-*Catalogue of Ships*   79
Horus/Orus   58, 59

Iamidae   82
Ibycus   49
Ilium   60
Mt. Imaus   123
Ionia   123
Isis and Osiris   59
Italy   38, 54

Lapiths   68
Lastheneia   50
Lasus of Hermione   99
Leandrius   38
Lebedus   38
Leophantus   38

Lepreon   79
Lesbos   27
Libya   54
Locri   41A
Lycia   65, 123
Lyconia   54
Lycurgus of Sparta   45

Maedica   54
Marathon   70
Marathus of Arcadia   70
Menedemus of Eretria   26 n.1
Metapontum   41A, 41B
Metrodorus of Lampsacus   96
Miltiades   81
Myson   38
Mytilene   27

Nausicaa   73
Neophron   67
Nicomachus   4
Nicostratus, son of Aristophanes, aka Philetaerus   103
Nile   126
Nilus   59
Ninus   60

Occelus of Lucania   53
Olympia   10, 85

Pamphylia   123
Pamphylus   38
Panchaea   124
Panaetius   5
Pausanias   79 n.1
Mt. Pelion   117
Pellene   9
Pelopidae   64
Peloponnesus   79, 123, 124
Penelope   89
Periander   38

Pericles **81**
Peripatetics/Aristotelians **13, 23,**
  31C, 53, 70
Perseus **61**
Persians/Medes **61, 75**
Phanias **4**
Pheidias, father of Dicaearchus **2**
Pherecrates of Phthia, character in
  Dicaearchus' dialogue set at
  Corinth **19**
Pherecydes of Samos **41A**
Philemon, comic poet **98**
Philetaerus, see Nicostratus
Philippus, son of Aristophanes
  103
Philip of Macedon **77**
Philochorus **46C**
-*Atthis* **46C**
Philocles, tragic poet **101**
Philonides, comic poet **104**
Phrygia **54**
Phrynicus, comic poet **104**
-*Muses* **104**
Piso **54**
Pithaida, daughter of Aristotle **4**
Pittacus of Mytilene **38**
Plato **5, 13, 21A, 21B, 25, 28,**
  38, 45, 46A, 46B, 46C, 47, 53,
  70, 86, 88
-*Phaedo* **21B**
-*Phaedrus* **48**
-*Protagoras* **38**
-*Republic* **88**
-*Rival Lovers* **47**
Platon, comic poet **104, 107**
-*Cleophon* **104**
-*Zeus Outraged* **107**
Plutarch **36**
-*Roman Sayings* **36**
Polybius **35, 117, 124, 125**
Pompey **8 n.1**

Poseidon **68**
Posidonius **117, 124**
Procilius **9**
Pteleum **64**
Pythagoras **21A, 38, 40, 41A,**
  41B, 42, 45, 53, 54
Pythagoreans **53**
Pytheas of Massilia **124**
Pythionike, Athenian courtesan **81**

Rome **9**

Samos **41A**
Samothrace **54**
Sardinia **123**
Scipio Africanus **35**
Sebosus **36**
Sesonchosis/Sesoster **58, 59**
Seven Wise Men **37, 38**
Sicily **123, 124**
Sicilians **105, 108, 109, 123**
Sicyonians **73**
Simmias **21B**
Socrates **25, 43, 45**
Solon **38**
Sophocles **61, 100, 112, 114**
-*Ajax* **113**
-*Oedipus Tyrannus* **101**
-*Tympanistai* **60**
Spain **54**
Sparta, Lacedaemon **2, 45, 73**
Stoics **5, 23, 28, 32**
Strato of Lampsacus **25**
Syrians **60**

Tarentum **41A**
Mt. Taurus **54, 123**
Teiresias **68**
Tellen **97**
Tenea **79**
Mt. Tetrica **54**

Thales   **21A, 38, 54**

Thebe   **65, 66**

Theophrastus   **4, 5, 13, 23, 33, 53, 86, 96**

-*In Reply to the Natural Philosophers*   **13**

Thero   **79** n.1

Theseus   **74**

Thrace   **54**

Thucydides   **70**

Thyestes   **54**

Timaeus   **6**

Tritia   **79**

Tyndaridae   **70**

C. Vestorius   **79**

Xenocrates of Chalcedon   **5, 13, 53**

Xenophon   **76**

Xerxes   **75**

Zeno of Citium   **54**

Zeus   **68**

Zopyrus of Magnesia   **93**

2

Dicaearchus on the Soul
and on Divination

R. W. Sharples

The problem I wish to discuss in this paper[1] can be stated simply enough. On the one hand, Dicaearchus is reported in some texts as having denied the very existence of the soul. On the other, he is said to have given the soul a part to play in divination. How are these conflicting reports to be reconciled?

The question is a significant one for several interlocking reasons. There has been much discussion in recent years[2] of Aristotle's position on what for us is the "mind-body" problem, but in the context of Aristotle's thought (leaving aside, for the moment only, the Active Intellect) rather the "soul-body" problem.[3] That discussion has in part been

---

[1] This paper was given successively at the Boulder conference on Demetrius and Dicaearchus, and to a seminar at the University of Edinburgh; I am grateful to all who contributed to the discussion, and especially to Victor Caston, who was the respondent at the conference, and to Jeff Carr, Paolo Crivelli, Bill Fortenbaugh, David Robinson and Dory Scaltsas.

[2] Comprehensively represented by the papers in M. C. Nussbaum and A. O. Rorty (eds.), *Essays on Aristotle's* De Anima (Oxford, 1992).

[3] The modern statement of the problem in terms of *mind* being above all due to Descartes; cf. Michael Frede, "On Aristotle's Conception of the Soul," in Nussbaum and Rorty (above, n. 2) 93–107, at 93–94.

stimulated by contemporary philosophical controversy, of which more later; and it is not only in connection with Aristotle that the question of the reducibility or otherwise of the psychological has been raised in the context of interpretations of ancient philosophy.[4] Moreover, since soul for Aristotle is form, discussion of the relation between soul and body in Aristotle is directly linked to the debate over whether ancient Peripatetics—first Aristotle's immediate colleagues and successors, and later Andronicus and Alexander of Aphrodisias—held materialist views which were essentially un-Aristotelian.[5] For all these reasons study of Dicaearchus' views on the soul seems both philosophically and philologically opportune. The present paper will in part be an investigation of the methods to be used in assessing ancient evidence, and of the grounds on which we may or may not be justified in dismissing any particular piece of it.

The apparent conflict stated in my first paragraph is indeed reminiscent of one much discussed in connection with another, and more famous, ancient philosopher: Empedocles, who on the one hand apparently interpreted thought materialistically,[6] and on the other believed in reincarnation. Much discussion of whether Empedocles was a "scientist" or a "mystic"—or, as some have suggested, was first one and then the other, in whichever order[7]—reflects the working out in the laboratory of antiquity of modern tensions and anxieties;[8] and in pursuing the modern literature on Dicaearchus one sometimes catches echoes of the

[4] Notably in David Sedley's seminal papers "Epicurus' Refutation of Determinism," *Syzetesis, Festschrift Gigante* (Naples, 1983) 11–51, and id., "Epicurean Anti-reductionism," in *Matter and Metaphysics*, ed. J. Barnes and M. Mignucci (Naples, 1988) 297–327. However, I do not think that his attribution to Epicurus of an emergentism that involves the causation of atomic swerves by mental events succeeds; see my "Epicurus, Carneades and the Atomic Swerve," *BICS* 38 (1991–1993) 174–90.

[5] Below, nn. 38–40, 44.

[6] Empedocles, frr. 105, 107, 109 DK.

[7] The views respectively of Bidez and of Diels and Kern; cf. W. K. C. Guthrie, *A History of Greek Philosophy*, vol. 2 (Cambridge, 1965) 124–25.

[8] In the light of D. O'Brien's comments in "Empedocles Revisited," *Ancient Philosophy* 15 (1995) 403–70 especially 437 and 441, I should perhaps emphasise that I am not claiming that the connection of an interpretation with particular more recent preoccupations is in itself any argument against it as an interpretation, nor yet that the particular point with which O'Brien is there concerned, the distinction (and also connection) between Empedocles' two poems in terms of their contents, is not established by convincing evidence. My claim is simply that anachronistic preoccupations can, and sometimes have, influenced the reporting and interpreting of earlier thinkers both in later antiquity and more recently (O'Brien agrees: 458), and that we should be aware of the possibility that this has happened in the case of Dicaearchus.

same issues. There has however been much less interest until relatively recently, at least in countries which have English as their primary language, both in post-Aristotelian philosophy in general, and in particular in Aristotle's own successors and in the doxographical tradition which will provide much of our evidence. It may be such incidental reasons that explain why Dicaearchus has been less of a cause célèbre than his fellow-Sicilian Empedocles.

Before coming to the central issue, however, it will be necessary to engage in some analysis of the ancient evidence for Dicaearchus' position.

1. A "Harmony" Theory of the Soul in Dicaearchus?

Ancient sources from the doxographical tradition—the pseudo-Plutarch *Placita*, Stobaeus, Theodoret—attribute to Dicaearchus an identification of the soul as a "harmony" or attunement of the four elements;[9] that is, presumably, though we are not explicitly told so, of earth, air, fire and water. Nemesius[10] gives a similar report, but immediately glosses it by

[9] [Plutarch] *Plac.* 4.2.5, Stobaeus *Ecl.* 1.49.1, Theodoret *Gr. aff. cur.* 5.18 (cf. app. **21A**). The view that soul is a harmony, with no further specification, is attributed to Dicaearchus by Hermias (below, n. 10) and by Meletius = *Anecd. Oxon* vol. 3 145.3 Cramer = **22** (for Meletius see H. Hunger, *Die hochsprachliche profane Literatur der Byzantiner*, vol. 2. Byzantinisches Handbuch 5.2 [Munich, 1978] 304).

[10] Nemesius *nat. hom.* 2, p. 17.10 Morani (Leipzig, 1987) = **21A**. The MSS of Nemesius in fact have not "Dicaearchus" but "Deinarchus"; "Dicaearchus" is Matthaei's substitution based on [Plutarch] and Stobaeus. Not surprisingly, a text dependent on Nemesius also has "Deinarchus" (Hermias *irris. gentil. philos.* 1 = H. Diels, *Doxographi Graeci* [Berlin, 1879] 651.13, cf. app. **21A**; the names from Nemesius according to Diels 262, but see also J. Mansfeld, "Doxography and Dialectic. The Sitz im Leben of the 'Placita'," *ANRW* II.36.4 [Berlin, 1990] 3056–3229, at 3072 n. 47). Theodoret too has not "Dicaearchus" but "Clearchus" (Theodoret *gr. aff. cur.* 5.18 p. 127.4 Raeder = Clearchus, fr. 9 Wehrli). "Clearchus" at any rate must be wrong, for Clearchus argued that the soul can be independent of the body (Clearchus frr. 7–8 Wehrli. H. B. Gottschalk, "Soul as *Harmonia*," *Phronesis* 16 (1971) 179–98, at 186–87 n. 26; P. M. Huby, "The Paranormal in the Works of Aristotle and his Circle," *Apeiron* 13 [1979] 53–62, at 57–58).

Morani retains "Deinarchus" in the text of Nemesius. Gottschalk argues (186–87 n. 26) that no such philosopher is known; actually this isn't *quite* true, for there was a Deinarchus who was a first-generation Pythagorean, recorded in Iamblichus' *Life of Pythagoras* (Iamblichus, *Vit. Pyth.* 36.267, p. 145.15 Dübner; R. Goulet (ed.), *Dictionnaire des Philosophes Antiques*, t. II [Paris, 1994] 617). There is however no other evidence to connect him with the theory of soul as harmony. But even if it is Dicaearchus who is the ultimate object of these reports, Mansfeld argues (3078) that "Deinarchus" and "Clearchus" are what Nemesius and Theodoret respectively wrote, and so should not be emended by editors of those authors' texts. Gottschalk argues (loc.

describing it as an attunement of the four primary qualities, hot, cold, wet and dry. To a certain extent these reports may give a not unreasonable characterisation of the *type* of view of the soul Dicaearchus held, in its general outline. But both the definition of soul as an attunement, and its identification as an attunement of the four elements, have been questioned. It is therefore necessary to consider these two points, in this order, at the outset. But it should be emphasised that they are both in a sense preliminary and ancillary to the main argument of this paper.

Cicero attributes to Dicaearchus, in a dialogue set at Corinth, the view that life—rather than soul; we shall return to this point later—is a power in a body "configured" in such a way that it has strength and sensation through a "natural blending" (*temperatio naturae*).[11] As Gottschalk has pointed out,[12] there is no reference to "harmony" or attunement either here or in a reference by Lactantius[13] to the soul as mortal for Dicaearchus. Cicero links Dicaearchus with Aristoxenus,[14] and Gottschalk suggests that the *term* "harmony" may have been transferred by the other sources from the latter to the former, while the actual borrowing in terms of theory may have been in the opposite direction. That is to say, Dicaearchus may have formulated a theory of the soul, or of life, as the arrangement of the body, and Aristoxenus, whose specifically musical interests are much better attested, may have borrowed the theory and applied the term "harmony" to it.[15] A theory of soul as "harmony" was indeed already attacked by Plato in the *Phaedo*,[16] and Plutarch describes

---

cit.) that Nemesius' "Deinarchus" shows that he is not dependent on a doxographical source; but if "Deinarchus" is indeed simply a mistake Nemesius may still be so dependent, albeit indirectly (cf. Mansfeld, 3078 n. 77. On Nemesius' sources, and his (indirect) connection with the doxographical tradition here, cf. Mansfeld 3076ff. and n. 70; H. Dörrie, *Porphyrios' Summikta Zetemata*, Zetemata 20 [Munich, 1959] 111–26). Just to add to the complexities, [Galen]'s *History of Philosophy* twice has "Diarchus," apparently not a personal name in regular use at all, in texts which seem secured by other parallels as referring to Dicaearchus, on the mortality of the soul and on divination respectively ([Galen] *hist. philos., Dox.* p. 613.15 = **28** and p. 639.27 = **30A**. The former passage was emended by Camerarius; Morani in his note on the Nemesius passage cited above seems to say that "Diarchus" should be kept, but it is not clear who this "Diarchus" would be. Mansfeld (3078, n. 77) suggests that "Deinarchus" and Theodoret's "Clearchus" (above) *may* be mistaken ancient attempts to correct "Diarchus"; but the context in [Galen] seems different from those in Nemesius and in Theodoret.

[11] Dicaearchus **19**. See below, n. 31.
[12] Gottschalk (above, n. 10) 179–98, at 184–86.
[13] Dicaearchus **29**.
[14] Dicaearchus **15–16**.
[15] Gottschalk (above, n. 10) 190.
[16] Plato *Phaedo* 91–94.

Dicaearchus as opposing Plato concerning the soul.[17] Even if Plutarch is right, however, it need not follow that Dicaearchus was defending the "harmony" theory in precisely the terms in which Plato attacked it.

What is important for our present concerns is indeed not so much the question whether Dicaearchus used the term "harmony" for the configuration that produces life, but rather the question how this configuration is to be understood. In the *Phaedo* the harmony theory, put forward by the Pythagorean Simmias in arguing against the immortality of the soul, is presented in terms of a tempering of the physical constituents of the body, and specifically of the extremes of the four primary qualities hot, cold, dry and wet.[18] As Gottschalk has pointed out,[19] for Aristoxenus at least there is no suggestion that "harmony" is to be understood as a relation between the *elements* that go to make up the body; it is rather the end-product of the activity of the living organism as a whole. The view attributed, though without use of the term "harmony," to Dicaearchus by Cicero in **19** is very similar; and Rohde and Gottschalk have therefore suggested[20] that Dicaearchus' view was like Aristoxenus' and that the doxographical tradition has attributed to him the idea of a harmony of bodily constituents through a confusion with the theory reported and criticised in the *Phaedo*. Indeed, as we have seen, Nemesius actually makes the harmony a harmony of the four primary qualities, as in the *Phaedo*.

The possible importance of this issue for our present concerns is that a "harmony of the whole organism" theory held by Dicaearchus might seem closer, at any rate, than a harmony-of-the-four-elements theory

---

[17] Plut. *adv. Colot.* 14 1115a = **13**. There is perhaps room for doubt whether Plutarch intends to attribute this motive to Dicaearchus as a historical fact, rather than just describing the relation between Dicaearchus' views and Plato's.

[18] Plato *Phaedo* 86bd. One solution to the conundrum of what Simmias, a Pythagorean, is doing there representing as Pythagorean a theory which excludes the immortality of the soul, has indeed been to suggest that a more general Pythagorean theory of the soul as a "harmony"—perhaps expressing the notion of degrees of virtue, or something of the sort—was replaced by a more narrowly physical theory (J. Burnet, *Plato's* Phaedo [Oxford, 1911] 82; id., *Early Greek Philosophy*, 4th ed. [London, 1930] 295f. But cf. R. Hackforth, *Plato's* Phaedo [Cambridge, 1955] 102–3). The concluding argument of Gottschalk's paper (above, n. 10, 190ff.) is that this did in a sense happen, but that the person who made the change, for the purposes of his own general argument, was Plato himself in the *Phaedo*.

[19] Gottschalk (above, n. 10) 183. Cf. also F. Wehrli, *Die Schule des Aristoteles* (Basel, 1967) 2^2:84.

[20] E. Rohde, *Psyche*, vol. 2, tr. W. B. Hillis (New York, 1966) 400 n. 52; Gottschalk (above, n. 10) 186–88.

would be to Aristotle's own hylomorphism, interpreted as stressing the unity in the compound individual of form, in this case soul, and body.[21]

2. Did Dicaearchus Deny the Existence of the Soul?

As we have seen, Cicero in *Tusculans* 1.21 = **19** reports Dicaearchus as denying the very existence of the soul. And while the doxographical tradition and Nemesius give alleged definitions of the soul by Dicaearchus—which presumably implies its existence in *some* sense— other texts too attribute to Dicaearchus a denial of the existence of the soul altogether. I shall henceforth refer to these texts as "the eliminativist reports." True, several others of them too are from Cicero,[22] and may have no value as evidence independently of **19**. If we believed in a Cicero who assembled his philosophical works from Greek sources by use of the ancient equivalent of scissors and paste, without ever letting his own thoughts interfere with the process, we might be able to argue that different Ciceronian texts constituted independent pieces of evidence; but in fact it is quite clear that Cicero, as one would in any case expect, associated certain doctrines with certain individuals in his own mind in such a way that they tend to recur.[23]

---

[21] Even Simmias' theory in the *Phaedo* does not presumably exclude the existence of more complex structures, first Aristotle's uniform and then his non-uniform parts, between the level of the four primary qualities on the one hand and the whole living creature on the other. But a theory of the harmony of the four primary bodies might seem to accommodate these less readily. Admittedly much depends on the detail in which such a theory is developed—precisely what doxographical summaries tend to obscure. Alexander of Aphrodisias has an account of the soul as the product of the mixture of the bodily elements which starts from the four simple bodies, indeed, but works upward through successively more complex structures before arriving at the level of the whole living organism, the form of which is the soul. See below, n. 42, also n. 68.

[22] Cic. *Tusc.* 1.24, 41, 51 = **14–16**; Cic. *Acad. pr.* 2.124 = **17**. (In the second of these passages I take it the sense of *ne condoluisse umquam videtur, qui animam se habere non sentiat* is that Dicaearchus felt no grief, since he was not aware that he had a soul [and feeling grief implies awareness of the soul], rather than, as J. E. King in the Loeb edition [Cambridge, Mass./London, 1927] has it, that he felt no grief "*at* not noticing that he had a soul" [my italics].)

[23] Cf., for example, the way in which he repeatedly cites together Aristo of Chios and Pyrrho: *On Ends* 2.43, 3.11–12, 4.43. J. M. Rist, *Stoic Philosophy* (Cambridge, 1969) 75 and n. 2; R. J. Hankinson, *The Sceptics* (London, 1995) 87. The claim that reports of particular doctrines in different passages in Cicero may just repeat the same material and are not independent of one another does not in any way conflict with the claim that he may not be as concerned as we might wish with connections between doctrines at-

As well as by Cicero, however, Dicaearchus' denial of the existence of soul is reported by Tertullian and by Sextus Empiricus. Tertullian[24] reports Dicaearchus as holding that the soul has no ruling part; Mansfeld[25] links this with the fact that Cicero too, in *Tusculans* 1.21, attributes to Dicaearchus a denial of the existence of mind before developing this to a general denial of the existence of soul, and suggests[26] that what we have in both texts is a reflection of a section of a discussion in the *Vetusta Placita* concerned with the location of the ruling part, rather than with the nature of the soul as such. Clearly Dicaearchus cannot have denied the very existence of the phenomena, such as thought, sensation and the initiation of movement, commonly ascribed to the ruling part; so the origin of these reports must be either that he denied that the ruling part had any specific physical location, being regarded as a function of the whole body, or that his denial of a substantial soul has caused him to be cited, in a list concerned with the location of the ruling part, as denying that this part existed at all (and hence, as it might seem to the compiler, *a fortiori* denying that it had any specific location). These explanations are not mutually exclusive.

Sextus in one text simply reports Dicaearchus as denying that the soul exists,[27] but in another reports his view as being that the soul is nothing but body in a certain state—*pôs ekhon sôma*, in Stoic terminology.[28] Stoic terminology is apparently present in Cicero's report in **19**, too, soul there being described as a power spread (*fusa*) throughout living

---

tributed to a single philosopher on diverse topics; see below in the final section of this paper.

[24] Tertullian *De anima* 15 = **25**. J. H. Waszink, *Tertullian: De Anima* (Amsterdam, 1947) 223, takes Tertullian's argument to be that Dicaearchus, Andreas and Asclepiades did away with the ruling part because they placed the senses in the mind, since the abolition of the distinction between sensation and the higher soul-faculties implies the abolition of the senses including the mind. This involves taking *dum* in a causal sense, and presents the abolition of the ruling part as an implication rather than an actual assertion; on the other hand Tertullian continues by saying that Asclepiades at least argued directly for the non-existence of the ruling part, by citing creatures that still live even when divided so that the part of the body thought to contain the ruling part of the soul has been removed.

[25] Mansfeld (above, n. 10) 3130; also 3163 on the parallel between Tertullian (following Soranus: Diels [above, n. 10] 206ff.; Waszink, ibid. 219; and Mansfeld 3068) and Sextus.

[26] Ibid. 3068; cf. 3099ff.

[27] Sextus *PH* 2.31 = **18**.

[28] Sextus *M* 7.349 = **24**. The Stoic language here is noted by L. Repici, *La natura e l'anima: saggi su Stratone di Lampsaco* (Torino, 1988) 14.

bodies,[29] though Movia has suggested that the language may rather reflect the influence of Strato's theory.[30] However that may be, the description in the same passage of life as a power of a body configured in
a certain way indicates that talk of a power extending through the body
must be understood metaphorically, and not as suggesting—as it would
for the Stoics or for Strato—soul as a separate substance or *pneuma*.

Cicero, as already noted, reports that Dicaearchus gave this view of
soul or life in two books of a three-book dialogue set at Corinth, and
placed it in the mouth of a character Pherecrates. Pherecrates, we are
told, was presented as a descendant of Deucalion, and Wehrli[31] suggests
that this was for the sake of an allusion to the origin of humans from
stones, after Deucalion's flood, as excluding any notion of soul as a
spiritual substance. And Julia Annas has described Dicaearchus' position as amounting to the claim that "our distinction between lifeless and
living things answers to nothing real,"[32] and has said that his tone suggests that his motive in discussing the soul was eliminativist rather than
reductivist.[33]

[29] Wehrli (above, n. 19) 1^2:45.

[30] G. Movia, *Anima e intelletto: ricerche sulla psicologia peripatetica da Teofrasto
a Cratippo* (Padua, 1968) 73.

[31] Wehrli (above, n. 19) 1^2:45. The question arises whether "Pherecrates" was indeed
a mouthpiece for Dicaearchus' own views. Cicero certainly took it so (**14–17**), and so
too do other authors (Sextus, above, nn. 27–28; Iamblichus, below, n. 34; Atticus, below,
n. 35; Simplicius, below n. 43). They can hardly all be dependent on Cicero; so if
"Pherecrates'" views have mistakenly been taken for Dicaearchus' own, either the mistake would have to have been made by Cicero and others independently, or else it goes
back to a common source. But it looks as if Cicero knew the Corinthian dialogue at first
hand (cf., as well as **19**, *ad Att.* 13.32 = **11B**, with Wehrli 1^2:44). Mansfeld (above, n.
10) 3129 and n. 336, argues that Cicero followed a doxographic source but consulted or
remembered the dialogue as well; *perhaps* a misinterpretation in the doxographic tradition could have led Cicero to fail to read the dialogue with a sufficiently open mind, but
this seems unlikely. Cicero was after all himself a writer of dialogues. Moreover, the arrangement described in **19**—review of opinions in the first book, followed by
"Pherecrates'" statement in the next two—does sound very much as if "Pherecrates" had
the major part of the work in order to put forward D.'s own thoughts (so Wehrli 1^2:45).
The pattern of the work would then reflect Aristotelian procedure in general, beginning
with a survey of *endoxa*, and in particular the three-book structure of Aristotle's own *De
anima*. Dicaearchus' dialogue *could* have ended without a definite decision on the points
at issue, but in that case the amount of space given to "Pherecrates" seems rather dispro-
portionate.—I am grateful to Bill Fortenbaugh for raising the issue discussed in this note.

[32] J. E. Annas, *Hellenistic Philosophy of Mind* (Berkeley and Los Angeles,
1992) 31.

[33] Ibid. 31 n. 43.

One wonders, however, whether this may not be too extreme a characterisation of Dicaearchus' position. To say that there is not a real *separate* thing that makes living bodies alive is one thing; to say that there is no real distinction between animate and inanimate another. Iamblichus gives Dicaearchus' view as an example of the claim that the body is ensouled while the soul has no existence of its own (*huparkhon*);[34] and Atticus describes Dicaearchus as doing away with the substance (*hupostasis*) of the soul.[35] Nemesius couples Dicaearchus with Aristotle, whose own definition of the soul as the entelechy of an organic body he gives accurately, and claims that Aristotle and Dicaearchus regard the soul as insubstantial, by contrast with Thales, Pythagoras and Plato.[36] It is therefore not surprising that some scholars have interpreted the ancient sources which say that Dicaearchus denied the existence of the soul as indicating only that he denied the existence of the soul as a separable substance in itself.[37] And it would be odd if, as our evidence at face value implies, Dicaearchus both denied the existence of the soul altogether and gave a definition of it as an attunement. Reports that present Dicaearchus as an eliminativist are therefore even more suspect than those attributing to him a definition of the soul as the attunement of the four simple bodies. In the case of the eliminativist reports we are dealing with an actual conflict between two sets of evidence (assuming indeed that the reports of Dicaearchus' definition of the soul, even if distorted, do rest on *something*), while in that of the reports of a harmony doctrine what may prompt doubt is the fact that references to an attunement of the primary bodies appear in only one group of our reports of Dicaearchus' views, most of them more or less closely linked with the doxographical tradition, coupled with the plausibility—and only the plausibility—of the suggestion that there has been influence from reports of Aristoxenus or from the theory of the *Phaedo*.

---

[34] Iamblichus ap. Stob. *Ecl.* 1.49.32 p. 367 W. = **23**.

[35] Atticus fr. 7.10, p. 63 des Places = **20**.

[36] Nemesius *nat. hom.* 2, p. 16.21ff. Morani = **21A**.

[37] Movia (above, n. 30) 76. Gottschalk (above, n. 10) 185 n. 24 points out that Atticus and Nemesius were wrong to deny that soul was substance for *Aristotle* (below), unless their point was that it did not have *separate* existence. Dörrie (above, n. 10) 112f., cited by Mansfeld (above, n. 10) 3079 and n. 81, held that Aristotle and Dicaearchus were coupled as holding that soul was *quality* rather than substance; Mansfeld notes (3080 n. 83) that, while this is not accurate for Aristotle, already in Boethus ap. Simpl. *in Cat.* 78.4ff. there is the suggestion that *eidos* might be quality or quantity.

3. Dicaearchus and Aristotle

The issue of whether the soul is to be defined in terms of the body or its arrangement was to recur later in the Aristotelian tradition. Andronicus[38] and Alexander of Aphrodisias[39] both identified soul with the product of the mixture of the bodily elements. Alexander in particular has been denounced by critics for un-Aristotelian materialism.[40] But the criticisms—or some of them—have tended to reflect a particular Thomistic understanding of soul in Aristotle. It is certainly not un-Aristotelian to assert that a given type of form can only be realised in a certain type of matter;[41] the question is which has priority in explanation, matter or form, or indeed the combination of the two.[42] While

[38] Galen *Quod animi mores* 44.18 Müller (*hepomenē*). Cf. P. Moraux, *Der Aristotelismus bei den Griechen*, vol. 1 (Berlin, 1973) 132–34; H. B. Gottschalk, "Aristotelian Philosophy in the Roman World," in *ANRW* II.36.2, ed. H. Temporini and W. Haase (Berlin, 1987) 1079–1174, at 1113.

[39] Alexander *De anima* 24.21–23 (*epi . . . gennōmenē*).

[40] P. Moraux, *Alexandre d'Aphrodise: Exégète de la noétique d'Aristote* (Liège and Paris, 1942) 29–62; H. Robinson, "Form and the Immateriality of the Intellect from Aristotle to Aquinas," in *Aristotle and the Later Tradition,* Oxford Studies in Ancient Philosophy, suppl. vol., ed. H. Blumenthal and H. Robinson (Oxford, 1991) 207–26, especially 214–18; also, from a different perspective, William Charlton, "Aristotle and the Harmonia Theory," in *Aristotle on Nature and Living Things: Philosophical and Historical Studies presented to David Balme*, ed. Allan Gotthelf (Pittsburgh, 1985) 131–50, at 134–36. But for a more sympathetic treatment cf. P. L. Donini, "L'anima e gli elementi nel *De Anima* di Alessandro di Afrodisia," *Atti dell'Accademia delle Scienze di Torino*, classe di scienze morali, storiche e filologiche 105 (1971) 61–107 (though Alexander's view is indeed here described as a wrong interpretation of Aristotle *De anima* 1.4. 408a24–26); also my reply to Robinson at *Classical Review* 43 (1993) 87–88, and "On Body, Soul and Generation in Alexander of Aphrodisias," *Apeiron* 27 (1994) 163–70; P. Accattino, "Generazione dell'anima in Alessandro di Afrodisia, *de anima* 2.10–11.13?," *Phronesis* 40 (1995) 192–201, and V. Caston, "Epiphenomenalisms, Ancient and Modern," *Phil. Rev.* 106 (1997) 309–63. (I am grateful to Professor Caston for the opportunity to discuss this paper with him in advance of its publication.)

[41] Aristotle *Physics* 2.9 200a8ff. (saws have to be made of iron). There is indeed the difference that iron can be used to make things other than saws, while in the case of an animal body, though its ultimate constituents can make up other things too, its proximate matter cannot—flesh and bone only occur in animal bodies. Cf. (but of non-uniform parts like hands) *Metaph.* Z 10 1036b24ff.; and below, n. 74.

[42] Cf. David Charles, "Matter and Form: Unity, Persistence and Identity," in *Unity, Identity and Explanation in Aristotle's* Metaphysics, ed. T. Scaltsas, D. Charles and M. L. Gill (Oxford, 1994) 75–105, at 78ff. Though regarding form as explanatorily and ontologically prior (103) Charles has no difficulty in proceeding through the type of ascending account (100ff.) which has been found objectionable in Alexander. Alexander explicitly argues that the compound derives its substantiality from that of form and matter (Alexander *De anima* 6.3–4).

Alexander's (and Andronicus') talk of a *product* may be unwise, it is not clear that Alexander wants, as some critics have argued, to deny the substantiality of form. And if "form" can be understood as "arrangement," it does not seem un-Aristotelian to suggest that the soul is the arrangement of the body—as a whole, rather than specifically of the four elements or four primary qualities. Of course such a doctrine will not provide critics with the sort of soul as a separate substance, material or immaterial, that will satisfy a Stoic or a Platonist respectively; but that does not mean that soul does not exist in the way an Aristotelian enmattered form does. Indeed, when Simplicius[43] reports Dicaearchus as denying soul for the same reason as the Eretrians who denied the existence of qualities because they had no *common* substantiality but existed only in particulars and compounds, the suggestion seems hard to resist that Dicaearchus' crime was not to believe in Platonic separable souls—just as some of the ancient, and perhaps also the modern criticisms of Alexander as an un-Aristotelian nominalist seem on examination to amount to little more than his failure to believe in transcendent Platonic Forms,[44] or just as the criticisms of Strato for denying teleology may to a large extent, as Repici has shown, reflect his *following* Aristotle in denying that the natural world is shaped by a conscious force.[45]

Certainly when sources report Dicaearchus as denying the immortality of the soul[46] they are saying nothing more than is implied by every-

[43] Simplicius, *in cat.* 216.12ff. = **26**.

[44] Simplicius, *in cat.* 82.22; Dexippus, *in cat.* 45.12. Cf. R. W. Sharples, "Alexander of Aphrodisias: Scholasticism and Innovation," in Temporini and Haase (above, n. 38) 1176–1243, at 1199, and references there.

[45] Plut. *Against Colotes* 14 1114F = Strato fr. 35 Wehrli; Cic. *On the Nature of the Gods* 1.35 = Strato fr. 33 Wehrli; cf. also id. *Academica Posteriora* 1.121 = Strato fr. 32 Wehrli; Repici (above, n. 28) 117–56. But cf. also M. van Raalte, "The Idea of the Cosmos as an Organic Whole in Theophrastus' *Metaphysics*," in *Theophrastean Studies*, *RUSCH* III, ed. W. W. Fortenbaugh and R. W. Sharples (New Brunswick, NJ, 1988) 189–215, at 203.

[46] Cic. *Tusc.* 1.77 = **27**, coupling Dicaearchus with Epicurus and citing Dicaearchus' *Lesbian Dialogues*; [Galen] *hist. philos.* 24 = **28**; Lactantius *Instit.* 7.13.7 = **29** (Dicaearchus, with Democritus and Epicurus, would retract his view if he saw a necromancer raising souls from the dead (!)). Mansfeld (above, n. 10) 3130, points out that this report in Cicero, by saying souls are mortal, implies that they *do* exist, contrary to Cicero's other reports; he also suggests (3129) that Cicero in those earlier passages has been influenced by a source which saw the denial of a ruling part (cf. above, nn. 24–26) as tantamount to denying the existence of the soul altogether. I suspect that in the later passage Cicero is simply, but significantly, careless with his language; in a context concerned with the immortality or otherwise of the soul, as opposed to a doxographical listing of views on the soul like that earlier in *Tusculans* 1, it is unim-

thing we have heard so far as Dicaearchus' view; and, while Aristotle himself may in fact have believed in individual personal immortality, it is rather difficult to reconcile it with his metaphysical views. (I am thinking here of Robinson's description of the Aristotelian soul as a single form part of which requires matter for its existence and part of which does not.)[47] And when Zeller, followed by Wehrli, links Dicaearchus' well-attested preference for the practical as opposed to the contemplative life[48] with his rejection of the Aristotelian immortal Active Intellect, I at least cannot help thinking that modern scholarship may be imposing on its fourth-century predecessors connections and preoccupations which they might not have readily recognised.[49]

The relation between Dicaearchus' view of soul and that of Aristotle himself has indeed been assessed in the most varied ways. Among the ancients, not only does Nemesius couple Dicaearchus and Aristotle as allegedly denying the substantiality of soul; Atticus too, in the passage already cited, reports Dicaearchus as "following Aristotle" in denying the substance of soul.[50] It is true that, as Movia points out,[51] the Platonism of such reporters as Atticus and Nemesius cuts both ways; they may be assimilating Aristotle to Dicaearchus, as equally unsatis-

---

portant whether a thinker denies the immortality of the soul because he says there is a soul but denies its immortality, or because he denies the soul exists at all—especially when, as we have seen, there is a certain amount of unclarity about just what constitutes "existing" in any case.

[47] Robinson (above, n. 40) 223. For a rather different account of Aristotle's doctrine of soul cf. Frede in Nussbaum and Rorty (above, n. 2), esp. 104–7.

[48] Cic. *ad Att.* 2.16.3 = **33**, against Theophrastus.

[49] E. Zeller, *Die Philosophie der Griechen* 2.2³ (Leipzig, 1879) 891; Wehrli (above, n. 19) 1²:50. I am not claiming that the suggested connection *cannot* be correct. But Aristotle's argument in *Nicomachean Ethics* 10.7–8 rests on the idea of a *nous* which is *god-like*, not on that of individual immortality; and Alexander at least, though denying individual immortality, did not exclude *theoria* from the good life, even if *Ethical Problem* 25 attributed to him suggests that practical and theoretical activity are both *parts* of the end (cf. R. W. Sharples, *Alexander of Aphrodisias: Ethical Problems* [London, 1990] 69 and n. 238).—I am grateful to Bill Fortenbaugh for discussion of this issue.

[50] Atticus, loc. cit. in n. 35 above. Des Places translates *hepomenos* by "being logical." There is a problem over the text; the MSS have *hê psukhê d' akinêtos houtôs. toigaroun hepomenos . . .*, which Stephanus emended to *. . . akinêtos. toutôi gar hepomenos . . . .* Des Places rejects the emendation, citing J. D. Denniston, *The Greek Particles*, 2nd ed. (Oxford, 1954) 566–67 for *toigaroun* normally coming as the first word in its clause (though Denniston notes this as an exception in Hippocrates and a partial exception in Lucian). But even so, the interpretation of *hepomenos* as "being logical" seems forced.

[51] Movia (above, n. 30) 83–84.

factory from a Platonist point of view, rather than the reverse.

Some modern scholars have asserted that Dicaearchus is entirely in agreement with Aristotle, apart from excluding the Active Intellect as an immortal element proper to the soul of each individual, as Alexander too was to do.[52] Others have argued that Dicaearchus misunderstood Aristotle,[53] or that his approach, while relating formal and material elements in Aristotelian fashion, reverses the direction of causation between the two. This is Gottschalk's view;[54] he not only draws an explicit comparison to the case of Alexander, already mentioned, but also connects Dicaearchus' view with a general decline of interest in the notion of form in the post-Aristotelian Peripatos, a trend whose reality it does indeed seem hard to deny.[55] Yet other interpreters, including Movia,[56] have argued that it is a mistake to approach Dicaearchus' views primarily in the context of Aristotle's *De anima*; the relevant context might rather be opposition to Plato,[57] and perhaps also to the theory of Aristotle's *Eudemus*. One is reminded of Glenn Most's argument that the discussion of teleology in Theophrastus' so-called *Metaphysics*, far from being criticism of Aristotle, is directed against Plato and reflects the developmental stages of Aristotle's own work.[58] And Dicaearchus and Aristoxenus' views have been linked with a Peripatetic interest in earlier theories[59]—whether genuinely Pythagorean, or mediated and modified by the *Phaedo,* perhaps does not matter here. The question whether Plato rather than Aristotle was Dicaearchus' target is in any case relevant to the historical question of Dicaearchus' attitude to and relations with Aristotle, rather than to the philosophical question whether Dicaearchus' view was such as to be liable to Aristotle's objections to a harmony theory.

[52] So, among others, Tennemann, Chaignet, Brink, Adorno. References at Movia (above, n. 30) 79–81.

[53] Ritter cited by Movia (above, n. 30) 82.

[54] Gottschalk (above, n. 10) 188–89 and n. 31.

[55] The tiny relative size of the "Metaphysics" section in FHS&G is one relevant indication.

[56] Movia (above, n. 30) 82–83.

[57] As suggested by Plutarch; above, n. 17. But how far Plutarch is drawing on positive information about the historical relationship between Dicaearchus and Plato, and how far he is simply influenced by the fact that Dicaearchus' recorded views were at variance with Plato's, must remain uncertain.

[58] A. Laks, G. W. Most and E. Rudolph, "Four Notes on Theophrastus' *Metaphysics*," in Fortenbaugh and Sharples (above, n. 45) 224–56, at 224–33.

[59] Movia (above, n. 30) 92–93; cf. Annas (above, n. 32) 30.

Victor Caston, in an as yet unpublished paper,[60] examines Dicaearchus' theory of soul in the context of an analysis of the Peripatetic tradition from Aristotle himself to Alexander, and argues that Dicaearchus' view of the soul was epiphenomenalist whereas Aristotle's was emergentist, in senses of both these terms which he carefully distinguishes;[61] both views can be classed as varieties of supervenience, but the crucial difference is the denial in epiphenomenalism of any causation by the psychic[62] *qua* psychic. As varieties of supervenience, epiphenomenalism and emergentism are both to be contrasted with, on the one hand, eliminativism, the denial that the term "soul" has any reference at all, and on the other with that form of dualism, found for example in Plato, which makes the soul a separate substance existing in its own right and not dependent on the body at all. The latter will henceforth be referred to as "substance-dualism."

Caston's evidence for regarding Dicaearchus as an epiphenomenalist where Aristotle is an emergentist rests in part on the criticism of the harmony theory by Aristotle himself which we will shortly come to, and also in part on a passage from Plutarch(?) *On Desire and Grief* reporting a discussion by Heraclides of Pontus which does not mention Dicaearchus and Aristoxenus by name, but which Caston interprets as alluding to their views for the sake of refuting them. It will be convenient to divide the passage into sections for the sake of subsequent discussion.

> (a) Some extend both belief and reasoning to the body outright, saying that the soul is not a cause at all, but that such things are brought about by the variation and quality and power of the body. (b) For some think that the book entitled *On the Things in Hades*, in which the account declares that the soul's existence is derived from (that of) substance, is not

[60] Above, n. 40.

[61] See also the discussions by Jaegwon Kim, "Epiphenomenal and Supervenient Causation," *Midwest Studies in Philosophy* 9 (1984) 257–70 = Jaegwon Kim, *Supervenience and Mind* (Cambridge, 1993) 92–108; "The Myth of Non-reductive Materialism," *Proceedings and Addresses of the American Philosophical Association* 63 (1989) 31–47 = *Supervenience and Mind*, 265–84; and "The Non-reductivist's Troubles with Mental Causation," in *Mental Causation*, ed. J. Heil and A. Mele (Oxford, 1993) 189–210 = *Supervenience and Mind*, 336–57. It is noteworthy that Kim regards a non-reductive physicalism as untenable; epiphenomenalist reductionism and dualism are the tenable options. And this seems to mean that he would side with Caston's epiphenomenalist Dicaearchus against Caston's emergentist Aristotle. But see further below, n. 76.

[62] In the ancient sense; Caston himself uses "mental" as more easily understood in the context of modern debate. Above, n. 3.

by Heraclides at all, others that it was composed to refute what had been said by others about the substance of the soul. (c) Well, whoever wrote it, it does away with the substance of (the soul) outright, since the body has in itself all the powers mentioned.

Plutarch(?) *On Desire and Grief* 5 =
Heraclides of Pontus fr. 72 Wehrli.[63]

The interpretation of the passage is indeed controversial; Sandbach, for instance, suggests that Heraclides might himself have attributed *consciousness* to the body while regarding the soul as a separate life-giving force, an "occult" notion of the soul for which there are precedents in Greek thought.[64] And even if the view represented in the passage is one that Heraclides was attacking rather than endorsing, its connection with Dicaearchus and Aristoxenus remains circumstantial; they are simply the most likely candidates for holding such a view at the appropriate time. But even if we concede these points, the question remains of how the passage is to be interpreted.

[63] (a) Ἔνιοι δ᾽ ἄντικρυς καὶ δόξαν καὶ διαλογισμὸν εἰς τὸ σῶμα κατατείνουσιν, οὐδ᾽ εἶναι αἰτίαν (οὐσίαν Pohlenz) ⟨τὸ⟩ (suppl. Bernadakis) παράπαν ψυχὴν (vulg.: ψυχῆς Laurent.) λέγοντες, ἀλλὰ τῇ τοῦ σώματος διαφορᾷ καὶ ποιότητι καὶ δυνάμει συντελεῖσθαι τὰ τοιαῦτα. (b) τὸ μὲν γὰρ Περὶ τῶν ἐν ῞Αιδου βιβλίον ἐπιγραφόμενον, ἐν ᾧ τὴν ψυχὴν τῇ οὐσίᾳ παρυπάρχειν ἀποφαίνεται ὁ λόγος, οἱ μὲν οὐδ᾽ εἶναι τὸ παράπαν Ἡρακλείδου νομίζουσιν, οἱ δὲ πρὸς ἀντιπαρεξαγωγὴν ⟨συν⟩τετάχθαι τῶν εἰρημένων ἑτέροις περὶ οὐσίας ψυχῆς· (c) ὅτῳ ⟨δ᾽ οὖν⟩ γεγραμμένον, ἄντικρυς ἀναιρεῖ τὴν οὐσίαν αὐτῆς, ὡς τοῦ σώματος ἔχοντος ἐν αὐτῷ τὰς εἰρημένας δυνάμεις πάσας. I am grateful to Victor Caston for bringing this passage to my attention, and for the opportunity to draw here on our discussions of it. F. H. Sandbach, who edited the text for the Loeb Plutarch, devoted two careful and balanced discussions to the question of the authenticity of the work. In his Loeb edition (Plutarch *Moralia*, vol. 15 [Cambridge, Mass., 1969] 32–35) he comes to the conclusion that "some may think" that similarities with Plutarch's authentic works make the genuineness of the treatise "probable," but that they may also be explained by its being by an associate of Plutarch. At the end of an equally careful discussion in "L'auteur du *De libidine et aegritudine*," *Revue de Philologie* 43 (1969) 211–16, he opts for its being genuine. (I am grateful to Victor Caston for drawing my attention to the latter discussion; see his paper in this volume.)— I have translated *parhuparchein* by "derives its existence from": the word is rare (only eleven occurrences for it and *parhuparxis* in the TLG CD-ROM "E" index), but the sense of "derivative" is suggested by the analogy of, e.g., Aristotelian "paronymy." However, one may note that the soul is said, in the middle part of the passage, to depend on *substance*, not on body (cf. below, at n. 72).
[64] Sandbach, Loeb ed. 46–47 n. See below, at n. 110.

(a) and (c) might seem to suggest an eliminativist view at least for those aspects of consciousness they discuss,[65] but (b) indicates some form of supervenience—the soul exists, but owes its existence to the body. If the passage were by Plutarch himself one might be tempted to suggest that the first and last sentences reflected Plutarch's own Platonic prejudices—a separate substantial soul or eliminativism being the only two real possibilities from his point of view—and would thus be no guide as to precisely what form of supervenience we should find in the middle part of the passage. Even if *On Desire and Grief* is not by Plutarch himself, it may be by an associate of his who would share his views (see above, n. 63). And in any case, our passage forms the second half of a rhetorical contrast with the view of those who attribute all consciousness, sensation included, to the soul rather than the body. (The example given of this is none other than the third head of the Lyceum, Strato, whom Plutarch himself, along with many other interpreters ancient and modern, certainly did regard as an un-Platonic materialist.) The author's desire, for the sake of rhetorical contrast at this point in his exposition, for a view attributing all consciousness to the body as opposed to the soul, might itself have the same effect as Platonist metaphysical assumptions in making him insensitive to the nuances of different forms of supervenience. And this means that we cannot safely use the fact that (a) and (c) suggest epiphenomenalism (or as I would argue, eliminativism), to interpret the middle sentence as evidence for epiphenomenalism rather than emergentism. Putting it another way, epiphenomenalism, as opposed to emergentism on the one hand and eliminativism on the other, may be the only position that provides a

---

[65] (a) being ambiguous between "the soul exists but is not a cause" and "the soul is not a cause and doesn't exist," and (c) being ambiguous between eliminativism and denial of both causal efficacy and substance-dualism. We might indeed argue that the first and last sentences must be interpreted in a non-eliminativist way because the middle part is clearly not eliminativist; but that is to presuppose that [Plutarch] is aware of the distinctions we are drawing.—"Extend" in (a) might be thought to suggest a non-eliminativist view, suggesting that belief and reasoning are *shared* by the soul and the body; but the context makes it clear that we are dealing with a view in which they are attributed to the body alone, and "extend" is probably to be interpreted as Plutarch(?)'s own contrast of the view he describes with others which as it were "confine" belief and reasoning to the soul; used from that point of view, "extend" need not imply that the particular thinkers referred to here themselves connect belief and reasoning with *both* soul and body, and as indicated that would conflict with the contrast between views involving the soul and views involving only the body which provides the context for the entire passage.

completely consistent reading of the *whole passage*; but is that clear evidence for the claim that Plutarch(?) himself intended epiphenomenalism rather than emergentism or eliminativism? The passage as a whole reflects Plutarch(?) rather than his source, and for that reason we cannot escape consideration of Plutarch(?)'s own understanding of the issues if we wish to use the passage as historical evidence. If on the other hand we base our argument for Dicaearchus' views only on the middle section (ii), then we cannot use the opening and closing sections as evidence for an eliminativist rather than an emergentist reading of this middle section.[66]

The major problem for the claim that, the Active Intellect apart, there is not really that much difference between Dicaearchus' and Aristotle's views on the soul is that Aristotle in *De anima* 1.4 explicitly *rejects* the notion of soul as "harmony." He gives a number of arguments for doing so, one of which is the point—essentially used already by Socrates in the *Phaedo*—that a "harmony" cannot be an efficient cause of motion.[67] It has been suggested above that the term "harmony" may not have been Dicaearchus' own but transferred by the tradition from Aristoxenus, and

---

[66] The question how far one can or should infer a position on a particular issue from the words of an author who may not have had that issue in mind in those terms raises questions that go to the heart of what we are doing in studying the history of philosophy; it also raises questions about the nature of philosophical debate between contemporaries. One person, notoriously, had no qualms whatsoever about seeing implications in people's words that they themselves were unaware of—namely, Socrates. In the present context, however, we are concerned with a slightly different issue: that of the relevance of a writer's awareness of the issues, or lack of it, not to our interpretation of his own thoughts, but to his reliability as a guide to the views of others.

[67] Aristotle *De anima* 1.4 407b32ff.; cf. Plato *Phaedo* 93A6–7. It is highly significant that S. Marc Cohen, "Hylomorphism and Functionalism," in Nussbaum and Rorty (above, n. 2) 57–73, regards the role of form as efficient cause as the major obstacle to a functionalist interpretation of soul in Aristotle (71–72). However, in the light of Aristotle, *De anima* 1.4 408b13–15, one wonders whether the question at 2.4 416a6–9 (below, n. 71) should be answered *not* by saying that it is a living creature's soul that holds it together, but that a living creature holds itself together and maintains itself by virtue of having a soul. Aristotle's other objections to the harmony theory include the observation that harmony is better applied to health or bodily excellences (cf. *Phaedo* 93Bff.), and the arguments—or assertions—that the soul is not a relation between or a combination of elements, and that it is difficult to assign to harmony what the soul suffers and does. Cf. also Aristotle, *Eudemus* fr. 45 Rose[3]; Wehrli (above, n. 19) 1[2]:46. Alexander expressly distinguishes his doctrine of soul (above) from a harmony theory: Alexander, *De anima* 24.18ff. But critics are not convinced that he draws the distinction radically enough. Cf. Donini (above, n. 40) 82–89, and Alessandro di Afrodisia, *L'anima: a cura di Paolo Accattino e Pierluigi Donini* (Rome, 1996) 146ff.; Charlton, loc. cit. in n. 40 above.

that the identification of the harmony as a harmony of the four elements is in any case dubious; but this simply means that, terminology apart, we are driven back to the question, in any case more interesting, whether Dicaearchus' *theory*, in so far as we can reconstruct it, succumbs to Aristotle's objections in the *De anima* passage. Gottschalk has argued[68] that Dicaearchus and Aristoxenus, in seeing the soul as a function of the *whole* organism, might have been seeking to answer *one* of Aristotle's objections to a *Phaedo*-style harmony theory, namely that if soul is a mixture of the bodily elements—i.e, the four primary elements or the four primary qualities—there will be different souls in different organs of the same body, since the proportion of the elements in each will be different.[69] And Aristotle does end his discussion by referring to the difficulties that there are in *rejecting* the harmony theory.[70]

The problem in assessing Dicaearchus' position is simply lack of evidence. At least for Alexander we have twenty-six quarto pages of Greek text setting out his general metaphysics of the soul, which make possible a detailed comparison between his position and Aristotle's, whatever exactly *that* was. For Dicaearchus we have, essentially, a number of statements that he denied the soul's substantiality or made it a disposition of the body; but the former are rendered suspect by their readiness to describe Aristotle too as denying the substantiality of the soul in the sense the critics apparently require, and the latter, using later terminology, look like recasting of Dicaearchus' presumed position in the light of later understanding, which may well have involved dropping his own qualifications and perspectives. As for our fullest report, Cicero's in **19**, just how much does it contain that is incompatible with essential Aristotelian doctrine? Only, I would suggest, the claim that *there is nothing* involved in a living creature apart from the body;[71] Aristotle, who in the

---

[68] Gottschalk (above, n. 10) 189. Repici (above, n. 28) 43 n. 62, apparently attributes to Gottschalk the view that the link between Dicaearchus' theory and Aristotle's discussion is justified only if Dicaearchus explicitly described the soul as a harmony; but for Gottschalk the point does not turn on the term *harmonia* (cf. 188), and Dicaearchus could be seen as responding to Aristotle's discussion even if he did not use the specific term "harmony." Gad Freudenthal, *Aristotle's Theory of Material Substance: Heat and Pneuma, Form and Soul* (Oxford, 1995) 43–44 n. 73, endorses the view that an attunement-of-the-whole-body theory would be proof against this objection by Aristotle.

[69] Aristotle *De anima* 1.4 408a13ff.

[70] Ibid. 408a24–28.

[71] Freudenthal argues that the question "what holds a living creature together, for Aristotle?" (above, n. 68, 15, citing Aristotle *De anima* 2.4 416a6–9; I am grateful to

Metaphysics regards all three of form, matter and the combination of the two as substance, would not have put the point quite like that. On the other hand, "body" is not the same as "matter," and in *Metaphysics* H6 Aristotle is prepared to regard even the question what unifies form and matter as an unreal question, on the grounds that there is really only one thing.[72]

The problem, if we try to take Aristotle's hylomorphism seriously, is that human beings are not typical compounds of form and matter, just because in their case the form has a separate name, "soul," and is contrasted with a term "body" which seems to designate, not indeed the *matter* as opposed to the form, but the compound as opposed to the form.[73] There has been much discussion recently of how "body," in the sense of "body potentially possessing life," can for Aristotle be defined independently of soul.[74] Our problem is the reverse one, of how, if the hylomorphic view is taken seriously, "soul" can be defined independently of "body," if "body" is understood—as it must be, if it is "a body potentially possessing life"—to include not just the material ingredients

---

Victor Caston, too, for drawing my attention to this passage) is to be answered in terms of natural heat and connate pneuma, *and* that from a *physical* point of view it does not matter whether one describes this as the operation of natural heat, or of nutritive soul using heat; though it may, he says, matter philosophically (34–35)—an issue he explicitly (68–69) declines to discuss. In other words, on the physical level at least Freudenthal regards the distinction between emergentism and epiphenomenalism as simply irrelevant. But see further below, n. 76.

[72] Cf. especially 1045b17ff. Robinson (above, n. 40) 215 sees Alexander's statement (*De anima* 6.3f. Bruns) that the combination of form and matter is substance as embodying the "reductionist" approach he objects to in Alexander; but Alexander is here qualifying his previous suggestion that form and matter are substances only because they are parts of the combination. See my discussion cited in n. 40 above. Walter E. Wehrle, "The Definition of Soul in Aristotle's *De anima* ii.1 is not Analogous to the Definition of Snub," *Ancient Philosophy* 14 (1994) 297–317, at 302–3 insists that the identity of form and matter in *Metaphysics* H6 is not strict identity; this is surely right (if it were not, we would, I take it, have eliminativism), but I shall argue below that it is not clear that Cicero's report of Dicaearchus' position should be taken at its eliminativist face value either.

[73] Cf. Wehrle, ibid., esp. at 310–16.

[74] The problem was given its classic statement by J. L. Ackrill, "Aristotle's Definitions of *psuche*," *Proc. Arist. Soc.* 73 (1972–1973) 110–33. Cf. especially B. Williams, "Hylomorphism," *Oxford Studies in Ancient Philosophy* 4 (1986) 189–99; S. Marc Cohen (above, n. 67); Jennifer Whiting, "Living Bodies," in Nussbaum and Rorty (above, n. 2) 75–91; C. Shields, "The Homonymy of the Body in Aristotle," *Archiv für Geschichte der Philosophie* 75 (1993) 1–30; Frank A. Lewis, "Aristotle on the Relation Between a Thing and its Matter," in Scaltsas, Charles and Gill (above, n. 42) 247–77.

but their arrangement into non-uniform parts.[75] Even if we leave aside the question of the survival of intellect without body, it may still be possible to stress the primacy of form and soul; a particular bodily configuration is both necessary and sufficient for life, but circularity is avoided because the *life* of a particular type of creature—a horse, say, or a human being—can be described independently of the bodily configuration which is indeed explained by the soul. That seems a thoroughly Aristotelian explanation;[76] it is not clear that there is anything in it that would be unacceptable to Alexander, and it is not even clear that it conflicts with Dicaearchus' view, unless we give Cicero's precise wording more credence than it perhaps deserves.

Cicero's report in **19** comes from a catalogue which promptly goes on to assert confidently that Aristotle himself identifies mind, or rather as it turns out soul in general, with the fifth element,[77] a fact that may lead us to suspect that the appearance of more detailed knowledge than is possessed by the other reports of Dicaearchus should not necessarily lead us to attribute to Cicero's report greater understanding or sympathy. On the face of it, Cicero in **19** represents Dicaearchus as an *eliminativist*; if we

[75] From an Aristotelian perspective as interpreted by Robinson, indeed, one should presumably argue that Dicaearchus' view as formulated by Cicero is topsy-turvy; rather than saying that there is nothing in a living creature except body, even if this is understood as "body potentially possessing life," we should say that there is nothing in a living creature except soul, both the part that requires matter and that which does not.

[76] It is at any rate how Alexander of Aphrodisias (?) *Quaestio* 2.8 answers the charge of circularity in Aristotle's definition of soul; cf. R. W. Sharples, *Alexander of Aphrodisias: Quaestiones 1.1–2.15* (London, 1992) 104–5, with the further corrective remarks at id., *Alexander of Aphrodisias: Quaestiones 2.16–3.15* (London, 1994) 96. And in the modern context, while Kim (above, n. 61) regards non-reductive physicalism as an unacceptable compromise, R. Van Gulick ("Who's in Charge Here? And Who's Doing All the Work," in Heil and Mele [above, n. 61] 233–56) argues that the privileging of "physical" explanations is in fact a mirage; there is no fundamental bedrock of physical explanation, and claims to the contrary undermine biochemical explanations no less than psychological ones. Van Gulick does not indeed want to argue that higher-level explanations are *superior* to lower-level ones; nevertheless, when he argues (251) that self-sustaining and self-reproductive patterns are real features of the world and causally potent, the parallel with Aristotelian form is striking. See also Fred J. Miller, Jr., *Nature, Justice and Rights in Aristotle's Politics* (Oxford, 1995) 336–46. In connection with Aristotle, at least, talk of "physicalism" should be seen only as stressing that the forms the "physicist" or natural philosopher studies are a part of nature or *phusis*, not as implying that matter is somehow *more* fundamental than form or soul.

[77] Cf. on this H. J. Easterling, "Quinta natura," *MH* 21 (1964) 73–85; Mansfeld (above, n. 10) 3083 n. 108 and 3130–31. It is true that just before the reference to Dicaearchus Cicero has reported Plato's view accurately from the Timaeus (*Tusculan Disputations* 1.20).

do not accept *that* interpretation of Dicaearchus, should we attach much weight to **19** as evidence for epihenomenalism rather than emergentism?

What does seem clear is that almost[78] the entire ancient Peripatetic tradition—including notably Aristotle,[79] Dicaearchus, Andronicus and Alexander—is in agreement in rejecting both the idea that the soul is a substance separate from the body, on the one hand, and a view that would completely eliminate the soul, on the other.[80] And this is in itself enough to create problems in connection with Dicaearchus' reported views on divination, with which the remainder of this paper will be concerned.

4. Dicaearchus and Divination—I

The reports we have of Dicaearchus' views on divination can be dealt with under three heads, which Martini indeed argued reflected three separate works.[81] Two of them offer few problems and can be dismissed pretty rapidly in the context of the present discussion. First, we know that Dicaearchus wrote a work on the oracle of Trophonius at Lebadaea in Boeotia. The procedure at this oracle is graphically described by Pausanias;[82] after preparations lasting for several days the person consulting the oracle was dragged by his feet into a subterranean chamber, after which he saw visions of the dead before eventually regaining his senses and the power to laugh. Plutarch adds that a certain Timarchus, after entering the chamber, seemed to feel himself being struck on the head in such a way that his soul left his body.[83] It is not too unreasonable to suppose that the procedures may have left room for a certain amount of sharp practice, perhaps with blunt instruments, on the part of the officials of the oracle, and that Dicaearchus' work may have

[78] But not perhaps quite all; Clearchus (above, n. 10) and Cratippus (below, n. 108) may be among the exceptions. (I am grateful to Victor Caston for emphasising this to me.)

[79] With a possible exception for an Active Intellect in the individual, if such there is.

[80] I am grateful to Victor Caston (above, n. 40) for discussion on this point. His paper outlines a debate within the Peripatetic tradition between epiphenomenalists and emergentists; but what is clear is that this debate takes place on the middle ground between the extremes of eliminativism on the one hand and a separate substantial soul on the other, which all the participants agree in rejecting.

[81] Martini at *RE* 5.1 (1903) 588.

[82] Pausanias 9.39.4ff.

[83] Plut. *De genio Socratis* 590b10.

been critical in tone; unfortunately, though, none of the six extant references to the work[84] relate to the actual subject of its title, most being
concerned rather with topographical details in the Peloponnese and in
Attica, presumably on the journey to the oracle; though we do also have
a reference which may be from it to an oracle at Elis where divination
took place by means of burnt offerings.[85]

Secondly, we know from Cicero that there was a "large book" by
Dicaearchus asserting that it was better not to know the future than to
know it.[86]

The third and most relevant, but also most contentious, group of reports relate to Dicaearchus' theory of divination through dreams and
altered psychic states, i.e. divine inspiration or *enthousiasmos*. Pseudo-
Galen and the pseudo-Plutarch *Placita* report, in virtually identical language, that "Aristotle and Dicaearchus" recognised divination of this
type because they held that the soul, though not immortal, had some
share in divinity.[87] The Aristotelian basis for this view is perhaps to be
found in *On Divination through Sleep*, where the traces of earlier im-
pressions may become apparent to the soul in sleep and may sometimes
indicate the course of future events, and where the "divine" nature of the
proceeding is explained, in terms reminiscent of the Hippocratic treatises, by the claim that nature as a whole is divine.[88] What is clear, however, is that the functioning of the soul involved in this process is for
Aristotle a sub-rational, rather than a supra-rational functioning.[89]

---

[84] **11 A–C, 79, 80, 81.**
[85] **82.**
[86] Cicero *De divinatione* 2.105 = **32.** For other treatments of the theme cf. A. S.
Pease, *M. Tullii Ciceronis De divinatione*, University of Illinois Studies in Language and
Literature 6.2–3, 8.2–3 (1920, 1923) 523.
[87] [Galen] *hist. phil.* 105, [Plut.] *plac.* 5.1 (= **30A–B**). Apart from variations in word
order the only difference is that [Plutarch] mentions prophetic ecstasy (*enthousiasmos*)
as well as dreams, while [Galen] does not. Cf. S. Pines, "The Arabic Recension of *Parva
Naturalia*," *Israel Oriental Studies* 4 (1974) 104–53, reprinted in id., *Studies in Arabic Versions of Greek Texts and in Medieval Science,* The Collected Works of S. Pines,
vol. 2 (Jerusalem/Leiden, 1986) 96–145, at p. 146 and n. 254 of the original pagination.
I am grateful to Inna Kupreeva for drawing my attention to this discussion.
[88] Aristotle *De div. per somn.* 2 463b14ff. Cf. Philip J. van der Eijk (ed.), *Aristoteles,
De insomniis, de divinatione per somnum,* Aristoteles Werke in deutscher Übersetzung,
14.3 (Berlin, 1994) 293–95, who compares "Hippocrates" *On the Sacred Disease* and
Airs Waters Places, but argues that in the Aristotelian context the nature in question is
to be understood as that of the individual human being; also id. 93 n. 137.
[89] Van der Eijk (ibid.) 91 contrasting Aristotle fr. 10 Rose (12a Ross), from the *De
philosophia,* if indeed, he remarks (89ff.), this gives Aristotle's own view. See further
below, n. 97.

And—the point that really concerns us here—there seems nothing in the account so far that is incompatible with what we have learned about Dicaearchus' view of the soul,[90] so long as we are prepared to allow that for him the soul existed to the extent that, even if it was not a separate substance, it was legitimate to speak of functions normally regarded as psychic and to attempt to talk of the relation of these to the body.

Where problems arise is with two of a series of three references to Dicaearchus in Cicero's *On Divination*.[91] The first of these, from the survey of the views of various philosophers at the beginning of the work, simply repeats what we know already, that Dicaearchus allowed only divination through dreams and ecstatic states (*furor*), without giving any further explanation.[92] But the second and third appear to attribute to Dicaearchus and to Cratippus, the Peripatetic friend of Cicero, the view that the mind can divine the future in these conditions because it is then free from the body and has nothing to do with it.[93]

At this point it may be useful to draw some distinctions, just because the ancient texts do not seem to draw them clearly. For Aristotle in *On Divination through Sleep*, as we have seen, prophetic dreams are explained by a sub-rational functioning of the soul in sleep. It will be helpful to label this view (A) and to distinguish from it both

> (B) the view that in dreams a rational part of the soul, while still located in the body, functions in a way that does not involve bodily organs, notably the senses

and also

> (C) the view that in dreams a rational part of the soul not only functions without the bodily organs but, because it is not tied to these organs or to

---

[90] Wehrli (above, n. 19) 1²:46 argues that Dicaearchus' reference to the soul's share in the divine is to be interpreted in the same way as Aristotle's reference to dreams being divine because nature is .

[91] K. Reinhardt, *Kosmos und Sympathie* (Munich, 1926) 269–70, argued that the account of divination at Plut. *Obsolescence of Oracles* 40 432cff. derived from Dicaearchus (cf. Huby [above, n. 10] 59); but cf. Moraux (above, n. 38) 244–45.

[92] Cicero *De div.* 1.5 = **31A**.

[93] Cicero *De div.* 1.113 = **31B**, and (less explicitly, but note *libere*) ibid. 2.100 = **31C**. The idea has classical antecedents; cf., in addition to Plato *Republic* 571d–572a (below, n. 96) and Aristotle fr. 10 Rose (below, n. 97), Pindar, fr. 116 Bowra and Xenophon *Cyropaedia* 8.7.21 (below, n. 97). E. R. Dodds, *The Greeks and the Irrational* (Berkeley and Los Angeles, 1951) 135 and nn.

the body at all, can travel away from the body and apprehend truths because it can travel in space, and conceivably in time as well.[94]

Following Dodds,[95] I shall label view (C) the "psychic excursion" view.
It is tempting to label view (B) as "dualistic," following van der Eijk,
but to do so may risk obscuring a further distinction. For if view (B) is
interpreted in terms of a radical mind-body dualism, there seems no reason why the rational part of the soul, or mind, referred to should have to
remain in the body during sleep, if indeed it makes any sense to talk
about its location anywhere. On such an interpretation the difference
between (B) and (C) would reduce to the point that in (C) it is supposed
that the relevant part of the soul has physical location and actually has to
travel on excursions to other places to perceive what is happening there,
whereas in (B) interpreted dualistically—let us call it (B2)—the mind, if
it functions through means independent of the senses and superior to
ordinary reasoning, can presumably (B2a) remain in the body while
having access to events remote in space and time,[96] or perhaps better
(B2b), on such a view the question whether it remains in the body or not
makes no sense because it is not the sort of thing to have a specific
location. More importantly for our present purpose, all our evidence
concerning Dicaearchus' theory of soul strongly suggests that view
(B2), just as much as (C), would be out of the question for him. So for
the moment we might consider another variant of (B), (B1), in which the
part or faculty of the soul involved in prophetic dreaming is one that is
as linked to the body as every other part of the soul, but is capable of
functioning without the senses, and is best able to do so in sleep. *How* it
functions in such a way as to divine the future remains obscure, but then
so it does on view (B2), unless indeed we reduce the absence of spatial

---

[94] I say "in time as well," because this seems to be required for dreams to be prophetic
through precognition. Cf. on this Huby (above, n. 10) 60. Attributing notions of *objec-
tive* time-travel to the ancient Greeks may seem anachronistic, but Plato in *Republic* 572a
can refer to the rational part of the soul in sleep seeing past, present and future (Dodds,
ibid. 135ff.), and we can seem to relive past events in dreams (ibid. 156–57 n. 1).
Theophrastus fr. 343 FHS&G refers to experiencing many more things in the course of
a dream than one could live through in a single year, but comes from a highly dubious
source; cf. R. W. Sharples, *Theophrastus of Eresus: Sources for his Life, Writings,
Thought and Influence. Commentary*, vol. 5: *Sources on Biology* (Leiden, 1995) 22–24.
[95] Dodds (above, n. 93) 141.
[96] This is perhaps Plato's view in *Republic* 571d–572a; above, n. 93.

location (B2b) to an omnipresence that would allow the soul to "see" things in the same way as in (C).[97]

[97] Aristotle seems to have put forward a view more like that attributed to Dicaearchus than that in *On Divination through Sleep* in his *De philosophia*, fr. 10 Rose (= Sextus Empiricus *M.* 9.20–22; compared with the views of Dicaearchus and Cratippus by van der Eijk [above, n. 88] 60 n. 43. See below, at n. 111):

> Aristotle said that the notion of gods originated among human beings from two origins, from the things that happen concerning the soul and from heavenly phenomena. From the things that happen concerning the soul, on account of the instances of inspiration and prophecy that it undergoes in sleep. For when, he says, the soul comes to be on its own in sleep, then it gets back its own proper nature and divines and foretells the future. It is also like this when undergoing separation from the body in death. At any rate he accepts the poet Homer's observation of this. For (Homer) made Patroclus, when dying, foretell the death of Hector, and Hector the end of Achilles. So it is from these (occurrences), (Aristotle) says, that people formed the notion that some divinity exists, which is in itself like the soul and understands all things. And also from heavenly phenomena.

> Ἀριστοτέλης δὲ ἀπὸ δυοῖν ἀρχῶν ἔννοιαν θεῶν ἔλεγε γεγονέναι ἐν τοῖς ἀνθρώποις, ἀπό τε τῶν περὶ ψυχὴν συμβαινόντων καὶ ἀπὸ τῶν μετεώρων. ἀλλ' ἀπὸ μὲν τῶν περὶ τὴν ψυχὴν συμβαινόντων διὰ τοὺς ἐν τοῖς ὕπνοις γινομένους ταύτης ἐνθουσιασμοὺς καὶ τάς μαντείας. ὅταν γάρ, φησίν, ἐν τῷ ὑπνοῦν καθ' ἑαυτὴν γένηται ἡ ψυχή, τότε τὴν ἴδιον ἀπολαβοῦσα φύσιν προμαντεύεταί τε καὶ προαγορεύει τὰ μέλλοντα. τοιαύτη δέ ἐστι καὶ ἐν τῷ κατὰ τὸν θάνατον χωρίζεσθαι τῶν σωμάτων. ἀποδέχεται γοῦν καὶ τὸν ποιητὴν Ὅμηρον ὡς τοῦτο παρατηρήσαντα· πεποίηκε γὰρ τὸν μὲν Πάτροκλον ἐν τῷ ἀναιρεῖσθαι προαγορεύοντα περὶ τῆς Ἕκτορος ἀναιρέσεως, τὸν δ' Ἕκτορα περὶ τῆς Ἀχιλλέως τελευτῆς. ἐκ τούτων οὖν, φησίν, ὑπενόησαν οἱ ἄνθρωποι εἶναί τι θεόν, τὸ καθ' ἑαυτὸ ἐοικὸς τῇ ψυχῇ καὶ πάντων ἐπιστημονικώτατον. ἀλλὰ δὴ καὶ ἀπὸ τῶν μετεώρων.

This text first describes the soul as functioning prophetically when on its own (καθ' ἑαυτήν) in sleep, in a way that could perhaps be interpreted as compatible with *On Divination through Sleep*, or at least—since it does refer to the soul "recovering its own nature" in sleep—in terms of (B1). (That there was no change in Aristotle's view and that he explained divination by a natural mechanism throughout is the thesis of J. Kany-Turpin and P. Pellegrin, "Cicero and the Aristotelian Theory of Divination by Dreams," in *Cicero's Knowledge of the Peripatos*, *RUSCH* IV, ed. W. W. Fortenbaugh and P. Steinmetz [New Brunswick, NJ, 1989] 220–45; cf., on this passage, 232.) However, the *De philosophia* fragment then goes on to say that something similar happens when the soul is separated from the body at death, this explaining how in Homer Patroclus and Hector, at the point of their own deaths, could prophesy those of Hector and Achilles respectively. Perhaps this can be interpreted in such a way that it does not imply that divination comes about through the soul's literally going on a "psychic excursion." To do this we would have to suppose that the actual point of comparison was not between psychic excursions in sleep and the soul's existing separately from the body *after* death,

Whether (B1) really makes any metaphysical sense I would not like to say. My immediate concern is rather to see whether Cicero's reports of Dicaearchus' theory of divination can be read in terms of (B1), and thus at least made compatible with what we know of Dicaearchus' views on the soul.[98] And, on the face of it, if we allow for a certain amount of rhetorical exaggeration on the part of Cicero, the reports of Dicaearchus' view that we have seen so far *could* be seen in these terms. No doubt in terms of (B1) to say, as Cicero does, that in sleep the mind has *absolutely* (*plane*) nothing to do with the body is an exaggeration—certainly if (B1) is to be compatible with the views of Dicaearchus for whom the body is in a sense the self. But to use "body" for "functions clearly recognisable as performed by obvious bodily organs," i.e., the senses, does not seem impossible.

---

but rather between the soul's functioning without reference to the body in sleep on the one hand and when it is *on the way out of* the body, death being imminent, on the other. The fact that "is separated" is in the Greek in the present tense (*khôrizesthai*) rather than the aorist could be seen as supporting this. (See now the discussion of this passage by John Glucker, "A Platonic Cento in Cicero," *Phronesis* 44 [1999] 30–44, at 41–42.) Xenophon (above, n. 93) uses the freedom of the soul in sleep as an argument for its survival apart from the body after death Whether Pindar fr. 116 Bowra (above, n. 93) should be understood as implying a literal separation of soul from body depends on whether the reference to death in the first line of the fragment should be understood as merely figurative in connection with sleep or as implying a real continuity between sleep and death; the latter seems far more likely (cf. Heraclitus fr. 26). Cf. also Aristotle *Eudemus* fr. 11 Ross (from al-Kindi), and other texts possibly from Aristotle *On Philosophy* discussed at Huby (above, n. 10) 55–56 and van der Eijk (above, n. 88) 92. See also Pines (above, n. 87) 140–43, where however the principal issue is not that of the separation of the soul from the body but that of the divine origin of dreams.

[98] Philip J. van der Eijk, "Aristotle on 'Distinguished Physicians' and on the Medical Significance of Dreams," in *Ancient Medicine in its Socio-cultural Context*, ed. Philip J. van der Eijk, H. F. J. Horstmanshoff, P. H. Schrijvers (Amsterdam, 1995) 447–59, at 455, indeed cites [Hippocrates] *De victu* 86 for the view that "when the body is at rest the soul, being set in motion and awake, administers its own household, and of itself performs all the acts of the body," and comments that "Aristotle . . . views the soul as the principle of organization of all bodily functions. . . . *It would be impossible* for Aristotle to say—as the writer of *Vict.* does—that in sleep the body is at rest but the soul works" (my emphasis). Yes: but my present suggestion (B1) claims only that one aspect of the soul's functioning can occur in sleep in separation from one aspect of the body's functioning, namely the senses. If all aspects of soul-functioning must have some physiological correlate, we ought in principle to be able to say what the bodily correlate of divinatory soul-activity is; but, the problem of access to events remote in time and/or space apart (see above, at the end of the previous paragraph), this seems no more of a difficulty in connection with divination than in connection with mental activity generally.

5. Dicaearchus and Divination—II

However, though we have reviewed the evidence in Cicero relating to Dicaearchus by name, we have not yet reviewed all the relevant passages in Cicero. And when we do it will become clear that the position sketched out in the preceding section, which may already have seemed like a desperate act of special pleading, cannot even be reconciled with Cicero's evidence in its entirety.

The problem is that in our passages Dicaearchus is coupled with Cratippus. And elsewhere in *On Divination* Cicero says that *Cratippus* explained divination in dreams, and oracular prophecy, by holding that human minds come "from outside"[99] and that the rational part of the mind (as opposed to that concerned with sensation, movement and desire)[100] functions best when most apart from (*absit a*) the body.

> I have set out as briefly as I could oracles from dreams and frenzy, which I had said did not involve skill. Both these kinds have a single explanation, which our Cratippus customarily uses: the minds of human beings are to a certain extent derived and drawn from outside—from which we understand that there is outside (us) a divine mind, from which the human (mind) is drawn. And of the human mind that part which possesses sensation, the power of movement, and desire is not separate from the influence of the body; but that part of the mind which shares in reasoning and intelligence is at its greatest strength when it is most apart from the body.[101]

[99] Presumably an echo of the *nous thurathen* of Aristotle *GA* 2.3 736b27ff. Cf. Moraux (above, n. 38) 231. But already Pindar, cited in n. 93 above, could refer to the part of the soul active in sleep as being the only part that comes from the gods.

[100] Cf. Moraux (above, n. 38) 229.

[101] *Exposui quam brevissime potui somni et furoris oracula, quae carere arte dixeram. quorum amborum generum una ratio est, qua Cratippus noster uti solet: animos hominum quadam ex parte extrinsecus esse tractos et haustos (ex quo intellegitur esse extra divinum animum, humanus unde ducatur); humani autem animi eam partem, quae sensum, quae motum, quae appetitum habeat, non esse ab actione corporis seiugatam; quae autem pars animi rationis atque intellegentiae sit particeps, eam tum maxime vigere, cum plurimum absit a corpore.* Cicero *De div.* 1.70.—H. Tarrant, "Recollection and Prophecy in the *De Divinatione*," *Phronesis* 45 (2000) 64–76, at 76 objects to the spatial reading (my "C") of this passage that "when it is most apart from the body" would imply, implausibly, that the soul is more affected by the body when only six kilometres away from it than when seven kilometres away. He also well observes (75) that "the question of precisely how the soul becomes free of bodily influence was unlikely to have been a matter of intense debate," and (76) that Cicero, *De div.* 1.113 (above, n. 93) is ambiguous as to whether the withdrawal from the body in question is

"Apart from" need not be understood in a literally spatial sense, but even if this is not the "psychic excursion" view (C) it certainly sounds more like (B2) than (B1). Cicero's understanding of Cratippus' position is presumably similar where Cratippus is cited alone and where Cratippus and Dicaearchus are cited together; and it is on the face of it entirely incompatible with everything we have heard so far about Dicaearchus' views on the soul.

Pease[102] cites Zeller and Rohde as saying that it is odd that Dicaearchus should couple belief in divination with disbelief in an *animus* separable from the body. He is correct about Rohde, who writes as follows:

> It remains very remarkable that Dicaearchus, who naturally knew nothing of a *separabilis animus*, *Tusculans* 1.21, nevertheless, believed not merely in *mantic* dreams—that would be just intelligible [citing Aristotle *On Divination through Sleep*]—but also in the prophetic power of *enthousiasmos*, which invariably presupposes the dogma of a special substance of the "soul" and its separability from the body.[103]

One may question whether Rohde is right in saying that *enthousiasmos* can only be understood in terms of a separation of soul from body;[104] even if one interprets it as "ecstasy," meaning that the inspired person has departed from their normal condition, it does not seem that this has to be understood as a spatial or even a metaphysical separation of part of the self from the rest.[105]

Zeller, on the other hand, though he does indeed say, as Pease indicates, that the combination of belief in divination with denial of a sepa-

---

literal (my "C") or metaphorical (my "B"). On this passage see also Pines (above, n. 87) 128–29, and 143 n. 239.

[102] Pease (above, n. 86) 58–59.

[103] *Psyche*, ed. cit. vol. 2 p. 512 n. 34. Rohde cites not only Cicero in *On Divination*, but also pseudo-Plutarch, who as we saw (**30B**: above, n. 87) attributed to Dicaearchus belief in divination not only through dreams but also through ecstatic states.

[104] He is certainly wrong to interpret in this way the term *enthousiasmos*, which refers to a divine power entering into and "possessing" the individual; on the difference between this conception and that of "ecstasy," cf. Dodds (above, n. 93) 70–71 and 80 n. 41.

[105] "*Ekstasis* did not originally involve (as Rohde assumed) the idea of the soul's departure from the body": Dodds (above, n. 93) 94 n. 84, citing Pfister. If indeed Dicaearchus had explained prophetic frenzy naturalistically in a similar way to Aristotle's explanation of dreams in *On Divination through Sleep*, he would be going beyond Aristotle in that work at least, for there is there no reference to ecstatic prophecy; but that is not unnatural given the subject of Aristotle's work. On Aristotle's position in earlier works see above, at n. 97.

rable soul is "striking," interprets Dicaearchus' account of divination naturalistically, as following Aristotle, and claims that Cicero in *On Divination* 1.113 = **31B** does not in fact attribute separation of soul from body to Dicaearchus himself.[106] There are two different points that Zeller could have had in mind here. First of all, Cicero's wording here does not absolutely have to be understood in terms of a soul that functions separately from the body. But since Cicero does explicitly attribute such a theory to Cratippus elsewhere in the treatise, it seems artificial to deny that this is the meaning of his words here.[107] Secondly, Zeller might have in mind the precise form of Cicero's statement: Cicero does not, indeed, say in so many words that Dicaearchus and Cratippus held the theory of prophecy through separation of soul from body, but first outlines the theory and then says that "therefore (*itaque*)" the two types of prophecy in question, that through dreams and that through divine inspiration, were approved by Dicaearchus and Cratippus. But, while this may not amount to a statement *expressis verbis* that Dicaearchus and Cratippus held this theory, it is in my view practically impossible to read it as implying anything else.

It seems, then, that Cicero's reports of Dicaearchus' views on divination *are* strictly incompatible with what we know from elsewhere of his views on the soul. Wehrli suggested[108] that *Cratippus* did believe in a soul that made psychic excursions from the body, and that Cicero has erroneously transferred Cratippus' view by association to Dicaearchus as well. It may not be irrelevant here that Cicero refers back to **31c** twice in what follows, but each time refers only to Cratippus and not also to Dicaearchus.[109]

Moraux suggested, though only tentatively, that Dicaearchus could have distinguished between a *soul* which is the body in a certain state, and a separate prophetic spirit entering the soul from outside—much as the Active Intellect enters the individual soul in Alexander of

---

[106] Zeller (above, n. 49) 891 and n. 4.

[107] Putting it another way: unless Cicero intended a distinction between Dicaearchus' views on divination and Cratippus', the fact that his wording does not absolutely rule out such a distinction, and the attribution of a soul that functions separately from the body view only to Cratippus, may be nothing more than a lucky coincidence—lucky, that is, for those who want to absolve him from the charge of attributing incompatible views, on the soul on the one hand and on divination on the other, to Dicaearchus. But then we have to ask, if Cicero did intend such a distinction, why does he give no clearer indication of it?

[108] Wehrli (above, n. 19) 1²:46; cf. Dodds (above, n. 93) 121 and n. 117.

[109] Cicero *De div.* 2.101 and 2.107–9.

Aphrodisias' interpretation of Aristotle's theory of intellect (the comparison is Moraux' own).[110] Van der Eijk, too, regards Dicaearchus as well as Cratippus as actually a dualist where divination is concerned,[111] presumably accepting a reconciliation of this with Dicaearchus' theory of soul in general along the lines suggested by Moraux. However, the theory of a separate prophetic spirit from outside hardly seems the most natural way to read Cicero's reports either of Dicaearchus or of Cratippus.

If Wehrli is right, it might seem easiest to suppose that Cicero was simply misinformed by Cratippus.[112] It is however clear, both from what Cicero says about the other aspects of Dicaearchus' writings on divination mentioned earlier, and from what he says about Dicaearchus' views on the nature of the soul, that he had direct acquaintance with at least some of Dicaearchus' works.[113] And the two conflicting theories, on the one hand the apparent attribution to Dicaearchus of an interpretation of divination in terms of a separable soul, and on the other the claim that Dicaearchus denied the existence of a soul at all, are both contained in works, albeit different works, by Cicero himself.

There seem to be three possibilities:

(a) Cicero simply copied mechanically, in the *Tusculans,* a source which told him that Dicaearchus denied the existence of the soul, and, in *On Divination*, one which told him that Dicaearchus explained divination in a

[110] Moraux (above, n. 38) 246. One may perhaps compare one way of reconciling the tension that was perceived between Empedocles' account of the soul and his belief in a reincarnated *daimon*, with the difference that the *daimon* is for Empedocles in some sense personal. Cf. G. S. Kirk and J. E. Raven, *The Presocratic Philosophers* (Cambridge, 1957) 358–61; contrast the second edition (G. S. Kirk, J. E. Raven and M. Schofield [Cambridge, 1983] 320–21), but cf. now A. Martin and O. Primavesi, *L'Empédocle de Strasbourg*, Strasbourg: Bibliothèque Nationale et Universitaire (Berlin, 1999) 90–95.

[111] He compares the views of both Dicaearchus and Cratippus to the dualist position suggested, in his view, by Aristotle *De philosophia* fr. 10 Rose; see above, n. 97, and Moraux (above, n. 38) 235–43.

[112] Glucker (above, n. 97) 40 n. 20, finds this implausible and suggests rather that Dicaearchus' views on the soul may have changed during his career. Cicero does not himself invoke the idea of such a development, and it would not be in the style of ancient philosophical interpretation to do so. So, even if Glucker is right, my argument in what follows for adopting (b) as the correct account of Cicero's procedure is unaffected. Van der Eijk (above, n. 88) 98–99 n. 152, suggests that an unpublished Arabic compendium of Aristotle's *Parva Naturalia* may reflect a "Hellenistic recension" relating to the dualistic interpretation of divination by Cratippus and (in his view) Dicaearchus.

[113] See also above, nn. 11, 31, 86.

way incompatible with this. Few, I think, will accept this view.

(b) Cicero has information about Dicaearchus, partly based on a study of Dicaearchus' own writings, on which he bases his statements about Dicaearchus' views, not just reproducing his sources mechanically; but he composes his works topic by topic, citing earlier philosophers with a view to what their views as he interprets them can contribute to his own argument, and does not see it as his task to investigate whether different areas of a philosopher's thought can be reconciled with one another, if such discussion is not germane to his immediate purpose.[114]

(c) Although Cicero does not go out of his way to explain how the views on divination he attributes to Dicaearchus are compatible with Dicaearchus' views on the soul as he presents them, he in fact holds that there is no incompatibility.

Whether Cicero held that there was no incompatibility in Dicaearchus' views as he reports them is a different question from whether there was in fact any incompatibility in Dicaearchus' actual views. But it is difficult to see, from the way in which Cicero actually reports Dicaearchus, how he could have supposed that there was no incompatibility. Thus we are driven back to (b). Cicero's approach to his material, while not the thoughtless and mechanical copying sometimes attributed to him by students of *Quellenforschung* in the past, is piecemeal rather than systematic. He was engaged—like many before and since—in philosophical debate rather than in historical reconstruction, and the question how Dicaearchus' or anyone else's alleged views on different topics were to be reconciled with one another simply did not trouble him if it was not germane to the immediate debate. If this is right, it has implications for our general understanding of Cicero's methods in his philosophical works.[115]

---

[114] Thus, in *On Divination* 1.113 and 2.100 the purpose of citing Cratippus and Dicaearchus is to draw the contrast between "natural" divination and "artificial" divination by omens; Cicero *could* have objected in Book 2 that Dicaearchus, given his views on the soul as reported in the *Tusculans*, had no business to be putting forward such a theory at all—but this would not be particularly helpful to his general argument.

[115] See also, on another aspect of this question, R. W. Sharples, "Causes and Necessary Conditions in the *Topica* and *De fato*," in *Cicero the Philosopher*, ed. J. G. F. Powell (Oxford, 1995) 247–71, at 271.

3

Dicaearchus' Philosophy of Mind [1]

Victor Caston

In recent years, controversy has raged over Aristotle's philosophy of mind. Many have thought it to have contemporary relevance, as an early form of functionalism. Others have argued that such rapprochement is impossible, even in principle—the overthrow of Aristotelian physics, they claim, puts his philosophy of mind forever beyond our reach.[2] Understandably, discussion has focused largely on central texts such as the *De anima*. But the debate would be better served by viewing Aristotle in his own context, especially in relation to members of his own school who worked on the topic, such as Dicaearchus and Aristoxenus. What we find is a debate *within* the Lyceum, parallel at numerous points to the current debate over mental causation—a debate, that is, within a broadly materialist framework about the reality and

[1] I would like to take the opportunity to thank Professor Robert Sharples of University College London very warmly for our extended correspondence, which I have found to be invaluable, as well as for his suggestion that I attend the conference.
[2] For the debate in general, see Martha C. Nussbaum and Amélie Oksenberg Rorty (eds.), *Essays on Aristotle's* De anima (Oxford, 1992), and in particular the challenge issued in the opening essay by Myles Burnyeat ("Is an Aristotelian Philosophy of Mind Still Credible?").

causal role of the mental.[3] What is distinctive about Dicaearchus and
Aristoxenus is that they reject the positions of *both* Aristotle *and* Plato,
in favor of one that closely resembles contemporary epiphenomenalism.[4]

The fragmentary nature of our evidence for Dicaearchus, of course,
makes for familiar difficulties. Without exception, his views are reported either (i) by hostile authors who are largely uninterested in the
nuances of different types of materialism; or (ii) by doxographers whose
main concern is to tabulate the voting records of philosophers on key
questions, and so lump together very different positions under a single
formula, often not in the original authors' phrasing. Discrepancies and
confusion are inevitable. Sifting through such reports requires good
judgement as well as a keen eye for detail and, in cases where the evidence does not admit of resolution, a willingness to withhold judgement.[5]

The critical question is whether such difficulties *are* genuinely intrac-
table. In the particular case at hand, I think they have been somewhat
overrated. Apparent conflicts dissolve on further scrutiny, and in many
instances we can explain why particular reports disagree in the way they
do. The picture which emerges is a philosophically coherent one, of
power and interest. Against both Plato and Aristotle, Dicaearchus accepts a version of the "harmonia" theory of the soul, essentially a form
of psychophysical supervenience (section I). In Aristotle's view, such a
theory leaves no room for mental causation, a result he finds unacceptable. But Dicaearchus rises to this challenge and accepts the inefficacy
of the mental, thus embracing a form of epiphenomenalism (section II).
Such views would conflict with any kind of spiritualism, a view which
has occasionally been ascribed to him. But the evidence adduced for
this claim requires no such conclusion (section III). In the end, then,
there is no good reason to doubt that Dicaearchus held epiphenomenalism firmly and unflinchingly. In this he shows philosophical integrity and courage—indeed, more so than many of our contemporaries.

---

[3] For my use of the terms "mental" and "physical" in relation to ancient authors,
see n. 9 below.

[4] I explore the history of this debate in "Epiphenomenalisms, Ancient and Modern," *Philosophical Review* 106 (1997) 309–63.

[5] See Professor Sharples' essay in this volume, which provides an excellent and
balanced survey of the state of our evidence and its various difficulties.

I. The *Harmonia* Theory of the Soul

In Plato's *Phaedo*, the Pythagorean Simmias famously objects that the soul would not be immortal if it were like the *harmonia* or tuning of an instrument (85E–86D). Though not one of the parts of an instrument, a tuning is nevertheless dependent upon them and their relation to one another. A given tuning will not exist unless an instrument is arranged in certain ways, but whenever the instrument is arranged in one of these ways, it will have that sort of tuning, necessarily, as a matter of nature. To claim that the soul is a *harmonia* of the body, then, is to claim that it depends in a similar way on the arrangement of bodily parts—in contemporary terminology, it is to claim that the mental *supervenes* on the physical.[6] If the soul is a *harmonia*, it will not exist apart from a functioning, living body, and its state or disposition is determined (ἔπεσθαι, 93A) by the state or disposition of the body underlying it.

A *harmonia* theory is clearly attributed to Dicaearchus in a number of fragments (**21A–B, 22**). Still, the attribution has been questioned: it is the result, allegedly, of a doxographical confusion, incorrectly assimilating Dicaearchus' views to those of his colleague Aristoxenus.[7] There seem to be two main grounds for this contention. First, a positive view like the *harmonia* theory seems to conflict with other reports, including one from Cicero, according to which Dicaearchus denied there was "any soul at all." Secondly, the attribution of a *harmonia* theory occurs only in late sources, many of whom seem confused over Dicaearchus' name. Cicero, in contrast, explicitly attributes such a theory only to Aristoxenus, even though he generally discusses the two philosophers in tandem.

It does not take much, however, to dissolve these apparent conflicts. Our best evidence suggests that all that Dicaearchus denied was the ex-

[6] For my use of "mental" and "physical," see n. 9 below. As for "supervenience," I take Simmias to be endorsing *strong* supervenience, which holds across possible worlds: necessarily, if any body *were* to possess a given "tuning," it *would* be in the corresponding mental state. For the classic discussion of different forms of supervenience, see Jaegwon Kim, "Concepts of Supervenience," *Philosophy and Phenomenological Research* 45 (1984) 153–76, reprinted in his *Supervenience and Mind: Selected Philosophical Essays* (Cambridge, 1993) 53–78. For more reflections on this notion, see also "Supervenience as a Philosophical Concept," *Metaphilosophy* 21 (1990) 1–27, reprinted in *Supervenience and Mind,* 131–60.

[7] H. Gottschalk, "Soul as *Harmonia*," *Phronesis* 16 (1971) 179–98, at 185–87. Dicaearchus is cited according to Mirhady (this volume) and Aristoxenus according to Wehrli (1967²). All translations are my own.

istence of a *substantial* soul that could exist separate from the body. But such a denial is compatible with a host of positive views about the soul, and certainly with one that identifies the soul with a *harmonia* of the body. To a dualist, of course, a *harmonia* theory might still seem *tantamount* to eliminativism, since from a dualist's point of view nothing short of a substantial soul could adequately account for mental phenomena. But then "eliminativism" functions less as a description than *as a critique*—an unacceptable consequence to which the view is thought to lead inexorably. Such evaluations are evident in the testimonia attributing total eliminativism when taken in their original context, Cicero and Atticus being the clearest examples (cf. the end of **15** and **20**, respectively).

More revealing still is Iamblichus' report (**23**), which in a single breath describes Dicaearchus both as *identifying* the soul with something bodily and as *denying* that the soul "can exist in any way at all." There is no need to trace this confusion back to Dicaearchus. The negative view Iamblichus reports is just the expression of a dualist's despair over the *harmonia* theory, much as before, and as such it can be discounted. But the positive view conforms to what else we know of the *harmonia* theory: it claims the soul is "something that has been naturally compounded or that belongs to the body like the state of being animate" (τὸ τῇ φύσει συμμεμιγμένον ἢ τὸ τοῦ σώματος ὂν ὥσπερ τὸ ἐψυχῶσθαι). Both alternatives recognize the reality of the mental. But they conceive of the mental as intimately related to the body, as its being structured in a certain way. Dicaearchus is not an eliminativist, then, in the sense of denying the existence of the mental in general.[8] What he denies is that there is any *substance* over and above the body. That is, he adopts a form of *monism*, which holds that mental states are just attributes of a single, bodily substance.[9]

---

[8] *Pace* Julia Annas, *Hellenistic Philosophy of Mind* (Berkeley, 1992) 31, esp. n. 43.

[9] Because the word "soul" has substantialist connotations, it will be useful to use a term like "the mental" to refer to the phenomena associated with the soul—the adjective "psychic," though cognate with the Greek word for soul, is too awkward given its ordinary associations. But we must be careful then to avoid Cartesian connotations: for the ancients, phenomena involving the soul can include nonintentional, vital phenomena like digestion and growth, as well as intentional and conscious states. *No assumption is made here as to whether the mental and the physical overlap or are mutually exclusive:* the terminology as I shall use it leaves open whether something mental might also be physical. Accordingly, I will use "physical" to designate the subject matter of the *lowest* level natural science concerned with inanimate objects—in, e.g., Aristotle's scheme, that would be the study of the four elements.

This characterization is supported by other passages. Sextus Empiricus, who elsewhere reports that Dicaearchus denies there is a soul (**18**), also ascribes to him the position that thinking (διάνοια) is "nothing other than the body in a certain state" (μηδὲν . . . παρὰ τὸ πῶς ἔχον σῶμα, **24**). Thinking is perfectly real on such a view. It is just not to be understood as the affect of a separate, substantial soul, but rather along the lines of the Stoic category Sextus alludes to, as the body modified in a certain way. It is thus the body itself which has the ability to think. Exactly the same point is reported by Plutarch, without attribution:

> Or is this the case: that the substance of the soul isn't anything at all, but the tempered body possesses the power of thinking and living?

> *Adv. Colot.* 1119AB

The reference to the "tempered" body (κεκραμένον), like Iamblichus' reference to its being "compounded" (συμμεμιγμένον), is a clear allusion to the terminology of the *harmonia* theory.[10]

This interpretation finds further confirmation in **19**, taken from Cicero's *Tusculan Disputations*. Cicero makes explicit that he is summarizing a speech from one of Dicaearchus' dialogues on the soul, a dialogue we know he had sent from Athens shortly before writing the *Tusculans*.[11] The main speaker, Pherecrates, finds it perfectly acceptable to speak about life, awareness, and action, as he does himself repeatedly (*vel agamus quid vel sentiamus . . . corporibus vivis . . . vigeat et sentiat*). His objection is instead to talk of "the soul or the spirit" (*animum vel animam*) and any derivative terminology that might be taken to imply them, such as "*animalia et animantes*"—thus, in Greek to "ψυχαί" and "ἔμψυχα," respectively (*not* "ζῷα", a point explicitly confirmed by Simplicius, **26**).[12] Unlike the contemporary eliminativist, then, Pherecrates assumes folk psychology *can* be accommodated within materialism, once mental states are properly reconceived as belonging to the body. The reason why is clear from his description of life as due to a power that is inseparable from the body and, in some sense, not even distinct from it. What Pherecrates objects to is not folk psychology, but a *metaphysical theory*, substantial dualism. And the surest

[10] Cf. esp. Plato *Phaedo* 86B7–C2, 86D2; Aristotle *De anima* 1.4 407b30–408a28.
[11] *Ep. ad Atticum* 13.32 = **11B**.
[12] I would like to thank David Sedley for discussion on this point.

way to remove temptation, he believes, is simply to obliterate any vestige of these words from our vocabulary: talk of "souls" and "spirits" must simply be eliminated. But once our mental vocabulary has been purified, there is no reason the rest of it cannot remain, suitably reconstrued. Compare our own attitude to the words "temperature" and "caloric." The former is acceptable, once properly redefined within statistical mechanics. The latter, in contrast, has no place and must—like "witch," "curse," and "hex"—be excised completely from our scientific vocabulary.

This nuanced position naturally leaves Dicaearchus ample room for a *harmonia* theory. According to Cicero, the "whole power by which we do or feel something" imbues the bodies of living things and is inseparable from them (*vimque omnem eam, qua vel agamus quid vel sentiamus, in omnibus corporibus vivis aequabiliter esse fusam nec separabilem a corpore esse*), since there is "nothing else apart from the body, just alone by itself, which is so configured that it lives and perceives by the tempering of its nature" (*nec sit quicquam nisi corpus unum et simplex, ita figuratum ut temperatione naturae vigeat et sentiat*). "The tempering of its nature," once again, is a clear allusion to the *harmonia* theory, and Pherecrates' claim is that a certain "tempering" and configuration of the body is *sufficient* for living, acting, and perceiving. Whether or not Dicaearchus felt comfortable referring to this as a "soul," he plainly acknowledges the reality of mental states and identifies our capacity for them with a *harmonia* of the body.

But we can make an even stronger case. First, the alleged conflict in our evidence attributing a *harmonia* theory to Dicaearchus is not peculiar to Dicaearchus. It is equally present in the evidence for his colleague Aristoxenus, who is uncontroversially recognized as a *harmonia* theorist. Aristoxenus is also reported as having "said that the soul is nothing at all"—in fact, both the *harmonia* theory and the rejection of the soul are attributed to Aristoxenus in Book I of Cicero's *Tusculans*, the very source which was alleged to have distinguished their views.[13] But given that *both* views are assigned to *both* thinkers, there is no longer any evidence to suggest their views have been wrongly assimilated, and so no basis for assigning one view to one and the other to the

[13] Cicero *Tusc. disp.* 1.22.51 (= Aristoxenus fr. 118) together with 1.10.19 (= fr. 120a), 1.11.24 (= fr. 119); cf. also Lactantius *Instit.* 7.13 and *De opif. Dei* 16 (= fr. 120c and 120d, respectively). Note that Lactantius only *infers* the denial of the soul from the *harmonia* theory at I.11.24.

other. The most straightforward hypothesis is that both thinkers shared a view later dualists could not distinguish from "eliminativism" (or, at any rate, did not wish to).

Secondly, the later tradition attributing a *harmonia* theory to Dicaearchus is more respectable than has been appreciated. Nemesius comments on Dicaearchus' *exact choice of words*: he says that Dicaearchus uses the word "*harmonia*" in place of (ἀντί) "tempering" or "concord," which is, he claims, what Dicaearchus in fact means (βούλεται λέγειν, **21A**). But this suggests, at least *prima facie*, that Nemesius depends on a source which attributes those very words to him. Now, it would be trivial to devise a story to undermine this evidence: it is always possible to concoct sceptical hypotheses to put such evidence in question. But the point is we no longer have *independent* reason to do so. Bare possibilties are not enough to reject uncontested evidence; if they were, nothing could stop such doubts from becoming all-corrosive. We should *not*, therefore, reject the tradition attributing a *harmonia* theory to Dicaearchus.

II. Dicaearchus and Aristotle on Mental Causation

None of this puts Dicaearchus at any great distance from Aristotle's views. Both are realists about mental states; both reject Plato's substantial dualism in the *Phaedo*; and both are in some sense material monists. But that still leaves plenty of room for disagreement. And Dicaearchus and Aristotle did disagree. They started a debate within the Peripatos that would continue among Aristotle's commentators centuries later.[14] What is at stake is whether there is *any causal role left for the mental qua mental to play*, once Platonic dualism has been rejected. Dualism obviously leaves ample scope for the mental in the production of behavior. But if the mental depends on the physical, how distinct can its contribution be? Can monism do justice to our intuitions about mental causation?

Aristotle is the first to level a charge along these lines. He accuses the *harmonia* theory of epiphenomenalism, of stripping the mental of all efficacy, a result he thinks unacceptable. He tries to restore the balance in his own theory, by arguing that some effects are due exclusively to the soul, without slipping back into dualism. But Dicaearchus is not per-

---

[14] See my "Epiphenomenalisms" (above, n. 4).

suaded. Instead, he reaffirms the *harmonia* theory over Aristotle's objections, candidly embracing the inefficacy of the mental. What we have is a dispute between materialists over mental causation, not monism.

To see this, we must clearly distinguish two issues: (1) the *ontological* relationship between body and soul and (2) their respective *causal* responsibilities. Attention is usually directed to the first question, since it is often assumed that if the mental depends on the physical for both its character and existence, it could not have any irreducible efficacy of its own *qua* mental, or equivalently, that if the mental does have such efficacy, it cannot depend on the physical in this way. But this does not in fact follow.

One might take the view, for example, that the physical is ontologically basic, in the sense that (a) every mereological part of a substance is physical and (b) once the physical characteristics of an object have been fixed, *eo ipso* so have the rest: the chemical, vital, mental, and even moral characteristics *supervene* on the physical.[15] Yet one might also hold that some of these higher-level characteristics were efficacious *without* themselves being *physical* powers: in particular, not all of the laws governing their behavior could be deduced from physical laws governing the lowest level. An atom-for-atom replica of Francis of Assisi, for example, would necessarily possess all the same properties and character traits; he would thus be every bit as inspiring as the real Francis. But on this view his inspirational power could not be captured, even in principle, by the laws of atomic physics—there would be genuinely new causal powers that *emerge*, necessarily, from the physical level without being reducible to that level. Such a position is easier to imagine with a relatively spare physics like Aristotle's, whose lowest level is limited to four elements, their four simple qualities, and their tendency to move towards their natural places. These powers cannot account for even the simple chemical phenomena described in *Meteorology* Book 4, not to mention phenomena involving life and consciousness,[16] and yet there is no other element in the sublunary world apart

[15] See esp. Geoffrey Hellman and Frank Thompson, "Physicalism: Ontology, Determination, and Reduction," *The Journal of Philosophy* 72 (1975) 551–64, for a precise characterization of these conditions (in their terminology "physical exhaustion" and "determination," respectively, the latter being equivalent to a form of what others have called "supervenience").

[16] *De an.* 2.4 416a6–b9; 1.3 406b15–25.

from these four.[17] These higher-level powers are thus *irreducible* for Aristotle, but *not* basic—they are powers, that is, which are ultimately *founded* on physical structures without *being* physical themselves.

Accordingly, the question of how different levels are related to one another *ontologically* must be separated from the question of how they are related *causally*. We should therefore distinguish the following positions:

(i)   the mental does *not* supervene on the body, but is efficacious
(ii) the mental supervenes on the body, but is *not* efficacious
(iii) the mental supervenes on the body, but is efficacious nonetheless.

The first position resembles a type of dualism, the second a contemporary version of epiphenomenalism, and the third either a kind of reductionism or a kind of emergentism, depending on whether the causal efficacy of the mental is *reducible* to the physical.[18]

The *harmonia* theory as stated in Plato's *Phaedo* (86B–C) is explicitly committed only to supervenience, and is thus compatible with either (ii) or (iii). But it is precisely supervenience that Socrates objects to. The state of the body, he argues, does *not* fix the state of the soul: the state of the soul can vary freely with respect to the body (92E–93A). Socrates, of course, also assumes that the soul is efficacious, giving him a dualism like (i) above. But his criticisms of the *harmonia* theory are purely ontological.[19] By cutting off monism at the root, he does not worry about efficacy.

Aristotle, in contrast, shows no concerns over supervenience. But as a result, the question of mental causation is critical. Epiphenomenalism and emergentism both accept supervenience—they differ only with regard to mental causation, and Aristotle's criticism is addressed to pre-

[17] *Metaph.* Z 17; *De gen. et corr.* 2.7 334b16–20; *Meteor.* 1.2 339a19–20, a27–28; *De part. anim.* 2.1 646b12–24.

[18] For a more detailed discussion of these positions, see my "Epiphenomenalisms" (above, n. 4). For a precise statement of different forms of epiphenomenalism, see Brian McLaughlin, "Epiphenomenalism," in *A Companion to the Philosophy of Mind*, ed. Samuel Guttenplan (Oxford, 1994) 277–88. For a lucid discussion of different forms of emergentism, see Jaegwon Kim, "'Downward Causation' in Emergentism and Nonreductive Physicalism," in *Emergence or Reduction? Essays on the Prospects of Nonreductive Physicalism,* ed. Angsar Beckerman et al. (Berlin, 1992) 119–38, and Brian McLaughlin, "The Rise and Fall of British Emergentism," in *Emergence or Reduction?,* 49–93.

[19] *Pace* Sharples (this volume). For a discussion of 92e–93a, see my "Epiphenomenalisms" (above, n. 4).

cisely this point. Tunings, he argues, cannot affect anything, while the soul preeminently can; therefore, the soul cannot be a *harmonia* (*De anima* 1.4 407b34–408a5). The objection is subtler than might first appear. For tuned *instruments* do affect other things, something Aristotle would not contest. His point is rather that musical instruments cannot affect anything *in virtue of* their tuning; when they produce effects, they do so *solely* in virtue of their physical powers. If we sometimes say that a minor key can make someone sad, that cannot strictly speaking be right. On his view, any "efficacy" we attribute to a tuning is parasitic on the physical powers of the instrument.

The situation is otherwise, Aristotle thinks, with living things: animals do genuinely produce effects in virtue of their soul. In fact, he is willing to claim even more strongly that the contribution of the mental is nonredundant in these cases—physical powers alone do not suffice to bring such effects about. If we were to consider the four elements in a plant apart from anything else, he argues, their tendency would be to separate and move to their natural places—these powers do not, on his view, balance each other out. But plants don't disintegrate; they remain unified wholes. There must, then, be a power holding them together that is not reducible to the elemental powers, and this, he concludes, is the soul (*De an.* 2.4 416b8–9; cf. a9–18). Human action similarly results from mental states, such as desire and thought, which function *qua* mental as "changed changers" and the "sources of change."[20] The body, in contrast, functions only as an instrument (ὄργανον), that by which desire effects change (ᾧ κίνει), something Aristotle distinguishes sharply from the changer itself.[21] In both cases, he insists the mental has a genuine causal role, which does not reduce to the efficacy of the body. But if he also believes these powers supervene on the body, as he seems inclined to,[22] then he is committed to the *emergence* of new causal powers. *Which* causal powers a body has will be determined by its elemen-

---

[20] *De an.* 1.3 406b24–5; 3.10 433b14–18 b27–30; *De motu anim.* 6 700b17–19, b35–701a1; 7 701a35; 10 703a4–6.

[21] *De motu anim.* 10 703a20, a28–29; *De an.* 3.10 433b19–27; *De brev. et long.* 4 469b1–2. Cf. *De an.* 3.10 433b14, 19; *De motu anim.* 7 701b2–3; 8 702a32–b11.

[22] The evidence suggests in fact that Aristotle does so in a way that avoids the notorious homonymy problems raised by Ackrill. He is committed to the generation, persistence, and demise of the soul supervening on changes in matter, where those changes are described independently of their being animated: see esp. *Phys.* 7.3 246a4–9; *De an.* 1.4 408a24–28; 1.5 411b7–9. See my "Epiphenomenalisms" (above, n. 4) for a full discussion.

tal makeup, from the "bottom up." But causation itself will run (in the relevant cases) from the "top down."

This is precisely where Dicaearchus comes in. Although he too rejects Platonic dualism, he cannot accept the idea of emergent causation. Instead he bites the bullet. He accepts Aristotle's claim that a *harmonia* cannot have causal powers. But he does not think that this is a reason to reject the *harmonia* theory; if anything, it is reason to change our views about the soul. He thinks that while there are mental events, they are completely inefficacious—their alleged effects are to be accounted for solely in terms of the powers of the body. Dicaearchus' position is that of the modern epiphenomenalist. He accepts material monism, but denies the efficacy of the mental.

The most explicit statement of this position can be found in a passage of *De libidine et aegritudine*, a treatise plausibly attributed to Plutarch:[23]

> Some straightforwardly extend belief and calculation into the body, saying that the soul is not a cause at all, but that it is rather by the difference, quality, and power of the body that such things come about. For some people think the book titled *On the Underworld*, in which it is argued that the soul is dependent on the substance, does not belong to Heraclides at all, while others [think] it was composed as a polemic against what others had said about the substance of the soul. But whoever wrote it, it destroys the substance of [the soul] straightaway, since the body possesses within itself all of the powers mentioned.

> *De lib. et aegr.* 5 p. 54.10–20 Pohlenz-Ziegler
> = Heraclides Ponticus fr. 72 Wehrli

Although Dicaearchus is not mentioned here by name, he is almost without a doubt the source of this view. The only person named in this connection, Heraclides Ponticus, could not have held it himself: he thought the soul was composed of light and travelled without the body through the Milky Way.[24] The only plausible hypothesis, as the ancient sources suggest, is that Heraclides presents the theory of a contempo-

---

[23] F. Sandbach shows that the arguments against authenticity cannot be sustained on pp. 32–35 of his edition of Plutarch *Fragments = Plutarch's Moralia*, Loeb Classical Library, vol. 15 (London, 1969) and at greater length in "Plutarque était-il l'auteur du *De libidine et aegritudine*," *Revue de Philologie* 43 (1969) 211–16. In the latter piece, he argues unequivocally for its authenticity.

[24] Frr. 96–100 Wehrli, together with fr. 92. See also H. Gottschalk, *Heraclides of Ponticus* (Oxford, 1980) 98–110, 153–55.

rary simply in order to criticize it. He is known, in fact, to have tangled with other Peripatetics of this period.[25] But Dicaearchus is clearly the target here. The view is strongly reminiscent of our other reports, especially **19** from Cicero, which similarly holds that mental states, while real, are due entirely to the body, which contains all of the powers normally ascribed to the soul. Nor is it accidental that proponents of this view are described here as "extending" or, more literally, "stretching" (κατατείνουσιν, 54.11) belief and reasoning into the body, a punning reference to the *harmonia* theory itself.

The position is straightforwardly epiphenomenalist. First, it rejects a substantial soul, without denying the reality of the mental altogether. The descriptions, in fact, strongly suggest supervenience: the soul is *dependent* on the substance (τῇ οὐσίᾳ παρυπάρχειν, 54.15), and various mental states "come about by the difference, quality, and power of the body" (τῇ τοῦ σώματος διαφορᾷ καὶ ποιότητι καὶ δυνάμει συντελεῖσθαι, 54.12–13). Second, it plainly rejects mental causation at the beginning and end of the passage: the soul is "not a cause in any way at all" (οὐδ' εἶναι αἰτίαν τὸ παράπαν, 54.11);[26] on the contrary, the body possesses "all these powers within itself" (ἐν αὐτῷ τὰς εἰρημένας δυνάμεις πάσας, 54.19–20).

The rejection of mental causation is significant. If the version of the *harmonia* theory in the *Phaedo* is just a supervenience thesis, compatible with either epiphenomenalism, reductionism, or emergentism, this version is not. Both emergentism and reductionism insist that there *is* mental causation: emergentism holds that some things come about

---

[25] According to DL 5.92 (= Heraclides fr. 176 Wehrli), he accused Chamaeleon of plagiarism.

[26] Reading αἰτίαν with the mss. The explicitly predicative use of εἶναι in this cannot naturally be construed as "is not a cause *and does not exist*" as Sharples suggests (this volume), which would rather have been expressed by "οὐδ' αἰτίαν οὐδ' εἶναι τὸ παράπαν."

Pohlenz' conjecture, οὐσίαν (followed by Ziegler and Sandbach), is unnecessary. Not only is the question about causal responsibility explicitly addressed in 54.12–13 and again at 54.19–20, but it is the point of *the whole treatise*: the present view is being contrasted with another, discussed in the preceding chapter, according to which all responsibility is assigned to the soul (4 53.10–54.9), and with the view discussed immediately afterwards, that the body and the soul are both held to be responsible (5–6 54.21–56.20). Chapter 8 57.23–58.19 argues that even when someone claims that the person as a whole is the agent, responsibility must still be assigned either to the body or the soul. I would like to thank Professor Sharples for extended correspondence on this passage, from which I have profited greatly, although we come to quite different conclusions.

solely in virtue of the mental, while reductionism holds that anything that comes about in virtue of the mental *eo ipso* comes about in virtue of the physical as well. Both, therefore, are straightforwardly incompatible with the present position, which holds that all events come about *solely* in virtue of the physical powers of the body and not at all in virtue of the mental. There is no ambiguity over the type of supervenience thesis involved.[27] The present position firmly embraces epiphenomenalism.

Nor is there any reason to doubt the reliablity of the *De libidine et aegritudine* regarding inefficacy. The treatise as a whole is concerned precisely with the question of causal responsibility—whether behavior occurs *in virtue of* the body or *in virtue of* the soul—and the author is worried about just the sort of nuanced case we are interested in. When, for example, he expresses sympathy for the Aristotelian view that it is the person who grieves and not the soul (7 56.23–57.10), he correctly insists that this does not resolve the question, once we distinguish between the agent and that *by which* the agent acts (8 58.3–19). And more generally, he realizes that a broadly materialist stance is compatible with a wide variety of positions on the causal efficacy of the mental and the physical. In fact, *all* of the philosophers he discusses are materialists: Democritus, Theophrastus, Strato, Aristotle, Zeno, Posidonius, Diodotus, and (if I am right) Dicaearchus. His main concern is not an ontological one, pitting dualists against materialists, but a *causal* one (8 58.3–6). The treatise does not show any signs of confusion on the question of causal responsibility.[28]

---

[27] Against Sharples' suggestion (this volume).

[28] Sharples (this volume) finds the treatise's claim that Strato ascribes all experience to the soul so implausible as to put the rest of its evidence in peril. But it is implausible only if one assumes the contrast between body and soul is a contrast between the material and the immaterial, which is quite inappropriate here; otherwise what is described is perfectly compatible with Strato's other views. Ancients who take the soul to be *a* body often distinguish it from "the" body, and Plutarch need not be presenting Strato as doing more than that here. Indeed, the passage in question seems only to be making a distinction between, in effect, the central nervous system and the rest of the body, and attributing experiences exclusively to the former.

Sandbach (above, n. 23) attacks the treatise's reliability on more questionable grounds, when he speaks of it as possessing "more of a sophistical nature, using various devices of rhetoric to adorn a superficial treatment of its subject. The author appears to be showing off to an audience of no great learning" (34). But what Sandbach calls "sophistical" is in fact something valued in good philosophy—a concern for nuance and precision on even the subtlest questions. We should remember that high-

But the author of *De libidine et aegritudine* draws a further, ontological conclusion at the end of our passage. The position, he claims, is an eliminativist one, which "destroys the substance of [the soul] straightaway" (ἄντικρυς ἀναιρεῖ τὴν οὐσίαν αὐτῆς, 54.18–19). This might appear to attribute to Dicaearchus a sweeping form of eliminativism, much as in our earlier testimonia. But like them, eliminativism would not be so much a report as an assessment. In fact, the author explicitly *infers* it from inefficacy: the position "destroys the soul's substance," he says, *because* (ὡς, 54.19) all causal powers belong to the body on this view—that is, because he thinks inefficacy is *tantamount* to eliminativism. He would be in good company, too. In his Presidential Address to the American Philosophical Association, Jaegwon Kim has attacked Donald Davidson's position, anomalous monism, along just the same lines. According to that position, Kim argues, the mental character of an event is "causally irrelevant." But then, he continues,

> [I]t's difficult to see what point there is in recognizing mentality as a feature of the world. I believe that if we push anomalous monism this way, we will find that it is a doctrine *virtually indistinguishable from outright eliminativism* ... anomalous monism, rather than giving us a form of nonreductive physicalism, is *essentially a form of eliminativism*. Unlike elminativism, it allows mentality to exist; but mentality is given no useful work and its occurrence is left wholly mysterious and causally inexplicable. *This doesn't strike me as a form of existence worth having*. (My emphasis)[29]

This argument presupposes a tight connection between causality and existence. Kim has in mind a particularly strong version of this, which he calls "Alexander's Dictum": *to be real is to have causal powers*.[30] The principle derives from Samuel Alexander's mocking *reductio* of epiphenomenalism in his emergentist work *Space, Time, and Deity*:

> [Epiphenomenalism] supposes something to exist in nature which has nothing to do, no purpose to serve, a species of *noblesse* which depends

---

handedness of this sort once consigned much of Plato's *Parmenides* to the realm of "parody."

[29] Cf. p. 270 of Jaegwon Kim, "The Myth of Nonreductive Materialism," in *Supervenience and Mind* (above, n. 6) 265–84. (Originally published in *Proceedings and Addresses of the American Philosophical Association* 63 [1989] 31–47.)

[30] For Kim's discussion of this principle, see p. 348 of "The Nonreductivist's Troubles with Mental Causation," in *Supervenience and Mind* (above, n. 6) 336–57.

on the work of its inferiors, but is kept for show and might as well, and undoubtedly would in time, be abolished.[31]

Both Kim and Alexander take such a picture to be absurd on its face; perhaps the author of *De libidine et aegritudine* does too. Faced with such ridicule, many, such as Davidson, would deny that the picture applies to their own theories.[32] But others, like Dicaearchus, would show more courage and just deny that it is absurd. Any epiphenomenalist worth his salt should be prepared to deny Alexander's Dictum. For whatever the importance of the causal, it is hard to see why we should believe it exhausts the real.

In any case, there is reason to think the author of the *De libidine et aegritudine* did *not* mean anything so sweeping when he claimed that the position "destroys the substance of [the soul] straightaway." A fully general eliminativism would in fact contradict the sentence immediately preceding, where the soul is recognized as something real, but *dependent* on the substance (τῇ οὐσίᾳ παρυπάρχειν, 54.15), and the repetition of the word "substance" in both sentences suggests that what is at stake is not existence, but the ontological category and status of the soul. Taken at its word, then, his conclusion need be nothing more than the correct observation that the position rejects *substantial* souls—that it is (once again) not eliminativist about the mental in general, but only eliminativist in a narrower sense, concerning substantial souls. Here the inference from the causal to the ontological is more plausible. It relies on the principle that while there may be inefficacious characteristics of a substance, no substance can be inefficacious itself. For that could occur only if none of its characteristics were efficacious either, but a wholly inefficacious substance is absurd.

III. Dicaearchus and Divination

Dicaearchus' interest in the mind was not limited to such issues, however: he also seems to have written on the topic of divination, oracles, and dreams (**11A–C, 30A–32, 79–81**). His attitude towards such phenomena need not, of course, have been credulous. But some scholars[33] have thought the evidence reveals a more favorable disposition than a

[31] *Space, Time, and Deity,* vol. 2 (London, 1927) 8.
[32] See Donald Davidson, "Thinking Causes" in *Mental Causation,* ed. John Heil and Alfred Mele (Oxford, 1993) 3–17.
[33] For references and detailed discussion, see Sharples (this volume).

materialist of his sort ought to have shown. Possible conflicts arise at
two points: first, statements that the soul, though mortal, has a certain
kind of "divinity," and secondly, the association of some of
Dicaearchus' views on divination with the spiritualism of the much later
Peripatetic Cratippus. In both cases, again, the conflicts are merely apparent. None of the evidence entails any inconsistency in Dicaearchus'
views.

According to two late doxographies, both Aristotle and Dicaearchus
appealed to dreams and inspiration on the grounds that soul, though
mortal, "has a share in the divine" (θείου δέ τινος μετέχειν, **30A** and
30B). This report is instructive, since relevant texts are available for
Aristotle. The comparison could not be more sobering. Aristotle does,
of course, famously speak of part of the human soul as "having a share
in the divine."[34] But we should be careful about what this means for
him. For he also speaks in his mature works of bees as "divine" (θεῖον),
not because they are infused with some spiritual principle, but because
they are intelligent and social.[35] And in his discussion of prophetic
dreams he expressly *denies* that such dreams are sent from the gods,
arguing that instead they are "daemonic" (δαιμόνια), since *all* of nature
is daemonic, though not divine (ἡ γὰρ φύσις δαιμονία, ἀλλ' οὐ θεία,
De div. per somn. 2 463b12–15). In fact, the veracity of such dreams is
purely accidental, he goes on to explain, due to the profuse number of
images such people generate: their "daemonic" character is nothing
other than this fecundity, which he compares with throwing dice
(463b15–21). These observations rely upon his thoroughly naturalistic
account of dream production (see his *De insomniis*, passim).

To speak of "sharing in the divine," then, need not conflict with materialism, and it certainly does not entail dualism. Dicaearchus need not
have meant anything more than Aristotle did; and given his other views,
he could not, on pain of contradiction. We have no independent reason
to think otherwise.

The more significant threat comes from the association of
Dicaearchus' views with those of Cratippus and in particular the view
that prophesy does not occur "unless the soul is loosened and empty,
having nothing at all to do with the body" (*nisi cum ita solutus est et
vacuus, ut ei plane nihil sit cum corpore*, **31B**) and "is moved loosely

---

[34] *Eth. Nic.* 10.7 1177b26–1178a8; *De part. anim.* 2.10 656a7–8; 4.10 686a27–28.
[35] *De gen. anim.* 3.10 761a5–6.

and freely" (*solute moveatur et libere*, **31C**). The evidence we considered earlier straightforwardly conflicts with such a claim, whether we construe this as involving the soul's leaving the body and travelling to other times or places; or the soul's functioning without the body; or even, should Tertullian be right (**25**), without the sense organs[36]—options (C), (B2), and (B1), respectively in Professor Sharples' enumeration.[37] The "power by which we act and are aware" is a power of the body, located in the same place and inseparable from its functioning (**19**). So understood, none of these views can be ascribed to him, if he is to be consistent.

Two equally simple, but drastic, solutions immediately present themselves. One would be to contend that all of our earlier evidence should not be attributed to Dicaearchus himself, but only to Pherecrates, a character in his dialogues. Given the way this evidence is presented, though—especially by Cicero, who had first-hand access to the dialogue—so extreme a solution seems unjustified. Pherecrates' speeches seem to have been given pride of place, without any significant opposition, as if they expressed Dicaearchus' own views; they were certainly understood as such by ancient writers. Alternatively, we could reject all the attributions concerning divination out of hand. But that, too, seems unreasonable, in the absence of evidence directly contesting these reports.

Instead, we should ask whether on closer scrutiny there is any genuine conflict in our evidence at all. Do our sources really assimilate Dicaearchus and Cratippus in the way we have been considering? All that our sources in fact attribute to Dicaearchus *explicitly* is (i) the view that the "soul has a share in the divine" and (ii) the view that there are only two forms of divination, in dreams and in *furor*. Regarding the latter we have only two passages, both from Cicero's *De divinatione* (1.113 = **31B**; and 2.100 = **31C**). When taken in context, though, it is clear **31B** does *not* attribute anything more to Dicaearchus than (ii)— the spiritualist explanation which immediately precedes it (*nec vero umquam . . . aut dormientibus*) and which requires the soul to be freed from the body, belongs to the speaker, Quintus Cicero. Dicaearchus is

---

[36] It is doubtful whether Tertullian is right, however. His assimilation of Dicaearchus' position with that of Asclepiades is surely due to a conflation of their neighboring reports in the doxography: Ps.-Plut. *Plac. philos.* 4.2.7–8 and Stob. *Ecl.* 1.49 (= Diels *Doxogr.* 387.5–9).

[37] See "Dicaearchus on Soul and Divination," this volume.

cited only to back up Quintus' *general* position limiting divination to dreamers and prophets.[38] **31C**, in turn, says only that the soul is "moved loosely and freely" in sleep, which is much vaguer and does not require any of the alternatives mentioned above. Like talk about the mind visiting distant times and places, this is almost certainly a dead metaphor for someone like Dicaearchus. If thoughts were described in earnest as "winged" (*Od.* 7.36) or darting through the universe like Hera (*Il.* 15.80), such phrases were not always taken so literally, especially by later, more urbane authors. When ps.-Longinus, for example, says that "the whole universe does not suffice for our ideas and reflections, but our thoughts often travel beyond the boundaries of the surrounding world" (*De subl.* 35.3), we know he is only speaking about the breadth of what we can think about, not shamanistic journeys. Why suppose Dicaearchus meant anything more?

Context suggests that we cannot rely on these passages as straightforward reports of Dicaearchus' views in any case. The speaker, Quintus Cicero, is trying to build up his case with authorities by namedropping, and it is to his advantage to force Dicaearchus into this pigeonhole. For his case will seem stronger if he can claim that his position is accepted by philosophers across the spectrum, especially those known to be hardheaded, like Dicaearchus, against expectations. The juxtaposition of Cratippus and Dicaearchus in this context is meant to be striking. But the mere appearance of agreement is all that is required for Quintus to score his rhetorical point. If Diceaerchus did speak of someone's soul as becoming "loosened and freed," he need not have meant anything like what Cratippus did.[39]

IV. Conclusion

Closer attention to our sources shows, then, that the alleged conflicts do not run very deep. There is good reason to think that Dicaearchus accepted the reality of mental activity, such as perceiving, thinking, and dreaming, even if he was unwilling to countenance talk of substantial souls. He appeals instead to the tempering or "tuning" of the body to explain mental capacities and activities, seeing them as inseparable from the body and fundamentally one. He is thus a mental realist and a

---

[38] If this is how E. Zeller's brief remark should be understood (*Die Philosophie der Griechen*, 3rd ed. [Leipzig, 1879–1892] 2.2 891 n. 4), I am in full agreement.

[39] See esp. *De div.* 1.70 and Sharples' discussion (this volume).

monist, squarely rejecting Platonic dualism. But he would have found Aristotle's position difficult to accept as well. For he seems to hold, not merely that mental activity depends on the state of the body, but that the body by itself is *causally responsible* for everything we might otherwise have assigned to the soul. He thus could not accept either reductionism or a nuanced emergentism like Aristotle's, both of which give a causal role to the mental, while tying it ontologically to the body. Instead, he seems to favor the straightforwardness of a position like epipheno-menalism, which makes mental activity dependent on the body, both causally *and* ontologically. That having been said, he could still admire these bodily powers as something very special, perhaps even "divine" in some urbane and etiolated sense; and, like his teacher Aristotle, he might well have tried to account for what appeared to be cases of pre-science on the naturalistic principles of his own system. But that hardly requires a departure from his other views and certainly not the heady spiritualism of a Cratippus.

In dealing with fragments, doubt easily becomes infectious. But this should not paralyze us. Often, with patient and watchful supervision, our sources can be healed

4

Principes Sapientiae: Dicaearchus' Biography of Philosophy

Stephen A. White

Nearly fifty years ago, Cornford's *Principium Sapientiae* (Cambridge, 1952) questioned prevailing views about the origins of Greek philosophy by exploring its affinities to religious speculation and prophecy. His book has won little favor among scholars, not least because he underestimates Presocratic conceptions of natural order.[1] But it continues a venerable tradition, which first flourished in the early Lyceum, of analyzing the nature of philosophy by tracing its origins. In particular, it resembles pioneering work by Dicaearchus. Cornford focused on speculative cosmology, whereas Dicaearchus was more interested in practical matters. But like Cornford, I shall argue, he tried to chart the evolution of philosophy by highlighting a series of epochal figures: the *principes sapientiae* of my title. This novel form of intellectual history, which I call the biography of philosophy, included elements of what we have since come to call biography: accounts of what people did and

---

[1] See the critical review by G. Vlastos, *Gnomon* 27 (1955) 65–76, reprinted in his *Studies in Greek Philosophy*, vol. 1 (Princeton, 1995) 112–23; cf. the sober discussion by G. E. R. Lloyd, "The Debt of Greek Philosophy and Science to the Ancient Near East," in his *Methods and Problems in Greek Science* (Cambridge, 1991) 278–98.

said. But he organized these accounts in a chronological sequence that revealed evolving conceptions of wisdom. His biographical work thus formed a history at once of the philosophical way of life and of progressively richer forms of philosophy.

First, a few words about our evidence and the interests and methods it indicates. By the lofty standards of the Lyceum, Dicaearchus was not a prolific writer. Pamela Huby rightly emphasizes how much has been lost.[2] But the only ancient list of his writings (in the Suda: **2**) names only three titles, and many of the twenty titles recorded elsewhere may well refer to parts of the same few works.[3] He also lacked the encyclopedic range of his more famous colleagues. Dialogues on the soul (**13–32**) addressed some abstract issues, though the dialogue form (**19, 27**) suggests a rather popular treatment. And work in geography (**116–27**, cf. **2**) shows an interest in applied science. But the rest of his attested work covered biography, government, and cultural or literary history. Most of this work, moreover, had a distinctly practical focus and a decidedly historical orientation. Cicero, who had access to many of his works (see **9–11, 19, 27, 78–79**), emphasizes the practical value of his political writings (*Leg.* 3.14: **86**, cf. **9**) and calls him ἱστορι-κώτατος (*Att.* 6.2.2: **79**)—if not literally "an excellent historian," certainly "very learned" (cf. **5, 7**, and Varro's *doctissimus*, *RR* 1.2.15: **55**). In fact, it is only for his views on the soul and divination that his name ever appears in doxographical reports.

Arguments from silence, of course, are never conclusive. But the extant testimony strongly suggests that Dicaearchus' primary interest was in βίοι, both lifestyles and individual lives. The work cited most often and most widely is *Life of Greece* (**1** no. 7a–f), which gave an historical account of the origins and development of Greek culture, but apparently also included biographical data (**58–77**). So did his work on poetry and festivals (**102–4**, cf. **85** and **47**). But the most substantial biographical material Wehrli grouped under the dual heading "Lebensformen, Biographien" (frr. 25–45; cf. **33–52**). Most of this material recounts the activities of individuals from the past. But Jaeger, in his seminal study "Über Ursprung und Kreislauf des philosophischen Lebensideals," pro-

---

[2] In this volume.

[3] Both **78** and **83** could well come from *Life of Greece* (cf. **76–77**), as could **39, 93–95, 105–10** (cf. **72**); and **74, 84–85, 112–15** could all come from a comprehensive study of musical contests (cf. **89, 90, 99**). For twenty possible titles, see J.-P. Schneider, in *Dictionnaire des Philosophes Antiques* 2 (Paris, 1994) 760–64.

posed that it derives instead from a work on a fundamental issue in ethics.[4] Taking his cue from a casual remark by Cicero (**33**, quoted in §V below), he argued that Dicaearchus composed an historical survey of political activity by earlier philosophers in order to show, in opposition to Aristotle and Theophrastus, that "die φρόνησις statt der σοφία [ist] die herrschende Macht in der menschlichen Seele" because "die Bestimmung des Menschen im πράττειν und nicht im θεωρεῖν [ist]."[5]

Jaeger's reconstruction, which depicts Dicaearchus as a thorough pragmatist whose opposition to the alleged intellectualism of his colleagues in the early Lyceum left its mark on *Magna Moralia*, is perceptive on many points. But it overlooks crucial evidence and misconstrues his aims. Jaeger, I shall argue, was right to ascribe an historical framework to Dicaearchus' work on the lives of philosophers and to maintain that it focused not on "individuality as such" but on representatives of an ideal type.[6] But he was wrong to identify this ideal as "the philosophical reformer and lawgiver" and to impute polemical aims to the work.[7] Rather than trying to settle an ethical debate simply by accumulating examples, Dicaearchus remained more faithful at once to history and to philosophy. His biography of philosophy presented neither a doxography of ethical theories nor a survey of competing ideals as in Aristotle's discussions of βίοι (*NE* 1.5, *EE* 1.5). Nor did it challenge the claim by Aristotle (*NE* 10.6–8, cf. 6.7, *MM* 1198b9–20) and Theophrastus (461, 481–82 FHS&G) that a philosopher's life is best, a politician's only second best. Rather, it showed that the cultivation of wisdom has both moral and intellectual dimensions (cf. Theophr. 479–80), and it sought to clarify the *relation* between theory and practice by examining the lives of earlier philosophers. Like his *Life of Greece*, it examined cultural evolution. But adopting a much narrower focus, it

[4] Originally in *Sitzungsberichte der Preussischen Akademie der Wissenschaft*, Phil.-hist. Kl. 25 (Berlin, 1928) 390–421; cited here from his *Scripta Minora* 1 (Rome, 1960) 347–93; an English translation is in his *Aristotle,* 2nd. ed. (Oxford, 1948) 426–61. For specific objections to Jaeger's account, see below, n. 32 and §VI.

[5] Ibid. 379.

[6] Ibid. 383 n. 1: "Die sogenannte Biographie erwächst aber nicht aus dem blossen Interesse für die Individualität als solche, sondern sie sucht im Leben der individuellen Vertreter die Ausprägung des Typus, also dessen was die philosophische Ethik unter βίος versteht und dessen Arten sie entwickelt." Cf. 381: "Die ältesten Vertreter der Philosophie sind offenbar auch für ihn [sc. Dicaearchus] die Repräsentanten eines Ideals, an denen die Philosophen der eigenen Zeit gemessen werden."

[7] Ibid. 384; cf. 385: "keinen blossen Theoretiker modernen Stils . . . sondern einen Staatsgründer und Gesetzgeber."

sought to analyze and describe the nature and origins of philosophy. While his colleagues in the Lyceum compiled histories of specific disciplines, Dicaearchus focused on the philosophical way of life itself. Or rather, since he approached his topic historically, he recounted the lives of philosophers in order to show how the pursuit of wisdom had developed over time. The result, which may have been entitled *On Lives* (named only once, DL 3.4: **47**), singled out those who introduced new conceptions of wisdom and its pursuit; it thus included biographical data. In so doing, it also marked out three stages in the evolution of philosophy, inaugurated successively by Pythagoras, Socrates, and Plato.

I. Canons of Wisdom

Many today take it for granted that philosophy began in Greece, and most modern histories of philosophy start with the Ionians.[8] But it is worth recalling that the story was not always so simple or so clear. Hippias, who compiled the first attested survey of earlier thought, started with the mythical poets Orpheus and Musaeus and the barely historical Hesiod and Homer, and he included barbarians alongside Greeks (Clem. *Strom.* 6.2.15: B6). Many centuries later, Diogenes Laertius still began by citing those who traced philosophy to foreign sources, such as the Persian Magi, the Babylonians or Chaldeans, and Egyptian priests (1.1–2). These accounts he promptly rebuts by crediting Musaeus with the first theogony and Linus with the first cosmogony (1.3–4). But he then returns to barbarians, and drawing primarily on work by Aristotle, Eudemus, and Clearchus (all more or less Dicaearchus' contempories), he outlines barbarian conceptions of the gods and cosmos (1.8–9). Evidently, debate about the origins of philosophy first flourished in the fourth century, and principally in the Lyceum.

At issue were rival conceptions of philosophy. Major advances in several fields of inquiry intensified discussion of the nature and aims of philosophy, and it is surely no coincidence that methical treatments of its history also began to appear.[9] Charting the origins and progress of a

---

[8] This picture, which owes most to Aristotle (esp. *Meta.* A), had rivals in antiquity and has dominated only since Hegel; see J. Mansfeld, "Myth, Science, Philosophy: A Question of Origins," *Studies in the Historiography of Greek Philosophy* (Assen, 1990) 1–21, who argues rather that philosophy began not with Ionian φυσιολογία but only when Heraclitus and Parmenides subjected earlier speculations to systematic critiques.

[9] Also the famously pessimistic etymology of the word, according to W. Burkert,

discipline is an effective way to characterize its scope and methods, as well as to organize and assess its results, and a history of philosophy provides at least an ostensive definition of philosophy itself. Apart from Aristotle's critiques of his predecessors, most of the early fruits of this labor are now lost, or preserved only indirectly and in fragmentary form. But even these meager remains are tantalizing. The Lyceum in particular spawned histories of several sciences as well as numerous monographs on individuals or groups. The first comprehensive treatment that is attested, in fact, is Aristotle's *On Philosophy*, and its contents challenge modern assumptions. Rigorous thinkers like Parmenides and Plato apparently bulked largest. But joining them were many earlier and more exotic forms of wisdom, including Persian, Chaldean, and Egyptian cosmologies (fr. 6 Rose; cf. *Meta.* A.1), Orphic verse (fr. 7), and the renowned maxims of the so-called sages (frr. 3, 4, 13).[10]

How far back Dicaearchus might have followed Aristotle here is hard to tell from our meager evidence. He did discuss some barbarian antecedents in his *Life of Greece*: the legendary Ninos he praised as "exceptionally shrewd" (συνέσει διάφορον) for unifying Ninevah long before the foundation of Babylon (**60–61**), and he singled out the legislation of Sesostris (or Senosret) in nineteenth-century Egypt (**58–59**).[11] We can no longer tell whether these assessments figured also in a scheme of specifically intellectual history. But it is presumably not fortuitous that he described the sages in precisely the same terms, as Diogenes Laertius reports at the end of his life of Thales (1.40: **37**).

> Damon of Cyrene, who wrote *On the Philosophers*, criticizes them all but especially the seven; Anaximenes says they all wrote poetry; and

"Platon oder Pythagoras? Zum Ursprung des Wortes 'Philosophie'," *Hermes* 88 (1960) 159–77.

[10] Though the practical connotations of "sage" (which reflect Dicaearchus' account, as we shall see) are plainly prejudicial and potentially misleading, I use the traditional label here for convenience.

[11] The only law Dicaearchus cites made practice of the crafts hereditary, which he might have seen as a forerunner of the principle of specialization that underlies Plato's *Republic* (see §V below). Sesostris is cited also by Aristotle for novel legislation and among those who "philosophize about government" (τοῖς περὶ πολιτείας φιλοσοφοῦσιν, *Pol.* 7.10 1329a40–b5); and Herodotus traces the origin of geometry to him (2.109). Contemporary work on Egypt by Hecataeus of Abdera may also have influenced Dicaearchus, though its date (probably shortly after 320) rules out influence on Aristotle; see O. Murray, "Hecataeus of Abdera and Pharaonic Kingship," *Journal of Egyptian Archaeology* 56 (1970) 141–71.

Dicaearchus says they were neither wise nor philosophers, but shrewd and skilled in lawmaking.

What Dicaearchus did attribute to "the sages" is fairly clear.[12] His first term (συνετούς) refers to practical insight (cf. *NE* 6.10), as expressed in wise maxims or sound decrees (as Bias of Priene was famous for fair judgment: Hipponax fr. 123, Heraclitus B39 and B104). His other term (νομοθετικούς) refers to skill in organizing society and its institutions (cf. *NE* 6.8), whether by statute or decree. But what Dicaearchus meant to deny is much less clear. He was plainly critical of prevailing views of these traditional exemplars of wisdom, and his criticism implies some sort of distinction between practical insight and action on one side, and wisdom and philosophy on the other. But instead of appealing to Cicero's casual remark that Dicaearchus ranked a "practical life" ahead of a "theoretical life" (**33**, quoted in §V below), we should ask what he meant by the labels he refuses to apply to the sages. The context in Diogenes points to larger issues. Cited beside Dicaearchus is Anaximenes, probably the contemporary who authored the so-called *Rhetorica ad Alexandrum*.[13] Both reject the tradition endorsed by Diogenes Laertius, and dozens of other authorities he cites, that the sages were wise: Anaximenes makes them out to be poets, and Dicaearchus says their insight was strictly practical. And neither stands alone. Not much later, Lobon of Argos discussed them in his work *On Poets*, and he either compiled or forged verses for at least six sages.[14] Poets, after all, had for centuries been considered paradigms of σοφία for their supposedly divine gifts of vatic vision and verbal facility as well as prodigious memory and practical insight.[15] Plato, on the other

---

[12] Dicaearchus probably did not think that every sage exhibited both traits (καί may be epexegetic); and the absence of celebrated lawmakers like Lycurgus and Charondas from his list of sages in **38** (contrast Ar. *Pol.* 2.7–9 and 2.12) suggests that he did not consider legislative skill a sufficient criterion; cf. n. 26 below.

[13] On Anaximenes, see H. Lloyd Jones and P. Parsons, *Supplementum Hellenisticum* (Berlin, 1983) fr. 45. This Damon cannot be identified with certainty; but C. J. Classen, "Zu zwei griechischen 'Philosophiehistorikern'," *Philologus* 109 (1965) 178–81, makes a strong case that he was a student of the late third-century Academic Lacydes; cf. T. Dorandi, in Schneider (above, n. 3) 607.

[14] *Supplementum Hellenisticum*, frr. 504–26.

[15] Cf. Aristodemus in Xen. *Mem.* 1.4.3; see M. Griffith, "Contest and Contradiction in Early Greek Poetry," in *Cabinet of the Muses*, eds. M. Griffith and D. Mastronarde (Berkeley, 1990) 185–207. Among the leading sages, only Solon is known to have composed poetry (which he calls σοφίη: fr. 13.52), though some well-known verses were sometimes ascribed to Cleobulus (DL 1.89–91). It is striking, in fact, that no

hand, evidently agreed with Dicaearchus. In the earliest extant reference to a group of *seven* sages, he has Socrates characterize them only as pious moralists (*Prot.* 342A–343C; cf. *Charm.* 164D–165A, *Hip. Maj.* 281c). Socrates also likens the "laconic" speech of Spartan warriors to the maxims of his seven sages. But the parallel is plainly ironic, offered only to bolster a pair of preposterous claims: that Sparta and Crete were home to the "oldest and most abundant φιλοσοφία of the Greeks" (342A7–8), and that Spartan hegemony was secured not by military training but by their φιλοσοφία (342B–C).

Dicaearchus' dispute over labels figured in an ongoing debate about the nature of wisdom and its cultivation that encompassed earlier *maîtres de sagesse*, from archaic poets and sages down to Socrates and the sophists. Early in the fourth century, Alcidamas lumped poets, statesmen, and philosophers together when citing Archilochus, Homer, and Sappho alongside the Spartan ephor Chilon and the archetypal theorists Pythagoras and Anaxagoras all as exemplars of wisdom (*Rhet.* 2.23 1398b11–20).[16] About the same time, Plato had Protagoras rank himself alongside poets, seers, and other experts as "sophists" (*Prot.* 316D–E); he also created a complex diachronic debate about wisdom and virtue pitting the philosopher Socrates against the sophist Protagoras against the poet Simonides (cf. 316D7) against the sage Pittacus (339–48). Similar debates long continued: Hermippus discussed the sages in his work *On the Wise,* but Hippobotus in his *List of the Philosophers* (DL 1.42; quoted in §II below). Yet a remarkably large proportion of what we hear about the sages comes from fourth-century sources. Diogenes Laertius alone cites dozens of authorities in his survey of eleven sages in Book 1. Some are little more than names.[17] Others clearly came later, though often only a generation or so (Satyrus,

---

poets, not even acknowledged masters of gnomic elegy, appear in lists or stories about sages: only the mythical Orpheus and Linus (called σοφός in Hesiod fr. 306) appear in Hippobotus' list (DL 1.42, quoted in §II below); and though Hermippus includes Simonides' rival, Lasus of Hermione, the text shows signs of interpolation (no other figure is identified by either city or father, yet three names are reported for Lasus' father; cf. Dicaearchus **99**).

[16] Only these six names can be securely ascribed to Alcidamas. He may also have named the three others Aristotle mentions (presumably all as statesmen): Solon, Lycurgus, and "the leaders at Thebes" (sc. Epaminondas and his associates); but the mention of Thebans suggests a date after 380, which would be rather late for Alcidamas.

[17] No reliable date can be assigned to Eleusis or Alexon (or Alexander?) of Myndos (1.29), Phanodicus (1.31: or perhaps Phanodemus the Atthidographer?), or Euanthes of Miletus and Archetimus of Syracuse (1.40).

Callimachus, Hermippus, Hieronymus, Hippobotus). But besides Dicaearchus and Anaximenes, he cites the histories of Ephorus (1.40: F181, 1.41: F182), chronicles by Leandrius of Miletus (1.28, 41), Andron of Ephesus (1.30), and Daimachos of Plataea (1.30; cf. *FGrH* 65), Plato (1.22) and Eudoxus (1.30) from the Academy, and Aristoxenus (1.42: fr. 86), Clearchus (1.30: fr. 70), Demetrius (1.22: 93 SOD, cf. 87 SOD), and Eudemus (1.23: fr. 144) from the Lyceum; and he could have cited Theophrastus (Plut. *Sol.* 4: fr. 583), Chamaeleon (Clem. *Strom.* 1.14.60: fr. 2), and Strato (*Strom.* 1.14.61: fr. 147) as well.

One explanation for the preponderance of fourth-century sources here is scholarly respect for seniority: older writers carried more authority, and to judge from extant testimony, very little had been written about the sages earlier.[18] But that hardly explains why discussion of the sages surged in the fourth century, especially in the Lyceum. This clearly reflects a newly self-conscious interest in the nature of philosophy, which in turn inspired research into its past, its origins, and its antecedents. In short, debate about the sages was part of an attempt to consolidate intellectual progress by defining and classifying distinct forms of knowledge. The debate also had implications for the value of different forms of knowledge. As widely accepted paragons of σοφία, the sages posed an implicit challenge to new conceptions of σοφία and the methods of its pursuit introduced by fourth-century philosophers.

One way to meet this challenge is to draw distinctions, as Aristotle does in his account of intellectual virtues in *NE* 6. Marking boundaries that Plato left unclear, he distinguishes theoretical, productive, and practical forms of knowledge, which he labels ἐπιστήμη, τέχνη, and φρόνησις (6.3–5). But before introducing his own account of σοφία, he reveals the great elasticity of this most honorific term by recounting three others (6.7).[19] Traditional usage equated σοφία with τεχνή quite

---

[18] D. Fehling, *Die sieben Weisen und die frühgriechischen Chronologie* (Bern, 1985) 9–18, argues that Plato invented the seven sages, primarily on the ground that *Protagoras* is the earliest extant depiction of the sages as a *group*; B. Snell, *Leben und Meinungen der Sieben Weisen* (Munich, 1971) 62–67, more plausibly proposes an earlier tradition of sympotic tales. In either case, Plato invented neither the category of sage nor its chronological unity.

[19] See G. E. R. Lloyd, *The Revolutions of Wisdom* (Berkeley, 1987) 83–108. His observation that "anyone could set himself up as a philosopher or sophist" (103) applies equally to "wise"; such claims rarely went unchallenged, of course, as the very elasticity of the terms encouraged controversy.

generally (even ditch-digging, as in the pseudo-Homeric *Margites*, 1141a12–16), and especially with "the most precise crafts" (exemplified by "Phidias the stonemason and Polyclitus the sculptor," a9–12);[20] and some equated σοφία with political skill (a20–b2). This trio recalls the three classes of putative σοφοί questioned by Socrates after Delphi pronounced none wiser than he (*Ap.* 21C–22E). Despite this diverse usage, Aristotle follows Plato's later view (cf. *Theaet.* 145E) that σοφία is restricted to "the most precise of the ἐπιστῆμαι": systematic knowledge derived from principles (1141a16–19), as of the eternal truths of cosmology studied by Anaxagoras and Thales (b1–8).

The homonymy Aristotle analyzes has historical roots, and though he ignores the issue here, his distinctions correlate with stages of cultural development.[21] His account in *Meta.* A.1 of the progress from technology to "liberal arts" and then theoretical speculation, which captures three of the four varieties of σοφία in *NE* 6, is explicitly developmental. A fuller account, in a passage from Philoponus that some have ascribed to Aristotle's *On Philosophy*, similarly explains that σοφία first designated technology, then successively the several arts, political skill, the natural sciences, and finally theology (*In Nicom.* 1.1: fr. 8b Ross). However, while this does correspond closely to material in Aristotle, Philoponus ascribes the fivefold account specifically to Aristocles, and a mention of ὑπερκόσμια in the fifth stage sounds suspiciously post-Aristotelian. It thus remains doubtful that Aristotle proposed a developmental scheme for conceptions of wisdom.[22] The first to offer an explicitly historical account centered on specific individuals was apparently Dicaearchus.

II. Gnomic Wisdom: The Sages

As modern debates about the literary canon illustrate, compiling lists of exemplars can be an effective way either to define or to challenge cultural authority. Ancient catalogues of the wise are a case in point, and as

[20] The daunting mathematical complexity of Phidias' architectural projects (including the Parthenon) and Polyclitus' celebrated "canon" of proportions suggests that Aristotle may have had a link to mathematics in mind.

[21] His examples in *NE* 6.7 do not suggest a chronological scheme: earliest is the legendary Margites (Aristotle considered *Margites* Homeric: *Po.* 4 1448b28–38); Thales substantially predates the rest, who all flourished in the mid-fifth century.

[22] Fr. 8b Ross appears neither in Rose nor in O. Gigon, *Aristotelis Fragmenta* (Berlin, 1987).

canons began to develop in the fourth century, rival lists proliferated.[23] So it is time to look more closely at those Dicaearchus denied were wise. Diogenes Laertius reports a veritable battle of the books involving several conflicting accounts (DL 1.41–42: **38**).

> There is also dispute about their number. Leandrius has Leophantus son of Gorgias, from Lebedos or Ephesus, and Epimenides the Cretan instead of Cleobulus and Myson. Plato in *Protagoras* has Myson instead of Periander, and Ephorus has Anacharsis instead of Myson, while still others list Pythagoras also. Dicaearchus supplies four accepted figures: Thales, Bias, Pittacus, and Solon; and he names six others from whom to select three:[24] Aristodemus, Pamphylus, Chilon of Lacedaemonia, Cleobulus, Anacharsis, and Periander. Some add Acusilaus son of Cabas or Scabas, from Argos. Hermippus in his *On the Wise* says there are seventeen who are put in various groups of seven: they are Solon, Thales, Pittacus, Bias, Chilon, <Myson>, Cleobulus, Periander, Anacharsis, Acusilaus, Epimenides, Leophantus, Pherecydes, Aristodemus, Pythagoras, Lasus (son of Charmantides or Sisymbrinus, or Chabrinus according to Aristoxenus) from Hermione, and Anaxagoras. Hippobotus in his *List of the Philosophers*: Orpheus, Linus, Solon, Periander, Anacharsis, Cleobulus, Myson, Thales, Bias, Pittacus, Epicharmus, and Pythagoras.

The number of candidates here is daunting: twenty-two different names altogether. Dicaearchus alone names ten, and it was not long before Hermippus and Hippobotus together doubled his total.[25] The four he singles out as "accepted" do appear in every known list. His list also backs up his emphasis on conduct and politics: all eight who can be identified were renowned for practical insight, all had engaged in public affairs, and most were known for little or nothing else.[26] Those he ex-

---

[23] For early canons in other fields, see R. Pfeiffer, *History of Classical Scholarship* (Oxford, 1968) 203–8.

[24] The subject of ἐκλέξασθαι, which could represent a quotation from Dicaearchus or simply the loose syntax so common in Diogenes, is unclear: did Dicaearchus report lists by others ("from whom *they* selected three"), and if so, who were "they"?

[25] Diogenes here cites his sources in chronological order, from Leandrius and Plato to Hippobotus.

[26] Not all were "lawmakers" in the same sense: only Solon is known to have introduced statutory reforms; Chilon, Sparta's model ephor, may have; Bias was renowned for adjudication (see §I above); Thales gave shrewd advice to the Ionians (Hdt. 1.170) and then Croesus (Hdt. 1.75); Pittacus, Periander, and Cleobulus were leaders in their own cities; Anacharsis was brother of a Scythian king, introduced Greek customs in

cludes, conversely, were best known for poetry (Epicharmus, Lasus, Linus, Orpheus) or speculation (Acusilaus, Anaxagoras, Pythagoras). His list is also chronologically unified: the eight identifiable figures all flourished in the sixth century, which accords with the claim of his colleague, Demetrius of Phaleron, that the group was first proclaimed wise by Delphi in 582 (dated by archon to the year Delphi inaugurated quadrennial games, DL 1.22: 93 SOD). But puzzles remain. Did Dicaearchus exclude Myson, whom Plato included and Hipponax had dubbed "most sensible" (DL 1.107: fr. 63), because he avoided public affairs (DL 1.107–8: Aristoxenus fr. 130)? And why did he include Aristodemus and Pamphylus, who appear on no other list and cannot be firmly identified?[27] Moreover, how can he call them wise at all when he denies in **37** that any sages were wise? And how can he include Thales when he also denies that any were philosophers? Did he disagree with Aristotle and the many others who considered Thales one of the first philosophers (*Meta.* A.3 983b20–21)?[28] Or did he reject the tradition, endorsed by Heracleides (ἰδιάστης, DL 1.25: fr. 45; cf. Cic. *De or.* 3.137), that Thales stayed out of politics? Answers to these questions can be found in a passage Jaeger overlooked from a short Greek work (Codex Vaticanus 435) of uncertain author and date that is dedicated to a Roman and bears the tentative title "Plutar<ch's or> Caecilius' Roman Maxims" (Πλουτάρ⟨χου ἢ⟩ Κεκιλίου ἀποφθέγματα ῾Ρωμαικά: **36**; indirect discourse is italicized).[29]

Scythia, and supposedly wrote on νόμιμα (DL 1.101); for the other two, see following note. Jaeger (above, n. 4) 381–84 suggests that Dicaearchus was the first to assemble these reports.

[27] Both names recur too frequently to identify either securely. Aristodemus is probably the Archaic font of maxims (see Pindar *Isth.* 2.9), or perhaps an earlier Spartan king, who would be chronologically anomalous but figured in Euripides' *Temenos*, which Dicaearchus discussed (if *POxy.* 2455 frr. 9–10 represents his work; cf. W. Luppe in this volume). Pamphylos is probably a Spartan also, perhaps the eponymous hero of a Dorian tribe (Hdt. 5.68). Two points favor Spartans: the names precede Chilon (unnecessarily identified as "Lacedaemonian": was the adjective originally plural?), and Dicaearchus would know them from working on his *Spartan Politeia* (**2**; cf. Hippias' recitations of Spartan genealogies, *Hip. Maj.* 285D–E).

[28] An important qualification is often overlooked: Aristotle pronounces Thales the founder only of "this type of philosophy," by which he means theories about material principles, hence at best the "second philosophy" of natural science. Diogenes evinces similar reservations when he presents Thales as the first of eleven sages in Book 1 but makes Anaximander the first philosopher in Book 2, and when he calls Thales a sage (1.13) but says only that he καθηγήσατο ("introduced" rather than "began") what he calls "Ionian philosophy" (1.122).

[29] The text survives only in one ms. of Synesius on a leaf bound between his letters

The Romans of old, my fine Sebosus, did not want to be reputed wise, so they did not hunt for reputation by cleverness in discourse or subtle and cogent maxims, which some Greeks employed and which are proclaimed more trustworthy than oracles: nothing in excess, follow god, waste no time, know thyself, a pledge brings bane, and the like. Presumably these do benefit those who are convinced, and there is something pleasant and attractive in their brevity of expression. But Dicaearchus thinks *not even these are the mark of wise men* [σοφῶν ἀνδρῶν], *since men of old never philosophized in discourse; wisdom back then, at any rate, was performing honorable deeds, and only in time did techniques of public speaking arise. Nowadays, anyone who argues cogently gets a reputation for being a great philosopher*; but in the old days, only the good man was a philosopher, even though he was not trained in standing up and speaking in public. For those men of old did not inquire whether or how one should engage in politics; rather, they did so honorably. Nor did they inquire whether one ought to marry; rather, they married the way one should and lived together with their wives. Those, he [sc. Dicaearchus] says, are deeds and performances of men who are wise, whereas these maxims are a vulgar affair. This is what I believe your ancestors as well were like: they wanted to be good men and they achieved this by their deeds; but incisive maxims and elegant phrases that could win a reputation for ingenuity [ὥστε περιττὰς εἶναι δοκεῖν] they neither performed nor knew. They used language just like their reasons for acting, not concisely worded but honorable, provided one considers the thought and refers each point to its utility rather than looking for display. [Roman exempla follow.]

The scope of this testimony is fairly unproblematic.[30] But its point is

---

and speeches; for text and discussion, see J. von Arnim, "Ineditum Vaticanum," *Hermes* 27 (1892) 118–30. The possibility of a disjunction in the lacuna ("Plutarch *or* Caecilius") makes ascription uncertain. Synesius himself is unlikely, given the favorable opinion of proverbs he expresses elsewhere (*Calvit. Enc.* 22: Aristotle fr. 13). Von Arnim dates the excerpt to the first or second century CE; and the ascription in the ms. makes Plutarch, who knew Dicaearchus' work (cf. esp. **35, 43, 45**; cf. **70** [*Thes.* 32] and *Thes.* 3, which echoes the conception of gnomic wisdom found here), the most likely author. But F. Egermann, *Sitzungsberichte der Akademie der Wissenschaften in Wien*, Phil-hist. Kl. 214.3 (Vienna, 1933) 53 n. 1 and 54 n. 1, argues that the addressee and hence the author were contemporary with Cicero; his case rests on identifying Sebosus with a travel-writer from the late Republic, which would afford a credible but hardly necessary motive for citing Dicaearchus, who was highly respected as a geographer.

[30] Dicaearchus is the only authority cited in the entire text, and indirect discourse following his name ensures that at least the gist of these lines comes from him. The following lines reiterate and expand the same points (complete with verbal echoes in ὀχλικοὶ λόγοι, and ἔργα and ἐπιτηδεύματα) before turning to Roman examples; the

not. At issue is what counts as wisdom, and the writer's main thesis is that deeds, not words, make a man wise. But his argument is complicated by three further contrasts: Romans vs. Greeks, wisdom of the past vs. pretense of the present, and maxims vs. discourse. The first, which clearly does not come from Dicaearchus, is what casts the sages in a negative light; hence, we must be wary of ascribing a similar opinion to him. The other two contrasts, which he is cited to support, each turn on historical changes. Unfortunately, they are formulated ambiguously. The crux is σοφῶν ἀνδρῶν. If this is a genitive of source, as Wehrli assumed, Dicaearchus denied either that the sages *coined* the maxims for which they were famous, or that they were really *wise*. The former denial, while not impossible, is highly implausible. Aristotle (fr. 3 Rose) and Clearchus (fr. 69) ascribed the famous "know thyself" to Pythian Apollo, and Theophrastus called it proverbial (fr. 738). Dicaearchus did discuss some less famous sayings (**44, 57, 68, 75, 97, 98**). But nowhere does anyone claim that no sage coined any maxims; and all seven sages whose sayings Demetrius of Phaleron collected (87 SOD) appear in Dicaearchus' lists in **38**. Hence, the alternative, that Dicaearchus denied the sages were wise, is more plausible. It would also harmonize with **37**, as would the denial here that the sages were philosophers. But here we find a crucial qualification: the sages did not philosophize "in discourse" (λόγῳ). This points to a third interpretation: if σοφῶν ἀνδρῶν is a genitive of characteristic, the claim is only that knowing maxims is not a sufficient condition for wisdom. Some did regard maxims highly: in the episode from Plato's *Protagoras* discussed above (*Prot.* 343A), Socrates remarks ironically that "both some today and some from long ago have recognized that being Laconic involves philosophy much more than physical training, since they know that the ability to utter sayings like that is the mark of a perfectly educated person."

Rejecting such claims, Dicaearchus maintains that wisdom requires good conduct: "wisdom back then [τότε] was performing honorable deeds." But since the sages did live honorably, how can he deny they were wise? If standards of σοφία changed; then he can consistently maintain that the sages were wise by *earlier* standards but not by *present* ones. At one level, usage simply changed. In the archaic period,

---

shift to direct discourse here is insignificant if von Arnim (ibid.) was right to emend φασίν (which has no antecedent) to φησίν, which is also supported by a parallel to φορτικόν in **48**.

good conduct and sage advice were necessary, and apparently sufficient conditions for the "gnomic wisdom" of the sages. Later, however, wisdom came to require skill in speaking (λόγων τέχνη) as well. Dicaearchus shows similar sensitivity to semantic change when he observes that even poets were once called wise (**39**): "the ancients considered the bard wise [τοὺς παλαιοὺς καὶ σοφὸν τὸν ᾠδὸν νομίζειν], as is clear from the one left with Clytemnestra" (cf. *Od.* 3.267–72, discussed also by Aristoxenus fr. 123).[31] Behind these shifts, however, he uncovers important continuity in two areas. First, "public speaking" (λόγοι ὀχλικοί) and "cogent argument" (πιθανῶς διαλεχθέντα) came to win a *reputation* for wisdom (note recurrent δοκεῖν, δόξα), just as pithy maxims had earlier. But second, in neither period was verbal dexterity sufficient for *genuine* wisdom, which always requires good conduct as well as sound speech. But why are sage maxims inferior to later forms of wisdom? Why did Dicaearchus deny the sages "philosophized in discourse" (λόγῳ)?

Dicaearchus' point here is not that the sages were wise but not philosophers. He refers indifferently to "wisdom back then" and "philosophers in the old days." The key is rather a contrast between maxims and λόγοι—between gnomic utterance and discursive argument or reasoning. The sages, after all, were famous for maxims, practical insight, civic leadership, and lawmaking, but not for "cleverness in discourse" (δεινότητι λόγων) or "arguing cogently" (πιθανῶς διαλεχθέντα). And maxims, decrees, and laws, while inherently general, are only isolated pronouncements, mere conclusions without reasons, explanation, or argument. Adopting the standards of his own era, Dicaearchus maintained that wisdom and philosophy require articulate reasoning. But he also required good conduct, which cleverness in argument hardly ensures. In short, a twofold conception of wisdom and philosophy underlies the contrast in **36**. The archaic sages led honorable lives, acting as "one

[31] Philodemus quotes this remark to illustrate the view that poetry can be morally instructive. That Dicaearchus shared this generally Peripatetic attitude is confirmed by his account of "skolia" as sympotic verse sung by "the most shrewd" (τῶν συνετωτάτων, **89**). This term echoes his description of the sages in **37**, which suggests in turn that he may have associated them with skolia, which were often gnomic: Ath. 15 694A–B (quoted by Wehrli on fr. 88 = **89**) presents the same account of skolia more fully (but without naming Dicaearchus), calls the singers "wise" as well as "shrewd," and adds that their verses were thought to contain "precepts and maxims useful for life" (παραίνεσίν τέ τινα καὶ γνώμην χρησίμην εἰς τὸν βίον); similar ideas may explain why Lobon ascribed gnomic verses to seven sages (see above, n. 14).

should" in civic and family affairs, but were unversed in arguments and speeches (μὴ ... ἀσκοῖτο λόγους). Many later figures, conversely, were skilled in "cogent argument," which won them a "reputation" for philosophy, but debated what to do in civic and family affairs because they had no insight into how to live.

The evidence for this distinction may be slender here. But it appears in other testimony, as we shall see, and it explains two otherwise puzzling implications of Dicaearchus' denial that the sages were either wise or philosophers (**37**).[32] If he did not recognize different usage of these terms, he could not consistently accept either the traditions he summarizes in **38**, which make Thales one of only four "accepted" sages, or the conclusions of his colleagues, which present Thales as a paradigm of specifically theoretical wisdom (*NE* 6.7) and a pioneer in the study of nature and number (Eudemus frr. 133–35, 143–45). But if Dicaearchus did understand λόγος in the way I suggest, he could endorse both traditions. In that case, all he need deny is that Thales established his ideas by arguments (λόγοι) or articulated them in speeches or writings (λόγοι). Both of these claims, in fact, were widely doubted then as now. Many denied that Thales had committed his discoveries to writing (DL 1.23–24), and the absence of texts left the details of his work in doubt. Many of his ideas, most notably his famous prediction of an eclipse, would sound like oracular pronouncements to the many who failed to understand their basis (cf. *Charm.* 164E, Lucr. 1.731–33); and though he was widely credited with some major insights in geometry and astronomy, no extant authority maintains that he offered any proofs for them.[33] In short, even his theoretical insights remained essentially "gnomic" like the practical insight of his fellow sages; or as Eudemus put it, "he discovered many things himself and laid the basis of many more for

---

[32] Jaeger (above, n. 4) argues that Dicaearchus ranked the sages alongside all later philosophers as paradigms of the same purely practical conception of both wisdom and philosophy; but he overlooks **36**, and despite quoting **37**, he ignores its denial that the sages were either wise or philosophers.

[33] When Proclus (*In Eucl.* 157, probably following Eudemus) says that Thales "showed" (ἀποδεῖξαι) that a circle is bisected by its diameter (which Euclid *posits* as Def. 17), he clearly does not have a rigorous "demonstration" in mind, since he goes on to describe an operation of superposition; cf. his contrast between Thales' "discovery" of Prop. 1.15 and its much later "*scientific* demonstration" (ἐπιστημονικῆς ἀποδείξεως, *In Eucl.* 352: Eudemus fr. 134). On the other hand, it is quite possible that Dicaearchus was among those who believed Thales had grasped the cause of eclipses; see A. Lebedev, "Aristarchus of Samos on Thales' Theory of Eclipses," *Apeiron* 23 (1990) 77–85.

those after him, handling some points quite generally [καθολικώτερον] and others quite empirically [αἰσθητικώτερον]" (fr. 133). His discoveries, many of which had clear practical applications, may even have been essentially technological, as Plato suggests (ἐπίνοιαι εὐμήχανοι εἰς τέχνας ἤ τινας ἄλλας πράξεις, *Rep.* 600A). Dicaearchus could thus maintain that Thales had investigated nature and mathematics, but deny that he had developed his ideas systematically or circulated them to a wider audience in written or "public" discourse.

III. Archaic Wisdom: Pythagoras

The chronological unity of the sages has nostalgic overtones. Their wisdom, it suggests, had not been rivalled since. But it also points to the origins of philosophy as we know it. Those who became known as sages mark an epoch: they were the earliest non-poets to win a lasting reputation for σοφία; yet they were also the last to do so before Pherecydes and Anaximander recorded their speculations in the first reliably attested prose.[34] Anaximander, of course, was considered Thales' intellectual heir, and Pherecydes in turn had reputedly taught Pythagoras. That brings us to a new paradigm of σοφία who also figured prominently in fourth-century debates about the origins of philosophy. According to Heraclides (fr. 88), Pythagoras had invented the very word.[35] Some gave him credit for geometrical discoveries that others ascribed to Thales (including perhaps the so-called Pythagorean theorem: DL 1.25, cf. Callim. fr. 191.59–61). He also appears, as we saw, in some lists of sages (**38**, quoted above). Yet Dicaearchus excludes him, which suggests that he did consider him both wise and a philosopher. Other evidence, though scanty, also suggests that his reasons for doing so rest on Pythagoras' use of λόγος.

Dicaearchus apparently discussed Pythagoras at some length. All that survives concerns his political activity and untimely death, and his

---

[34] The advance of literacy also led to the first written laws; see K.-J. Hölkeskamp, "Written Law in Archaic Greece," *PCPhS* 38 (1992) 87–117. In calling the sages συνετούς τινας καὶ νομοθετικούς, Dicaearchus may have had in mind primarily oral precepts, decrees, and customs rather than inscribed statutes; maxims could also have quasi-legal force, as shown by the Peisistratid ploy of having them inscribed on herms throughout Attica; see pseudo-Plato, *Hipparchus* 228C–229B, and H. A. Shapiro, *Art and Cult Under the Tyrants in Athens* (Mainz, 1989) 125–32.

[35] See Burkert (above, n. 9).

novel theories only indirectly.[36] This led Jaeger to infer that Dicaearchus assimilated Pythagoras to his own (supposedly purely practical) conceptions of wisdom and philosophy.[37] But the evidence supports a rather different picture. The most significant testimony comes from Porphyry, who cites Dicaearchus for his account of Pythagoras arriving in Croton and delivering a series of "public speeches" (*VP* 18–19: **40**).

> When he reached Italy and came to Croton, says Dicaearchus, the arrival of this ingenious [περιττοῦ] man who had travelled far and whose own nature was also well endowed by fortune—for he was tall and free-minded in appearance and possessed consummate grace and charm in his voice and character and all else—his arrival so impressed the people of Croton that, after he had captivated the ruling elders with his many fine arguments [πολλὰ καὶ καλὰ διαλεχθείς], the leaders requested him to deliver again precepts on youth to the young people, then to the children assembled from the schools, and finally to the women in a meeting specially arranged for him.

When Pythagoras spoke to the civic leaders of Croton, he so "captivated" (ἐψυχαγώγησε) them that he was not only permitted but actually "requested" (κελευσθείς) to address the rest of the city, and in three separate gatherings. Dicaearchus thus depicts Pythagoras as a man whose natural gifts and wide experience gave him not only a charismatic presence, but above all, immense moral authority. This focus on moral advice (παραινέσεις) and public instruction recalls the sages. But Pythagoras differed from them in two important ways: he addressed his teaching directly to large audiences, and he used the rhetorical tactic of tailoring his speeches to different audiences as he addressed in turn the council, ephebes, children, and women.[38] In short, whereas the sages were lawmakers, he was a public speaker and teacher. Porphyry did not record what if anything Dicaearchus said about the content of these

---

[36] His peculiar religiosity appears in two reports: **41A–B** describes his fasting to death in a temple of the Muses (cf. the death of Socrates in **43**); and **42** summarizes the legend of his previous incarnations (DL 8.5; cf. Heraclides fr. 89), which Dicaearchus must have dismissed since he denied the soul survives after death (**14–20, 23–29**).

[37] Jaeger (above, n. 4) 384–89.

[38] Antisthenes also thought this instance of Pythagoras' rhetorical skill a mark of his σοφία; and he argued that Homer considered Odysseus wise because being πολύτροπος means being δεινὸς διαλέγεσθαι and knowing how to tailor each λόγος to its audience, which only the wise can do (Sch. *Od.* 1.1: fr. 187 Giannantoni). Plato, in a context showing Pythagorean influence (*Gorgias* 502D), complains that Athenian democracy ignores this rule. **35** may also be relevant here.

speeches, though the legendary Pythagorean rules of secrecy suggest that little was said about speculative topics or his novel ideas about souls.[39] What Dicaearchus clearly did highlight is Pythagoras' "captivating" rhetoric and arguments, the like of which Croton had apparently never heard before. Indeed, in the only other passage where Porphyry names Dicaearchus as his source (for Pythagoras' flight from Croton to Caulonia, then Locri, Tarentum, and Metapontum), we find Pythagoras refused sanctuary at Locri for two quite telling reasons: the Locrians had no interest in new laws, and they had heard that Pythagoras was "a wise and clever man" (*VP* 56: **41A**). In short, Dicaearchus characterized him as having both what he ascribed to the sages in **37** and what he denied them in **36**. Like the sages, Pythagoras enjoyed a reputation for practical insight and political activity (as in **41A**), but like the philosophers of later eras, also for articulate argument (διαλεχθείς, **40**) and clever and forceful speaking (δεινόν, **41A**).

No extant text shows Dicaearchus calling Pythagoras a philosopher. But extant testimony does ascribe to Pythagoras what he expects of philosophers in **36**: both honorable conduct and persuasive discourse. Pythagoras and his later followers were assigned a very prominent part in fourth-century accounts of philosophy. How much of this Dicaearchus endorsed is now unclear. But it would be highly anomalous if he refused to call him a philosopher, at least in some sense of the term. He need not have endorsed the legend that Pythagoras coined the word, much less the famous but surely apocryphal tale from Heraclides that explains its point with an Olympic parable (*Tusc. Disp.* 5.8–10: fr. 88). Unlike Heraclides, Dicaearchus apparently took a dim view of the grandiose tales then circulating and presented a remarkably sober narrative.[40] Porphyry ranks him among his most reliable sources (ἀκριβέστεροι, *VP* 56: **41A**; cf. ἀκριβῶς, **56A**); and Gellius says he reported the multiple incarnations of Pythagoras only as what the man

---

[39] In the following lines, Porphyry reports that Pythagoras attracted numerous companions (ὁμιλητάς) but says that it is impossible to know what he taught them, due to their rules of secrecy. The only teaching he is willing to ascribe even here (τοῖς συνοῦσιν) concerns the immortality and transmigration of souls (*VP* 19), doctrines Dicaearchus rejected. This caution suggests that he is still following Dicaearchus; see W. Burkert, *Lore and Science in Ancient Pythagoreanism* (Cambridge, Mass., 1972) 122–23. For plainly fictitious versions of the Croton speeches, probably derived from Timaeus (see Burkert, 104 n. 37), see Iambl. *VP* 37–57.

[40] See H. Gottschalk, *Heraclides of Pontus* (Oxford, 1980) 143; cf. Burkert, ibid. 106.

himself was wont to claim (*dictitasse*), adding scornfully that his preceding incarnation had been as a courtesan (**42**). This critical attitude, however, did not prevent Dicaearchus from recognizing that Pythagoras had advanced beyond the sages in his endeavor to spread his ideas. In a word, he was a teacher; and what he taught, as Plato puts it in *Republic* 10, was a βίος or way of life (ὁδόν τινα βίου or τρόπον τοῦ βίου, 600B; cf. Alcidamas in DL 8.56). For Dicaearchus, this marked a radically new conception of wisdom and a new stage in his history—or rather biography—of philosophy.

The Pythagorean βίος or way of life involved two major innovations, each closely connected to fourth-century debates about wisdom. Rather than use civic institutions to promulgate his insights, as the sages had, Pythagoras tried to shape people's conduct by education; and as Dicaearchus also reported (**41A**), he attracted a body of companions who shared his interests (ἑταίρων and φίλων). This cultivation of character and devotion to learning fully warrants the label "philosophy"; for whatever doctrines or practices Pythagoras taught, his commitment to learning itself implies a consuming interest that it would be natural to call "love of wisdom."[41] Similarly, anyone who had special expertise in these studies and ventured to teach others would be naturally called a σοφιστής, whether or not he specialized in the rhetorical skills we now associate with the term. Thus Plato has the preeminent sophist Protagoras present himself as only the latest in a long line of "sophists" or teachers that includes poets, seers, medical men, and experts in music (*Prot.* 316D–317B), where the only shared feature he mentions is "educating people" (317B4–5). Moreover, one of the main differences between the sages and Pythagoras in Dicaearchus' account is the latter's skill in public speaking and persuasion. It is therefore hard not to infer that he considered Pythagoras both a philosopher and a sophist, though the absence of explicit testimony precludes certainty.[42] What is clear is

[41] See the range of φιλο-terms Aristotle uses when discussing rival βίοι in *NE* 1.8 (1099a7–16); his observation that doing what we "love" makes life enjoyable indicates the force of these terms.

[42] The earliest reference to Pythagoras as a "sophist" is by Herodotus (4.95, from which Them. *Or.* 23 286bc evidently derives). What exactly he meant by the term is unclear, in part because he seems to apply it to sages (1.29); but it is suggestive that he presents Pythagoras as the *teacher* of Zalmoxis, and the only others he calls "sophists" are "exegetes" of Dionysian rites (2.49; cf. the Orphics in *Prot.* 316D); cf. Burkert (above, n. 39) 210–11. When Aristotle called the sages "sophists" (*De phil.* fr. 5), he probably had in mind the moral *instruction* supplied by their maxims, much as Phainias probably did when he applied the term to some poets (fr. 10).

that Dicaearchus assigned Pythagoras a decisive role in the development of moral education. Wisdom henceforth was something for adults to pursue as a way of life, and the Pythagorean life of teaching and study long remained a model of the philosophical life. The end of the Archaic period thus coincides with the origin of philosophy as Dicaearchus understood it.

IV. Dialectical Wisdom: Socrates

To indicate the difference between archaic and contemporary wisdom, the author of the letter to Sebosus (**36**) depicts the sages as honorable public servants but complains that philosophers in his own day merely debate "whether to engage in politics" (εἰ πολιτευτέον). Plutarch, who clearly fell on the later side of this divide, wrote an essay late in life addressing the more specific question "Whether an older man should engage in politics." Near the close of the essay, he draws an analogy between politics and philosophy to help explain his belief—and practice—that good citizens engage in politics even outside of official capacities (*An seni resp. ger.* 26 796C: **43**).

> Above all, we must remember that engaging in politics is not limited to holding office, serving as an envoy, shouting in an assembly, and raving around the podium, saying and writing the things most people think characteristic of engaging in politics, just as they no doubt think those who discourse from a lectern and publish their lectures in books engage in philosophy. But people overlook the constant political activity [or citizenship] and philosophy observed regularly in daily deeds and actions. After all, they say those who go back and forth in the porticoes are strolling [περιπατεῖν], as Dicaearchus used to say, but not those who walk to the farm or a friend. Engaging in politics is like engaging in philosophy. Socrates, at any rate, engaged in philosophy not by putting out benches or holding a chair or offering regular lectures or strolling with colleagues, but rather even when he happened to be socializing, or at parties, on campaign, in the market, and finally, bound in prison when he drank the poison. He was the first to exhibit a life engaged in philosophy at every time, in every part, and in absolutely all situations and activities.

The boundaries of what here should be ascribed to Dicaearchus are problematic. But there are good reasons for thinking that the description of Socrates, which explains his joke about walking, also comes from him, and I shall assume that it does.[43] What then is his point? To Jaeger and others who dwell on Cicero's melancholy jests about the rival claims of theory and practice (**8**, quoted below and **33**), the close analogy drawn here between politics and philosophy may seem odd. But context points in another direction. The crucial contrast here is not between action and theory, but rather between an activity performed to achieve something else and the same activity performed for its own sake. Specifically, the passage contrasts occupations and vocations (in the moral or religious sense): doing something *for a living,* and doing it *as a way of life.* This is plainly the contrast Plutarch draws in the political sphere. He concedes that popular usage, then as now, equates politics with what "career" politicians do, which he summarizes by describing the four main areas of ancient government (administration, diplomacy, legislation, and litigation). But in keeping with the thesis of the entire essay, he argues that law-abiding citizens who serve the interests of the city in unofficial capacities are also engaged in politics (cf. 796D). He then points to a parallel difference in philosophy, which popular usage again equates with what paid teachers do: lecturing, publishing, and talking to colleagues. But the case of Socrates, who was universally considered a philosopher, shows that professional activities are unnecessary. He engaged in philosophy in all manner of settings, among friends at their homes, away on military service, and downtown in the agora. But what did he do that made this philosophy?

Plutarch's own contrast between politicians and private citizens turns on differences between public and private action. But Dicaearchus' description of Socrates' activities, which depicts both public and private scenes (the army and the agora as well as drinking parties), points in a different direction. Philosophy, it implies, can be done both in private and in public; an institutional setting is only incidental. Plutarch's thesis, after all, is not that politicians *never* serve their cities well, only that

---

[43] The joke turns on a contrast between walking as a means (to get somewhere) or as an end in itself (strolling); and the analogy implies that people also practice politics and philosophy both ways. If περιπατεῖν had acquired its doctrinal connotations (from Aristotle's habit of strolling while lecturing, according to Hermippus fr. 45: DL 5.2; but cf. Hesychius and Suda s.v. Aristotle), the joke also suggests that philosophy is studied for its own sake in the Lyceum. But Dicaearchus' mention of στοαῖς, which probably predates its doctrinal sense (though the etymology at DL 7.5 echoes his ἀνακάμπτοντας), suggests he was characterizing philosophers and students in general (cf. *Euthyd.* 273A, *Eryxias* 392A, Alexis frr. 151 and 206); in that case, the joke itself implies the contrast that follows.

official standing is neither necessary nor sufficient for civic service. The same contrast appears in Cicero's remarks in a letter to Atticus (*Att.* 2.12.4 = 30.4 SB: **8**): "You're right to like Dicaearchus: he's a splendid person and a far better citizen than those unjust officials of ours. [Greetings from Terentia.] Cicero the philosopher embraces the politician Titus." The letter is dated 19 April 59. Cicero, a supremely active politician who had spent his entire adult life (nearly thirty years) in official capacities, ironically dubs himself a "philosopher" because his virtual exile from Rome under the Triumvirate that had recently seized power left him more leisure for study.[44] Atticus, whose equestrian rank and business interests, as well as his personal and philosophical preferences for Epicureanism, kept him out of government, he styles a "politician" not because he held any office, but because at that time his dynamic social life inside the Roman beltway involved frequent discussion of politics. A recent letter from him had even reported hobnobbing with Clodia (2.12.4; cf. 2.14.1, a week later), whose brother Clodius had been instrumental in driving Cicero out of Rome. In the same vein, Cicero calls Dicaearchus, a learned scholar who was excluded by his alien status from political office in Athens, a much better "citizen" than the corrupt politicians then running Rome. Cicero obviously singles out Dicaearchus for his name, which affords a sly pun.[45] But the gibe is all the weightier given Cicero's high regard for him as a political thinker (**9, 10, 11B, 86**, cf. **79**). Both Cicero and Plutarch, then, associate Dicaearchus with a distinctly unconventional conception of politics. Plutarch even assimilates this conception to Dicaearchus' account of Socrates. It thus appears that Dicaearchus accepted the picture of Socrates drawn in Plato's early dialogues, including the claim in *Gorgias* that Socrates, despite avoiding official business, was a true politician because he always sought what was best in all he said and did (521D; contrast Callicles' derisive charges, 484C–486D). In short, Dicaearchus singled out Socrates as a model philosopher primarily because he devoted his life to the pursuit of wisdom and virtue.

---

[44] Most assume that Cicero calls himself φιλόσοφος. But W. S. Watt, "Notes on Cicero, *Ad Atticum* 1 and 2," *CQ* 12 (1962) 252–62, adduces parallels that strongly suggest this refers to Cicero's son, though allowing that he was simply "attributing to him his own philosophical interests and pursuits" (258). For the point of calling Atticus πολιτικόν, see Shackleton Bailey's note ad loc.

[45] The pun is double-barrelled: the Triumvirs were not only unjust leaders (ἀδικαίαρχοι) but also held office (ἀρχή) unjustly, thanks to corrupt elections.

If Plutarch, and apparently Dicaearchus as well, did not condemn professional politicians as a class, then it is surely implausible that either meant to disparage teachers wholesale.[46] The point in **43** is rather that being a professor, like knowing maxims, is neither necessary nor sufficient for being a philosopher. Why, then, did Dicaearchus consider Socrates a philosopher? Surely because of what he is shown doing in all known dialogues, whether by Plato or other Socratics: examining fundamental problems in the conduct of life through dialectical argument. Recall the portrait of Socrates in **43**. The final image plainly alludes to *Phaedo*, where Socrates passes his entire last day in prison arguing with his friends, about the very topics Dicaearchus discussed at length in his own dialogue on the soul (**13–32**).[47] But the preceding images evoke several other Socratic dialogues: "chance" encounters with young men as in *Lysis*, *Charmides*, and *Phaedrus* (which Dicaearchus also discussed, DL 3.38: **48**);[48] symposia as dramatized by both Plato and Xenophon; military service as reported in *Laches* and *Symposium*; and conversations in the agora as recreated in *Euthyphro* and recalled in *Apology* and Xenophon. Philosophy and the pursuit of wisdom as depicted in these works center on the same two factors central to Dicaearchus' account of Pythagoras: good conduct and sustained discussion. The former aligns Socrates with what Dicaearchus said about both the sages and Pythagoras. The latter corresponds to what he found new in Pythagoras. But there are also important differences. Dicaearchus presented Pythagoras as a persuasive public speaker and a teacher of esoteric doctrines, but apparently not as a proponent of open debate or methodical argument. What Dicaearchus considered new in Socrates, it seems, was essentially twofold: he employed dialectical argument in discussions of conduct, as Aristotle also reports (*Meta.* A.6 987b1–4, cf. M.4 1078b23–29); and he pursued his inquiries in all realms of life, public and private alike. As the first to integrate these factors in a methodical examination of how to live, Socrates introduced

---

[46] Wehrli (51; cf. 52 on fr. 31 = **36**) needlessly suspects polemics against Theophrastus, whose lectures were famously well attended (DL 5.37).

[47] **22** even suggests direct criticism of arguments in *Phaedo*; cf. H. Gottschalk, "Addenda Peripatetica," *Phronesis* 18 (1973) 91–100.

[48] He criticized *Phaedrus* for its "vulgar style" (τὸν τρόπον τῆς γραφῆς ὅλον ἐπιμέμφεται ὡς φορτικόν; cf. K. Gaiser, *Philodems Academica* (Stuttgart, 1988) 338–40. He may also have objected to its "juvenile subject" (μειρακιῶδες πρόβλημα); this charge precedes mention of Dicaearchus, but if its target is the dialogue's focus on love and pederasty, the criticism corresponds to views reported in **49** and **83**.

a new conception of wisdom and exemplified a new form of the philosophical life.

V. Systematic Wisdom: Plato

Like Pythagoras before him, Socrates so impressed some of his contemporaries that they tried to imitate him in deed and in word. Also like Pythagoras (Porph. *VP* 57–58), he committed none of his ideas to writing.[49] But unlike Pythagoras, he was apparently quite willing to share his ideas with any and all, and after his death, several of his followers began to circulate written recreations of his conversations in a novel literary form soon labelled "Socratic λόγοι" (Arist. *Po.* 1447b8–13; cf. *On Poets* fr. 72). This once again transformed philosophy, as Dicaearchus recognized, for the last exemplary philosopher he discussed is the one Socratic most responsible for this change. His treatment of Plato apparently included elements of biography in the modern sense: Plato's early activity in athletics, painting, and poetry (DL 3.4: **47**),[50] the origins of the Academy (**70**), and at least some of the students he attracted (**50**). Plato's writings were also covered: besides ascribing to him verse in several genres (dithyramb, lyric, and tragedy: **47**), Dicaearchus criticized his *Phaedrus* (DL 3.38: **48**; see n. 48 above). But the most substantial evidence, and the most intriguing, is from Philodemus, whose history of the Academy quotes Dicaearchus at length, both praising Plato's dialogues and crediting him with "doing more than anyone else to advance philosophy—and to undermine it" (*Acad.* col. 1.1–2.7, excluding col. Y= **46A** and **46C**).[51]

---

[49] Porphyry may still be following Dicaearchus here in denying Pythagoras left any writings; all that intervenes after **41A** is an alternative version of Pythagoras' death. For telling arguments that later reports that Pythagoras wrote books are unreliable and anachronistic, see Burkert (above, n. 39) 239–40.

[50] Wehrli cites parallels to support including in **47** a preceding account of Plato's education; this may derive from Dicaearchus, but it should be noted that Wehrli omits an intervening passage that cites Alexander's *Successions* and Neanthes, who (along with many others) may instead be its source.

[51] The relevance of this text, which greatly enlarges Wehrli's fr. 45 (= col. 2.4–7), was first shown by K. Gaiser, "La biografia di Platone in Filodemo: nuovi dati dal *PHerc* 1021," *Cronache Ercolanesi* 13 (1983) 53–62; his later book develops and modifies his views (above, n. 48) 307–66. Gaiser's analysis is very instructive but rests on a highly conjectural text that at key points is inconsistent with the papyrus; for discussion, see T. Dorandi in this volume, and for the text, see his *Filodemo: Storia dei filosofi* (Naples, 1991) 125–28 and 203–11. What I translate is Dorandi's duly conservative text, minus what is too lacunose to construe but with three modest supplements:

". . . from the available material he [sc. Plato] further renewed all of it [sc. philosophy] once again, and for this reason he added the enchanting cadences in his dialogues. But he also introduced many new things of his own, and thereby—if one must honestly describe what happened— he did more than anyone else to advance philosophy and to undermine it; for he converted virtually unlimited numbers of people to it [sc. philosophy] through the composition of his dialogues, but he also made some people engage in philosophy superficially by diverting them to a patent . . . ." He also says that ". . . [1 line] . . . provided a prelude to philosophy, so that neither having learned . . . and nothing . . . learn, not only count themselves among the philosophers but also . . [c. 6 lines] . . . persuaded, so that some people, while drawn to him, believe they have an adequate defense for their own ignorance; or rather . . . since they alone recognize the . . . of the noble and wisest teacher . . . [c. 3 lines] . . . generosity . . . equals." While this is the sort of thing Dicaearchus has written, Philochorus in the sixth book of his *Atthis* mocked . . .

The initial claim that Plato "renewed philosophy again" (ἐπανε-καίνισε πάλιν) confirms that Dicaearchus organized his work chrono-logically, and that he discussed at least two earlier forms or stages of philosophy (both its first and its renewal). Moreover, the passage again highlights two innovations. First, Plato composed elegant dialogues (λόγοι refers at once to the dialogues and to the arguments they record), which greatly "increased" philosophy by "converting" many new students to its study. The second innovation is very different: Plato "under-mined" (κατέλυσε) philosophy by "diverting" (ἐκτρέπων) many students to a "superficial" form of philosophy.[52] This remarkable verdict, which Dicaearchus pauses to excuse by pleading a need for candor (παρρησίας) much as Aristotle does before criticizing Plato's form of the good (*NE* 1.6 1096a13–17), was apparently explained more fully in the following lines. The passage is lamentably lacunose but it suffices to indicate a striking parallel to Dicaearchus' accounts of the sages in **36**

Gaiser's ἐ[πᾴδο]υσ[αν in 1.3, Mekler's φιλ[οσόφων in 1.25, and αὐ]τοὺς καταριθμε[ῖν in 1.25–26.

[52] See J. Barnes, "Philodemus and the Old Academy," *Apeiron* 22 (1989) 139–48 on 147, for this interpretation of Dorandi's κατέλυσε, rather than the favorable verdict Gaiser based on κατήνυσε (which Dorandi rules out). The following lines elaborate this charge if supplements proposed by Gaiser and Praechter are correct: φανερὰν ἐκτρέ[πων εἰς] τρι[βήν] ("diverting [students] to what is patently a [mere] routine"; cf. *Gorg.* 463B4, 501A7, *Rep.* 493B, *Phdr.* 260E) would charge Plato with fostering technical expertise without moral virtue or understanding.

and of Socrates in **43**. There he contrasts true moral insight with pretentious discourse; here he observes that Plato was a "noble and very wise
teacher," but complains that many of his students remained seriously
ignorant.[53] What was his basis for this charge?

The text is too meager to afford a definitive answer. But supplemented
with other testimony, it strongly suggests that the charge involved
Plato's revolutionary approach to some very traditional problems.
Dicaearchus focuses his praise on the dialogues but his criticism on new
ideas that Plato introduced (πολλὰ ἐπεισηνέγκατο ἴδια) and on the superficial study (ἐπιπολαίως φιλοσοφεῖν) he allegedly promoted.[54] The
most likely target of the first complaint, especially for someone familiar
with Aristotle's critique of Plato for turning Socrates' search for definitions of moral terms in a new but fruitless direction (see *Meta.* A.6; esp.
ἴδια at 987a31), is Plato's "separation" of universals from phenomenal
particulars. As I observed at the outset, there is little sign that
Dicaearchus worried much about ontology. But a more pragmatic objection, and one more in keeping with his generally practical orientation, is
ready to hand. Just as Aristotle argued that even if there is a form of the
good, it is useless for conduct (*NE* 1.6 1096b30–1097a13), so
Dicaearchus may have worried that Plato's theoretical proposals would
have little or no practical benefit. Cicero associates just such concerns
with his name in another letter to Atticus slightly later than the one
quoted in §IV (*Att.* 2.16.3 = 36.3 SB: **33**, on or about 30 April 59).

> I have finally made up my mind. Since your friend Dicaearchus and my
> dear Theophrastus are so opposed that your man puts τὸν πρακτικὸν
> βίον far ahead of everything whereas mine puts τὸν θεωρητικόν first,
> each shall approve my conduct. I do think I have done quite enough for

[53] Dicaearchus charged many of Plato's converts with failing to learn or understand
(μήτε μεμαθηκότας, μηδὲν . . . μαθεῖν) and yet "believing they have an adequate defense (or rationale?) for their own ignorance" (ἱκανὸν ἔχειν πρόβλημα τῆς ἰδίας ἀμαθίας
νομίζουσιν). The following lines about "the wisest teacher" seem to contain a very similar
charge: Gaiser (above, n. 48) 335 cites a close parallel at *Phaedo* 90C, where Plato warns
that practice (διατρίψαντες, cf. 1.18 τρι[βήν?) in "contradictory arguments" often leads
people to imagine they "alone" (cf. 1.39) are "wisest" (cf. 1.40) and to adopt
(κατανενοηκέναι, cf. 1.41 κατανοοῦντες) scepticism and "misology."

[54] The opening passage exhibits a sustained antithesis. Barnes (above, n. 52) points
out that the twofold verdict εὔξησεν/κατέλυσε is explained by the following contrast
(προετρέψατο μέν/ἐπιπολαίως δέ); the same contrast also appears in the opening lines
(ἐπανεκαίνισε/ἐπεισηνέγκατο, also marked by μέν/δέ). The first term in all three
pairs involves literary aspects of the dialogues; the second involves their content.

Dicaearchus. Now I am turning my attention back to this other group who not only permit me leisure but reproach me for not having always maintained leisure. So let's apply ourselves, my dear Titus, to those splendid studies and return at long last to what we never should have left.

Cicero, who studied philosophy intensely in his youth, does not say that Dicaearchus saw no value in theoretical studies. The position Cicero ascribes to him is simply that action matters most (*longe omnibus anteponat*). Cicero, in a letter to his closest friend, may have spoken loosely. But I think we can press his words a bit further. If Dicaearchus valued action most, he must have objected to ignoring practical matters entirely, and to pursuing theoretical studies without regard to anything else. But this does not imply any objection to research that yields practical benefits or has useful applications. If we now return to Philodemus, we can see better how this demand bears on Plato. The text of cols. 1–2 translated above was written continuously in two successive columns. But Philodemus apparently decided at a later stage to append some further material that occupies a column directly on the reverse side (col. Y). Both Gaiser and Dorandi place this passage between cols. 1 and 2. But in the absence of any sign in the text where it was to be inserted, it should probably be treated separately.[55] It may even come from a different source (none is named in the extant lines). But whatever its origin, the passage addresses a topic closely related to Dicaearchus' critique, which is surely why Philodemus chose to add it. After mentioning the "progress in mathematics" that resulted from a program of research directed by Plato, the passage singles out advances in purely theoretical disciplines but finds nothing comparable in the applied fields of optics and mechanics (*Acad.* Y.1–33 = **46B**).[56]

---

[55] See Dorandi in this volume. The lacunose state of the papyrus precludes certainty, but *pace* Gaiser (above, n. 48) 76–77, whose arguments are at best inconclusive, it is very likely that cols. 1 and 2 should be read continuously: no sign survives to indicate that col. Y belongs between them (as 2.38 indicates where col. V belongs, and 6.26/7 where col. T belongs); μέν in 1.42 can be answered by δέ in 2.1; and though δε also appears in Y.1, the editorial παρέγραψα strongly suggests a fresh start. Why Philodemus added col. Y is less clear: it may come from another source, or simply elsewhere in Dicaearchus' book. Dorandi is cautiously agnostic about the source for col. Y, but Gaiser (above, n. 48) 347, is probably right to infer that Dicaearchus drew on work by Eudemus: col. Y corresponds with Proclus' summary of Eudemus (fr. 133) on several points, but merely summarizes what is there covered in much greater detail.

[56] The text translated is again Dorandi's, minus lacunose sections but with two

. . . I inserted: "Much progress," he says, "had also been recognized in mathematics at that time, since Plato was designing a program and posing problems, and the mathematicians were investigating them intensely. Accordingly, the theory of proportion first reached maturity then, as did the problems in definition, since Eudoxus and his associates replaced the old-fashioned approach of Hippocrates [sc. of Cos]. There was also much progress in geometry, since the method of analysis was created as well as the use of lemmas for deciding what is provable, and in general problems in geometry were much . . . optics and mechanics not at all . . . [c. 2 lines] . . . lots of scavengers . . . things for themselves; for there was virtually another . . . of students, and from this harvest they each picked out their own private part without sharing . . . [c. 9 lines] . . . they detached from necessities . . . about beneficial things . . .

Dicaearchus credits Plato with organizing a program of research (ἀρχιτεκτονοῦντος μὲν καὶ προβλήματα διδόντος) that for the first time established firm foundations for several fields of mathematics. Hence the mention of a "*theory* of proportion" (μετρολογίαν), and the emphasis on definitions (ὁρισμούς) and the methods of "analysis" and "*diorismos*," which yielded proofs more methodical and systematic than the "primitive" efforts (ἀρχαισμόν) of earlier geometry. Some of these points recall ideas sketched in Plato's dialogues (methodical study of irrationals in *Theaetetus* 147D–148B; an obscure example of *diorismos* in *Meno* 87A–B, cf. *Phaedo* 78B) and recounted (no doubt more fully) by Eudemus in his history of geometry (fr. 133).[57] But the claim that Plato framed the program for this work points clearly to *Republic* 7, where Plato outlines a radically new approach to number, plane and solid geometry, astronomy, and harmonics (521–31).[58] His goal, roughly put, was to transform these fields into systematic sciences by deriving all theorems rigorously from basic principles. But the way

---

minor changes: I translate αὐτῶν (instead of αὑτῶν) in Y.21, and Schenkl's ἰδ[ιωτικὸν] in Y.23.

[57] See G. E. R. Lloyd, "The *Meno* and the Mysteries of Mathematics," *Phronesis* 37 (1992) 166–83; Lloyd glosses *diorismos* as "establishing the *conditions on the given* for a solution to a problem to be possible" (his italics).

[58] For a sympathetic assessment and further references, see G. Vlastos, "Observation in Plato's Astronomy" in *Studies*, vol. 2 (above, n. 1) 223–46. Gaiser (above, n. 48) supplements col. 1.18–21 to yield a similar account by Dicaearchus: [θεὸς τὸν ἀριθμὸν] καὶ τὴ[ν τ]ῶν ἄσ[τρων ὄψιν τ]οῦ φιλ[οσο]φεῖν ἐνδόσιμον ἔδω[κεν]; his reconstruction, while intriguing, is highly conjectural and not entirely consistent with Dorandi's readings.

he proposes to achieve this goal requires ignoring or at least bracketing the practical needs and uses that had allegedly driven previous work. This new focus, and the general disdain Plato expresses for utility as well as observation and empirical methods, also supplies a target for the complaints that Philodemus records. Why was there little progress in the applied fields of optics and mechanics? The explanation offered here seems to be that Plato's program ignored what Ben Franklin called "useful knowledge," which led his colleagues to "detach [sc. their work] from necessities" (ἀπήρτησαν τῶν ἀναγκαίων).

The accuracy of this critique is irrelevant here. The problematic origins of **46B** also preclude certainty about its author. But Dicaearchus did discuss the origins of Plato's Academy (**70**) and at least some of the students he attracted (**50**). It was presumably his critical account of Plato in **46A** that prompted Philodemus to append this account. Moreover, these complaints would come naturally from someone as interested in applied mathematics as Dicaearchus was. Not only was he identified by some as a "geometer" (**2**), but as Paul Keyser shows, he was also responsible for some major advances in geography that had lasting influence.[59] Most of these involve applications of geometry (a term that was applied also to surveying and geography, as **2** shows): astronomical observations that confirm the earth's sphericity (**121**), estimates of the shape (**122**) and size (**124**) of the Mediterranean οἰκουμένη, establishment of a meridian latitude (**123**), and calculations of altitude (**118–20**, cf. **2**). His measurements of mountains, in fact, not only involved some sort of instruments (ὀργανικῶς) but also exploited theorems in optics (**120**), one of the very fields **46B** accuses Plato's colleagues of neglecting. By Dicaearchus' standard of practical utility, then, the revolution Plato instigated in science and mathematics had mixed results. Great progress was made in rigor, but the gap between theory and practice yawned wider. The foolish or vicious could already parrot sage maxims, deliver impressive speeches, or engage in dialectical debate. Now, like parasites or scavengers (σπερμολόγων, **46B**), they were also enabled and even encouraged to construct systematic theories without regard for practical affairs or the proper conduct of life.

This verdict brings me to one more item concerning Plato. Plutarch recounts a discussion, at a dinner celebrating Plato's birthday, of

[59] In this volume; cf. Wehrli's observation (76) that "*mathematische* Höhenberechnungen lassen sich aber vor D. nicht nachweisen" (italics added).

whether god does geometry (*QC* 8.2, cf. 8.1 717A). A Spartan first summarizes the argument in *Republic* 7 that study of mathematics diverts the mind from physical phenomena (quoting 527E at 718D), which he illustrates by describing how Plato reproached the leading mathematicians of his day (Archytas, Eudoxus, and Menaechmus are named) for using empirical methods to solve the famous problem of the Delian cube (718C–F).[60] The speaker thus agrees with Dicaearchus on two points of fact, though they disagree sharply about the merits in each case: Plato favored a strictly theoretical approach to mathematics, and he spurned mechanical methods (ὀργανικὰς καὶ μηχανικὰς κατασκευάς at 718E, echoing both the charge in col. Y.17 that "mechanics" languished under Plato's supervision, and Theon's description of Dicaearchus' own work as ὀργανικῶς, **120**).[61] Where Plutarch stood on these issues does not matter here (but see 719F–720C). What is significant is that he then has Florus, his Roman patron (whose name he had adopted), respond by defending the application of mathematics to practical affairs (719A–B); and his defense, which is prefaced by a claim Dicaearchus made about Plato (**45**), focuses on politics.

> You helped us, Florus said, by offering this argument not as your own but in common. For you gave us a way to refute its claim that geometry is necessary not for gods but for us. For of course god has no need of mathematics as a tool to turn his thought away from generated things and redirect it to the real beings; those depend on god and are with and about god. But see whether you haven't missed something closely related to you in Plato's enigmatic claim [sc. that god always does geometry], given that he mixes Lycurgus in with Socrates no less than

---

[60] For the problem and its ancient solutions (including one by Eratosthenes in his *Platonicus*), see T. Heath, *A History of Greek Mathematics,* vol. 1 (Oxford, 1921) 244–70. Its name arose from the story that the Delians received an oracle to build an altar twice as large as one they already had; which altar this was is not recorded, though it is worth noting that Dicaearchus apparently discussed the famous Delian "altar of horns" (Plut. *Thes.* 21: **74**).

[61] The Delian problem offers a third point of contact: the problem is to double a given cube, which is the analogue in solid geometry to the much simpler problem in plane geometry that Plato uses to exhibit recollection in *Meno* 82–85; following that passage, Plato introduces and illustrates the method of *diorismos* (cf. Y.15), which the Delian problem also famously exemplifies, since its solution was recognized to depend on solving a clearly defined preliminary problem (find two mean proportionals in continuous proportion).

Pythagoras, as Dicaearchus thought.[62] For you surely know that Lycurgus banished numeric proportion from Sparta for being democratic and populist, and introduced the geometric proportion that suits a moderate oligarchy and constitutional monarchy. For the former distributes what is equal numerically, but the latter distributes rationally according to merit: instead of mixing everything together, it provides a clear discrimination between the helpful and troublesome people, using no balances or lotteries but the difference between virtue and vice, so that everyone receives what suits them.

Dicaearchus here presents Plato as endebted to earlier philosophy (cf. ἐνδεχομένων, *Acad.* col. 1.1 = **46A**), and in particular, to the two other figures he singled out as exemplary philosophers. Plato's primary debt, he implies, is to Socrates, presumably not only as the protagonist of his dialogues but also as the dialectician and moral exemplar portrayed therein. Socrates thus lies behind the new literary form Plato gave to philosophy, the dialectical method he continued, and the moral values he championed. A debt to Pythagoras is also intelligible, though we can no longer tell whether Dicaearchus emphasized similarities in their educational and political proposals, shared interests in theoretical speculation and especially mathematics (as emphasized by Aristotle *Meta.* A.6), or some combination of these. But Lycurgus is a new element in the picture.[63] What did Dicaearchus think Plato owed to the legendary Spartan lawmaker? His main point was surely political. Dicaearchus, who wrote about the Spartan *politeia* (**2**), must have recognized the laconizing features of Plato's own *Politeia*: its class divisions, systematic military training, comprehensive paternalism, and pervasive social and economic conformism (including communal dining: **87**). But Plutarch explains Plato's debt to Lycurgus in very general and abstract terms, describing the Spartan *politeia* as an embodiment of geometric equality. Ascribing a mathematical blueprint to Lycurgus, who predates

---

[62] Osann's emendation <ὡς> is surely necessary; but it leaves unclear what Plutarch ascribes to Dicaearchus. Gaiser (above, n. 49) 318 ascribes to Dicaearchus only the widely shared idea that Plato drew on Pythagoras and Socrates. But I follow Jaeger (above, n. 4) 389–91, who argues that he mentioned all three figures, since Plutarch would have cited him only if he went beyond the standard view. On the other hand, this leaves unexplained the provisional tone of ᾤετο, as Jaeger concedes.

[63] Aristotle, who singles out Heracliteanism alongside Pythagoreans and Socrates as the three decisive influences on Plato's ontology (*Meta.* A.6, M.4; cf. DL 3.8), says nothing about debts to Lycurgus, political or otherwise.

even the pre-philosophical sages, is plainly anachronistic.[64] Similar claims, however, were made by Plato, who associates geometric proportion with the rule of reason and virtue (*Gorg.* 508A) and pronounces Sparta its closest historical approximation (*Rep.* 8 544–50, *Laws* 3 691–93). Ranking it first after the ideal, he characterizes Spartan timocracy as the "mean" between monarchy and democracy (547C–D, 550B6), whereas democracy embodies numeric equality (558C). *Laws*, besides reasserting that Sparta exemplified the mean between monarchy and democracy (3 693D–694B), ascribes divine insight to its founding lawmaker (surely Lycurgus: 691E, 696A–B) and expects Magnesia to exemplify the same mean, which Plato explicitly ties to geometric proportion (6 757). The substance of Plutarch's assessment is thus authentically Platonic.[65] It was also familiar to Aristotle (*Pol.* 2.6, esp. 1265b26–33; cf. 1266a1–7), and surely to Dicaearchus as well. And he had good reason to discuss these issues.

Dicaearchus evidently shared Plato's admiration for the Spartan constitution. His ideal, which he probably articulated in his aptly entitled *Tripoliticus*, was a "mixed constitution" that combined elements of monarchy, aristocracy, and democracy and later became known as "Dicaearchic" (**88**). But as Aristotle reports, Sparta was considered by many the model of mixed systems (*Pol.* 1265b31–1266a1, 4.9 1294b13–41; cf. *Laws* 4 712D–E). Whether Dicaearchus adopted either of the two rival accounts of the Spartan mixture summarized by Aristotle is no longer clear, though his account of its austere common meals (**87**, from *Tripoliticus*) suggests he agreed with those who thought this a democratic element in the Spartan βίος (1265a41, cf. 1271a32–37). But that he did consider Sparta a form of mixed constitution is very likely.[66] And that his account of its *politeia* was generally favorable is implied by a later Spartan law that required all ephebes to

---

[64] Cf. *Tusc. Disp.* 5.7; Dicaearchus presumably agreed with Aristotle that it was ἀσκεπτότερον τῶν χρόνων to imagine, as some did, that Lycurgus was a near contemporary of the sages (*Pol.* 2.12 1274a25–31).

[65] Plutarch echoes *Laws* 757 on many points. For the history of these ideas, which were widely associated with Archytas, see F. D. Harvey, "Two Kinds of Equality," *Classica et Mediaevalia* 26 (1965) 101–46.

[66] The format of his Πολιτεία Σπαρτιατῶν (**2**) is unrecorded, but even if it emphasized institutions (as in *Ath. Pol.*), it probably also discussed wider social and educational factors (as Xenophon's did), if not the Spartan βίος or "way of life" as a whole. If so, Dicaearchus' claim that Plato borrowed from Lycurgus had an ethical basis as well, since the product (and ostensibly the goal) of Lycurgan legislation was a very distinctive way of life not unlike what Plato's own *Politeia* envisioned.

hear his work read every year in a veritable civics lesson (**2**). On the other hand, his assessment of Plato's *"politeia"* (in *Republic*, and perhaps also in *Laws*) was evidently critical (**88**). What exactly he criticized, and how his objections squared with his admiration for Sparta, is nowhere reported. But a likely explanation, I suggest, is that he endorsed many of the laconizing features in Plato's proposals, including his program of physical and literary education, but rejected his program of higher education for "philosopher-kings" because of its strictly theoretical focus. In underscoring Plato's debt to Lycurgus (**45**), then, Dicaearchus highlighted features he approved in Plato's model society, while excluding features he considered flawed (**46B**). If he also advanced the mathematical explanation that follows in Plutarch, as the context suggests he did,[67] then he also pinpointed an awkward tension in Plato: while deprecating applied mathematics, he analyzes social and political systems mathematically. Lycurgan Sparta in particular illustrates the political benefits of applied mathematics, and in a sphere very dear to Plato. Dicaearchus thus singled out Sparta as an application of mathematics that Plato himself deeply admired.

Plato's "renewal" of philosophy, according to Dicaearchus, had three central features. The novel form and literary charm of his dialogues brought philosophy to the attention of much wider audiences and attracted many more to the pursuit of wisdom (**46A** and **50**). His bold methodological proposals helped revolutionize mathematics and paved the way for systematic theory (**46B**). And the community he founded in the Academy (cf. **50, 70**) created a hospitable setting for sustained study and research. One result was a new way of life: the academic philosopher. In Plato and many of his colleagues, this devotion to wisdom embraced both moral and intellectual virtues. But while attracting many who shared his ideal, Plato also opened another way for philosophy and morality to diverge, as Dicaearchus observed (**46A**). Just as gnomic insight, captivating rhetoric, and subtle dialectic can be mimicked or exploited by the foolish or corrupt, so can systematic theory. None of these intellectual attainments entails moral insight or virtuous conduct, which remain the essential basis of genuine wisdom. Plato's own program, Dicaearchus worried, even encouraged this divorce, primarily because he advocated theoretical study for its own sake and disdained the ap-

[67] A parallel may lurk in *Acad.* col. 2.3–4, which Gaiser plausibly supplements as προ[ίε]το [ἴσοι]ς ἴσα; though the context is lost, this would be a clear application of geometric equality.

plied sciences. In so doing, Plato reversed what Dicaearchus considered the true order of priority: the ultimate justification for all inquiry, he held, is practical. Progress in philosophy, as in earlier stages, came at a price.

VI. Philosophy Matured

The βίος of Plato brought Dicaearchus' biography of philosophy down to the recent past. The history of philosophy had continued since, as had progress in many fields of inquiry, especially in the Lyceum. But the philosophical way of life and the conception of wisdom introduced by Plato had not changed; and these, not doctrinal disputes, were the focus of Dicaearchus' biography of philosophy. Or so the surviving evidence suggests. Most scholars have assumed that he covered other figures as well; and Jaeger proposed that he composed a "systematic" survey of political activity by earlier philosophers.[68] But there is no evidence that anyone but the sages, Pythagoras, Socrates, and Plato figured prominently in his work.[69] The extant testimony, in fact, contains only one certain mention of another philosopher; but it is only to report that Empedocles' *Purifications* were once recited at Olympia, and it is explicitly ascribed to a different work (entitled *Olympic*, **85**). Crönert proposed, and Jaeger accepted, that **52** mentions Heraclitus; but the supplement is highly conjectural and rightly discounted by Wehrli.[70] Others have suspected that the "old man in Elea" named in **71** was a philosopher.[71] But even so, he could have received only passing mention, perhaps in connection with Plato or Pythagoras; and again, the remark more likely comes from a different work, probably one of the dialogues, since the phrase is quoted for its exemplary prose rhythm (*On Style* 182).

---

[68] Jaeger (above, n. 4) 381–84.

[69] Wehrli suggests **69** figured in Dicaearchus' account of Pythagoras; see below, n. 85.

[70] Even if sound, the reference need have no bearing on the scope of Dicaearchus' work, since he could have named Heraclitus alongside the sages for his "riddling aphorisms" (cf. *Theaet.* 180A, Lucr. 1.638–44), or Pythagoras for his esoteric ideas (cf. the Suda life, which reports that he studied with the Pythagorean Hippasus).

[71] His identity is uncertain: Mueller proposed Xenophanes; Wehrli suggests Pythagoras as an alternative; other plausible candidates include Parmenides (cf. πρεσβύτην, *Parm.* 127B2), Archytas, and even Plato's "Eleatic stranger" (identified by some as Parmenides: *POxy.* 3219 fr. 2; but dismissed at DL 3.52).

Neglect of other philosophers is readily explained, however, if Dicaearchus thought no others had introduced new ways of cultivating wisdom or embodied new conceptions of philosophy. Parmenides and Empedocles, for example, advanced radically new theories, which earned each a prominent place in doxographies. But besides clothing their thought in epic verse and adopting the stance of visionary seers, both associated closely with Pythagoreans, whose philosophical way of life Dicaearchus may well have thought they adopted.[72] Especially odd on Jaeger's hypothesis is the absence of Protagoras, who was close to Pericles and helped design a legal system for Thurii (DL 9.50: Heraclides fr. 150). But he was also notorious for charging his students fees (*Prot.* 328b, cf. DL 9.52), which puts him on the wrong side of Dicaearchus' contrast between professional teachers and devoted philosophers (**43**); and even if Dicaearchus agreed with those who considered him the father of dialectic ("the Socratic form of argument," DL 9.53), he is quite unlikely to have considered Protagoras an exemplar, much less the originator of the Socratic βίος and its consuming cultivation of moral knowledge and wisdom. On the other hand, if the aim of Dicaearchus' work was to isolate distinctive conceptions of philosophy, the omission of these and other earlier philosophers is only natural. A polemical survey of politically engaged thinkers, such as Jaeger proposed, would be far more comprehensive. So too would a doxographic survey of earlier theories. But whereas histories that chart the dialectical progress of philosophical views and arguments tend to follow the evolutionary model of gradualism, the attempt to discern distinct stages in intellectual history favors a focus on boundaries and the model of punctuated equilibrium.

Paucity of evidence precludes certainty here. But three striking parallels favor my hypothesis that Dicaearchus' biography of philosophy highlighted only three individuals. One comes from *Magna Moralia*, which Jaeger thought endebted to Dicaearchus for its alleged preference for "the practical life." Dispensing with the surveys of competing values and βίοι that open Aristotle's *NE* and *EE*, this work begins with a critique of earlier philosophical accounts of virtue (1.1 1182a10–31). But instead of offering a comprehensive survey, it criticizes the views of

[72] Iambl. *VP* 166; for Parmenides, cf. *VP* 267 (where the Sch. trace both dialectic and rhetoric back to Pythagoras via Parmenides and Empedocles respectively), 104, 135; for Empedocles, cf. DL 9.21 and 8.54–55 (containing B129).

only three figures. Not only are these the same three we know
Dicaearchus discussed; the survey also suits his treatment of them.[73]
Like Aristotle, it faults Socrates for over-intellectualizing virtue and
Plato for tying virtue to ontological issues of "the good" that are alien to
ethics. But unlike Aristotle, who names Socrates as the first moral theorist (*Meta*. M.4 1078b17–30) and favors cautious references to
"Pythagoreans" (rather than their founding figure),[74] it singles out
Pythagoras himself as the first moral theorist and as the source of an
application of mathematics to ethics, in fact the very focus on proportional equality that Dicaearchus ascribes to him in **45** and portrays him
following in **40** when adapting his speeches to different audiences.
Moreover, the historical format of the survey, which is unparalleled in
other extant work on ethics from the early Lyceum, also fits
Dicaearchus' approach closely. Jaeger may well have been right, then,
to suspect his influence behind this three-stage survey, which adopts the
very same model of punctuated equilibrium as Dicaearchus did.

Two much later parallels point the same way. Diogenes Laertius, after
discussing Plato's life, discusses his writings at some length (3.47–66)
before summarizing his doctrines. After distinguishing various types of
dialogues, and before describing how Thrasyllos arranged them in te-
tralogies, he draws an intriguing analogy between progress in philosophy and drama (3.56).

> Just as long ago the chorus in tragedy first acted all alone, but later
> Thespis invented a single actor to allow the chorus a break, then
> Aeschylus added a second, and Sophocles completed [συνεπλήρωσεν]
> tragedy with a third, so too in philosophy discourse [ὁ λόγος] was first
> only about nature, Socrates added ethics second, and Plato perfected
> [ἐτελεσιούργησε; cf.Them. *Or*. 27 337b] philosophy by adding dialec-
> tic third.

Diogenes cites no source for this analogy, and it would be rash to
ascribe it to Dicaearchus. But several points suggest his influence.[75] The

---

[73] Although the author and date of *MM* are notoriously controversial, there is much
evidence to support Jaeger's suggestion (above, n. 4) 365–79, that it was composed
late enough to be influenced by Dicaearchus, either late in the fourth or early in the
third century. See I. Düring's review of F. Dirlmeier, *Magna Moralia* (Berlin, 1958) in
Gnomon 33 (1961) 547–57, esp. 557; cf. C. Rowe, "A Reply to John Cooper on the
Magna Moralia," *AJP* 96 (1975) 160–72.

[74] On Aristotle's caution, see Burkert (above, n. 39) 29–30.

[75] H. Tarrant, *Thrasyllan Platonism* (Ithaca, 1993) 89–90 and 105–6, suggests that

three-stage scheme, with its focus on pivotal figures and on Socrates and Plato in particular, corresponds closely to what we know about his work. All this became commonplace, of course, and here it is tied to a threefold division of philosophy into physics, ethics, and logic that is elsewhere traced back to the fourth century but nowhere explicitly to Dicaearchus.[76] But while the analogy differs from Dicaearchus on some points, it bears his stamp at others. First, it matches his account of the development of tragedy, for it is explicitly on his authority that later scholars ascribed the third actor to Sophocles rather than Aeschylus (**100**).[77] The analogy likewise follows his account of the origin of philosophy: just as tragedy began when Thespis transformed choral poetry by introducing the first actor, so philosophy began not with the maxims of the sages but with the first λόγος or "reasoned discourse" (cf. **36, 37, 40, 43**). Finally, the last stage follows his account both in ending with Plato and in crediting him with "perfecting" philosophy (cf. ἐπὶ κορυφὴν τότε πρῶτον, **46B**, cf. **46A**).

The same analogy appears again in Themistius (*Or.* 26 316d–319a), who recounts the progress of philosophy in greater detail and in terms that correspond quite closely to Dicaearchus' work. After outlining the development of tragedy in similar terms (316d),[78] he describes four suc-

---

the whole analogy goes back to Aristophanes of Byzantium. But he may in turn have taken it from Dicaearchus, whose work on drama and lyric he certainly used (**101, 103–4, 110, 113–15**); see Pfeiffer (above, n. 23) 193, cf. 181 and 222.

[76] Sextus (*Adv. math.* 7.16) says the "founder" (ἀρχηγός) of the trichotomy was "in principle" (δυνάμει) Plato (cf. Cic. *Ac.* 2.19) "but explicitly [ῥητότατα] Xenocrates and those from the Peripatos." Aristotle mentions the trichotomy casually (*Top.* 1.14 105b19–29, *Rhet.* 1.2 1358a17–20), and Cicero (*Fin.* 5.9–11) adds that Theophrastus also used it; so it was apparently available to Dicaearchus, though we have no evidence that he did follow it.

[77] Aristotle says the same in *Poetics* 4 1449a15–19. But Hellenistic scholars may not have known this (the famous story about the loss of Aristotle's treatises suggests they did not); and even the learned Themistius says Aristotle ascribed the third actor to Aeschylus (*Or.* 26 316d). Modern scholars follow Dicaearchus; see B. Knox, "Aeschylus and the Third Actor," *AJP* 93 (1972) 104–24. But claims about numbers of actors— certainly modern claims, and presumably ancient ones as well—rest on the evidence of extant plays; debates about priority thus depend on didascalic records, which both Aristotle and Dicaearchus used.

[78] Besides adding a few details, Themistius contradicts Diogenes and Dicaearchus (and *Po.* 4) in ascribing the third actor to Aeschylus (cf. previous note). Yet he cites Aristotle as his source. Assuming he is not simply confused, the best explanation is that he drew on Aristotle's *On Poets* rather than *Poetics*, which was not much read in antiquity: apart from these two passages in Themistius, the earliest evidence for knowledge of *Poetics* is from the late fifth century; and while *Or.* 27 337b parallels *Po.*

cessive stages that echo Dicaearchus at several points. Themistius starts with the antecedents or "seeds" of philosophy, which he identifies as "a few sayings of Thales and the other sages, which still now fill walls and tablets" (317a); and while acknowledging the utility of these maxims, he emphasizes their limitations by pointing out that they contain only "as much insight [νοῦς] as two words can, and are devoid of confirmation, like orders, and instructive [sc. only] for a small part of virtue" (317b). Two developments then mark the first stage of philosophy: Thales receives some of the credit because he proposed the first naturalistic explanations of celestial phenomena (317b); but since he expressed his ideas obscurely like a prophet (προεφήτευσεν) and formulated nothing in writing, Anaximander is also named for composing the first written λόγος (317bc). Another stage began with Socrates, who was the first to examine practical matters methodically (318a), and the first to share his λόγοι openly with anyone "over tables, in the shops, and at the gymnasia" (318b).[79] Philosophy finally reached full maturity when Plato united its disparate branches in a coherent system (318c–319a) and introduced a new type of λόγος, his "captivating and inspiring" dialogues (319a). Themistius, signalling his own primary philosophical affiliation, goes on to assign further innovations to Aristotle: the trichotomy of philosophy (319b), technical treatises (319b–d), and formal logic (320a). But apart from this supplement, his account corresponds to Diogenes' analogy at every point. It also follows Dicaearchus, not only in singling out the sages, Socrates, and Plato, but also in focusing on the form rather than the content of their thought.[80] At some points, Themistius even echoes Dicaearchus' phrasing.[81] Thus, however much

---

1449b6–7, 1448a33, and 1449a11–12, it contains information not found there. The contradiction in Aristotle could then be explained if he changed his view between writing the dialogue and the treatise, perhaps thanks to Dicaearchus' research. At any rate, Themistius follows the same scheme of three stages, each introduced by Thespis, Aeschylus, and Sophocles (though he adds Euripides, just as he adds Aristotle to his account of philosophy).

[79] Themistius describes interrogations of a general, a demagogue, a rhetor, and a poet (318bc), evoking in turn *Laches*, *Rep.* 1, *Gorgias*, and *Ion*.

[80] The one difference reflects the trichotomy of philosophy: like DL 3.56, Themistius starts with physics, rather than the first philosophical βίος, hence substitutes Thales and Anaximander for Pythagoras.

[81] Especially in his treatment of Plato: ἐπεισηνέγκατο appears in 319a and **46A**; καινοτόμος (318c) echoes ἐπανεκαίνισε (col. 1.2); 319a highlights Plato's rhythmic prose as in col. 1.4 (cf. DL 3.37: Arist. fr. 73 Rose); and 318d parallels the renewal described in **46A**.

this scheme was reworked by Themistius and Diogenes or their sources, the parallels with Dicaearchus' work support the hypothesis that he too distinguished four stages and counted only three as philosophy.

One more passage from Themistius, which contains his only explicit reference to Dicaearchus (**6**), complements this scheme and confirms the possibility of direct influence. Responding to charges that he had misused philosophy in public life, Themistius aligns himself with four famous philosophers from the distant past (*Or.* 23 285a–d). He opens his defense by claiming that wisdom and philosophy, like most good things, tend to evoke resentment in those who lack them (284d–285a), and he backs up his claim by recalling hostile reactions to Pythagoras, Socrates, Plato, and Aristotle. With one addition (again readily explicable), his list matches Dicaearchus' three paradigms. But two further points of correspondence are more telling: Themistius here presents Pythagoras as the first philosopher (cf. ἀρξάμενον and τοῖς ἀπ' ἐκείνου, 285a); and he gives the same account of his peregrinations and death as Dicaearchus did (**41A**).[82] In short, Themistius here follows Dicaearchus closely for the one period where he diverges from his account in *Or.* 26. Pythagoras, of course, suits his interest here in persecuted philosophers, whereas Thales and Anaximander do not. But the shift also reflects his own choice of philosophical models (285d).[83] Both the list itself, then, and its explicit rationale correspond to the account I reconstructed for Dicaearchus. Here, moreover, Themistius lists Dicaearchus himself among writers (albeit critics of Aristotle) whose works could still be read (285c). The possibility of direct influence is thus clear. One final point increases its probability.

Both Themistius and Diogenes Laertius describe the evolution of philosophy in three stages. Both also recognize crucial differences between philosophy and the gnomic insight of the sages. And both

---

[82] The itinerary (from Samos to Croton, then Locri, Tarentum, and finally Metapontum) matches **41A**. So does the treatment of Cylon, which contradicts Aristotle fr. 191 and Aristoxenus fr. 18; see Burkert (above, n. 39) 117. And the death-scene (in a shrine of the Muses after fasting forty days) follows **41A–B**.

[83] And perhaps the wider audience to which this speech was addressed: both *Or.* 23 and 26 answer the same complaints and were apparently composed about the same time; but the proem of *Or.* 23 addresses the general public, whereas the proem to *Or.* 26 (which seems to refer to 23 as delivered πρώην, 311c) addresses a smaller audience of the learned. For date (357–359) and background, see J. Vanderspoel, *Themistius and the Imperial Court* (Ann Arbor, 1995) 106–11 and 236–40.

knew Dicaearchus' work, at least indirectly.[84] The parallels could be mere coincidence. But another explanation is much more likely. Wehrli collected twenty-three testimonia under the heading περὶ βίων (frr. 25–46, including 35a and b). If we exclude frr. 37–38 = **69**,[85] every item comes from writers who knew the history of philosophy well. Some wrote histories themselves: Diogenes, Porphyry, and Philodemus. The rest had read quite widely: Cicero, Plutarch, Themistius, Gellius, and the author of *On Style* (who cites many lost works of fourth-century philosophy). This striking affinity invites the inference that Dicaearchus' work on the evolution of philosophy long remained both a popular work for serious students of philosophy and a major source for subsequent histories of philosophy. To what extent his "biography of philosophy" influenced these histories, whether by helping define the parameters of philosophy or simply by supplying useful information about its founding fathers, we can no longer tell. But its use by Diogenes and apparently by Themistius, nearly seven centuries after its composition, shows that its influence was lasting.

Two lines of development stand out in the four stages of the "biography of philosophy" that I have ventured to reconstruct. These two strands reflect two related but distinct forms of λόγοι (a term which looms large in the testimony I have examined): first, the degree of articulation and argument; second, types or modes of dis-

---

[84] Besides being our only sources for the analogy with tragedy, they both report the obscure tale of Axiothea (**50**: DL 3.46; cf. Them. *Or.* 23 295c).

[85] **69** recounts Teiresias and Caenis changing sex. Wehrli suspected they figured in Dicaearchus' account of Pythagoras, perhaps to ridicule his claims about prior incarnations (cf. **42**). But neither is ascribed to a specific work and both probably belong elsewhere. The source is Phlegon, who recounted several similar tales (*FGrH* 257 F 36.4–10), but he cites Hesiod in each case, which points to wider poetic traditions. The Hesiodic *Melampodia* (fr. 275), about the legendary prophet whom Herodotus credited with introducing divination into Greece (2.49), told a similar tale about Teiresias; and since **69** provides an *aition* for his powers of divination, it may well come from Dicaearchus' work on that topic (cf. **30–32**). Or Teiresias could have figured in *Life of Greece* (cf. the exegesis of Hesiodic myth in **56A**). That is also a likely source for the tale of Caenis: after changing her sex, she became a proverbially sacrilegious king named Caeneus, whom Theophrastus discussed in *On Kingship* (fr. 600 FHS&G; cf. Hesiod fr. 87, Pindar fr. 128f). Or Dicaearchus may have discussed Caenis/Caeneus in his work on plays for the Dionysia (**99**, cf. **100–4**): two comedies entitled *Caenis* are attested, both from the first half of the fourth century, one by Antiphanes (subject of a monograph by Demetrius of Phaleron, 118 no. 11 SOD) and another (probably later) by Araros, whom Dicaearchus numbered among the sons of Aristophanes (**103**).

course (cf. Them. *Or.* 26 316d–319a). Dicaearchus portrayed all of his paradigms as living virtuous lives; moral virtue he evidently considered an essential part of wisdom. But all of them also exhibit intellectual virtues. The sages acquired a reputation for wisdom not only for the way they lived but also because they helped others live honorably by formulating their insights in memorable maxims and general rules or laws. But their proposals were *disiecta membra* neither explained nor supported by argument, and they remained essentially practical figures. Pythagoras, however, developed a more comprehensive model of conduct, and he sought for the first time to elaborate and promulgate his ideas both in public speeches and in private instruction. His revolutionary way of life, with its new methods of education and study, thus marks the first stage of philosophy. Socrates in turn, whose methodical questioning brought new rigor to moral debates and thoroughly integrated education and conduct, advanced a new conception of wisdom. His way of life also exemplified a new form of its devoted pursuit, and hence a richer form of philosophy. Finally, with the advent of Plato, who established the framework for systematic theory and composed dialogues that converted many to theoretical studies, Dicaearchus found the first "compleat philosopher." That is not to say that he endorsed Platonic doctrines. On the nature and powers of the soul, we know he did not; and we have seen that he criticized Plato for exalting pure theory without regard to its practical applications. Yet he did credit Plato with completing philosophy through the new literary form of his dialogues, his organization of the Academy, and his systematic conception of wisdom.

Dicaearchus did not imagine that Plato or anyone since had discovered a philosophical panacea. Philosophical methods, like sage insights, are always liable to misuse and abuse, and innumerable questions remained for further study. But solutions to specific problems and the accumulation of wider knowledge were not the focus of his "biography of philosophy." Rather, by focusing more narrowly on the pursuit of wisdom itself, he described how philosophy had evolved as a series of thinkers introduced new ways to cultivate learning and virtuous conduct. As an intellectual historian, then, Dicaearchus was neither a triumphalist nor a primitivist, and neither optimist nor pessimist *tout court*. But his account did reveal progress in philosophy. Casting a critical eye over the course of Greek thought, he singled out three pivotal figures; and by describing the strengths and weaknesses of their philosophical methods, he tried to show how each transformed prevailing conceptions of wisdom and enriched the intellectual and educational resources of Greek culture.[86]

[86] I am very grateful for comments and criticism I received at the Colorado Conference and in colloquia at Cornell University and the University of Washington. Special thanks to Tiziano Dorandi for help with Philodemus and to Carl Huffman for help with Pythagorica.

5

Dicaearchus' Historical Anthropology

Trevor J. Saunders

Antecedents

It is a sad paradox that what seems to have been a central theme, or *the* central theme, in the historical anthropology of early and classical Greece survives only in accounts that are either brief, or lacunose, or diluted. I mean the thesis that from some primitive stage mankind has progressed materially, technologically, socially, legally, and morally, *by its own efforts exclusively*, to the point where a civilised life in a *polis* has become possible. A brief source would be a summary in the *Anonymus Iamblichi* (6); a lacunose source would be the pitifully few relevant fragments of Democritus (DK B30, B144, B154). By "diluted" I mean (a) the admixture of gods as givers of resources or skills or virtues as *gifts* to mankind, as in Protagoras' "great speech" in Plato's dialogue of that name; (b) the presence of moral miserabilism, i.e. the theme of moral decay, in spite of, or indeed because of, material and technological progress from initial ignorance and poverty (e.g. in Plato, *Laws* III *ad init.*). That the gods appear *pari passu* with men themselves as the cause of progress is perhaps not too worrying, as "double determination" is common in Greek thought; and in any case the gods can of course always be rationalised: even in the *P.V.*, Prometheus, while

237

claiming to have "given" (446, cf. 506) all crafts etc. to men, consistently says (458, 460, 469, 482, 489, 503) that he "found" or "marked out" or "showed" them, which, if one wants to insist on men's own efforts, betokens at any rate some work in learning. Of miserabilism, often called moral "primitivism," we have only one full-blown example, Hesiod's myth of the five ages/races. In his account, however, mankind's original condition was not hardship but effortless abundance of resources, and the sequential changes in technology are not presented, at least not explicitly, as the *causes* of moral decline; and there is some moral recovery at stage 4, the age of heroes. Hesiod in fact displays a double primitivism, moral and material. It is not, I think, until Diodorus Siculus' celebrated account (I *init.*), in the first century B.C., which draws on heaven knows what sources, that we have a non-fragmentary, full-scale historical anthropology entirely disinfected of gods and primitivism of either kind.

"But," you may protest, "you miss the joker in the pack: Aristotle." The objection is only half true. Aristotle did indeed collect a great deal of material we should now call historical anthropology, as distinct from history political and constitutional, notably in his *Nomima Barbarika*.[1] But so far as we can tell, the material remained raw: it was not systematically exploited to produce a connected and principled anthropology, either progressivist or primitivist or some mixture, from earliest times to his own day. There is nothing comparable to Protagoras' *On the State of Things in the Beginning*—if indeed this work did extend right down to the fifth century.

Nevertheless, Aristotle does write several scattered passages in which he accepts and exploits the *progressivist* tradition:

(i)   In his chapter devoted to Hippodamus, II viii, he asks whether it is desirable to encourage changes in laws. Yes, he says, at least *prima facie*, on the analogy of skills and customs; for they certainly have changed for the better through history, and it would be silly to stick to the quaint practices (he gives examples) of early folk, who were probably rather witless (1268b31–1269a8).

(ii) Similarly, in Book VII (1329b25ff.), he blesses research to discover good constitutional practices, on the analogy of the historical discoveries of things which meet our physical needs and serve our comforts (cf. 1264a1–5, 1331a1–2, *EN* 1098a23–26).

---

[1] For an evaluation, see G. Huxley, "On Aristotle's Historical Methods," *GRBS* 13 (1972) 157–69.

These two passages, and others like them (e.g. fr. 53 Rose), incorporate the assumptions and results of the optimistic tradition of anthropology, which is obviously ready-made for Aristotle's teleology. So too does (iii), the star exhibit, *Pol.* I ii, his celebrated historical description of the growth of human organisation from the primitive pairings through houshold and village to the *polis*. Clearly this constitutes anthropology of a kind; but its focus is essentially political. Aristotle tells how in response to a naturally inbuilt ὁρμή man gradually met, in a series of authority-structures, the totality of his needs and comfort, and achieved "happiness," εὐδαιμονία, in a political framework which allows him to fulfil his complete potentiality as a human being. This brilliant reconstruction is highly schematic and highly selective: specific material conditions, the food supply, technical skills, benefactors, gods—all are either ignored or mentioned only sketchily or by implication. Aristotle does not even tell us *how* men progressed—their state of mind, their experiments and methods, their successes and failures etc.; but it is clear that they did so progress, and by their own efforts. The central point is this: he is not a primitivist in either sense. He believes neither that early men lived a life of material abundance, nor that there was a general moral decline through history. That men often make poor moral judgements and inflict disaster on themselves and others is of course admitted *passim* in his ethical and political works; but that does not make him a primitivist. It is after all integral to his teleology that things can "get in the way" of the final perfection of any process.

The *Bios Hellados*: Problems of Interpretation

So much by way of preliminaries, which I hope are not controversial; at any rate, I shall utilise them as we proceed. It is now time to approach Dicaearchus,[2] and to ask, "what made him *tick*, as an anthropologist?" I am not here enquiring what his sources were: obviously they were many and various, as a skim through the "fragments" will show; indeed, as a collector of information he seems to have been a veritable magpie. In particular, I have not the space to go into the relationship of his historical anthropology to the historical anthropology employed by Theophrastus in his denunciation of animal sacrifice, also reported by

[2] References to Dicaearchus are to the edition of Mirhady, which is Chapter 1 in this volume.

Porphyry, and at vast length. There are important similarities and differences; but here I concentrate on interpreting Dicaearchus alone. Nor do I enquire about the overall economy and structure of his *Life of Greece*. It is clear enough, as we shall see, that it started with a description of the very first men (though how, if at all, it distinguished early Greek men from early other men, is obscure); then it described the life of hunters and shepherds as the next stage, then that of farmers as the next. What course it then took is not so clear. The several passages relating to Oriental cultures make plausible C. Müller's thesis in the last century that before further Greek material there was a consideration of the debt of Greek culture to Oriental (PW 1903 548–49). Reconstruction beyond this point I leave to others.[3]

My central concern is, then, "what controlling assumptions or principles or purposes guided Dicaearchus' narrative?" The question sounds as if it ought to be easy to answer: "*Peripatetic* principles, of course." But the plain fact is that we simply do not know whether Aristotle's optimistic teleology was some sort of orthodoxy in the writing of history by Peripatetics when Dicaearchus was at work. Were there really Peripatetic *canons* of historiography? Even if there were, was Dicaearchus attempting to conform to them, or to modify them, or to pursue some independent line? Was he, even, a primitivist of some kind? E. R. Dodds certainly supposed so: he speaks of his having "idealised early man in a way which would surely have surprised [his] master," and of a decisive "shift of value judgement."

In fact, in the fairly few studies that have been made of the *Bios Hellados* there is a pronounced but not universal tendency to take passage **56A** at face value, as evidence that Dicaearchus was indeed precisely that: a primitivist.[4] I shall argue that this view of him is mistaken.

---

[3] See W. Ax's paper in this volume.
[4] E. R. Dodds, *The Ancient Concept of Progress* (Oxford, 1973) 16–17. Cf. E. Passamonti, "Dicearco di Messina: Nota di E. P., presentata dal S. Ferri," *Rendiconti della Reale Accademia dei Lincei* 208, IV 7 (1891) 243; A. O. Lovejoy and G. Boas, *Primitivism and Related Ideas in Antiquity* (Baltimore, 1935) 93–96; F. Wehrli, *Die Schule des Aristoteles*, vol. 1 (Basel, 1944) 56; B. Gatz, *Weltalter, goldene Zeit und sinnverwandte Vorstellungen* (Hildesheim, 1967) 156–57; L. Edelstein, *The Idea of Progress in Classical Antiquity* (Baltimore, 1967) 134–35, 139; G. Bodei Giglioni, "Dicearco e la riflessione sul passato," *Riv. Stor. Ital.* 98 (1986) 629–52. Agnostic: F. C. Seeliger in Roscher's *Lexicon*, vi 409. Critical of Porphyry's reliability: E. Graf, *Ad aureae aetatis fabulam symbola*, Leipz. Stud. z. Class. Philol. 8 (1885) 45–47.

56A: Structure and Theme

Of the many pieces which could with more or less reason be printed under the title *Bios Hellados*, the following are relevant for our purposes: **53**, the first half of **54, 55, 56A–B**, and **58**. The most important is **56A**. It comprises most of Porphyry, *De Abstinentia* IV 2. Wehrli omits the chapter's opening sentence and its last two; but he ought to have printed the whole of it, with IV 1 as well. For IV 1 outlines Porphyry's purposes in IV 2, and tells us why it takes the shape it does; and the final two sentences of IV 2 betray the *parti pris* with which it is written.

The formal or technical status of **56A** is far from clear. Porphyry presents the whole thing as Dicaearchus' own account; he says φησί in lines 6 and 43 and ἀφηγούμενος and ἐξηγούμενος in lines 5 and 51; of Dicaearchus' methods he says he wrote "succinctly and accurately," that he "collected" material, and that he "went through it." But nothing in the passage tells us anything about the degree, if any, to which Porphyry is quoting directly, nor about the degree to which the passage is summary, abridgement, selection, rewriting, insertion, or expansion. Note that, at the end of his account in 584A of Theophrastus (i.e., at *de Abst.* II 32 iii), Porphyry admits to having made certain additions and abbreviations to Theophrastus' text. One wonders, but cannot know, what liberties he has taken in **56A** of Dicaearchus (cf. below, n. 9).

At this point it will be useful to clear up a point of punctuation and translation, in lines 15–16. In his line 9, Wehrli prints a full stop, and Patillon and Segonds, in the recent Budé text, print a semi-colon. But that leaves εἰ δεῖ . . . ἀνάγειν as a long protasis in dire need of an apodosis. Surely a mere comma is needed (adequately translated by "-" in the Budé), and εἰ = εἴπερ, "since it is the case that" [we have to interpret myth in historical and rational terms].[5]

In IV 1 Porphyry undertakes to pursue what he calls certain "particular" or "specialised" enquiries, notably (i) into the belief that there is benefit to be gained from eating meat, and (ii) into the thesis that no race, and no wise individual, has ever rejected the practice. It is impor-

[5] In what tone of voice is εἰ δεῖ to be said? Grudgingly? ". . . if one *has* to rationalise this fanciful material, the only material we have for this early period, it being impossible to use it in any other way, since it is clearly unhistorical as it stands?" But grudgingly or not, Dicaearchus evidently accepts the obligation, so "since" seems natural. "If" would leave open the possibility that rationalisation might *not* be necessary.

tant to realise that his purpose, in interpreting Dicaearchus' text, is restricted to finding evidence contrary to these two propositions. He is not interested in the wider question, which *we* ask, "was Dicaearchus a primitivist or a progressivist?" If he had wanted to present him as an out-and-out primitivist, he would scarcely have allowed to survive in his account of him some fairly strong progressivist points which he evidently found in his text; or he would have at least explained them away. But he is wholly indifferent to them, as we shall see.

56A is articulated on the basis of the three historical stages in the food-supply of the Greek race: (A, lines 5–38) the Golden Age, in which men simply ate the spontaneous produce of the earth, without having to labour for it; (B, 39–47) the pastoral stage, characterised by mastery of animals, and the eating of their flesh, which I take to be implied by "laid hands on" (ἥψαντο, 28); and (C, 47–49) the agricultural stage. It is immediately obvious, from the length and elaboration of A, that it is the Golden Age that primarily interests Porphyry; for a high proportion of the description of A is devoted to the technicalities of certain features of B, which were absent from A: he is keen to establish that A did not have certain disbenefits of later stages. Only when he has done that, does he formally enumerate B, at 39, ὕστερον. So in a sense it would be possible to regard B (and C, come to that: note γεωργικήν in 20) as starting as early as 19, with οὐ γάρ.

This basic threefold development in terms of the source of the food-supply is surely genuinely Dicaearchean, and as far as I can tell it is original to him. Jerome attributes stage A to him in **56B** (on what evidence?), Varro B and C in **55**; and the full scheme is attributed to him by Varro in **54**–but with very different emphases.[6] That fragment states, indeed, that the earth's produce emerged spontaneously; but we hear nothing of the *goldenness* or ideality of stage A (it is simply termed "natural"), nothing about Hesiod and how to interpret myth, nothing about the later adoption of meat-eating, nothing about the illnesses thus induced, and nothing about the growth in possessions, competition, injustice, and warfare. Primitivism, if such there was in Dicaearchus, has been filtered out. Varro's chief concern is to dwell on the *dignitas* possessed by the pastoral life, which for that reason was evidently *better*

---

[6] Cf. the perceptive account in B. Reischl, *Reflexe griechischer Kulturenentstehungslehren bei augusteischen Dichtern*, Diss. Ludwig – Maximilians Universität München (1976) 90–96 of Varro's relationship to Dicaearchus.

than the "natural" one; and this he does at length. In sum, the interpretation he puts on Dicaearchus is progressivist.

It is significant that Varro mentions two things we would have assumed anyway, but which have largely dropped out of Porphyry's report: (a) the non-lethal use of animals for their milk, and for their exteriors, as in shearing sheep, for clothing (though of course the use of actual skin does involve the animal's death).[7] Porphyry's account is skewed, because he is overwhelmingly concerned with meat-eating; the nearest he gets to the other uses of animals is in 29–30. (b) The notion that the historical sequence is not a series of discrete stages, but that B retains elements of A, and C elements of both. This progressivist point is made explicitly by Varro in **54** (cf. the progressivist *utilitas*), but only vaguely by Porphyry in **56A**: by "noticing" what was "useful" men arrived at stage C. Porphyry, anxious to dwell on the bodily ills and on the moral and social decline caused by meat-eating, inevitably mutes the idea of material progress; but he does not eliminate it. In view of all this, it becomes difficult to regard Dicaearchus as a primitivist across the board.[8] For can a primitivist believe, as Dicaearchus evidently does, that initally man did not have enough to eat, and that later he won greater material resources by "noticing" what was "useful"?

56A: Rationalisation of the Golden Age

I now turn to the crucial sentences at the start of **56A**, down to line 9, ἔμψυχον. Their core theme is: "Dicaearchus says the ancients slaughtered no living thing." One must, I think, accept that as a genuinely Dicaearchean position, though whether it had a Pythagorean inspiration, and whether he dwelt on it with Porphyry's messianic zeal, is much less certain—indeed wholly improbable, in my view, or Porphyry

[7] Graf (above, n. 4) 46 argues that "touch, laid hands on" (**56A**.40) is a clever piece of ambiguity on Porphyry's part: *tangere / pro cibo uti,* only the former practices (taming etc.) being found (in whatever words) in Dicaearchus.

[8] My respondent, Teun Tieleman, argues that *summum* (**54**.7) must be evaluative: "highest in rank." But surely it has the same meaning as in *summa memoria* in line 5 ("as far back as memory goes"), and is merely chronological: "remotest in time." Similarly *secundam* (*vitam*) in 8, *tertio* in 16, and *superioribus* in 18 simply mark the stages of an historical sequence. The word *descendere*, which appears four times, is also purely chronological; it does not signify any sort of decline; cf. Reischl (above, n. 5) 93 (*summus gradus* = "die erste Stufe," 95).

would have reported as much,[9] probably at some length. Further, if Dicaearchus did not believe in the immortality, or even the existence, of the soul, how could he have espoused a Pythagorean-style disapproval of meat-eating?[10] And for what it is worth (very little), in **87** he reports meat-eating at Sparta without disapproval. At the very least, however, the absence of meat-eating from stage A is a sound inference from what is evidently his belief in the rest of the piece, namely that it is only in stage B, the pastoral life, that animals were conquered. But caution is needed. The quotation from the *Works and Days* does not say explicitly that meat-eating was absent from the Golden Age (and indeed the possibly spurious line 120 mentions flocks); one has to infer it, on the assumption that the quotation describes the *only* mode of food-getting in that age. I assume that the inference is Dicaearchus' inference, and that the point has been highlighted by Porphyry for his own purposes.

The core theme is much elaborated by a fulsome description of the excellence of the ancients' way of life, and a comparison between them and men of the present day. Most of the account is a single sentence, long, highly participial, and confusing. The main verb is φησί, and a string of participles intervenes before the infinitive in indirect speech, μηδὲν φονεύειν ἔμψυχον. The other infinitive, νομίζεσθαι, is to be taken, unavoidably I think, with ὡς in the sense of ὥστε; and the two following participles belong to that consecutive construction: παραβαλλομένους are the ancients, ὑπάρχοντας the moderns. There is a tangle of problems. First, what is the nuance of καί before ἐγγύς? The recent Budé, citing Plato, *Philebus* 16C, takes it as epexegetic/consequential: "de ce fait, proches des dieux": "ancient *and so* in virtue of this fact born near gods." Ancientness, on this view, *entails* being born near gods. The Budé translation then effectively inserts a further καί in front of βελτίστους, and treats the τε . . . καί clause as merely two further items in a list of the ancients' attributes. Or perhaps the editors took the τε itself as linking on to what went before: "the ancients and therefore born near gods and best by nature and livers of the best life." It is hard to know.

But there is another way of taking καί and the τε . . . καί clause: ". . . says that the ancients were born actually/in fact close to gods, *in virtue*

---

[9] Cf. M. Patillon and A. Ph. Segonds, *Porphyre, De l'Abstinence* = Budé ed., t. III, livre IV (Paris, 1995) xiv–xv.

[10] Cf. Graf (above, n. 4) 45.

of being best by nature and livers of the best life . . . ." That is, the τε . . . καί clause is by way of giving *a reason* for the claim "born near gods"; and the historical consequences of that reason are then elaborated at length, starting with ὡς. For καί as "actually" see Denniston *Greek Particles* s.v., II C: it calls attention to something a little surprising or even crucial, which is then justified by the τε . . . καί clause. Exploiting the explanatory function of brackets, I translate: "In presenting the ancient life of the Greeks he says that the men of old were born actually close to gods (they were best by nature and lived the best life, so that they are regarded as a golden race when compared with men of today, who are made of adulterated and low-grade matter), and killed no living thing." This is of course tendentious; but so is any translation of such awkward and ambiguous Greek.

On the face of it, Dicaearchus makes four claims about the ancients:

(i)   that precisely in virtue *either* of their ancientness *or* of their nature etc., they were born "near" gods, either chronologically or in some other sense;
(ii)   that they were best by nature;
(iii) that they lived the best life;
(iv)   that they were constituted of better "matter" than men of the present day.

But for two complementary sets of reasons, one set negative and the other positive, I am sceptical that such claims can be those of Dicaearchus himself. Negatively, in the mouth of a pupil of Aristotle they are very strange indeed. (i) Dicaearchus evidently believed the species man is eternal: it has no beginning, but has existed always (see **53**, which attests a Peripatetic orthodoxy on the matter). In what sense, then, can the ancients be "born," except from men even more ancient? There cannot, despite what **56A** says in line 36, have been any men who were *first*, literally—though the meaning *could* be "the first we are considering." And how can men of an early era be "close to," i.e., presumably "clos*er* to" gods than men of a later era, chronologically? All men of any era look equally "close to" the gods. Or perhaps "close to the *birth* of the gods" is meant. If that is so, how can the moral qualitites of one era differ from those of another, in so far as those qualities depend on men's being ancient or modern, and so in a different relationship to the *birth* of the gods? These obscurities may be brushed aside, however, if "near gods" is taken to have no real or functional or chronological reference to gods, and to be only a way of saying "very virtuous." That would indeed point to a plain primitivistic thesis of a moral kind, perhaps unlikely in a Peripatetic, but still possible in one of an independent turn of mind. But even then there are awkward questions to ask, e.g., "what accounts for the transition to stage B occurring at one time and not another?"

Claims (ii) and (iii), that the ancients were best by nature and lived the best life, are mysterious. For can a Peripatetic claim that whole generations of men can have different φύσεις, as distinct from acquired social and moral characteristics? Individuals certainly can: one man's natural endowments fit him to be a master, and another's fit him to be a slave (*Pol.* I vi etc.). Aristotle's own description of early men as "witless," *if* it is a reference to their φύσις, rather than to their acquired knowledge and skills (surely the more probable reference), would nevertheless presuppose an *improvement* in φύσις across the generations, whereas Dicaearchus' text here assumes a deterioration. Or perhaps Dicaearchus means, by "best nature" and "best life," moral simplicity or lack of corrupt sophistication (cf. Plato, *Laws* 679C), or even "ignorance is bliss" (cf. **32**)—but that is again simply not Aristotelian. As for the "best life" itself, it is of course, according to Aristotle, life based on moderate, not meagre, resources, lived by a citizen in a *polis*, an institution which obviously early man did not have. Specifically, I ask again, can the "best" life be one in which you do not have enough to eat?

(iv) The notion that different generations of men are constituted from different "matter" seems to me equally fishy. Is there *any* sense in which it could be consistent with Aristotle's biology? Does "matter" mean menstrual fluid? Dicaearchus' point *might* be that the superior diet of early human beings caused superior *menses* in their women. That would be very interesting; but it is a great deal to squeeze from the text.

To turn to my positive reasons, and to pull out of the hat the rabbit whose ears have no doubt long been visible, claims (i)–(iv) make fine sense if they are taken to be, in plain and sober prose, reports and summaries of features of Hesiod.[11] (i) "Ancient and near gods" I take to be a reproduction, using the same verb, γίγνομαι, of Hesiod's own attempt to locate the origin of early men (*WD* 108): ὡς ὁμόθεν γεγάασι θεοὶ θνητοί τ' ἄνθρωποι, i.e, they were "near" gods in that they lived the same kind of life in early times. This is followed immediately by a description of how the gods had *created* (110) the first men, the golden race, who then lived *like* gods (ὥστε θεοί 112), in the time of Cronus,

[11] Graf (above, n. 4) 45.

i.e., in the Golden Age. The Phoenicians of the *Odyssey* are also "near-gods" (V 35, ἀγχίθεοι, and VII 205). Ἐγγὺς θεῶν is simply a prose version of that.[12] As for (ii) and (iii), the men of Hesiod's Golden Age obviously were indeed best in nature and lived the best life of the five he enumerates. The clincher is (iv): the "matter" is obviously the iron in the constitution of the men of today and κίβδηλος "counterfeit," while it can be used in a moral sense, is precisely the adjective used to describe inferior metal, especially coins. And ὕλη is of course just the word a Peripatetic would instinctively use in reference to the basic stuff from which something is made.

You may reasonably ask, "So what?" Dicaearchus "relates" this stuff, and "says" it: he must therefore be committed to primitivism, and prays Hesiod in aid. But the point is absurdly simple. If I relate to you the story of Adam and Eve and the tree of knowledge in the Garden of Eden, in my own and not biblical style, and you repeat or summarise it for me, prefacing it by identifying its immediate source by the words "you say," that is literally accurate; but you do not (I trust) mean to imply that I believe it.[13] Pretty obviously, in the text which Porphyry has in front of him, Dicaearchus is engaging in the old game, a constant habit of the Master, of assuming that myth and poetry, as well as common reputable opinions, ἔνδοξα, and the work of early philosophers, contain some kernel of truth, which one often proceeds to winkle out (lines 35–38 have another instance of the same thing). But plainly you cannot do that without referring to or summarising or quoting the author you propose to interpret. It therefore looks as if Dicaearchus first summarised, in his own words and concepts, Hesiod's myth of the five ages, with special reference to the Golden Age, and then quoted the three and a half lines relating to his special interest, the food supply. And he inserted, in lines

[12] Some simplification could be achieved by taking γεγονότας (**56A**, line 6) as simply "were," rather than "(having been) *born*"; but that would lose a reference, surely probable enough, to Hesiod's account of the *creation* of men.

[13] Indeed, "he says" in Porphyry guarantees nothing: the whole of the long first sentence of **56A** could at an extreme be mere Porphyrean *invention*, justified only by Dicaearchus' citation of Hesiod. Consider the medley of quotation, paraphrase, and exegesis of Plato *Theaetetus* 173C–174A, at I 37, which has φησί *ter* (cf. J. Bernays, *Theophrastus' Schrift über Frömmigkeit* [Berlin, 1866]; W. Pötscher, *Theophrastos ΠΕΡΙ ΕΥΣΕΒΕΙΑΣ* [Leiden, 1964] 1–14; and J. Bouffartigue and M. Patillon, *Porphyre, De l'Abstinence*, Budé ed., t. I, livre I [1977] xxv–xxxvii, on Porphyry's general handling of his sources). On the other hand, the quasi-technical ὕλη does suggest that in **56A** Porphyry did have a source, a Peripatetic one.

36–38, the point that this story of the Golden Age is the *historical explanation* why men of today think (wrongly, as it turns out) that the life of early man was bliss compared to their own.

What Dicaearchus means to achieve is to present the life of early men as autarkic, a good thing in Aristotle's political philosophy, but to present it as only minimally autarkic. Porphyry, to whom abstention from meat is wonderful and highly desirable, is anxious to find an authority that will justify placing it in a wonderful and highly desirable context—a *godlike* autarkic life (cf. *Eudemian Ethics* 1244b8, 1249b16). By accident or design he writes in such a way as to give the impression that Dicaearchus too so placed it.

At any rate, Porphyry himself, in lines 15ff., makes very clear that Dicaearchus does not endorse Hesiod at face value. In fact, in this line we pass from narrative, ἀφηγούμενος, to interpretation, ἐξηγούμενος. The pivotal term, whether it be Dicaearchus' *ipsissimum verbum* or Porphyry's summary, is τοιοῦτον. The right nuance would be caught by translating, "after that fashion," "of that ilk," or "in that category," or "has similarities to." The word's essential purpose is to introduce a restriction: Dicaearchus' ancients lived a life in some important respect or respects *like* that of Hesiod's, but not in all respects like it. Each is an autarkic life, in which food is simply "there" for the taking, and men have no toil or trouble. But Hesiod's men live a life of luxury, whereas Dicaearchus' do not, as emerges later. The two lives are species of a single genus, the autarkic. The restriction is made necessary by the methodology I have outlined, which is set out for us in lines 16–17: ". . . since one has on the one hand to take it [life under Cronus] as having happened[14] and as not having received a pointless name, but on the other to jettison the excessively mythical element and reduce it to natural terms by means of reason." And an example of what he means by reason occurs immediately: claiming, very much in the traditional

---

[14] Teun Tieleman interestingly suggests, as an "educated guess," that Dicaearchus is here engaging in Euhemerism: Cronus was an historical ideal king (cf. **58**), later treated as a god by Hesiod, whose beneficent and happy reign is now rationalised by Dicaearchus. But that does nothing to make Dicaearchus a primitivist: he himself cannot have supposed such a reign to have led to a life of felicity, since lines 28–29 tell us that men did not have enough to eat. Tieleman also notices, though he sees that nothing would hinge on the point, that technically αὐτόν in line 16 could refer to Cronus, not to the βίος under him. But in that case, why the ado about naming? That the Golden Age was in *some* respect (rudimentary autarky) appositely called golden, is relevant; but that Cronus was appositely called Cronus would in this context be a mysterious claim.

progressivist manner, that early men did not "yet" have either the skill of farming or any other, and so could not have got their food that way, he reasons reasonably (εἰκότως, cf. 35); that *since* they survived nevertheless (cf. Euripides, *Suppl.* 199–200), they must have got it in some other fashion, by just taking what (little) emerged spontaneously. Hesiod's text is simply a mythical and idealised description of that mode of life.[15]

The Medical Connection

Dicaearchus now makes an easy transition from a lack of toil to a lack of disease. His argument, if Porphyry reports him correctly, is again inferential. In stage A, precisely because there could have been no over-eating, or eating of foods "stronger than nature," *therefore* no περιττώματα, "excesses" or "residues," which (*inter alia?*) cause disease, could have arisen. Who are the "most finished" doctors?[16] It seems certain that they do not include Hippocrates; at any rate the term περίττωμα occurs nowhere in that corpus. But it is prominent in Aristotle's biological works (see the masterly summary in A. L. Peck's Loeb edition of the *Generation of Animals*, pp. 65–67). To simplify, residues are what is left over (*GA* 724b26) after the processes of digestion and nourishment are complete, or left incomplete because of some defect in the food. Some residues are natural and useful (e.g. semen and menstrual fluid); others are useless, and are excreted; but others again are actually harmful, and can in divers ways cause disease—though

[15] *Pace* W. K. C. Guthrie, *In the Beginning* (London, 1957) 76, Dicaearchus is not really concerned to "*accommodate* [my italics] an essentially romantic and poetic view of the state of early man to the more realistic theories." His procedure is to cut it down to size, by isolating and *reinterpreting* its one element of truth: autarky. That is not to *accommodate* romance; it is to kill it. As Guthrie himself puts it in the same sentence, he gives us "the Golden Age stretched almost to breaking point."

[16] The "sophisticated" (χαρίεντες) doctors in Aristotle (e.g. *Div. Somn.* 463a3–7) seem to be those whose methods are not simply empirical, but who study medicine in the wider context of natural science (P. J. van der Eijk, "Aristotle on 'Distinguished Physicians' and on the Medical Signficance of Dreams," in *Ancient Medicine in its Socio-Cultural Contest*, vol. II, eds. P. J. v. d. E., H. F. J. Horstmanshoff, P. H. Schrijvers [Amsterdam, 1995] 447–57). Obviously the same point could be conveyed by "most finished," γλαφυρώτατοι: these doctors relate health to dietetics (cf. Hipp. *Reg.* I ii). On the other hand, in a socio-political context, "finished" seems to mean "exact, neat, delicate, elaborate (laws etc.)," like a spider's web (see Aristotle *HA* 623a8ff., *Pol.* 1271b20ff., 1274b7–8; T. J. Saunders, *Aristotle, Books I and II*, translated with a commentary [Oxford, 1995] 158–59). The point may then be that Dicaearchus' doctors distinguish *multiple* causes of περιττώματα; see below.

there is less evidence for this latter point than one would expect: I am aware of only seven passages, three in the *Problems* (out of many, apparently[17]), one in *On Sleeping and Waking*, one in *On Length of Life*, but two in the *GA* itself (725a4ff., 738a27–33)—and of course our present passage, for what it is worth.

What, then, is going on in our present passage? It has in common with ch. III of *On Ancient Medicine* the notion of a kind of fight between the constitution of the body and the food it ingests: "strong" food apparently overcomes the strength of the digestive process (cf. *On Plants* 822a25ff.), and causes illness. Thus far, one could ascribe to Dicaearchus a conflation of Hippocratic and Peripatetic thought: περιττώματα are the intermediate step between poor digestion and disease. But Anonymus Londinensis (V 37ff.) attributes the same conflation to Hippocrates himself, with the additional point that the residues give rise to breaths, φῦσαι, the immediate cause of disease—and all this, allegedly, on the authority of Aristotle. A little later, however, Anonymus claims (VII 37ff.) that these opinions were *not* the opinions of Hippocrates.

Now it is commonly supposed that Anonymus is reproducing, or at least summarising, the work of one Meno, who according to Galen compiled a collection of medical opinions, which was labelled as being by Aristotle (who, one assumes, supervised its production). Anonymus may then have been available to Dicaearchus. But the common story is very likely wrong:[18] Manetti throws strong doubt on the relevance of Meno, and argues, from a close inspection of the papyrus, that Anonymus wrote in the first century A.D. In that case, we are simply left guessing at Dicaearchus' sources: "wide reading in Aristotle and Hippocrates" will be as much as one could say.

However, to hedge my bets, let me adopt briefly the usual hypothesis about Anonymus' date. *If* he wrote about the end of the fourth century B.C., and *if* he drew on Meno, and *if* Dicaearchus had one or both of them in front of him, then knowing περιττώματα to be Aristotelian, and being in no better position than we to see through the fog Anon./Meno/Aristotle/Hippocrates (not to mention Euryphon and Herodicus, both of Cnidos, who also believed in residues, IV 20ff., as well as the Hippo-

---

[17] Van der Eijk, ibid. 53 n. 57.
[18] See D. Manetti, "Note di Lettera dell' Anonimo Londinese," *ZPE* 63 (1986) 57–74, cf. 83 (1990) 219–33; Id. "Autografi e incompiuti: il caso dell' Anonimo Londinese, P. Lit. Lond. 165," *ZPE* 100 (1994) 47–59.

cratic Dexippus of Cos, XII 14, and Aegimius, XIII 18), he blandly and discreetly described his medical authority as "the most finished doctors." At any rate, Dicaearchus' *elaboration* (see note 15 above) of the causes of residues may derive from Anonymus, who (V 39ff.) lists three features of food that are productive of περιττώματα: (i) (excess) quantity, (ii) variety, (iii) "strength," i.e., resistance to digestion. Of these Dicaearchus certainly has the first and last; and if "enough of the acorn" in line 37 indicates that monotony as well as frugality of diet disappeared in stage B, he has all three. There are, then, *two* possible points of contact between Dicaearchus and Anonymus: the "conflation" of thought about the role of περιττώματα, and the plurality of their causes.

Far more important, however, is the *use* Dicaearchus makes of his medical material.[19] The treatise *On Ancient Medicine*, which so far as I know is the only other work to give an extended treatment to medicine in an historical anthropology, finds its origin in dietetics. It posits that early men had the same diet as animals: the produce of the earth, fruits, wood, grass. In spite of their being inured to such a diet, raw, unmixed, and having great "powers," they suffered grievously, and in time, by trial and error, they arrived at the diet suitable for their nature—by e.g. grinding, kneading, and baking wheat; and medicine prescribes such practices in the promotion of health. Dicaearchus himself says nothing about medicine (or perhaps Porphyry edited that theme out of his text); but he inverts the sequence of events. The disease-free stage is the "interpreted" Golden Age, and it is now stage B that contains the unsuitable "strong" foods, conspicuously meat, presumably, that cause disease. What happened at stage C is not clear; but if we put γεωργικήν (20) together with γεωργικόν (49), we might suppose that the farming life too generated illness through bad diet. Does not all this, then, amount to a primitivist account of dietetics and disease?

I think not. I believe Dicaearchus' dietetics are teleological, like Aristotle's. In *Politics* I viii and ix Aristotle gives a long account of various modes of obtaining food, including the pastoral and the agricultural, Dicaearchus' stages B and C. He proceeds, however, ahistorically: at the present day all modes are practised simultaneously, some by some people and some by others, and different combinations of them by different people, in accordance with suitability and in response to necessity. Yet some historical reference is perhaps implicit in his account; for

---

[19] P. H. Schrijvers, "Intertextualité et polémique dans le *De Rerum Natura* (V 925–1010); Lucrèce vs Dicéarque de Messene," *Philologus* 138 (1994) 288–304.

"response to necessity" is of course a key concept in progressivist his-torical anthropology. However that may be, Aristotle draws a parallel (1256b7ff.) between nature's provision of food to species and her supply of it to the *individuals* of each species. In the latter case, there are two stages: that in which nature supplies food gratuitously, before the as yet young animal can fend for itself (mother's milk in the case of human be-ings and other mammals), and that in which she "supplies" food (fruits, crops, etc.) for it to acquire for itself later. It does not take much extrapo-lation from that *schema* to suppose that the species man also must have had a stage when food was supplied for it gratuitously, when it was not yet able to fend for itself by mastery of the skills of exploiting animals and agriculture. This is, I hazard, the point of Dicaearchus' stage A: it is the first step in a teleological progression; skills, as he says, come later. Perhaps he regarded his own *sequential* account of the food supply as superseding Aristotle's own ahistorical one and wished to present the βίος of the species on the model of the βίος of the individual.

In *Pol.* I x medicine takes its place without special remark beside the art of acquisition as one skill providing a good, namely health. But the recognition of that which calls for medicine, namely disease, does not make Aristotle a primitivist. On the contrary, he is aware that there has been progress in medicine (1268b35ff.). Similarly, to suppose that dis-ease arose at stage B, when men were unused to meat, and ate it raw, and/or too much of it, does not make a primitivist of Dicaearchus. Any disadvantage at any stage will make the preceding stage, when it was absent, look better; and Dicaearchus, unless he was quite unscrupu-lously selective, cannot have failed to acknowledge the rise of medicine, along with the other skills. In fact, his own medical passage in **56A** is at once diagnosis and remedy. It is Porphyry again, who has stressed the evils of stage B, to the exclusion of the remedies, in order to make the non-meat-eating stage A look ideal.

Moral and Social Questions

I have left little space to deal with the development of strife in stage B and presumably C. Dicaearchus' story, if indeed the glowing account in line 33 is his own words and not Porphyry's rhetoric, is that in stage A the low level of resources, and the lack of need to work to obtain them,

[20] Guthrie (above, n. 15) 76.

entailed peace and friendship; it was only when resources increased to the stage where they were worth competing for that strife arose (cf. Plato, *Laws* 679B7–C2). There is something charmingly quaint about this; and it is easy to make the point, as Guthrie (above, n. 15) 76 in effect does, that one can as readily quarrel about a berry as about a banquet. (Read carefully, however, 30–32, esp. τοσαύτην, may leave open the possiblity of minor dispute even in the Golden Age; cf. also **57**.) Yet Dicaearchus' *schema* is not unintelligent. His point, I conceive, is an intellectual one. So long as one's conception of need is only of basic need, and all one's basic needs are met automatically (this is the hypothesis of the Golden Age), then one does not compete for more. But the resources of that age, it seems, though sufficient for survival, leisure and friendship, were not abundant; they could indeed be scarce. One had no need to compete for necessities, but more than necessities was not available; life was frugal (cf. Theophrastus 584A line 26). Men somehow began then to distinguish between sufficient and more than sufficient; note ἐφιεμένοις (34): in stage B they "aimed at" or "desired" great things—and before one can aim at or desire something one has to have a certain conception of it; note also κατανοοῦντες (48), the conception of the means useful to getting more than the basic resources of the Golden Age. It is not difficult to imagine how the need for effort, absent during that age, led to competition, strife, and war.

All this has some parallel in the anthropology of Aristotle himself. In *Pol.* I ii *init.* the household was founded to satisfy "daily needs," the village for "more than daily needs"; and he has an intellectualising explanation of the desire to obtain great wealth. In I viii–ix he distinguishes (i) *natural* modes of acquisition, i.e., taking what nature offers, by farming etc., and exchanging the produce for other produce to meet local shortages; (ii) *un*natural modes, i.e., trade and usury. What makes the difference between natural and unnatural is sufficiency and more than sufficiency: the natural kinds aim to supply goods sufficient for life, the unnatural ones to gain unlimited wealth, by false analogy with skills such as medicine, whose aim is to produce unlimited health. These distinctions, retrojected into the remote past in an account of the food supply, could have been Dicaearchus' broad inspiration. I suggest, therefore, that his account of the origin of greed and war is far more respectable, and peripatetically orthodox, than the version we get of it in Porphyry.

As for greed, **58** has a report that Sesonchosis (Sesostris, a king of Egypt) laid down a law that no one should desert his father's τέχνη; for he took this to be the start of πλεονεξία. Does "start" mean we have to locate this law in stage B, where πλεονεξία did apparently arise? It seems to presuppose, like στάσεις (30), some kind of structured society; but a structured society is not the focus of **56A**.

Conclusion

I conclude briefly. Having navigated as best I can the twin reefs of our ignorance—the degree of Dicaearchus' Aristotelianism, and the degree of trust we may place in Porphyry's report of him—I judge Dicaearchus to be certainly not a primitivist, glorifying a life of hardy but bare subsistence; but neither is he a progressivist across the board. Rather he is what I would call an *ironic* progressivist,[21] who sounds quite modern. More men have been killed by attacks by men, he claims in **78**, than by any other calamity. We nowadays, who are acutely aware that, e.g., successful drugs are all too apt to have side-effects, or that increased longevity produces demographic problems, must respond sympathetically to Dicaearchus' belief that a better food-supply generated disease, and that greater material resources, far from satisfying men, led to war between them.[22] In short, what impresses me most about Dicaearchus' historical anthropology is his keen sense of irony and paradox.

This paper was read to the Conference of Project Theophrastus at Boulder in September 1995, and subsequently to the North Eastern Classical Research Seminar at Newcastle upon Tyne. I am grateful to members of both audiences for fruitful comments and suggestions, and especially to my respondent at Boulder, Dr. Teun Tieleman.

---

[21] Cf. Reischl (above, n. 5), who uses the term "ambivalente Aszendenz," and J. Haussleiter, *Der Vegetarismus in der Antike* (Berlin, 1935) 62–63.

[22] Notice also the irony in "the same life" (43), if indeed these words are Dicaearchus', and not part of a tendentious report by Porphyry, designed to link meat-eating and war; cf. the penultimate sentence of IV 2, and Budé (above, n. 9) xv, following Graf (above, n. 4) 46; also Budé (above, n. 13) xxx. R. Hirzel, ΑΓΡΑΦΟΣ ΝΟΜΟΣ, Abh. d. K. S. Ges. d. Wiss., Phil.-hist. cl. 20.1 (Leipzig, 1903) 88 detects irony in Dicaearchus' description of the Golden Age.

6

Dikaiarchs Βίος Ἑλλάδος und die
Philosophie des vierten Jahrhunderts

Eckart Schütrumpf

Nach einer weit verbreiteten Deutung[1] beschrieb Dikaiarch in seinem Βίος Ἑλλάδος[2] das Leben der Menschen der Frühzeit in einer idealisierenden Weise und vertrat damit einen Primitivismus, der sich so schlecht mit dem Fortschrittsdenken seines Lehrers[3] zu vertragen scheint. Demgegenüber hat sich T. Saunders[4] gegen eine simple Deutung dieser Schrift des Dikaiarch als primitivistisch ausgesprochen. Er argumentiert, daß gewisse ihm von Porphyrios, dem Gewährsmann des ausführlichsten Berichtes, zugeschriebene Auffassungen eher mit Vorsicht zu benutzen seien; bestimmte Annahmen des Dikaiarch über Kulturentwicklung seien auch mit peripatetischen Grundüberzeugungen unvereinbar; er weist ihm daher eine paradoxe oder

---

[1] Z. B. H. Schwabl, "Zum antiken Zeitaltermythos und seiner Verwendung als historiographisches Modell," *Klio* 66 (1984) 405–15, 411.

[2] Für die Fragmente dieses Werkes s. **53–77**. Der Titel ist bezeugt in **1** no.7a–f.

[3] S. E. Schütrumpf, *Aristoteles Politik,* Buch II–III, übersetzt und erläutert, in *Aristoteles Werke in Deutscher Übersetzung,* Bd. 9, Teil II (Berlin und Darmstadt, 1991) Anm. zu II 5 1264a2.

[4] Dicaearchus' Historical Anthropology, dieser Band S. 237–54.

ironische[5] Einstellung zum Fortschritt zu. Saunders hatte nicht
beansprucht, die Quellen Dikaiarchs zu untersuchen, und nur einzelne
ausgewählte Aspekte des uns erhaltenen Werkes, besonders die
medizinischen Vorstellungen, zu zeitgenössischem Gedankengut in
Beziehung gestellt. Einige der Probleme, die ihm schwer lösbar
erscheinen (z.b. S. 245), erklären sich jedoch leicht oder erledigen sich
völlig vor dem Hintergrund der bei Dikaiarch vorausgesetzten
Vorstellungen, die wir bei Denkern des vierten Jahrhunderts finden.
Klarheit über die Deutung der Gedanken und Absicht des Dikaiarch läßt
sich eher gewinnen, wenn man in umfassenderer Weise seine Tendenz,
die Methodik und die Auswahl der von ihm berücksichtigten
Erscheinungen in die Tradition oder zeitgenössische Diskussion um
Fortschritt stellt und von anderen Äußerungen besonders des vierten
Jahrhunderts zu den gleichen oder verwandten Fragen abgrenzt. Ein
solcher Ansatz soll hier verfolgt werden.

Wir besitzen zwei indirekte Wiedergaben von Dikaiarchs Darstellung
der verschiedenen Stufen menschlicher Zivilisationsentwicklung. **54**,
aus Varros *Rerum Rusticarum* Buch II, bietet nur den allerknappsten
Bericht. Nach meiner Deutung hat Varro am stärksten den überkommen
Argumentationszusammenhang für seine Zwecke verändert. Der zweite
Bericht (**56A**) stammt aus Porphyrios *De abstinentia* IV 2, einer
Schrift, die die Enthaltsamkeit von Fleischgenuß propagiert. Er ist weit
detaillierter als derjenige Varros, insbesondere für die erste
Entwicklungsstufe. Man hat zu bedenken gegeben, daß Porphyrios,
bewußt oder unbewußt, Dikaiarchs Darstellung in einer Weise
wiedergegeben haben könnte, wie sie seiner Intention entsprach,
nämlich zu zeigen, daß der Genuß von Fleisch Ungerechtigkeit
gegenüber Tieren und ein Symptom der Ungerechtigkeit, die jeden
Bereich des gesellschaftlichen Lebens durchdringt, ist. Eine solche
Skepsis[6] scheint jedoch unangebracht, wie ich unter Hinweis auf
ähnliche Vorstellungen in Texten, mit denen sich Dikaiarch berührt,
nachzuweisen versuchen werde.

Ich beginne mit Varros Darstellung (**54**), die nach zwei
Gesichtspunkten geordnet ist: *origo* und *dignitas*. Unter *origo* unter-

---

[5] Schon R. Hirzel, ΑΓΡΑΦΟΣ ΝΟΜΟΣ (Leipzig, 1900) (Abh. Königl. Sächs. Ges.
Wiss XX,1) 88, hatte Ironie in der Zuweisung von Glück an diese Menschen, die alle
Tugend, höhere Intelligenz und Arbeit vermissen lassen, erkennen wollen.

[6] U.a. von F. Wehrli, *Die Schule des Aristoteles*: I, *Dikaiarchos* (Basel, [2]1967) 56,
der bestreitet, daß für Dikaiarch der vegetarische Gedanke eine Rolle gespielt habe.

scheidet Dikaiarch drei Entwicklungsstufen: die älteste, in der die Menschen von dem lebten, was die Natur bereitstellt, ohne daß sie selber eingreifen oder sich abmühen mußten. Die zweite Stufe des Lebenserwerbs (vita) ist die der Hirten, die wilde Tiere fingen, einpferchten und zähmten. Die dritte Stufe ist durch den Übergang zum Ackerbau charakterisiert, in der aber Wesenszüge der beiden früheren erhalten blieben.[7] Diese Abfolge ist auch in dem von Porphyrios auf Dikaiarch zurückgeführten Gedankenzusammenhang enthalten, sie kann als dikaiarchisch gelten. Ihre früheste Stufe enthält Züge der goldenen Zeit,[8] die beiden anderen begegnen auch vor Dikaiarch.[9]

Dies waren Entwicklungsstufen der Vergangenheit, aber es scheint, daß für Dikaiarch die Entwicklung dabei nicht zu Ende kam, denn Varro erwähnt eine weitere, ja weitreichende Entwicklung: "processerunt longe, dum ad nos perveniret."[10] Wir wissen nicht, wie Dikaiarch den Entwicklungsstand des zeitgenössischen Griechenlands[11] bezeichnete. Spiegelte seine Beschreibung das Sentiment, das er nach Porphyrios als das der 'Späteren' angab, die von vielen Übeln, Kriegen und internen Auseinandersetzungen, heimgesucht wurden und sich nach den segensreichen Bedingungen der Vergangenheit zurücksehnten (**56A.** 29ff.)?

Jede neue Entwicklungsstufe ist bei Varro durch Formen des Wortes *descendere* beschrieben.[12] Man könnte darüber streiten, ob er bei Dikaiarch ein Dekadenzmodell gefunden hat oder lediglich die Angabe

[7] Das ist ein Nebeneinander verschiedener Erwerbsweisen, nicht notwendigerweise ihre Kombination, die schon Aristot. *Pol.* I 8 1256b2–7 als "novità maggiore" eingeführt hatte: G. Cambiano und L. Repici, "Cibo e forme di sussistenza in Platone e Dicearco," in O. Longo und P. Scarpi, *Homo Edens. Regimi, Miti e pratiche dell'alimentazione nella civiltà del Mediterraneo* (Verona, 1989) 86.

[8] S. generell B. Gatz, *Weltalter, goldene Zeit und sinnverwandte Vorstellungen.* Spudasmata 16 (1967).

[9] Die früheren Griechen, die von *Weidetieren* lebten, *bearbeiteten* noch nicht das *Land*: Thuk. I 2, 2. Die Hirten, die die große Flut überlebt hatten (Plat. *Ges.* III 678Eff.), wandten sich viele Generationen später dem Ackerbau zu (680E). Die zeitliche Abfolge von nomadischer Hirtenwirtschaft und Ackerbau ist auch aristotelisch: *Pol.* VII 10 1329b14.

[10] Ist vielleicht *pervenirent* zu lesen?

[11] **77** (aus Bíος 'Ελλάδος B. III) und **76** zeigen, daß Dikaiarch sich auf Ereignisse des 4. Jahrh.s bezog.

[12] Die Wahl des Wortes *inviolata* (**54–58**) für den Zustand der Erde im frühesten Stadium scheint emotional stärker geladen und die Folie zur späteren Entwicklung, in der Menschen weder Tiere noch einander schonten, zu bilden.

einer zeitlichen Abfolge.[13] Eindeutig ist auch nicht **55**, wo Varro unter Berufung auf Dikaiarch Ackerbau einem 'inferior gradus aetatis' als Weidewirtschaft zuweist.[14] Eine Deutung, daß Dikaiarch ein Dekadenzmodell vertrat,[15] wird durch **58** (*Schol. vetus* Apollon. Rhod. IV 272–74) gestützt, wonach Sesonchosis ein Gesetz gab, das untersagte, daß jemand eine vom Vater ererbte *technē* aufgab, da dies der Anfang von Habgier sei — das Aufgeben von Nahrungserwerb, wie ihm Hirten nachgehen, um stattdessen Ackerbau zu treiben, wäre ein Beispiel für das Aufgeben einer überkommenen *technē*, um größeren Gewinn zu machen.

Dieses Argument, daß Habgier den Übergang zu einer neuen Entwicklungsstufe erklärt, wird besonders deutlich im Bericht des Porphyrios zum Ausdruck gebracht (**56A**), fehlt aber bei Varro **54**. Die Erklärung dafür mag wohl darin zu suchen sein, daß Varro die beiden Aspekte *origo* und *dignitas* auseinanderhielt, der Gesichtspunkt des *Wertes*—oder Unwertes—der Entwicklungsstufen wurde daher nicht bei der Darstellung ihres *Zustandekommens* erörtert. Diese Trennung von *origo* und *dignitas* erlaubte es Varro, unter *dignitas* seine eigenen Einsichten und Beobachtungen, etwa solche, die auf der lateinischen Sprache beruhen, vorzutragen, ohne die Wiedergabe von Dikaiarchs Erklärung des Ursprungs damit zu beeinträchtigen. Bei *origo* war er einfacher und wohl getreuer Berichterstatter, die Bemerkungen zur *dignitas*, die Römisches enthielten, können dagegen nicht auf Dikaiarch zurückgehen und sind der deutlichste Hinweis, daß Varro hier seine eigenen Wege geht.

Man muß beachten, daß Varro sich diesem Thema von einer Seite nähert, zu der es keine Entsprechung bei Dikaiarch gibt: die Überlegenheit der Menschen, die auf dem Lande wohnten, über die Stadtbewohner (II 1). Varro überträgt geradezu dikaiarchische Motive auf diese Gegenüberstellung: Die Lebensform (*vita*) der Landbewohner ist älter als die der Stadtbewohner und ist besser (III 1,1–4). Göttliche

---

[13] So T. J. Saunders (oben, Anm. 4) 243 mit Anm. 8..

[14] Varro gebraucht *summus* für die früheste Stufe. Die gewöhnliche Bedeutung von *summus* zur Bestimmung der Zeit ist 'letzte' (*Oxford Latin Dictionary*, ed. P. G. W. Glare [1982] s.v. 5), für die Bedeutung 'früheste' zitièrt *OLD* s.v. 2 d nur die vorliegende Stelle. Das Wort mag gewählt sein, um die Vorstellung des Abstiegs (descendisse) auszudrücken.

[15] Wehrli (oben Anm. 6) 56, weist zurecht darauf hin, daß in sophistischen Darstellungen wie auch bei Theophrast die Frühzeit nüchterner geschildert wurde.

Natur gab die Ländereien, menschliche Kunst baute Städte.[16] Varro kann zeitlich nicht hinter Ackerbau zurückgehen, und so entspricht dieser in seiner Beschreibung (*göttliche Natur*) Dikaiarchs erstem Stadium, das im Mythos das Zeitalter des *Kronos* war, in dem Menschen entsprechend der *Natur*[17] und noch ohne *technē* lebten. Das Attribut, das Varro städtischer Ansiedlung zuweist (*ars humana*), hatte Dikaiarch entsprechend für Ackerbau gebraucht: *technē* (γεωργικὴ τέχνη **56A**.20).

Dikaiarchs Annahme von Lebensstufen und seine Bewertung war so verschieden von derjenigen Varros, daß dieser den Bericht über den Ursprung, der sich an Dikaiarch orientierte, einerseits und seine Wertung andererseits auseinanderhalten mußte. Dies legt nahe, daß erst Varro diese Trennung von *origo* und *dignitas* vorgenommen hat, um Römisches und seine eigene Wertung in seine Erörterung der verschiedenen landwirtschaftlichen Bemühungen einzubringen. Diese Trennung hat allerdings zur Folge, daß wir bei Varro nicht erfahren, wie nach Dikaiarch die *Qualität* der einen Stufe dafür verantwortlich war, daß man nach etwas anderem sucht und so eine neue Stufe erreichte, die innere Logik dieses Ablaufes ist so nicht mehr einsichtig. Alles deutet darauf hin, daß die wertneutrale Darstellung der Entwicklungsabfolge bei Varro auf seine Unterscheidung von *origo* und *dignitas* zurückzuführen und nicht Dikaiarch zuzuschreiben ist.

In dem Abschnitt zur *dignitas* spricht Varro von dem hohen Ansehen, dessen sich die Hirten erfreuten: die berühmtesten Männer der Vorzeit waren Hirten. In der Tat nennt er hier niemanden aus dem goldenen Zeitalter, aber das muß nicht heißen, daß er deswegen dem Hirtenleben den Vorzug vor dem natürlichen gab und Fortschritt positiv beurteilte.[18] Da Varro von Männern sprach, die *illustrissimi* waren, d.h. sich durch besondere Leistungen ewigen Ruhm erwarben, mußte er bei seinem Preis der Alten (*antiqui*, **54**.27) die Menschen der ersten, naturgemäßen Stufe, denen alles in den Schoß fiel und die für ruhmeswerte Taten keine Notwendigkeit oder Motivation kannten,[19] übergehen. Verlangen nach Ehre (φιλοτιμία) kommt ja erst in der zweiten Stufe auf (**56A**).

Von diesen Einschränkungen abgesehen, spricht aber auch der Abschnitt zur *dignitas* für eine Dekadenztheorie: hier belegt Varro das

---

[16] III 1, 4 . . . *divina natura dedit agros, ars humana aedificavit urbes.*
[17] *naturalem*, **54**.7.
[18] Saunders (oben, Anm. 4) 242f..
[19] E. Martini, s.v. Dikaiarchos, *RE* V 1 (1903) 548.

hohe Ansehen, dessen sich—auf der dem Ackerbau vorausgehenden Stufe—Hirten und damit auch Weidetiere erfreuten, an sprachlichen und mythischen Beispielen.[20] Die Hochschätzung der Vergangenheit ist darin erhalten, daß er die berühmtesten Männer der Vorzeit—er nennt Herakles—als Hirten identifizierte. Diese übermenschlichen Gestalten kennzeichnen eine der Gegenwart überlegene Vorzeit, und dies ist die der Hirten. Varros Verweis auf Herakles legt nahe, daß auch hier Dikaiarch seine Quelle war. Denn Dikaiarch schreibt Herakles die Gründung der Stadt Thebe in Lykia zu (**64**)—dies ist die Gegend in Klein Asien, wo nach dem Bericht zur *origo* in **54** das Hirtenleben "auch jetzt noch"[21] anzutreffen war. Herakles' Rolle in Lykia, dessen Gesellschaft selbst in der Gegenwart noch nicht über die Hirtenkultur hinausgekommen war, paßt völlig zu seiner Beschreibung bei Varro zur *dignitas* der verschiedenen Kulturstufen. Diese Hirtenkultur bildete einen noch stärkeren Gegensatz zur Verstädterung, gegen die sich Varro aussprach.

Porphyrios' Referat von Dikaiarchs Βίος Ἑλλάδος (**56A**) ist weit ausführlicher als die Bemerkungen Varros zur *origo*, besonders für die Beschreibung der ersten Stufe. Er bemerkt zuerst, daß die Menschen, die damals lebten, die besten natürlichen Anlagen hatten und sich des besten Lebens erfreuten. Sie töteten kein lebendes Geschöpf. Nach Porphyrios' Darstellung hatte Dikaiarch diese erste Stufe menschlicher Entwicklung mit dem goldenen Zeitalter, d.h. dem Leben unter Kronos, gleichgesetzt. Er griff aber nicht einfach auf diesen Mythos als von der Tradition überkommenes und zur Benutzung bereitliegendes Modell der Idealisierung der Vergangenheit zurück, sondern setzte bei dem Bewußtsein der späteren Generationen an, deren unglückselige Lebensbedingungen (vgl. auch **56A**.34–35) die Vergangenheit wie Gold erscheinen lassen—nach einer auch sonst belegten Ausdrucksweise.[22]

---

[20] Die goldenen Äpfel (*mala*, griech. μῆλα), die Herakles von den Hesperiden gebracht haben soll, waren in Wirklichkeit Ziegen und Schafe (μῆλα). Die Benutzung der Sprache reflektiert wohl eher Varros wissenschaftliches Interesse als das des Dikaiarch, aber rationalisierende Umdeutung des Mythos schreibt ihm auch Porphyrios **56A**.11 zu, sodaß Varros Vorgehen dem Dikaiarchs nicht sehr fern steht.

[21] Etiam nunc, **54**.19 = Varro II 1,5. Die Denkform, die Frühzeit aus gegenwärtigen Verhältnissen rückständiger Völker zu erschließen oder die Richtigkeit der Rekonstruktion an ihnen zu bestätigen, ist vor Dikaiarch auch sonst belegt: Thuk. I 5, 3 μέχρι τοῦδε, vgl. 6, 6; Aristot. *Pol.* I 2 1252b20 καὶ νῦν ἔτι, ebenso Theophr. 584A 5, 5; 21,4 FHS&G.

[22] Plat. *ep.* 7 324D7: ὁρῶν δήπου τοὺς ἄνδρας ἐν χρόνῳ ὀλίγῳ χρυσὸν ἀποδεί-ξαντας τὴν ἔμπροσθεν πολιτείαν.

Diese Kennzeichnung 'golden' stellt die Brücke zum goldenen Zeitalter her. Den Rückgriff auf die goldene Zeit vollzog Dikaiarch also nicht direkt und unmittelbar, sondern auf dem Umweg über die Menschen späterer Generationen, die ein Gegenbild zu den eigenen schlimmen Erfahrungen entwarfen und die Vergangenheit sozus. vergoldeten. Die Dichter, wie Hesiod, haben nach Dikaiarch lediglich diesem verbreiteten Sentiment Ausdruck gegeben und den Gegensatz zur beklagenswerten Gegenwart übertrieben. Dikaiarch las Hesiod[23] als ein aufgeklärter, moderner Mann, der den Mythos wenn überhaupt,[24] dann nur in einer naturwissenschaftlich erklärten Form akzeptierte und seine Übertreibung auf sinnvolle Verhältnisse zurechtstutzte.[25] In der Tat stellte die Erde alle Güter bereit,[26] denn die Menschen konnten noch nichts anbauen. Das Angebot an Nahrung war entsprechend eher bescheiden. Die Menschen lebten in Muße, hatten noch nicht die Erfahrung von Schmerz und waren frei aller Sorgen — Dikaiarch gibt hier im Einklang mit seiner rationalisierenden Deutung der früheren Dichtung eine wissenschaftliche Erklärung unter Berufung auf medizinische Experten,[27] die Gesundheit auf Mäßigung in der Nahrung zurückführten.[28] Zu dieser Zeit gab es auch keinen Krieg oder inneren Kampf. Es herrschten Frieden und Freundschaft unter den Menschen. Dieses Leben erschien späteren Generationen attraktiv, die vielen Unannehmlichkeiten ausgesetzt waren, was die Folge ihres Verlangens nach Dingen, die über die Notwendigkeiten des einfachen Lebens hinausgingen, war.[29]

---

[23] Auch Aristoteles geht auf den Dichter Hesiod zurück, vgl. *Pol.* I 2 1252b10, aber nicht, indem er ihn als vorwissenschaftlichen Zeugen einer auf andere Weise begründbaren richtigen Erkenntnis anführt, eine solche Argumentation eher *Met.* Λ 8 1074a38ff.

[24] Das ist der Sinn von εἰ δεῖ λαμβάνειν μὲν αὐτὸν ὡς γεγονότα . . . **56A**.16.

[25] εἰς τὸ διὰ τοῦ λόγου φυσικὸν ἀνάγειν, **56A**.17–18.

[26] Vgl. **54** *quae inviolata ultro ferret terra*. Aus diesem Sammeln von Früchten konnte man eine vegetarische Lebensweise entnehmen, dies ließ sich schon aus Hes. *op.* 116–19 ablesen, vgl. H. Schwabl, *Klio* 66 (1984) 411. Zum Vegetarismus in Vorstellungen vom goldenen Zeitalter s. Gatz (oben, Anm. 8) 165–71.

[27] Saunders (oben, Anm. 4) 249ff. hat dies weiter verfolgt.

[28] Vgl. T. J. Tracy, *Physiological Theory and the Doctrine of the Mean in Plato and Aristotle* (Chicago, 1969).

[29] τοῖς δὲ ὑστέροις ἐφιεμένοις μεγάλων καὶ πολλοῖς περιπίπτουσι κακοῖς . . . **56A**.34–35. Diese zusätzlichen Begierden sind die Ursache für die unmittelbar danach beschriebenen Übelstände (für den Zusammenhang zwischen Gier und verheerenden Folgen vgl. Theogn. 45; 50), wie umgekehrt das Fehlen solcher begehrenswerter Güter Frieden sichert: Dikaiarch **56A**.29–30.

Die nächste Stufe, die der Hirtenkultur, verdankt entsprechend ihr Entstehen der Unzufriedenheit mit dem frugalen Leben der Vorväter. "Uns reicht es mit den Eicheln"[30] soll der Schlachtruf des Mannes gewesen sein, der den Wandel herbeiführte[31] und bessere und abwechslungsreichere Nahrung wünschte. Tiere bildeten jetzt eine Grundlage der Nahrungsbeschaffung.[32] Mit dem jetzt erworbenen Reichtum kam es zu Kämpfen. Der Konflikt entstand, als einige den Ehrgeiz entwickelten, den Besitz anderer an sich zu reißen, und dazu Helfershelfer um sich scharten — sie bildeten eine Bande von Dieben, die Weidetiere stahlen — während andere ihren Besitz schützen wollten. Die Gesellschaft wurde gespalten, es standen sich diejenigen gegenüber, die aggressiv andere ihres Besitzes beraubten, und die, die sich selber gegen solche Versuche wehrten.

Diese Menschen, die ständig versuchten, das was nützlich ist, zu entdecken, nahmen dann die Lebensform von Ackerbau an. Porphyrios hat wenig darüber zu sagen, man muß annehmen, daß mit ihren gesteigerten Begierden ihre sozialen Beziehungen noch schlimmer gestört wurden. Porphyrios schließt mit der Bemerkung, Dikaiarch habe das Leben der frühesten Menschen als das glücklichste angesehen.

In dieser Entwicklungsgeschichte der βίοι ist 'Leben' in einem sehr eingeschränkten Sinne gebraucht: als die spezifische Form der Beschaffung und Versorgung mit den für das Leben erforderlichen oder wünschenswerten Gütern, in erster Hinsicht mit Nahrung. In anderen philosophischen Erörterungen bildet dieser Aspekt von Leben wohl den Ausgangspunkt der Entwicklung des Menschengeschlechts, z.B. im Mythos des Protagoras in Platons *Protagoras*,[33] der jedoch dann sofort in eine andere Richtung geht: er hebt ganz auf die Organisation der Gemeinschaft und die sozialen Beziehungen ab,[34] die aber ganz

---

[30] Ebenso Theophr. *De pietat.* 584A 5, 6 FHS&G, aber bei einem weniger radikalen Übergang, demjenigen von wilden Früchten zu kultivierten.

[31] Dikaiarch hat demnach das Motiv des πρῶτος εὑρετής verwandt, vgl. **58**: Sesonchosis erfand die Nutzung von Pferden für das Reiten. Für die Suche nach dem 'protos heuretes' im Peripatos vgl. Aristoteles' Sammlung von Erfindungen, εὑρήματα 63 Rose.

[32] ζῴων ἥψαντο **56A**.40. Bei Dikaiarch findet sich nicht die Zwischenstufe von Kannibalismus, wie bei Theophr. *De piet.* 584A 27, 1 FHS&G.

[33] Nachdem Prometheus das Feuer von Hephaistos und Athene gestohlen hatte, τὴν μὲν οὖν περὶ τὸν βίον σοφίαν ἄνθρωπος ἔσχεν: 321D3, vgl. E3; 322A6: Erfindung von Behausung, Kleidung, Schuhen, Lagerstätten καὶ τὰς ἐκ γῆς τροφάς; B3 ἡ δημιουργικὴ τέχνη αὐτοῖς πρὸς μὲν τροφὴν ἱκανὴ βοηθὸς ἦν.

[34] "Sie lebten zerstreut, gründeten Städte," 322A, B, vgl. Isokr. 3, 6; 15, 254.

unabhängig von der Sicherung der Nahrung dargestellt werden. Auch der Anon. Jambl. setzt die Sicherung der Lebensbedürfnisse voraus und leitet sofort zur Qualität des Zusammenlebens, das auf Gesetze angewiesen ist, über.[35] Dikaiarch unterscheidet sich von ihnen darin, daß er die Form der Nahrungsquelle nicht nur auf jeder neuen Entwicklungsstufe betrachtet, sondern sie für ihr Aufkommen verantwortlich macht. Sie erklärt auch die zunehmende Zerstörung sozialer Beziehungen.

Es ist nicht auszumachen, ob Dikaiarch sich damit kritisch gegen Protagoras gewendet hat, aber der Unterschied in der Betrachtungsweise ist deutlich: Man kann nach Dikaiarch nicht sagen, daß zu irgendeinem Zeitpunkt die Versorgung gesichert sei und man sich nun Gerechtigkeit und den zwischenmenschlichen Beziehungen zuwenden müsse, die Arten der Nahrung(sbeschaffung) bilden vielmehr die Grundlage aller Stufen der Kulturentwicklung. Und Gerechtigkeit ist viel stärker materiell begründet, Dikaiarch weist die Auffassung zurück, daß Gerechtigkeit, die die Beziehungen zwischen Menschen regelt, ein rein ethisches oder rechtliches Ordnungsprinzip sei.

Näher kommt der Darstellung des Dikaiarch schon Aristoteles in *Pol.* I 8 bei der Einführung seiner Unterscheidung natürlicher und unnatürlicher Erwerbsformen: ἀλλὰ μὴν εἴδη γε πολλὰ τροφῆς, διὸ καὶ βίοι πολλοὶ καὶ τῶν ζῴων καὶ τῶν ἀνθρώπων εἰσίν· οὐ γὰρ οἷόν τε ζῆν ἄνευ τροφῆς, ὥστε αἱ διαφοραὶ τῆς τροφῆς τοὺς βίους πεποιήκασι διαφέροντας τῶν ζῴων.[36] Dies ist genau die Rückführung verschiedener Formen von Leben auf die unterschiedlichen Arten des Nahrungserwerbes wie bei Dikaiarch. Wenn Aristoteles hierbei nicht Menschen eine Sonderstellung einräumt, sondern für seine Argumentation gleichwertig die Nahrungsbeschaffung von *Tieren* als Beispiel benutzen kann, so liefert dies einen willkommenen Hinweis auf den konzeptuellen Zusammenhang: seine Zoologie. In *Hist. anim.* I 1 (487a11ff.) behandelt er die Charakteristika, nach denen man Tiere voneinander unterscheiden kann, das erste ist der Unterschied in ihren

[35] πᾶσα δε ἡ ζωὴ αὐτοῖς εὕρηται καὶ τὰ τεχνήματα πρὸς ταύτην, σὺν ἀλλήλοις δὲ εἶναι αὐτοὺς κἂν ἀνομίᾳ διαιτᾶσθαι οὐχ οἷόν τε, H. Diels und W. Kranz, *Die Fragmente der Vorsokratiker*, 3 Bde. (Berlin, ¹¹1961) 89 6,1 (Bd. 2, 402).
[36] 1256a19. Auch die Ausdrucksweise 'leben von': 1256a35, a39 τὸ δὲ πλεῖστον γένος τῶν ἀνθρώπων ἀπὸ τῆς γῆς (ζῇ) hat ihre Entsprechung bei Dikaiarch **54** (Varro): viverent homines ex his rebus quae . . . ferret terra, vgl. Arist. VI 4 1318b10: der beste Demos lebt von Ackerbau oder als Hirten.

264   Dicaearchus of Messana

Lebensweisen (αἱ δὲ διαφοραὶ τῶν ζῴων εἰσὶ κατά τε τοὺς βίους . . .);
diese Unterschiede ergeben sich wiederum aus den unterschiedlichen
Orten, an denen sie leben. Bei den Tieren, die im Wasser leben, trifft er
die folgende Unterscheidung: . . . ἔνυδρα δὲ διχῶς, τὰ μὲν ὅτι τὸν βίον
καὶ τὴν τροφὴν ποιεῖται ἐν τῷ ὑγρῷ, καὶ δέχεται τὸ ὑγρὸν καὶ
ἀφίησι, τούτου δὲ στερισκόμενα οὐ δύναται ζῆν, οἷον πολλοῖς
συμβαίνει τῶν ἰχθύων· τὰ δὲ τὴν μὲν τροφὴν ποιεῖται καὶ διατριβὴν
ἐν τῷ ὑγρῷ . . . (487a16–20). Hier findet man, wie das auch im
Abschnitt *Pol.* I 8 ausgedrückt war, eine Unterscheidung der
Lebensformen, wie sie sich aus der Nahrung, von der sie leben, und der
Art ihres Erwerbs ergibt, und auf diesen Zusammenhang verweist
Aristoteles häufig.[37]

Man könnte einwenden, daß diese biologische Betrachtungsweise
allein Dikaiarchs βίοι nicht gerecht wird, da er über die drei Formen
von Nahrungsbeschaffung hinausgeht, wenn er die damit
einhergehenden sozialen Beziehungen von Freundschaft oder Krieg
behandelt. Aber Aristoteles geht in seinen zoologischen Schriften auch
darauf ein: nach *Hist. anim.* IX 1 608b19ff. herrscht Krieg unter Tieren,
die im gleichen 'Revier' und von der gleichen Nahrung leben: Πόλεμος
μὲν οὖν πρὸς ἄλληλα τοῖς ζῴοις ἐστίν, ὅσα τοὺς αὐτούς τε κατέχει
τόπους καὶ ἀπὸ τῶν αὐτῶν ποιεῖται τὴν ζωήν· ἐὰν γὰρ ᾖ σπάνιος ἡ
τροφή, καὶ πρὸς ἄλληλα τὰ ὁμόφυλα μάχεται . . .[38] Bei Mangel an
Nahrung kämpfen selbst Tiere der gleichen Art gegeneinander, m.a.W.:
sie verhalten sich nicht anders als Menschen, deren elementare
Bedürfnisse oder weitergehende Begierden nicht befriedigt sind. Gibt
es dagegen genug Nahrung, dann leben selbst die wildesten Tiere in
Frieden miteinander,[39] sie erfreuen sich des gleichen Friedens, den bei
Dikaiarch Menschen in der frühesten Zeit hatten, als die Erde alles in
ausreichendem Maße hervorbrachte.[40] Der Unterschied liegt darin, daß
das Verhalten der Tiere ganz von dem Nahrungsangebot abhängt,
während die Menschen mit Gier bzw. der Kontrolle solcher Begierden

[37] 487b33–488a20; IX 34 620a5ff.; 41 628b13.
[38] Vgl. auch 609a22ff.; 609b28ff.; 610a13ff.
[39] 608b28ff. Wenn man Nahrung reicht, kann man wilde Tiere zähmen, wie es in
Ägypten die Priester mit Krokodilen tun.
[40] Es ist wichtig, daß bei Dikaiarch Auseinandersetzungen nicht mit dem Besitz von
Land, sondern schon demjenigen von Tieren beginnen, s. G. Bodei Giglioni, "Dicearco
e la Riflessa sul Passato," *Riv. Stor. Ital.* 98 (1986) 639.

den Mangel oder das ausreichende Angebot an Nahrung und die damit gegebenen sozialen Beziehungen selber schaffen.

Es wird deutlich, daß Dikaiarch und Aristoteles in der grundlegenden und elementaren Einteilung von Lebensformen entsprechend der Art der Nahrung und ihrer Beschaffung übereinstimmen, sodaß man den Eindruck gewinnt, Dikaiarch habe diesen Teil seiner Konzeption von Aristoteles übernommen. Diese Einteilung ist deswegen elementar, da sie zunächst einmal Unterschiede im Tierleben nach Aristoteles' zoologischen Schriften erklärt. Ein Abschnitt in Aristoteles' *EN* illustriert dies: bei seinem Versuch, menschliche Arete zu bestimmen, beginnt er mit dem irrationalen Seelenteil: τοῦ ἀλόγου δὲ τὸ μὲν ἔοικε κοινῷ καὶ φυτικῷ, λέγω δὲ τὸ αἴτιον τοῦ τρέφεσθαι καὶ αὔξεσθαι· τὴν τοιαύτην γὰρ δύναμιν τῆς ψυχῆς ἐν ἅπασι τοῖς τρεφομένοις θείη τις ἄν ... (I 13 1102a32ff.). Das Seelenvermögen, das die Beschaffung und Aufnahme von Nahrung kontrolliert, findet sich in allen, die Nahrung zu sich nehmen, es wird aber in *EN* I beiseitegelassen, da es ungeeignet ist, das spezifische Menschliche zu bestimmen, das vielmehr in der Verwirklichung der ethischen und dianoetischen Qualitäten und letztlich dem theoretischen Leben besteht.

In anderer Beziehung geht Aristoteles über die elementaren Bedingungen in dem berühmten Kapitel *Pol.* I 2 hinaus, wo er ebenfalls drei Entwicklungsstufen auf unterschiedliche Formen der Versorgung zurückführt. Aber er spricht nicht von einer Versorgung mit unterschiedlichen Gütern, sondern einer zunehmenden Verbesserung der Versorgung, die auf der zweiten Stufe auf längere Frist[41] und auf der letzten in vollkommenster Weise gesichert werden kann. Außerdem stellt Aristoteles diese Entwicklung in ihrer Wechselwirkung mit den Unterschieden in der sozialen Organisation (Haus; Dorf; Stadt) oder Herrschaftsformen dar. Bei Dikaiarch sind dagegen die unterschiedlichen Lebensformen zunächst nichts anderes als die unterschiedlichen Quellen der Nahrungsversorgung und sind als solche gekennzeichnet: nomadisches–landbearbeitendes Leben (**56A**.39 und 49). Mit diesem geradezu materialistischen Ansatz geht eine Bewertung der dadurch bedingten menschlichen Beziehungen einher: Gesteigerte Bedürfnisse entzweien Menschen. Während Dikaiarch somit soziale Beziehungen insofern berücksichtigt, als er von Frieden und Freundschaft der Menschen der goldenen Zeit spricht und dem den

---

[41] χρήσεως ἕνεκεν μὴ ἐφημέρου, 1252b16.

Zwist der späteren Epochen entgegenhält, sieht er doch keinen Zusammenhang zwischen der Entwicklung der Versorgung und sozialen Organisationsformen:[42] in dieser Hinsicht scheint er keinen Unterschied beim Übergang von der nomadischen Kulturstufe der Hirten zur sesshaften der Ackerbauer festgestellt zu haben.

Indem Dikaiarch von den sozialen Organisationsformen absieht, ignoriert er die soziale Teleologie, die das beherrschende Element der Betrachtung der Erwerbsweisen bei Aristoteles ist. Deren natürliche Form muß "einen reichlichen Vorrat an Gütern, die für das Leben unerläßlich und für die staatliche und häusliche Gemeinschaft nützlich sind . . . bereitstellen."[43] Dikaiarch interessiert nur der erste Teil, 'Leben', nicht die Form der Gemeinschaft, letztlich der Staat, der mit der Vollkommenheit der Versorgung auch das beste Leben ermöglicht. Wir finden nichts wie die aristotelische Vorstellung eines höchsten Gutes, das nur in den am weitesten entwickelten Formen menschlicher Gemeinschaft, der polis, ereicht werden kann. Dikaiarchs Interesse gilt dagegen ausschließlich den elementarsten Bedürfnissen der Ernährung,[44] seine Erklärung der zwischenmenschlichen Beziehungen baut darauf auf — in einer Weise, wie es Aristoteles ebenfalls nicht akzeptiert hätte.

In *Pol.* II 7 nimmt Aristoteles kritisch zu Phaleas von Chalkedon Stellung, der in gewisser Hinsicht viel mit Dikaiarch gemein hat: während Phaleas nicht Zivilisationsstufen der Vergangenheit erörterte, ist er doch einer der Theoretiker, die, wie Aristoteles behauptet (1266a36), eher von lebensnotwendigen Erfordernissen ausgehen. Phaleas hatte inneren Krieg auf die ungleiche Verteilung dieser notwendigen Güter zurückgeführt. Aristoteles wies dies als eine zu simple Erklärung, die darüberhinausgehende Motive menschlichen Handelns ignoriere, zurück. Wenn Dikaiarch die Lebensformen nach der Art der Beschaffung der elementarsten Mittel zum Überleben, der Nahrung, unterschied, und Frieden mit der einen, Krieg der anderen in Verbindung brachte, dann stimmt er eher mit Phaleas überein als mit Aristoteles. Entsprechend dessen Kritik an Phaleas könnte man Dikaiarchs vorrangiges Interesse an Nahrung und den Methoden ihrer Beschaffung genauso als eine simplifizierende Erklärung menschlicher

---

[42] Anders Giglioni (oben, Anm. 40) 634; sie schreibt dem nomadischen Leben schon erste Gesetze zu (638), aber daß sich **57** oder **58** darauf beziehen, bleibt spekulativ.

[43] *Pol.* I 8 1256b26ff.

[44] Fast wie in dem Sprichwort: "der Mensch ist, was er ißt."

Entwicklung bezeichnen. Es gibt zusätzliche Gründe, Dikaiarch als einen "Fundamentalisten" zu deuten, der—zumindest für seine Darstellung der Entwicklung menschlicher Zivilisation—sich mit elementaren Erklärungsmustern begnügte und auf fortgeschrittenere Elemente, etwa die aristotelische soziale Teleologie, verzichtete. Dies wird deutlich, wenn man Dikaiarchs Darstellung der ersten Stufe menschlicher Zivilisationsentwicklung mit aristotelischen Vorstellungen vergleicht.

Die frühste Stufe menschlichen Lebens

Daß nach Dikaiarch Menschen im Zeitalter des Kronos nicht weit über den Tieren lebten, zeigt sich daran, daß sie noch keine technē besaßen,[45] diese wurde erst auf der nächsten Entwicklungsstufe erfunden.[46] Aristoteles nahm an, daß die Natur einige der Aufgaben, die sie begann, nicht vollenden konnte, sie beließ Menschen hungernd und voll anderer Bedürfnisse, sodaß sie technē entwickeln mußten. Deren Funktion ist damit dadurch bestimmt, daß sie dort helfen soll, wo die Natur allein nicht ihre Aufgabe erfüllen kann—als Beispiel führt er den Ackerbau an.[47] Daß Menschen ohne technē nicht in befriedigender Weise leben können, steht für ihn außer Zweifel. Der Mensch ist auf technē angewiesen, schon um zu überleben, erst recht um gut zu leben.[48] Technischer Fortschritt ist eine unverzichtbare Notwendigkeit für ein Leben, das wirklich verdient, menschlich genannt zu werden, ein Leben, in dem der Mensch seine Potentialität voll erfüllt.

Sind die Lebensverhältnisse in Dikaiarchs erstem Entwicklungsstadium ebenfalls von Mangel gekennzeichnet, der die Entwicklung von technē zu einer Notwendigkeit macht? Zweifellos nicht. Während er die Lebensdingungen der ersten Entwicklungsstufe als kärglich beschreibt, zwingen sie doch keinesfalls die Menschen dazu, durch

[45] **56A**.20, das folgende μήθ' ἑτέραν μηδεμίαν (τέχνην) könnte sich auf das Zähmen von Tieren beziehen, welches eine techne ist: Isokr. 2, 12–vgl. Dikaiarch später **56A**.40–42.
[46] **56A**.40 κατανοήσαντες: sie erkannten Unterschiede zwischen Tieren, weshalb sie einige zähmten (dies als *technē*, s. vorige Anm.), vgl. l. 34 κατανοοῦντες, was zum Ackerbau führt–aristotelisch gesprochen tritt *technē* hinzu, wo die Natur alleine nicht ausreicht–sein Beispiel ist Ackerbau: *Protr.* B 13 Dü., s.u.
[47] *Protr.* B 13 Dü. Generell s. *Pol.* VII 17 1337a1; *Phys.* II 8 199a15.
[48] *Pol.* IV 4 1290b39ff.

Erfindungen ihre armseligen Verhältnisse zu verbessern[49]—es war nicht Unterernährung oder andere mit Gesundheit verbundene Gründe, die zwangen, andere Nahrung zu suchen. Für Dikaiarch war das Leben in der ersten Entwicklungsstufe gesund,[50] er vertritt eher eine idealistische Vorstellung von der ersten Entwicklungsstufe. So ist die zweite Stufe auch nicht das Ergebnis von Bedürfnissen, die man besser befriedigen mußte, sondern von neuen und verfeinerten Ansprüchen und Begierden,[51] deren Erfüllung Probleme brachte, die man vorher nicht kannte. Saunders sieht das anders: "For can a primitivist believe . . . that initially man did not have enough to eat, and that later he won greater material resources by 'noticing' what was 'useful'?"[52] In der Tat ist bei Dikaiarch die dem Unfang nach angemessene (μετρία) Nahrung doch in den meisten Fällen eher knapp (ἐλάττων, **56A**.28ff.). Aber bei Dikaiarch ist dies der Gegensatz zu dem späteren Zustand, als man nach vielem trachtete (34). In der aristotelischen Tradition macht das eher knappe Maß an Nahrung Sinn: die richtige Mitte ist nicht mathematisch bestimmt, vielmehr erscheint der Endpunkt, zu dem man der Natur nach stärker strebt, weiter von der Mitte entfernt, diese liegt näher bei dem anderen Extrem (*EN* II 8 1109a12ff.). Wenn man bei Nahrung gewöhnlich eher nach Überfülle verlangt, dann ist nach diesem Verständnis der eher kärgliche Zustand der angemessenere. Daß das spätere Angebot an raffinierter Nahrung, die nicht nur Gesundheitsschäden, sondern auch Kriege nach sich zieht, als Fortschritt zu betrachten sei, wie es Saunders möchte, widerspricht dem ganzen Gedankengang.[53] Im Gegenteil: in einer Schrift *Über den Untergang der Menschen* hatte Dikaiarch ausgeführt, daß mehr Menschen voneinander als von allen Katastrophen oder Angriffen von Tieren

[49] Vgl. Giglioni (oben, Anm. 40) 650, die richtig Dikaiarch auch den sophistischen Theorien von der Entwicklung der Menschen, die mit χρεία einsetzten, gegenüberstellt.

[50] In *Gulliver's Travels*, Part IV, ch. 3, beschreibt J. Swift den Aufenthalt Gullivers bei den Houyhnhnms, wo er von Hafer leben mußte, den er zu einer Art Brot machte: "It was at first a very insipid diet, though common enough in many parts of Europe, but grew tolerably by time; and having been often reduced to hard fare in my life, this was not the first experiment I had made how easily nature is satisfied. And I cannot but observe, that I never had one hour's sickness while I stayed in this island." Gulliver ist ehrlich genug zuzugeben, daß er bisweilen seine Diät durch einen Hasen oder Vogel bereicherte.

[51] Vgl. Giglioni oben, Anm. 40) 650; ebd. 635 notiert sie diesen Unterschied zwischen Dikaiarch und den Begründern der politischen Ökonomie im 18. Jahrhundert.

[52] Saunders (oben, Anm. 16) 243.

[53] S. auch Giglioni (oben, Anm. 40) 635.

umkamen (**78**)—das würde nicht durch die Lebenserleichterungen technischen Fortschritts aufgewogen.

Der früheste Zustand ist für Dikaiarch der gesündeste, friedlichste und glücklichste. An diesem Punkt weicht er somit grundlegend von Aristoteles ab, der den frühesten Bedingungen inhärente Mängel zuschreibt[54] und entsprechend die ersten Schritte, sie zu überwinden, nicht von moralischer Dekadenz belastet darstellt. Für Aristoteles war auch der Besitz landwirtschaftlicher Produkte naturgemäß, nur der von Geld widernatürlich (*Pol.* I 8–9). Bei Dikaiarch spaltet dagegen schon der Besitz in nomadischen und dann erst recht agrarischen Gesellschaften die Menschen und ist für Erscheinungen wie Krieg verantwortlich. Anders gesagt: während bei Dikaiarch die sozialen Probleme schon zu dem Zeitpunkt beginnen, als der Mensch zum ersten Male seine Lebensverhältnisse verbessern wollte und nur die goldene Zeit von diesen Übeln frei war, liegt bei Aristoteles der Naturzustand weniger weit zurück, denn die agrarische Form der Güterbeschaffung ist naturgemäß (*Pol.* I 8), und diese Menschen leben anständig.[55] Aristoteles, dem sicherlich die Vorstellungen einer goldenen Zeit bekannt waren, hat einen ihrer Züge, nämlich in Muße ohne Mühe zu leben, vom goldenen Zeitalter, dem auch Dikaiarch sie zuschreibt, auf die Stufe, die bei Dikaiarch darauf folgt, übertragen, das nomadische Leben: ἡ γὰρ ἀπὸ τῶν ἡμέρων τροφὴ ζῴων ἄνευ πόνου γίνεται σχολάζουσιν, *Pol.* I 8 1256a32. Das Ideal bleibt, aber es liegt nicht in einer so ungreifbaren Ferne wie bei Dikaiarch.

Es ist unbestreitbar, daß Dikaiarch in seiner Beurteilung der frühesten Entwicklungsstufe nicht Aristoteles folgt.[56] Ich glaube, daß man die Tradition, der er sich anschließt, identifizieren kann. Zu seiner Beschreibung der Vorzüge des goldenen Zeitalters, wie sie bei Porphyrios erhalten ist, nämlich Gesundheit, Frieden, Freundschaft, gibt es eine genaue, beinahe wörtliche Parallele in Platons *Rep.* II, der Darstellung der ersten Gesellschaft: καὶ οὕτω διάγοντες τὸ βίον ἐν εἰρήνῃ μετὰ ὑγιείας... γηραιοὶ τελευτῶντες... (372D), und wenige Zeilen vorher berührte er ihre sozialen Beziehungen.[57] Falls Dikaiarch

---

[54] Für Aristoteles waren die Menschen der Vergangenheit primitiv: *Pol.* II 8 1268b38.
[55] VI 4 1318b9ff., 1319a19ff.
[56] Vgl. Giglioni (oben, Anm. 40) 641.
[57] ἡδέως συνόντες ἀλλήλοις, 372B8, vgl. C1 εὐλαβούμενοι... πόλεμον. Dikaiarchs Erklärung dafür, daß es noch keinen Krieg gab, nämlich, daß man nichts besaß, worum man streiten könnte, ist die gleiche wie bei Plat. *Rep.* IV 422D. Die Um-

diesen platonischen Abschnitt kannte–ich werde später nachweisen, daß er zu einem beträchtlichen Teil von Platon beeinflußt war—dann mag ihn dabei die Tatsache angezogen haben, daß Platon der *Nahrung* dieser Menschen beträchtliche Aufmerksamkeit schenkte (θρέψονται, b1). Sie bestand aus Weizen und Gerste. Der Mitunterredner Glaukon ist mit diesem Speiseplan unzufrieden, er vermißt ὄψον im Sinne von Fleisch (C2), was Sokrates veranlaßt, ihrer Nahrung ὄψον hinzuzufügen, jedoch in anderem Sinne,[58] als den Brotbelag, der in Oliven, Käse, Zwiebeln, Salat und anderen Produkten wie Bohnen und schließlich natürlich Eicheln bestand–nach Dikaiarch war "Uns reicht es mit den Eicheln" der Schlachtruf des Mannes, der die zweite Stufe menschlicher Entwicklung einführte, eines Mannes, der genauso unzufrieden mit dem frugalen Leben des goldenen Zeitalters war wie Glaukon in Platons *Rep.* unzufrieden mit der Nahrung des ersten Staates ist. Die Menschen dieses ersten Staates in Platons *Rep.* waren Vegetarier,[59] das einzige tierische Produkt, das Platon erwähnt, ist Käse. Diese Menschen brauchten für ihre Versorgung noch keine Tiere zu töten, genau wie dies im goldenen Zeitalter bei Dikaiarch der Fall war. Diese Charakteristik der goldenen Zeit ist also philosophisches Gedankengut des frühen vierten Jahrhunderts,[60] es ist nicht erst Porphyrios, der dies entdeckte.[61] In dem aufgedunsenen Staat, der bei Platon auf den ersten folgt, ißt man Fleisch, und Platon sieht sofort als unvermeidliche Begleiterscheinung das Aufkommen von Ärzten, die die nun auftretenden Krankheiten behandeln,[62] die Gesundheit des früheren Stadiums, das er wie Dikaiarch preist, war verlorengegangen. Es gibt einen anderen Zug im ersten Staat in Platons *Rep.*, der auf das goldene Zeitalter hindeutet: diese Menschen starben gesund in hohem Alter, was die Variation eines

---

kehrung dieses Motivs bei der Erklärung innerer Auseinandersetzungen oder Kriegen mit Nachbarn aus großem oder wertvollen Besitz ist aber älter, vgl. Thuk. I 2, 4.

[58] Vgl. J. J. Adam, *The Republic of Plato*, edited with critical notes, commentary, etc., with an introduction by D. A. Rees, 2 vols. (Cambridge, ²1965) I zu 372C17.

[59] Vgl. Adam Kommentar zu 372B9.

[60] Also außerhalb der Pythagoreer oder Orphiker (vgl. dazu Plat. *Leg.* VI 782C), hinzukommt Theophrast *De pietat.*, s.u. Anm. 80.

[61] **56B** (Hieron. *Adv. Iovin.* II 13), eine von Porphyrios unabhängige Überlieferung, schrieb ebenfalls dem frühesten Stadium bei Dikaiarch Enthaltsamkeit von Fleischgenuß zu: nullum comedisse carnem.

[62] II 373C4–D2, vgl. III 405A.

Aspektes des goldenen Zeitalter in Hesiods Beschreibung des Lebens unter Kronos darstellt.[63]

Ein etwas klareres Bild von Dikaiarchs *Bios Hellados* im Verhältnis zur Tradition sollte sich damit ergeben haben: seine Rückführung von Lebensformen auf unterschiedliche Arten der Nahrungsversorgung deckt sich beinahe wörtlich mit aristotelischen Äußerungen. Dagegen war Dikaiarch in anderen Beziehungen, etwa der Vorstellung vom besten Leben (s.o. S. 266), kein Aristoteliker. Nach meiner Deutung der erhaltenen Fragmente des Βίος Ἑλλάδος ging Dikaiarch in wichtigen Annahmen seiner Anthropologie eigene Wege. Denn während er die Vorstellung vertrat, daß die Menschheit eine Anfangsstufe aufgab, die Züge des hesiodeischen goldenen Zeitalters besaß, reflektierte Aristoteles über eine solche Stufe überhaupt nicht, *naturgemäß* war bei ihm allein die agrarische Erwerbsform von Hirten und Ackerbauern, die bei Dikaiarch die weit minderwertigeren Lebensformen der folgenden Stufen repräsentieren.[64] Dikaiarchs Auffassung über das erste Stadium menschlicher Entwicklung stimmt eher mit dem platonischen in *Rep.* II überein.

Platonischen Einfluß in Dikaiarch hatte schon Wehrli[65] angenommen, wenn er über die Entwicklung von Früchtesammeln zu Herdenbesitz und Ackerbau bemerkte, daß Dikaiarch "die sittliche Problematik dieser Entwicklung bei Platon (*Leges* III 678E: über Krieg und Aufruhr) vorgezeichnet fand." Platon beschrieb dort die Wirkung der großen Flut, die beinahe alles zerstörte: die Städte am Meer und in der Ebene wurden ausgelöscht.[66] Die gesamte Kenntnis technischer Erfindungen ging verloren (678C7). Nur die Tiere, die auf den Bergwiesen weideten und bescheidene Versorgung mit Lebensnotwendigem brachten,[67] überlebten zusammen mit den Hirten.

Diese Flut vernichtete nicht nur technische Errungenschaften, sie änderte auch das moralische Klima der Gesellschaft: während die

---

[63] *Op.* 113: dem goldenen Geschlecht blieben die Plagen des Alters erspart.

[64] Richtig Giglioni (oben, Anm. 40) 644.

[65] "Dikaiarchos von Messene," in H. Flashar, *Grundriss der Geschichte der Philosophie,* begründet v. F. Ueberweg, *Die Philosophie der Antike.* Band 3, *Ältere Akademie, Aristoteles-Peripatos* (Basel und Stuttgart, 1983) 537; s. auch Giglioni (oben, Anm. 40) 635; 645 Anm. 49 und W. Ax (dieser Band) S. 287.

[66] 677C, vgl. *Tim.* 22D6ff.; Arist. Π. Φιλοσοφ. fr. 8 Ross (*OCT*) S. 76.

[67] 677E9ff.; später hatten diese Menschen mehr: 679Aff.

Zivilisation vor der Flut viele Beispiele von Tugenden wie Lastern kannte (678A8ff.), werden die Menschen der Hirtengesellschaft "gut" genannt (679B7ff.) — man könnte sagen, sie lebten noch in einem Zustand der Unschuld, in dem sich die Möglichkeit, Schlechtes zu wählen, noch nicht bot. Platon behauptet, daß es unter ihnen weder Krieg noch inneren Kampf gab (678E6ff.; 679B4; D7) — dies ist ein wichtiges Motiv Dikaiarchs. Nach Platon freute man sich, die Mitmenschen zu sehen,[68] d.h. man erfreute sich der Freundschaft, von der Dikaiarch gesprochen hatte.

Platon beschrieb diese bessere Gesellschaft der Vergangenheit als Folie der Übel der Gegenwart. Dies wird daran deutlich, daß er bei der Vergangenheit hervorhebt, daß die Probleme der Gegenwart *fehlten*: weil man genug Nahrung (Milch und Fleisch) hatte, gab es noch *nicht* die extreme Armut, weshalb man *keine* Zwietracht kannte. Das *Fehlen* von Silber und Gold bewirkte, daß *niemand* sehr reich werden konnte. Da die Menschen weder arm noch reich waren, gab es *nicht* die Laster, die mit diesen beiden Besitzlagen verbunden sind (679Aff.).[69]

Während bei Platon die Vergangenheit attraktive Züge besitzt, war doch die große Flut, die ja das Überleben nur gerade der ältesten Zivilisationsstufe sicherte, kein ungetrübtes positives Ereignis, etwa in dem Sinne, daß man so mit einem Schlage der späteren Degeneration enthoben wurde—eine Zerstörung Sodoms—, vielmehr gingen wichtige Errungenschaften, wie Staatsverfassungen, verloren. Das gilt auch auf einer elementareren Ebene: Menschen mußten in der Kultur, die die Flut überlebte, für ihren Unterhalt arbeiten, aber nur die primitivsten Mittel standen ihnen zur Verfügung, während die fortgeschritteneren Methoden, die ihre Arbeit leichter und effizienter machten, verloren gegangen waren. Es gibt in diesem Zusammenhang von Platons *Gesetzen* nicht die Regierung des Kronos, die man bei Dikaiarch findet, kein Zeitalter, in dem die Erde selber alle Güter bereitstellte.[70] Die früheste Stufe, zu der Platon zurückgehen kann, die Hirtengesellschaft,[71] besitzt zwar einige Züge des goldenen Zeitalters, aber es wird doch so dargestellt, daß der primitive Zustand der materiellen Bedingungen Verbesserungen geradezu verlangte oder

---

[68] 678C5ff., cf. E9: ἠγάπων καὶ ἐφιλοφρονοῦντο ἀλλήλους.

[69] Diese Erklärung moralischer, und impliziert sozialer Probleme kommt derjenigen des Phaleas von Chalkedon nahe, s. oben S. 266f.

[70] Vgl. Cambiano und Repici (oben, Anm. 7) 85. Auf die Zeit unter Kronos geht Platon später im Mythos von *Gesetze* IV 713C ein.

[71] Eine frühere wird nicht in Erwägung gezogen, s.o. S. 269 zu Aristot. *Pol.* I 8.

gebot. Die Menschheit mußte wieder von vorn anfangen und Schritt für Schritt[72] ihr Los verbessern, um den Stand der Entwicklung wieder zu erreichen, den ihre Vorfahren schon besaßen. Platon gibt somit eine eher ambivalente Beschreibung der Vergangenheit,[73] die nebeneinander lobenswerte (moralische Unschuld) wie unzureichende Bedingungen aufwies. Man findet keine Spur dieser Ambivalenz bei Dikaiarch, der eine klare Trennungslinie zwischen dem goldenen Zeitalter auf der einen und den Entartungsformen auf der anderen Seite, angefangen mit der Hirtengesellschaft, zog. Man übersieht Wichtiges, wenn man Dikaiarchs Vorstellung menschlicher Kulturentwicklung auf Platons *Gesetze* zurückführen möchte.

Platon kehrte in den *Gesetzen* häufig zu Themen zurück, die er in früheren Werken behandelt hatte und die ihm wichtig waren, die Spekulation über menschliche Kulturentwicklung ist eines dieser Themen. Statt bei Dikaiarch den Einfluß der platonischen *Gesetze* anzunehmen, glaube ich, daß man eher in seinem *Politikos* das Vorbild für Dikaiarchs Vorstellung von der Vergangenheit finden kann. Das Thema dieses Dialogs ist die Klärung des Wissens des Herrschers (βασιλικὴ τέχνη bzw. ἐπιστήμη, 258Eff.). Bei der Widerlegung der Auffassung, ein König sei der Hirte seines Volkes, bemerkt Platon, daß eine solche Rolle in einer anderen Periode zutraf—Periode in der wörtlichen Bedeutung eines Zyklus' kosmischer Bewegung (274E10). In diesem früheren Zyklus regierte Kronos,[74] während die gegenwärtige Periode mit der des Zeus gleichgesetzt wird (272B2). In dem früheren Zyklus hatten die Menschen Naturen, die über denjenigen der anderen Periode standen,[75] gegenüber den Tieren sind sie ein göttlicheres

---

[72] Οὐκοῦν προϊόντος μὲν τοῦ χρόνου . . . εἰς πάντα τὰ νῦν καθεστηκότα προελήλυθεν πάντα; . . . Οὐκ ἐξαίφνης γε, ὡς εἰκός, κατὰ μικρὸν δὲ ἐν παμπόλλῳ τινὶ χρόνῳ, 678b5ff., vgl. Dikaiarch **54**: *gradatim descendisse ad hanc aetatem.*
[73] Vgl. P. Vidal-Naquet, "Plato's Myth of the Statesman, the Ambiguities of the Golden Age and of History," in *The Black Hunter*, übers. von A. Szegedy-Maszak (1986) 298.
[74] 271C4ff., 272B, vgl. 269A6.
[75] Die Überlegenheit dieser Männer der Vergangenheit ist bei Plat. *Pol.* 273B7ff. auch dadurch ausgedrückt, daß die Verschlechterung von allem unter dem neuen Zyklus kosmischer Bewegung beschrieben wurde, vgl. auch *Rep.* VIII 546C5ff. Für Dikaiarch s. **56a**.6. Seine Annahme, daß Menschen verschiedener Entwicklungsstufen unterschiedliche Naturen haben, erscheint Saunders (oben, Anm. 4) S. 246 bei einem Schüler des Aristoteles 'mysterious'. Aber vgl. Aristoteles *Poet.* 2 1448a17 βελτίους τῶν νῦν. Die Vergangenheit, auf deren Begebenheiten sich die Sujets der Tragödie beziehen sollten, besaß Menschen, die besser sind, als man sie heutzutage findet.

Geschlecht.[76] Das war die Zeit, als Menschen alles ohne eigenes Zutun zufiel (πάντα αὐτόματα γίγνεσθαι τοῖς ἀνθρώποις).[77] Sie lebten von der Erde, die Früchte in reichlichem Maße produzierte,[78] Ackerbau gab es noch nicht (272A1–4). Platon fügt später hinzu, daß die Menschen sich der Muße erfreuen (B9).

Die Frage, ob das Leben dieser Menschen glücklicher als das der Gegenwart war, wird aufgeworfen und positiv beantwortet. Ein Grund für diese Beurteilung liegt darin, daß es keinen Krieg oder inneren Kampf gab (271E2). Die Menschen schlossen in ihre Unterhaltungen, die philosophischer Natur waren, auch Tiere ein (272B9ff.). Und später heißt es: οὔτε ἀλλήλων ἐδωδαί (271E1). Einerseits bedrohten Tiere nicht Menschen,[79] andererseits enthielten sich auch Menschen des Genusses jeglichen Fleisches. Die vegetarische Lebensweise, die schon beim ersten Staat von *Rep.* II beschrieben wurde, ist hier prononzierter zur Sprache gebracht und mit dem spezifischen Verhältnis zwischen Menschen und Tieren in Verbindung gebracht.[80]

Dieser Mythos (274E) in Platons *Politikos*[81] kommt Dikaiarch näher als jeder bisher betrachtete Text: in beiden Fällen ist die früheste Periode diejenige unter Kronos (vgl. **56A**.15). Die Menschen standen den Göttern näher. Damals hatte man Muße (Plat. *Polit.* 272B9; **56A**.20–21). Kein Lebewesen wurde getötet.[82] Nach der Bedeutung, die dieser Gedanke bei Platon findet, muß es damit weniger überraschen, daß auch Dikaiarch, der in so vielem mit Platon übereinstimmt, diesen Zug herausstellte—es besteht damit umso weniger Grund, dies erst als Porphyrios' Entstellung anzusehen, s.o. 270. Es gab keinen Krieg oder inneren Kampf.[83] Das Leben der Vergangenheit war glücklicher als das der folgenden Stufe (272B3ff.; **56A**.50), es war auf jeden Fall viel besser als das der Gegenwart.

In *Pol.* 272A3 καρποὺς δὲ ἀφθόνους hatte Platon zweifellos Hes. *op.* 117f. καρπόν δ᾽ . . . ἄφθονον im Sinne, Dikaiarch zitiert diese Zeilen. Er scheint jedoch direkt auf Hesiod zurückgegriffen zu haben, wenn er

---

[76] 271E5–7. Plat. mochte schon an Hes. *op.* 108 gedacht haben.
[77] 271D1, vgl .E4f.; 272A; 274C2.
[78] 272A3: καρποὺς δὲ ἀφθόνους; vgl. C6: ἐμπιμπλάμενοι σίτων ἄδην.
[79] Wie im anderen Zyklus: 274B8; vgl. *Prot.* 322B.
[80] Theophr. 584A22,1 FHS&G erklärt mit der Freundschaft mit allem, was verwandt war, daß man nichts, auch nicht Tiere, tötete.
[81] Vgl. Cambiano und Repici (oben, Anm. 7) 84; Vidal-Naquet (oben, Anm. 73) 291f.
[82] **56A**.9; vgl. o. 270 mit Anm. 59.
[83] **56A**.29; Plat. *Pol.* 271E2.

Eigenschaften des Lebens dieser Männer erwähnt, die sich nicht bei Platon finden, die aber Hesiod erwähnt hatte. Mit ἄνευ πόνων καὶ μερίμνης (**56A**.22) hat Dikaiarch ganz eindeutig Hes. *op*. 113 νόσφιν ἄτερ τε πόνου καὶ ὀιζύος wiedergegeben. Bei Hesiod ist dieser Zug in der Weise erklärt, daß Menschen nicht den körperlichen Niedergang hohen Alters erleiden, sondern schließlich ein friedliches Ende finden. Es liegt nahe, daß Dikaiarch, der zum Leben ohne Schmerzen und Sorgen im goldenen Zeitalter als nächsten Zug nennt, daß sie von Krankheit verschont blieben (**56A**.22–23), die Anregung dafür von Hesiods Schilderung der Gesundheit des goldenen Geschlechts empfing. Aber er las Hesiod als ein wissenschaftlich gebildeter Mann, der im Mythos den vorwissenschaftlichen Ausdruck durchaus richtiger Einsichten sah und die mythologische Übertreibung auf die natürlichen Gründe zurückführte (s.o. Anm. 25). Zu dieser Rationalisierung des Mythos fügt sich gut die medizinische Erklärung, die deswegen besonders paßt, weil sie einen Zusammenhang zwischen *Natur* und *Nahrung* herstellt (**56A**.26–29). Bei seiner Rückführung der Übertreibung des Mythos auf sinnvolle Verhältnisse beschrieb Dikaiarch das Leben des goldenen Geschlechtes nicht als eines von Überfluß, sondern Kargheit.[84]

Versucht man die Stellung des Dikaiarch zur Tradition zu bestimmen, so zeigt sich, daß die einzelnen Elemente seiner Entwicklungsphilosophie in ganz unterschiedlichen Zusammenhängen bei seinen Vorgängern vorgegeben sind. Die Rückführung von Lebensformen auf Nahrungsversorgung hat wörtliche Parallelen in aristotelischem biologischem Denken. Aber während für Aristoteles diese Zusammenhänge sozusagen die animalische Grundlage bildeten, über die Menschen mit Erfindungen und verschiedenen Entwicklungen, u.a. der sozialen Organisation, hinauszugehen hatten, um die spezifische Form menschlichen guten Lebens möglich zu machen, setzt Dikaiarch diesem Fortschrittsdenken ein Dekadenzmodell entgegen. Die ursprüngliche Lebensordnung, die auf die Einfachheit der Nahrung zurückgeführt wurde, war natürlich und ist der gegenwärtigen vorzuziehen. In dieser Deutung der Entwicklung ließen sich enge Übereinstimmungen mit platonischen Vorstellungen nachweisen. Man könnte geradezu sagen, daß Dikaiarch aristotelisches biologisches Denken mit platonischer Dekadenztheorie verbindet. Daß Dikaiarch dabei spezifische eigene

---

[84] σπάνις **56A**.29, cf. 35–36. S.o. 268 zur Mitte.

Akzente setzte, z.B. in der gleichsam naturwissenschaftlichen Erklärung der frühesten Vergangenheit, wurde im einzelnen hier dargelegt.

Bei Dikaiarch bietet das so neuinterpretierte goldene Zeitalter, dessen Kennzeichen nicht mehr der Überfluß mythischer Phantasie, sondern Kargheit eines einfachen Lebens wurde, eine eher realistische Lebensform. Es scheint, daß Dikaiarch mehr geben wollte als nur seine Theorie vergangener Entwicklung, seine Darstellung des Wandels der Lebensweisen enthielt ja moralische Urteile über menschliche Verhaltensweisen, die wiederum soziale Mißstände erklärten. Hier hilft eine Gegenüberstellung mit Platon, der im 7. Brief (326B6) seinem Mißfallen über das als glücklich gepriesene Leben in Syrakus Ausdruck verleiht. Als ersten Zug dieses Lebens nennt er u.a., daß man lebe, indem man sich zweimal am Tag an den Tafeln fülle. Kein Staat könne in Ruhe leben, wenn Menschen glauben, sie müßten alles auf reichliches Essen und ähnliche Genüsse im Übermaß vergeuden. Platon bezieht sich hier auf einen βίος (B7; C1), den er für die moralische Krise und politische Misere verantwortlich macht.

Ich möchte Dikaiarchs Primitivismus so als paradigmatisches Modell deuten. Es enthielt die Moral, daß Verhaltensweisen, sich mit wenigem zufrieden zu geben, ein sorgenfreies Leben verheißen, und dies konnte als naturgemäß sogar nach dem Erkenntnisstand zeitgenössischer Medizin begründet werden. Die Zustände der Vergangenheit sind somit nicht ein für allemal verloren, der Mythos vom goldenen Zeitalter war ja nur eine dichterische Übertreibung medizinisch erklärbarer Tatsachen. Jeder, der maßvoll und gesund lebt, konnte für sich das goldene Zeitalter wieder entstehen lassen.[85]

Eine Parallele gibt es bei Aristoteles: in seiner Darstellung der zeitlichen und rangmäßigen Abfolge der Erwerbsweisen ist die agrarische ursprünglich und naturgemäß (*Pol.* I 8), in anderem

---

[85] Vgl. Plat. *Rep.* X 608B1: die Verfassung, die man in sich selber hat. Vgl. Vidal-Naquet (oben, Anm. 73) 289 zum "Leben in der Zeit des Kronos" als Slogan für philosophische und religiöse Sekten, die mit der herrschenden Ordnung nicht zufrieden waren, vgl. 297. Wehrli (oben, Anm. 6) 57 verweist darauf, daß Gehorsam gegenüber der Natur, die alles Nötige gewährt, zur gemeinsamen Lehre der hellenistischen Schulen wird, vgl. Giglioni (oben, Anm. 40) 651, sie vergleicht Hor. *od.* III 16, 42–44. Genügsamkeit bei der Nahrung ist besonders ein Grundzug der kynischen Lehre, vgl. Krates von Theben bei DL VI 90 = Demetrios von Phaleron, 58A/B SOD; Teles in O. Hense, *Teletis Reliquiae* (Tübingen, [2]1909) 41, 3ff.

Zusammenhang begründet sie die beste Demokratie.[86] Eine naturgemäße, von der Entwicklung verdrängte Erwerbsweise behält ihre Bedeutung als Richtschnur für die Gestaltung der Gegenwart. Bei Dikaiarch braucht man nicht vorauszusetzen, daß er die älteste Lebensform in großem Stile wiederherzustellen empfehlen wollte. Er gibt ja zu, daß sich ursprüngliche Züge später erhalten haben.[87] Die Rückkehr zu gesunden Verhältnissen blieb also auch für einzelne eine Wahl, selbst wenn nicht alle dem folgten. Dies fügt sich gut in den Gesamtcharakter des Βίος Ἑλλάδος, dessen beherrschender Zug ja das Absehen von sozialen Organisationsformen war.

[86] VI 4, vgl. 1319a20, gegenübergestellt extreme Demokratie IV 12 1296b28ff., vgl. III 4 1277a39ff.
[87] *. . . ex duobus gradibus superioribus retinuerunt multa*, **54.**

7

Dikaiarchs Bios Hellados und Varros De vita populi Romani

Wolfram Ax

Dikaiarch aus dem sizilischen Messene, geb. um 376 v. Chr., neben Theophrast und dem ihm nahestehenden Aristoxenos einer der ältesten Schüler des Aristoteles, erlitt als Schriftsteller das gleiche Schicksal wie fast alle seine Nachfolger im Peripatos. Obwohl später, insbesondere von den Römern, hochgeschätzt, ging, was er schrieb, verloren, und nur noch wenige Spuren geben heute Auskunft über sein philosophisches Werk. 118 Testimonien und Fragmente hat Wehrli in der bislang maßgeblichen Textsammlung "Die Schule des Aristoteles" zusammentragen können, darunter allerdings verschwindend wenig Wörtliches.[1] Dennoch läßt sich wenigstens in Umrissen immer noch nachvollziehen, in welchen Werken und in welchen Schwerpunkten sich seine Philosophie niedergeschlagen hat.[2]

---

[1] Vgl. F. Wehrli, *Die Schule des Aristoteles. Texte und Kommentar*, Bd. 1: *Dikaiarchos* (Basel/Stuttgart, 1967). Eine frühere Textsammlung stammt von Carl Müller, *Fragmenta Historicorum Graecorum*, Bd. II (Paris, 1848) 225–68.

[2] Vgl. zu Dikaiarchs Leben und Werk: F. Martini, "Dikaiarchos 3) Peripatetiker," *RE* V.1 (1903) 546–63, F. Wehrli, "Dikaiarchos 3)," *RE Suppl.* 11 (1968) 526–34, S. E. Smethurst, "Cicero and Dicaearchus," *TAPA* 83 (1952) 224–32 und zuletzt G. Bodei Giglioni, "Dicearco e la riflessione sul passato," *Rivista storica Italiana* 98 (1986) 629–52.

Da ist zunächst ein Werk Περὶ ψυχῆς / *Über die Seele* in 6 Büchern mit zwei Dialogen zu je drei Büchern mit Schauplatzwechsel (Korinth und Lesbos) wie später in Ciceros *de finibus* (**1** nos. 1–4). Ein weiterer Dialog von mindestens zwei Büchern mit dem Titel *Abstieg in das Heiligtum des Trophonios* behandelte Probleme der Mantik (**1** nos. 8a–d). Von den folgenden nicht (in einem Fall nicht sicher) dialogischen Schriften werden drei weitere der Ethik zugerechnet: *Über das Opfer in Troja* (**1** no. 9)—gemeint ist das Achilleusopfer Alexanders—, *Über die Zerstörung der Menschen* (**1** no. 10) und Περὶ βίων / *Über Lebensformen* (**1** no. 5) mit unbekannter Buchzahl. In den Bereich der Kulturgeschichte gehören lt. Wehrli die drei Bücher Βίος Ἑλλάδος/Leben Griechenlands (**1** nos. 6–7), die gleich im Zentrum unserer Überlegungen stehen werden.[3] Die politischen Schriften (**1** nos. 11–13) enthalten eine möglicherweise dialogische *Verfassung der Spartaner*, eine Schrift Τριπολιτικός (*Dreierverfassung*), wenn nach einer Vermutung Wehrlis beide Titel nicht ein und dieselbe Schrift meinen,[4] und drei weitere, allerdings ebenfalls nicht zweifelsfreie *Verfassungen der Pellenier, Korinther und Athener.*[5] Zu nennen sind weiter, ohne sie hier noch im einzelnen auszuweisen, einige Schriften zu Kulten und Festen (**1** nos. 14–16), Philologisches zu Homer, Alkman und zu Sprichwörtern (**1** no. 18) und zum Schluß natürlich die später viel genutzten geographischen Schriften (**1** no. 19), die *Erdbeschreibung*, die *Pinakes* (Landkarten) und die *Vermessungen der Berge in der Peloponnes* (**1** nos. 20–21).

Auch wenn diese uns soeben noch zugänglichen Werke sicher nicht das Gesamtwerk Dikaiarchs repräsentieren—es existiert leider kein Schriftenverzeichnis—, so zeigt sich doch auch schon in dem, was uns geblieben ist, das typische Bild der Spezialisierung auf bestimmte Gebiete und Einzelaspekte in der Nachfolge des Aristoteles. In der Physik interessieren ihn als Detailgebiete die Psychologie und die Mantik, vor allem aber natürlich die Geographie, die er zu einem bedeutenden Schwerpunkt ausbaute. Auch in der Ethik fehlen die großen systematischen Entwürfe, statt dessen wird neben Einzelproblemen ein starkes Interesse an Fragen konkreter Lebensführung

---

[3] Vgl. F. Wehrli, "§21. Dikaiarchos von Messene," in *Ältere Akademie Aristoteles Peripatos*. Die Philosophie der Antike, Bd. 3, ed. Hellmut Flashar (Basel/Stuttgart, 1983) 535. Ebenda 537 firmieren sie dann allerdings unter den Schriften zur Ethik.

[4] Vgl. Wehrli (oben, Anm. 1) 64; (oben, Anm. 2) 532 und (oben, Anm. 3) 537.

[5] Vgl. Wehrli (oben, Anm. 1) 64f. und (oben, Anm. 2) 532.

deutlich, das zu biographischen (wie bei Aristoxenos) und allgemein kulturhistorischen Arbeiten führt. In der Politik konzentriert er sich auf Sparta, in der Literaturwissenschaft auf zwei Autoren. Die Logik, Sprachphilosophie und Rhetorik scheinen ganz zu fehlen. So ist es nicht verwunderlich, daß Dikaiarch in der späteren Lehrtradition vor allem als Geograph, Kulturhistoriker und politischer Schriftsteller gewirkt hat.[6] Daß er dabei durchaus eigenständige Ansichten auch gegen die eigene Schultradition vertrat, ist bekannt, so in den Prinzipien seiner Psychologie und in der expliziten Bevorzugung der *vita activa* vor der *vita contemplativa* gegen Aristoteles und Theophrast.[7]

Im folgenden Beitrag werde ich mich ausschließlich Dikaiarchs kulturhistorischer Schrift Βίος Ἑλλάδος zuwenden. Ich versuche zunächst das Werk selbst, soweit das noch möglich ist, zu beschreiben. Dann werde ich zweitens seiner Wirkung nachgehen, und zwar vor allem der Frage, inwieweit die Schrift *de vita populi Romani* des M. T. Varro den Einfluß Dikaiarchs erkennen läßt. Zunächst also zum *Bios Hellados* selbst, und zwar in der Reihenfolge der Aspekte (1) Aufbau und Inhalt, (2) Titel, (3) Literarische Gattung und (4) Gesamttendenz:

ad (1): Der Titel ist weitgehend, die Buchzahl des Werks (3 Bücher) völlig zweifelsfrei.[8] Nur 20 Texte haben sich erhalten, wovon die weitaus meisten, nämlich 11, so gut wie sicher dem ersten Buch angehören.[9] Trotz dieses äußerst kargen Bestandes lassen sich doch noch Inhalt und Aufbau der Schrift in großen Zügen und in einigen Einzelheiten rekonstruieren.[10] Ich gebe zunächst ein tabellarische Übersicht:

---

[6] Vgl. dazu die unter Anm. 2 genannte Literatur.

[7] Vgl. dazu z.B. Wehrli (oben, Anm. 3) 538.

[8] Seltsamerweise wird die Schrift in den Dikaiarchfragmenten nirgendwo unter dem heute üblich gewordenen Titel *Bios Hellados* zitiert. Es existieren mehrere Varianten. Welcher Titel original ist, läßt sich wohl nicht mehr absichern. Jason von Nysa, wie Varro ein Nachfolger Dikaiarchs (s.dazu unten Anm. 55) nannte sein Werk lt. Herodian (*Gramm.Graec.* III 1, 274,2) ὁ βίος τῆς Ἑλλάδος.

[9] Kein Fragment gehört sicher in das zweite Buch (Die beiden Erwähnungen des zweiten Buches in **59** und **60** sind wohl fehlerhaft). Nur ein Fragment (**77**) kann ohne Zweifel, zwei weitere (**76** und **70**) könnnen mit großer Wahrscheinlichkeit dem dritten Buch zugeschrieben werden. Sechs Fragmente (**58, 63, 65, 67, 72** und **73**) sind in ihrer Zuweisung ungesichert.

[10] Vgl. dazu Müller (oben, Anm. 1) 232ff.; Martini (oben, Anm. 2) 548f.; Wehrli (oben, Anm. 1) 63f.; Id. (oben, Anm. 2) 530f.; Id. (oben, Anm. 3) 537.

Buch 1: 11 sichere Fragmente

1. Kulturgeschichte der Urzeit (Vom Urzustand bis zum Ackerbau)
   —Die Menschheit ist ohne Anfang   **53–54**
   —Kulturentstehung in drei Schritten   **55–56B**
   1. Naturzustand, goldene Zeit unter Kronos
      (vita naturalis, ὁ ἐπὶ Κρόνου βίος)
   2. Hirtenleben
      (vita pastoralis, ὁ νομαδικὸς βίος)
   3. Ackerbau
      (agri cultura, γεωργικὸν εἶδος)
      Zu 2.: Kein Teilen beim Essen   **57**

2. Orientalische Kulturen vor Griechenland
   —*Ägypten*: Sesonchosis /Sesostris
      —Ständegesetze/Erfinder des Reitens   **58**
      —Chronologie   **59**
   —*Babylonien*: Chaldaios, Gründer Babylon Chaldäer **60–61**

3. Kulturgeschichte Griechenlands: Anfang
   —3 Städte Nestors bei Homer, Thamyrissage
      (Musikgeschichte?)   **63**

Buch 2: Kein sicheres Fragment

Buch 1, 2 oder 3: 6 unsichere Fragmente
Kulturgeschichte Griechenlands: Fortsetzung
   —Gentilizisch-politische Verbände: Patra, Phratria
      und Phyle   **64**
   —Gründung des kilikischen Theben durch Herakles   **65–67**
   —Übermäßiger Gebrauch von Kastagnetten im
      kultischen Tanz und Gesang der Frauen   **72**
      (Alkman, Musikinstrumente)
   —Erfindung bestimmter Tanzformen (Ballspiel)
      und vielleicht anderer sportlicher Übungen   **73**
   —Medea nicht von Euripides, sondern von Neophron
      (Tragödie)   **62**

Buch 3: 3 Fragmente

Kulturgeschichte Griechenlands bis auf die eigene Zeit
—Agesilaos' Tochter und Mutter des Epameinondas
    unbekannt. (Schlichtheit der spartanischen
    Lebensführung? Moralische Vorzüge von Frauen?)   **76**
—Philipp von Makedonien geht ohne Frauen in den Krieg.
    Dareios mit 360 Nebenfrauen (Orientalische
    Üppigkeit?)   **77**
—Etymologie des Namens Akademos (Heros der
    platonischen Akademie; Philosophie)   **70**

Aus dieser Übersicht wird unmittelbar evident: Dikaiarchs Kulturgeschichte war nicht systematisch, also etwa nach Sachgebieten wie
Kleidung, Ernährung, Spiel, Sport o.ä., sondern primär historisch
angelegt. Dabei wählt sie den denkbar größten zeitlichen Rahmen: vom
Urzustand der Menschheit bis auf die eigene Zeit.[11] Mit welchen
Einschnitten dieser geschichtliche Ablauf gegliedert war, ist jedoch nur
noch im gröbsten Umriss nachvollziehbar. Völlig unklar ist ferner, ob
auf einer unteren Gliederungsebene auch systematische Aspekte eine
Rolle gespielt haben. Allenfalls das erste Buch zeigt hier deutlichere
Konturen: Es begann mit Problemen der Anthropogenese—ob vorher
auch die Kosmogonie und Zoogonie behandelt wurde, wissen wir
nicht—, und zwar offensichtlich mit einer Parteinahme für die
Anfangslosigkeit der Menschheit.[12] Darauf folgte die dreistufige
Kulturentstehung vom ursprünglichen Naturzustand (1) über das
Hirtenleben (2) zum Ackerbau (3). Der eigentlich historische Teil
begann mit einer Beschreibung der orientalischen Kulturen vor
Griechenland, zunächst wohl der Ägyptens mit dessen sagenhaftem
König Sesonchosis oder Sesostris; vielleicht wurde auch Assyrien
behandelt,[13] sicher aber Babylon mit dessen Gründerkönig Chaldaios
und den nach ihm benannten Chaldäern.[14] Noch im ersten Buch muß

[11] Vgl. **55**: *Dicaearcho, qui, Graeciae vita qualis fuerit ab initio, nobis ita ostendit.*
[12] Zum Problem vgl. Wehrli (oben, Anm. 1) 56.
[13] Vgl. die Erwähnungen des Gründers von Ninive, Ninos, in **60** und **61**.
[14] Hier hat sich übrigens ein bis in einzelne Zahlen nachvollziehbarer
chronologischer Rahmen erhalten, der die Zeit vom Beginn der ägyptischen Geschichte
bis zur ersten Olympiade in Griechenland in vier Epochen meist mit genauen
Zahlenangaben einteilt (**59**): Von Horus zu Sesostris (ohne Zeitangabe), von Sesostris
zu Neilos (2500 Jahre), von Neilos zur Eroberung Trojas (7 Jahre) und von da zur ersten

dann die Kulturgeschichte Griechenlands eingesetzt haben, mit welchem Beginn und nach welcher Ratio läßt sich aufgrund des einzigen Fragments (**63**) nicht mehr feststellen. Es bezeugt Dikaiarchs Kritik an der Erwähnung dreier Städte Nestors im homerischen Schiffskatalog, die, verbunden mit der Thamyrissage, vielleicht in einen musikgeschichtlichen Zusammenhang gehört.[15] Was dann im weiteren Verlauf der Abhandlung noch in das erste oder schon in das zweite Buch fällt, muß ebenfalls ungeklärt bleiben. Sicher ist der chronologischen Ausrichtung entsprechend zuerst über die mythische Frühzeit Griechenlands berichtet worden (Gene, Phratrien, Phylen; Herakles' Brautwerbung und Gründung des kilikischen Theben; Kultische Tänze und Gesänge, Kastagnetten; Tanz). Der Übergang zur historischen Zeit[16] bleibt uns verborgen, jedoch deutet die Tatsache, daß Dikaiarch die Erfindung bestimmter Formen des Tanzes und vielleicht auch sportlicher Übungen den Sikyoniern zuschreibt (**73**) auf das 6. und, daß er die Tragödie Medea dem Euripides abschreibt (**62**)[17] auf das 5. Jhdt. v. Chr. Das dritte Buch hat dann offensichtlich vor allem dem 5./4. Jahrhundert (Agesilaos/Epameinondas) und der Zeit Diakaiarchs selbst (4. Jhdt.) gegolten, wie man noch aus den Fragmenten über Philipp II von Makedonien und Alexander (**77**) und über die platonische Akademie (**76**) erschließen kann.

Soviel zum zeitlichen Rahmen. Welche Themen Dikaiarch für seine Kulturgeschichte wählte, ist natürlich bei den überaus spärlichen Resten, deren Auswahl zudem noch vom Überlieferungszufall abhängt, nicht mehr zufriedenstellend zu beantworten. Deutlich hebt sich der Komplex der Kulturentstehungslehre (**53–55**) ab, ebenso der Abschnitt der orientalischen Völker vor Griechenland (**58–60**). Im Bereich der eigentlichen griechischen Kulturgeschichte begegnen Fragen der

---

Olympiade (436 Jahre), insgesamt also 2943 Jahre.Das ergibt nach unserer Zeitrechnung für Sesostris 3719 v. Chr. und für den Fall Trojas 1212 v. Chr., wenn man für die 1. Olympiade von 776 v. Chr. ausgeht. Es muß auch eine Zählung nach Königen gegeben haben. Vgl. **60** und **61**: Chaldaios, der 14. König nach Ninos. Leider wissen wir nicht, inwieweit diese Chronologie auch zur Disposition des ersten Buches gedient hat.

[15] Vgl. Wehrli (oben, Anm. 1) 61.

[16] Der Unterschied "mythisch-historisch" wird hier nur vermutungsweise eingebracht, er ist für Dikaiarch noch nicht bezeugt, wohl aber später für Varro (s.u. Anm. 63).

[17] Nach Wolfgang Luppe, "Zu Dikaiarchos Fr. 63 Wehrli," *RM* 135 (1992) 94–95 gehört **62** allerdings in das erste Buch. In diesem Fall müßte Euripides in einem chronologisch anderen Zusammenhang erwähnt worden sein.

allgemeinen Lebensführung (**57**: Verhalten beim Essen, **76**: Schlichtheit), ein gewisser Schwerpunkt scheint bei Beobachtungen im fraulichen Bereich gelegen zu haben (**65–66**: Werbungsagon, Hochzeit; **72**: Verhalten beim Kult, **76**: Unbekanntheit bedeutender Frauen; **77**: Mitführen von Frauen im Krieg, Philipp/Dareios). Weiter werden Probleme der Sozialordnung (**64**: Verwandtschaftsverbände im frühen Griechenland, **58**: ständische Ordnung per Gesetzgebung in Ägypten) behandelt, der politische Bereich also durchaus miteinbezogen. Von den einzelnen Kulturbereichen müssen Musik (Instrumentalmusik, Gesang **72**, Anfänge der Musik **63**), Tanzformen/ Ballspiel, also wahrscheinlich auch Sport (**63, 73**), Dichtung (**62**) und Philosophie (**70**) ebenfalls gebührende Beachtung gefunden haben.[18]

Im Zusammenhang mit dieser Themenwahl werden Interessen Dikaiarchs deutlich, die ihn klar in die peripatetische Tradition stellen. Er interessiert sich für Dichtung (Euripides, **62**), arbeitet gern Dichterzitate ein (Hesiod, Sophokles, Alkman, Homer), die er zur Stützung seiner Argumentation (**56A, 60, 72**) anführt, die er dabei aber auch rationalisiert (besonders deutlich bei Hesiod **56A**) und kritisiert (Homer **63**) und erklärt gern Sprichwörter (**56a** und **57**). Das alles paßt gut zu seinen auch sonst bezeugten *literaturwissenschaftlichen und philologischen* Interessen.[19] In der Herleitung von Sprichwörtern wird außerdem ein *aitiologischer* Zug erkennbar, dem er auch bei anderen Themen nachgibt, z.B., wenn er Völkernamen etymologisch ableitet (Chaldäer von Chaldaios **60, 61**), die Etymologie des Wortes "Akademie" liefert (**70**) oder Städtegründungen erwähnt, die in unserem spärlichen Material immerhin dreimal belegt sind (Herakles–Theben **65**; Ninos–Ninive, Chaldaios–Babylon **60, 61**). Daß damit natürlich auch ein *ethnographisch-geographisches* Interesse bezeugt ist, ist bei einem Autor wie Dikaiarch nicht verwunderlich (vgl. **60, 61** zwei Völker mit dem Namen Chaldaioi). Hierher gehört dann auch seine für den sonstigen Peripatos ebenfalls bezeugte Vorliebe für *Heuremata*, z.B. die Ständeordnung des Sesostris, dessen Erfindung des Reitens (**58**) und die Erfindung bestimmter Tanzformen durch die Sikyonier (**73**). Nicht vergessen darf man die *chronologischen* Interessen, die für uns im altorientalischen Teil noch erkennbar sind.[20]

[18] Vgl. Wehrli (oben, Anm. 1) 64.
[19] Vgl. Wehrli (oben, Anm. 3) 537f.
[20] Vgl. oben Anm. 14.

Ich kann hier nicht weiter auf die vielfachen Probleme des Aufbaus und der einzelnen thematischen Aspekte eingehen und muß stattdessen auf Wehrlis Kommentar verweisen. Allerdings muß ich wenigstens zum Komplex der Kulturentstehungslehre bei Dikaiarch etwas sagen, weil sich darin grundsätzliche Tendenzen in der Anlage und Zielsetzung seines Werkes zu verbergen scheinen. Die Forschung ist deshalb auch besonders intensiv auf diesen Punkt eingegangen.[21] Problematisch ist zunächst die Einordnung des dikaiarchischen Modells der drei Entwicklungsstufen Urzeit, Hirtenleben und Ackerbau in die frühere Lehrtradition. Ferner wäre zu bestimmen, ob Dikaiarchs Modell im Sinne einer moralisch neutralen, zivilisatorisch-technischen Aszendenz (Rohe, tierhafte Anfänge mit schweren Mangelzuständen, Überwindung der Mangelszustände durch zivilisatorische Höherentwicklung) mit der Folge einer positiven Wertung der letzten Epoche oder als ein auf moralischen Wertungen beruhendes Dekadenzmodell zu deuten ist, demzufolge die letzte Epoche (in der ja der Autor noch selbst lebt) im Vergleich zu einer idealisierten, paradiesischen Frühzeit doch wohl negativ einzuschätzen wäre. Nach der Antwort auf diese Frage wäre schließlich noch zu klären, welche Folgen sich daraus für den "ideologischen" Unterbau, die moralische Deutung des kulturhistorischen Ablaufs ergeben, die Dikaiarch seinem Werk zugrundelegt.

Die communis opinio in der Frage nach der Lehrtradition, in der Dikaiarchs Kulturentstehungslehre steht, ist vor allem von Wehrli geprägt worden.[22] Die Abfolge Hirtenleben-Ackerbau, führt er mit dem Verweis auf Thukydides I 2 auf sophistische Vorläufer zurück. Ob diese Parallele wirklich ausreicht, um sophistischen Einfluß auf Dikaiarch zu unterstellen, bleibt fraglich.[23] Sehr viel tragfähiger ist dagegen Wehrlis

[21] Vgl. Wehrli (oben, Anm. 1) 56–58; Id. (oben, Anm. 2) 530f.; Id. (oben, Anm. 3) 537; Martini (oben, Anm. 2) 548f.; Bodo Gatz, *Weltalter, goldene Zeit und sinnverwandte Vorstellungen*, Spudasmata XVI (Hildesheim, 1967) 156f.; Bernhard Reischl, *Reflexe griechischer Kulturentstehungslehren bei augusteischen Dichtern*, Diss. München (Augsburg, 1976) 90ff. und Bodei Giglioni (oben, Anm. 2). Weitere Literatur zur Kulturentstehungslehre Dikaiarchs im Beitrag von Trevor Saunders in diesem Band.
[22] Vgl. Wehrli (oben, Anm. 1) 56; Id. (oben, Anm. 2) 531 und id. (oben, Anm. 3) 537.
[23] Weder läßt sich m.E. das Thukydideskapitel I 2 zweifelsfrei auf sophistische Quellen zurückführen, noch kann man daraus eine eindeutige Reihenfolge der Kulturstufen *Hirtenleben /Ackerbau* im Sinne Dikaiarchs ableiten. Die Unterschiede zwischen Thukydides und Dikaiarch betont auch schon Bodei Giglioni (oben, Anm. 2) 644f. Dagegen sieht P. H. Schrijvers, "Intertextualité et polémique dans le *de rerum natura* (V 925–1010). Lucrèce vs. Dicéarque de Messène," *Philologus* 138 (1994) 288–

Hinweis auf Platons Nomoi III 677Bff., wo in ähnlicher Abfolge auf ein Stadium des Hirtenlebens der Ackerbau folgt mit entsprechenden moralischen Implikationen.[24] Hier scheint tatsächlich ein Traditionsstrang erfaßt, dem sich Dikaiarch verpflichtet fühlte. Trotzdem bleibt die systematische Eingliederung des Dreischritts in den Kontext der Kulturentstehungslehre Dikaiarchs Verdienst oder ist zumindest erstmals bei ihm belegt.

Das zweite Problem liegt, wie gesagt, in der Zuordnung von Dikaiarchs Modell zu den verschiedenen Typen von Kulturentstehungslehren.[25] Drei Typen werden gewöhnlich unterschieden: die mythische Deszendenz (z.B. Hesiods Weltzeitalter in den Erga), die sophistisch-atomistische Aszendenz (Protagoras, Demokrit u.a.) und die spätere "dialektische" Synthese von Deszendenz und Aszendenz (erkennbar in der Vulgata des 2./1. Jhdts v. Chr., z.B. Poseidonios, Diodor, Lukrez).[26] Im Fall Dikaiarchs liegt die Schwierigkeit darin, daß sein Dreistufenmodell in zwei Fragmenten überliefert ist, die durchaus unterschiedliche Typenzuordnungen zulassen (**54** Varro und **56A** Porphyrios) und daher sorgfältig miteinander verglichen werden müssen, bevor man sie für Dikaiarch auszuwerten versucht.[27] Varro und Porphyrios referieren zweifellos beide Dikaiarchs Dreischritt, aber es ist evident, daß sie dabei ihr Referat den eigenen Darstellungszielen oder Anschauungen angepasst und so umgefärbt haben, daß ihre Quelle, Dikaiarch, nicht mehr klar genug erkennbar wird. Wie Reischl

---

304, 293 und 302, Anm. 33 die Abhängigkeit Dikaiarchs in **56A** von Thukydides durch Formulierungsparallelen gesichert, die jedoch m.E. nicht tragfähig sind. Ein ähnlich systematischer Dreischritt wie bei Dikaiarch läßt sich außerdem in den bekannten sophistisch-atomistischen Kulturentstehungslehren (Protagoras VS 80 C 1, Demokrit VS 68 B 5) nicht nachweisen, und wenn Dikaiarch, jedenfalls nach **56A**, das hesiodeische Dekadenzschema (wenn auch mit sophistischer Rationalisierung, wie Wehrli sagt) adaptiert, so sollte man bedenken, daß er sich damit, wie Wehrli (oben, Anm. 1) 56 selbst zugibt, in einen prinzipiellen Gegensatz zur sophistischen Aszendenztheorie setzt.

[24] Vgl. Wehrli (oben, Anm. 1) 56f., Id. (oben, Anm. 2) 531 und id. (oben, Anm. 3) 537 und dazu noch die Hinweise von Gatz (oben, Anm. 21) 150. Bodei Giglioni (oben, Anm. 2) 643 sieht eher Unterschiede zu Platon.

[25] Vgl. dazu Gatz (oben, Anm. 21) 144ff. und Reischl (oben, Anm. 21) 1ff.

[26] Vgl. dazu Gatz (oben, Anm. 21) 161 und Reischl (oben, Anm. 21) 1.

[27] Dies hat, soweit mir bekannt, erstmals Reischl (oben, Anm. 21) 88–96 geleistet. Gatz (oben, Anm. 21) 157 und Bodei Giglioni (oben, Anm. 2), stützen sich zu einseitig auf Porphyrios (**56A**). Skeptisch gegenüber Porphyrios ist auch Francesco Della Corte, "L'idea della preistoria in Varrone," *Atti del Congresso Internazionale di Studi Varroniani,* 2 vols. (Rieti, 1976) I:111–36, 128, zu Varros Zeugnis vgl. ebenda 129f.

überzeugend herausgearbeitet hat, erscheint Dikaiarchs Modell bei Varro (**54**) als rein aszendente Variante, in der es ausschließlich um den technisch-zivilisatorischen Fortschritt im Nahrungserwerb in drei Kulturstufen geht, deren höchste der Landbau ist (Natürlicher Urzustand = Keine Nahrungsvorsorge, vegetarische Ernährung; Hirtenstufe = Nahrungsvorratswirtschaft im vegetarischen Bereich durch Sammeln von Früchten, im tierischen Bereich durch Domestikation; Agrikultur = künstliche (vegetarische) Nahrungserzeugung durch Landbau). Daß dies von Varro als eine Reihe des technischen Fortschritts gedacht ist, zeigt deutlicher noch **55**. Von einer eventuell damit verbundenen moralischen Dekadenz ist bei Varro keine Rede, obwohl gerade ihm sonst kulturkritische Ansätze nicht fremd sind. Vor allem wird der Urzustand bei ihm nicht idealisiert und mit dem goldenen Zeitalter unter Kronos gleichgesetzt wie in Porphyrios Bericht. Dies mag seinen Grund darin haben, daß Varro für seine *res rusticae* nur auf die zivilisatorisch-technische Seite auschließlich der agrarischen Kulturentwicklung abhob und andere Züge seiner Vorlage beiseite ließ.[28]

Anders Porphyrios (**56A**). Hier erscheint Dikaiarchs Modell als eine für die spätere Vulgata typische Kombination von technisch-zivilisatorischer Aszendenz und deren Bewertung als einer physischen und moralischen Deszendenz: Der Bios der ersten Menschen unter Kronos—das goldene Geschlecht Hesiods wird zur Erläuterung herangezogen, aber zugleich auch rationalisiert—gilt hier ebenfalls als die zivilisatorisch niedrigste, aber anders als bei Varro als die Stufe physisch und moralisch gesehen höchster Lebensqualität. Diese Menschen, standen noch den Göttern nahe, waren von Natur aus gut, hatten die beste Art der Lebensführung, die Nahrung wuchs von selbst (das berühmte Automaton-Motiv), d.h. sie wendeten keinerlei agrarische (und auch sonst keine) Technik an, hatten also Muße und keine Mühe und Sorge. Ihre genügsame Diät hielt sie gesund. Es gab keinen Besitz, also auch keinen Streit und keinen Krieg. Besonderer Nachdruck wird dabei, wie im gesamten folgenden Text, auf den Verzicht auf die Tötung von Tieren, also auf die vegetarische Ernährung der Menschen dieser Epoche gelegt (Bezeugt auch durch **56B**). Dementsprechend entsteht auf der zweiten Stufe, dem νομαδικὸς βίος, in dem erstmals Tiere getötet und domestiziert werden, Zwietracht und Krieg durch Besitz. Die dritte Stufe, das γεωργικὸν εἶδος, wird nicht

---

[28] Vgl. Reischl (oben, Anm. 21) 94–96.

näher charakterisiert, dafür noch einmal das Glück der Frühzeit
gepriesen unter erneuter Erwähnung der Enthaltung vom Fleischgenuß.
Obwohl Porphyrios, wie das häufige φησὶν und die größere
Detailgenauigkeit besonders in der Hesiodpassage zeigt, näher am
Originaltext zu referieren scheint als Varro, ist auch hier im Hinblick
auf die Authentizität des Wortlautes und die Vollständigkeit der
Wiedergabe der Lehre Dikaiarchs Vorsicht geboten.[29] Insbesondere ist
das Merkmals des Vegetarismus der goldenen Frühzeit, das Porphyrios
so betont, strittig. Hat schon Dikaiarch, wie in der Seelenlehre vielleicht
auch hier den Pythagoreern folgend, in der Tötung von Tieren eine Art
"Sündenfall" der Menschheit gesehen, der zum moralischen Niedergang der Folgeepochen führte ? Wie schwer hier eine Antwort zu geben
ist, zeigt Wehrli, der im Kommentar 1967 dem Gedanken des
Vegetarismus für Dikaiarchs Kulturentstehungslehre jede Bedeutung
abspricht, ihn aber später doch wieder als dekadenzauslösenden Faktor
nach dem Vorbild von Theophrasts *de pietate* auch für Dikaiarch
zuläßt.[30]
Wie dem auch sei—Porphyrios scheint insgesamt doch insofern
Dikaiarch vollständiger wiederzugeben als Varro, als Dikaiarch in
seiner Kulturentstehungslehre am Anfang des *Bios Hellados* nicht nur
den technisch-zivilisatorischen Fortschritt im Nahrungserwerb
beschrieb, sondern eine, wie Reischl sich ausdrückt, "ambivalente
Aszendenztheorie" vertrat,[31] die unter partieller Verwendung des
poetischen Weltzeitaltermythos Hesiods den Gedanken gleichzeitiger
physischer und moralischer Dekadenz (Krankheit, Luxusstreben/
Habgier/Krieg etc.) einbrachte, wohl in der Absicht, nicht nur den
technischen Fortschritt, sondern auch die Übel in der Welt zu erklären.
Es ergibt sich daraus die bereits erwähnte weitere Frage, welche
Reichweite dieser Gedanke im Gesamtwerk Dikaiarchs hatte, ob er z.B.
nur auf die Urperiode der Menschheitsgeschichte beschränkt oder für
den gesamten im *Bios Hellados* beschriebenen historischen Ablauf
bestimmend war. Mir scheint das erste zuzutreffen, denn der Dekadenz-
gedanke dominiert die gesamte Darstellung keineswegs so wie bei
Hesiod, etwa in dem Sinne, daß die Zeit von der Entstehung der
höchsten Kulturstufe, der Agrikultur, bis zur Zeit des Autors selbst
ständig als ein moralisch verkommenes Jammertal vorgestellt würde.

[29] Vgl. oben Anm. 28.
[30] Vgl. Wehrli (oben, Anm. 1) 56 und id. (oben, Anm. 3) 493 und 537.
[31] Vgl. Reischl (oben, Anm. 21) 93.

Im Gegenteil, es gibt später ja auch moralische Verbesserungen (57–59) und Lobenswertes (76 und 77). Aus dem Kulturmodell Dikaiarchs läßt sich m.E. jedenfalls nichts für die moralische Gesamttendenz des Werkes ableiten.[32] Soviel zum Aufbau und zum Inhalt der Schrift, mit deren Hilfe sich schon manches zu seinen Spezifika ermitteln ließ.

ad (2): Mehr kann sicher noch aus der im *Titel* verborgenen Begriffsgeschichte des Wortes βίος und seiner Verbindung mit Ἑλλάδος gewonnen werden. Die Bedeutungen von βίος zur Zeit Dikaiarchs lassen sich leicht an Aristoteles' Gebrauch des Wortes ablesen. Es bedeutet hauptsächlich (1) *Lebensdauer, -zeit* (2)*Lebensunterhalt* (victus) und (3) *Lebensweise, -führung*.[33] In der dritten Bedeutungs-gruppe ist im menschlichen Bereich die Übertragung des βίος-Begriffs vom Individuum auf den Staat ganz selbstverständlich. Die in der Ethik entwickelten Prinzipien der Lebensführung gelten für das menschliche Individuum wie für den Staat und seine Verfassung in gleicher Weise, ja die Verfassung (πολιτεία) ist die Lebensform, -führung (βίος) des Staates (*Politik* 4.11 1294a40 und 7.3 1325b30–32). Obwohl die Verbindung von βίος mit einem konkreten Staat m.W. bei Aristoteles nicht belegt ist, führt von hier aus kein weiter Weg zum βίος Ἑλλάδος Dikaiarchs, den man dann im Sinne von *Über die Lebensführung/Lebensweise Griechenlands* verstehen könnte.

Aber man kommt, was eventuelle Vorläufer Dikaiarchs im Gebrauch von βίος betrifft, durchaus über Aristoteles hinaus, nämlich bis zu den Vorsokratikern und zwar in den Umkreis ihrer für Dikaiarch ja so wichtigen Kulturenstehungslehre.[34] Hier trifft man auf Stellen, die von einem kollektiven βίος der Menschen reden, der sich in Stufen höher entwickelt. Z.B. spricht Kritias von einem anfänglich ungeordneten, tierischen Bios der Menschen ohne Recht und Gesetz (Kritias VS 88 B

---

[32] Hier möchte ich eher der vorsichtigen Skepsis Wehrlis (oben, Anm. 1) 64 folgen als der Zuversicht Bodei Giglionis (oben, Anm. 2), die ja, wie schon gesagt (Anm. 28), von 56A aus die moralische Gesamttendenz des Werkes ermitteln zu können glaubt.

[33] In diesen Bedeutungen kann es sich mit Mensch, Tier und Pflanze (*Gen. an.* 736b13) verbinden (exemplarische Zusammenstellung von βίοι von Mensch und Tier in *Politik* I 8). Dabei wird βίος immer auf Gattungen bezogen (z.B. maximale Lebensspanne der Pferde 576a29; Lebensunterhalt der Adlerjungen 619b27; verschiedene Arten der Lebensführung (βίοι) des Menschen. Belege bei Bonitz, Index Aristotelicus, s.v. βίος) Eine Verbindung von βίος mit einer individuellen Person (etwa βίος Ἀρχύτα wie bei Aristoxenos) ist jedoch, wenn ich nichts übersehen habe, bei Aristoteles nicht belegt.

[34] Vgl. die Hinweise bei Gatz (oben, Anm. 21) 146ff. und oben Anm. 22.

25), ähnlich auch Demokrit-Diodor (VS 68 B 5, II 135, 33ff., 136, 12). Besonders beziehungsreich ist hier der Palamedes-Komplex. Palamedes, der Förderer des zivilisatorischen Fortschritts der Menschheit par excellence (Kriegskunst, Recht, Buchstabenschrift, Maße und Gewichte, Rechnen u. a.), rühmt sich bei Gorgias (VS 82 B 11a §30, II 301, 23ff. D.-K.) den menschlichen Bios in Griechenland entscheidend verbessert zu haben. Und in dieser Motivtradition stoßen wir auch auf den m. W. n. ersten und ältesten Beleg der Junktur Ἑλλάδος βίος. Es ist das Aischylosfragment 181a Radt aus der Tragödie Palamedes.[35] Palamedes sagt dort:

ἔπειτα πάσης Ἑλλάδος καὶ ξυμμάχων βίον διῴκισ' ὄντα πρὶν
πεφυρμένον θηρσίν θ' ὅμοιον, πρῶτα μὲν τὸν πάνσοφον ἀριθμὸν
εὕρηκ' ἔξοχον σοφισμάτων.

Dann ordnet ich des ganzen Hellas wie auch der Mitkämpfer Leben, das zuvor verworren war und Tieren gleich. Zuerst erfand die Zahl ich, die Allweise, aller Wissenschaften trefflichste.

Kein Zweifel, Dikaiarch stellt sich mit seiner Titeljunktur über Aristoteles hinaus auch in die vorsokratische Tradition der Kulturentstehungslehre, die βίος im Rahmen eines aszendenten technisch-zivilisatorischen Entwicklungsmodells als *Kulturzustand, Zivilisationstufe* o.ä. verstanden wissen will, und so könnte man den Titel seiner Schrift auch mit *Über die Kultur, Zivilisation Griechenlands* wiedergeben. Die Schrift selbst war dann als eine Kultur- bzw. Zivilisationsgeschichte Griechenlands gedacht.

Wenn im vorsokratischen βίος–Begriff das Merkmal der Kulturentstehung und –entwicklung, also ein historisches Moment immer schon mitgegeben ist, so ist damit noch nicht das Merkmal des vollständigen historischen Ablaufs der griechischen Kultur von den Anfängen bis auf die Zeit des Autors erklärt. Hier könnte eine neue Bedeutung von βίος eine Rolle gespielt haben, die mit der Entstehungsgeschichte der Biographie von Individuen im Peripatos nach Theophrast zusammenhängt. βίος bedeutet hier nicht mehr nur *Lebensführung*, sondern auch *individueller Lebensverlauf, Lebensgeschichte* und in deren Folge auch *Beschreibung dieses Lebens-*

---

[35] Radt versieht das Fragment zwar mit zwei Sternen (nicht für Aischylos belegt), hält es aber doch für echt.

verlaufes, Biographie. Es ist nun eine alte These Fr. Leos, daß Dikaiarchs *Bios Hellados* von dieser Entwicklung beeinflußt ist und in dieser Schrift analog zur Individualbiographie nicht nur die Lebensführung, sondern auch die "Lebensgeschichte" eines Volkes beschrieben werden sollte.[36] Dikaiarch hätte also, wenn diese Vermutung stimmt, im komplexen Spiel begrifflicher Assoziationen die vorsokratische zivilisatorische βίος-Bedeutung (*Zivilisationsstufe, Kulturzustand*) mit der ethisch-politischen des Aristoteles (*Lebensweise,-führung*) und der neuen biographisch-literarischen Bedeutung (*Lebensgeschichte*) verbinden wollen. Ob diese These stimmt, wird gleich zu prüfen sein. Seinen Werktitel müßten wir allerdings in jedem Fall wegen seiner zweifellos auch historischen Nebenbedeutung als *Lebensweise, Kultur Griechenlands in ihrem vollständigen historischen Verlauf* oder einfacher, wie ja schon oft geschehen, als *Kulturgeschichte Griechenlands* paraphrasieren und sein Werk selbst entsprechend verstehen.

ad (3): Solche Beobachtungen lenken den Blick, wie schon angekündigt, auf die Frage, welche Rolle der *Bios Hellados* Dikaiarchs im Gefüge verwandter *literarischer Gattungen* spielt. Offenbar muß diese Schrift im Hinblick auf ihren Gattungscharakter als etwas völlig Neues bewertet werden, ist doch kein Werk gleichen Titels und auch keine irgendwie anders betitelte monographische Behandlung der Kulturgeschichte Griechenlands vor ihr bekannt.[37] Auf eine Archegetenrolle Dikaiarchs deuten, wie schon häufiger vermerkt wurde, auch die Nachahmungen seines Werkes durch Schriften gleichen Titels von Jason von Nysa (4 Bücher βίος τῆς Ελλάδος)[38] und von Varro (*de vita populi Romani*). Doch worin genau besteht eigentlich das Novum dieser Schrift, das sie von anderen, verwandten Gattungen absetzen könnte?

Wenn dieses Novum, wie oben erläutert, in der erstmaligen Übertragung der Gattungskriterien der Einzelbiographie auf die Vita eines Volkes liegen sollte, hätten wir als erste verwandte Gattung die

---

[36] Vgl. Friedrich Leo, *Die griechisch-römische Biographie nach ihrer literarischen Form* (ND Hilsheim, 1901) 99, Albrecht Dihle, *Studien zur griechischen Biographie* (Göttingen, 1970) 71, Wehrli (oben, Anm. 1) 63 und id. (oben, Anm. 3) 537.

[37] Vgl. Dihle, ibid. 71: "das erste und bedeutendste kulturgeschichtliche Werk der Antike."

[38] Zu Jason s. unten Anm. 54.

Biographie heranzuziehen. Vorstufe der im frühen Peripatos entstandenen biographischen Literatur ist bekanntlich die theoretische
Systematik der Bioi (Lebensweisen, Berufe) in der aristotelischen Ethik
und Politik. Schon bei Theophrast verdichtet sie sich zu einer nur dem
Titel nach bekannten monographischen Behandlung der Lebensformen,
in der sicher viel konkretes biographisches Material zur Exemplifizierung der verschiedenen Lebensformen verarbeitet war.[39] Faßbarere
Spuren solcher Bioi-Sammlungen finden sich aber erst bei Dikaiarch
selbst und besonders bei dessen Zeit- und Schulgenossen Klearch von
Soloi (geb. vor ca. 340 v. Chr.). Von Dikaiarch stammt eine mindestens
zwei Bücher umfassende Schrift Περὶ βίων, die jedoch für uns leider
nur noch ein Schemen bleiben muß.[40] Sie behandelte allgemeine
Fragen der Lebensführung sicher mit einem für die Römer später so
attraktiven Plädoyer für den (insbesondere politischen) βίος
πρακτικός. Desweiteren muß die Schrift—wahrscheinlich unter
Beschränkung auf Philosophen—unter dem leitenden Aspekt des βίος
πρακτικός Beispiele für verschiedene Lebensführungen, also Ein-
zelbiographien enthalten haben, vielleicht über die Sieben Weisen,
Pythagoras, Sokrates und Platon. Von den Fragmenten dieses Werks aus
führt noch keine Brücke zum *Bios Hellados,* wohl aber von den
Fragmenten des gleichnamigen Werks περὶ βίων von Klearch in
mindestens acht Büchern.[41] Laut Wehrli stellte Klearch "Biographien
als *Veranschaulichung prinzipiell möglicher Daseinsformen* dar."
Dabei erwähnt Wehrli zwei wichtige Unterschiede zur Biographie von
Individuen: "Das Leben des Einzelnen brauchte dabei n i c h t
v o l l s t ä n d i g erzählt zu werden; andererseits kamen g a n z e
V ö l k e r wie Lyder und Perser, sowie Städte des kleinasiatischen
Ostens und Westens zur sittengeschichtlichen Behandlung."[42] Für uns
ist hier vor allem der zweite Unterschied von großer Bedeutung. Die
peripatetische βίοι-Literatur zur Zeit Diakaiarchs und Klearchs war
also zur Exemplifizierung ihrer Typen von Lebensführungsarten
keineswegs auf die Vitae von Einzelpersonen festgelegt, sondern es
konnten auch kollektive "Sitten, Gebräuche, Lebensweisen" von

---

[39] Vgl. Leo (oben, Anm. 36) 98 (Diog. Laert. 5, 42: 3 Bücher περὶ βίων). Schriften
dieser Art gab es aber lt. Leo, 98, auch schon in der Akademie, z.B. von Xenokrates.
[40] Vgl. **1** no. 5 und **33–52** und Wehrli (oben, Anm. 3) 536f.
[41] Vgl. Klearch bei Fritz Wehrli, *Die Schule des Aristoteles.* Bd. 3, 2nd. ed. (1969)
frr. 37–62 und Wehrli (oben, Anm. 3) 549f.
[42] Vgl. Wehrli (oben, Anm. 3) 549f. Hervorhebung von mir.

ganzen Völkern und Städten beschrieben werden, wie im Fall Klearchs solche der Spartaner, Lyder, Milesier, Skythen, Tarentiner und Meder. Von hier aus ist es natürlich sehr leicht, eine Brücke zu Dikaiarchs *Bios Hellados* zu schlagen: Die Schrift steht grundsätzlich in der Tradition der im Peripatos erstmals bei Theophrast faßbaren und dann im Peripatos besonders gepflegten βίοι-Literatur, die Arten von Lebensweisen, Typen der Lebensführung, Sitten, Gebräuche etc. zum Gegenstand hatte und diese mit Hilfe von Beispielen individueller und kollektiver Lebensführung illustrierte. Das Neue an Dikaiarchs Schrift wäre von dieser Gattungstradition her gesehen l e d i g l i c h d i e K o n z e n t r a t i o n a u f d i e m o n o g r a p h i s c h e B e h a n d l u n g e i n e s e i n z i g e n k o l l e k t i v e n B i o s, n ä m l i c h a u f d e n V o l k s b i o s G r i e c h e n l a n d s.

Mit dieser Einordnung des *Bios Hellados* als eines Sonderfalls der Gattung Περὶ βίων ist allerdings noch nicht die unzweifelhafte Absicht Dikaiarchs erklärt, den Bios Griechenlands auch in seinem vollen historischen Ablauf zu beschreiben, denn auf Vollständigkeit in diesem Punkt war es ja, wie bereits erwähnt, in der Περὶ βίων-Literatur offenbar nicht angekommen. Ich habe schon erwähnt, daß Leo diese Eigenart des *Bios Hellados* auf eine Übertragung von Darstellungsprinzipien der Einzelbiographie zurückführte.[43] Für den individuellen Bios, wie er sich bei Aristoxenos herausbildete, war es nämlich sehr wahrscheinlich konstitutiv, daß nicht nur die Lebensführung, der Charakter der behandelten Person, sondern auch die vollständige Lebensgeschichte eines Menschen beschrieben wurde.[44] Dikaiarch wäre dann von hier aus dazu angeregt worden, in Übertragung des Persönlichkeitsbegriffs aus der individuellen Biographie nicht nur den "Charakter," die Lebensführung (βίος) des griechischen Volkes, sondern auch dessen Lebensgeschichte, "Biographie" darzustellen. So plausibel diese Erklärung zunächst zu sein scheint—sie verliert für mich bei näherer Betrachtung doch erheblich an Überzeugungskraft. Es mag durchaus sein, daß Dikaiarch bei der Wahl des Begriffes βίος für den Titel seiner Schrift auch unter

---

[43] S. oben Anm. 37.

[44] Vgl. dazu Dihles Definition der Biographie: *Sie* (die Definition) *besagt, daß man von Biographie als literarischer Gattung nur sprechen kann, wenn das Leben eines Menschen als ganzes ins Auge gefaßt, in seinem Ablauf, . . ., dargestellt und als Verwirklichung eines moralisch bewerteten Charakters interpretiert wird, . . .* in Albrecht Dihle, *Die Entstehung der historischen Biographie* (Heidelberg, 1987) 8.

dem Einfluß der ihm sicher bekannten Biographien des Aristoxenos und vielleicht auch seines eigenen biographischen Material in seiner Schrift Περὶ βίων stand und daher auch die Komponente *Lebensverlauf, Biographie* im Titel mitschwingt. Ob damit aber das Merkmal des historischen Ablaufs, so wie es sich dann in der Schrift selbst zeigt, ausreichend erklärt ist, möchte ich deshalb bezweifeln, weil dieser Ablauf kaum zu einer Biographie, sondern viel eher zu einer anderen Gattung paßt, und zwar zur Historiographie, genauer zur U n i v e r s a l g e s c h i c h t e.

Bei dem von mir bereits anfangs erläuterten historischen Ablauf in: *Anthropogenese (vielleicht sogar Zoogonie)—Kulturentstehung in drei Stufen—Orientalische Kulturen—Griechenland: mythische Zeit— historische Zeit bis auf die Gegenwart des Autors* drängt sich m. E. die Analogie zur Universalgeschichte förmlich auf. Bekanntlich ist das Jahrhundert Dikaiarchs auch das Jahrhundert der ersten Universalgeschichte, ich meine die 30 Bücher Ἱστορίαι des Ephoros von Kyme (entstanden etwa von 350 bis 330). Sie reichten von der Rückkehr der Herakliden bis auf die Zeit des Autors, wobei nicht nur die Geschichte Griechenlands, sondern auch die barbarischer Völker miteinbezogen wurde. Universalgeschichtliche Ansätze zeigen auch die ebenfalls zur Zeit Dikaiarchs entstandenen *Philippica* oder Φιλιππικαὶ Ἱστορίαι des Theopomp von Chios (geb. 378/377 v. Chr.). Obwohl vom Thema her auf Philipp von Makedonien und seine Zeit beschränkt, griff diese Schrift doch weit darüber hinaus und behandelte Weltgeschichte im Sinne von fr. 25 Jacoby: αἵ τε τῶν Ἑλλήνων καὶ βαρβάρων πράξεις. Es ist nun mehr als wahrscheinlich, daß sich Dikaiarch von diesen neuen Tendenzen in der Historiographie seiner Zeit bei seinem Plan hat anregen lassen, eine Kulturgeschichte Griechenlands zu schreiben. Die Ähnlichkeiten sind frappant, wenn man spätere universalgeschichtliche Darstellungen zum Vergleich heranzieht, die man aufgrund ihres Erhaltungszustandes besser überblicken kann als die Werke des Ephoros und des Theopomp. Ich meine vor allem Diodors (1. Jhdt. v. Chr.) *Bibliotheke* in 40 Büchern, die ja in der Tradition der Universalgeschichte des 4. Jhdts. steht. Der zeitliche Rahmen einer Universalgeschichte reicht gewöhnlich von den Anfängen bis auf die Zeit des Autors, bei Diodor vom Anfang der Welt bis zum Jahre 54 v. Chr. (so auch bei Nikolaos von Damaskus). Das gleiche Prinzip ist, wie wir gesehen haben, auch in Dikaiarchs *Bios Hellados* eingehalten. Der inhaltliche Ablauf bei Diodor liest sich streckenweise fast wie ein

Inhaltsverzeichnis der Schrift Dikaiarchs: Kosmogonie, Zoogonie, Kulturentstehungslehre (vielleicht nach Demokrit) (Buch 1), dann drei Bücher über barbarische, insbesondere orientalische Völker (B. 1–3), nämlich Ägypten (B. 1), Assyrer (u.a. Ninos), Chaldäer und andere Völker (B. 2–3). Ab Buch 4 folgen dann die Griechen, zuerst die mythische Zeit in B. 4–6, dann von 7–17 die historische Zeit vom trojanischen Krieg bis zum Tod Alexanders u. s. f. bis zu Caesars Expedition nach Britannien 54 v. Chr. Eine derart weitgehende Parallele kann m. E. nicht auf Zufall beruhen, sondern liefert ein beredtes Zeugnis für den Einfluß der Universalgeschichte auf den *Bios Hellados* Dikaiarchs.

Von der Gattungsgeschichte der Historiographie her gesehen ergibt sich also ein zweites Novum der Schrift Dikaiarchs: Er ging von der βίοι-Literatur aus und konzentrierte sich dabei auf einen einzigen Bios, den Bios Griechenlands. Dabei war er aber auch an der vollständigen Erfassung der historischen Dimension seines Gegenstandes interessiert und versuchte ihm dadurch gerecht zu werden, daß er sich der Darstellungsmittel der Universalgeschichte seiner Zeit bediente. Er wollte nicht einfach nur den Bios, die Lebensweise, die Sitten und Gebräuche Griechenlands, sondern e i n e U n i v e r s a l g e s c h i c h t e G r i e c h e n l a n d s u n t e r d e m A s p e k t s e i n e s B i o s, a l s o e i n e K u l t u r g e s c h i c h t e G r i e c h e n l a n d s i m v o l l e n S i n n e d e s W o r t e s s c h r e i b e n.[45] Dikaiarchs Schrift dürfte demnach kaum als das Ergebnis einer Übertragung von Prinzipien der Einzelbiographie (Charakter und Lebensgeschichte), sondern als eine Art Mischgattung zwischen der peripatetischen περὶ βίων-Literatur und der zeitgenössischen Universalgeschichte zu verstehen sein.[46]

[45] Es handelt sich hier wohlgemerkt nur um eine erste vorläufige Vermutung, die durch weitere gründliche Prüfung der Beziehungen zwischen der Universalgeschichte von Ephoros bis Diodor und Dikaiarchs *Bios* abgesichert werden muß, eine wichtige Aufgabe, die im Rahmen dieses Beitrages nicht geleistet werden kann. Ich habe daher hier auf Einzelnachweise und Literaturangaben verzichtet.

[46] Zu prüfen wäre ebenfalls noch das Verhältnis des *Bios Hellados* zur Ethnographie und weiterer verwandter Gattungen. Vgl. dazu Albrecht Dihle, "Zur hellenistischen Ethnographie," in *Grecs et Barbares, Entretiens VIII*, 205–39 (Vandoeuvres-Genève, 1962) 205–39; Klaus E. Müller, *Geschichte der antiken Ethnographie und ethnologischen Theoriebildung*, 2 Bände (Wiesbaden, 1972/1980) I:213–18 (Dikaiarch) und II:26–42 (Varro); und Albrecht Dihle, *Die Griechen und die Fremden* (München, 1994).

ad (4): Abschließend komme ich zur Frage, ob unsere Fragmente des *Bios Hellados* eine Gesamttendenz, eine Art zentraler Aussage erkennen lassen. Diese Aussage könnte—bei einer Sitten- und Kulturgeschichte ein naheliegender Gedanke—in eine kritisch-moralisierende Richtung zielen. Die Spärlichkeit unserer Überlieferung läßt hier jedoch m. E. keine sichere Antwort zu. Es läßt sich nämlich, wie schon gesagt,[47] auf der Basis unserer Fragmente nicht nachweisen, ob eine moralisierende Betrachtung, wie sie unzweifelhaft in **56A** vorliegt, das gesamte Werk durchzog. Die sonstigen Fragmente verhalten sich in diesem Punkt neutral und lassen sich ebensogut aus einem rein kulturaitiologischen Interesse erklären. Wenn man dennoch an einer moralischen Gesamttendenz des Werks festhalten will, bleibt nur die Möglichkeit, sich auf **56A** zu stützen und dessen Aussage auf das gesamte Werk zu extrapolieren. Diesen Weg ist vor allem G. Bodei Giglioni gegangen. Für sie ist der *Bios Hellados* ein Denkmal des Kulturpessimismus in der Zeit geographischer Expansion und politischer Krisen des 4. Jhdts. Aus einem Gefühl der Enttäuschung über die krisenhafte Gegenwart sei eine idealisierende Aufwertung der Frühzeit entstanden, verbunden mit dem moralischen Apell vor allem zur Vermeidung von Krieg und Gemetzel, zum Vegetarismus, zur Reduktion der Bedürfnisse überhaupt im Sinne eines "Zurück zur Natur," Idealen, die von den Menschen der Vorzeit beispielhaft vorgelebt worden seien. Diese Tendenz verbinde Dikaiarch mit anderen philosophischen Richtungen seiner Zeit wie den Kynikern und Epikureern. Dikaiarch wäre, so gesehen, eine frühe Stimme im Chor hellenistischer Enthaltsamkeitphilosophen.[48] Gegen diese Auffassung scheint mir eher Skepsis angebracht, ganz einfach deshalb, weil, wie schon gesagt, die wenigen außer **56A** uns verbliebenen Fragmente eine derartig dezidierte Aussage nicht ausreichend stützen können. Ich möchte mich in diesem Punkt doch eher Wehrli anschließen, der dem *Bios Hellados* zwar einen durchgehenden moralischen Gesichtspunkt unterstellt, sich aber außerstande sieht, unseren Resten eine einheitliche Konzeption in dieser Hinsicht abzugewinnen.[49]

---

[47] S. oben S. 290.
[48] Vgl. Bodei-Giglioni (oben, Anm. 2) passim, besonders 650f.
[49] s. oben S. 290 mit Anm. 33.

Nach der Beschreibung des Werkes selbst komme ich nun, wie
angekündigt, zu meinem zweiten Punkt, der *Nachwirkung* des *Bios
Hellados*. Daß Dikaiarchs Philosophie allgemein sich auch noch im
intellektuellen Rom des ersten Jahrhunderts vor Chr. ungebrochener
Aufmerksamkeit erfreute, ist bekannt und z.b. für Cicero ausführlich
von Smethurst dargestellt worden.[50] Nachwirkungen speziell des *Bios
Hellados* hat man allerdings bisher ausschließlich für Varro
behauptet.[51] Vor allem galt es als ausgemacht, daß Varros titelgleicher
Schrift *de vita populi Romani* (= *vpR*) in vier Büchern, die man
gewöhnlich auf das Jahr 43 v. Chr. datiert, Dikaiarchs *Bios* Modell
gestanden hat.[52]

Vor einer vergleichenden Betrachtung beider Schriften, die sich von
daher sofort anbietet, sind jedoch zwei präzisierende Vorbemerkungen
nötig. Zunächst ist Vorsicht geboten, wenn man Varros Schrift
ausschließlich und direkt auf Dikaiarchs *Bios Hellados* zurückführt.
Zweifellos kannte Varro Dikaiarchs Schrift aus eigener Lektüre, wie die
beiden Erwähnungen in den *res rusticae* beweisen,[53] und, obwohl er sie
in unseren Fragmenten von *vpR* nicht nennt oder zitiert, läßt sich doch
allein die Verwendung des Originaltitels in lateinischer Übersetzung
kaum anders als ein Hinweis auf sein peripatetisches Gattungsvorbild
verstehen. Dennoch ist auch ein zeitgenössischer Einfluss auf Varro
nicht auszuschließen, ja sogar recht wahrscheinlich. Es gab nämlich,
wie schon erwähnt, zur Zeit Varros auf griechischer Seite noch eine
weitere titelgleiche Kulturgeschichte in der Folge Dikaiarchs, und zwar
die vier Bücher *Bios Hellados* des Stoikers Jason von Nysa-eines
Enkels des Poseidonios und dessen Nachfolger in der Schulleitung ab
ca. 50 v. Chr.[54] Zwar läßt sich eine relative Chronologie der Schriften

---

[50] Vgl. Smethurst (oben Anm. 2). Zur Wirkung auf Lukrez vgl. jetzt Schrijvers
(oben, Anm. 23) mit dem wichtigen Hinweis (294, Anm. 15) auf Elizabeth Rawson,
Intellectual Life in the Late Roman republic (London, 1985), die den Einfluß Dikaiarchs
auf Atticus, Cicero und Varro sehr hoch einschätzt (Vgl. Rawsons Index s.v.
Dicaearchus).

[51] Dazu muß nach Schrijvers (oben, Anm. 23) jetzt auch Lukrez gestellt werden.

[52] Vgl. z.B. Hellfried Dahlmann, "Terentius 84," *RE Suppl.* 6 (1935) 1172–1277,
1244; Wehrli (oben, Anm. 1) 64; oder Reischl (oben, Anm. 21) 84, 90–96.

[53] Vgl. Varro, *res rusticae* 2,1,3 (= **54**) und 1,2,15 (= **55**). Dazu wird *ling. Lat.*
5,108f. gezogen. Vgl. dazu Dahlmann (oben, Anm. 52) 1245, dagegen Wehrli (oben,
Anm. 1) 64.

[54] Jasons Fragmente sind nicht gesammelt. Nur ein Fragment (nicht aus dem *Bios
Hellados*) bei Jacoby FGH III C 1 Nr. 162 (S. 182). Werkübersicht im Suda-Artikel s.v.
Ἰάσων (II p. 605). Ich habe bisher erst ein Fragment aus dem vierten Buch des *Bios
Hellados* gefunden: Herodian, *Gramm. Graec.* III 1, 274, 2–10 Lentz. Es handelt von der

Varros und Jasons nicht mehr herstellen, aber die doppelte Parallele im
Titel und in der Buchzahl (4 Bücher) ist für mich so auffallend, daß ich
eine direkte Beziehung zwischen beiden Schriften annehmen möchte.[55]
Wenn Varro in diesem Fall der Nehmende gewesen sein sollte, hätte er
sich nicht nur von der älteren peripatetischen Tradition, sondern auch
von dem an den Peripatos anknüpfenden ethnographischen und
kulturhistorischen Interesse der zeitgenössischen Mittleren Stoa seit
Poseidonios beeinflussen lassen.[56] Dazu paßt gut seine Tendenz, auch
in anderen kulturhistorischen Schriften wie etwa in *de gente populi
Romani* zeitgenössische Quellen, hier Kastor von Rhodos für die
Chronologie, heranzuziehen.[57]

   Zweitens muß man für einen Vergleich zwischen Dikaiarch und Varro
nicht nur *vpR,* sondern, wie man gleich sehen wird, auch noch *de gente
populi Romani* (= *gpR*), eine Schrift in ebenfalls vier Büchern, in oder
kurz nach dem Jahre 43 v. Chr. entstanden, heranziehen. Beide
Schriften sind offenbar chronologisch und thematisch, von der
Titelgebung und von der Buchzahl her als eine sich gegenseitig
ergänzende Einheit gedacht, die erst zusammen den von Dikaiarch als
gattungstypisch vorgeprägten Rahmen einer Kulturgeschichte
abdecken.[58] Für Dikaiarch erstreckte sich der Gegenstand "Kulturgeschichte Griechenlands" zeitlich von den Anfängen der Menschheit bis
auf seine Zeit. Dies erfüllen erst beide Schriften Varros gemeinsam,

---

Gründung Alexandrias. Die Buchzahl 4 ist durch den Suda-Artikel gesichert. Die
Verfasserschaft Iasons von Nysa wird für den *Bios Hellados* allerdings auch
angezweifelt. Vgl. jetzt Peter Steinmetz, "§41. Die Stoa in der Mitte und zweiten Hälfte
des ersten Jahrhunderts vor Christus," in *Die hellenistische Philosophie. Die
Philosophie der Antike,* ed. Hellmut Flashar, Bd 4/2 (Basel, 1994) 706f.,
Werkbeschreibung 709, 714f. Fragmente.

[55] Diese These ist neu, sonst werden beide Autoren nur selten nebeneinander
erwähnt, ohne die Frage ihrer Beziehung zueinander zu erörtern (vgl. z.B. Martini [oben,
Anm. 2] 549, Schanz-Hosius, *Geschichte der römischen Literatur* I 566 und Wehrli
[oben, Anm. 1] 64). Möglich ist natürlich auch die gleichzeitige Nutzung Dikaiarchs
durch Jason und Varro unabhängig voneinander. Dagegen spricht aber die auffällige
Parallele der gleichen Buchzahl. Bei gegenseitiger Abhängigkeit kommt wohl allein eine
Abhängigkeit Jason–Varro, nicht Varro–Jason in Frage.

[56] Vgl. E. Wendling, "Zu Posidonius und Varro," *Hermes* 28 (1893) 335–53 und
Jürgen Malitz, *Die Historien des Poseidonius,* Zetemata 79 (München, 1983) 7, Anm.
18; 23; 25, Anm. 166; 47, Anm. 98 und 82, Anm. 57. Dazu Della Corte (oben, Anm. 27)
134 und A. La Penna, "Alcuni concetti base di Varrone sulla storia Romana," *Atti del
Congresso Internazionale di Studi Varroniani,* 2 vols. (Rieti, 1976) II:397–407, 406ff.

[57] Vgl. Dahlmann (oben, Anm. 52) 1240f.

[58] So schon Della Corte (oben, Anm. 27) 130.

denn *gpR* reicht von den Anfängen bis in die römische Königszeit, *vpR* dann von den römischen Königen bis zur Zeit Varros. Auch thematisch bilden beide Schriften eine Einheit, indem sie am Leitfaden der politischen Epochengliederung eine vorwiegend aitiologisch orientierte Darstellung kultureller (öffentlicher und privater) Einrichtungen, Sitten und Gebräuche liefern. Und, obwohl es anders als bei Dikaiarch zwei Leitaspekte der Darstellung gibt, die zur Trennung des kultur-historischen Kontinuums in zwei Schriften geführt haben, nämlich *gens* und *vita*, ist der gemeinsame Herkunftsbereich der Titelmetaphorik doch auch ein Zeichen für die Zusammengehörigkeit beider Schriften.[59] Schließlich dürfte auch die gleiche Buchzahl nicht auf Zufall beruhen. Dies alles spricht für eine Synopse beider Schriften mit Dikaiarchs *Bios*. Für den Vergleich mit Dikaiarch ist vor diesem Hintergrund übrigens schon jetzt festzuhalten, daß direkte stoffliche (nicht methodische) Parallelen, wenn überhaupt, dann nur in *gpR* zu erwarten wären, etwa in den beiden ersten Griechenland gewidmeten Büchern, denn *vpR* behandelt ausschließlich die römische, nicht die griechische Kulturgeschichte.

Ich führe also den Vergleich mit beiden Schriften Varros durch und beginne mit einer kurzen Beschreibung von *gpR*. Die Schrift umfaßte vier Bücher und ist, wie schon gesagt, nicht vor 43 v. Chr. geschrieben. Ca. 23 sichere Fragmente haben sich erhalten.[60] Ihr Ziel ist es, wie schon die Titelmetapher zeigt, dem römischen Volk—der Familien-geschichte eines Individuums vergleichbar—seinen Platz in seiner *gens*, der "Völkerfamilie," anzuweisen, es also in eine im engeren Sinne genealogische und darüberhinaus in eine allgemein mythologie- und kulturgeschichtliche Reihe zu stellen, die von den Anfängen der Menschheit bis zu dem Punkt reicht, wo die individuelle Lebens-geschichte des *populus Romanus*, seine *vita* also, beginnt. Die dazu nötige Chronologie entnahm Varro, wie schon gesagt, Kastor von Rhodos, der in seinen sechs auf synchronische Vergleichung zielenden

---

[59] *Gens* und *vita* sind ja beide vom Individuum auf das Volk übertragene Metaphern (*gens* = "Familien"geschichte, *vita*: Individuelle Geschichte eines Volkes).

[60] Grundlegend Plinio Fraccaro, *Studi Varroniani. De gente populi Romani libri IV* (Padova, 1907), die Fragmente pp. 247–86. Die Fragmente auch bei Peter HRR II 10ff., nach dem sie hier zitiert werden. Vgl. außerdem noch Dahlmann (oben, Anm. 52) 1237–42; Lily Ross Taylor, "Varro's *De Gente Populi Romani*," *CP* 29 (1934) 221–29; Della Corte (oben, Anm. 27) 126ff.; und K. E. Müller (oben, Anm. 46) II:29f. Terminus post quem der Schrift ist 43 v. Chr., weil f. 9 Peter Hirtius und Pansa, die Konsuln des Jahres 43, erwähnt werden.

Büchern *Chronica* eine vielleicht nur tabellarische Übersicht von den assyrischen Königen bis zum Jahre 61/60 geliefert hatte.[61] Von Kastor stammt vielleicht auch Varros Dreigliederung der Menschheits-geschichte in drei Epochen, in das *"adelon"* (von den unbekannten Anfängen der Menschheit bis zur Sintflut des Ogyges, bzw. -os, bis 2376 v. Chr. also), das *"mythicon"* (von der Sintflut bis zur ersten Olympiade, also von 2376 bis 776 v. Chr.) und das *"historicon"* (von der ersten Olympiade bis zur jeweiligen Jetztzeit des Autors, also von 776 bis im Fall Varros 43 v. Chr.).[62] Man weiß allerdings nicht genau, wie sich diese drei Spatien auf die vier Bücher von *gpR* verteilt haben. Die Darstellung reichte insgesamt, der Konzeption der Schrift entsprechend, von den Anfängen der Menschheit zu Beginn des ersten Buches bis zur Gründungszeit Roms im vierten Buch, wobei es unklar bleiben muß, ob das vierte Buch schon mit der Frühphase der Königszeit, also im wesentlich mit Romulus, endete oder noch die gesamte Königszeit bis zur Vertreibung der Könige 510 v. Chr. einschloß.[63] Wenig Sicheres läßt sich auch zur Binnengliederung sagen. Wie f. 5 Peter zeigt, kann das *adelon* nur sehr kurz einleitend behandelt worden sein, denn dort heißt es, daß Varro seine Darstellung mit der ogygischen Flut, also mit dem spatium *mythicon* ab 2376 begonnen habe. Durch f. 14 P. erfahren wir, daß der trojanische Krieg das zweite Buch abschloß, nach Varros Rechnung also das Jahr 1176 erreicht ist. Da das *mythicon* aber bis zur ersten Olympiade reichte, muß sich dessen Beschreibung noch weit in das dritte Buch erstreckt haben, wie ja auch die Erwähnung Olympias im f. 15 P. beweist, das ausdrücklich für das dritte Buch bezeugt ist. Vielleicht fand Varro mit dem Epochendatum 776, der Grenze zwischen dem *mythicon* und dem *historicon*, sogar einen geeigneten Schlußpunkt für das dritte Buch, um dann mit der Gründung Roms als einem der ersten wichtigen Ereignisse

[61] Vgl. zu Kastor *RE* 20, 2 (1950) 1463f; Dahlmann (oben, Anm. 52) 1240f., Kl. Pauly s.v. Kastor.

[62] Zur Chronologie der Schrift vgl. vor allem Dahlmann (oben, Anm. 52) 1237–41. Das von Censorin überlieferte Schema der drei Epochen (f. 3 P.) geht laut Reischl (oben, Anm. 21) 88, Anm. 5 auf Eratosthenes zurück (vgl. Jacoby, Frg. gr. Hist. 241, Komm. 709 1 c). Vgl. auch Jacques Poucet, "Temps mythique et temps historique. Les origines et les premiers siècles de Rome," *Gerion* 5 (1987) 69–85.

[63] Zur Unklarheit der Verhältnisse am Ende des vierten Buches vgl. Dahlmann (oben, Anm. 52) 1239. Die Erwähnung von Hirtius und Pansa in f. 9 Peter als Endpunkt der chronologischen Berechnungen Varros bedeutet natürlich nicht, daß auch die Schrift *gpR* in der Zeit Varros endete. Dieser Zeitpunkt ist erst mit dem vierten Buch von *vpR* erreicht.

der historischen Zeit im vierten Buch fortzufahren. Doch muß dies Spekulation bleiben. Die einzelnen Bücher waren dem griechischen Vorbild entsprechend nach Königslisten gegliedert, das erste und zweite Buch behandelte u.a. die thebanischen, sikyonischen, argivischen und athenischen Könige bis zum trojanischen Krieg. Inwieweit die orientalischen Völker einbezogen wurden, ist nicht mehr auszumachen, unzweifelhaft liegt jedoch der Schwerpunkt auf der griechischen Geschichte.[64] Das dritte Buch begann wahrscheinlich mit den italischen Königen, zunächst mit den Königen von Laurentum, denen dann die latinischen Könige und die Könige von Alba Longa folgten. Die Gründung Roms und die Liste der römischen Könige stand dann vielleicht am Anfang des vierten Buches.

Es ging in dieser Schrift natürlich auch um die Frage der physischen Abstammung des *populus Romanus*, wobei die Hauptlinie der varronischen Genealogie der troisch-latinische Ursprung des römischen Volkes, wie man sie später allgemein, etwa bei den augusteischen Dichtern, wiederfindet, gewesen sein dürfte. Aber *gpR* war ebenso sicher auch eine Kulturgeschichte im weiteren Sinne des Wortes, in der das römische Volk über die physische Verwandtschaft hinaus in eine "kulturidentische" Reihe mit anderen Völkern, insbesondere mit den Griechen, gestellt wurde.[65] In dieser Kulturgeschichte wurden nicht wie in der Historiographie die *res gestae* beschrieben, sondern es standen die Herkunft der *instituta*, der (öffentlichen und privaten) Einrichtungen, Sitten, Gebräuche etc. im Vordergrund, wie Servius anläßlich einer bestimmten von den Spartanern und Kretern übernommenen Tischsitte der *maiores* (f. 21 P. Im-Sitzen-Essen) sogar ausdrücklich feststellt: *ut Varro docet in libris de gente populi Romani, in quibus dicit, quid a quaque traxerint gente per imitationem.* Dazu paßt die Erwähnung altitalischer Disziplin allgemein (f. 20 P.) und weiterer kulturhistorische Details aus der römischen Frühzeit bei

---

[64] Es ist den Fragmenten nicht sicher zu entnehmen, ob Varro der orientalischen Geschichte einen eigenen Abschnitt widmete. Dahlmann (oben, Anm. 52) 1241 glaubt an einen Wegfall der assyrischen Geschichte. Varro wird orientalische Ereignisse eher in der Art des Augustinus synchron-vergleichend in seine Darstellung eingeflochten haben wie z.B. die ägyptische Geschichte in f. 12 oder 13 P. Die griechische Geschichte scheint jedenfalls den Vorrang gehabt zu haben.

[65] Dahlmann unterscheidet beide Aspekte (oben, Anm. 52) 1237, 1239 und 1242 nicht deutlich genug. Klarer formuliert K. E. Müller (oben, Anm. 46) II:30. Allerdings scheint Varro eine physische Abstammung der Römer auch von der Griechen in Erwähnung gezogen zu haben. Vgl. Augustinus, *Civ.* 18, 14 und Benedetto Riposati, *M. Terenti Varronis de vita populi Romani* (Milano, 1972) 268.

militärischen Ehrungen (f. 22 P.) und bei Wagenrennen (f. 23 P.). Ein deutliches kulturaitiologisches und insbesondere namens-etymologisches Interesse ist ein weiteres Indiz für eine kultur-geschichtliche Orientierung wie z.b. die Etymologien der Namen Athens (f.7 P.), des Areopag (f. 8 P.), des Serapis (f. 13 P.), des Beinamen Lykaios (f. 17 P.) und des Aventin (f. 18 P.) zeigen.[66] Eine der gesamten Schrift zu unterstellende "Ideologie" im Sinne einer moralisch-kritischen über die rein kulturhistorische Wissensver-mittlung hinausgehende Gesamtaussage, wie man sie, wie wir gleich sehen werden, für *vpR* ermitteln kann, läßt sich m.E. aus den Fragmenten von *gpR* nicht sicher entnehmen. Sie ist aber in den rombezogenen Teilen auch nicht auszuschließen, wo unverkennbar der *mos maiorum* wie in *vpR* behandelt wurde (f. 20–22 P.)

Die Schrift *vpR*, wie *gpR* vier Büchern umfassend, muß zwischen 49 und 32 v. Chr. entstanden sein. Meist wird sie aber aus den schon erwähnten Gründen in die zeitliche Nähe von *gpR*, also in das Jahr 43 v. Chr. gerückt.[67] 129 Fragmente, überwiegend von Nonius bewahrt, zählt Riposati in seiner immer noch grundlegenden Ausgabe von 1939.[68] Ich habe schon gesagt, daß *vpR* in mehrfacher Hinsicht die Entsprechung und Fortsetzung von *gpR* darstellt. Schon die Titelmeta-pher *vita*—wie *gens* aus der Sphäre des menschlichen Individuums auf das Kollektiv *populus* übertragen—ist in chronologisch komple-mentärer Weise so auf *gens* bezogen, daß jetzt nach der "Familien-geschichte" der individuelle Lebensverlauf des römischen Volkes beschrieben werden soll.[69] Entsprechend setzt *vpR* im ersten Buch da ein, wo *gpR* aufgehört hatte, nämlich mit dem Beginn der römischen Königzeit, wobei das Maß der Überschneidung mit dem vierten Buch von *gpR* nicht mehr deutlich wird, und führt dem Muster Dikaiarchs folgend die Darstellung bis auf die Zeit des Autors (49/48 v. Chr.)

---

[66] Das besonders häufige Hervortreten des Komplexes "Apotheose bedeutender Menschen" in den Fragmenten von *vpR* sollte man vorsichtiger als Dahlmann (oben, Anm. 52) 1239 direkt auf Varro selbst zurückführen, denn hier spielt auch die Exzerption des Augustinus eine erhebliche Rolle, der in *civ. Dei* natürlich besonders an solchen Fällen interessiert war.

[67] Vgl. Dahlmann (oben, Anm. 52) 1243 und Riposati (oben, Anm. 65) 84–86.

[68] Vgl. Riposati (oben, Anm. 65), Abhandlung und ausführliche Kommentierung der Fragmente 3ff., die Fragmente selbst 247–86. Vgl. zu *vpR* besonders auch noch Dahlmann (oben, Anm. 52) 1243–46; Reischl (oben, Anm. 21) 84f., 91f., 107–29; und K. Müller (oben, Anm. 46) II:30–32.

[69] Vgl. Dahlmann (oben, Anm. 52) 1237.

fort. Damit ist natürlich hier die universalhistorische Perspektive zugunsten einer Konzentration auf die rein römische Geschichte aufgegeben.[70]

Die Binnengliederung der vier Bücher ist noch recht gut erkennbar. Auf die Königszeit im ersten Buch (wohl 753–510) folgte die frühe römische Republik des 4./3 Jhdt. (510 bis vielleicht 264, Galliereinfall, Samnitenkriege, Pyrrhus) im zweiten Buch, dann im dritten das 3./2. Jhdt, also die Zeit der punischen Kriege, sicher des zweiten bis zur Schenkung des Attalos (264?–133 v. Chr.). Das vierte Buch reichte schließlich von den Gracchen (133 v. Chr.) bis zum Bürgerkrieg zwischen Caesar und Pompeius (49/48 v. Chr.). In diesen historisch-chronologischen Rahmen wird nun thematisch die Kulturgeschichte des römischen Volkes eingearbeitet, ein Verfahren, das wir ja schon von Dikaiarch her kennen. Auf Varros Beschreibung der vielfältigen öffentlichen und privaten Bräuche, Einrichtungen und Lebensbedingungen des populus Romanus kann ich hier nicht im einzelnen eingehen.[71] Sie umfaßt in großer Spannweite im öffentlichen Bereich ökonomische und soziale Verhältnisse, religiöse Kulte, Tempelbauten, Kalender, politische Ämter, Militaria, national- und völkerrechtliche Riten u.a.m. und im privaten Bereich Familienleben, insbesondere Rolle der Frau, Hochzeitsbräuche, Grabriten, Hausanlage, Hausrat, Speisen, Getränke, Kleidung etc. Daß auch hier wieder ein ausgeprägtes kulturaitiologisches und insbesondere namensetymologische Interesse am Werk ist, dürfte bei einem Autor wie Varro kaum verwundern.[72]

Mit *vpR* hat nun aber Varro zweifellos eine anders als in *gpR* auch aus den erhaltenen Fragmenten noch klar erkennbare generelle Wirkung erzielen wollen. Diese Gesamttendenz der Schrift ist bereits so eingehend von Dahlmann und vor allem von Reischl herausgearbeitet worden, daß ich mich hier kurz fassen kann.[73] Reischls ausführliche Interpretation der Fragmente von *vpR* hat ergeben, daß Varro hier keineswegs nur kulturgeschichtliches Wissen vermitteln wollte,

---

[70] Aber das gilt ja auch schon für Dikaiarch, dessen *Bios Hellados* ja auch in eine Kulturgeschichte ausschließlich Griechenlands ausmündete.

[71] Vgl. Riposatis detaillierte Übersichten im Inhaltsverzeichnis XI–XV und zu den einzelnen Büchern (oben, Anm. 65) I:91–93, II:164f., III:194f. und IV:231.

[72] Vgl. Dahlmann (oben, Anm. 52) 1243f. und Reischl (oben, Anm. 21) 86f.

[73] Vgl. Dahlmann (oben, Anm. 52) 1243f. und Reischl (oben, Anm. 21) vor allem 107–29.

sondern Kulturgeschichte mit Kulturkritik verband, mehr noch, seine "kulturgeschichtliche Forschung als einen Beitrag zur moralischen Erneuerung des römischen Volkes"[74] verstand. In Fortsetzung ähnlicher Tendenzen schon bei Ennius und Cato maior wollte Varro vor allem den altrömischen *mos maiorum*, die Schlichtheit, Anspruchslosigkeit, Einfachheit des Lebensstils der Vorfahren und deren moralische Integrität in einen tadelnden Gegensatz zum dekadenten Luxusstreben, zur Hab- und Machtgier, zur selbstzerstörerischen Aggressivität der eigenen Zeit setzen, um so dem allgemeinen moralischen Verfall seiner Gegenwart durch Besinnung auf die Tugenden der römischen Frühzeit entgegenzuwirken. Diese Absicht ist von jener damals verbreiteten Vorstellung eines dekadenten Verlaufs der römischen Geschichte seit dem zweiten Jhdt. v. Chr. veranlaßt, der auf schädliche äußere Einflüsse und vor allem auf den Wegfall außenpolitischer Bedrohung mit der Folge eines überhöhten Wohlstandes zurückgeführt wurde, eine Vorstellung, wie man sie, von Polybios und Poseidonios vorbereitet, im ersten Jhdt. nicht nur bei Varro, sondern bald danach auch bei Sallust vorfindet.[75]

Ich komme nun am Schluß meines Beitrages zur Frage der Wirkung von Dikaiarchs *Bios Hellados* auf beide kulturhistorische Schriften Varros. Die Forschung hat sich, soweit ich sehe, in diesem Punkt fast nur zu *vpR* geäußert.[76] So steht es z.B. 1935 für Dahlmann außer Frage,[77] daß der *Bios Hellados* Varros "großes griechisches Vorbild" gewesen sei, aber dieses Vorbild liefere ihm nur den wissenschaftlichmethodischen Rahmen, den er auf seinen römischen Gegenstand übertrage.[78] Alles andere weise eher auf einen hohen Grad an Eigenständigkeit Varros. Es gebe in *vpR* weder Erwähnungen Dikaiarchs noch inhaltliche Berührungspunkte, es sei denn, man würde vermuten, daß Varro das dikaiarchische Dreistufenmodell nicht nur in den *res rusticae* und *ling.Lat.* 5, 105ff., sondern auch am Anfang von *vpR* behandelt habe.[79] In der moralisierenden, nationalen Gesamtten-

---

[74] Vgl. Reischl (oben, Anm. 21) 102 in der Kapitelüberschrift.

[75] Vgl. Reischl (oben, Anm. 21) 129ff.

[76] Mit Ausnahme von Della Corte (oben, Anm. 27) 130 (s. o. Anm. 60) natürlich, der ja, wie schon bemerkt, eine Aufteilung des bei Dikaiarch gebotenen Stoffes auf beide Werke Varros vermutet, also eine Wirkung des *Bios* auch auf *gpR* unterstellt, wie ich finde, zu Recht.

[77] Vgl. Dahlmann (oben, Anm. 52) 1244f.

[78] Zu diesem Punkt sind Dahlmanns Ausführungen (1244f.) unklar formuliert.

[79] So vermutet Dahlmann (oben, Anm. 52) 1245. Das Verhältnis der beiden *res rusticae* - Stellen (1, 2, 16 und 2,1,3f.) zu *ling.Lat.* 5, 105ff. ist ein kompliziertes

denz der Schrift sieht Dahlmann sogar eine besondere Leistung Varros, mit der er sein Vorbild Dikaiarch übertrifft, dessen Kulturgeschichte "allein das objektive Ziel der Kenntnis, nichts Tendenziöses darüber hinaus hatte." Diesem Urteil schließt sich Riposati 1939 voll an.[80] Er sieht ebenfalls nur die Methode von Dikaiarch übernommen, ansonsten überall Eigenständigkeit, und in der "visione nazionale moralizzante"[81] sogar mit Dahlmann einen wesentlichen Vorzug Varros gegenüber Dikaiarch. Der differenzierteste Vergleich, den ich kenne, stammt von Reischl. In einer eingehenden Analyse der Fragmente von *vpR* (unter stützendem Einbezug von Fragmenten aus den menippeischen Satiren) wird die zeitkritische Gesamtaussage der Schrift, wie ich sie schon erläutert habe (Stichwort: *mos maiorum*), neu erarbeitet.[82] Der Vergleich von *vpr* mit Dikaiarchs *Bios Hellados* folgt dann 117f: Varro habe, so Reischl, gewöhnliche, alltägliche Vorgänge des Lebens bevorzugt, Dikaiarch die großen Themen der Kulturgeschichte (Sozialverbände, Musik, Tanz, Dichtung, Philosophie). Varro stelle genauer dar und verwende die Etymologie als heuristische Methode weitaus intensiver als Dikaiarch. Varro habe mit der historischen Zeit, Dikaiarch mit den Uranfängen der Menschheit begonnen und dabei dem Orient besondere Anerkennung zukommen lassen. Varro habe einen übergreifenden Gesichtspunkt, eine einheitliche Konzeption (im Sinne Dahlmanns), Dikaiarch dagegen nicht (im Sinne Wehrlis). Er sei also, so das Fazit (118), gewiß in der Idee, die Biographie seines Volkes zu verfassen, von Dikaiarch bestimmt. Im Resultat habe er aber "andere Akzente, einheitliche Gesichtspunkte gesetzt, die Geschichte in klar moralisierender Absicht zum Sittenspiegel für die Gegenwart werden lassen."[83]

Sonderproblem, auf das ich hier nicht eingehen kann. Vgl. außer Dahlmann (oben, Anm. 52) 1244f. noch Riposati (oben, Anm. 65) 264 und Reischl (oben, Anm. 21) 89ff. Eine Behandlung des Dreistufenmodells in *vpR* weist Riposati (oben, Anm. 65) 264f. zurück. Reischl geht auf dieses Probem nicht ein. Ich glaube mit Della Corte (oben, Anm. 27) 130, wenn überhaupt, dann an eine Darstellung in *gpR*.

[80] Vgl. Riposati (oben, Anm. 65) 82 und 264–69.

[81] Ebenda 264.

[82] Vgl. Reischl (oben, Anm. 21) 102, bes. 107ff. Der Komplex der von Dikaiarch beeinflußten Urzeitdarstellung in den *res rusticae* und *ling. Lat.* 5, 105, der bei Reischl 88ff. zur Annahme einer reinen Aszendenztheorie bei Varro im Gegensatz zur ambivalenten Aszendenztheorie bei Porphyrios/Dikaiarch führt, kann hier beiseite gelassen werden, weil Reischl ihn nicht zu *vpR* in Beziehung setzt.

[83] Vgl. Reischl (oben, Anm. 21) 118.

Dieses Ergebnis bisheriger Forschung zur Rezeption Dikaiarchs bei Varro kann nach den vorangehenden Überlegungen eigentlich in keinem Punkt zufriedenstellen. Grundsätzliche Bedenken habe ich schon früher angemeldet (fehlende Berücksichtigung zeitgenössischer Quellen, Synopse beider Schriften *gpR* und *vpR* mit Dikaiarchs *Bios Hellados*). Es werden außerdem zu weitreichende Schlüsse aus den wenigen Fragmenten gezogen und die verwendeten Begriffe zu wenig überdacht, insbesondere der Begriff "Methode." Gehen wir das Ergebnis im einzelnen durch: Varro soll Dikaiarch gefolgt sein, aber nur in der Methode, sonst sei er eigenständig. Dies ist im Prinzip wohl richtig, aber was heißt "Methode"? Dikaiarchs Methode besteht darin, aus einem universalhistorischen Ansatz heraus den vollständigen historischen Ablauf der Menschheitsgeschichte von den Anfängen bis zur Gegenwart des Autors zugrundezulegen und auf dieser Grundlage ein auch zahlenmäßig bestimmtes chronologische Gerüst bereitzustellen, in das die nationale Kulturgeschichte als Hauptziel der Darstellung eingebettet wird. Zweifellos hat Varro diese Methode übernommen, aber er erfüllt die mit dem Gattungsvorbild gegebenen methodischen Bedingungen nicht allein mit *vpR*, sondern erst mit beiden Schriften zusammen. Er hat also keinen von Dikaiarch verschiedenen Zeitausschnitt gewählt (Reischl). Warum Varro dabei aber genauer als Dikaiarch vorgegangen sein und die Etymologie intensiver genutzt haben soll (Reischl), läßt sich m.E. aus den Fragmenten nicht begründen.[84]

Die Eigenständigkeit Varros wird zunächst daraus abgeleitet, daß keine Erwähnungen Dikaiarchs und keine inhaltlichen, thematischen Berührungspunkte vorliegen. Wieder liegt der Fehler in der einseitigen Berücksichtigung von *vpR*. Ich habe schon gesagt, daß solche direkten Bezüge wegen der stofflichen Parallelität nur in *gpR* zu erwarten wären, und, wenn sie auch dort nicht zu beobachten sind, so kann das einfacher Überlieferungszufall sein. Immerhin scheint aber *gpR* f. 3 Peter, in dem die Streitfrage der Anfangslosigkeit berührt wird, wie sie für Dikaiarchs *Bios Hellados* u. a. auch von Varro bezeugt ist (**53–54**), dafür zu sprechen, daß Dikaiarchs Urzeitlehre nicht nur in den *res rusticae*, sondern auch am Anfang von *gpR* von Varro behandelt worden ist.[85] Was *vpR* betrifft, so kann ein Autor, der die römische Kulturgeschichte

---

[84] Auch Dikaiarch verwendet ja die Etymologie **60** und **70**, wie oft, läßt sich natürlich nicht mehr entscheiden, ebenso wenig, wie "genau" Dikaiarch vorging.

[85] Vgl. dazu oben Anm. 80.

zum Gegenstand seiner Schrift gewählt hat, nicht gut konkrete thematische Parallelen zu seinem griechischen Vorbild aufweisen. Aber es gibt doch auch Themengleichheit in einem abstrakteren Sinne, ich meine gleiche kulturgeschichtliche Themenbereiche, und hier gibt es durchaus Parallelen zwischen Varro und Dikaiarch (Ständische Ordnung, Gentilizische Verbände, Tischsitten, Verhalten der Frau z.B.), die sich vielleicht noch vermehren ließen, wenn wir mehr von Dikaiarchs *Bios Hellados* erhalten hätten. Warum Dikaiarch eher die großen und Varro eher die alltäglichen Themen vertreten haben soll (Reischl), will mir ebenfalls nicht einleuchten, denn Varro behandelt ja doch auch politische, religiöse und soziale Themen von hohem Rang mit großer Ernsthaftigkeit und Dikaiarch auch "niedrigere" Themen, z.b. Eßsitten in **57**. Auch hier kann der Überlieferungszufall wieder eine Rolle spielen. Das Fehlen des orientalischen Bereichs bei Varro (Reischl) wird übrigens wieder durch den synchronistischen Einbezug des Orients in *gpR* wieder wettgemacht.[86]

Eigenständigkeit, ja sogar Überlegenheit über Dikaiarch wird Varro vor allem wegen der deutlich zutage tretenden kohärenten Gesamttendenz seiner Schrift zugesprochen. Hier gilt es nun m.E. besonders vorsichtig zu sein. Daß wir dem *Bios Hellados* keine einheitliche Gesamtkonzeption abgewinnen können, liegt, wie schon erläutert, vor allem an der Spärlichkeit der Zeugnisse, die es einfach nicht erlauben, hier wie Bodei Giglioni eindeutige Aussagen im Sinne einer Extrapolation des **56A** auf die gesamte Schrift zu machen.[87] Ausgeschlossen ist sie deshalb aber keineswegs. Dikaiarch könnte ebenso wie Varro durchaus ein Kulturkritiker, ein *laudator temporis acti* gewesen sein. Wir wissen es eben nur nicht genau. Es ist jedenfalls keineswegs gesichert, daß Dikaiarch nur neutrale Wissensvermittlung, und darüber hinaus nichts Tendenziöses im Sinne hatte (Dahlmann). Außerdem ist es eigentlich eine banale Selbstverständlichkeit, daß der Autor einer römischen Kulturgeschichte entsprechend den besonderen Bedingungen seines Gegenstandes eigene Tendenzen und Wirkungs- absichten verfolgt. Ich kann darin noch keine Eigenständigkeit oder Überlegenheit Varros über Dikaiarch erkennen.

Was ich bis jetzt kritisch gegen die frühere Forschung vorgebracht habe, scheint Varros kulturhistorische Schriften wieder mehr in die

---

[86] S. oben S. 302 mit Anm. 65.
[87] S. oben S. 297.

Nähe seines Vorbildes zu rücken und scheint die Eigenständigkeit ihres Autors zugunsten einer vor allem methodisch, aber auch thematisch und "ideologisch" treuen Nachfolge Dikaiarchs einzuschränken. Wir dürfen aber nicht vergessen, daß es auch Unterschiede zwischen beiden Kulturgeschichten gibt und daß Varro zusätzlich zeitgenössischen Einflüssen ausgesetzt war, die die Wirkung des Vorbilds Dikaiarch wieder relativieren könnten. Ich kann hier die Probleme nur streifen, die, wenn das bei unserer Überlieferungslage überhaupt möglich ist, erst von weiteren Forschungen geklärt werden müssen.

Man würde, was die Abhängigkeit Varros von Dikaiarch betrifft, sehr viel klarer sehen, wenn man genauer wüßte, was er der peripatetischen, von Dikaiarch ausgehenden Linie und was er der stoischen Linie Poseidonios-Jason verdankt. Der Aufbau der Kulturgeschichte Varros mit ihrer stofflichen Verteilung auf zwei Schriften in je vier Büchern und ihrer aspektuellen Trennung in *gens* (Vorgeschichte) und *vita* (Geschichte) wirkt wesentlich differenzierter als die drei Bücher Dikaiarchs, die beides in nur einer Schrift abdecken. Hier könnten zeitgenössische Vorbilder eingewirkt haben, man denke etwa an die erwähnten vier Bücher *Bios Hellados* des Jason von Nysa. Allerdings läßt sich nur für den Aspekt βίος ein griechisches Pendant in vier Büchern finden, leider keines in vier Büchern mit dem *gens* entsprechenden γεννεά.[88] Vom Titel her hat Dikaiarchs *Bios Hellados* also offenbar nur auf den Teil der Kulturgeschichte Varros eingewirkt, der die eigentliche Vita des Volkes behandelt. Vielleicht ist hier ebenfalls zeitgenössischer Einfluß am Werk gewesen. Außerdem ist in der Titelgebung Varros wegen der Kombination mit *gens* die individual-biographische Metaphorik wieder stärker als bei Dikaiarch betont, obwohl ihm sämtliche anderen Bedeutungen von βίος/vita (Lebens-unterhalt, Lebensführung, Zivilisationsstufe, Biographie) natürlich ebenfalls geläufig sind. Was den Gattungscharakter der Kultur-geschichte Varros angeht, so hat er hier nicht wie Dikaiarch eine neue Gattung aus einer Mischung der Peri-Bion-Literatur und der Universalgeschichte erst schaffen müssen, sondern er konnte auf ein fertiges Gattungsmuster, eben den *Bios Hellados* selbst zurückgreifen. Die universalgeschichtliche Komponente seines Unternehmens muß allerdings nicht allein auf dem Weg über den *Bios Hellados* Dikaiarchs zu ihm gelangt sein, sondern hier gab es möglicherweise ebenfalls

---

[88] So schon Dahlmann (oben, Anm. 52) 1241.

zeitgenössische Einflüsse, und zwar von römischen Autoren. Ich meine vor allem die 3 Bücher *Chronica* des Cornelius Nepos (54 v. Chr.) und speziell für *vpR* den *liber annalis* des Atticus (47 v. Chr.). Von der Stellung der Kulturgeschichte Varros in seinem Gesamtwerk her ist zum Schluß noch festzuhalten, daß er seiner systematisch angelegten Enzyklopädie römischer Altertümer, den *Antiquitates*, eine chronologisch verlaufende Kulturgeschichte des römischen Volkes an die Seite stellen wollte.

Diese letzten, natürlich noch durch weitere Forschungen abzusichernden Bemerkungen wollten davor warnen, die Wirkung Dikaiarchs auf Varro vorschnell als eine ausschließliche und direkte Beziehung zu verstehen. Vielmehr wird sein Einfluß in einem Ausmaß, das wir leider nicht mehr voll übersehen können, nur mittelbarer, von zeitgenössischen Zwischeninstanzen überdeckter Art gewesen sein. Varro war nämlich bei aller Pietät den literarischen *maiores* gegenüber doch auch ein durchaus moderner Autor, der zeitgenössische Tendenzen (Kastor von Rhodos, Jason, Nepos, Atticus) gerne aufgriff. Davon unberührt, ist er ein Zeuge der ungebrochenen Wirkung von Dikaiarchs *Bios Hellados* in Rom in der Mitte des ersten Jhdts. v. Chr.

8

The *Controversia* between Dicaearchus and Theophrastus about the Best Life

Pamela M. Huby

I The Material Available[1]

I open with a warning about the nature of our material. We have a limited number of passages from, or references to, a fairly large body of written works by Dicaearchus. In the case of the discussion of the harmony theory of the soul there is at least enough for us to be able to work out something interesting, if not entirely coherent, but with most of the rest we have but a few pieces of the jigsaw puzzle and it is tempting to try to fit them together even though in fact they may be unrelated. We even have to be wary of any particular arrangement. In some cases an author gives us the title and even the individual book number on which he is drawing, and this provides a reliable starting point for assigning the passage to a certain group, but in others every editor must use his own judgment to assign a passage to one group or another, having himself decided on the number and name of these groups, and he is unlikely to be correct in every case. Wehrli tended to cut his material to the bone,

---

[1] References to Mirhady (this volume) are in bold type. References to Wehrli are to *Die Schule des Aristoteles,* vol. 1 (Basel, 1944/1968).

311

and in several cases only a fuller quotation makes the point at issue clear.[2]

In the case of our present subject, the supposed disagreement between Theophrastus and Dicaearchus, there is no book title, and indeed no quotation. The sole passage directly bearing on it is **33** = 481 FHS&G,[3] from a letter of Cicero to Atticus (2.16 of the middle of 59 BC). The opening words of the excerpt—*qua re incumbamus, o noster Tite, ad illa praeclara studia, et eo unde discedere non oportuit aliquando revertamur* ("Wherefore, dear Titus, let us apply ourselves to those splendid studies and at last return to the place from which it was not proper ever to depart" [Fortenbaugh's translation])—enable us to see the context in which Cicero places this matter. It is in connection with his own turning from an active life, which he has been leading, to a leisured one and the pursuit of certain studies, a course in accordance with the views of Theophrastus, whereas Dicaearchus had recommended an active life. The full letter opens with a discussion of Caesar's proposals for land distribution in Campania, and also mentions the activity of Pompey, at this time a member of the so-called first triumvirate, and the end of the letter returns to various public problems. In 2.17, written soon after 16 (May 59), Cicero is still concerned with Pompey, but at the end and the beginning seems to expect to continue a quiet way of life with what he calls, using the Greek term, *adiaphora* (indifferent things). We must not follow this hare too far, but it is a sign of Cicero's

---

[2] One passage should probably be eliminated. Themistius (*Sophistes* 285 = **6**) refers to four enemies of Aristotle: Cephisodorus who was a disciple of Isocrates and attacked Aristotle in four books, Euboulides, the logician and author of the liar and other paradoxes, who is said by Diogenes Laertius (2.108) to have been a critic of Aristotle on many points, and Timaeus, presumably the historian from Sicily who spent most of his life in Athens and who was criticised on many counts by Polybius, including the fact that he attacked Homer, Aristotle and Theophrastus (*Histories* 12.11.5 and 12.23.8). The fourth supposed critic of Aristotle is named as Dicaearchus, but there are grave doubts about this. Düring, *Aristotle in the Biographical Tradition,* Studia Graeca et Latina Gothoburgensia 5 (Göteborg, 1977) 388, accepts Luzac's suggestion that the man meant was Demochares, who attacked the philosophers in Athens in 306, being then in his fifties and so old enough to have attacked Aristotle. (Düring is unwilling to change the text of Themistius because he thinks it may have been Themistius who was mistaken). Whereas for the others mentioned there is other evidence for atttacks on Aristotle, there is none in the case of Dicaearchus, unless we think that in writing on the Seven Wise Men (see below) Dicaearchus was attacking Aristotle's *On Philosophy*. We should probably ignore this particular passage.

[3] FHS&G = *Theophrastus of Eresus: Sources for his Life, Writings, Thought and Influence,* ed. W. Fortenbaugh, P. Huby, R. Sharples and D. Gutas (Leiden, 1992).

eclecticism that he can here bring in a notorious Stoic term, and in this way refer to a quiet life in which he has abandoned the pursuit of virtue in the political field. Like most politicians Cicero led a chequered life, sometimes in the thick of things and sometimes not. In his particular case there was the complication that he was an outstanding orator, who could play a part on the public scene, though not in a political way, even at a time when he was not active politically.

The upshot of all this is that all we have is a passing reference to a difference of opinion between Theophrastus and Dicaearchus, and little more can be extracted from the remains of either: for Theophrastus pseudo-Plutarch, *De placitis philosophorum* 874F = 479 FHS&G, from the doxographical work which is part of our evidence for Aetius, talks of Aristotle and Theophrastus and almost all the Peripatetics as holding that "the perfect man must be one who both contemplates realities and engages in right actions" (Fortenbaugh's translation). Cicero, *De fin.* 5.73 = 480A and 5.11 = 482 and Ambrose, *De officiis ministrorum* 2.2 = 480B, also mention both Aristotle and Theophrastus, but none of them distinguishes between the two of them, and they can be ignored for our purposes. Theophrastus did write on the happy life (*beata vita*), as witness Cicero, *De fin.* 5.86 = 475 5.11 = 482 and 5.12 = 498, and probably *Tusc. Disp.* 5.24–25 = 493, but he seems to have been much more concerned with the life of an individual affected by ill-fortune, following up some things that Aristotle said in his *Ethics*.[4] It is true that all of relevance that we have from him are passages selected because they bear on the place of fortune in men's lives, and there may have been much more, but otherwise there survive only snippets from Athenaeus (489 and 552B FHS&G) and an anonymous lexicographer (494A) which do not help.

For Dicaearchus we have **8**, also from Cicero's *Letters to Atticus,* 2.12 (19 April 59), which repeats rather than adds to the point of **33**, but is also puzzling; Cicero describes Dicaearchus as *luculentus homo et civis haud paulo melior quam isti nostri adikaiarchoi. Luculentus* can mean "rich" but here probably no more than "fine," and *adikaiarchoi* is primarily a pun. So we have: "a fine man and a citizen in no small degree better than those unjust rulers of ours." The word *civis* is puzzling, because, like the majority of the Peripatetics, Dicaearchus was an outsider in mainland Greece, and there is little evidence of his having spent

[4] E.g. *EN* 1.10 1100a4–9; 7.13 1153b19–21.

time in his home town, Messina.[5] So what did Cicero mean by calling him a *civis*? We will return to that question later. In **34** (*Ad Att.* 7.3 of 9 Dec. 50, nearly ten years after 25 and 27) Cicero refers to "that matter on which you say that you do not agree with Dicaearchus." The point of this has been disputed, but Shackleton Bailey[6] says that it must have been in answer to Cicero's rueful confession in 7.1 that he wished he had stayed in Cilicia. Bailey thinks Atticus said something like this: "You would have done better to have stayed there, for I hold that Dicaearchus was wrong to advocate the active life, and in the present situation there is more trouble in Rome than in Cilicia."

It is also at first sight a puzzle that the Epicurean Atticus is supposed to be a supporter of the active, non-philosophical life (**33**): as an Epicurean he would be expected to avoid politics, and in fact he lived very much on the sidelines as compared with Cicero, making his home in Athens for many years, though he did move to Rome in 65 and helped Cicero in many ways. But, as Michèle Ducos says,[7] he was a Roman as well as an Epicurean, and he clearly was a political animal, taking an active interest in Cicero's political affairs.

Much has been made of one small passage, a passing reference in one of Cicero's letters: we are constantly told of the well-known dispute between Dicaearchus and Theophrastus, and several attempts have been made to amplify the story in different directions: even the sober Regenbogen[8] refers to the *Streit* between Theophrastus and Dicaearchus and says that it was famous in ancient times. Fortenbaugh[9] and Donini[10] interestingly relate it to views about the existence of the soul and intellect, while F. Müller's study of Cicero's *De republica*,[11] with Dicaearchus in mind, relates the discussion of the best way of life in the Peripatos to the question of the origins of philosophical thought

---

[5] Little is known of Dicaearchus' life. J. P. Schneider, in *Dictionnaire des philosophes antiques,* ed. R. Goulet, vol. II (Paris, 1989–) 760–64 thinks he was born about 376, which would make him rather older than Theophrastus.

[6] *Cicero's Letters to Atticus,* vol. III (Cambridge, 1968) 289–90.

[7] *Dictionnaire des philosophes antiques,* vol. I (above, n. 5) 664.

[8] *RE* suppl. 11 (1968) col. 1481 under *Peri bion.*

[9] *Quellen zur Ethik Theophrasts* (Amsterdam, 1984) 202–4.

[10] *La Philosophia Greca dal VI al IV Secolo, Storia della Philosophia III* (Milan, 1975) 352.

[11] "Das Problem Theorie-Praxis in der Peripatos-Rezeption von Ciceros Staats-schrift," in *Cicero's Knowledge of the Peripatos, RUSCH* IV, ed. W. W. Fortenbaugh and P. Steinmetz (New Brunswick, NJ, 1989) 101–13.

(104).[12] This may be correct, but I wish to apply a more sceptical approach.

II Cicero's Part

Much of our information about Dicaearchus comes from Cicero and other Latin authors, Tertullian, Lactantius, Gellius, Censorinus, Varro, Pliny, and Martianus Capella,[13] and **36**, though in Greek, is addressed to a Roman. Cicero, however, is ambivalent about him. While in **33** he has Theophrastus as his own friend, with Dicaearchus as that of Atticus, elsewhere, *Tusc. Disp.* 1.77 = **27**, Dicaearchus is Cicero's *deliciae meae* (my darling)—here in connection with Dicaearchus' arguments for the mortality of the soul. Again in *Ad. Att.* 8.4.1 = **7** of 22 Feb. 49 about Dionysius, the tutor of his son who has turned out to be ungrateful, Cicero says that he has written a very polite letter to him, adding that he might have been sending an invitation to Dicaearchus or Aristoxenus, not a "chatterbox and incompetent teacher" (Shackleton Bailey).

Where did Cicero get his information? In many of his philosophical works he used doxographical material,[14] but the case of Dicaearchus is different. It is clear from Cicero's correspondence with Atticus that the two of them had access to a number of works of Dicaearchus still in circulation: in *Ad Att.* 2.2 = **9** (60 BC) Cicero says he was holding the constitution of Pellene in his hands and had a large pile of Dicaearchus' works at his feet, and thinks he has the constitutions of the Corinthians and the Athenians in his house in Rome; in 13.31 = **11A** (May 45), fifteen years later, he particularly wants "those three books" which Shackleton Bailey thinks are the *Descent*.[15] Cicero has been expecting a visit from Atticus, but now thinks that he will be delayed, and is in a hurry for those books. In 13.32 = **11B** (also 45) he wants Dicaearchus' works called *On the Soul* and the *Descent* from Atticus, and also asks for the *Tripoliticus* and the letter to Aristoxenus. At this stage he may

[12] Wehrli (p. 50) thinks his frr. 29 = **43** and 31 = **36** are connected with this matter, and he may be right, but it is not obviously so.

[13] Cicero's interest in Dicaearchus is noticed also by W. Görler, "Cicero und die 'Schule des Aristoteles'," in *RUSCH* IV (above, n. 11) 250–51, but mainly from the point of view of the form of the dialogue.

[14] See *RUSCH* IV (above, n. 11) passim, esp. David Runia, "Aristotle and Theophrastus Conjoined in the Writings of Cicero," 29–33.

[15] That is, the *Descent into the Cave of Trophonius:* Trophonius had an oracle near Lebadeia in Boeotia.

have been planning the *Tusculan Disputations,* and in that work, at 1.21 = **19** he has a quotation from Dicaearchus. In 13.33 = **11C** (also 45) he says that he has received the *On the Soul* and is waiting for the *Descent.* Cicero was, then, directly acquainted with a large number of the works of Dicaearchus, whom he greatly admired in spite of his occasional preference for Theophrastus. These were not only philosophical works: at *Ad Att.* 6.2 = **79** of 50 BC, Cicero indicates that he has drawn on Dicaearchus for the information, or misinformation, that all states in the Peloponnese had a sea coast. The reference appears to be to *De republica* 2.8, which Cicero claims to have taken over from Dicaearchus "in so many words."[16] But in spite of all this background all we really learn from Cicero at **33** is that Dicaearchus much preferred the practical life to the theoretical, while Theophrastus was of the opposite persuasion.

Cicero, then, had access to, and in some cases owned, a number of works of Dicaeachus. But with a few exceptions it is difficult to relate them to anything he wrote. It seems to be the same for Theophrastus. In the same month as he asked for the various constitutions of Dicaearchus, December 60, Cicero also asked Atticus to send him Theophrastus' *On Ambition* from Quintus' library (*Ad Att.* 2.3 = 436.21 FHS&G). In *De div.* 2.1 Cicero says that he has written six books on the republic, using Plato, Aristotle, Theophrastus, and *tota Peripateticorum familia* ("the whole school of the Peripatetics," which surely must include Dicaearchus[17]). In the case of Theophrastus it is not easy to be sure from the evidence we have what other books Cicero actually knew. I am inclined to think, however, as does Gigon,[18] that he also had the work on happiness, *De beata vita,* quoted in the *De finibus,* and, if Gellius is right (1.3.10–12 = 534 FHS&G), Cicero also knew and used the *De amicitia,* though it is not possible to find many traces of it in his own *Laelius* or *De amicitia.* The upshot of all this is that Cicero did have some works of Theophrastus and Dicaearchus in his hands, but it is very difficult to go further. Nowhere in any of his other references to

[16] **10** = 13.30.2, which Shackleton Bailey puts just after 13.31, but both on 28th May 45. Cicero has an idea for a conference at Olympia *more Dicaearchi familiaris tui,* "in the way of your friend Dicaearchus." Bailey refers to Dicaearchus' *Olympikos, Panathenaikos, Korinthiakos* and *Lesbiakos.*

[17] Solmsen, "Die Theorie der Staatsformen bei Cicero de re publ. I," *Philologus* 88 (1933) 338 argued that the *De republica* was based on Dicaearchus.

[18] "Theophrast in Cicero's *De finibus,*" in *RUSCH* IV (above, n. 11) 183.

either Theophrastus or Dicaearchus does he mention a controversy between them. There are places where it might have come in, and if he was aware of it in 59 BC as an important matter it is unlikely, with his remarkable memory, that he would have forgotten it later. Nor is there any positive reference in any of our other material. In Stobaeus *Anth.* 2.31.124 = 465 FHS&G, without attribution beyond the name of Theophrastus, there is a passage in a protreptic vein which complains that men take great care over all other matters of life but do not worry about the best way of life. There is no positive doctrine here, but one could imagine that it was followed by arguments about the best way of life. Again 476 FHS&G, from a gnomologium written in the fourteenth century for school use, attributes to Theophrastus the statement that it is difficult to decide on the best way of life, and even more difficult to stick to it. But it is not said what the best way of life is.

III Controversia

What can we deduce from the word *controversia*? Need it mean anything more than a difference of opinion?[19] We may compare the opening of **38** where Diogenes Laertius (1.41) uses the word *stasiazetai* about the number of the Seven Wise Men (which appears to mean the names of those who made up that number); this can hardly mean more than that Diogenes, or his source, found different views in different sources. Hicks renders it "nor is there any agreement," and I myself would be happy with "difference of opinion" for *controversia*. It is true that Cicero uses the expression *tanta controversia,* which might suggest something on a larger scale, but there is a complete absence of any other direct evidence to support it.

How did Cicero get his knowledge even of this? In view of the fact that he had available so many of the works of Dicaearchus it seems possible that that knowledge also came directly from those particular works, though it cannot be ruled out that it came, for instance, from Antiochus. There is no evidence of a work by Dicaearchus which attacked Theophrastus, nor for one by Theophrastus which attacked Dicaearchus, and the information in **33** must come from someone who was able somehow to compare the views of the two. This might force us

---

[19] *Controversia* is a common word in Cicero and other Latin writers. *Brutus* 18.62 has *controversia est inter scriptores de numero annorum,* which seems very similar to the usage here.

back to a doxographical work, but it could equally be Cicero himself, though the latter, in writing to Atticus, takes it for granted that Atticus too knows about this *controversia*.

Whatever the situation was, the background is likely to be Aristotle's discussion of the good life, and D. Frede[20] suggests (96 n. 31) that Theophrastus and Dicaearchus may have been concerned with something referred to in *Pol* 7.1 1323a22, where Aristotle says that he has said enough about the best life in his exoteric works, rather than with something in one of the *Ethics*. But were they, as it were, engaged directly with one another in a "set piece" argument, or did they just write independently supporting different forms of life? Did they, perhaps, engage in a philosophical "joust" on the subject of the good life, before their assembled colleagues, and did someone then record it all?[21] But it is equally possible that each wrote separately on this matter. What we know of their works suggests very different styles: Dicaearchus appears to have been more discursive than Theophrastus, though Theophrastus had his discursive moments, and there are a number of possible homes for whatever arguments Dicaearchus may have given. Indeed he may not have given any arguments at all, but just stated his preference for the active life, which Aristotle does, after all, still honour. Aristotle's views are confusing, but D. Frede[22] (82–83) has shown that he favoured "leisurely" political activity as much as anything else. Further, for him there are two possible kinds of theoretical life, that of the contemplation of God, and that of study. Clearly it was the latter that Cicero was interested in. At *De fin.* 5.11 = 482 FHS&G he equates the contemplation and examination (*cognitio*) of things (*rerum*) with the life of the gods, and "things" here must mean things in the world; and at *Tusc. Disp.* 1.44–45 = 484 FHS&G he refers explicitly to astronomy.

---

[20] "Constitution and Citizenship: Peripatetic Influence on Cicero's Political Conceptions in the *De re publica*," in *RUSCH* IV (above, n. 11) 77–100.

[21] Gilbert Ryle, "Dialectic in the Academy," in *New Essays on Plato and Aristotle,* ed. R. Bambrough (London, 1965) 55, renamed "The Academy and Dialectic," in *Collected Papers* 1, ed. G. Ryle (London, 1971) 103, talks of "moots that are held, so to speak, on Wednesday evenings between a young Coriscus and a young Theophrastus, with the not very old Aristotle or Xenocrates acting as coach, umpire and time-keeper." In "Dialectic in the Academy," *Aristotelian Dialectic Proceedings of the Third Symposium Aristotelicum* (Oxford, 1965) 75 and *Collected Papers* 1, 121–22 he thinks that written records of argument-sequences were kept and the arguments worked upon.

[22] Above, n. 20.

On the basis of **33** we might have concluded that Dicaearchus rejected the life of study in favour of that of action, but we know that he wrote a great deal, and that some of it was theoretical, like the discussion of the "harmony" theory of the soul. In any case there is a query about what style of life should be regarded as that of action. For Aristotle it seems to have been a life of political activity, and while in **33**, Cicero uses the word *praktikos* of Atticus' way of life as the alternative to *theoretikos* of his own, in **8** the same Cicero refers to himself as *philosophos* but Atticus (Titus) as *politicos,* in effect equating the practical with the political life and the theoretical with the philosophical. In 479 FHS&G from pseudo-Plutarch, the doxographical passage, a distinction is made between subjects which are "theoretical," like whether the sun is a living thing, and whether the universe is infinite, and "practical" like how one should live, bring up children, rule and make laws. But both of these are subjects of study, not actions.

IV   Different Directions

If we are to explain Cicero's silence about our *controversia* elsewhere than in his letters we should perhaps look in different directions, away from the more strictly ethical and philosophical matters about which he wrote so much. Dicaearchus may for example have dealt with the matter in his *On Lives,* that mysterious genus of works. Diogenes Laertius 5.42 lists an *On Lives* in three books for Theophrastus, which Regenbogen 1481 thinks resembled the work of Clearchus, but nothing is known of its contents. Works called *On Lives* were also written by Heraclides Ponticus, Clearchus, and Strato. It is only for Clearchus that we have much information: he was clearly a favourite of Athenaeus, and among other works Athenaeus gives us a number of quotations from his *On Lives* which ran into at least eight books. Most quotations are given in Athenaeus' Book 12 and are from Clearchus' Book 4.[23] The emphasis is on examples of luxury and licentiousness from all over the world, given in considerable detail. While connected with "vices," which in theory might lead on to a discussion of "virtues," it is difficult to see them as mainly concerned with the question of the best kind of life. One might relate them to Theophrastus' *Characters,* although that

---

[23] Wehrli's 37–39, 41–43a, 44–51a, 51d–55, and 57–62 are all from Athenaeus. Cf. the Index of Texts and Passages in this volume.

is not known as *On Lives*,[24] or to his "little golden book" on marriage, of which we would know nothing were it not for the interest in virginity of fourth-century Christians and the decision of Jerome to quote at length from it (*Adversus Jovinianum* 1.47–48 = 486 FHS&G). By such a chance we know quite a lot about the work, but by no means all. In particular, was it serious, or was it part of a set of arguments on different sides?[25] It would be in tune with the tone of what survives for Theophrastus to have also argued that it is best for the wise man not only to remain unmarried, but also to refrain from political life and devote himself to his studies, and if he did that might give a basis for Cicero's remarks, whether Theophrastus' arguments were meant seriously or not. But we do not know.

To return to Dicaearchus' *On Lives,* Diogenes Laertius 3.4 = **47** refers to the first book of that work for the report that Plato engaged in wrestling at the Isthmian games. This is all that we can be sure of, though several other remarks about Plato could well be from the same source.[26] But we are left with no clear idea of what the *On Lives* was like. This work must be distinguished from Dicaearchus' *Life of Greece,* named in **60** and **63** (both Stephen of Byzantium), **58** and **59** (Scholiasts), **72** and **77** (Athenaeus) and **62** (Hypothesis of the *Medea*), itself rather puzzling as it seems to cover much more than Greece alone. It is also listed by the Suda (under Dicaearchus: II 1062 Adler = **2**; cf. **1** no. 7a–f) as one of the two named books by Dicaearchus. The excerpts from it are largely factual, and although we have to allow for the interests of the excerptors it seems unlikely that there was room in it for a theoretical discussion of the value of different styles of life. That might send us back to the *On Lives,* but it is safer to confess our ignorance.

---

[24] R. Müller (above, n. 11) 103 and 112 n. 3 and 6 makes some relevant points.

[25] See W. W. Fortenbaugh, "Theophrastus, the *Characters* and Rhetoric," in *Peripatetic Rhetoric after Aristotle, RUSCH* VI, ed. Fortenbaugh and Mirhady (New Brunswick, NJ, 1993) 24–25.

[26] Oswyn Murray, *Early Greece,* 2nd ed. (London, 1993) 166, writing in connection with what is supposed to be from Aristotle's *Constitution of the Spartans* (see below, n. 36) says: "It was common in antiquity to quote one's main source of information for a subsidiary detail: originally the technique may have been an attempt to make a false claim to originality without losing the reputation for learned research; but by Plutarch's day its was a mere stylistic device." To follow this through is beyond the scope of this paper, but it does raise new possibilities which should at some stage be considered.

V Seven Wise Men

Another possibility for Cicero's ultimate source is Dicaearchus' accounts of the Seven Wise Men, though this is not easy material. On the one hand there is an entirely factual approach: from Diogenes Laertius 1.41–42 = **38** we learn that Dicaearchus paid attention to identifying the seven sages, accepting four names, Thales, Bias, Pittacus and Solon, and, with admirable caution, giving six other possibles, of which three were to be selected. But he also (Diogenes 1.40 = **37**) raised a theoretical matter, denying that they were either wise or philosophers, but saying rather that they were clever men (*sunetoi*) and lawgivers. Wehrli points us to *Laelius* or *De amicitia* 2 where Cicero makes Fannius say to Laelius that men think that Laelius is the only wise man of his time. Cato was esteemed as wise for his all-round ability, and Atilius for his ability in civil law, but Laelius is wise in a different sense, not only for his *natura et moribus* (nature and character), but also for his *studio et doctrina* (interest in study and learning): he is wise not as the common herd think, but as do those (unnamed) who define it so strictly that they are not even prepared to call the Seven Wise Men truly wise; Socrates was the only wise man in Athens, judged the wisest even by the oracle of Apollo. Is Dicaearchus behind this? But Cicero himself admitted several senses for *sapiens*. Aristotle also discussed several meanings of *sophos* in his *De philosophia,* fr. 8 Ross, in which Philoponus (*In Nicom. Isag.* 1.1) lists five senses that Aristotle said were used by the men of old: a) the invention of devices for living better, b) the skills to produce beautiful things, c) of the Seven Wise Men, the ability to devise laws, d) the work of scientists, and e) the knowledge of things divine. Since this was an exoteric work of Aristotle we would expect Dicaearchus to have known it, but it is not easy to relate it directly to what he said. Philoponus introduces his report with a long account of the disasters which Aristotle said had overwhelmed mankind, and this resembles in some ways Dicaearchus' account of the ways in which men perish (Cicero *De off.* 2.5.16 = **78**), though it does not draw Dicaearchus' moral that many disasters are caused by men themselves, and the relationship between the two is not clear. Plutarch, *An seni gerenda respublica* 26 796C = **43** which, in spite of doubts, is probably from Dicaearchus,[27] is also relevant: it says that Socrates was a philosopher,

---

[27] C. Natali, *Bios theoretikos* (Bologna, 1991) 142 on **43** says there have been doubts about how much of Dicaearchus is here, some limiting it to the meanings of

although his way of life was different from the accepted one for philosophers. Although the reference here is to philosophy, not to wisdom, the tone of this passage is such as to make it likely that it was by Dicaearchus. But much of its content is trivial: Socrates did not stand on a pedestal or sit on a throne or have a set hour for teaching, but in the whole of his life displayed his philosophy. Is Dicaearchus here rejecting completely Plato's picture of Socrates as a thinker, or just objecting to the "philosophical" trimmings of his contemporaries? In Codex Vat. 435 = **36** Dicaearchus expands on what philosophy is, and says that in the past only the good man was a philosopher. They did not then enquire whether one should indulge in political matters and how, but actually did it well, and did not ask if one should marry, but actually married.[28] One might see more serious digs at Dicaearchus' contemporaries here, perhaps especially Theophrastus, who did ask if the wise man should marry (486 FHS&G), though in what spirit is uncertain, and we may tentatively suppose that Dicaearchus wanted to draw a contrast between those who called themselves philosophers in his own time, and those whom he regarded as the true philosophers of the past. These were people who took part in politics, and married, and behaved well. But we are left with the question why he would not allow that the Seven Wise Men, whoever they were, were wise and philosophers.

He seems indeed to have turned his attention to some so-called philosophers of the past as well as those of the present: in **37** he denies both wisdom and philosophy to the Seven Wise Men; in **36** he denies the name of wise to the Greeks who coined terse saws like "Know thyself" and adds that those of old did not philosophise *logôi* (verbally?), but that wisdom was then the practice of noble deeds, but later it became the art of popular speaking (*logoi ochlikoi*). Of the examples given, "Know thyself" and "Nothing too much" are particularly associated with Delphi,[29] but they were also discussed by Aristotle in his *De*

---

peripatos, but Natali accepts that what follows the reference to Dicaearchus is all genuine.

[28] The passage was found by von Arnim (*Hermes* 27 [1892] 119f.) as an odd page in a manuscript mainly devoted to Synesius, written in a fourteenth-century hand. After the quoted passage, he goes on to examples from Roman history: Appius and Pyrrho, Kaeso and the Carthaginians, and finally Romulus and Remus. Von Arnim notes a similarity to Diodorus, who like Dicaearchus was a Sicilian, but was a younger contemporary of Cicero.

[29] The sayings of Delphi were widespread in the Greek area. The recent excavations at Ai Khanum on the Oxus have recovered an inscription which says that Clearchus set

philosophia, frr. 3 and 4 Ross. "Know thyself" and "Nothing too much" and the obscure remark about pledges are all there, and it is clear that there were many disputes about their origins. Some ascribed them to some of the Seven Wise Men. Aristotle himself, as reported by Synesius (*Calvitii Encomium* 22 85c [the first passage in *De philosophia* 8 Ross]) said that these short sayings were fragments of the philosophy of the ancients preserved after great disasters through their "conciseness and cleverness" (Ross). We have probably returned, then, to Aristotle's *De philosophia,* though Synesius does not name it, and perhaps Dicaearchus is attacking it, though again the position is unclear.[30] "And nowadays he who speaks persuasively is seen as a great philosopher, but in times of old the good man alone was a philosopher." Wehrli continues the quotation to the final sentence in which the word *phesi* (he says) occurs: "These," he says, "were the deeds and practices of men who were wise, but these utterances (i.e., the apothegms) are a tiresome thing." There seems to be a polemic here again against both men of Dicaearchus' own time, and some earlier ones. It worries me a little that among his contemporaries are, on this view, those who go in for popular speaking, but the words *logoi ochlikoi* are vague and we need not think of people like the second sophists or anything of that kind.

It seems, then, that Dicaearchus objected to the activities of his contemporaries, possibly just those in the Peripatos, but possibly also the general philosophical community particularly centred on Athens, allowing them the name of philosophers but devaluing it with a contrast

---

them up there. This Clearchus has plausibly been identified with Theophrastus' and Dicaearchus' contemporary: if so it confirms an interest in those sayings by the Peripatos. It has become possible to reconstruct a list of those sayings by the use of various pieces of evidence, particularly an inscription from the town of Miletopolis, but also, for example, from Stobaeus. The lists are not identical either in format or in substance, but they give us a good idea of the nature of the lists. Some have been influenced by Christianity, and that given by Stobaeus is given each in only two words.

We all know "Nothing too much" and "Know thyself," and have accepted these as profound distillations of Greek thought. But what of the rest? Homespun morality at best: educate your children, praise virtue, obey the law, revere your ancestors, and so on. It is hardly surprising that Dicaearchus thought these unworthy of a true philosopher. For a convenient account of Ai Khanum and Delphic maxims in general see F. W. Walbank, *The Hellenistic World* (London, 1992) 60–61, 270.

[30] Theophrastus (Stobaeus *Anth.* 3.21.12 = 738 FHS&G) said that "Know thyself" was a proverb, but Clearchus said it was given by the god (Apollo?) to Chilon, and most people thought that it was invented by Chilon. Theophrastus seems to have been treating a proverb as something of which the origin was unknown, possibly agreeing with Aristotle that it was a survival from the very distant past.

with the men of the past who had lived upright lives and served their communities, concluding that if his contemporaries were correctly called philosophers these early sages should not be so called; I suggest that there was some work in which Dicaearchus both wrote about the Seven Sages and expressed his preference for the practical life, that is, the life of an upright citizen. Wehrli assigns the Wise Men passages to his section on *Lebensformen* and biography, but no book titles are to be found here, except at **47** about Plato, which was in the first book of the *On Lives;* they could, for example, belong to the next section, devoted to the three books of the *Life of Greece.* We can only guess. Someone somewhere knew this work and also knew at least one place where Theophrastus expressed a different opinion, and compared the two. Cicero and Atticus may or may not have known these original works.

VI Dicaearchus' Life and Works

There is some inconsistency in Cicero's attitude to Dicaearchus. On the one hand he is settling for a quiet life in the spirit of Theophrastus, but on the other he is asking for the works of Dicaearchus, and apparently intending to use them in his writing. But this inconsistency is inevitable. Dicaearchus was a writer: otherwise he would not have come into the picture. But he was not only a writer. Some of his activities could be seen as practical but non-political, like his measuring the height of mountains, and producing a map of the world, and others as political but not practical like his constitutions of various Greek states. Living as he did at a time when the Macedonians put an end to the independence of Greece the opportunities for a traditional political life were limited, but he could write constitutions, and it is to these that I would like to turn. He clearly wrote several: we are told of constitutions by him of Athens, Sparta, Corinth, and Pellene, the latter being a small town near Corinth but belonging to Achaea, and it was some of these that attracted Cicero's enthusiasm. Were they the reason why Cicero called him *civis*? About them two important questions have to be asked: how were they related to Aristotle's collection of constitutions, and what were they like? If they were part of Aristotle's collection, and if Dicaearchus did, as is said, write a *Constitution of the Athenians* (Cicero *Ad Att.* 2.2 = **9**), the *Constitution of the Athenians* that we possess should be his. There have always been doubts about the authorship of that work. Rhodes[31] does not believe that Aristotle wrote it.[32] But there is a difficulty in supposing it was the work by Dicaearchus admired by Cicero: in this one case we know what it was like. It has been dated to 328–325 and is a dry work, and it is difficult to imagine Cicero being excited by it. It is useful to pure historians, and to detailed constitutional specialists, but Cicero? But if this was by Dicaearchus,[33] it is reasonable to accept that other works in the collection were by him, such perhaps as the constitutions of the Pellenians and the Corinthians also mentioned in **9**, but the evidence is inadequate: the Aristotelian? *Constitution of the Pellenians* has only one fragment, 567 Rose, and that is, like the *Constitution of the Athenians,* on a dry factual matter about the men employed to hunt for the property of exiles. The *Constitution of the Corinthians* has two possible fragments, 516 and 517, though neither actually names its source, and they are not informative.

We are left with one exciting possibility, the *Constitution of Sparta,* or rather *of the Spartans.* This work is in fact named only in **2**, from the Suda, and it is there said that it was read out annually to the young men of Sparta for some time;[34] it is not one that Cicero said he had, though he did ask for the *Tripoliticus,* to be discussed later. Was this *Constitution of the Spartans* the *Constitution of the Lacedaimonians*[35] attributed to Aristotle? Was Dicaearchus the author of the one of which we have fragments in Rose 532–45?[36] In several of these the author sets Aristotle alongside other writers who hold different views on the matter in question, but Dicaearchus is not mentioned at all. In view of the supposed popularity of his work with the Spartans this is odd, unless he did write

---

[31] *A Commentary on the Aristotelian Athenaion Politeia* (Oxford, 1981) 62–63.

[32] Murray (above, n. 26) 30 says: "some of the political analyses are so crass and some of the documents so blatantly forged that many modern scholars have wanted to believe that the work was compiled by a rather unintelligent pupil of Aristotle."

[33] See W. Görler (above, n. 13) 251 and n. 18.

[34] The Suda (II 1063 Adler) lists a second Dicaearchus who actually was a Spartan. He is said to have been a *grammatikos* and a student of Aristarchus (second century BC). Could there have been some confusion here?

[35] The Spartans called themselves Lacedaimonians because they were the inhabitants of Lacedaimon.

[36] In Rose's fragments it is called the constitution of the Lacones or the constitution of the Lacedaemonians.

the one attributed to Aristotle. Oswyn Murray[37] 166ff. attributes a passage from Plutarch's *Life of Lycurgus* 6 (536 Rose, extended) *in toto* to Aristotle's *Constitution of the Spartans*.[38] It includes a document giving a decree containing "the earliest surviving written Greek political constitution," a commentary, and a short passage from Tyrtaeus. Aristotle or Dicaearchus?

What is meant by a constitution? In one sense, there can be only one constitution for any given place at any one time, and an account of it will just detail the existing laws and arrangements. There cannot be two such contemporary constitutions of, say, Athens, and what we have in the second part of the *Constitution of the Athenians* is of that kind. So where there are said to be several constitutions of one place these must be of a different kind, and we do have examples of these. The oldest is the pseudo-Xenophontic *Constitution of the Athenians* by the man known as the "Old Oligarch," written about the beginning of the Peloponnesian War and arguing that that constitution is well adapted to the interests of the democratic party. In contrast the genuinely Xenophontic *Constitution of the Spartans* is a eulogy of the Spartan constitution, and such a work as might have been read out annually to the young Spartans.

If the work attributed to Aristotle is by Dicaearchus, and if the numerous passages where no title is given are all from it, what can we learn? It seems to have been very much on the same lines as the *Constitution of the Athenians,* but our sources are not of the kind to pick out much beyond facts. There is a lot about Lycurgus from Plutarch, and much from scholia and lexicographers. Murray thinks the Plutarch passage discussed above resembles the *Constitution of the Athenians*.[39] That suggests that the *Constitution of the Spartans* was also dry.[40]

[37] Above, n. 26.

[38] In contrast to what he says about the *Constitution of the Athenians,* Murray takes it for granted that this work was by Aristotle, and goes on to argue that since Aristotle was an intelligent man it should be possible to make sense of what Plutarch says.

[39] Rose (*ad* 567) says that Cicero had the *Constitution of the Pellenians* among his books, referring to *Ad Att.* 2.2 and implicitly identifying Dicaearchus' work with Aristotle's. He does the same for the *Constitution of the Corinthians* (*ad* 516) and that of the Athenians (*ad* 381).

[40] The Spartan constitution was however a sensitive matter. For example Pausanias, the exiled king of Sparta, wrote a propaganda pamphlet on the constitution of Lycurgus, the original Spartan law-giver, at the beginning of the fourth century, and in *Pol.* 7.14 1333b18 Aristotle, in his own account of the Spartans, refers to constitutions by Thibron and others, suggesting that there were many.

Wehrli thinks that the *Tripoliticus,* in which Cicero expressed his interest, was identical with the *Constitution of the Spartans.* **88** is a report by Photius (*Bibl.* 37) from an anonymous Byzantine author of a dialogue on politics, who refers to an *eidos politeias Dikaiarchikon* ("a Dicaearchic form of constitution")—a mixed constitution.[41] It was a mixture of monarchy, aristocracy, and democracy in their pure forms. Clearly there are similarities between such a constitution and that of Sparta, but it could also have been an ideal constitution like that of Plato. We may bring in here **86** from Cicero's *De legibus* (3.13–14). There it is clear that the *veteres* of the opening are Stoics, and that Cicero is contrasting their theoretical approach to politics with that of Plato and his successors, including Dicaearchus, who wrote "with a view to things useful for the people and citizens." This broad front covers much variety, and we could suppose that Dicaearchus wrote in a number of genres, in particular an ideal constitution, the *Tripoliticus,*[42] and several items in Aristotle's collection.

According to our evidence Theophrastus wrote no constitutions, but he did write a work called *Laws,* which ran to 24 books and is frequently quoted. Perhaps there was a division of labour in the Peripatos by which Theophrastus did laws, and Dicaearchus did constitutions. It is still puzzling that Cicero was apparently so enthusiastic about the latter.[43] Could we understand Cicero's interest if we reflect that there are

---

[41] 594 FHS&G is an obscure passage from Philodemus' *Rhetoric* 6 (P. Herc. 832 – *BT* vol. 2 p. 57.7–20) which speaks of Aristotle collecting laws along with Theophrastus and a large number of constitutions, but it is entirely open whether Theophrastus was involved in the latter.

[42] Josephus *Contra Apionem* 1.220–21 says that the author of the *Tripoliticus,* whom he leaves unidentified, but says is not Theopompus, attacked the constitution of the city of Thebes. Further, Pausanias 6.18.5 says that the *Trikaranus* was written by Anaximenes of Lampsacus and attacked Athens, Sparta, and Thebes. Anaximenes distributed it widely under the name of Theopompus to discredit the latter. The fact that both Josephus and Pausanias mention Thebes and Theopompus suggests that the *Tripoliticus* and the *Trikaranus* may be identical, and had nothing to do with Dicaearchus.

[43] These constitutions have turned up in Egypt. Our *Constitution of the Athenians* was discovered in Egypt in 1890, and there is also a papyrus from Memphis now in St. Petersburg (Pack[2] 2089), written at the beginning of the third century AD with a list of books, almost certainly from a private library, miscellaneous and arranged with no obvious order, which lists not only Aristotle's *Constitution of the Athenians* but also his *Constitution of the Neapolitans,* along with Theophrastus' *On Temperance* (= 436 no.9c FHS&G) and a variety of other works. It is difficult to understand what attraction these two constitutions would hold for those inhabitants of Memphis. Or was it a school?

I cannot resist quoting from Blass' preface to his Teubner edition of the *Constitu-*

similarities between his times and those of the Peripatetics? In both an established order was coming to an end, old freedoms were being lost, and a "dictatorial" rule was being established. This was to some extent understood: Cicero, when he came to write his speeches against Antony, called them "Philippics" after Demosthenes' speeches against Philip.[44] The parallels between the fourth century BC in Greece and his own time were certainly clear in Cicero's mind by the end of his life, when he wrote the "Philippics," but when did the awareness start? Already, in his own consulate of 63, Rome was in trouble, and Cicero had to deal with Catiline. Pompey was an independent source of trouble, and one could see the old order threatened as the old order in Greece was threatened by the Macedonians. But we cannot go further because we know so little of the contents of Dicaearchus' works.

Things in this account have not fitted well together. I have explored various areas where Dicaearchus might have said something about the best life, that is, the Seven Sages, the ideal constitution, and his apparent criticism of his fellow philosophers. The Suda **2**, describes him as *philosophos, rhetor* and *geometres* (here surely a land-measurer), and while the first and last epithets are supported by our evidence, that of rhetor is puzzling. The Suda's reliability is not great, but is there something here?

---

tion of the Athenians p.v: *Fingamus nobis animo hominem in abdito aliquo angulo Aegypti viventem, qui cum libelli huius Aristotelei amantissimus esset, neque mercari poterat eius exemplum neque nancisci allud quam truncatum illud* ("Let us imagine a man living in an obscure corner of Egypt, who greatly loved this little book of Aristotle, but could neither buy a copy of it nor get hold of anything except this truncated one"). This supposed devotion is also puzzling.

[44] In *Ad Att.* 12.9 of 46 Cicero calls Lucius Marcius Philippus, consul of 56, husband of Caesar's niece and stepfather to the future Augustus, "son of Amyntas" after the father of Philip of Macedon.

9

Neues aus Papyrus-Hypotheseis
zu verlorenen Euripides-Dramen

Wolfgang Luppe

Bevor hier über Euripides-Hypotheseis selbst gesprochen wird, seien ein paar Überlegungen über die Autorschaft dieser mythologischen Inhaltsangaben geäußert. Es liegt nahe anzunehmen, daß sowohl die zahlreichen Papyrusfunde aus einer alphabetisch nach dem Anfangsbuchstaben der Titel angeordneten Sammlung mythologischer Inhaltsangaben von Euripides-Dramen als auch der bisher einzige Papyrusfund aus einer gleichartigen Sammlung von Inhaltsangaben von Sophokles-Dramen,[1] bei denen jeweils (neben dem mit οὗ / ἧς / ὧν ἀρχή eingeleiteten Zitat des ersten Verses) der Titel ὑπόθεσις in der Überschrift erscheint, identisch sind mit dem durch Sextus Empiricus (2. Jahrh. n. Chr.), Adv. Math. III 3, für Dikaiarchos bezeugten Werk Δικαιάρχου τινὰς ὑποθέσεις τῶν Εὐριπίδου καὶ Σοφοκλέους μύθων (**112**).

Diese Annahme wird dadurch bekräftigt, daß die Hypothesis im Codex Laurentianus (12. Jahrh.) der "Alkestis" die Überschrift trägt

---

[1] P. Oxy. 3653 (2.Jh. n.Chr.) Hypotheseis zu Ναύπλιος καταπλέων, Νιόβη (mit teilweise erhaltener Überschrift . . . ἧ]ς ἀρ[χὴ] ἥδε· Zitat-Rest, ἡ δ᾽ ὑπόθεσις) und vermutlich (vgl. den Verf., *ZPE* 60 [1985] 11) Οἰδίπους Τύραννος.

ὑπόθεσις 'Αλκήστιδος Δικαιάρχου (**115A**), da sich diese Hypothesis
aufgrund eines Papyrusfundes eindeutig als gekürzte Fassung der in
besagter Hypotheseis-Sammlung enthaltenen "Alkestis"-Hypothesis
erweist.[2]
Hinzu kommt, daß in Handschriften des "Rhesos," dessen Hypothesis, wie ein Papyrusfund gezeigt hat, in jener Hypotheseis-
Sammlung mitenthalten war, in einer Debatte um zwei verschiedene
Prologe dieses Dramas bemerkt wird:

ὁ γοῦν Δικαίαρχος ἐκτιθεὶς τὴν ὑπόθεσιν τοῦ 'Ρήσου γράφει κατὰ
λέξιν οὕτως· " <---> νῦν εὐσέληνον φέγγος ἡ διφρήλατος" (**114**);

denn Zitat des Anfangsverses neben der Darlegung (ἐκτιθεὶς) der
betreffenden Hypothesis ist gerade das entscheidende Kennzeichen
jener Hypotheseis-Sammlung. Vervollständigt man das ausdrücklich
wörtlich angeführte Zitat, das schwerlich aus dem bloßen Anfangsvers
des Dramas bestanden haben kann (deshalb die Annahme einer Lücke),
zu < 'Ρῆσος, οὗ ἀρχή ·> νῦν εὐσέληνον φέγγος ἡ διφρήλατος, so wäre
dies das wörtliche Zitat der Einleitung dieses Dramas in jener
Sammlung. Und das wörtliche Zitat des Dikaiarchos dient in dieser
Debatte ja als Beweis dafür, daß es noch einen anderen — als den in
unseren Handschriften enthaltenen — Prolog gegeben hat. Die Kürze
des Zitats braucht neben ausdrücklichem κατὰ λέξιν m.E. keine
Bedenken zu erregen: Aus der Hypotheseis-Sammlung war nur dies zu
entnehmen, weil darin diesbezüglich nichts weiter gestanden hat. Vorausgesetzt, diese Sammlung war ein Werk des Dikaiarchos, war ein
solches Zitat ein exakter Beweis.[3]
    Die Überlieferungslage scheint mir also dafür zu sprechen, daß dieses
Sammelwerk der Hypotheseis zu Euripides- und Sophokles-Dramen
ein Werk des Dikaiarchos ist.
    Nun wird dagegen geltend gemacht, es handele sich dabei um eine
fälschliche Zuschreibung eines Werkes, das erst im ersten oder zweiten
Jahrhundert n.Chr. verfaßt worden wäre.[4]
    Es gibt für diese Annahme ebensowenig einen Beweis wie eine
Widerlegung. Ich meine, man sollte zunächst der Überlieferung
vertrauen. Das Mißtrauen beruht darauf, daß man bloße mythologische

---

[2] P. Oxy. 2457 = **115B**, vgl. den Verf., *Philologus* 126 (1982) 10–16.
[3] Vgl. dazu den Verf., *ZPE* 84 (1990) 11–13.
[4] Vgl. vor allem J. Rusten, *GRBSt* 23 (1982) 357–67.

Inhaltsangaben einem Schüler des Aristoteles wie Dikaiarchos nicht zutraut, d.h. sie für unter seiner Würde erachtet. Dabei ist zweierlei zu beachten. Erstens sollte man bei der geringen Kenntnis, die wir tatsächlich von den Werken des Dikaiarchos haben, vorsichtig sein mit der Einschätzung, welcher Art ein jeweiliges Werk von ihm gewesen ist. Zweitens ist zu prüfen, was denn ein solches Werk der mythologischen Inhaltsangaben, dessen Gestalt uns durch die Papyrusfunde hinreichend bekannt geworden ist, zu seiner Zeit tatsächlich darstellte.

Es bestand neben dem Zitat des ersten Verses ausschließlich aus der Darstellung des Mythos in dem jeweiligen Drama, ohne daß auf dessen szenische Gliederung eingegangen wird. Es ist reine Mythenwiedergabe. Es wird keinerlei Vergleich zu andersartiger Darstellung des betreffenden Mythos in irgendeiner Literaturgattung gegeben. Es wird nichts über die Plazierung im Agon, nichts über die Zeit der Aufführung gesagt (abgesehen von der relativen Chronologie in dem Falle, daß es zwei Dramen desselben Titels gab, wie das bei der Überschrift Φρῖξος πρῶτος und Φρῖξος δεύτερος deutlich wird[5]).

So sei auf die Gründe, die m.E. für die Echtheit sprechen könnten, hier nochmals eingegangen.[6]

Zu bedenken ist in diesem Zusammenhang u.a. der Umfang des Werkes. Die bloße Nacherzählung der Mythengestaltung bei Euripides umfaßte, wie sogleich gezeigt werden wird, vermutlich 2 Rollen = 2 Bücher. Das umfangreichere Dramenwerk des Sophokles läßt demnach mindestens 3 Bücher Mythenwiedergabe erwarten. 5 Bücher mythologischer Inhaltsangaben sind ein beachtliches Werk. Kritische Auseinandersetzung mit der jeweiligen Mythengestaltung und Vergleiche mit anderen Darstellungen hätten dieses Werk sehr umfangreich und gewiß weniger übersichtlich gemacht. Die systematische Auflistung der Aufführungsfakten einschließlich der Plazierung der jeweiligen Konkurrenten war ohnehin durch ein anderes Werk, Aristoteles' Διδασκαλίαι, gegeben. — Kann man dem Dikaiarchos nicht zubilligen, in einem solchen, zwangsläufig umfangreichen Werk sich darauf beschränkt zu haben darzulegen, wie

---

[5] Möglicherweise weist auch **101** auf eine derartige Zählung, vgl. dazu den Verf., *Hermes* 119 (1991) 467–69 (ὥς φησι Δικαίαρχος zu beziehen auf εἰσὶ δὲ καὶ οἱ 'πρότερον', οὐ 'τύραννον' αὐτὸν (sc. den betreffenden "Oidipus") ἐπιγράφοντες.

[6] Dargelegt von mir in *Aristoteles, Werk und Wirkung*, 1. Bd., *Aristoteles und seine Schule*, hrsg. von J. Wiesner (Berlin/New York, 1985) 610–12. Vgl. auch M. Haslam, *GRBSt* 16 (1975) 151–55.

jeder der beiden Dramatiker in den einzelnen Dramen die betreffende Sage gestaltet hat? Hat Dikaiarchos doch offenbar, was er zu den Aufführungen zu sagen hatte, in einer anderen kleineren, ein Buch umfassenden Schrift περὶ Διονυσιακῶν ἀγώνων dargelegt (**99**: Δικαίαρχος ἐν τῷ περὶ Διονυσιακῶν ἀγώνων)?

Setzt man ferner voraus — worauf auch die der Identifizierung dienende jeweilige Angabe des ersten Verses zu weisen scheint—, daß ein gesicherter Bestand des Oeuvres der beiden Dichter noch nicht vorlag, sondern es Dikaiarchos war, der diese Bestandsaufnahme gemacht und sie durch Zitieren des ersten Verses sowie Wiedergabe des mythologischen Inhalts gesichert hat, wäre das eine dem Aristoteles-Schüler von vornherein unwürdige Leistung? Man könnte zugleich auch die alphabetische Reihenfolge als Ordnungsprinzip als "Erfindung" des Dikaiarchos deuten.

Ich meine also, man sollte mit der Deutung der Hypotheseis-Sammlung als "Pseudo-Dikaiarchos" vorsichtig sein.

Und nun zu einigen Einzelheiten dieser Schrift, dem eigentlichen Anliegen dieses Beitrages.

Die große Zahl von Papyri — von denen in der Zwischenzeit mehr als ein Dutzend publiziert worden ist —, die Teile dieser Sammlung von Euripides-Hypotheseis enthalten, haben uns eine Menge von Informationen über ungefähr zwanzig Dramen des Euripides gebracht, die verloren sind. (Dabei sind die unechten Tragödien "Rhadamanthys," "Rhesus" und "Tennes" miteingeschlossen.)

Durch den Zufall der Funde besitzen wir vor allem Reste von solchen Papyri, die Teile von Hypotheseis enthalten, die sich auf Dramen beziehen, deren Anfangsbuchstabe des Titels A ist oder ein Buchstabe aus dem zweiten Teil des Alphabets von M an.

Allein die Hypothesis des Ἀλέξανδρος ist fast vollständig erhalten, auch ein umfangreicher Teil des Anfangs der Hypothesis des Αἴολος und der Αὔγη ist gefunden worden. Was die Hypothesis des Παλαμήδης betrifft, der zweiten Tragödie der Trojanischen Trilogie Ἀλέξανδρος – Παλαμήδης – Τρῳάδες, so werde ich darüber im weiteren Teil dieser Ausführungen sprechen, ebenso, wie ich über die Identifizierung eines Fragments der Πελιάδες-Hypothesis handeln werde.

Von den uns verlorenen Dramen mit dem Anfangsbuchstaben aus dem zweiten Teil des Alphabets besitzen wir — abgesehen von den

beiden soeben genannten mit Π anlautenden Titeln — hauptsächlich
Reste der Hypotheseis folgender Dramen:

vom Ῥαδάμανθυς das Ende der Hypothesis,
vom Σκείρων und den Σκύριοι in beiden Fällen den Anfang der
   Hypothesis,
vom Συλεύς Anfang und Ende der Hypothesis — mehr über dieses
   Satyrspiel sogleich —,
vom Τέννης das Ende der Hypothesis.
Es liegen umfangreiche Teile von vier Tragödien über den Herakliden
   Τήμενος und seine Kinder vor.
Von den Tragödien Ὑψιπύλη, Φαέθων und Φιλοκτήτης besitzen wir
   in jedem Fall den Mittelteil der Hypothesis,
von den beiden Φρῖξος in jedem Fall sowohl Anfang als auch Ende
   der Hypothesis.
Und es gibt noch mehrere kleine Fragmente weiterer Tragödien.

Es kann nicht Aufgabe dieses Beitrages sein, den Inhalt aller dieser
Teile darzulegen. Aber ich möchte einige m.e. besonders interessante
Erkenntnisse und Probleme als Beispiele besprechen.

Solche Erkenntnisse sind m.e. vor allem aus den zahlreichen
Fragmenten der Sammlung von Euripides-Hypotheseis P. Oxy. 2455 zu
gewinnen, die im 27. Band der Oxyrhynchos-Papyri von 1962 enthalten
sind. Dieser Papyrus betrifft solche Titel, deren Anfangsbuchstabe zum
zweiten Teil des Alphabets gehört, genauer gesagt, die von M–X
reichen (also Hypotheseis von Dramen von Μήδεια – Χρύσιππος). Wie
ich glaube, umfaßte diese Sammlung ursprünglich zwei Rollen, von
denen uns in P. Oxy. 2455 nur Fragmente der zweiten Rolle vorliegen.
Für diese Annahme könnte sprechen, daß sich unter den sehr zahlreichen Fragmenten dieses Papyrus kein einziges Bruchstück befindet, das
auf einen Dramen-Titel geht, der mit einem Buchstaben aus der ersten
Hälfte des Alphabets beginnt. Auch vom Umfang her wäre diese
Annahme akzeptabel: Wir haben mit ungefähr 80 Dramen des
Euripides zu rechnen. Bei 80 Dramen und einer durchschnittlichen Hy-
pothesis-Länge von etwas über einer Kolumne in diesem Papyrus
ergäbe sich ein Umfang von über 40 Kolumnen für jede der beiden
Rollen. Das entspräche etwa dem Umfang einer Dramen-Rolle.
Zu diesem Hypotheseis-Papyrus im einzelnen:

Anhand eines neuen Photos konnte von mir fr. 18 identifiziert werden.[7] Dort läßt sich nämlich in Zeile 15 κα[τέθ]ηκεν εἰς λ[έ]βη[τα herstellen, "setzte in einen Kessel." Damit ist ein Stichwort zu einer bekannten Sage gegeben, nämlich der von den Pelias-Töchtern. Als Objekt zu κα[τέθ]ηκεν läßt sich dann κρ[ιόν, "Widder" (Z.13 Ende) verifizieren. Steht doch in der Inhaltsangabe des entsprechenden Euripides-Dramas bei Moses Chorenensis, p. 550f. Nauck[2]: *nempe ut Medea laniatum arietem in lebetem coniecerit.*

Es geht in diesem Hypothesis-Bruchstück also ganz offensichtlich um Medeias Versprechen, den alten Pelias zu verjüngen, was sie zuvor an einem Widder exemplifizierte. Wir haben es also hier zweifellos mit der Hypothesis zu den "Peliades," einer der Tragödien der ersten Aufführung des Euripides zu tun.

Diese Annahme wird durch die Fundumstände bestätigt: Auf der Rückseite von diesem fr. 18 befand sich nämlich zunächst noch ein kleines Bruchstück — jetzt fr. 141 —, das Barrett als Teil der bekannten "Orestes"-Hypothesis identifiziert hat. Vermutlich haftete dieses kleine Bruchstück an der Stelle, wo es sich ursprünglich innerhalb der Rolle befand. Die dem Alphabet nach späteren Hypotheseis befanden sich weiter im Inneren der Rolle. So lag folglich auf der Ὀρέστης-Hypothesis ein im Alphabet folgendes Stück. Das könnte sehr gut die Πελιάδες-Hypothesis gewesen sein.

An Einzelheiten läßt sich nun zeigen, daß offenbar die ausführliche Schilderung dieser Geschichte bei Diodor IV 51/52 sich an Euripides' Darstellung orientiert.

Bei Diodor heißt es, als von der Verjüngung des Pelias gesprochen war, ἐκπληττομένου δὲ τοῦ βασιλέως τὸ παράδοξον τῶν λόγων ("als der König erstaunt war über das Widersinnige der Worte"). Am Anfang einer Zeile von fr. 18 steht δοξον, das war also παρά]|δοξον.

Diodor berichtet τρεφομένου γὰρ κριοῦ πολυετοῦς κατὰ τὴν οἰκίαν ("ein sehr alter Widder wurde in dem Haus gehalten"). Im Papyrus folgt auf κρ[ιὸν nach einer kurzen Lücke ἤδη. Man könnte an etwas wie κρ[ιὸν γὰρ παλαιὸν]| ἤδη denken. Diodor sagt μυθολογοῦσι τὴν Μήδειαν κατὰ μέλη διελοῦσαν τὸ σῶμα τοῦ κριοῦ καθεψῆσαι ("man erzählt, Medeia habe den Leib des Widders zerteilt und ge-

[7] *Anagennesis* 3 (1983) 125–41, und *ZPE* 60 (1985) 16–20.

kocht"). An der entsprechenden Stelle des Papyrus steht καταμ[, also ist vielleicht κατὰ μ[έλη διεῖλεν zu ergänzen. Entsprechend heißt es in der eben genannten Inhaltsangabe bei Moses Chorenensis *laniatum arietem*. Die Zeilenlänge in diesem Papyrus ist aus den anderen Fragmenten bekannt. Der betreffende Absatz der Hypothesis könnte also gelautet haben:

καὶ τὸ [δοκοῦν εἶναι παρά]Ιδοξον ὥς ἐστιν δυ[νατὸν μηχανή]Ιμασιν
δείξασα· κρ[ιὸν γὰρ παλαιὸν]Ι ἤδη λα[βο]ῦσα κατὰ μ[έλη διεῖλεν
καὶ]Ι κα[τέθ]ηκεν εἰς λ[έ]βη[τα καὶ καθεψήσασα Ι ἐποίησεν ἄ]ρνα,

". . . und nachdem sie, daß das widersinnig zu sein Scheinende möglich ist, durch Tricks gezeigt hat; sie nahm nämlich einen Widder, der schon alt war, zerlegte ihn, legte ihn in einen Kessel, kochte ihn und machte ihn zu einem Lamm."

Ging es hier im wesentlichen um die Zuordnung eines Hypothesis-Fragments zu einem bekannten Euripideischen Dramen-Titel, so lassen sich m.E. aus anderen Fragmenten dieses Papyrus neue Erkenntnisse über bisher teilweise unbekannte Dramen-Titel gewinnen. Und zwar erstens für die Tragödien aus dem Sagenkreis der Herakles-Nachkommen, speziell der Temeniden. Als diesbezügliche Titel sind uns aus Zitaten und aus der Titelliste P. Oxy. 2456 bekannt: Τήμενος und Τημενίδαι, ferner der nach dem ältesten Temenos-Sohn benannte Ἀρχέλαος und der Κρεσφόντης, betitelt nach dem Sohn des gleichnamigen Temenos-Bruders. Das sind allein vier Dramentitel dieses Sagenkreises, den Euripides also besonders bevorzugt hat. Nun zeigen m.E. die Fragmente jenes Hypotheseis-Papyrus, daß dies noch nicht alle diesbezüglichen Euripides-Titel sein können, die es gegeben hat. Wir haben nämlich aus jenem Papyrus vier größere Hypotheseis-Fragmente, die von Temenos bzw. den Temeniden handeln. Von diesen kann aber keines zum Ἀρχέλαος oder zum Κρεσφόντης gehören, da diese Titel ja mit einem Buchstaben aus dem ersten Teil des Alphabets beginnen, unser Papyrus aber, wie die zahlreichen Fragmente zeigen, nur solche des zweiten Teils des Alphabets umfaßt. Jene größeren Fragmente sind fr. 9, fr. 10 und fr. 11 und dazu noch P. Michigan 1319, ein Fragment, das sich durch Überschneidung mit dem kleinen Fragment 107 unseres Oxyrhynchus-Papyrus als ein solches Hypothesis-Fragment erwiesen hat.[8] Vier entsprechende Hypotheseis-Fragmente also für nur zwei Titel, "Temenos" und "Temenidai"? Es scheint unmöglich, alle diese vier Hypotheseis-Fragmente in nur zwei Hypotheseis unterzubringen. Dagegen sprechen der Inhalt und der Umfang dieser Fragmente; denn der Gesamtumfang einer Hypothesis ist relativ beschränkt, umfaßt in jenem Papyrus jeweils ohne Überschrift etwa 30–40 Zeilen, wie ich früher zu verdeutlichen gesucht habe.[9] Die vier Stücke umfassen jeweils ungefähr ein Drittel einer Hypothesis.

Fr. 9 und fr. 10 erzählen zudem ausführlich jeweils dieselbe Begebenheit, die Aufteilung der Peloponnes an die entsprechenden Herakles-Nachkommen, wobei Argos dem Temenos zuteil wird, Messenien dem Kresphontes, Sparta den Aristodemos-Söhnen. Ich zitiere den diesbezüglichen Textabschnitt in der von mir[10] e.g. ergänzten Form:

Fr. 9   διι[α]ν[είμα]ντο[ς] δὲ τοῦ Ὀ[ξύ]λου τὴν Πελοι[πόννησον εἰς] μέρη
τρία, τ[ὴν μ]ὲν Ἀργείl[αν ἀπήιτησ]ε Τή[με]ν[ος] πρεσ[βύ]τατος l
[ὤν, τὴν δὲ] Μεσσηνίαν ἔ[λα]βεν Κρ̣[εσφόνl]της ---], τὴν δ[ὲ]
Λακ[ωlνίαν οἱ Ἀριστο]δήμ[ου] παῖδες.

"Als Oxylos die Peloponnes in drei Teile geteilt hatte, forderte Temenos als der Älteste die Argolis, Messenien nahm Kresphontes, Lakonien die Söhne des Aristodemos."

Fr. 10   Τήμενος μερίσ[ας l τὴν χώραν, ἣν εἰλή]φει, παρ᾽ ἑκόντων τ[ὸ
Ἄρlγος ἑλόμε]νος ἐκλ[ή]ρωσεν· ἔλαχεν [δὲ̣ l Κρεσφόντ]ης τὴν
Μεσσηνίαν, τοῖς [δὲ̣ l Ἀριστοδήμου] παισὶν — Namen — [Σπάρ]τη
[προσέπεσ]εν̣ τῷ κλήρῳ.

"Als Temenos das Land, das er erobert hatte, geteilt hatte, verloste er es, nachdem er sich unter Zustimmung Argos genommen hatte. Es erlangte Kresphontes Messenien, den Aristodemos-Söhnen . . . fiel Sparta durch das Los zu."

---

[8] Identifiziert von A. Harder, *ZPE* 35 (1979) 7–14.
[9] *ZPE* 72 (1988) 27–30.
[10] *Prometheus* 13 (1987) 193–203.

Das kann unmöglich zweimal in ein- und derselben Hypothesis erzählt sein, zumal der Sachverhalt sich in Einzelheiten in beiden Fragmenten deutlich voneinander unterscheidet: Hier teilt Oxylos — dort teilt Temenos.

Von eben diesen Teilen der Peloponnes ist auch in fr. 11 berichtet:[11] hier ist aber offenbar die Teilung schon vorausgesetzt, aber andererseits ist dieses Fragment nach Anordnung und Wortlaut offensichtlich der Beginn einer Hypothesis; denn größerer Zeilenabstand zu Anfang des Fragmentes und Worttrennung erweisen den Anfang dieses Fragments m.E. als einen Hypothesis-'Kopf'.

Dafür spricht auch die ausführliche Vorstellung einer Person in diesem Fragment, die gerade für den Beginn einer Hypothesis bezeichnend ist: Τεισαμε]νὸς υἱὸς ὢν Ὀρέ[στου καὶ υἱδοῦς | Ἀγαμέ]μνονος, βασιλεὺς [---. Teisamenos schickt offenbar einen Späher in die an die Temeniden bereits aufgeteilten Gebiete der Peloponnes: ἀπ|έπεμ]ψεν κατάσκοπον εἰς Σπάρτ[ην καὶ | κατὰ Μ]εσσήνην. Dieses Fragment kann also schwerlich aus derselben Hypothesis wie fr. 9 oder fr. 10 stammen.

Von Weitergabe der Königsherrschaft des Temenos an den tüchtigsten seiner Söhne, also schon von der nächsten Generation, ist andererseits in jenem mit fr. 107 sich überschneidenden Michigan-Papyrus die Rede:

Τήμενος, ὁ τῶν Ἡρακλειδῶν πρεσβύτατος, τὴν βασιλείαν ἔφησεν παραδώσειν τῷ κατὰ μάχην ἀριστεύσαντι τῶν υἱῶν.[12]

Meines Erachtens können also die beiden uns bekannten Titel Τήμενος und Τημενίδαι nicht die beiden einzigen diesbezüglichen Dramen des Euripides gewesen sein, deren Titel mit einem Buchstaben aus dem zweiten Teils des Alphabets begann. Es muß mindestens noch ein weiteres Drama der Temenos-Sage von Euripides gegeben haben. Gab es vielleicht Τημενίδαι πρῶτοι und Τημενίδαι δεύτεροι, wie derselbe Papyrus durch Überschrift eindeutig bewiesen hat, daß es einen Φρῖξος πρῶτος und einen Φρῖξος δεύτερος gegeben hat? Das erschiene mir als die einfachste Lösung. (Die Möglichkeit eines zweifachen Τήμενος ist ausgeschlossen durch den zufällig in fr. 8

---

[11] Zu diesem Fragment vgl. den Verf., *APF* 41 (1995) 25–33.

[12] Es überschneidet sich von dem hier zitierten Satz ην βασιλ und μαχη. Zu den weiteren Überschneidungen vgl. zuletzt den Verf., *ZPE* 49 (1982) 15–19.

erhaltenen Titel Τήμενος, οὗ ἀρχή.) Eine andere Möglichkeit wären Τημενίδες, Töchter des Temenos. Steht doch bei Stobaios in allen seinen Zitaten, wo er den Titel im Dativ angibt, Τημενίσιν, was man bisher als Fehler ansieht. Freilich wissen wir nur von einer Temenos-Tochter namens Ὑρνηθώ. Oder sollte es etwa irgendeinen anderen Titel für das betreffende Drama gegeben haben, dessen Anfangsbuchstabe in der zweiten Hälfte des Alphabets zu suchen wäre? Aber daß der Titel einer Tragödie des Euripides, die noch der Verfasser der Hypotheseis gekannt hätte, uns gänzlich unbekannt geblieben wäre, ist relativ unwahrscheinlich. (Bei einem Satyrspiel ist ein solcher Totalverlust eher denkbar, dazu sogleich.) Der Titel bleibt ungewiß, ein weiteres solches Drama außer den Τήμενος und Τημενίδαι betitelten scheint mir jedoch aufgrund der besagten Hypotheseis-Fragmente gewiß.

Noch ein weiteres Drama des Euripides, dessen Titel zweifach vertreten war, glaube ich aus diesem Hypotheseis-Papyrus erschließen zu können, und zwar ein Satyrspiel. Bei Satyrspielen ist die Annahme des Verlustes eines Titels an sich von vornherein weniger problematisch; denn ohnehin sind offensichtlich einige Satyrspiel-Titel des Euripides zu vermissen. Wir wissen nämlich — von dem erhaltenen Κύκλωψ abgesehen — nur von 6 Satyrspielen, die nachweislich nach Alexandria gelangt sind, da uns aus ihnen Fragmente zitiert sind, Αὐτόλυκος, Βούσειρις, Εὐρυσθεύς, Σίσυφος, Σκείρων, Συλεύς. Durch Athenaios erfahren wir, daß es zwei Αὐτόλυκοι, Αὐτόλυκος A und Αὐτόλυκος B, gegeben hat (X 413C Εὐριπίδης ἐν τῷ πρώτῳ Αὐτολύκῳ λέγει — es folgt fr. 282 N²). Bastianini und ich haben kürzlich in einer Schülerübung eines Wiener Papyrus — als zweites Zeugnis — als Überschrift einer Hypothesis Αὐτόλυκος A identifiziert.[13] Daneben kennen wir noch den Titel eines Satyrspiels, das zu Zeiten der Alexandriner verloren war, die Θερισταί, wie die 'Medeia'-Hypothesis unserer Handschriften zeigt (τρίτος Εὐριπίδης Μηδείᾳ, Φιλοκτήτῃ, Δίκτυι, Θερισταῖς σατύροις. οὐ σῴζεται). Bekanntlich wird aus Satyrspielen viel seltener zitiert als aus Tragödien. Von einer Reihe von Satyrspielen einiger Tragiker haben wir nur je ein einziges Zitat. Fehlte dies, fehlte oftmals unsere Kenntnis von dem betreffenden Satyrspiel völlig. Wir lesen in der vita des Euripides, daß acht Satyrspiele des Euripides bewahrt worden wären (p. 4 Schwartz: σῴ

---

[13] *Analecta Papyrologica* I (1989) 31–36.

ζεται δὲ αὐτοῦ ..., σατυρικὰ δὲ η'). Wir kennen die Zeit dieser vita nicht. Nur wenn die Feststellung für den Autor der Euripides-Hypotheseis Gültigkeit hat, wäre ein weiteres Satyrspiel ausgeschlossen. Aber ich meine, der Autor der Hypotheseis könnte früher sein als diese vita. Oder es gab Verwirrung durch die gleichartigen Titel verschiedener Satyrspiele. Vielleicht nämlich wurden zwei Aufführungen eines Satyrspieles mit demselben Titel als *ein* Stück gezählt.

Soweit allgemein zur Satyrspiel-Überlieferung, nun zurück zu unserem Papyrus: In den letzten Zeilen einer Hypothesis — auf fr. 8 — steht eindeutig καὶ τὸν Συλέα. Das ist also das Ende einer Hypothesis zum Συλεὺς σατυρικός. (4 Zeilen danach endet diese Hypothesis mit einer nicht vollbeschriebenen Zeile, und darauf folgt der nächste Titel: Τήμενος, οὗ ἀρχή.)

Aber in fr. 5 haben wir noch einen Schluß einer Hypothesis eines mit Σ anlautenden Titels. (Denn auf diesen Hypothesis-Schluß folgt als weiterer Σ-Titel auf demselben Bruchstück die Σθενέβοια-Hypothesis.) In dieser — der "Stheneboia"-Hypothesis vorausgehenden — Hypothesis ist vom Auftritt des Herakles die Rede: ἐ]πιφαν[εὶ]ς δ' Ἡρα[κλῆς.[14] Die einzige Tragödie, deren Titel neben der Σθενέβοια noch mit Σ anlautet, sind jedoch lediglich die Σκύριοι, in denen es um die Abholung des Achilleus nach Troja geht. (Der Anfang dieser Hypothesis ist uns durch einen anderen Papyrus bekannt.) Es kann sich bei fr. 5 also nur um ein Satyrspiel handeln, wie gesagt, eines mit Σ anlautenden Titels. Dem entspricht übrigens auch der Auftritt des Herakles. Ist Herakles doch eine häufige Figur im Satyrspiel. Man hat an den Σκείρων gedacht, dessen Hypothesis-Anfang wir besitzen. Aber der "Skiron" gehört in die Theseus-Sage. Daß Euripides in der bekannten Sage den attischen Heros durch Herakles ersetzt hätte, erscheint jedenfalls abwegig. (Natürlich kann nicht absolut ausgeschlossen werden, daß Herakles am Ende des Skiron-Satyrspiels auftritt, als Theseus den Skiron bereits getötet hatte, aber es ist zumindest höchst unwahrscheinlich.) Dann bliebe unter den dem Titel nach bekannten Satyrspielen, dessen Titel außerdem noch mit Σ anlautete, nur der Σίσυφος. Da man von dessen Inhalt so gut wie nichts

---

[14] ἐπιφανεὶς bezeichnet in den Hypotheseis auch das Auftreten einer Person, vgl. Hyp. Orestes Ἠλέκτρα δὲ Ἑρμιόνην ἐπιφανεῖσαν ἔδωκεν εἰς χεῖρας αὐτοῖς ... ἐπιφανεὶς δὲ Μενέλαος ... .

weiß, kann man natürlich alles unter diesen Titel stellen. Und so ist es auch geschehen.

Aber es scheint einen anderen Anhaltspunkt zu geben: Außer der Erwähnung des Herakles steht in diesem Bruchstück -μ]ενος ὑπ[ὸ] τοῦ ϹΥ[. Danach bricht die Zeile ab. Das einfachste wäre ὑπὸ τοῦ Συ[λέως. Dann stammt auch dieses Schlußstück einer Hypothesis, wie das von fr. 8, aus einer Συλεύς-Hypothesis. Da Herakles' Auftritt erst fünf Zeilen vor dem Ende der Hypothesis erwähnt ist, dürfte ein großer Teil dieses Syleus-Satyrspieles vor diesem Auftritt spielen, was nicht erstaunlich wäre. Es gab dann zwei Satyrspiele dieses Titels, Συλεὺς πρῶτος und Συλεὺς δεύτερος, genauso, wie es einen Αὐτόλυκος πρῶτος und einen Αὐτόλυκος δεύτερος gegeben hat. Dazu noch folgende Überlegungen:

Von der Existenz zweier Αὐτόλυκος betitelter Euripideischer Satyrspiele wußten wir bis vor kurzem (s.o.) allein durch jenes eine Zitat bei Athenaios (von insgesamt vier). Wäre es da verwunderlich, wenn wir von zwei Συλεύς-Satyrspielen ein entsprechendes Zitat nicht haben? Bei 20 aus den beiden Φρῖξος-Dramen mit Titel gegebenen Zitaten steht nur bei zweien der Zusatz δεύτερος. Den 17 Zitaten aus dem ersten "Hippolytos" mit bloßem ἐν Ἱππολύτῳ (oder ähnlich) steht ein einziges — fr. 442 N^2 — mit der Angabe ἐν Ἱππολύτῳ καλυπτομένῳ gegenüber. Der Συλεύς wird uns aber insgesamt überhaupt nur dreimal ausdrücklich mit Titelangabe zitiert (fr. 692–94 N^2). So steht der Annahme eines zweiten Συλεύς aus dieser Sicht nichts im Wege.

Wir haben in dem Straßburger Papyrusfragment 2676 Aa, das aus derselben Rolle stammt, noch den Anfang einer 'Syleus'-Hypothesis. (Der entscheidende Teil des Titels, der über die Duplizität des Titels entschiede, ist nicht erhalten.) Gab es zwei Συλεύς-Satyrspiele, könnte jenes Bruchstück sowohl zum Συλεύς A als zum Συλεύς B gehören.[15]

Bis jetzt habe ich einen Fund nicht erwähnt, der in meinen Augen sensationell ist. Ich meine einen langen Papyrusstreifen aus der Hypothesis zu dem verlorenen ersten "Hippolytos," dem sogenannten Καλυπτόμενος oder Κατακαλυπτόμενος, P. Mich. 6222A.[16] Dieser Papyrus zeigt, daß dieser 'Hippolytos' in derselben Weise wie der zweite, der sogenannte Στεφανίας, in Troizen spielt und teilweise in seinem Inhalt mit dem zweiten übereinstimmt, auch was die Verfluchung und den Tod des Hippolytos betrifft. Der bedeutsame

---

[15] Vgl. dazu den Verf., *Anagennesis* 4 (1986) 223–43.
[16] Vgl. dazu den Verf., *ZPE* 102 (1994) 23–39.

Punkt ist eine Szene, die nach meiner Meinung eine andere Interpretation des Beiwortes Καλυπτόμενος erfordert als man bisher angenommen hat, d.h. daß diese Tragödie mit diesem Beiwort versehen worden wäre, weil Hippolytos, geschockt von Phaidras schamlosem und ehebrecherischem Anbieten ihrer selbst, sich aus Scham verhüllt hätte. Denn in dem Papyrus lesen wir in unmittelbarer Nähe τὴν Ἱπ]πολύτου στολήν und ἐκέλευσε[ν . . . (κατα)κα]λυψάμενον . . . καθίσαι. Jemand spricht also über die Kleidung des Hippolytos und ordnet an, daß jemand sich hinsetzt, nachdem er einen Teil von sich — ich meine, sein Gesicht bzw. seine Augen — verhüllt hat. Ich sehe keine andere Interpretationsmöglichkeit dieses Wortlautes, als daß jemand eine Person auffordert, vorzugeben, Hippolytos zu sein. Und ich vermute, der Zweck dessen ist es, Phaidra zu prüfen, die daraufhin, getäuscht beim Zusammentreffen mit dieser verhüllten Person, ihre Leidenschaft in Gegenwart dieses vermeintlichen Hippolytos kundtut und so ihr Verlangen gegen ihre Absicht einer Öffentlichkeit preisgibt. Als Person, die sie prüfen will, kommt m.E. Theseus in Frage, der nach Verdammung seines Sohnes mißtrauisch geworden ist. Demnach muß der Ἱππόλυτος (κατα)καλυπτόμενος ein falscher Hippolytos sein, nämlich eine Person, die zum Zwecke der Täuschung Phaidras vorgibt, sie wäre Hippolytos. Natürlich bin ich mir dessen gewiß, daß es Bedenken geben wird, diese Interpretation anstelle der früheren — lediglich auf Vermutung aufgrund des Beititels beruhenden — zu akzeptieren.

Ein anderer Michigan-Papyrus, der noch unveröffentlicht ist, enthält das Ende der Παλαμήδης-Hypothesis. Dieses zeigt, daß am Ende der Tragödie Nauplios, Palamedes' Vater, auf der Bühne erschien und dem Agamemnon drohte, Rache für die Ermordung seines Sohnes zu nehmen. Außerdem scheint deutlich zu werden, daß Palamedes' Bruder Oiax von den Griechen ins Meer geworfen und in letzter Minute durch die Nereiden gerettet worden war.

Soweit einige Gedanken zu den Euripideischen Papyrus-Hypotheseis, die uns so viele neue Erkenntnisse von wichtigen Teilen verlorener griechischer Literatur, nämlich von zahlreichen Euripides-Dramen, erbracht haben.

10

La Tradizione Papirologica di Dicearco

Tiziano Dorandi

I. Tra gli autori peripatetici i cui frammenti sono stati raccolti dal Wehrli nell'ormai classica raccolta *Schule des Aristoteles* quello che piú ha beneficiato di un rinnovato esame della tradizione papirologica è, senza dubbio, Dicearco. La silloge di Wehrli registrava tre passi estratti da opere di Filodemo. Nella sezione: "Über Lebensformen, Biographien," lo studioso riportava una brevissima testimonianza, recuperata dalla *Academicorum historia* (F 45 = **46C**); in quella: "Homerfragen" alcune linee dal *De musica* (F 93 = **39**). Tra gli: "Unbestimmbares, Unechtes, Unsicheres," infine, un frustulo lacunoso (F 118 = **52**) dal *De Stoicis*.[1]

II.1. La prima testimonianza—dalla *Academicorum historia*—era limitata da Wehrli alle sole parole: τοιαῦτα γεγραφότο[ς Δ]ικαιάρχου Φιλόχ[ο]ρος ἐν τῷ τῆς Ἀτθ[ί]δ[ος] ἕκτω[ι] παρέπαι[σεν] ἐπὶ το ... e cosí laconicamente commentata: "In fr. 45 ist der Inhalt des D.-Zitates nicht mehr feststellbar."[2] Qualche anno fa, con felice intuizione, Gaiser è, tuttavia, riuscito a dimostrare non solo che il testo che precede quella frase deve essere restituito a Dicearco, ma che si tratta anche di una

---

[1] Cf. T. Dorandi, *Testimonia Herculanensia*, in *CPF* I 1* (Firenze, 1989) 36s.
[2] Wehrli, *SdA* 1.55.

343

citazione letterale, derivata, con buona probabilità, dai capitoli del Περὶ βίων dedicati a Platone.[3]

Per intendere come Gaiser sia giunto a formulare la sua ipotesi, sono necessarie alcune premesse generali sulla particolare natura del Papiro di Ercolano 1021, il rotolo cioè che tramanda la *Academicorum historia* di Filodemo.[4] Il *PHerc.* 1021 conserva la "copia di lavoro," il brogliaccio di Filodemo, come confermano le peculiarità della scrittura dall'esecuzione disordinata, le tecniche librare irregolari, le aggiunte, le espunzioni, i passi ripetuti, i segni che indicavano trasposizioni, inserzioni, probabili guasti testuali e il fatto stesso che si tratti di un papiro "opistografo." Nel mettere insieme questa che potremmo ben definire una raccolta di materiale approntata in vista della stesura della sua opera sull'Academia platonica, il metodo di lavoro di Filodemo non era stato molto diverso da quello di Plinio il vecchio descritto dal nipote, Plinio il giovane: *liber legebatur, adnotabat, excerpebat.* Filodemo aveva letto le sue fonti, aveva indicato con segni i passi che gli sembravano utili per la sua opera, ne aveva fatto *excerpta.* La compilazione era avanzata per gradi con cambiamenti, correzioni e aggiunte seriori, che si erano stratificate l'una sull'altra. Il risultato, quale leggiamo oggi sul *PHerc.* 1021, è una raccolta non sempre omogenea di estratti talora riprodotti alla lettera, talora rielaborati in varia misura, derivati da piú antichi autori che avevano scritto su Platone e sulla sua scuola. Una parte di questi appunti, per effettiva mancanza di spazio sul *recto* del rotolo, Filodemo aveva sistemati sul *uerso*: sono le colonne indicate con le lettere dell'alfabeto da Z a O, oggi non piú leggibili sull'originale, ma conservate dall'apografo oxoniense del papiro.[5] Nel tentativo di ricostruire la successione dei capitoli dell'opera, si deve tenere conto che queste colonne, che contengono integrazioni aggiunte da Filodemo in momenti successivi, vengono a incunearsi nel tessuto

---

[3] Una prima notizia della scoperta Gaiser dette nella *Neue Zürcher Zeitung* del 6 novembre 1981, 33–34. Essa venne ripresa e confermata dal medesimo nel suo articolo "La biografia di Platone in Filodemo: Nuovi dati dal PHerc. 1021," *Cronache Ercolanesi* 13 (1983) 58–62 e, infine, nel volume: *Philodems Academica. Die Berichte über Platon und die Alte Akademie in zwei herkulanensischen Papyri* (Stuttgart e Bad Cannstatt, 1988) 97–100, 307–66.

[4] Per una piú dettagliata analisi, cf. T. Dorandi, *Filodemo. Storia dei filosofi: Platone e l'Academia* (Napoli, 1991) 109–13 e id., "Den Autoren über die Schulter geschaut. Arbeitsweise und Autographie bei den Antiken Schriftstellern," *Zeitschrift f. Papyrologie u. Epigraphik* 87 (1991) 11–17.

[5] Cf. Dorandi, ibid. 108s.

narrativo principale secondo criteri e modalità variabili, da determinare, di volta in volta, a partire da elementi interni. Fondandosi su queste premesse, Gaiser ha, per primo, correttamente compreso che, nel caso di quell'opera specifica, nella redazione tramandata dal *PHerc.* 1021, esiste una interrelazione fra l'ordine di successione delle colonne e le singole fonti riportate da Filodemo, spesso nel loro dettato originale. Per la determinazione delle fonti, Gaiser applica, con ottimi risultati, al materiale raccolto da Filodemo il metodo della stratificazione genetica. Il rapporto fra la successione delle colonne e l'alternarsi delle fonti porta a presupporre tre strati nella formazione compositiva della *Academicorum historia.* La sezione su Dicearco—che corrisponde alle colonne 1*, 1, 2.1–5, con l'inserimento posteriore della col. Y, tra le colonne 1 e 2—dovrebbe esser fatta risalire, secondo lo studioso, già al primo livello della stratificazione.[6]

Questi, in breve, i motivi e gli argomenti sui quali Gaiser fonda la sua attribuzione di quella pericope testuale al Περὶ βίων di Dicearco. L'ampio brano che comprende le colonne 1*-1–2.5 mostra una compatta unità testuale,[7] la cui paternità è esplicitamente indicata alla fine (col. 2.4–5): τοιαῦτα γεγραφότο[ς Δ]ικαιάρχου. I cinque frammenti finora noti dalla *Vita* di Platone (F 40–44 Wehrli = **45–50**) troverebbero tutti una corrispondenza nelle pagine estrapolate da Filodemo; la lingua stessa del brano si conforma all'uso del filosofo peripatetico e cosí pure la descrizione dei progressi delle scienze esatte nella scuola di Platone (col. Y), che Dicearco poté avere derivati dalla storia della matematica scritta da Eudemo di Rodi (F 133 Wehrli), fonte, a sua volta, del compendio che leggiamo nel Commento agli *Elementi* di Euclide di Proclo. L'unico motivo che potrebbe essere addotto contro la paternità dicearchea, cioè la positiva descrizione di Platone fautore di un *bios theoretikos* piuttosto che di un *bios praktikos*, è riconosciuto da Gaiser piuttosto come un elemento indicativo della obiettività del biografo peripatetico.

Se l'individuazione e la delimitazione dell'estratto è risultata relativamente facile, ben piú complessa e perfino frustrante si presenta la ricostruzione di quel testo a causa dello stato gravemente lacunoso di larghe parti. Gaiser ha cercato con ammirevole maestria di restaurare il

[6] Gaiser (*supra*, nota 3) 76s., 87–96.
[7] S. Mekler, *Academicorum philosophorum index Herculanensis* (Berlin, 1902/1958) 29 scorse tracce di Dicearco anche nella col. V, ma Gaiser (*supra*, nota 3) 101–3 ha convincentemente dimostrato che fonte di questo passo è piuttosto Filocoro.

frammento nella sua quasi totalità con risultati che, seppure soddisfacenti dal punto di vista sintattico-grammaticale e anche contenutistico, devono, purtroppo, essere presi in considerazione con estrema cautela, proprio perché basati, piú di una volta, su tracce fin troppo labili e frutto talora piú di interpretazione presupposta che di una concreta realtà testuale.[8]

Parallelamente alle ricerche di Gaiser, Lasserre aveva sviluppato l'ipotesi che nella parte iniziale della *Academicorum historia* filodemea fossero da individuare, semmai, resti del Περὶ Πλάτωνος dell'allievo di Platone Ermodoro di Siracusa, che a sua volta avrebbe mediato quelle informazioni dall'omonimo scritto dell'altro discepolo della Academia, Filippo di Opunte.[9]

Le colonne prese in considerazione da Lasserre sono in numero maggiore rispetto a quelle ritenute da Gaiser: X/Z, 3/5, Y, 1*, 1–2.5 del *PHerc.* 1021 e il fr. 13 del *PHerc.* 164 (il secondo esemplare, purtroppo molto frammentario, della *Academicorum historia* di Filodemo[10]). Da Ermodoro sarebbero derivate a Filodemo le informazioni sui viaggi di Platone in Sicilia (col. X/Z), sull'ultima notte del filosofo (col. 3/5), sulla sua scuola e lo sviluppo delle scienze esatte (col. Y), sui suoi dialoghi (1*-1–2.5). Gli estratti avrebbero formato due insiemi, il primo dei quali riuniva tutte le notizie sulla vita di Platone, il secondo esponeva l'attività di Platone nell'Academia. La lunga citazione da Ermodoro sarebbe stata preceduta e interrotta da una avvertenza di Filodemo stesso all'inizio della col. X (ll. 1–5), che Lasserre cosí ricostruisce (a partire dai risultati di Mekler e Crönert): οὐ]κ ἀπει[κότως ἐπι]ǀτεμὼ[ν οἷ]ς ἄλλοι συν[ῆιδο]ν ἐ[πι]τρέχω τὰ γεγραμμένα περὶ Π[λ]άἰτωνος ἄπ[α]νθ᾽ ὑπογράψας ἔχονǀτα οὕτως e interpreta: ". . . en retranchant, non sans raison, les passages sur lesquels s'accordaient d'autres auteurs, je passe en revue tout son ouvrage sur Platon et j'en reproduis les grands lignes de la manière que voici." Una frase che Gaiser intende, invece, come premessa di Filodemo a introduzione del suo resoconto della sola esperienza siciliana di Platone.[11]

---

[8] Cf. T. Dorandi, *Gnomon* 63 (1991) 300–6.

[9] Cf. F. Lasserre, "Hermodore de Syracuse dans PHerc. 1021 et 164?," *Cronache Ercolanesi* 13 (1983) 63–74; Id., "Le barbare, le grec et la science selon Philippe d'Oponte," *MH* 40 (1983) 175–77 e *De Léodamas de Thasos à Philippe d'Oponte. Témoignages et fragments* (Napoli, 1987) 601–5, 668–69.

[10] Sui rapporti fra i due manoscritti, cf. Dorandi (*supra*, nota 4) 103–13.

[11] Gaiser (*supra*, nota 3) 165 e 391s.

Contro molte congetture di Lasserre possono essere richiamate, in linea di massima, le critiche già mosse da Gaiser:[12] L'autore con cui colloquia Filippo di Opunte in col. 5.36–39 era un suo più giovane contemporaneo, cioè Neante di Cizico e non Ermodoro; le notizie sul soggiorno di Platone in Sicilia derivano, per esplicita dichiarazione di Filodemo stesso (col. X 1–5), da diverse fonti, tra le quali forse anche Ermodoro; in col. X 7 è detto che Platone, alla morte di Socrate, aveva ventisette anni, mentre da Ermodoro (in Diogene Laerzio 3.6) sappiamo che ne aveva ventotto; non è affatto certo che Ermodoro avesse scritto un'opera Περὶ Πλάτωνος; l'ipotesi che in col. 1.41 fosse indicato Filippo di Opunte è fondata sul solo supplemento: δια[δόχου; i paralleli fra la col. Y 2–17 e il commento di Proclo al I libro degli *Elementi* di Euclide sui quali Lasserre fonda principalmente la sua ipotesi di una derivazione dell'intera sezione da Ermodoro tràmite Filippo di Opunte, sono invece sintomatici, per Gaiser, di una comunanza di fonte piuttosto con Eudemo di Rodi.[13]

Pure limitata dalle gravi lacune e dalle incertezze di lettura, l'acquisizione del nuovo frammento a Dicearco prospettata da Gaiser ha incontrato una positiva accoglienza[14] e risulta, per diversi motivi, meglio fondata della attribuzione a Ermodoro avanzata da Lasserre.

Resta, comunque, un aspetto che merita di essere riconsiderato, quello cioè della effettiva estensione della citazione di Dicearco. Per quanto riguarda la col. 1*, l'estrema frammentarietà consiglia di non prendere posizione o di assumere un atteggiamento perlomeno scettico di fronte alle integrazioni di Gaiser. Ben più complesso è, invece, il caso della col. Y per la quale Burkert, contro Gaiser,[15] ha messo in dubbio la paternità dicearchea e ha ne suggerito, con sostanziali e convincenti argomenti, una attribuzione a Filippo di Opunte.[16] Innanzitutto, il verbo

---

[12] Gaiser (*supra*, nota 3) 89–91. Cf. M. Isnardi Parente, *MH* 46 (1989) 153; T. Dorandi, *Prometheus* 15 (1989) 191s. e id. (*supra*, nota 4) 86s.

[13] L'idea è sviluppata da F. Ferrari, *Rivista di Storia della filosofia* 48 (1993) 352–53. Contro la paternità di Eudemo, senza tenere presente il passo filodemeo, si dichiara C. Eggers Lan, "Eudemo y el 'Cátalogo de geómetras' de Proclo," *Emerita* 53 (1985) 127–57. Cf. Lasserre (*supra*, nota 9) 613–17.

[14] Rinuncio a dare una dossografia delle voci favorevoli e indico, di volta in volta, soltanto i contributi di coloro che si sono dichiarati contrari.

[15] Gaiser (*supra*, nota 3) 76s.

[16] W. Burkert, "Philodems Arbeitstext zur Geschichte der Akademie," *Zeitschrift f. Papyrologie u. Epigraphik* 97 (1993) 92–94 e *Platon in Nahaufnahme. Ein Buch aus Herculaneum* (Stuttgart u. Leipzig, 1993) 24–34.

παρέγραψα (Y 1) indica con chiarezza l'inizio di un nuovo estratto, che Filodemo aveva fatto sistemare sul *uerso* del rotolo in aggiunta e parallelamente alla citazione da Dicearco, che continua, invece, e si conclude con le linee iniziali della col. 2. Il brano contiene una interessantissima descrizione del progresso della matematica e del ruolo giocato da Platone in questo processo. Sotto la guida di Platone con funzioni di architetto (ll. 4–5: ἀρχιτεκτονοῦντος . . . Πλάτωνος), la teoria delle misure (μετρολογία) e i problemi delle definizioni (ὁρισμοί) raggiunsero il piú alto livello, dopo che Eudosso ebbe rinnovati i metodi antiquati di Ippocrate di Chio; anche la geometria, grazie all'introduzione del metodo della analisi e di quello delle determinazioni (διορισμοί) progredí; né rimasero trascurate l'ottica e la meccanica (ll. 1–17). Il resto della colonna è troppo lacuno perché si possa ricavarne qualcosa di sicuro né si può fare affidamento sui tentativi di ricostruzione acuti, ma assai ipotetici di Gaiser e di Lasserre:[17] sembra di intuire un contesto polemico contro σπερμολόγοι, che pensavano, nel loro piccolo, soltanto alla propria "raccolta" (ll. 20ss.) e di intravedere un accenno al problema (ll. 32–33) dell' "utile" (ὀνήσιμα) e del "necessario" (ἀναγκαῖα). In questa colonna non c'è niente, dunque, che riconduca a Dicearco, che, tra l'altro, non mostrò mai interesse alcuno per le scienze matematiche. Anche la supposizione di Gaiser che gli stretti paralleli della col. Y con il *Commento a Euclide* di Proclo ne indichino una fonte comune in Eudemo pone gravi aporie: difficilmente Eudemo, in quanto peripatetico, avrebbe espresso un simile giudizio su Platone. La fonte di entrambi i luoghi—un autore platonico, vissuto forse prima di Eudemo—non può essere che Filippo di Opunte, come già aveva intuito Lasserre. Filippo, dunque, e non Dicearco è l'autore dell'estratto sul progresso della matematica nella col. Y che Filodemo riproduce nel suo dettato letterale.[18]

　　Un breve accenno, infine, alla recente suggestione di Voutiras, secondo cui dalle linee iniziali di col. 2 si dedurrebbe solo che fine di Filodemo era quello di contrapporre un perduto resoconto dossografico di Dicearco relativo al pensiero della antica Academia e a Platone—non citato alla lettera—alla parallela rappresentazione del sesto libro della

[17] Cf. Dorandi (*supra*, nota 4) 207–10.
[18] L'ipotesi che fonte della col. Y sia Eudemo è stata ripresa con argomenti, a mio avviso, non convincenti, da L. Torraca: A. Tepedino Guerra e L. Torraca, *Etica e astronomia nella polemica epicurea contro i Ciziceni*, in *Epicureismo greco e romano*, a c. di G. Giannantoni e M. Gigante (Napoli, 1996) 1.149–50 n. 102.

Atthis di Filocoro (Φιλόχ[ο]ρος ἐν τῷ τῆς Ἀτθ[ί]δ[ος] ἕκτω[ι] παρέπαι[σεν] κ.τ.λ.): tra le due fonti, Filodemo avrebbe considerato la testimonianza di Dicearco piú attendibile e da preferire a quella di Filocoro.[19]

Se si escludono—per i motivi sopra indicati—le colonne 1* e Y, questi i contenuti del nuovo frammento di Dicearco, a partire dal testo che ho stabilito nella mia edizione dello scritto filodemeo cercando di mantenermi, nei limiti del possibile, quanto piú aderente ai resti tramandati e rifiutando qualsiasi esegesi che parta da pericopi testuali interamente o in larga misura integrate. Dicearco dava una valutazione positiva dell'opera di Platone: un rinnovamento della filosofia, l'euritmia dei dialoghi, il progresso della ricerca filosofica. La composizione dei dialoghi aveva sortito un benefico effetto protrettico e aveva spinto innumerevoli lettori a filosofare, taluni seppure in maniera superficiale perché sviati dalla apparenza esteriore.[20] Venivano in seguito menzionati alcuni discepoli che avevano ritenuto avere una scusa sufficiente della propria ignoranza o piuttosto essere in possesso della virtù (?), in quanto soli conoscitori del genuino pensiero del nobile e sapientissimo maestro, Platone (1). Alla rappresentazione dell' importanza e del valore della filosofia di Platone in Dicearco, Filodemo faceva seguire (col. 2.4–5: τοιαῦτα γεγραφότο[ς Δ]ικαιάρχου) larghi estratti dai libri V e VI dell'*Atthis* di Filocoro (coll. 2 e V) relativi alla organizzazione dell'Academia, alla vita di Platone e alla fondazione di una comunità filosofica nella città di Asso in Troade dopo la sua morte.

II.2. In un altro passo della *Academicorum historia*, Filodemo aveva citato Dicearco. Il nome dello scrittore peripatetico si legge infatti nel frammento 22 del *PHerc. 164*,[21] che già il Mekler[22] era riuscito a collocare in corrispondenza della col. 11.17–21 del *PHerc. 1021*. La supposizione, confermata da Gaiser,[23] mi sembra attendibile nonostante la lacunosità del passo. Filodemo riportava la citazione da Dicearco— mediata probabilmente attraverso Ermippo—nel *Bios* di Cherone di

---

[19] E. Voutiras, "Sokrates in der Akademie: Die früheste bezeugte Philosophenstatue," *Mitt. Deut. Arch. Inst. (Ath. Abt.)* 109 (1994) 146–55. L'ipotesi su Dicearco si inserisce in un piú vasto contesto volto a dimostrare che nella col. 2 della *Academicorum historia* di Filodemo si conserva la prima e piú antica testimonianza sicura dell'esistenza di una statua di Socrate nell'Academia.

[20] Interpreto cosí seguendo J. Barnes, *Apeiron* 22 (1989) 146s.

[21] Cf. Dorandi (*supra*, nota 4) 179 e 255.

[22] Mekler (*supra*, nota 7) XXs.

[23] Gaiser (*supra*, nota 3) 219 e 496s.

Pellene, atleta illustre, discepolo di Platone e Senocrate e poi tiranno spietato della sua patria.[24] La lacunosità del luogo impedisce di determinare il contesto in cui esso ricorreva e i motivi che potevano averne consigliato l'utilizzazione.

II.3. Una probabile testimonianza delle *Questioni omeriche* di Dicearco si legge in un frammento del *De musica* di Filodemo.[25] Il riferimento a Dicearco si colloca in un contesto polemico incentrato su un dibattito relativo al *melos* e alla musica. Filodemo riferisce, per poi criticarla, l'opinione del suo avversario stoico Diogene di Babilonia secondo cui la musica ha un valore educativo e risulta utile in quanto può disporci a tutte le virtù. Un esempio del potere educativo della musica—ammette Diogene—lo fornisce Dicearco, quando sostiene che l'aedo per gli antichi è sapiente, come lo αἰοδὸς ἀνήρ al quale Agamennone aveva affidato la moglie Clitemestra: niente, infatti, poté Egisto sulla donna finché l'aedo le fu vicino e lei ne ascoltò il canto (ll. 20–29).[26] Lo stoico elenca poi fra gli altri poteri (δυνάμεις) del *melos* quello di far cessare le contese sia fra gli uomini sia fra gli animali e cita a conferma un luogo di Archiloco sul potere ammaliatore della poesia aedica e sulla sua capacità rasserenatrice (ll. 38–39).[27] La recente suggestione[28] che anche queste argomentazioni e il frammento stesso di Archiloco derivino a Diogene di Babilonia dalle *Questioni omeriche* del nostro filosofo peripatetico non è improbabile.

II.4. Piú incerta è la presenza di una nuova testimonianza di Dicearco in un passo ancora dell'opera *Sulla musica* filodemea, prospettata dalla Rispoli.[29] Filodemo, in un contesto polemico, critica le idee di un

---

[24] Il passo manca nella raccolta di Wehrli dedicata a Dicearco, ma è raccolto tra i frammenti di Ermippo (F 89).

[25] Phld. *De mus.*, *PHerc.* 1572, fr. 2.20–39 (= **39**: limitato alle ll. 20–29). L'ultima edizione del passo filodemeo è quella di G. M. Rispoli, *Il primo libro del* περὶ μουσικῆς *di Filodemo*, in *Ricerche sui Papiri Ercolanesi* 1, d. F. Sbordone, 236–43 (Napoli, 1969) (fr. 37). Esso sarà riproposto da D. Delattre nella sua edizione del De musica di Filodemo come col. 43. Per la delimitazione del frammento dicearcheo, cf. M. Gigante, "Filodemo e Archiloco," *Cronache Ercolanesi* 23 (1993) 5–10.

[26] Cf. Hom. *Od.* 3.267. La stessa esegesi ritroviamo nel F 123 W. di Aristosseno e nel 144 SOD di Demetrio del Falero. Cf. F. Montanari (in RUSCH vol. 9).

[27] Archil. F 253 West. Una piccola, ma insidiosa lacuna (l. 39) ostacola la comprensione del testo. Una storia "sistematica" del frammento ha tracciato Gigante (*supra*, nota 25). Lo studioso suggerisce di integrare: κηλῶ⟨ν⟩ται δ' ὅτις | [ἀστ]ῶν ἀοιδαῖς e interpreta: "Siano ammaliati ciascuno dei cittadini dai canti," "Siano ammaliati i cittadini dai canti."

[28] Gigante (*supra*, nota 25) 8.

[29] Phld. *De mus.*, *PHerc.* 225, fr. 22.14–20. Il frammento, dopo G. M. Rispoli, *La*

avversario che riteneva la poesia la prima forma in cui la saggezza si era espressa e i poeti i primi saggi e avanza la teoria secondo cui la poesia, come forma del linguaggio umano, precedette la prosa (cosí deve essere intesa la inusitata espressione: ἔμμετρος ῥητορική alla l. 18 [= 40] e l'ἄμετρον di l. 20 [= 42]).[30] Quest'ultima concezione, in particolare, sottesa alle parole dell'avversario di Filodemo mostra evidenti rapporti con la tesi sull'origine e l'evoluzione del linguaggio attestata in tre passi di Varrone, Strabone e Plutarco[31] per i quali la critica moderna ha supposto una fonte peripatetica, identificata talvolta in Dicearco.[32] In entrambi i casi, la conoscenza poetica si configura come la piú antica forma di sapienza, che col tempo si trasformò in prosa, e al poeta è attribuita la qualifica di saggio. La ἔμμετρος ῥητορική viene interpretata come πρώτη σοφία nel senso che, in questa fase della civiltà, il poeta è ritenuto importante per la sua esperienza qualificata del linguaggio metrico, che gli consente di esprimere la σοφία. Ma il frammento di Filodemo fornirebbe anche due indicazioni supplementari: confermerebbe una origine peripatetica del trattato, fonte comune a tutti e quattro gli autori, e consentirebbe di determinare che fine dell'avversario era quello di mettere in rilievo, quale strumento espressivo e paideutico, la musica ancor prima della poesia. In questa affiorante e insistente mescolanza di antropologia e storia della cultura, che individua nella musica una forma di saggezza ben piú antica della poesia, può essere indicata—secondo la Rispoli—una prova complementare a favore dell'ipotesi di identificare in Dicearco l'ignoto filosofo bersaglio delle critiche di Filodemo nel frammento del *De musica*.

---

saggezza poetica, in *Atti XVII Congr. Intern. Papirologia* (Napoli, 1984) 2.543–49, è stato riedito da D. Delattre, *Cronache Ercolanesi* 19 (1989) 133 (indicato come: col. 101* 32–43). Con sostanziali cambiamenti esso sarà riprodotto dal Delattre nella sua edizione del *De musica* di Filodemo. Ringrazio l'autore per avere messo cortesemente a mia disposizione il testo dei due luoghi filodemei quale da lui stabilito. La ricostruzione del testo presenta ancora diverse incertezze. La paternità dicearchea, condivisa da Gaiser (*supra*, nota 3) 97, è ritenuta assai incerta da Delattre.

[30] Rispoli, ibid. 544.

[31] Varrone, *ap.* Isid., *Orig.* 1.38.2 (= F 319 Funaioli); Strab. 1.2.5ss. e Plut. *De Pyth. orac.* 405D–406F. St. Schröder, *Plutarchs Schrift De Pythiae oraculis*. Text, Einl. u. Komm. (Stuttgart, 1990) 53 richiama anche Max. Tyr., *Diss.* 4.3.

[32] Una discussione dei testi e della bibliografia in Rispoli (*supra*, nota 29) 544–48. Per Schröder, ibid., che non conosce il contributo della Rispoli, Plutarco e gli altri tre autori dipendono da una fonte comune che finora non è stato possibile identificare con certezza. Nessuno di questi passi compare nella raccolta di Wehrli.

II.5. Il nome di Dicearco compare anche in un frammentino incerto dello scritto *Sugli Stoici* di Filodemo, dal quale niente si ricava.[33] Quanto mai dubbia l'illazione di Crönert[34] che proponeva di integrare διὰ | τοῦ 'Hρα]κ[λε]ιτου (1. 1s.) e supponeva che la menzione di Eraclito, in un'opera polemica contro gli Stoici, dovesse essere fatta in un contesto polemico.

II.6. Se si lasciano da parte le *hypotheseis* a drammi di Euripide e di Sofocle,[35] la presenza di Dicearco nei papiri di provenienza egizia è pressoché nulla. Il nome del filosofo peripatetico è stato, infatti, intravisto da Page in alcuni frustuli estremamente mutili di un *Trattato di poesia lirica*, conservato dal *POxy.* 2506.[36] Il fatto che nel **102** Dicearco fosse accostato a Alceo porterebbe a ipotizzare l'eventuale traccia di una testimonianza dello scritto Περὶ 'Aλκαίου.[37]

III. Queste in sintesi i risultati della mia indagine sulla tradizione papirologica di Dicearco. Due nuovi testi sono stati individuati. Il primo, estratto dalla sezione su Platone dell'opera *Sui generi di vita* (Περὶ βίων) contiene concrete informazioni sulla recezione del pensiero platonico e sulla Academia. L'acquisizione del frammento, seppure decurtato di una parte sostanziale rispetto alla originaria estensione definita da Gaiser, può ritenersi ormai accertata. Il secondo, ancora di non troppo sicura assegnazione, contiene significativi complementi di carattere antropologico e storico-culturali rispetto al resto della tradizione a proposito della concezione che la musica rappresenta una forma di saggezza piú antica della poesia. Se si accetta la paterntà dicearchea, si potrebbe supporne, in via del tutto ipotetica, una sua eventuale derivazione dal Βίος 'Ελλάδος. La revisione dei frammenti sicuri e già riuniti da Wehrli ha consentito di ampliare l'estensione di uno con la citazione di un verso di Archiloco e di progredire nell'interpretazione dei rimanenti. Dubbia rimane la presenza del nome di Dicearco nei frustuli di *POxy.* 2506.

---

[33] Phld. *De Stoicis*, *PHerc.* 339 e 155, fr. 15 Dorandi (dal *PHerc.* 155 = **52**). Cf. T. Dorandi, "Filodemo. Gli Stoici (*PHerc.* 155 e 339)," *Cronache Ercolanesi* 12 (1982) 104 e 129.

[34] W. Crönert, *Kolotes und Menedemos* (Leipzig, 1906; Amsterdam, 1965) 192, *s.v.* Dikaiarchos. *Contra*, Wehrli *SdA* 1.80.

[35] Cf. W. Luppe, in questo volume.

[36] Riproposti, da ultimo, da F. Montanari, *CPF* I 1** (*supra*, nota 1) 30–32: 44 1T(?) = **111**.

[37] Cosí Page, *ad loc.*, richiamando i **105–110**.

11

The Geographical Work of Dikaiarchos

Paul T. Keyser

Despite the exiguity of the remains, it appears that one can determine the focus of Dikaiarchos' work on geography. In this brief survey of the sherds, I try to summarize his interests and accomplishments in a synoptic way, placing them in their proper historical context. (Two possible new texts are discussed.)

I. Heights of Mountains

118: Dicaearchus uir in primis eruditus regum cura permensus montis ex quibus altissimum prodidit Pelion MCCL passuum, ratione perpendiculi nullam esse eam portionem uniuersae rotunditatis colligens. (Pliny, *HN* 2.162)

119: καὶ ἔστι μὲν τῆς Κυλλήνης τὸ ὕψος ἔλασσον σταδίων ιε', ὡς Δικαίαρχος ἀναμεμετρηκὼς ἀποφαίνεται. τοῦ δὲ Σαταβυρίου ἐλάσσων ἐστὶν ἡ κάθετος σταδίων ⟨η'⟩. (Geminus, *Elem. Astr.* 17.5)

120: δέκα δὲ σταδίων ἐστὶν ἡ τῶν ὑψηλοτάτων ὀρῶν πρὸς τὰ χθαμαλώτατα τῆς γῆς ὑπεροχὴ κατὰ κάθετον, καθὰ Ἐρατοσθένης καὶ Δικαίαρχος εὑρηκέναι φασίν, καὶ ὀργανικῶς δὲ

ταῖς τὰ ἐξ ἀποστημάτων μεγέθη μετρούσαις διόπτραις
τηλικαῦτα θεωρεῖται. (Theon Smyrnaios, *Math.* [124 H.])

The altitude of the peaks in mountainous Greece was already an issue
for the Presocratics. Anaximenes (fr. A7.6 DK[11] = Hippolytos, *Ref.*
1.7.6) attempted to explain the setting of the sun and its rising using an
aition entirely independent of the earlier mythical stories: the sun is hid-
den by high mountains which ring the flat disk of the Earth. This was
presumably itself an analogy derived from local Greek experience: as
one draws closer to western foothills, sunset on a given day of the year
seems to (and indeed does) fall at ever earlier times (the corresponding
phenomenon for sunrise in the east also of course). The shape of the
Earth, according to Demokritos (fr. A94 DK[11] = Aëtios 3.10.5) and
Archelaus (fr. A4.4 DK[11] = Hippolytos, *Ref.* 1.9.4), was that of a bowl
inside of which we dwell. Plato's picture in *Phaedo* 108D–110B (compare even *Tim.* 34) is similar, although the bowl is there but one of many
dimples in the spherical Earth.

Earlier estimates for the heights of mountains were extreme.[1]
Herodotos 4.184 records that Mt. Atlas is said to be so high that one
cannot see its peak, but it is the Caucasus that he calls the highest mountains of all: Hdt. 1.203. I would cite particularly Aristotle, *Meteorologica* 1.13 (350a28–35), who gives as the height of the Caucasus the
"fact" that their peaks are lit for a third part of the night before dawn,
and after sunset. But Aristotle has here (350a28–b14) an almost
Presocratic or Platonic view of the local topography, according to
which high mountains ring Greece and the Mediterranean frog-pond on
all sides: the Caucasus to the East, the Pyrenees to the West, the (fictive)
Rhipaeans to the North, and the Ethiopian highlands to the South.[2]

Such was the background of Dikaiarchos' interest; his own context
may have provided a motivation as well (to be discussed below).

---

[1] Wilhelm Capelle, *Berges- und Wolkenhöhen bei griechischen Physikern* =
ΣΤΟΙΧΕΙΑ 5 (Leipzig and Berlin, 1916) 3–15.

[2] The Rhipaian ("Gusty") Mts. lay far to the North already in the fifth century B.C.E.,
according to four writers: Hekataios of Miletos, *FGrHist* 1 F 194 (Strabo 7.3.6);
Hellanikos, *FGrHist* 4 F 187 (Clem. Alex. *Strom.* 1.15.72.2); the geographer Damastes
of Sigeion, *FGrHist* 5 F 1 (Stephanos Byz., s.v. "Hyperborians"); and fourth
Hippokrates, *Airs Waters Places* 19 (2.74 L.), who may have imagined them as a high
escarpment at the edge of the Skythian plain: Jacques Desautels, "Les monts Riphées
et les Hyperboréens dans le traité Hippocratique Des Airs, des Eaux et des Lieux," *REG*
84 (1971) 289–96.

Dikaiarchos seems to me to have made use of a newly-developed scientific method by which for the first time ever the heights of the mountains could be accurately determined.[3] The new method was optical, as explained in **120** μετρούσαις διόπτραις, which probably refers to a mirror, as in Euclid, *Optics* 19 (see Fig. 1).[4] The older method, which involved no mirror or sighting instrument, and so would not be described as performed with a *dioptra*, is explained in Euclid, *Optics* 18: similar triangles are determined using only a *gnomon* to measure heights. This method seems to require that one use the sun's rays in such a way that one would have to be east or west of the mountain, near sunset or sunrise respectively. (That restriction would apply to ordinary objects also, but it is relatively far easier to position oneself correctly with respect to a building than with respect to a mountain.) This method was quite old; and Eudemos in his history of geometry thought it went back to Thales (as it well could have).[5]

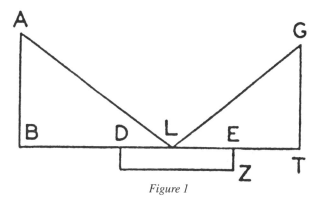

Figure 1

[3] Contrary to Fritz Wehrli, *Die Schule des Aristoteles*, vol. 1: *Dikaiarchos* (Basel, 1944) *ad loc.*, and to Per Collinder, "Dicaearchus and the 'Lysimachian' Measurement of the Earth," *Sudhoffs Archiv für Geschichte der Medizin* 48 (1964) 63–78. Capelle (above, n. 1) 17–18 takes "*dioptra*" seriously, but does not cite Euclid.

[4] The *dioptra* was any of a wide variety of sighting instruments; the plural is doubtless a generalising one. For a *dioptra* only slightly later than Dikaiarchos, see Albert Lejeune, "La dioptre d'Archimède," *Société Scientifique de Bruxelles. Annales, Série 1: Sciences Mathématiques, Astronomiques et Physiques* 61 (1947) 27–47.

[5] Thales fr. A20 DK[11] = Eudemos, *Geom.* fr. 87 Sp. (from Proklos *In Euklid. Geom.* [352.14 Fr.]): the theorem that triangles with one side and the two adjacent angles equal are themselves equal, and application of that theorem to determining the distance of ships at sea (the known length being along the shore). Thales, fr. A21 (Pliny *HN* 36.82 + Plut. *Conv. Sap.* 2 [147A]) and fr. A1.27 (D.L. 1.27), also measured the heights of the pyramids using their shadow and a gnomon—this is exactly the method of Euclid *Optics* 18.

The new method of Euclid, *Optics* 19, proceeded as follows. The rise from base of the mountain (B in the figure) to its peak (A in the figure) was determined from a known height (probably of a gnomon; GT in the figure) and known distances (that to the base of the mountain, LB in the figure,[6] and that to the known height, LT in the figure), by the means of similar triangles (ALB and GLT in the figure). The triangles could be known to be similar because of the equal-angle reflection law of light. (The angles ALB and GLT in the figure are to be formed by a "vision ray" falling from the eye G onto the mirror DE at the point L, and extending thence to the peak A.)[7] Again, this is just as Theon records Dikaiarchos explaining (**120**): τὰ ἐξ ἀποστημάτων μεγέθη. Since Euclid here is the first to mention the equal-angle reflection law of light (citing his own [lost] *Catoptrics*), and is also the first to mention this method of determining heights, I suggest that Euclid (or a contemporary) was the first to discover the law and the method. Dikaiarchos may have been the first to apply it to measuring the heights of mountains, long a topic of wonder and myth.

However he did it, his method seems to have tended to generate some sort of systematic error (perhaps a sighting error), and in fact the values recorded are ca. 1/6 (17%) high. The following table will make this clear.[8] It should be noted that the modern heights are computed from sea level, while Dikaiarchos' were measured as rise from base. Since his peaks all rise from near sea level, if he measured from an inland base, the systematic error would actually be slightly larger than that given in Table 1.[9]

[6] This distance would have been determined by the simple techniques of horizontal surveying (known even to the Egyptians) of three or four points on a plain around the mountain, and geometrical computation from those.

[7] Vision rays are geometrically equivalent to light. They were the standard ancient theory of light at this time (Epicurean *eidola* notwithstanding): see Paul T. Keyser, "Cicero on Optics (*Att.* 2.3.2)," *Phoenix* 47 (1993) 67–69 at n. 11.

[8] Following the plausible emendation η' of G. Aujac for the numeral ι' in Geminos.

[9] Elevations and locations of mountains are determined from the gazetteer of the *Times Atlas of the World*, 8th ed. (London 1990). For the length of the *passus* in Pliny, I use 1 *pes* = 29.6 cm (and 5 *pes* = 1 *passus*): see Fr. Hultsch, *Griechische und römische Metrologie*, 2nd ed. (Berlin 1882) 30–31, 44–45, 697. For the stade, I use the standard "Olympic" stade of 177.6 m: see Hultsch 48–64, 696–99; C.F. Lehmann-Haupt, "Stadion (2)," *RE* 3A (1929) 1931–63; and Aubrey Diller, "The Ancient Measurements of the Earth," *Isis* 40 (1949) 6–9. If we were to use "Eratosthenes' stade" of 157.5 m for Kyllene and Atabyrion, we would find equivalent heights of 2362 m and 1260 m, respectively—very close to the modern values. But I think it most improbable either that Dikaiarchos used Eratosthenes' value, or that later authors bothered to convert.

Table 1

Dikaiarchos' Measurements of Mountain-Heights

Peak (Region)	Dikaiarchos' Height	Modern Altitude
1 Pelion (Thessaly)	1250 *passus* = 1850 m	1547 m (+20%)
118 = Pliny 2.162	? <10 st.> → + 15%	(39°24' N 23°03' E)
2 Kyllene (Arkadia)	15 st. = 2664 m	2376 m (+ 12%)
119 = Gem. 17.5		(37°56' N 22°24' E)
3 Atabyrion (Rhodes)	<8> st. = 1421 m	1215 m (+ 17%)
120 = Gem. 17.5		(36°12' N 26°52' E)
4 Olympos (Lykia)	2000 *passus* = 2960 m	2366 m (+ 25%)
Dik.?– = Sallust,	? <15 st.> → + 13%	(36°32' N 30°26' E)
Hist. fr. 2.82 M.		

I have tentatively added Lykian Olympos to the list of mountains measured by Dikaiarchos, on the grounds that the error is not out of line for his work (especially if Sallust's source in fact recorded 15 stades, and Sallust simply converted that to a round number of *passus*), and that the mountain is in the general region in which he made measurements (and see §II). (Similarly, for Pelian, if we convert Pliny's 1250 *passus* to stades, using his own formula in *HN* 2.85, we get 10 stades, which gives a height, 1776 m, much closer to the modern value—but we do not know that Pliny's 1250 *passus* was obtained in this way.)

It is to be noted as well that the four (or three) peaks attributable to Dikaiarchos are all close to or on his own line of "zero" latitude (see §III below). Nonetheless, the only explicit reference to a region where he made measurements is the Peloponnesos, according to the *Suda* entry "Dikaiarchos" (**2**), listing a title "Measurements of Mountains in the Peloponnesos." Geminus does record a measurement on Rhodes.

The source of the systematic error is of some interest. In Figure 1, the lengths GT (of the gnomon itself) and LT (from the foot of the gnomon to the center of the mirror) are unlikely to have been

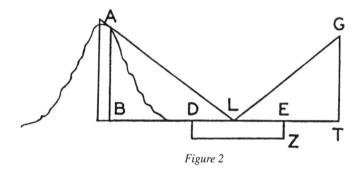

Figure 2

mismeasured, as they were nearby and short.[10] The errors in the distance to the (inaccessible) interior base of the mountain are more likely to be random (though large) than systematic. I make two suggestions for the source of this systematic error (both may have been operating). In Fig. 2, one notes that for most mountains, Dikaiarchos would have been sighting to the "military crest," unexpectedly closer to his position, so that the apparent height would be increased. But not all mountains have this shape (the Matterhorn being a famous exception). In Fig. 3, one notes that the air at lower elevations contains more water vapor, and would thus have a higher index of refraction, so that the ray from the mirror to the peak, assumed straight by Dikaiarchos, would have in fact bent in such a way as to produce a systematic overestimate of the height (temperature inversions of one sort or another might also have produced a similar effect). But the amount of overestimate would be less than 1% due to humidity.[11]

After Dikaiarchos, others also measured the heights of mountains, presumably by more or less the same method, though there are traces of only a few (and most are probably mere guesses). Strabo 8.6.21 records that the height of the Acrocorinth was 3.5 stades, but gives no authority; since the number is precise and accurate, it may be a measurement. Plutarch, *Aemil. Paul.* 15.6, preserves an epigram by a Xenagoras son of Eumēlos celebrating his measurement of the height (10 stades plus

[10] The gnomon would have to have been recorded as, say, 7 (or more) feet long, when it was really 6 feet long, to generate the sort of error noted above. Equivalently, the distance LT would have to have been recorded as, say, 5 1/7 feet (or less) long, when it was really 6 feet long.

[11] Even high humidity only increases the index of refraction of air by about 0.6%, and the excess height is proportional to that increase in index of refraction.

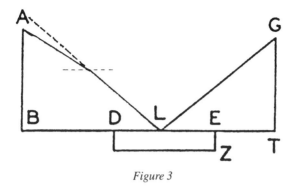

Figure 3

96 feet) of Macedonian Olympos,[12] possibly the rise from base, and probably the source of the remark in Apuleius (*Socr.* 8) and Martianus Capella (2.149) that Olympos is 10 stades tall. Less reliably, D.S. 2.13.2 and 7 (= Ktesias, *FGrHist* 688 F 1.13.2, 7) records excessive values for the rise from base (εἰς/πρὸς ὕψος ἀνατεινο-) of two peaks in modern Iran, Bagistanos (mod. Tāq-e Bostan) and Orontes (mod. Kūh-e Alvand). One suspects that Ktesias was not relying on measurement. For Kyllene we have two records of its height later than Dikaiarchos: Strabo 8.8.1 records that "some say" the perpendicular height is 15 stades, others 20 stades; while Apollodoros of Athens, *On the Gods* (*FGrHist* 244 F 130), states that it was 9 (Olympic) stades, less 80 feet, high (i.e., 5320 Greek feet). The latter is presumably a measurement of the rise from base. Finally, Pliny is pretty clearly guessing, or recording the length of the ascent, when he claims that the height of the Thracian Haimos (mod. Musala) is 6 Roman miles (Pliny 4.41);[13] even more absurd is his value for the Alps: 50 Roman miles (Pliny 2.162).

Moreover, it is recorded that later geometers improved on Dikaiarchos' method, and that mountain heights could be measured was known even into late antiquity.[14] Eratosthenes (fr. II.A.2 B) continued Dikaiarchos' work, and may be the source of one or both of the

---

[12] Plutarch (as he notes, *Aemil. Paul.* 15.3 and 16.2) is here following Polybios (29: lost), and a letter of P. Cornelius Scipio Nasica Corculum, cos. 162 B.C.E., cos. II 155 B.C.E., on the war against Perseus, in 168 B.C.E. The epigram is doubtless from Polybios; cp. Capelle (above, n. 1) 21–23.

[13] Compare the tall tale about Haimos in Polyb. 34.4 = Livy 40.21.2 = Strabo 7.5.1.

[14] The Xenophon cited by Alexander Polyhistor (*FGrHist* 273 F 72; cp. perhaps F 19.36) for Ἀναμέτρησις τῶν ὀρῶν probably wrote about ὄρων: Capelle (above, n. 1) 23.

Table 2
Later Measurements and Guesses of Mountain-Heights

Peak (Region)	Height (*Italics = Guesses*)	Modern Altitude (* = rise from base)
1 Acrocorinth Strabo 8.6.21	3.5 st. = 622 m (by ?)	575 m (+ 8%)
2 Olympos (Macedonia) Plut. *Aemil.* 15.6	10 st. + 96 ft. = 1804 m (by Xenagoras)	* 1900 m (+ 5%) (35°44' N 27°11' E)
3 Kyllene (Arkadia) Apollod. *Gods* fr. 130	9 st. - 80 ft. = 1575 m (by ?)	* 1400 m (+ 12%) (37°56' N 22°24' E)
4 Kyllene (ibid.) Strabo 8.8.1	15 st. = 2664 m (by ?)	2376 m (+ 12%) (ibid.)
5 Bagistanos (Iran) Ktesias fr. 1.13.2	*17 st. = 3020 m*	* 2100 m (+ 44%) (34°22' N 47°08' E)
6 Orontes (Iran) Ktesias fr. 1.13.7	*25 st. = 4440 m*	* 1800 m (+ 150%) (34°40' N 48°32' E)
7 Kyllene (Arkadia) Strabo 8.8.1	*20 st. = 3552 m*	2376 m (+ 49%) (37°56' N 22°24' E)
8 Haimos (Thrace) Pliny 4.41	*6000 passus = 8880 m*	2925 m (+ 200%) (42°10' N 23°35' E)
9 Alpes Pliny 2.162	*50,000 passus = 74,000 m*	!!

anonymous measurements in Table 2 above.[15] In 62 C.E., Heron describes an improved method (*Dioptra* 13), by which the heights even of inaccessible mountains could be surveyed. In the second century C.E.,

[15] In fact the measurement of Kyllene in Apollodoros is exactly 10 of Eratosthenes' stades; equivalently, the given value of nine stades less eighty feet, if computed with Eratosthenes' stade, would give 1396 m, very close to the modern value of the rise from base.

the historian and philosopher Arrian, *Physika* (as preserved in Stobaios 1.31.8 [246.14 W.]), recorded that by these methods a maximum height of 20 st. (3552 m) had been determined; evidently measurements had not been taken in India. Even as late as the fourth century, according to Kleomedes, *Caelest.* 1.7.121–30 (cp. 2.1.345–52), and the sixth century, according to Philoponos, *In Meteor.* 1.3 (27.9 H.), the method of measurement was known and in use; Philoponos adds that the greatest height so determined was 12 st. (possibly referring to rise from base).

II. Sphericity of the Earth

121: formam totius terrae . . . rotundam globosam etiam Dicaearchus asseuerat. namque ortus obitusque siderum non diuersus pro terrae eleuatione uel inclinationibus haberetur, si per plana diffusis mundanae constitutionis operibus uno eodemque tempore supra terras et aequora nituissent, aut item si emersi solis exortus concauis subductionis terrae latebris abderetur. (Mart. Cap. 6.590–91)

Dik.?: καὶ μὴν εἰ πλατεῖ καὶ ἐπιπέδῳ τῷ σχήματι ἐκέχρητο ἡ γῆ, δέκα μυριάδων ἡ ὅλη ἂν τοῦ κόσμου διάμετρος ἦν. τοῖς μὲν γὰρ ἐν Λυσιμαχίᾳ κατὰ κορυφῆς ἐστιν ἡ τοῦ Δράκοντος κεφαλή, τῶν δ᾽ ἐν Συήνῃ τόπων / ὑπέρκειται ὁ Καρκίνος. τοῦ   60 δὲ διὰ Λυσιμαχίας καὶ Συήνης ἥκοντος μεσημβρινοῦ πεντεκαιδέκατον μέρος ἐστὶν ἡ ἀπὸ τοῦ Δράκοντος μέχρι Καρκίνου περιφέρεια, ὥς γε διὰ τῶν σκιοθηρικῶν δείκνυται. τὸ δὲ τοῦ ὅλου κύκλου πεντεκαιδέκατον πέμπτον τῆς διαμέτρου γίνεται. ἂν τοίνυν ἐπίπεδον ὑποθέμενοι τὴν γῆν καθέτους ἐπ᾽ αὐτὴν ἀγάγωμεν ἀπὸ / τῶν ἄκρων τῆς   65 περιφερείας τῆς ἀπὸ τοῦ Δράκοντος ἐπὶ Καρκίνον ἡκούσης, ἐφάψονται τῆς διαμέτρου, ἢ διαμετρεῖ τὸν διὰ Συήνης καὶ Λυσιμαχίας μεσημβρινόν. ἔσται οὖν τὸ μεταξὺ τῶν καθέτων μυριάδων δύο· δισμύριοι γὰρ ἀπὸ Συήνης εἰς Λυσιμαχίαν στάδιοι. ἐπεὶ οὖν πέμπτον τῆς ὅλης διαμέτρου τοῦτο τὸ διάστημα, δέκα μυριάδων ἡ ὅλη / τοῦ μεσημβρινοῦ   70 διάμετρος γενήσεται. δέκα δὲ μυριάδων τὴν διάμετρον ἔχων ὁ κόσμος τὸν μέγιστον ἕξει κύκλον μυριάδων τριάκοντα· πρὸς ὃν ἡ γῆ στιγμιαία οὖσα πέντε καὶ εἴκοσι μυριάδων ἐστίν, ὁ δὲ ἥλιος ταύτης πολυπλασίων ἐστίν, ἐλάχιστον τοῦ οὐρανοῦ μέρος ὑπάρχων. πῶς οὐχὶ καὶ ἀπὸ τούτων φανερὸν ὅτι μὴ οἷόν τε ἐπίπεδον εἶναι τὴν γῆν; (Kleomedes, *Caelestia* 1.5.57–75)

The hypothesis of the sphericity of the Earth was first advanced in the late fifth century, probably around 420 B.C.E.[16] This was accepted by Plato (see the *Phaedo* passage already cited), and by Aristotle, *De caelo* 2.14 297a8–8b20. The status of the theory around 300 B.C.E. is relevant; to this point I return below.

Aristotle (*De caelo* 2.14 297b31–8a9) in fact uses just the argument that Dikaiarchos later did: that the fixed stars visible to an observer moving north or south on the Earth change (*inclinationibus* = latitudes). Wehrli argues that Dikaiarchos referred to the difference in rising times apparent to one going east or west (and, evidently, correctly taking account of the 4 minutes per day shift due to annual motion!). Indeed, moving from Athens (at ca. 23° 45' E) to, say, Side in Pamphylia (about 7.5° further east) would generate one half of one (equinoctial) hour difference in rising or setting times of the fixed stars.[17] But the earliest reliable measurement of longitude (a necessary prerequisite for any such determination of the difference in rising times) was not made until over three centuries later (by Heron in 62 C.E.: see *Dioptra* 35). Moreover, I doubt if either *eleuatione* or *inclinatione* can possibly refer to motion in longitude (east/west).

A generation before Dikaiarchos, Pytheas of Massilia had made further confirming measurements of this effect of latitude on the appearance of the fixed stars, traveling as far north as the Shetland Islands (T29 R. = Mart. Cap. 6.608–9).[18] He observed the angle of the pole and reported corresponding lengths of longest days of the year (the standard way of reporting latitude at the time): T5 R. = Strabo 2.1.18; T18a R. = Pliny 2.186–87; and T18b R. = Mart. Cap. 6.595.

Pliny 2.162 (**118**) explicitly states that the reason Dikaiarchos undertook his measurements was to establish that mountains did not signifi-

---

[16] A complex issue, into which I hope to delve at another time. In summary, there is no good evidence (though much bad evidence, of course) for an earlier publication of the theory, and there is plenty of corroborating evidence that theories of the shape of the Earth before this invariably assumed a more or less flat Earth.

[17] Similarly, 7.5° (or one half hour) west of Athens one finds Locri, and 15° (or one hour) east of Athens one finds Edessa.

[18] See C. H. Roseman, *Pytheas of Massilia: On the Ocean* (Chicago, 1994).

cantly affect the sphericity of the earth.[19] A dispute about the evidence for the sphericity of the Earth, despite the long and weighty acceptance of that model, might have been relevant to Dikaiarchos, given the contemporary emergence of Epicureanism. Epicurus after all had used Anaximenes' old idea that the sun sets by going behind remote high mountains at the edge of the Earth (cp. Epicurus *Pyth.* 92). That would explain Dikaiarchos' interest in mountain heights—if Aristotle's (probably tralaticious) claims in *Meteor.* 1.13 were allowed to stand, the Caucasus would indeed do for such a sun-hiding mountain range. On the other hand, it may be that Dikaiarchos was also attempting to show that nearby mountains were of relatively little height, in order to support a "dimpled-Earth" model such as had been held by Plato (and perhaps Aristotle). If local mountains were no more than 15 stades tall, then the Mediterranean area could well be deep in a dimple (ringed by the Caucasus, the Rhipaeans, the Pyrenees, and Mt. Atlas and the Ethiopian highlands, perhaps). That is consistent with a likely interpretation of **126** (below §III).

Did Dikaiarchos himself make a measurement of the *size* of the Earth? Kleomedes 1.5.57–75 in the fourth century C.E. refers to an unattributed and undated measurement of the meridian Lysimachia-to-Syene as 1/15 of the circumference (which would yield 30 myriad stades for the total). This measurement must be post-309/308 B.C.E., the foundation of Lysimachia.[20] It is perhaps prior to Archimedes who mentions an estimate of 30 myriad stades for the circumference (*Aren.* 1.8).[21] Another possible, but by no means certain, date *ante quem* would be the more accurate measurement of Eratosthenes, giving 25 myriad stades.[22] Collinder rightly points out that the particular measurements recorded in Kleomedes seem rather careless. The star said to be at zenith at Lysimachia is in fact off by 12.5° (about 1/7 of a right angle, and

---

[19] Later, Eratosthenes (fr. II.A.2 B = Simplic. *In de Caelo* 2.14 [549.32 H.]) also made such measurements for this reason.

[20] D.S. 20.29; J. Weiss, "Lysimachia (4)," *RE* 13.2 (1927) 2554–56.

[21] Of course, Archimedes may be referring to some other measurement which merely happened to give the same value (or even only a value close to 30 myriad stades, which Archimedes then rounded off to 30 myriads). But Archimedes takes the 30 myriad stades as the agreed and only existing value.

[22] In fact measurements, even in modern times, need not converge monotonically to the correct value: Poseidonios' measurement (fr. 202 E–K) gave 18 myriad stades, far too small, but was considered authoritative even by Columbus.

easily measurable using the ancient instrument, a gnomon).[23] The arc of meridian is not in fact 1/15 of the circle, but about 1/22 (a large and easily measurable difference).[24] Such inaccuracy becomes less and less explicable the later the measurement is put, but it is not impossible that Dikaiarchos might have assigned the measurement to a less careful assistant (or even made a rather poor measurement himself). Given his era, it is likely that Kleomedes was using some rather early authority as his unnamed source here; later authors (such as Eratosthenes and Poseidonios) Kleomedes usually cites by name. In sum, an early source is likely, but not certain.

I believe the decisive argument is this: in order for someone to have made the measurement at all, there must have been professional connections between Lysimachia and Egypt. Before the Roman conquest of the eastern Mediterranean (a period too late for a source for Kleomedes or for a measurement of such inaccuracy), the only time such a thing was politically possible was when Ptolemy was an ally of Lysimachos (299 to ca. 281 B.C.E.), or more likely earlier when Ptolemy and Lysimachos were allies of Cassander ruler of Greece including the Peloponnesos (308 to 302 B.C.E.).[25] Both periods are only consistent with an attribution of this measurement of the size of the earth to Dikaiarchos (for or else we must believe that there was an otherwise unattested coeval of Dikaiarchos also interested in the size of the earth and also connected with Lysimachos and Ptolemy).[26] Given then that the measurement is by Dikaiarchos, the later period seems less likely, as Dikaiarchos is attested to have been a coeval of Aristoxenos,

[23] P. Collinder 1916 (above, n. 3 = 1964) rightly compares Aristotle's measurement, *Meteor*. 2.5 362b10–12, of the constellation Corona, close to the zenith at Athens (within 2 or 3 degrees).

[24] The third difficulty pointed out by Collinder need not be decisive: the distance Lysimachia to Syene is given as 2 myriad stades, when in fact it is close to 1 myriad stades. But accurate measurements of long distances in antiquity were notoriously difficult, and are often off by as much, even far later.

[25] I rely here and in the following sentences on the *Cambridge Ancient History* 6 (1927; repr. 1964) 489–504 and 7, sec. ed. (1984) 39–61. The era is not well represented in extant sources, and is complex, so caution is warranted.

[26] Theophrastos won't do, as he remained in Athens; Straton is likewise ruled out. It is not impossible that there was another such person, only very unlikely. Hugo Berger, *Geschichte der Wissenschaftlichen Erdkunde der Griechen*, 2nd ed. (Leipzig, 1903) 370–73 attributes this to Dikaiarchos, arguing from the *termini* provided by the measurements of Archimedes and Eratosthenes, and by the destruction of Lysimachia "nach dem Tode des Lysimachos" by the Thracians (but that is dated to ca. 200 B.C.E.), which was not rebuilt until 196 B.C.E.: cp. Weiss (above, n. 20).

and so would have been about seventy-five (in the earlier period, he would have been about sixty); moreover, at least in 299–288 B.C.E. Demetrios was the ruler of the Peloponnesos, Dikaiarchos' adopted homeland, and no ally of Lysimachos or Ptolemy.

This earlier date (305 ± 3 B.C.E.) is also consistent with the known locations of the mountains measured by Dikaiarchos: in Thessaly and Arkadia ruled by Cassander 311–302 B.C.E., and in Rhodes nominally free at the time but influenced by Ptolemy.[27] Only at this time was it politically possible for Dikaiarchos to have done this, and only at this time could it be said that he measured mountains *cura regum* (**118**), meaning Cassander and Ptolemy.[28] Furthermore, the dating of Dikaiarchos' measurements of mountains to 305 ± 3 B.C.E. is consistent with his use of Euclid, *Catoptrics*, that author being dated only to the reign of Ptolemy.

I conclude that the measurement of the earth's circumference as 30 myriad stades, recorded in Kleomedes, is indeed by Dikaiarchos, sponsored by Lysimachos and Ptolemy. Furthermore, both it and his measurements of the heights of mountains were carried out in 305 ± 3 B.C.E., the latter sponsored by the kings Cassander and Ptolemy.

III. Map of the Earth; Latitude Zero Line

122: οἱ μὲν οὖν παλαιοὶ τὴν οἰκουμένην ἔγραφον στρογγύλην, μέσην δὲ κεῖσθαι τὴν Ἑλλάδα καὶ ταύτης Δελφούς. τὸν ὀμφαλὸν γὰρ ἔχειν τῆς γῆς. πρῶτος δὲ Δημόκριτος πολύπειρος ἀνὴρ συνεῖδεν ὅτι προμήκης ἐστὶν ἡ γῆ, ἡμιόλιον τὸ μῆκος τοῦ πλάτους ἔχουσα. συνήνεσε τούτῳ καὶ Δικαίαρχος ὁ Περιπατητικός. (Agathemeros, pr. 2)

123: Δικαίαρχος δὲ ὁρίζει τὴν γῆν οὐχ ὕδασιν, ἀλλὰ τομῇ εὐθείᾳ ἀκράτῳ ἀπὸ στηλῶν διὰ Σαρδοῦς Σικελίας Πελοποννήσου Καρίας Λυκίας Παμφυλίας Κιλικίας καὶ Ταύρου ἑξῆς ἕως Ἰμάου ὄρους. τῶν τοίνυν τόπων τὸν μὲν βόρειον, τὸν δὲ νότιον ὀνομάζει. (Agathemeros, pr. 5)

---

[27] If we include Lykian Olympos among the mountains Dikaiarchos measured, even Lykia fits here too, for Ptolemy briefly controlled it in 308–306 B.C.E., and not again until 296 B.C.E. and after.

[28] Cassander only declared himself "king" in 306 B.C.E., and Ptolemy in 304 B.C.E.; but Dikaiarchos could have made his measurements in, say, 307 B.C.E. supported by both, and yet have the support of his work be credited to the two rulers as kings retrospectively in the tradition.

124: Πολύβιος δὲ τὴν Εὐρώπην χωρογραφῶν τοὺς μὲν ἀρχαίους ἐᾶν φησι, τοὺς δ᾿ ἐκείνους ἐλέγχοντας ἐξετάζειν Δικαίαρχόν τε καὶ Ἐρατοσθένη τὸν τελευταῖον πραγματευσάμενον περὶ γεωγραφίας καὶ Πυθέαν, ὑφ᾿ οὗ παρακρουσθῆναι πολλούς. ... Ἐρατοσθένη ... Πυθέᾳ δὲ πιστεύειν, καὶ ταῦτα μηδὲ Δικαιάρχου πιστεύσαντος. ... Ἐρατοσθένους δὲ εἴρηται ἡ περὶ τὰ ἑσπέρια καὶ τὰ ἀρκτικὰ τῆς Εὐρώπης ἄγνοια. ἀλλ᾿ ἐκείνῳ μὲν καὶ Δικαιάρχῳ συγγνώμη, τοῖς μὴ κατιδοῦσι τοὺς τόπους ἐκείνους. ... ἀποφάσεις, ἃς ποιοῦνται περὶ τῶν ἐν τοῦτοις τοῖς τόποις διαστημάτων καὶ ἐν ἄλλοις πολλοῖς. ... τοῦ γοῦν Δικαιάρχου μυρίους μὲν εἰπόντος τοὺς ἐπὶ στήλας ἀπὸ τῆς Πελοποννήσου σταδίους, πλείους δὲ τούτων τοὺς ἐπὶ τὸν Ἀδρίαν μέχρι τοῦ μυχοῦ, τοῦ δ᾿ ἐπὶ στήλας τὸ μέχρι τοῦ πορθμοῦ τρισχιλίους ἀποδόντος, ὡς γίνεσθαι τὸ λοιπὸν ἑπτακισχιλίους τὸ ἀπὸ πορθμοῦ μέχρι στηλῶν. (Strabo 2.4.1–2)

125: Δικαίαρχος δὲ καὶ Ἐρατοσθένης καὶ Πολύβιος καὶ οἱ πλεῖστοι τῶν Ἑλλήνων περὶ τὸν πορθμὸν ἀποφαίνουσι τὰς στήλας ⟨τοῦ Ἡρακλέους⟩. (Strabo 3.5.5)

79: Peloponnesias ciuitates omnes maritimas esse hominis non nequam sed etiam tuo iudicio probati Dicaearchi tabulis credidi. is multis nominibus in Trophoniana Chaeronis narratione Graecos in eo reprehendit, quod mare tantum secuti sunt nec ullum in Peloponneso excipit. (Cicero, *Ad Atticum* 6.2.3)

First we must clarify Agathemeros' confusion in **122**. He has misunderstood Dikaiarchos as agreeing with Demokritos about the shape of the Earth. In fact while Demokritos made the Earth flat and oblong (fr. B15 DK[11] = Agathemeros), Dikaiarchos held the Earth to be spherical (**121**, above §II). What then did Dikaiarchos mean? He refers to the *oikoumene*, i.e., the inhabited known land-mass (and in fact that is the word used here). The οἰκουμένη itself (not the Earth as a whole) was oblong. Later Eratosthenes agreed (fr. II.C.18 B = Strabo 1.4.5) and so it became a standard teaching. The idea is also in Aristotle, *Meteor.* 2.5 362b12–30; the ratio of the oblong varied in different authors.

All of the these fragments very likely refer to the *Periodos Gēs*, Dikaiarchos' description of the world. It was adorned with maps, as Cicero informs us (**79**), which were thus probably the earliest careful ("scientific") maps of the world attempted in the Mediterranean area. (Already Babylonians drew schematic maps of the flat, round Earth, and there may well have been many similar sketches before Dikaiarchos.)

As for the oblong shape of the *oikoumene*, Dikaiarchos' latitude zero (**123**) also became the standard device from Eratosthenes on. One presumes Dikaiarchos determined this line from records of the observations of the elevation of the pole (equivalently, the length of the longest day of the year) at the various sites. It ran through Sardinia, Sicily, the Peloponnese, Karia, Lykia, the Tauros, and the "Imaos," usually interpreted as the Himalayas. There must have been some error for Sardinia, for it lies north, not west of Sicily; moreover the latitude of the "Imaos" is likely to have originated with one of the philosophers in Alexander's retinue, and hence must be somewhere in Persia, Bactria, or the Indus.[29] As noted above (§I), all of the mountains for which Dikaiarchos is known to have determined altitudes lie close to or on this line; he may well have also made the measurements of latitude, at least for the Peloponnesos, Karia and Lykia (he is said to have been ignorant of the western regions: **124**). One could thus remark that by inventing this latitude zero, Dikaiarchos may be credited with inventing the notion that the Mediterranean Sea was the "center" (perhaps the central dimple) of the spherical Earth.[30]

Two details (**125** and **124**) are worth attention. Dikaiarchos located the famous mythical Pillars of Herakles at the Strait of Gibraltar, an identification which itself became standard, though not undisputed. Moreover (**124**), he recorded a number of distances, all extant ones being measured from the Peloponnese (his adopted home country). Two are seriously misestimated: to the Strait of Gibraltar is a myriad stades (which would be about 1800 km; in fact it is about 2400 km), and to the end of the Adriatic gulf is greater than that (i.e., greater than about 1800 km; in fact it is just half the first distance, i.e., about 1150 km).[31] Again,

[29] There are several suspects: Nearchos (see Arrian *Indica* 25.4–8), Onesikritos (Pliny 2.183–85), and the source used by Diodoros of Sicily, 2.35.2 (probably Megasthenes).
[30] As pointed out by Stephen A. White at the conference. But the name "Mediterrane-" first occurs apparently over five centuries later in Solinus 23.14 (ca. 210 C.E.), and compare Isidore *Origines* 13.16.1; "inner sea" is the usual Greek name (to the Romans it became "our sea").
[31] Compare n. 22 above. Given the accuracy of the third estimate, one may suppose that it is based on autopsy, while these two were based on hearsay of some sort.

as for **123**, it would seem that Dikaiarchos did not make the measurements in the "west" himself. The third (and shortest) distance is remarkably close: to the Strait at Sicily is three thousand stades, which would be about 530 km: it is in fact about 550 km.

Dikaiarchos' measurement of the whole length and breadth of the *oikoumene* is not preserved (only his ratio of 3/2 is: see **122**).[32] Berger argues that we may be able to infer a probable set of values: Dikaiarchos made the distance Meroë-Syene half a myriad stades, and the distance from Lysimachia to the Arctic Circle (said to be the limit of habitation by his recent predecessor Pytheas) he made one and a half myriads, for a total north-south extent of four myriad stades (thus the east-west was six myriad stades).[33] Perhaps.

IIII. The Nile (126); Tides (127)

126: ἀλλὰ καὶ Δικαίαρχος ἐν Περιόδῳ Γῆς ἐκ τῆς Ἀτλαντικῆς θαλάττης τὸν Νεῖλον ἀναχεῖσθαι βούλεται. (Ioannes Lydos, *Mens.* 4.107 = Seneca, *NQ* 4A, fr. 6 G.)

128: (πῶς ἀμπώτιδες καὶ πλήμμυραι γίνονται) ⟨Δικαίαρχος⟩ ὁ Μεσσήνιος ἡλίῳ καὐτὸς τὴν αἰτίαν ἀνατίθησι, καθ' οὓς μὲν ἂν τόπους γένηται τῆς γῆς πλημμύροντι τὰ πελάγη, ἐξ ὧν δ' ἂν τύχῃ παραποστὰς ὑποσυνέλκοντι. ταῦτα δὲ συμβαίνειν περὶ τὰς ἑῴας καὶ τὰς μεσημβρινὰς ἐκκλίσεις (Stobaios 1.38.2 [252 W.].)

Dikaiarchos claimed that the source of the *rise* of the Nile (a chestnut for two more millennia) was the Atlantic Ocean (**126**).[34] The suggestion that the Atlantic be the source of the Nile predates Aristotle's animadversions on rivers (in *Meteorologica* 1.13 349b23–351a18), and reaches back to Hekataios (*FGrHist* 1 F 302; cp. Herodotos 2.21, 23) and before him to Homer, *Iliad* 21.194–97. The Egyptians held almost

---

[32] If Dikaiarchos had made the Peloponnese the geometrical center of the *oikoumene* (as did those before Demokritos, see **122**), then the length of the *oikoumene* would have to have been just twice the distance Peloponnese—Gibraltar of a myriad stades. Thus the whole length would have been two myriad stades, far too small. But Dikaiarchos did not make Greece or Delphi the geometrical center.

[33] Berger (above, n. 26) 374–76. For Pytheas on the habitability of the the arctic circle, see Strabo 2.5.8.

[34] As Berger (above n. 26) 376–78, points out, ἀναχεῖσθαι can only mean *superfundi*, not *effundi*.

the same belief, that Nūn the primeval Ocean was the source of the life-giving Nile (cp. D.S. 1.37.7).[35] Dikaiarchos went back not to the Egyptians or to Hekataios, but perhaps to the idea of Euthymenes of Massilia, who had observed a Nile-like river, containing crocodiles and flowing out of west Africa into the Atlantic (probably the Senegal), from which he thought the Nile took its mysterious rise (Seneca, *NQ* 4A.2.22: *Nilus fluit maior . . . minorque . . .*).

What is the explanation of Dikaiarchos' peculiar idea? I suspect that he was assuming that the Atlantic Ocean was at a higher level than the Mediterranean, so that water could flow into the "other" Nile, and then come down the Egyptian Nile. First, Aristotle had said that the Red Sea was higher than the land of the Nile (a canal from the Nile to that sea was abandoned when it was realised that the canal would flood the land: *Meteor.* 1.14 352b22–31). In the generation after Dikaiarchos, a similar theory about the seas was promulgated by Straton of Lampsakos (*fl.* 287–269 B.C.E.). He seems to have argued that the current in the Bosporos from the Black Sea into the Aegean, and the current in the Straits of Gibraltar, from the Atlantic into the Mediterranean, could both be explained as flows due to differences in level of the basins (Strabo 1.3.4–5).[36] Secondly, the idea that one river might have two outlets remote from one another was widely believed in Dikaiarchos' era, for the case of the Hister (a river considered very similar to the Nile: Herodotos 2.26, 33–34). The periplus (of ca. 360 B.C.E.) attributed to Skylax records this belief (§20);[37] as does Aristotle, *History of Animals* 8.13 598b15–18, claiming that the τριχίας fish swims up the Hister from the Black Sea, and down the other arm of the Hister to the Adriatic; so too does Theopompos, *Philippica* (*FGrHist* 115 F 129 = Strabo 7.5.9), writing perhaps around 330 B.C.E. Even two generations after Dikaiarchos, Apollonios of Rhodes made use of this belief to get his Argonauts out of the Black Sea (4.282–93, 323–26).

---

[35] See A.B. Lloyd, *Herodotus: Book II*, v. 2 (Leiden, 1976) 100–1 ad 2.21.

[36] I am indebted to Sylvia Berryman for drawing my attention to this theory of Straton. To us the theory seems as irrational as it did to Strabo; but note that Straton does assume that the mechanism of flow was "downhill" from a higher basin to a lower, and recall that the first writer to explain liquid flow was Ktesibios of Alexandria, who flourished after Straton (i.e., ca. 270–260 B.C.E.): A.G. Drachmann, *Ktesibios, Philon and Heron: A Study in Ancient Pneumatics* (Copenhagen, 1948) 1–20.

[37] For the date of [Skylax], see Paul Fabré, "La Date de la Rédaction du Périple de Scylax," *Les Études Classiques* 33 (1965) 353–66.

Like many other Greeks and Romans with some acquaintance with the outer Ocean, Dikaiarchos sought to explain the un-Mediterranean ebb and flux of that water. The tides were explained by Plato (*Phaedo* 111E4–112B1) as the breathing of the living Earth. Aristotle thought that winds were the efficient cause of ebbs and fluxes of the sea (cp. *Meteor.* 2.8 367a20–b7), at least for what we call not tides but tsunamis. Pytheas connected tides in the Atlantic with the phases of the moon (T26 R. = Aëtios 3.17.3); he also noted that they were greater in wider seas (T19 R. = Pliny 2.217).[38] Much later, in the mid-second century B.C.E., Seleukos of Seleucia explained the tides as due to large-scale atmospheric motions initiated by the moon (Strabo 3.5.9);[39] Poseidonios in the first century B.C.E. also connected them with the moon (Strabo 3.5.8).[40]

Dikaiarchos chose a theory of solar attraction (**127**): evidently he was arguing from a peripatetic model of evaporation according to which the sun (or heat in general) attracts water. His thought is not entirely clear, as the preserved fragment refers to ἐκκλίσεις (at dawn and noon), which ought to be some sort of deflections: but of what?[41] Aristotle, *Meteor.* 2.8 366a13–23 uses the word of the change of direction of the wind at dawn. The sea winds in the Mediterranean do indeed suffer an *ekklisis* at dawn and noon, but also at sunset: has the sunset *ekklisis* fallen out of the text? The word is used in an astronomical sense, of the moon's deflection from a simple circular orbit, by Plut. *Fac. Orb. Lunae* 16 929C2. But no-one is recorded as having thought that the sun had such *ekkliseis*. Probably Dikaiarchos meant the winds; he may have decreased the *ekkliseis* to two in order to match the number of tides. We should recall that even now tides are complex to explain in detail, and the observed motions of water vary greatly depending on the sea and coast.[42]

---

[38] The latter point also in [Arist.] *Problemata* 23.17 933b5–10, without attribution (though almost certainly from Pytheas).

[39] H. Gossen, "Seleukos (38)," *RE* 2A.1 (1921) 1249–50; W. Kroll, "Seleukos (38)," *RE* S. 5 (1931) 962–63; Berger (above, n. 26) 561–62. This is the Seleukos who followed Aristarchos in advocating heliocentricity.

[40] Fr. 217 in L. Edelstein and I. G. Kidd, *Posidonius* I (Cambridge, 1972), and II (1988) 767–76.

[41] Hippokrates *Joints* 62 (4.264 L.) calls the defect in cases of club-foot an *ekklisis*; and the word is found in a list of causes of unnatural humours: *Humours* 1 (5.476 L.). The word is a favorite of Epiktetos, who uses it of "inclinations of the will" over sixty times.

[42] Cp. J. Oliver Thomson, *History of Ancient Geography* (Cambridge, 1948) 204–5.

V. Spuria (12)

Passing in the manuscripts as by Dikaiarchos is the torso of a verse periegesis of Greece addressed to "Theophrastos" (in 150 iambics; *GGM* 1.238–43), and three extracts from a prose work of the same sort (*GGM* 1.97–110). The verse has been shown to be by Dionysios son of Kalliphon (of unknown date) through the discovery of an acrostic in the first 23 lines giving his name.[43] The three prose extracts are probably by Herakleides "Criticus" (ca. 245 ± 15 B.C.E.), since a verbatim quotation from one, made by Apollonios, *Mirabilia* 19 (ca. 100 B.C.E.), is attributed to Herakleides; his work was called *On the Cities in Greece*.[44] How either the iambs or the prose came to be assigned to Dikaiarchos one cannot say for certain; given his date, may we suspect that Herakleides in his (lost) preface referred to his recent predecessor, leading to the confusion?

VI. Summary

It is clear that, so far as we are informed, Dikaiarchos' main interest lay in what we would call physical geography. He is not recorded to have been concerned with chorography or topography or the sort of geography practiced by Herodotos and by "Hippokrates" in *Airs, Waters, and Places*. His focus is in keeping with Aristotle's in the *Meteorologica*, as well as with his own reputed materialism. For example, Dikaiarchos may well have been interested in measuring the heights of mountains so as to bring them within the grasp of his naturalistic *logos*—previously they had been mythically tall, their summits the foci of cult and the abodes of gods; now they were just tall piles of rock.[45] The rise of the Nile and the reflux of the sea were famous *paradoxa*, held to prove the inexplicability of the natural world; Dikaiarchos evidently sought to extend the rule of human reason over these as well. There is an interesting *lack* of influence of the journeys of Alexander: one might have expected information about the mountains or rivers of that area, or more about the extent of the *oikoumene* in that direction than the mere reference to the latitude zero passing through the Himalayas (but perhaps that is

---

[43] H. Berger, "Dionysios (115)," *RE* 5.1 (1903) 971–72.
[44] H. Daebritz, "Herakleides Criticus," *RE* 8.1 (1912) 484–86.
[45] Capelle (above, n. 1) 37–38.

merely the misfortune of poor preservation). All of these fragments could fit comfortably into one book on the nature of the Earth (Περίοδος Γῆς), and I am inclined to suspect that apparent references to other titles are in fact descriptions (titulature was hardly fixed in ca. 305 B.C.E., prior to the founding of the Library).

Indeed it is appropriate to remark that we seem to have lost a great deal (whether there were several books, or one book encompassing his whole work). Given Dikaiarchos' materialism, one might speculate that Byzantine Christians consigned his works (like most of those of Epicurus) to death by neglect (cp. **29** = Lactantius, *Inst. Div.* 7.13.7). But well into the Christian era, as late as Nemesios (Dikaiarchos **21A**), Simplicius (Dikaiarchos **26**), and Stephanos of Byzantium (**60, 63, 64**) one could obtain some of Dikaiarchos' works.[46] Rather it may have been a more subtle and pernicious factor: neglect of and indifference towards science and its history. Certainly he was not lost due merely to replacement by later writers such as Eratosthenes: he was readily available to Cicero, and in any case what book is supposed to have replaced his work on measuring mountains?

[46] Perhaps even as late as Photios (**88**), the *Suda* (**89**), and Eustathios (**61**): but it is very hard to be sure these authors were citing directly. Photios is not here summarizing the *Politeia Spartiatōn*, merely referring to it.

Index of Ancient Sources
for Articles 2–11

AESCHYLUS
Palamedes
  fr. 181a Radt   291
Prometheus vinctus
  446–506   237–8
AËTIUS
Placita philosophorum
  3.10.5   354
  3.17.3   370
AGATHEMERUS
Geographiae informatio
  pr. 2, 5   365–6
ALEXANDER
APHRODISIENSIS
De anima
  6.3f. Bruns   161 n.72
  6.3–4   152 n.42
  24.18ff.   159 n.67
  24.21–3   152 n.39
Problemata
  25   154 n.49
ALEXANDER POLYHISTOR
Fragmenta
  FGrH 273 F 72   359 n.14
ALEXIS
Fragmenta
  PCG 151, 206   215 n.43

AMBROSIUS
De officiis ministrorum
  2.2 (*PL* 16 col.104A–B)   313
ANAXIMENES
Fragmenta
  SH 45   200 n.13
  VS A7.6   354
ANONYMUS IAMBLICHI
  VS 89 6.1   263 n.35
ANONYMUS LONDINENSIS
  IV 20ff.   250
  V 37ff.   250
  V 39ff.   251
  VII 37ff.   250
  XII 14   251
  XIII 18   251
ANTISTHENES
Fragmenta
  187 Giannantoni   211 n.38
APOLLODORUS
ATHENIENSIS
Fragmenta
  FGrH 244 F 130   359–60
APOLLONIUS
PARADOXOGRAPHUS
Mirabilia
  19   369

APOLLONIUS RHODIUS
Argonautica
4.282–93, 323–6   371
APULEIUS
De deo Socratis
8   359
ARCHELAUS
Fragmenta
VS A4.4   354
ARCHILOCHUS
Fragmenta
253 West   350 n.27
ARCHIMEDES
Arenarius
1.8 (2.247 H.)   363
ARISTOTELES
Topica
1.14 105b19–29   231 n.76
Physica
2.8 199a15   267
2.9 200a8ff.   152 n.41
7.3 246a4–9   184 n.22
De caelo
2.14 297a8–8b20   362
2.14 297b31–298a9   362
De generatione et corruptione
2.7 334b16–20   183 n.17
Meteorologica
1.2 339a19–20, 27–8   183 n.17
1.13   363
1.13 349b23–351a18   368
1.13 350a28–35   354
1.13 350a28–b14   354
1.14 352b22–31   369
2.5 362b10–12   364 n.23
2.5 362b12–30   366
2.8 366a13–23   370
2.8 367a20–b7   370

De anima
1.3 406b15–25   182 n.16
1.3 406b24–5   184 n.20
1.4 407b30–408a28   179 n.10
1.4 407b32ff.   159 n.67
1.4 407b34–408a5   184
1.4 408a13ff.   160 n.69
1.4 408a24–8   184 n.22
1.4 408a24–6   152 n.40
1.4 408b13–15   159 n.67
1.5 411b7–9   184 n.22
2.4 416a6–b9   182 n.16
2.4 416a6–9   159 n.67,160 n.71
2.4 416a9–18   184
2.4 416b8–9   184
3.10 433b14–18   184 n.20
3.10 433b14, 19   184 n.21
3.10 433b19–27   184 n.21
3.10 433b27–30   184 n.20
De divinatione per somnum
1 463a3–7   249
2 463b12–15   190
2 463b14ff.   164 n.88
2 463b15–21   190
De longitudine et brevitate vitae
4 469b1–2   184 n.21
Historial animalium
1.1 487a11ff.   263
1.1 487a16–20   263–4
1.1 487b33–488a20   264 n.37
6.22 576a29   290 n.33
8.13 598b15–18   369
8.39 623a8ff.   249 n.16
9.1 608b19ff.   264
9.1 608b28ff.   264 n.39
9.1 609a22ff.   264 n.38
9.1 609b28ff.   264 n.38
9.1 610a13ff.   264 n.38

9.34 620a5ff.   264 n.37
9.34 619b27   290 n.33
9.41 628b13   264 n.37
De partibus animalium
2.1 646b12–24   183 n.17
2.10 656a7–8   190 n.34
4.10 686a27–8   190 n.34
De motu animalium
6 700b17–19,
   b35–701a1   184 n.20
7 701a35   184 n.20
7 701b2–3   184 n.21
8 702a32–b11   184 n.21
10 703a4–6   184 n.20
10 703a20, a28–9   184 n.21
De generatione animalium
1.18 724b26   249
1.18 725a4ff.   250
2.3 736b13   290 n.33
2.3 736b27ff.   169 n.99
2.4 738a27–33   250
3.10 761a5–6   190 n.35
Metaphysica
1   198 n.8
1.1   199, 203
1.3 983b20–1   205
1.6   225, 225 n.63
1.6 987a31   220
1.6 987b1–4   217
7.10 1036b24ff.   152 n.41
7 17   183 n.17
12.8 1074a38ff.   261 n.23
13.4   225 n.63
13.4 1078b17–30   230
13.4 1078b23–9   217
Ethica Nicomachea
1.5   197
1.6 1096a13–17   219

1.6 1096b30–1097a13   220
1.7 1098a23–6   238
1.8 1099a7–16   213 n.41
1.10 1100a4–9   313 n.4
1.13 1102a32ff.   265
2.8 1109a12ff.   268
6.3–5   202
6.7   197, 202, 203 n.21, 209
6.7 1141a9–b8   203
6.8   200
6.10   200
7.13 1153b19–21   313 n.4
10.6–8   197
10.7–8   154 n.49
10.7 1177b26–1178a8 190 n.34
Ethica Eudemia
1.5   197
7.12 1244b8   248
8.3 1249b16   248
Politica
1.2   239, 253, 267
1.2 1252b10   261 n.23
1.2 1252b16   265 n.41
1.2 1252b20   260 n.21
1.6   246
1.8–11   253
1.8–9   251, 269
1.8   263, 264, 269,
                272, 276, 290 n.33
1.8 1256a19   263 n.36
1.8 1256a32   269
1.8 1256a35   263 n.36
1.8 1256a39   263 n.36
1.8 1256b2–7   257 n.7
1.8 1256b7ff.   252
1.8 1256b26ff.   266 n.43
1.10   252
2.5 1264a1–5   238

2.5 1264a2	255 n.3	2 1448a17	273 n.75
2.6	226	3 1448a33	232 n.78
2.6 1265a41	226	4 1448b28–38	203 n.21
2.6 1265b26–33	226	4 1449a11–12	232 n.78
2.6 1265b31–1266a1	226	4 1449a15–19	231 n.77
2.6 1266a1–7	226	5 1449b6–7	232 n.78
2.7–9	200 n.12	*De disciplina*	
2.7	266	fr. 63 Rose	262 n.31
2.7 1266a36	266	*Eudemus*	
2.8 1268b31–1269a8	238	fr. 11 Ross	168 n.97
2.8 1268b35ff.	252	fr. 45 Rose	159 n.67
2.8 1268b38	269 n.54	*De philosophia*	
2.9 1271a32–7	226	fr. 3 and 4 Ross	323
2.9 1271b20ff.	249 n.16	fr. 3 Rose	199, 207
2.12	200 n.12	4	199
2.12 1274a25–31	226 n.64	5	213 n.42
2.12 1274b7–8	249 n.16	6, 7	199
3.4 1277a39ff.	277 n.86	8	271 n.66, 321, 323
4.4 1290b39ff.	267 n.48	8b Ross	203 n.22
4.9 1294a40	290	10	164 n.89, 167 n.97,
4.9 1294b13–41	226		213 n.42
4.12 1296b28ff.	277 n.86	13	100, 206 n.29
6.4 1318b9ff.	263 n.36,	53 Rose	239
	269 n.55	*De poetis*	
6.4 1319a19ff.	269 n.55	fr. 72 Rose	218
6.4 1319a20	277 n.86	fr. 73	232 n.81
7.1 1323a22	318	*Protrepticus*	
7.3 1325b30–2	290	B13 Düring	267 nn.46, 47
7.10 1329a40–b5	199 n.11	*De Pythagoreis*	
7.10 1329b14	257 n.9	fr. 191 Rose	233 n.82
7.10 1329b25ff.	238	*Politiae*	
7.10 1331a1–2	238	*Atheniensis*	
7.14 1333b18	326 n.40	fr. 381 Rose	326 n.39
7.17 1337a1	267 n.47	*Corinthiensis*	
Rhetorica		516	325, 326 n.39
1.2 1358a17–20	231 n.76	517	325
2.23 1398b11–20	201	*Lacedaemonia*	
Poetica		532–45	325
1 1447b8–13	218	536	325

Pellenensis
567   325, 326 n.39
[ARISTOTELES]
De plantis
2.1 822a25ff.   250
Problemata
23.17 933b5–10   370 n.38
Magna Moralia
1.1 1182a10–31   229
1.34 1198b9–20   197
ARISTOXENUS
Fragmenta
18 Wehrli   233 n.82
86   202
118   180 n.13
119   180 n.13
120a   180 n.13
120c, d   180 n.13
123   208, 350 n.26
130   205
ARRIANUS
Indica
25.4–8   367 n.29
Physika
ap. Stobaeum, *Ecl.* 1.31.8   361
ATHENAEUS
Deipnosophistae
10 413C   338
15 694A–B   208 n.31
ATTICUS
Fragmenta
fr. 7.10,
    p. 63 des Places   151 n.35
BOETHUS
ap. Simplicium, *In Arist. Cat.*
78.4ff.   151 n.37
CALLIMACHUS
Iambi
fr. 191.59–61   210

CHAMAELEON
Fragmenta
2 Wehrli   202
CICERO
De amicitia
2   321
Ad Atticum
2.2   315, 324, 326 n.39
2.3   316
2.12   313
2.12.4   216
2.14.1   216
2.16   312
2.16.3   154 n.48, 220–1
2.17   312
6.2   316
6.2.2   196
6.2.3   366
7.1   314
7.3   314
8.4   315
12.9   328 n.44
13.30   316 n.16
13.31   315, 316 n.16
13.32   150 n.31, 179 n.11, 315
13.33   316
Brutus
18.62   317 n.19
De divinatione
1.5   165 n.92
1.70   169, 169 n.101, 192 n.39
1.113   165 n.93, 169 n.101,
             171, 173 n.114, 191
2.1   316
2.100   165 n.93, 173 n.114,
                                191
2.101   171 n.109
2.105   164 n.86
2.107–9   171 n.109

De finibus
1.35 — 153 n.45
2.43 — 148 n.23
3.11–12 — 148 n.23
4.43 — 148 n.23
5.11 — 313, 318
5.12 — 313
5.73 — 313
5.86 — 313
De legibus
3.13–14 — 327
3.14 — 196
Lucullus
121 — 153 n.45
124 — 148 n.22
De natura deorum
5.9–11 — 231 n.76
De oratore
3.137 — 205
De officiis
2.5.16 — 321
De republica
2.8 — 316
Tusculanae Disputationes
1.10.19 — 180 n.13
1.11.24 — 180 n.13
1.21 — 148, 149, 170, 316
1.22.51 — 180 n.13
1.24, 41, 51 — 148 n.22
1.44–5 — 318
1.77 — 153 n.46, 315
5.7 — 226 n.64
5.8–10 — 212
5.24–5 — 313
CLEARCHUS
Fragmenta
7–9 Wehrli — 145 n.10
37–62 — 293 n.40

37–9, 41–43a, 44–51a,
51d–55, 57–62 — 319 n.23
69 — 207
70 — 202
CLEMENS ALEXANDRINUS
Stromata
1.14.60–1 — 202
1.15.72.2 — 354 n.2
6.2.15 — 198
CLEOMEDES
Caelestia
1.5.57–75 — 361–3
1.7.121–30 — 361
2.1.345–52 — 361
CODICES
Laurentianus
32.2 — 329
Vaticanus Graecus
435 (*Hermes* 27 [1892]
119ff.) — 205, 322
CRITIAS
VS 88 B25 — 290–1
CTESIAS
FGrH 688 F
1.13.2, 7 — 359–60
DAIMACHUS PLATAEEUS
Fragmenta
FGrH 65 — 202
DAMASTES SIGEUS
Fragmenta
FGrH 5 F 1 — 354 n.2
DEMETRIUS PHALEREUS
Fragmenta
58A–B SOD — 276 n.85
87 — 202, 207
93 — 202, 205
118 n.11 — 234 n.85
144 — 350 n.26

DEMETRIUS RHETOR
De elocutione
182   228
DEMOCRITUS
Fragmenta
VS 68 A94   354
VS 68 B15   366
VS 68 B30   237
VS 68 B144   237
VS 68 B154   237
VS 68 B 5 D   287 n.23, 293
DEXIPPUS
In Aristotelis Categorias
45.12   153 n.44
DIODORUS SICULUS
Bibliotheca
1 init.   238
1.37.7   369
2.13.2, 7   359
2.35.2   367 n.29
4.51–2   334
20.29   363 n.20
DIOGENES LAERTIUS
Vitae philosophorum
1.1–2   198
1.3–4   198
1.8–9   198
1.13   205 n.28
1.22   202, 205
1.23–4   209
1.23   202
1.25   205, 210
1.27   355 n.5
1.28   202
1.29   201 n.17
1.30   202
1.31   201 n.17
1.40   199, 201 n.17,
                     202, 321

1.40–1   204
1.41–2   204, 317, 321
1.41   202
1.42   201, 201 n.15, 202
1.89–91   201 n.15
1.101   205 n.26
1.107–8   205
1.122   205 n.28
2.108   312 n.2
3.4   198, 218, 320
3.6   347
3.8   225 n.63
3.37   232 n.81
3.38   217, 218
3.46   234 n.84
3.47–66   230
3.52   228 n.71
3.56   230, 232 n.80
5.2   215 n.43
5.37   217 n.46
5.42   293 n.39, 319
5.92   186 n.25
6.90   276 n.85
7.5   215 n.43
8.5   211 n.36
8.54–5   229 n.72
8.56   213
9.21   229 n.72
9.50   229
9.52   229
9.53   229
DIONYSIUS KALLIPHONTIS
FILIUS
Fragmenta
  GGM 1.238–43   371
EMPEDOCLES
Fragmenta
  VS 31 B129   229 n.72
  VS 105, 107, 109   144 n.6

EPHORUS
Fragmenta
　FGrH 70 F 181–2　　　202
EPICURUS
Ad Pythoclem
　92　　　　　　　　　363
ERATOSTHENES
Fragmenta
　II.A.2 Berger　359, 363 n.19
　II.C.18　　　　　　366
　FGrH 241　　　301 n.62
EUCLIDES
Catoptrica　　　356, 365
Elementa
　Def. 17　　　　209 n.33
　Prop. 115　　　209 n.33
Optica
　18　　　　　　　　355
　19　　　　　　　355–6
EUDEMUS RHODIUS
Fragmenta
　133–5 Wehrli　209, 209 n.33,
　　　　　　　　　　210
　133　　221 n.55, 222, 345
　143–5　　　　　　209
　144　　　　　　　202
Geometria
　fr. 87 Spengel　　355 n.5
EURIPIDES
Supplices
　199–200　　　　　249
Temenos　　　　205 n.27
GALENUS
Quod animi mores
　44.18 Müller　　152 n.38
[GALENUS]
De historia philosophica
　24 (DG p. 613–16
　　Diels)　146 n.10, 153 n.46

　105 (DG p. 639.
　　27–9)　　　　164 n.87
GELLIUS
Noctes Atticae
　1.3.10–12　　　　316
　4.11.14　　　　212–13
GEMINUS
Elementa astronomiae
　17.5　　　　　353, 357
GORGIAS
Fragmenta
　VS 82B11a.30　　　291
HECATAEUS
Fragmenta
　FGrH 1 F 302　　　368
　FGrH 1 F 194　　354 n.2
HELLANICUS
Fragmenta
　FGrH 4 F 187　　354 n.2
HERACLIDES CRITICUS
Fragmenta
　GGM 1.97–110　　　371
HERACLIDES PONTICUS
Fragmenta
　45 Wehrli　　　　205
　72　　　　　156–7, 185
　88　　　　　210, 212
　89　　　　　211 n.36
　150　　　　　　229
　176　　　　　186 n.25
HERACLITUS
Fragmenta
　VS 22 B39　　　　200
　VS 22 B104　　　200
　VS 22 B26　　　168 n.97
HERMIAS
*Irrisio gentilium
philosophorum*
　1　　　　　　145 n.10

HERMIPPUS
Fragmenta
  45 Wehrli   215 n.43
  89   350 n.24
HERODIANUS
De prosodia catholica
  GG 3.1.274.2–10   298 n.54
  GG 3.1.274.2   281 n.8
HERODOTUS
Historiae
  1.29   213 n.42
  1.75   204 n.26
  1.170   204 n.26
  1.203   354
  2.21, 23   368
  2.26, 33–4   369
  2.49   213 n.42, 234 n.85
  2.109   199
  4.95   213 n.42
  4.184   354
  5.68   205 n.27
HERON
Dioptra
  13   360
  35   362
HESIODUS
Opera et Dies
  108–12   244, 246–9
  108   274 n.76
  113   271 n.63, 275
  116–19   261 n.26
  117f.   274
  120   244, 246–9
Fragmenta
  87   234 n.85
  275   234 n.85
  306   201 n.15

HESYCHIUS
Lexicon
  s.v. Aristoteles   215 n.43
HIERONYMUS
Adversus Jovinianum
  1.47–8   320
  2.13   270 n.61
HIPPIAS
Fragmenta
  VS 86 B6   198
HIPPOCRATES
De aëre aquis et locis   371
  19 (2.74 L.)   354 n.2
De articulis
  62 (4.264 L.)   370 n.41
De humoribus
  1 (5.476 L.)   370 n.41
De prisca medicina
  3   250
Regimen
  1.2   249 n.16
[HIPPOCRATES]
De victu
  86   168 n.98
HIPPOLYTUS
Refutatio omnium
Haeresium
  1.7.6   354
  1.9.4   354
HIPPONAX
Fragmenta
  63 West   205
  123   200
HOMERUS
Ilias
  15.80   192
  21.194–7   368

Odyssea
3.267–72   208
3.267   350 n.26
5.35   247
7.36   192
7.205   247
[HOMERUS]
Margites   203
HORATIUS
Carmina
3.16.42–4   276 n.85
IAMBLICHUS
ap. Stobaeum, Ecl.
1.49.32 p. 367 W.   151 n.34
De vita Pythagorica
36   145 n.10
37–57   212 n.39
104   229 n.72
135   229 n.72
166   229 n.72
267   229 n.72
IOANNES LYDOS
De mensibus
4.107   368
IOSEPHUS
Contra Apionem
1.220–1   327 n.42
ISIDORUS HISPALENSIS
Origines
13.16.1   367 n.30
ISOCRATES
Orationes
2.12   267 n 45
3.6   262 n.34
15.254   262 n.34
LACTANTIUS
De opificio dei
16   180 n.13

Divinae institutiones
7.13   153 n.46, 180 n.13
Institutiones divinae
7.13.7   372
LIVIUS
Ab urbe condita
40.21.2   359 n.13
LOBON OF ARGOS
Fragmenta
SH 504–26   200 n.14
[LONGINUS]
De sublimitate
35.3   192
LUCRETIUS
De rerum natura
1.638–44   228 n.70
1.731–3   209
MARTIANUS CAPELLA
*De nuptiis Philologiae et
Mercurii*
2.149   359
6.590–1   361
6.595   362
6.608–9   362
MAXIMUS TYRIUS
Dissertationes 4.3   351 n.31
MELETIUS
*Anecdota graeca
Oxoniensa*
vol. 3 145.3 Cramer   145 n.9
NEMESIUS
De natura hominis
2, p. 16.21ff. Morani   151 n.36
2, p. 17.10   145 n.10
PAPYRI
Pack²
2089   327 n.43
PHerc: vid. PHILODEMUS

PMich
  1319   335
  6222A   340
POxy
  2455   205 n.27, 333
  2456   335
  2457   330 n.1
  2506   352
  2676Aa   340
  3219   228 n.71
  3653   329 n.1
PStrassb
  2676Aa   340
PAUSANIAS
Periegesis Hellados
  6.18.5   327 n.42
  9.39.4ff.   163 n.82
PHAINIAS
Fragmenta
  10 Wehrli   213 n.42
PHILODEMUS
Academicorum historia
  PHerc 164 fr. 13   346
  PHerc 164 fr. 22   349
  PHerc 1021 col. T   221 n.55,
                             344–6
  PHerc col. V   221 n.55, 349
  PHerc col. X/Z   346–7
  PHerc col. X 1–5   346, 347
  PHerc col. X.7   347
  PHerc col. Y   221, 221 n.55,
                223, 227, 345–6,
                         348 n.18
  PHerc col. Y.1   221 n.55, 348
  PHerc col. Y.1–33   221–2
  PHerc col. Y.2–17   347
  PHerc col. Y.9   231
  Pherc col. Y.15   224 n.61
  PHerc col. Y.17   224

PHerc col. Y.21   222 n.56
PHerc Y.23   222 n.56
PHerc col. 1*   347
PHerc col. 1*–1–2.5   347
PHerc col. 1–2.5   345–6
PHerc col. 1.1–2.7   218–19,
                    221, 221 n.55
PHerc col. 1   221, 221 n.55,
        223, 227, 232 n.81, 345
PHerc col. 1.1–18   220 n.54
PHerc col. 1.1   225
PHerc col. 1.2   232 n.81
PHerc col. 1.4   232 n.81
PHerc col. 1.10   231
PHerc col. 1.17–18   219 n.52
PHerc col. 1.18–21   222 n.58
PHerc col. 1.36–8   220 n.53
PHerc col. 1.39–41   220 n.53
PHerc col. 1.41   347
PHerc col. 1.42   221 n.55
PHerc col. 2   221, 221 n.55,
                       345, 348–9
PHerc col. 2.1   221 n.55
PHerc col. 2.1–17   348
PHerc col. 2.3–4   227 n.67
PHerc col. 2.4–7   218 n.51
PHerc col. 2.4–5   345, 348–9
PHerc col. 2.20ff.   348
PHerc col. 2.32–3   348
PHerc col. 2.38   221 n.55
PHerc col. 3–5   346
PHerc col. 5.36–9   347, 349
PHerc col. 6.26–7   221 n.55
PHerc col. 11.17–21   349
De musica
PHerc 225, fr.
  22.14–20   350 n.29
PHerc 1572, fr.
  2.20–39   208, 350 n.25

Rhetorica
6 (PHerc 832–BT 2
   p. 57.7–20)   327 n.41
De Stoicis
  PHerc 155, fr. 15   352 n.33
  PHerc 339   352 n.33
PHILOPONUS
In Aristotelis Meteorologica
  1.3 340a24 p. 27 H   361
In Nicomachi Isagogen
  1.1   203, 321
PHLEGON
Fragmenta
  FGrH 257 F 36.4–10   234 n.85
PHOTIUS
Bibliotheca
  37   327
PINDARUS
  fr. 116 Bowra   165 n.93
Isthmia
  2.9   205 n.27
  fr. 128f.   234 n.85
PLATO
Apologia
  21C–22A   203
Charmides
  164D–165A   201
  164E   209
Epistulae
  7 324D7   260 n.22
  7 326B6–C1   276
Euthydemus
  273A   215 n.43
Gorgias
  463B4   219 n.52
  484C–886D   216
  501A7   219 n.52
  502D   211 n.38
  508A   226

  521D   216
Hippias Major
  281C   201
  285D–E   205 n.27
Leges
  3   237
  3 677Bff.   287
  3 677C   271 n.66
  3 677E9ff.   271 n.67
  3 678A8ff.   272
  3 678B5ff.   273 n.72
  3 678C5ff.   272 n.68
  3 678C7   271
  3 678E   271
  3 678Eff.   257 n.9
  3 678E6ff.   272
  3 678E9   272 n.68
  3 679Aff.   271 n.67, 272
  3 679B4   272
  3 679B7ff.   272
  3 679B7–C2   253
  3 679C   246
  3 679D7   272
  3 680E   257 n.9
  3 691–3   226
  3 691E   226
  3 693D–694B   226
  3 696A–B   226
  4 712D–E   226
  4 713C   272 n.70
  6 757   226, 226 n.65
  6 782C   270 n.60
Meno
  82–5   224 n.61
  87A–B   222
Parmenides
  127B2   228 n.71
Phaedo
  78B   222

85E–86D	177	321D3	262 n.33
86B–D	147 n.18	321E3	262 n.33
86B–C	183	322A–B	262 n.34
86B7–C2	179 n.10	322A6	262 n.33
86D2	179 n.10	322B	274 n.79
90C	220 n.53	322B3	262 n.33
91–4	147 n.16	328B	229
92E–93A	183, 183 n.19	339–48	201
93A6–7	159 n.67	342A–343C	201
93Bff.	159 n.67	343A	207
108D–110B	354, 362	*Respublica*	
111E4–112B1	370	2 372B1	270
Phaedrus		2 372B8	269 n.57
260E	219 n.52	2 372B9	270 n.59
Philebus		2 372C1	269 n.57
16C	244	2 372C2	270
Politicus		2 372C17	270 n.58
258Eff.	273	2 372D	269
269A6	273 n.74	2 373C4–D2	270 n.62
271C4ff.	273 n.74	3 405A	270 n.62
271D1	274 n.77	4 422D	269 n.57
271E1	274	6 493B	219 n.52
271E2	274, 274 n.83	7 521–31	222
271E4f.	274 n.77	7 527E	224
271E5–7	274 n.76	8 544–50	226
272A1–4	274	8 546C5ff.	273 n.75
272B	273 n.74	8 547C–D	226
272B2	273	8 550B6	226
272B3ff.	274	8 558C	226
272B9ff.	274	9 571D–572A	165 n.93,
273B7ff.	273 n.75		166 nn.94, 96
274B8	274 n.79	10 600A	210
274C	274 n.77	10 600B	213
274E	274	10 608B1	276 n.85
274E10	273	*Theaetetus*	
Protagoras		145E	203
316C–D	201, 213 n.42	147D–148B	222
316D–317B	213	173C–174A	247 n.13

180A	228 n.70	*Adversus Colotem*	
Timaeus		14 1114F	153 n.45
22D6ff.	271 n.66	14 1115A	147 n.17
34	354	21 1119A–B	179
[PLATO]		*Vitae*	
Eryxias		*Aemilius Paulus*	
392A	215 n.43	15.3	359 n.12
Hipparchus		15.6	358, 360
228C–229B	210 n.34	16.2	359 n.12
PLINIUS		*Lycurgus*	
Naturalis historia		6	325, 326
2.85	357	*Solon*	
2.162	353, 357, 359–60, 362	4	202
2.183–5	367 n.29	*Theseus*	
2.186–7	362	3	206 n.29
2.217	370	21	224 n.60
4.41	359–60	32	206 n.29
36.82	355 n.5	[PLUTARCHUS]	
PLUTARCHUS		*De libidine et aegritudine*	
Morales		4	186 n.26
Septem sapientium convivium		5	185–6, 189
2 147A	355 n.5	7	156–7, 187
De Pythiae oraculis		8	186 n.26, 187
405D–406F	351 n.31	*De placitis philosophorum*	
De defectu oraculorum		4.2.5	145 n.9
40 432Cff.	165 n.91	4.2.7–8	191 n.36
De genio Socratis		5.1	164 n.87
590B10	163 n.83	874F	313
Quaestiones convivales		POLYBIUS	
8.1 717A	224	*Historiae*	
8.2 718C–F	224	12.11.5	312 n.2
8.2 719A–B	224	12.23.8	312 n.2
8.2 719F–720C	224	34.4	359 n.13
An seni respublica gerenda sit		POPHYRIUS	
26 796C–D	214–15	*De Abstinentia*	
26 796C	321	1.37	247 n.13
De facie in orbe lunae		2.32	241
16 929C2	370	4.1–2	241, 254 n.22

4.2   256
Vita Pythagorae
  18–19   211
  19   212 n.39
  56   212
  57–8   218
POSIDONIUS
Fragmenta
  fr. 217 E-K   363 n.22, 370
PROCLUS
In Euclidis Elementa I
  157 Fr.   209 n.33
  352   209 n.33, 355 n.5
PROTAGORAS
Fragmenta
  VS 80 C1   287 n.23
PYTHEAS MASSILIENSIS
Fragmenta
  T5 R.   362
  T18a, b   362
  T19   370
  T26   370
  T29   362
SALLUSTIUS
Historiae
  fr. 2.82 Maurenbrecher   357
SCHOLIA
In Apollonii Rhodii Argonautica
  4.272–4   258
In Homeri Odysseam
  1.1   211 n.38
[SCYLAX]
Periplus
  20 (*GGM* 1.26)   369
SENECA
Naturales quaestiones
  4A 6 Gerke   368
  4A 2.22   369

SEXTUS EMPIRICUS
Adversus mathematicos
  7.16   231 n.76
  7.349   149 n.28
  9.20–2   167 n.97
Pyrrhoniae hypotyposes
  2.31   149 n.27
SIMPLICIUS
In Aristotelis Categorias
  82.22 Heiberg   153 n.44
  216.12ff.   153 n.43
In Aristotelis De caelo
  549.32 Heiberg   363 n.19
SOLINUS
Collectio rerum mirabilium
  23.14 (p.105
      Mommsen)   367 n.30
SOLON
Fragmenta
  13.52   201 n.15
STOBAEUS
Anthologium
  1.31.8   361
  1.38.2   368
  1.49   145 n.9, 191 n.36
  2.31.124   317
  3.21.12   323 n.30
STRABO
Geographica
  1.2.5ff.   351 n.31
  1.3.4–5   369
  1.4.5   366
  2.1.18   362
  2.4.1–2   366
  2.5.8   368 n.33
  3.5.5   366
  3.5.8   370
  3.5.9   370

7.3.6	354 n.2	23 286bc	213 n.42
7.5.1	359 n.13	23 295c	234 n.84
7.5.9	369	26	233, 233 n.83
8.6.21	358, 360	26 311c	233 n.83
8.8.1	359, 360	26 316d–320a	231–2,
STRATO			231 n.77, 232 nn.79,
Fragmenta			81, 235
32 Wehrli	153 n.45	27 337b	230, 231 n.78
33	153 n.45	*Sophistes*	
35	153 n.45	285	312 n.2
147	202	THEODORETUS	
SUDA		*Graecorum affectionum curatio*	
s.v. Aristoteles	215 n.43	5.18	145 n.9, n.10
s.v. Dicaearchus	320,	THEOGNIS	
325 n.34, 328, 357		*Elegiae*	
SYNESIUS		45; 50	261 n.29
Calvitii Encomium		THEON SMYRNAEUS	
22	206 n.29	*De utilitate mathematicae*	
22 85c	323	124 H.	353–4, 356
STEPHANUS BYZANTIUS		THEOPHRASTUS	
Ethnica		*Fragmenta*	
s.v. Hyperboreoi	354 n.2	343 FHS&G	166 n.94
TELES		436 no.9c	327 n.43
Diatribae		436.21	316
41.3ff. Hense	276 n.85	461	197
TERTULLIANUS		465	317
De anima		475	313
15	149 n.24	476	317
THALES		479	313, 319
Fragmenta		479–80	197
VS 11 A1.27	355 n.5	480A	313
VS 11 A20	355 n.5	480B	313
VS 11 A21	355 n.5	481–2	197
THEMISTIUS		481	312
Orationes		482	313, 318
23	233 n.83	484	318
23 284d–285a	233	486	320, 322
23 285a–d	233	489	313

493	313	VARRO	
494A	313	*De lingua Latina*	
498	313	5.105ff.	305–6
534	316	5.108f.	298 n.53
552B	313	*De re rustica*	
583	202	1.2.15	196, 298 n.53
584A	241, 253, 260 n.21,	1.2.16	305 n.79
	262 nn.30, 32,	2	256
	274 n.80	2.1	258
594	327 n.41	2.1.3f.	305 n.79
600	234 n.85	2.1.3	298 n.53
738	207, 323 n.30	2.1.5	260 n.21
THEOPOMPUS		3.1.1–4	258
Fragmenta		XENAGORAS EUMILI FILIUS	
FGrH 115 F 25	295	ap. Plutarchum, *Vita Aemilii*	
FGrH 115 F 129	369	*Pauli*	358
THUCYDIDES		XENOPHON	
Historiae		*Cyropaedia*	
1.2	286	8.7.21	165 n.93
1.2.2	257 n.9	*Lacedaemonia politia*	326
1.2.4	270 n.57	*Memorabilia*	
1.5.3	260 n.21	1.4.3	200 n.15
1.6.6	260 n.21	[XENOPHON]	
		Atheniensis politia	326